PSP™ GAME CREATION FOR TEENS

MICHAEL DUGGAN

Course Technology PTR

A part of Cengage Learning

COURSE TECHNOLOGY
CENGAGE Learning™

Australia • Brazil • Japan • Korea • Mexico • Singapore • Spain • United Kingdom • United States

COURSE TECHNOLOGY
CENGAGE Learning™

PSP™ Game Creation for Teens
Michael Duggan

Publisher and General Manager,
Course Technology PTR: Stacy L. Hiquet

Associate Director of Marketing:
Sarah Panella

Manager of Editorial Services:
Heather Talbot

Marketing Manager: Jordan Castellani

Senior Acquisitions Editor: Emi Smith

Project Editor: Jenny Davidson

Technical Reviewer: Parker Hiquet

Copy Editor: Mike Beady

Teen Reviewer: JT Hiquet

Interior Layout Tech: MPS Limited, a Macmillan Company

Cover Designer: Mike Tanamachi

Indexer: Sharon Shock

Proofreader: Sandi Wilson

For product information and technology assistance, contact us at **Cengage Learning Customer & Sales Support, 1-800-354-9706**

For permission to use material from this text or product, submit all requests online at **www.cengage.com/permissions**
Further permissions questions can be emailed to **permissionrequest@cengage.com**

PSP is a trademark of Sony Computer Entertainment Inc. in the United States and other countries.

All other trademarks are the property of their respective owners.

All images © Cengage Learning unless otherwise noted.

Library of Congress Control Number: 2010936647

ISBN-13: 978-1-4354-5784-3

ISBN-10: 1-4354-5784-6

Course Technology, a part of Cengage Learning
20 Channel Center Street
Boston, MA 02210
USA

Cengage Learning is a leading provider of customized learning solutions with office locations around the globe, including Singapore, the United Kingdom, Australia, Mexico, Brazil, and Japan. Locate your local office at: **international.cengage.com/region**

Cengage Learning products are represented in Canada by Nelson Education, Ltd.

For your lifelong learning solutions, visit **courseptr.com**

Visit our corporate website at **cengage.com**

Printed by RR Donnelley. Crawfordsville, IN. 1st Ptg. 12/2010

Printed in the United States of America
1 2 3 4 5 6 7 12 11 10

ACKNOWLEDGMENTS

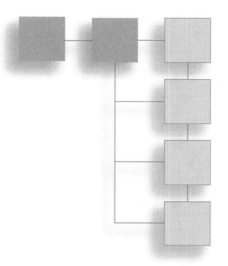

Thanks to Emi Smith, Jenny Davidson, Parker Hiquet, Mike Beady, JT Hiquet, and all the staff at Cengage Learning who helped in the creation of this book. Thanks to Krystal Duggan, Levi Ward, and Hayley Mainord for giving me time to work on this book. Thanks to Sony, Adobe, and all the Flash developers who have come before who set the standard for making PSP Flash homebrew games.

ABOUT THE AUTHOR

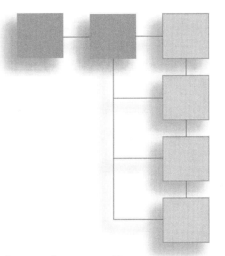

Michael Duggan is an author and illustrator by trade, as well as a college instructor in digital media and game design. He created core curriculum for game development at Bryan College and North Arkansas College and is the author and illustrator of *The Official Guide to 3D GameStudio*; *Torque for Teens*, Second Edition; *Web Comics for Teens*; *2D Game Building for Teens*; and *Wii Game Creation for Teens*. Michael spends most of his free time drawing children's books and making cartoon animations and games. He currently resides in northern Arkansas. For more information about the author, go to MDDuggan.com.

CONTENTS

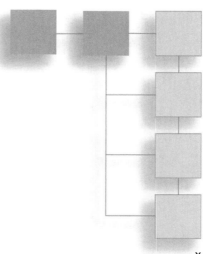

INTRODUCTION

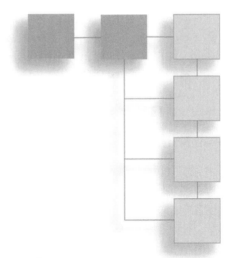

Games have come a long way since their inception far in our past.

The tools we have used in our game play have changed, as well, from knuckle bones to cards to board games to early arcade games to today's spiffy video game consoles. The progression has been a lengthy one. Now hardware advances are even changing the way we play games, such as handheld devices you can take anywhere and play games with complex mechanics and graphics in the palm of your hand. As anyone who has tried it can tell you, handheld game devices have made games fun again, in a whole new way!

A seventh-generation handheld game system, the Sony PlayStation Portable (PSP) competes primarily with the Nintendo DS.

With a strong PSP fanbase, independent game developers started creating Flash games to be played through the PSP. Using Adobe Flash, anyone with a little know-how can create electronic games to be played on the Sony PSP. That means that you, too, can make games for the PSP, no matter your age, income, or skill level.

Welcome to *PSP Game Creation for Teens*! This book will help you learn about the booming video game industry and the techniques it takes to make your electronic game ideas come to life.

This book is written in a tutorial format, so that as you read you don't just process information but you put it to immediate use and get hands-on learning to reinforce the knowledge.

Throughout this book, you will start by learning how to draw on paper, then on the computer, and put your work into the Adobe Flash program. Using Flash, you will see what it takes to create animations and cartoons. Then you will learn ActionScript and how to make animated video games using Flash. Finally you will learn how to publish these games for PSP users to play.

It's hoped you will continue to use the skills you learn within these pages to springboard your game-development talents into making dozens of electronic games!

WHAT YOU WILL LEARN FROM THIS BOOK

In *PSP Game Creation for Teens* you will learn about the electronic game industry, its history, the process by which video games and cartoons are made, and how you can make your very own games for the Sony PSP using Adobe Flash.

The PSP is one of the most popular video game handhelds from one of the gaming industry titans, Sony Computer Entertainment, and Adobe Flash allows you to make games for users of the PSP. This is not only a fantastic method for someone wanting to learn how to build electronic games, but *PSP Game Creation for Teens* will break it down for you in easy-to-understand techniques.

WHO SHOULD READ THIS BOOK

Anyone who is interested in working in the game industry, who likes playing video games and would like to make their own, or someone who is interested in making games as a hobby and doesn't know where to start, will find the contents of this book useful.

The following text goes over the specifics of creating cartoons and video games with Adobe Flash, with the express intent of publishing them for use with the Sony PSP, but it also covers the very real day-to-day responsibilities game developers have to deal with. This helps you to further understand and prepare yourself for the ever-growing game industry.

Note

As this book is about designing computer art and games, you should have some experience with computers beforehand! It is not required that you be a computer nerd, but you need to know the difference between a file and a folder, how to drag-and-drop, and how to double-click.

How This Book Is Organized

Here are some specifics about the chapter breakdown for this book.

Chapter 1: Where Did It Come From?—Before leaping into game production, this introductory chapter gives you a quick run-down on the history of the video game industry, its progression, classic genres of games, and the origins of digital animation that made all this possible.

Chapter 2: What Is It?—This chapter shows you the name-brand history behind the Sony Computer Entertainment company and the development of their PlayStation Portable (PSP) handheld system, as well as the history and importance of the Adobe Flash software.

Chapter 3: The Flash Tools You'll Need—This chapter delves into Adobe Flash, the multimedia editing tool you will use to create your animations and video games. You'll learn how Flash works and how to move around in the Flash software interface.

Chapter 4: Drawing It Out—A large part of Flash game development is learning how to draw, and even if you're not an artist yourself, this chapter can teach you how to get the art you imagine onto your computer screen.

Chapter 5: Get It Moving—This chapter starts you on the path to animation by putting your computer art skills to the test. You will learn how animation is made possible and how it happens in Flash.

Chapter 6: Make Up a Decent Story—In this chapter, you'll learn how to conceive heroic characters and weave stories around them to make your animations more compelling and entertaining.

Chapter 7: Frame the Scene—This chapter shows you how to design scenes in Flash for your audience to explore. It covers staging, composition, and digital storytelling.

Chapter 8: Make It Scream—This chapter covers sound recording, editing, composition, and the use of royalty-free sound effects libraries to bring audible life to your silent animations.

Chapter 9: Project A: Your First Animation—This chapter tells you how to put it all together and make a quick Flash animation of your own. You will make a short animation from start to finish.

Chapter 10: Game On!—Before getting down-and-dirty and creating your electronic game, it's best to know some jargon and what *not* to do. In this chapter you will also construct your game outline, which is kind of like a blueprint for the game you want to make.

Chapter 11: Accept the Challenge—This chapter enlightens you on conceiving game characters and missions for them to go on. Games are different from stories, because games are interactive, and this chapter will help you build interactive entertainment.

Chapter 12: Where in the World?—Game worlds are as vastly dissimilar from one another as can be, and their composition exploratory in nature. Find out how to come up with game environments in this chapter.

Chapter 13: Project B: Your First Game—This chapter tells you how to put it all together and make a Flash game every bit your own.

Chapter 14: Project C: Your Next Game—After finishing your first Flash game, you should look at what other games you can make for the PSP, because there are so many options.

Chapter 15: Spread It Around—This chapter shows you how to publish your Flash animations and games online and share your creations with PSP users.

COMPANION WEB SITE DOWNLOADS

You may download the companion Web site files from www.courseptr.com/downloads. Please note that you will be redirected to our Cengage Learning site.

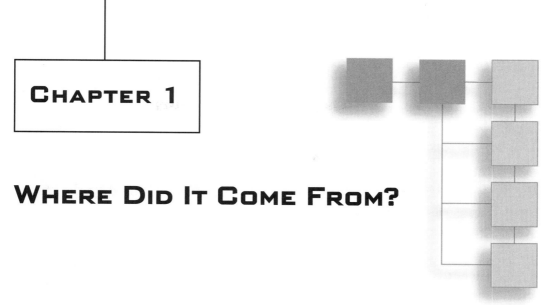

Chapter 1

Where Did It Come From?

In this chapter you will learn:

- How animation got started
- How to make a flipbook
- What traditional animation is and how it differs from digital animation
- How video games got started
- How Flash can be used to create animation and video games

By "it," I mean digital cartoons and computer games, in general. To understand how to make animated movies and games, it's best to know where they came from and what has been done before. A brief review of the history of animation and video games will better prepare you, and perhaps provide you with some inspiration, for making your own PSP (PlayStation Portable) media. Or, as the proverb goes, you will know what has come before so as to be better equipped for what comes next.

You may be more interested in creating your own animations, but if you don't know the history of animation, and how it got started, how do you expect to make your own mark?

This chapter will teach you where cartoons got their start and how video games came to be. The next chapter will teach you about the history of Sony and their PlayStation Portable handheld console.

HISTORY OF ANIMATION

Do you believe that the Cartoon Network or Walt Disney invented cartoons? Then you'd be wrong. Animation has been around an awfully long time, and while Walt Disney and the Cartoon Network have contributed to the look of our modern-day cartoons, they borrow from a long history of moving pictures.

A 4,000-year-old Egyptian mural shows wrestlers in battle. The artist depicted the action by drawing a series of movements much like a modern-day comic strip, but because there was no way back then of viewing the pictures in motion it could not very well be called a cartoon.

In 1896, New York newspaper cartoonist James Stuart Blackton interviewed famed inventor Thomas Edison. Edison, inventor of the lightbulb and electric power distribution, was then busy experimenting with moving pictures. During their discussion, Blackton did some quick sketches of Edison. Edison was so impressed by Blackton's speed and skill that he asked Blackton to do a whole series of them, which Edison then photographed. Later, in 1906, Edison and Blackton released *Humorous Phases of Funny Faces*, a short animated picture that used close to 3,000 "flickering drawings." The first of its kind, this picture was the forerunner of today's cartoons.

Among the first-ever beloved cartoon characters was Felix the Cat, a simply drawn black-and-white cartoon feline who, in the 1920s, became nearly as popular as the irrepressible Charlie Chaplin. Felix and another silent-film character, Betty Boop, whom you may have seen on some Hot Topic merchandise, were really trendy animated characters in the days before talkies.

In 1928, Mickey Mouse surpassed Felix the Cat in popularity by starring in the first-ever animated cartoon to incorporate moving pictures and synchronized sound in *Steamboat Willie*, made my Walt Disney. Mickey was created by Walt Disney and was based on a pet Disney had adopted and kept in his Kansas City studio. Disney's mouse was originally called Mortimer Mouse until Lillian Disney suggested that "Mickey" sounded better.

Walt Disney had plans for a full-length feature film, which his family and friends dubbed "Disney's Folly" and unsuccessfully pressured him to drop, because they felt it would drive him to bankruptcy. Disney astounded everyone in 1934 when his company released the first English-speaking full-length animated feature film. It contained drama and comedy, involved professional voice talents and an orchestrated soundtrack, and was an 83-minute-long masterpiece called *Snow White and the Seven Dwarfs*.

No one at the time could believe it. Disney animator Ward Kimball once recalled, "You can have no idea of the impact that having these drawings suddenly speak and make noises had on audiences at that time. People went crazy over it."

The critical and financial success of *Snow White and the Seven Dwarfs* helped launch the Golden Age of Animation, during which Disney's company produced movies they are still known for today, including *Pinocchio*, *Bambi*, *Dumbo*, and *Fantasia*.

Indeed, some 80 years after the release of *Steamboat Willie*, Disney (shown in Figure 1.1) remains the most famous cartoon filmmaker of all time, even though he passed away in 1966. His corporation, The Walt Disney Company, nets about $35 billion every year.

Figure 1.1
Walt Disney is still a legend, even today.

HOW THEY MAKE PICTURES MOVE

The *Persistence of Vision theory* states that human beings (that is, you or I) compile flashes of images in time to create seamless perception in order to survive. In other words, flickering images can seem to be one continuous image in motion. This scientific theory forms the basis of moving pictures, including cartoon animation.

Thaumatropes and Flipbooks

This theory was beautifully illustrated by a clever optical contraption called a *thaumatrope*. A thaumatrope is a disc held between two pieces of string or mounted on the end of a pencil that could be quickly twirled, making both sides of the disc blur together until they look like a faultless scene. Though originally a scientist's tool, the thaumatrope quickly became a cute toy kids got at Christmas.

Similar to the thaumatrope was a novelty called a flipper book, or *flipbook*, which appeared worldwide in 1868. If you held a flipbook in one hand and used the other hand to flip the pages of the book, the drawings on the pages would create the illusion of continuous action. Figure 1.2 shows an example of a flipbook.

Figure 1.2
An example of a flipbook.

Exercise 1: Creating a Flipbook

One of the best ways to experiment with the Persistence of Vision theory is to create your own flipbook. Anyone can make a small flipbook—it's not that hard. You might have made something like it before in grade school. Here's how:

1. Plan your animation beforehand. Keep it short and sweet, because otherwise you will have more to draw, more paper to fill up, and more time to put in than you might want to devote.

2. Find a blank notebook containing unlined paper. You can use a pad of tracing paper, which works faster, but if you are using unlined notebook paper or a sketchbook, here's what you do: Close the notebook and, using a Sharpie or pen, draw one or more black marks across the top of all of the pages in the book. These can be your placement guides.

3. Open the notebook and, on the first page, draw the picture you want to start with.

4. Trace the picture onto the next page, this time making subtle changes to it as you do.

5. Repeat the last step, drawing page after page and adding subtle changes to the image each time, until you get to the end of your animation.

6. Now, close the book and hold one end closed with one hand and flip the pages with the other—notice how your illustration seems to be animated! That's all there is to it.

Animation Techniques

Although equipment and materials have improved over the years, the way animated cartoons are made has changed very little.

A motion picture is a sequence of tiny pictures called *frames*. The Persistence of Vision theory enables us to see continuous movement where there are actually multiple still images.

You make a film by taking photos of thousands of segments of action. These photos are combined into one extensive filmstrip, with each photo comprising a single frame. A projector shines light through each frame as the filmstrip rolls from beginning to end, magnifying the image on each frame onto a screen. Each frame is held still in front of the light just long enough to see it. Then a shutter comes down while the next frame is positioned. The frame rate change happens so quickly you don't even notice the individual frames or the shutter speed. Indeed, without the shutter between frames, the film would look like one long blur.

There are typically 24 to 30 frames for each second of film, with the average frames per second (fps) for television being 27. Although the perceptual difference between 12fps and 24fps is negligible, most media producers believe that higher frame rates result in more fluid viewing and industry standards must be kept up with.

Although digital filmmaking has since replaced the need for filmstrips and shutters with computer technology, thousands of individual frames still show action, but the speed and order in which they are shown are controlled by computer programs.

Traditional Animation

The main difference between traditional animation and digital animation is the use of computers. *Traditional animation* does not use computers to effectively create 2D animation; instead, artists draw and paint each frame by hand. They draw images onto cels, which were originally celluloid sheets, and layer them with backdrops and other animated elements. This is why traditional animation is sometimes called cel animation.

What follows is a breakdown of the traditional animation process.

First, the cartoon animator breaks each scene down into different movements, as shown in Figure 1.3. Each animator works on drawing one movement at a time. Each picture drawn is called an *extreme*, and each extreme is numbered. The numbers on the extremes tell the other animators how many extra stages need to be drawn in between to complete the whole action.

The animator has a chart representing what will happen during each split second of film, including sound effects and voiceovers, and frame numbers to reveal the pacing speed. The movements drawn have to match up, or synch, to the recorded sound.

Once all of the extremes are drawn by one group of animators, they are passed off to other members of the animating team to do all of the drawings in

Figure 1.3
One example of motion breakdown, by Ronald Fong.

between the extremes; these members are called *in-betweeners*. The numbers on the extremes show the in-betweeners how many pictures need to be drawn.

Animators, especially in-betweeners, work on a flat box with a glass surface, called a light box, to draw the frames (see Figure 1.4). Light shining up through

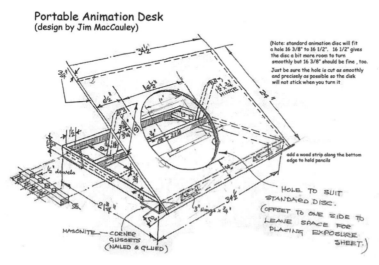

Figure 1.4
A guide for making a portable light box for animators, designed by Jim MacCauley.

the glass surface of the light box lets the artist stack several sheets of paper on top of one another and still see the papers underneath. This is an efficient way to trace over characters to make minute changes to demonstrate motion. It works more efficiently than using tracing paper or roughly copying images using guidelines like you would with flipbooks.

The finished drawings, the extremes, and the in-betweens are then traced onto transparent cels. Each cel is turned over and painted on the back so that the brush strokes are not apparent from the front.

In the old days, the cels, when dry, went to shooting, where they were photographed one by one on a rostrum camera. The rostrum camera took stop-motion pictures and combined them into one reel of film. Background scenery was painted on long rolls of paper and laid on the plate of the cartoon camera with the cels placed on top. The background scenery could be rolled to either side on rollers. As the camera took pictures, this made the character look as if it was moving across the background.

Nowadays, this type of camera is obsolete, replaced by digital scanners.

This may sound tedious and time-consuming, and in many ways it is. If you could go back in time and watch a studio work to produce a single cartoon before the advent of computer technology, your mind would be boggled. To get from simple hand drawings to animated features is often a laborious process involving many animators and long months of effort. It took the developers of *The Secret of NIMH* (1982) over two years to make that charming animated film, which is shown in Figure 1.5.

Today, most animators use a combination of traditional and digital animation, with a heavy emphasis on the digital, but Walt Disney Animation Studios returned to traditional hand-drawn animation with *The Princess and the Frog* (2009) and several companies have since followed suit.

Traditional animation is the oldest and most historically fashionable form of animation. Many people claim that there is more of a human touch, and, therefore, more appeal in hand-drawn animations. This is something you should remember when you embark on animation yourself.

Figure 1.5
The Secret of NIMH (1982) only used traditional animation.

Digital Animation

Two-dimensional animation principles have changed little as the industry has switched from traditional to digital media, but today digital animation is aided by computer technology, making the need for special cameras and cel painting nearly obsolete.

Instead, figures are created and edited digitally using bitmap or vector graphics. This animation approach involves automated computer versions of such traditional animation techniques as in-betweening (now called *tweening*), morphing, onion-skinning, and rotoscoping.

There are even some very popular cartoons that are created completely on computers that never have to leave the digital environment. These shows are produced by skilled digital animators and include such programs as *Foster's Home for Imaginary Friends*, *The Powerpuff Girls*, *South Park*, *The Grim Adventures of Billy & Mandy*, and *El Tigre: The Adventures of Manny Rivera*.

There are several 2D animation software applications used to make cartoons, with probably the most popular being Adobe Flash.

Other programs, like Toon Boom Studio (www.toonboom.com), Anime Studio (www.anime.smithmicro.com), and DigiCel Flipbook (www.digicelinc.com) (see Figure 1.6.), can output files for the Web, television, or video with ease and many of them have a similar look and feel that allows you to acclimate to them quickly.

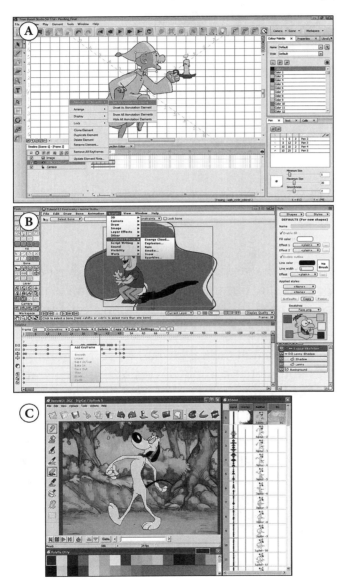

Figure 1.6
(A) Toon Boom Studio, (B) Anime Studio, and (C) DigiCel Flipbook.

The following are prices for the software packages shown in Figure 1.6:

- **Toon Boom Studio** (www.toonboom.com): $329
- **Anime Studio** (www.anime.smithmicro.com): $49 for the Debut version
- **DigiCel Flipbook** (www.digicelinc.com): $298 for the Studio version

Adobe Flash Used in Digital Animation   You may already be familiar with Adobe Flash, because of the countless Flash animations you see on the Web, like the ones at Newgrounds.com. Many animators employ Flash to produce content for Internet distribution because Flash allows them to release projects well under file size limitations.

Look at the Flash interface shown in Figure 1.7.

When it comes to Flash animated cartoons, also called *webtoons*, the first noted use was in 1999 when *Ren & Stimpy* creator John Kricfalusi set out to bring cartoons to the Web. Soon after, webtoons began popping up everywhere.

Some webtoons became so trendy, due in part to programming networks like MTV and G4, that they have appeared on national television. These include

Figure 1.7
The Adobe Flash interface.

Figure 1.8
Comic carnage is typical in the Flash-made cartoon *Happy Tree Friends*.

Happy Tree Friends (shown in Figure 1.8) and the politically minded *Jib-Jab* shorts. Some webtoons, like James Farr's *Xombie* and Jonathan Ian Mathers' *Foamy the Squirrel*, became DVD productions with popular comic merchandise and toy lines.

HISTORY OF VIDEO GAMES

Animation laid the path for the graphical games that would come later. As you can probably tell, video games wouldn't be the same without those pretty animations.

Games have evolved from board and tabletop games to the tiny worlds of primitive 8-bit graphics to the high-quality next-generation landscapes of games that make even Hollywood directors envious. Electronic games, like cell phones, e-mail, digital cameras, and faux-hawk haircuts, are still very new to our society, even though you may have grown up playing them and can't imagine a world without them. Yet electronic games haven't been around that long. In fact, they didn't really start to take off until the 1970s.

Even so, video games have quickly risen to a competent entertainment medium, right alongside books, movies, music, and artwork. The game design industry, in fact, is the largest growing industry in America today.

ABI Research, an independent technology market research firm, estimates that video game sales from 2005, around $32.6 billion, are going to double to around $65.9 billion in 2011. Right now, sales of video games have topped sales of CDs, videos, and DVDs—making more money than either the movie or music industry. This global economic expansion has ushered in a need for skilled programmers and talented game artists. Game design schools have sprung up all across the world to meet the rising demand for game development.

A single game may take a team of 20 to 300 or more individual programmers, artists, animators, sound engineers, and directors—and may cost upward of $500,000 (usually around $50 million for a big triple-A title) to make. A game design team is often funded by a game publisher, such as Microsoft, Nintendo, Electronic Arts, or Activision, for exclusive publishing rights. Once the game is made, it must hit the store shelves running and make as much money in the first month as possible or it might wind up in the bargain bins or (gasp!) returned to the manufacturer.

Will Wright, the creator of *The Sims* and *Spore*, said in an article for *WIRED Magazine* that "games have the potential to subsume almost all other forms of entertainment media. They can tell us stories, offer us music, give us challenges, allow us to communicate and interact with others, encourage us to make things, connect us to new communities, and let us play. Unlike most other forms of media, games are inherently malleable... And more than ever, games will be a visible, external amplification of the human imagination."

Console Games

In 1961, Digital Equipment Corporation donated their latest computer to the Massachusetts Institute of Technology (MIT). It was called the Programmed Data Processor-1, or PDP-1. Compared to most computers at the time, the PDP-1 was comparatively modest in size, only as big as a large automobile!

Like most universities, MIT had several campus organizations, one of which was the Tech Model Railroad Club, or TMRC. TMRC appealed to students who liked to build things and see how they worked. They programmed for the PDP-1 for fun.

Steve Russell, nicknamed "Slug," was a typical science-fiction-loving nerd who joined TMRC. He put nearly 6 months and 200 hours into completing an interactive game where two players controlled rocket ships. Using toggle switches built into the PDP-1, players controlled the speed and direction of their ships and fired torpedoes at each other. Russell called his game *Spacewar!* Thanks to "Slug," this game launched a whole new trend amongst programmers and became the predecessor for future arcade games.

Entrepreneur Nolan Bushnell saw *Spacewar!* and turned it into the first coin-op arcade game, called *Computer Space*, in 1971. *Pong* and *Asteroids* followed shortly thereafter.

Pong, some people argue, was the first game created, as it appeared in 1958 as a table tennis game on an oscilloscope built by Willy Higinbotham at the Brookhave National Labs in New York; it was later demonstrated on a console in 1972 by Magnavox and "appropriated" by Atari in the same year. But most tech historians agree that *Spacewar!* really started the video game industry. You can see an early arcade poster for *Pong* in Figure 1.9.

After the success of his *Computer Space* coin-op game, Nolan Bushnell, along with Ted Dabney, went on to found Atari, which, roughly translated, means "Watch out, I win!" or "Check!" in the Japanese board game *Go*. Bushnell later

Figure 1.9
An early Atari poster advertising the arcade version of *Pong*.

left Atari to start a chain of pizza parlors with arcade games right inside them; he originally called his pizza arcade Pizza Time Theater, but the company eventually changed its name to Chuck E. Cheese.

Atari started with arcade games but eventually became better known for their console games, which they continued making, one right after the other, bringing video games into people's homes for the first time in history. You can see an Atari home console system in Figure 1.10.

Then a curious thing happened: sales plummeted and the game industry slumped. Console sales bottomed out in 1983, causing everyone to question whether the industry could ever recover.

Several theories for this slump have been supposed, one of which says that with so much market saturation, development studios were pressured to crank out games quickly. This led to imitative, low-quality titles.

One of the worst was the Atari game *E.T.* It was a rush job put out for Christmas to tie in to the Steven Spielberg movie and ended up with millions of units being sent back to the factories and later buried in a landfill, which is totally understandable if you've ever played the game. The game had lousy graphics, incomprehensible rules, and no storyline whatsoever.

Figure 1.10
The Atari CX2600-A console system is similar to the one I owned in the 1980s.

You can even see the Wintergreen video for "When I Wake Up," inspired by this game, on YouTube at www.youtube.com/watch?v=8Rt_3_bQVJU.

Thankfully, the video game industry recovered. In 1985, the video game "Golden Age" began. With the advent of technical innovations, and with Nintendo, SEGA, Sony, and Microsoft entering the console race, the bar was raised, much to the delight of players. The substance and number of titles released with neat features quadrupled along with sales. Games went from being coded straight on the medal to being distributed on cartridges to being burnt on CD-ROMs or DVDs, evolving along the way from chunky 8-bit graphics to the next-generation photo-realistic images we see today.

At the time of this writing, the industry is dominated by three console giants: Microsoft (Xbox), Sony (PlayStation), and Nintendo (GameCube and Wii), who are all involved in the current console wars (see Figure 1.11). The future of the console wars depends on the consumer, mainly kids and teenagers.

Figure 1.11
A common sight in many American homes. This rack has an Xbox, Xbox 360, GameCube, PlayStation 2, and PSP on it. Most gamers cannot settle for just one console.

Computer Games

Consoles aside, the first computer game was the text-based *Colossal Cave*, but it wasn't until Donald Woods expanded the idea and made Infocom's *Zork* in 1979 that programmers everywhere were inspired to make their own computer games.

One of these developers was Roberta Williams, who, next to *Centipede* originator Dona Bailey, was one of the first female game designers. Roberta Williams launched the Sierra On-Line company with her husband. Back in the day, they'd package their computer games, distributed on floppy disks, in Ziploc baggies while sitting at their kitchen table.

Most of these early computer games were adventure games, also known as text-parser games, because players had to type in two-word combinations to interact with the game world, such as "walk north" or "get sword." Here was a typical, and rather sad, example of text adventure game play:

```
> kill monster
Be more specific?
> stab monster
Do not understand "stab"?
> hit monster
Hit monster with what?
> hit monster with sword
You are not currently equipped with "sword".
> run away
The monster's hideously long tentacles wrap around you, squeezing your torso
until you can no longer breathe. You have died. Your quest ends here.
```

As the level of graphics in computer games grew, mostly due to the invention of DirectX and Direct3D libraries, so did adventure games, replacing text choices with picture icons. LucasArts™ produced graphical point-and-click adventure games (sometimes not-so-lovingly referred to as "hunt-the-pixel" games) like *Maniac Mansion* and *Secret of Monkey Island* and set the standard for the genre. These games evolved into today's adventure and hunt-the-pixel games, of which *A Vampyre Story* is one example, as seen in Figure 1.12.

Networked computer games started when Rick Blomme made the very first multiplayer games at the University of Illinois in 1961. He used a software program still popular today for use with electronic-based education; it is called

Figure 1.12
A not-so-typical point-and-click adventure game is *A Vampyre Story*, published by Crimson Cow.

PLATO. His early games were mostly based on *Star Trek* or *Dungeons and Dragons*, but they were still not *true* online games because they were played over a network, such as a LAN, and not the Internet.

It wasn't until 1979 that some fellows in Essex in the United Kingdom created the first Multi-User Dungeon, or MUD, on Arpanet (the system that would later become the Internet). MUDs instantly became popular role-playing game communities on college campuses everywhere and the precedent for modern online games. MUDs, like the earliest adventure games, were text-based, and it wasn't until nearly 20 years later they started incorporating graphics.

Players today can immerse themselves in role-playing or strategy games played online, such as Blizzard Entertainment's *World of WarCraft*. With the sheer number of homes possessing computer technology and broadband or DSL connectivity, it's no surprise that computer games are just as popular as ever. There are many games with downloadable content that supplements and extends replayability. There are map editors, mod communities, machinima, patches, wallpaper, desktop goodies, and loads more available on the Internet for these games.

Here is an interesting bit of trivia. According to a 2007 report from the market research NPD Group, among kids aged 2 to 17 who play games online, an average of 39 percent of their time is spent playing games online as opposed to offline. Kids ages 15 to 17 spend even *more* time online than that and are considered superusers, or players who spend 16 hours or more per week on gaming. That is as much time as most adults spend at a part-time job!

Flash Games

Just as Adobe Flash became the predominant building environment for digital animations, a lot of Web-based games have started using Adobe Flash to make games, because of the ease of file publishing and online distribution. Strangely enough, the forerunners to using Flash to make games were advertisement companies making animated banners for commercial Web sites.

The types of Flash games now hitting the Internet closely imitate the older console games of the 1980s. There are several *Tetris* and *Pac-Man* clones, but these can be seen as rudimentary experiments testing the technology, because Flash's ActionScript coding language allows for endless versatility. Although Flash focuses primarily on two-dimensional bitmap and vector art, it has the potential for three-dimensional rooms and objects, and many users have had success making 2D/3D hybrid games with it.

Because Flash is an all-in-one kit for creating vector art; putting together bitmap art, audio, and video; and programming interactive functionality, it is ideal for game designers, especially when Flash ports to so many devices, including mobile and handheld devices and any hardware that has an Internet connection and browser interface.

Several multiplayer games built with Flash have become mainstream market games, such as *Dofus* (www.dofus.com), *Habbo* (www.habbo.com), *Disney's Club Penguin* (www.clubpenguin.com), *The Continuum* (www.thecontinuum.com), and *Neopets* (www.neopets.com).

WHAT'S NEXT?

That was certainly a lot of information to take in at once, I know. So get yourself a drink, take a breather, and get ready to learn about Sony and their PSP handheld console system, and the Adobe Flash program you'll use to make games you can play on your PSP.

CHAPTER 2

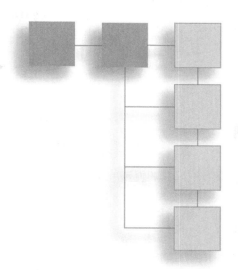

WHAT IS IT?

In this chapter you will learn:

- What game systems Sony has released
- Where the PSP comes from
- How the PSP works
- Where Flash came from and how it's used
- How you can break into the PSP developer market

By "it," I mean the Sony PSP (PlayStation Portable) and the Adobe Flash program. What is the Sony PSP, and where did it come from? How did Flash become so important to game developers? The answers to these questions are what you will learn in this chapter. The rest of the book will show you how to use them.

A LOOK AT SONY

Sony Computer Entertainment, Inc. (SCEI) is a video game company that specializes in multiple areas of game development, and (as you can probably guess) is a subsidiary of Sony, the major electronics company.

SCEI was established on November 16, 1993, in Tokyo, prior to the launch of the first PlayStation (PSX) video game console system. The logo, which is shown in Figure 2.1, has been used since 1994.

Figure 2.1
The SCEI logo.

Kicking It PS-Style

Sony Computer Entertainment (SCE) produces the PlayStation video game consoles and handhelds.

PSX

Sony's first widely recognized home console release was the PlayStation (code-named the PSX, later nicknamed the PSOne). The PSX was originally developed to be a CD-ROM drive add-on for Nintendo's Super Nintendo Entertainment System (SNES) video game console. This was in response to Sega's Sega CD, released 1992. When the prospect of releasing the game system as an add-on for the SNES dissolved, Sony decided to redesign the machine into a stand-alone unit, which they called the PlayStation.

Figure 2.2
The first Sony PlayStation machine, the PSX.

The PSX was released in Japan on December 3, 1994, and later in North America on September 9, 1995. You can see a picture of the PSX in Figure 2.2.

PlayStation 2 (PS2)

One of the highest selling home console systems of all time, SCE's second home console, the PS2 was released in Japan on March 4, 2000, and later in North America and Europe in October and November 2000, respectively.

The PS2 was the first-ever video game console to have DVD playback functionality included straight out of the box.

Today, it has sold up to 150 million units worldwide. You can see a picture of the PS2 in Figure 2.3.

PlayStation 3 (PS3)

The newest home console in the PlayStation family, and Sony's entry in the seventh-generation of consoles, the PlayStation 3 (PS3) was launched in November 2006. It includes unique proprietary hardware, including a graphics processing unit called the Reality Synthesizer (RSX), co-developed by Sony and Nvidia.

Figure 2.3
The second Sony PlayStation machine, the PS2.

PS3 also supports *Blu-ray disc* technology. Blu-ray disc derives its name from the blue-violet laser used to read the disc. Blu-ray disc is an optical disc storage medium developed in 2002 to supersede the standard DVD format. Blu-ray is used for high-definition video, PS3 video games, and other data, with up to 25-gigabyte single-layered or 50-gigabyte dual-layered discs. Many people believe that Blu-ray is the way of the future and will one day completely replace regular DVDs.

Another feature the PS3 heralded was Sony's exclusive *PlayStation Network*, an online multiplayer gaming and digital media delivery service provided and run by SCE for use with the PS3 and PSP game consoles. As of February 12, 2010, there were over 40 million registered PlayStation Network user accounts worldwide. You can see the logo for the PlayStation Network in Figure 2.4.

The PS3, as shown in Figure 2.5, competes with Microsoft's Xbox 360® and Nintendo's Wii as one of the three top video game console systems today.

The PS3's American release was so dramatic, it was fraught with violence. Reports surrounding its American debut include one customer getting shot, campers robbed at gunpoint, customers shot in a drive-by shooting with BB guns, and sixty campers fighting tooth and nail over ten game systems.

Figure 2.4
The logo for the PlayStation Network.

Figure 2.5
The third Sony PlayStation machine, the PS3.

PSP

The PSP is SCE's first major foray into the field of handheld gaming, which has always been dominated by Nintendo. The PSP was officially unveiled at the Electronic Entertainment Expo (E3) conference in 2004 and released in Japan on December 12, 2004, and in North America on March 24, 2005.

Sales of the PSP have, with some exceptions, lagged behind those of its competitor, the Nintendo DS. Nevertheless, the console is "the most successful non-Nintendo handheld game system ever sold" writer Matt Matthews said in his article "Opinion: What Will the PSP Do in 2009?" posted on Gamasutra.com, December 2008.

The PSP, shown in Figure 2.6, has seen two major redesigns since its initial launch. The redesigns included a smaller size, more internal memory, a better quality liquid crystal display (LCD) screen, and a lighter weight.

The PSP allows access to the PS3 game console from a remote location using the PS3's WLAN capabilities, a home network, or wireless router and PSP's built-in *Remote Play*. Features that can be utilized through Remote Play include photos, slideshows, music, and videos.

Figure 2.6
The Sony PlayStation Portable, or PSP.

Figure 2.7
The latest redesign of the Sony PSP is the smaller, lighter PSP Go.

A new design, the PSP Go, was released at the end of 2009. It has a 3.8" LCD that slides up to reveal the main controls underneath. The PSP Go is 45% lighter and 56% smaller than the original PSP. It also supports Bluetooth® wireless connectivity and is meant to exist completely digital, meaning all media must be downloaded or transferred to the device, which has 16 gigabytes of internal Flash memory storage.

You can see an image of the PSP Go in Figure 2.7.

This book will give you the skills and know-how to make Flash games that you can play on the Sony PSP.

Sony Software Development

Sony Computer Entertainment Worldwide Studios (SCE WWS) is a subsidiary of SCE. It is a group of video game developers fully owned by SCE, that primarily build games for Sony consoles.

The internally owned Sony studios in the SCE WWS include the following:

- **Bigbig Studios** (Europe)—makers of *Pursuit Force* and *MotorStorm: Arctic Edge*

- **Cambridge Studio** (Europe)—makers of *MediEvil*, *PlayTV*, and *PlayStation Home* with SCE London Studio

- **Clap Hanz** (Japan)—makers of *Everybody's Golf* and *Everybody's Tennis*

- **Evolution Studios** (Europe)—makers of *MotorStorm* and *World Rally Championship*

- **Guerrilla Games** (Europe)—makers of the *Killzone* series

- **Incognito Entertainment** (United States)—makers of *Warhawk* with SCE Studios Santa Monica, the *Twisted Metal* series, *Downhill Domination*, and *Calling All Cars*

- **Japan Studio** (Japan)—makers of *Ape Escape*, *Siren*, *LocoRoco*, and *Patapon*

- **Liverpool Studio** (Europe)—makers of *Wipeout* and *F1*

- **London Studio** (Europe)—makers of *SingStar*, *Eyetoy*, and *PlayStation Home* with SCE Studio Cambridge

- **Media Molecule** (Europe)—makers of *LittleBigPlanet*

- **Naughty Dog** (United States)—makers of *Crash Bandicoot*, the *Jak & Daxter* series, and the *Uncharted* series

- **Polyphony Digital** (Japan)—makers of *Gran Turismo*, *Motor Toon Grand Prix 2*, *Tourist Trophy*, and *Omega Boost*

- **San Diego Studio** (United States)—makers of *NBA*, *MLB: The Show*, and *Modnation Racers*

- **Santa Monica Studio** (United States)—makers of *Kinetica*, the *God of War* series, and *Warhawk* with Incognito Entertainment

- **Sony Bend** (United States)—makers of *Syphon Filter* and *Resistance: Retribution*

- **Sony Online Entertainment** (United States)—makers of *EverQuest*

- **Team ICO** (Japan)—makers of *Shadow of the Colossus*, *Ico*, and *The Last Guardian*

- **Zipper Interactive** (United States)—makers of the *SOCOM: U.S. Navy SEALs* series

Since its inception in 1993, SCE has also built up a large stable of third-party developers who often collaborate with them in a variety of manners, from publishing to funding to co-development. These companies are not owned or under contract with SCE.

They include partners such as Insomniac Games (makers of the *Ratchet & Clank* series), Sucker Punch Productions (makers of the *Sly Cooper* series), and Quantic Dream (makers of *Heavy Rain*).

A Look at Adobe Flash

Adobe Flash is a multimedia program designed specifically for creating animated and interactive content on the Web.

Flash began as FutureSplash, which former American graphics and web-development software house Macromedia acquired in 1997. Shortly after acquiring it, Macromedia shortened the name "FutureSplash" to "Flash."

Macromedia's top rival, Adobe Systems, obtained Flash from Macromedia when Adobe Systems bought out Macromedia on December 3, 2005. Adobe Systems, Inc. is an American software company headquartered in San Jose, California. Adobe Systems has historically focused on the creation of multimedia and creativity software packages, with a more recent foray into rich Internet application software development.

Adobe Flash, currently a part of the Creative Suite 5 (CS5) package (as seen in Figure 2.8), combines motion, graphics, sound, and interactive functionality in a format proficient for a web page.

Flash has long been a popular tool for making cartoons and games, and what you learn from this book will serve you in developing Flash games and animations for the Web and other platforms just as much as making games for the Sony PSP.

Flash on the Web

Since its introduction in 1996, Flash technology has become the premier tool for adding animation and interactivity to web pages.

Figure 2.8
Adobe Flash CS5.

Shockwave Files (SWFs)

The earliest web pages were incredibly bare: just text with web links on a gray background. That was all the original Web browsers could show. There were no images, special typefaces, or colors.

As web artists saw the potential to do more, from file sharing to e-commerce to entertainment to games, they bellowed for more tools. Static images (ones that didn't move), colors, and typefaces were implemented first. Later, motion rolled out in the form of animated GIF images and SWFs.

SWFs have the .swf file extension, often pronounced "swiff."

Early SWFs appeared ground-breaking, though they were rarely seen because the program used to make them (Macromedia Director) was too complex for everyone to master and because the files it produced were too hefty to be sensible on most web pages.

Today, Flash is the most popular program for creating rich multimedia experiences, in part because it's so versatile and easy to use. Flash also creates small enough SWFs to be useful on a wider number of web pages.

SWFs Used for Entertainment

There are numerous ways Flash can enrich a Web site. Its greatest strength lies in entertainment.

There is simply no better tool for creating an animated web cartoon. Flash has also been used to make cartoons you may have seen on television, such as *Mucha Lucha!, Foster's Home For Imaginary Friends, Atomic Betty*, and more.

More advanced users of the software can create compelling games with Flash.

Places like Newgrounds.com (www.newgrounds.com) showcase both animations and games (as seen in Figure 2.9).

You can use SWFs to create buttons to navigate around a site or make an entire Web site. Several software products, hardware devices, and systems can display SWFs.

Drawbacks of Using SWFs

Flash sounds tempting to use for just about everything, doesn't it? Unfortunately, Flash makes a lot of sense for an entertainment or game site, but for a more mainstream site such as MSN (www.msn.com) or BBC News (http://news.bbc.co.uk)—or for an informative site such as Behind the Name (www.behindthename.com) or AAA Math (www.aaamath.com)—simple text and static graphics work better. Visitors to these sites prefer the more direct experience of a conventional HTML web page, without any flashy animation or moving graphics.

Other Programs Used to Make SWFs

There are a number of other software packages available that can create output in the .swf file format.

Figure 2.9
Updated daily, Newgrounds.com is a host site for loads of Flash content.

Among these are the following:

- **Anime Studio** (http://anime.smithmicro.com)—This program, used in the making of *South Park*, is useful for making animated movies and then exporting them out to SWF or movie files. The Debut version costs $49, while the Pro version costs $199.

- **KoolMoves** (www.koolmoves.com)—KoolMoves is trying to give Flash a run for its money. At $49 and with 3D model importability and ActionScript 3.0 integration, KoolMoves is one of the better bargain alternatives.

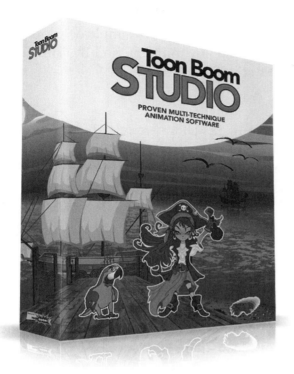

Figure 2.10
Toon Boom Studio.

- **Toon Boom Studio** (www.toonboom.com)—Toon Boom Studio (see Figure 2.10) has been around a while. Its primary focus is on making 2D animated movies. It can also export those movies to SWF files. Toon Boom Studio costs $329.

- **Toufee** (www.toufee.com)—Toufee is a browser-based program that lets you create short Flash animations using pictures, photos, or videos you have on your Desktop. You can add text and transition effects. Toufee is free to try and subscriptions cost $59 per year.

These front ends often provide additional support for creating cartoons, with tools more tailored to traditionally trained animators.

Flash is still the most versatile software used to make SWFs, because it not only creates animated cartoons but also interactive media and electronic games using its scripting language *ActionScript*. ActionScript is a very simple object-oriented programming language specific to the Flash environment, and by "simple" I mean you don't have to be a rocket scientist to use it.

The Flash Player

To exhibit Flash content, a web user must install a particular piece of software called a *plug-in*. The necessary Flash plug-in is called Flash Player. Flash Player is free, and approximately 98% of all web users already have some version of it installed on their computer. Flash is an integrated development environment, or IDE, while Flash Player is a virtual machine used to run Flash files over a Web browser.

The PSP, since firmware 2.70 on, has a Flash Player plug-in built into its Web browser. This is what enables you to play Flash games on the PSP.

How Flash Can Go Fast

If you've ever surfed the Internet using a slow browser, you might have noticed how some pages took longer to download than others. File size has a huge influence on how fast web pages display.

Used well, Flash can create relatively small SWFs that are easy-to-download and rich with animation, sound, and interactivity. Besides its built-in file compression function, there are two reasons why Flash can go so fast: because it uses vectors and because it uses reusable symbols.

Vector versus Bitmap

Vector graphics are one reason why Flash files are so small. Flash is a vector-based graphics program.

There are two basic types of graphics you can create on a computer: *bitmap* or *vector*. Most web pages display bitmap graphics in either JPEG or GIF formats, but with vector format there are several advantages.

A bitmap (often called raster) image file is composed of tiny squares (or pixels) of color information, which when viewed together create an illusion that we perceive as a photograph or other piece of artwork (see Figure 2.11). You may have seen pixels if you've ever zoomed in on an image in a graphics program such as Photoshop. Generally, one GIF or JPEG image is composed of thousands of pixels.

Figure 2.11
A close-up look at a bitmap image.

Graphics come with instructions, and the instructions a GIF or JPEG image give to your computer are, "Make this pixel that color, that pixel that color, and so on..."

A vector image tells your computer, "Make this geometric shape, and make it this color, and make it good." By "make it good" I mean that vector images are unique in their display quality. A vector shape will always look snappy whether resized smaller or bigger—even if it's resized to the dimensions of a billboard.

A bitmap can look pretty good, but it almost certainly won't look so good enlarged like that.

See Figure 2.12 for a comparison.

Flash highlights vector graphics but supports bitmap graphics too. Bitmaps are still better at reproducing photographs, which is one reason bitmaps are still used in making roadside billboards, while vectors have the digital edge in rendering type and shapes.

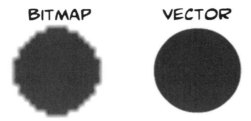

Figure 2.12
The comparison between bitmap and vector graphics.

Importance of Flash Symbols

A Flash *symbol* is any reusable object created and used within the Flash program. A symbol can be reused throughout your project. There are three categories of symbols, based on their function: Graphics, Buttons, and Movie-clips. We'll get into these later.

A copy of a symbol used in a movie is called an *instance*, which can have its own independent properties, like color, size, and functionality, different from the original symbol. All symbols used in a Flash project are stored in the Library from where you can drag-and-drop new instances of the symbols into your movie. When a symbol is edited, all of its constituent instances are updated automatically, but changing the effects or dimensions of a single instance of a symbol will not affect the original symbol or other instances.

Using Flash symbols is crucial to the file size of your project. The Flash file size depends largely on the file size of all of the content (including graphics, video, audio, text, and more) you employ in your Flash project. Here, the major advantage of using symbols is that a symbol's size is taken into consideration only once, no matter if it's used a thousand times within the project! Unused symbols in your Library are not counted at all in the final file size of your project. This is the true power of Flash.

The three categories of symbols are described as follows:

▪ **Graphic symbols**—Graphic symbols are reusable static images that are used primarily to create animations. Any drawn vector or imported bit-map image or combination thereof can be converted into a single graphic symbol. You can also place text in a graphic symbol.

- **Button symbols**—Button symbols are used for timeline navigation. Similar to buttons you might've seen on other Web sites, you can click the buttons to take you forward or back in the Flash project or make things happen within the project. Button symbols are useful for providing interactivity in a Flash project.

- **Movieclip symbols**—Movieclip symbols are reusable pieces of Flash animation. They're like having a Flash within a Flash, because they consist of their own timeline and can have embedded graphic symbols, button symbols, or other movieclip symbols inside them.

The three symbol types are used throughout Flash, and the more you use these symbols, the smaller your SWFs will be, making the SWFs port easier to other platforms.

WHAT'S NEXT?

In the next chapter, you'll open up Adobe Flash and navigate its interface, getting used to the workspace. Once you know how to get around in Flash and develop vector images, we'll concentrate on how to draw. There's a lot of ground to cover before you can make Flash games for the PSP, but we'll get to it eventually.

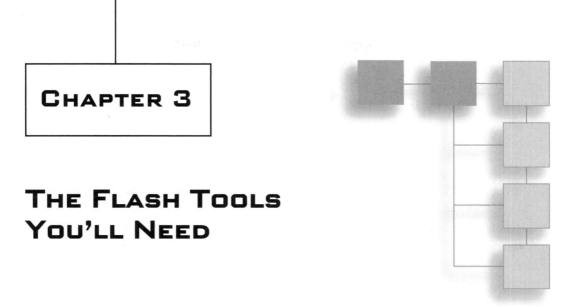

CHAPTER 3

THE FLASH TOOLS YOU'LL NEED

In this chapter you will learn:

- What makes Flash such a versatile tool for you to use
- How to find your way around the Flash application
- How to draw, color, and modify vector art objects on the Stage
- How to use layers, layer folders, and text in your Flash document
- How to import bitmap graphics from outside sources to use in your movie

The Adobe Flash program is the one piece of software you will learn to use to make animations and games for the Sony PSP. There are other programs out there that can make SWFs, and there are other (more complicated) programs for making PSP games, but for ease of use and adaptability Adobe Flash is hands-down the best you can use for making homebrewed PSP games.

In this chapter you will learn how to use Flash. This is crucial, as you will make Flash movies and games for the PSP later in this book.

TAKE A TOUR OF THE FLASH PROGRAM

If you are familiar with other graphics programs, especially those programs within the Adobe Creative Suite (such as Photoshop or Illustrator), you will be way ahead of most of us in learning Flash.

To use Flash, all you need is a personal computer, the Flash software, and a browser with the latest version of the Flash Player installed. If you can't get a copy of Flash and aren't sure you want to buy it yet, Adobe provides a free 30-day trial version you can download from their Web site: www.adobe.com/downloads. Once you've installed Flash, you should have everything you need.

For this book, we will be using Adobe Flash CS5, as that is the most recent edition of the Flash program at the time of this writing. If you are using an older, or more recent, edition of Flash, you should still be able to do all of the lessons in this book. The only difference will be where certain commands or panels or tools are located, as the workspace varies between Flash editions. Otherwise, all of the Flash editions work practically the same. If you find yourself stuck, however, search Google® for the answer.

Now that you have a working copy of Flash, open up the Flash program and go to File > New to start a new document from scratch. Be sure, for now, to make a new Flash document using ActionScript 2.0. ActionScript 2.0 is the scripting language version we will be using later in this book to program our games. Although you can make games in ActionScript 3.0, and we'll look at that, 2.0 is fine for doing typical app creation.

There are four main parts to the Flash program: the Stage, the Timeline, the menu bar, and panels. See Figure 3.1 as we discuss each of them.

All of Flash Is a Stage

First, there's the Stage where you assemble everything you want seen in your Flash product. The Stage is your main workspace in Flash. You can draw, select, and reposition artwork here. Although it's not a perfect preview of your finished movie, the Stage does display where objects are placed and how they change according to the Timeline.

Flash provides you a workspace surrounding the Stage to place stuff on while you are working. Stuff you've moved off of the Stage will not appear in your final product.

Take a Look at the Timeline

Accompanying the Stage is the Timeline, which is where you determine what happens when. The Timeline, as the name implies, shows you a scale of time for when events can take place within your movie.

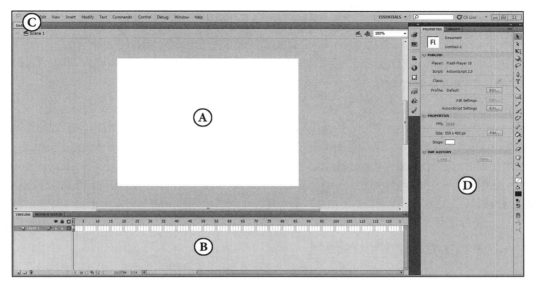

Figure 3.1
(A) The Stage, (B) Timeline, (C) the menu bar, and (D) panels.

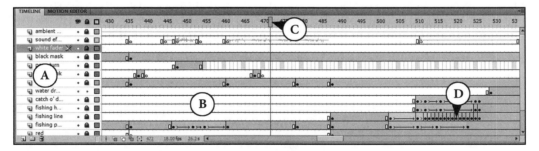

Figure 3.2
(A) Layers, (B) frames, (C) playhead, and (D) keyframe.

The Timeline window is really composed of two main sections: the layers section where content is stacked according to virtual depth and the frames section where content is planned in frames (see Figure 3.2).

In the layers section of the Timeline, you can label and organize your stacks of frame rows. You can also lock or hide individual layers. Each frame on the Timeline, indicated by cells from left to right, represents an increment of time.

The moveable red frame indicator, also called the playhead, determines what frame is currently shown on the Stage. Special frames, called keyframes, mark changed views on the Stage. Dots, arrows, comments, and other markings indicate what is happening from frame to frame.

Beneath the Timeline are a few important buttons. The first will center the current frame in the Timeline. The others are for the onion skin feature, which allows you to view/edit multiple frames at once. The numbers to the right of these indicate the current frame number, the frame rate (how fast the movie is set to flow), and how much time has elapsed up to the current frame number.

What's on the Menu Bar?

The menu bar—which you may be familiar with in other programs—appears at the top of the program window and displays command categories. The menu bar gives you access to many of the program's features. Click on a category to pull down a menu to select from a list of commands.

For instance, to open a new document in Flash you can go to File > New. Over the course of this text you will be told to select a command from the menu bar in this fashion. The command will start with the main menu's categories (in this case, File) and may be followed by a submenu, ending with the command itself (in this case, New).

Most menu items have keyboard shortcuts. Shortcuts save you time for commands you use frequently. They are usually displayed alongside the menu commands so that you can easily remember the ones you want to. Not every command, however, has a shortcut.

Panels

Most of the controls you need to change elements on the Stage and Timeline are found in the last part of Flash, the panels. *Panels* are small windows that can float or remain docked in the Flash workspace. Each panel has controls dedicated to specific tasks such as selecting tools, changing colors, or writing actions for selected objects. You can open new panels from the Windows category on the menu bar.

The upper right corner of most panels has a minus-sign symbol used to minimize or collapse the panel and an X symbol to close the panel. Directly under those is an arrow symbol you can click to bring up the panel options list specific to that panel. Several panels have white boxes for input where you designate object properties like color code or line thickness. Many of these input boxes are accompanied by sliders or drop-down menus, so you don't have to remember what to type.

You can group panels in Flash to suit the way you work. To do this, just drag a panel's tab and release it over the top of another panel's name tab. To separate them, or to undock a panel, simply drag one panel's tab away from those of the other panels. Once you have several panels opened the way you want them, you can save that arrangement by going to Window > Workspace > Save Current. Anytime after that, you can select your workspace from the Window > Workspace submenu to instantly rearrange the panels to the saved arrangement.

There are two main panels you will use time and again.

The first panel you'll become very familiar with is the Tools panel. By default, it appears on the right-most side of the Flash workspace. The Tools panel has every tool on it that you use in Flash production, displayed as icons. If you hover over a tool icon, a tool tip will pop up to tell you the name of that tool. Most tools work just like you'd think they work. The Brush tool lets you paint on the Stage, and the Text tool lets you write words on the Stage. We'll look at the tools in a moment.

The second most commonly used panel is the Properties panel, shown in Figure 3.3. This context-sensitive panel shows up automatically in most default workspaces, and with it you can alter the properties of the movie or individual objects selected on the Stage.

Tip

Never be afraid to try something you haven't before in Flash. Anything you draw, erase, delete, change, or otherwise modify can be undone with a single command. Choose Edit > Undo (Ctrl+Z for Windows or Cmd+Z for Macintosh) and the last thing you did in Flash will be undone as if it never even happened. You can repeat this command, too, thereby undoing more than one successive modification.

Figure 3.3
The Properties panel.

How to See the Stage Best: Visibility

While working, you may need to zoom in to see some minor detail or zoom out to see "the big picture." There are various tools in Flash that allow you to alter the way you view your Stage, without altering the Stage or the project output.

The Zoom Tool

The Zoom tool, found on the Tools panel, lets you enlarge the view of the Stage area. It looks like a magnifying glass. Click to select the Zoom tool and click your cursor anywhere on the Stage to zoom in to that area for a closer look. Click more than once to enlarge the view even more. Click and drag to define a rectangular marquee and release, and the view will zoom to cover the area you selected with the marquee.

To zoom back out again, or reduce the view, hold down the Alt (or Option) key on your keyboard before you click with the Zoom tool.

The Hand Tool

To move your view around the Stage, you can click on the scroll bars and sliders on the edges of the Stage, or select and use the Hand tool. The Hand tool, by far, is much quicker and more precise.

Click to select the Hand tool from the Tools panel and your cursor becomes a hand. Just like you would with artwork on your desk, click and drag the hand cursor on the Stage to reposition your view of the work area.

You can also activate the Hand tool at any time during production. No matter what tool you are using, if you press and hold down the Space bar, your cursor will temporarily change into the Hand tool. As soon as you let go of the Space bar, your cursor will revert to whatever tool you were using previously.

Magnification

Current magnification is displayed in the upper right-hand corner of the Stage. A published movie will normally be displayed at 100% in a Web browser window. Anything less than 100% gives you a wider, less detailed view. A value greater than 100% gives you a larger, close-up view. To zoom to an exact percentage, type the number in right there at the upper right-hand corner of your Stage and then press the Enter (or Return) key on your keyboard. Pull down the menu next to the percentage box for preset magnification values.

Rulers and Guides

In most cases you may feel comfortable aligning objects on the Stage by eye, but other times you may want more exactness than that. When that is the case you can use rulers, guides, or a grid (shown in Figure 3.4).

Select View > Rulers option and two rulers will appear at the top and left side of the Stage. These rulers are used as a reference for positioning and aligning objects on the Stage. Click on either ruler and drag a guide, or blue line running from one side of the Stage to the other, onto the Stage. Drag an existing guide to reposition it; or drag it back into the ruler to remove it. Guides are light-colored guidelines to help you align objects vertically or horizontally. They do not show up in your published movie. Once you have placed any guides you want, you can hide or lock them under the View > Guides submenu.

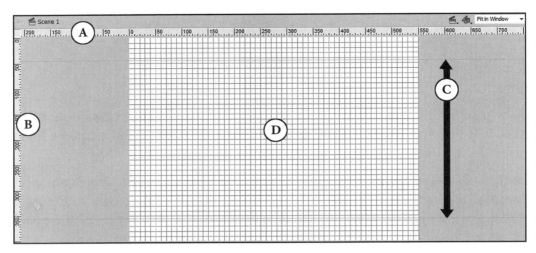

Figure 3.4
(A) Top ruler, (B) side ruler, (C) guidelines, and (D) a grid.

A grid works a lot like guides, except it covers the entire Stage, looking much like graph paper. You can show or hide the grid, and turn its Snap to feature on or off. The Snap to feature will help you align objects to your grid or guides, even if they are hidden.

How to Draw Vector Art in Flash

Drawing in Flash is reasonably straightforward.

Anything you draw in Flash becomes a vector shape. Vector, as we looked at in the last chapter, is a big bonus to Flash users over bitmap or raster images, because vector is (a) scalable, and (b) the quality is not resolution-dependent, meaning it will never look grainy or blurry when magnified.

For simple drawings, use the Pencil, Brush, or Pen tools, as shown in Figure 3.5. Choose one of them and start clicking and dragging around on the Stage. That's fundamentally all you need to do to draw in Flash by hand.

Tip

Some Flash users swear that drawing is made much easier using a Wacom or similar brand digital pen tablet. Digital pen tablets (see Figure 3.6) give you a surface to "write" on with a digital stylus, much like doodling with a regular ballpoint pen. The stylus operates the same as a computer mouse, but with the ease and efficiency of a pen. If you have one to try out and practice on, you might find a digital pen tablet to be useful to you, too, but if you don't, you will have to practice and get better at managing with a computer mouse.

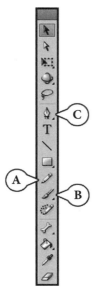

Figure 3.5
The (A) Pencil tool, (B) Brush tool, and (C) Pen tool.

Figure 3.6
A Wacom digital pen tablet.

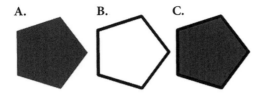

A.   B.   C.

Figure 3.7
An object with a (A) fill, (B) stroke, and (C) both fill and stroke.

Using the Drawing Tools

Every shape created in Flash is vector and can have a fill or stroke, or both (see Figure 3.7). The fill refers to the solid area inside a shape. The stroke outlines a shape or acts as the border of the shape. The Brush tool creates fill-only shapes, and the Pencil tool creates stroke-only shapes. The Pen tool creates shapes with both fill and stroke. You can use the Paint Bucket tool to add or modify the fill of a shape.

Drawing with the Pencil Tool

Use the Pencil tool to depict straight and curved lines. Click and shift the mouse in any direction on the Stage. Your line doesn't have to be straight unless you want it that way. Can you draw a perfect circle or straight line? Don't worry; most people can't. The Pencil tool can help.

You don't have to draw an entire line in one motion, either. You can extend a line with the Pencil tool. Starting from one end of an existing line segment, draw where you want to extend it.

Try drawing a polygon with five sides using the Pencil tool. Draw it somewhere on your Stage, but be sure to leave room to add other shapes besides this one. Also, close your edges so there's no gap or opening along the edges of your polygon.

When you're done, save your Flash file (by going to File > Save) as Basics.fla.

Drawing with the Brush Tool

The Pencil tool creates a line with a steady thickness, a stroke. Use the Brush tool to make a solid shape, or fill. Just click down the mouse and draw in the

Stage. As you paint with the Brush tool, all touching or overlapping shapes of the same color will merge into a single shape.

Try drawing a wavy line or two with the Brush tool, somewhere on your Stage beside the polygon you made. Try alternating between scrawling fast and slow with the Brush tool, because, if you notice, the Flash program does something fancy with the brush stroke when you do. Leave room for one more object to be placed on your Stage.

Save your work when you're done.

Smooth and Straighten Those Lines

Underneath the Options section of the Tools panel, you can tell your drawing to Smooth or Straighten (see Figure 3.8).

Use the Selection tool (the black arrow at the top of the Tools panel) to select your wavy line you made with the Brush tool. It should have tiny dots filling its surface to show you that it is selected. Then click on Smooth two times to see how the wavy line changes. Press Ctrl+Z (or Cmd+Z) twice to remove these changes. Click on Straighten two times to see the alterations there, too. Notice what these operations do to transform the shape of your object.

You also have a Smoothing option in the Properties panel whenever you're painting with the Brush tool. The Smoothing value ranges from 0 to 100. 0 is practically as straight and hard-edged as the Pencil tool, while 100 gives you warped brush lines that almost look like they were composed with a calligraphy pen.

Experiment with Brush lines of varying Smoothing values.

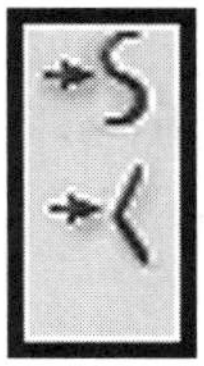

Figure 3.8
The Smooth and Straighten options refine your Pencil or Brush tool lines.

Drawing with the Pen Tool

If you are familiar with another vector-based program from Adobe called Illustrator (also part of the Adobe Creative Suite), you may recognize the Pen tool, because the Pen tool is one of the key elements of vector drawing in Illustrator. Sometimes the Pen tool is called the Bezier tool, which is the name of the paths it creates with points and handles. You use the Pen tool to draw lines and shapes by clicking and dragging from point to point.

You can set the fill and stroke colors of the objects you make with the Pen tool in the Properties panel. Here, you can also set the width of the stroke (border) and the way the stroke looks. You can even make the stroke look like a dashed or wavy line, rather than a straight one. Do this by pulling down the drop-down menu list beside Style in the Properties panel.

If you are satisfied with the work you make with the Pencil and Brush tools, you don't have to use the Pen tool. But if you draw a lot, and want to make perfect reproductions or commercial artwork, it will be worth it to you to practice and learn how to use the Pen tool.

The Pen tool lets you draw paths to create your shapes by interconnected anchor points, kind of like drawing a dot-to-dot image. The Pen tool gives you more control over the minute details of every curve and angle by adjusting using each anchor point's handles. The handles are the rays that jut off from anchor points. You won't be able to see the handles unless you have an anchor point selected. The way you select the anchor points is as you're making them or with the Subselection tool, the white arrow icon on the Tools panel, second to the Selection tool, or black arrow icon.

When you draw with the Pen tool, you generate points with either curved or straight lines between them, depending on what type of point you create. Refer to Figure 3.9 to see what kinds of points you can have.

To create a corner anchor point, simply click with your mouse and a new point will appear. This point will have no handles, because any line coming out from it will be straight and therefore need no adjustment. You can move it about by using the Subselection tool.

To create a curve anchor point, when you click your mouse on the location of your anchor point, don't immediately let go; drag a little, until you see the

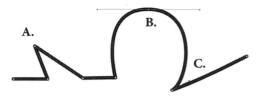

Figure 3.9
(A) Corner anchor point, (B) curve anchor point, and (C) Bezier corner point.

connecting lines between your points begin to curve and two antennae-like handles appear on either side of the point. You can use the Subselection tool to grab these handles and drag them to control the size and angle of the curves to either side of the point.

There's also a combination of the two called a Bezier corner point, which is an anchor point that has a straight line to one side and a curve to the other side. To create one of these, you first need an anchor point that is corner-only; a Bezier point created immediately adjacent to that one will automatically be a Bezier corner point with only one handle and a curve to only one side, because one side of it connects to a corner point.

Any lines drawn, whether in a closed shape or just an open path, will be stroked with your selected stroke color. When you close a path (by clicking on your starting point; you'll know you're about to close your path because a small circle will appear to the right of your Pen tool mouse cursor), it will automatically fill with whatever fill you have set in your Properties panel. You can use the Paint Bucket tool to change this, or just select your finished shape and change the fill options in the Properties panel.

Try out the Pen tool now. Make sharp- and round-cornered objects. The objects don't have to look like anything. The main reason to have you play with the Pen tool now is to get a little practice with it. Note how it operates.

When you're done, save your work.

Other Drawing Tools

The Oval and Rectangle tools are fairly straightforward. After selecting one of these tools, click and drag with your cursor on the Stage to create a circular or rectangular shape. These tools create shapes with both a fill and a stroke. Hold down the Shift key on your keyboard while dragging to constrain the shapes to a perfect circle or square.

In whatever area you have left on the Stage, create some oval and rectangle shapes.

The Eraser tool is the opposite of the Brush tool. It removes, or erases, anything you click and drag your cursor over, both fills and strokes.

From this tool's options, found at the bottom of the Tools panel, the Eraser Shape offers different sizes and shapes for the Eraser.

You can double-click on the Eraser tool icon to automatically clear everything on the Stage.

Try erasing part of your wavy lines you created with the Brush tool and the geometric shapes you created with the Oval and Rectangle tools. See how the Eraser tool works.

Save your work when you're through.

Tip

Flash has the option to take any line or stroke you've drawn and convert it to a fill instead, affecting its behavior and how various Flash drawing tools and their settings operate on them. To do this, select the fill you want to convert, and click Modify > Shape > Convert Lines to Fills.

Select the Right Object: Selection Tools

To alter an object in Flash you need to first let the program know you want to modify it by selecting it. Selecting an object makes it active and allows you to move or transform it in a number of different ways. There are four main tools you use to select and modify objects on your Stage: the Selection tool, the Subselection tool, the Lasso tool, and the Free Transform tool (see Figure 3.10).

Using the Selection Tool

The Selection tool, also called the Arrow tool (because it is looks like a little black arrow), is active by default whenever you first launch Flash. It's used for selecting, reshaping, moving, and deleting objects. Select an object on the Stage with the Selection tool before applying an effect to it. For some objects, you can simply click on some objects to select them.

Figure 3.10
The (A) Selection tool, (B) Subselection tool, (C) Lasso tool, and (D) Free Transform tool.

If you click on a fill, the fill itself will become selected (which is displayed by a pattern of tiny white overlaid dots). If you click on a stroke, the stroke by itself will become selected. If you double-click on the fill the nearest or connecting stroke will also become selected, or vice versa.

Hold down the Shift key before you click on objects to select multiple objects at once.

You can also click down and drag diagonally to define a rectangular marquee that selects an area. A marquee is a dotted preview of the area that will be selected when you release the mouse button.

Using the Subselection Tool

Flash lets you manipulate lines and shapes in two different ways. Remember the Pen tool? It's different from the other drawing tools in that it uses anchor points and handles to define its shape. The Subselection tool allows you to reshape any object, but with the points and handles of the Pen tool.

Rope 'Em, Cowboy: Using the Lasso Tool

Not everything you want to select fits in a rectangular marquee. The Lasso tool allows you to make an irregular-shaped selection. Select the Lasso tool from the Tools panel and click and drag in any path on your Stage to select the area you want. You can move or delete what you select or modify it with another tool.

Tip

Even if you start with the Selection tool and switch to using the Lasso tool, you can combine these selections. You can add to a current selection by pressing the Shift key before clicking on an unselected object to add it to the selection. Shift-click again on a selected object to drop it from the current selection.

Using the Free Transform Tool

After selecting the Free Transform tool from the Tools panel, click on an object and that object will sprout a frame with handles at the corners and sides (see Figure 3.11). You can resize, rotate, and distort an object by moving the various handles and sides of the frame. Watch your mouse cursor carefully, because it will indicate what transformation will occur to your object when you start clicking and dragging from the current cursor position.

Color Me Pretty in Flash

Up to now we've just looked at drawing in Flash with little regard to color. You can choose colors before drawing new objects, or change the colors of existing objects. There are several ways to select colors.

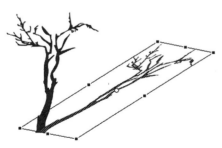

Figure 3.11
Using the Free Transform tool.

Figure 3.12
Color swatches for both the stroke and fill can be found on the Tools panel.

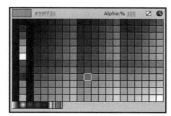

Figure 3.13
The color grid pop-up window helps you choose colors.

Colors on the Tools Panel

Every object in Flash, as mentioned previously, can have either a stroke or a fill or both. The stroke has its own color, and so does the fill.

From the Colors section of the Tools panel, shown in Figure 3.12, click on the fill or stroke swatch, or sample square of color, and a color grid will pop up, like the one in Figure 3.13, allowing you to pick a color. The preferred color will apply to whichever tool, such as Pencil, Brush, or Pen, you have active, or if you have an object selected, it will change the object's components to this color.

Using the Color and Swatches Panels

You can also choose colors with the Color and Swatches panels (found under the Window category on the menu bar) as you would from the Tools panel, but with a few more options.

To specify colors from the Color panel, enter numeric values or click in the color rainbow. Select a color from the grid of color swatches on the Swatches panel just as you would from the pop-up color grid accessed from the Tools panel.

Tip

Flash only uses web-safe colors, which means a color palette that displays well on most media, but especially over the Internet. These colors each have a corresponding alphanumeric representation, called a hexadecimal; for instance, the color black is #000000, red is #FF0000, and blue is #0000FF. You can see visible hexadecimal color charts online at http://html-color-codes.com and http://www. webmonkey.com/2010/02/color_charts.

Using the Eyedropper Tool

After you have created an object, it is unlikely that you would commit to memory its exact colors, especially hex colors, when you might just want to use those same colors somewhere else for a new object. In this case, use the Eyedropper tool (it looks like an eyedropper) from the Tools panel.

With the Eyedropper tool, click to select a color from an existing object on the Stage and it will apply the color to whatever tool or object you might have selected.

Using the Paint Bucket Tool

The Paint Bucket tool can add a fill shape inside an empty stroke or change the color of an existing fill. The Paint Bucket tool works with both solid fills and gradients.

The options for the Paint Bucket tool control just how tolerant the flood fills are. The options are found at the very bottom of the Tools panel. If you set it to Don't Close Gaps (the perfect circle icon, which is the default), then the Paint Bucket tool will only work to fill completely enclosed areas of a shape (that is, shapes that are completely bounded by a line with no broken spaces). But if you set it to Close Small Gaps, it will ignore small breaks in the bounding lines to fill the enclosed area. Close Medium Gaps and Close Large Gaps will cause the Paint Bucket tool to ignore larger and larger spaces in the bounding lines and treat them as enclosed areas.

Because you just created a polygon object that has closed edges on the Stage, use the Paint Bucket tool to fill it with any color you like.

Using Gradient Fills

A gradient fill is a gradual change in tone or color, including at least two different colors. Gradients add dimension and depth to your 2D artwork when used appropriately—and because Flash is a vector-based application, you can use a few smart gradients for shading while still retaining a relatively small file size for your published movie.

You apply a gradient fill just like you would a solid color fill. Choose an existing gradient, a blue, red, or green one, from the fill color grid or Swatches panel and use the Paint Bucket tool to add it to an existing object you have on the Stage to see what a gradient fill is and what it does.

To adjust the positioning and shape of the gradient, choose the Gradient Transform tool, hidden behind the Free Transform tool.

Tip

> Any time you see a little black arrow at the bottom right corner of an icon button in the Tools panel, it indicates that there are other tools hidden behind the one shown. This helps organize and simplify the Tools panel. To reveal and select tools hidden behind one another, click and hold down on the icon until the other tools reveal themselves, then move your cursor over one of them before letting go. Likewise, many tools have keyboard shortcuts that can greatly speed up your selection process once you've memorized them.

Using the Gradient Transform tool, select your gradient-filled object on the Stage and watch it sprout controls for adjusting the position and shape of the gradient's shading (see Figure 3.14). These take some playing with to understand how they work. One control sets the center point of the gradient, another its fall-off limits. Another control sets the rotational axis. Try clicking and dragging these controls in various directions to see what happens to your gradient.

Be sure and save your work when you're done.

Manipulating More Than One Object

Once you've created an object in Flash, you can draw over it to change it. Any tool does the job. Use the same color to add a shape, or use a different color to create a second adjacent shape. You could also select an object, copy it (via Edit > Copy on the menu bar), and paste a duplicate of it (via Edit > Paste on the

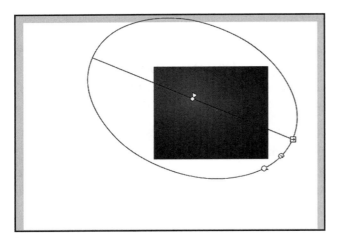

Figure 3.14
Using the Gradient Transform tool to change the visible gradient fill of an object.

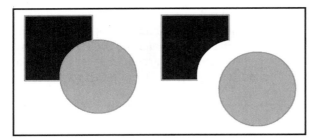

Figure 3.15
Combining unlike objects cut into and away from each other.

menu bar). Note that to copy-and-paste quicker you can use the shortcut keys Ctrl+C and Ctrl+V (Windows) or Cmd+C and Cmd+V (Mac).

If you place a new object over a same-color object, they merge into a single shape. Place a shape of a different color over an object, and it will cut into the other shape—as shown in Figure 3.15.

The 7-Layer Burrito: Using Layers in Flash

If you have used other graphics programs, such as Photoshop, you may be familiar with the use of layers.

Layers work like overlays and are an important organizational tool in Flash. They are based on the concept of overlays in classic graphic design. Overlays are clear sheets of plastic (celluloid or acetate sheets) laid over one another to create a composite image. Each sheet contains a graphic object, allowing other layers below to show through outside of that object.

You can create one layer for an imported bitmap image and another for a cartoon character you want to show in front of that bitmap image. So if you want a side-view of a rabbit walking in front of some trees but want a bush passing by in front of his bouncy stride, you would put the bush on the top-most layer, the rabbit in the middle, and the trees in the bottom-most, or furthest, layer.

Here are some reasons for adding layers:

- To be sure one object appears in front, or on top, of another.
- To distinguish between different elements on the Stage.
- To animate an object on the Stage (animations should be on separate layers).
- To prevent one graphic from merging into another or accidentally editing one object when working with another.
- To systematize all your elements for easier editing, especially if another Flash artist is planning to follow behind you or you are working on a project with someone else.
- To separate frame actions, labels, or sound from other elements in the same movie.

Layers are found on the Timeline. The left side of the Timeline lists the layer names with their corresponding frames to the right. Each layer on a Timeline matches a layer appearing on the Stage. The contents of layers at the top of the list appear in front of the layers lower on the list.

Choose Insert > Layer to add a new layer to the Timeline. Conveniently, below the layer names are a few buttons that make it easy for you to add or remove layers. Create as many layers as you need. There's no limit, but the more layers you create, the more you will have to manage as you edit the Flash file.

You can also organize your layers into layer folders. Add a layer folder to the Timeline as you would a standard layer. Add other layers to it by dragging their names over the folder. You cannot add frames to layer folders, just other layers.

By default, Flash names new layers with numbers (Layer 1, Layer 2, Layer 3, and so on). If you are only using two or three layers, those default names will do fine. When you start working with lots of layers, that's when you might want to consider naming them something specific so you will remember what goes on each layer. Identifying the contents of a layer by using specific layer names goes a long way to improve organization. To rename a layer, double-click on the current name to select it, and when you see the text highlight or a typing cursor appear, type in the new name you want the layer to have. Press Enter (or Return) to save your name change.

The order of the layers determines what appears on top or behind. The top-most layer in the Timeline will appear on top of everything else on the Stage, while the bottom-most layer in the Timeline will appear behind everything else on the Stage. To change the order of a layer, click and drag the layer (by the layer name) up or down in the list.

You can also show or hide layers, and lock or unlock layers; these buttons are found just to the right of the layer names, as shown in Figure 3.16. The Show/ Hide icon looks like an eyeball and the Lock/Unlock icon looks like a key lock. You can hide layers to uncover what lies beneath, and click again to reveal that layer again. You can lock a layer and it will still be visible, but you cannot

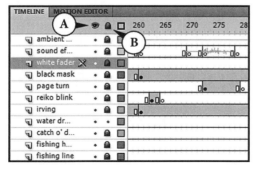

Figure 3.16
The (A) Show/Hide icon and (B) Lock/Unlock icon.

inadvertently move or edit anything on that layer. When you want to edit a locked layer, click the icon to unlock it.

Try using layers now.

Make a separate layer for each of the major objects you created on your Stage. Then select the objects on the Stage one at a time. Cut them (either by going to Edit > Cut, Ctrl+X, or Cmd+X). Cutting objects essentially copies and deletes the selected objects. Switch to one of your new layers by clicking on its layer name in the Timeline. Then go to Edit > Paste in Place. The Paste in Place command will paste the object last placed in the Clipboard to the same place on the Stage it was originally. Do this with each of your objects, so that they exist on separate layers.

Try turning layer visibility on and off to see the objects disappear and reappear. You should also practice changing layer names. Give each new layer a descriptive name, such as the name of the object residing on that layer. Keep your layer names short and untruncated. For instance, if you have a rectangle shape on one layer, you might name that layer Rectangle, and if you have some wavy lines on another layer, you might name that layer WavyLines.

When finished with layers, save your Flash file again.

S-P-E-L-L It Out: Typing in Flash

You can use text for just one word, a caption, a block of information, a business logo, or for several paragraphs. Flash can create text much richer than what appears on standard HTML pages, because Flash uses vector type. Flash does not limit you in choice of fonts (typefaces), either, so you can use any font found on your computer while building your movie.

To add or edit text in a Flash movie, choose the Text tool from the Tools panel. Click it anywhere on the Stage, then type from your keyboard, and you will see what you type appear right there on the Stage. Click down, drag, and release with the Text tool to automatically constrain the text to a specific text box width. Otherwise, the text will continue on a straight line until you press the Enter (or Return) key.

You might want to put your type on a new layer, and you might want to name your new layer Text so you know what's on it. Type the phrase "This is my work," somewhere on your Stage using the Text tool.

When you have completed typing, you will have a new text box, which you can position anywhere you like with the Selection tool just like any other object on the Stage.

With the Text tool, you can select individual words or characters in a text block and use the Text options that appear in the Properties panel to modify them (shown in Figure 3.17). You can change the font to whatever is available on your computer and make it big or small. You can change the color of the text here as well. The text color is considered the same as the fill color in Flash, so you can change the fill color on any panel to affect the selected text.

Other text options are available in the Properties Inspector panel for more advanced dynamic text features. There are three options here: Static Text, Dynamic Text, and Input Text. Use Static Text unless you need to implement dynamic behavior through ActionScript code or user input boxes.

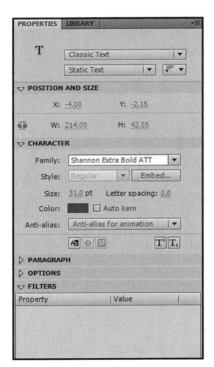

Figure 3.17
The Text options in the Properties panel.

Lastly, you can choose Modify > Break Apart to convert a text block into vector shapes that can be reshaped, painted, and modified just like other Flash vector art. However, once you convert a text block into a vector shape, you will not be able to edit it as text again. You will usually use this option only when you're ready to add fancy animation to each of the letters in your text.

Save your Flash file when done with your text.

Scene It Once, Scene It Twice

Besides using symbols and layers to organize your Flash file, you can also use scenes. Scenes are like blank slates. When you add a new scene to your existing Flash document, you are essentially adding a whole new Flash document to your existing one. Your project properties, such as the size of the Stage and the background color, remain the same, but you are presented with a blank Stage and empty Timeline to work from, and this new scene is added onto your existing project, as a continuation of it.

Many Flash artists discourage the use of scenes if you're aim is to make a video game or other complex, scripted application. The reason for this being that when Flash publishes your Flash file to an SWF that can be used on the Web, Flash recombines the scenes so that they're all added into one giant scene. Basically, the frames from consecutive scenes are combined to the frames of the primary scene, so that you end up with one big scene. This is all right in most cases and won't hurt anything, but if you have ActionScript relating to frame 23 of your Flash file, Flash won't know if you're talking about Frame 23 of Scene 1 or Scene 8 anymore, so your script can get broken.

With that in mind, you still may want to use scenes to make your work easier. Let's try it now. In your Basics.fla document, go to Window > Other Panels > Scene (Shift+F2) to open the Scene panel. Every Flash document has at least one scene. The default name of this scene is Scene 1. You should see Scene 1 here, in the Scene panel.

At the bottom of the Scene panel, you have three important icons: Add Scene, Duplicate Scene, and Delete Scene. Click the Add Scene icon; it's the one that looks like a piece of paper with the corner folded up. Name your new scene Smiley. To rename a scene, simply double-click on its name, and when the highlight and text cursor come up type the new name you want. Store your changes by pressing the Enter (or Return) key.

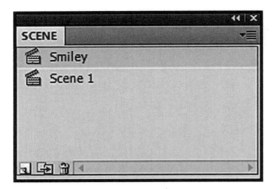

Figure 3.18
The Scene panel after adding your Smiley scene.

Note that, by default, your new scene is placed after Scene 1. You can drag and drop the scenes to swap them back and forth. The topmost scene will always go first when the Flash movie is played, and so on. For now, put Smiley on top of Scene 1.

Compare your Scene panel to Figure 3.18.

Make sure the Smiley scene is active, and that you're looking at a blank Stage and Timeline. Save your Basics.fla file.

Adding Bitmap Graphics

You've already seen the benefits of drawing using the Flash vector art tools. That's one way to add graphics in Flash, and many Flash animators (including the bunch that make *Happy Tree Friends* and *Neurotically Yours*, featuring Foamy the Squirrel) use vector art by itself. Vector art is smooth, and it can be resized and played with without ever losing its original graphic quality.

However, there will be times you want to use bitmap graphics in your animation. Or you want to scan in your artwork and convert it to vector so you can add it to your animation. You can do all this, too, with Flash. Flash accepts several varieties of bitmap graphics.

There are two quick ways to bring bitmap graphics into Flash. The first is to use the Import command in Flash, and the other is to drag and drop or copy and paste it into Flash.

Import Bitmap Graphics to Flash

Assuming you have first saved an image, you could choose File > Import to Stage and a dialog box would pop up. You would navigate through that dialog until you locate and select the desired image file. Then click the Open button and the desired image will appear on the Stage.

Another way to import bitmap graphics onto your Stage is to copy and paste them from another graphics editing program, like Photoshop, or to drag and drop them from your Desktop or another window into your open Flash program window. These are handy shortcuts to know, but they don't work every time.

To import artwork, an unlocked layer must be active. Upon import, the artwork will be placed on the Stage in the active, or presently selected, layer. You can resize, rotate, or move your bitmap image as you would any other object on the Stage.

Let's try it now. Open up your Web browser and go to Google. Be sure to restrain your search to images only by clicking on the Images button in the top-left corner of the Google window. This will let you navigate only search-appropriate web images.

Search for "smiley face." You should see somewhere in the neighborhood of 910,000 results (this number was from a search conducted in July 2010 and may vary). Find a smiley face image that looks like the typical smiley face button. Make sure it has a plain white background surrounding it. See Figure 3.19 for an example.

Click on the image once to see the page it is from and click it again to be taken to the image by itself. When you are satisfied with the image you've found and want to borrow it (for learning purposes only, as any other reason can be

Figure 3.19
An example of the kind of smiley face image you should browse for.

misconstrued as plagiarism!), right-click on it, and (depending on your current browser and operating system), choose to copy the image.

Return to Flash. In the Smiley scene, paste your image using Ctrl+V, Cmd+V, or Edit > Paste, whichever works for you.

Breaking Apart Bitmap Graphics

If you choose Modify > Break Apart (Ctrl+B or Cmd+B), you can reduce the image to an editable version of itself. This makes it easier to use the bitmap as a fill object, meaning that you can use the Eyedropper tool to copy the fill and use the Paint Bucket tool to paint the object as a fill into any shape. This is useful when filling an entire background with a tileable image, such as grass or rock. We don't want to do this with our smiley face, however, so don't use the Break Apart command on it just yet.

Converting Bitmap to Vector

Sometimes you might want to apply vector attributes to a bitmap image. After you have a bitmap image in Flash, you can convert it into a vector image by choosing the Modify > Bitmap > Trace Bitmap command. Do so now. A dialog box will pop up with various settings. You can experiment with these values here. Depending on the bitmap image you are converting, this may help improve file size or the appearance of the artwork. You can also use it to create an interesting effect.

Color threshold will do its best to emulate the original colors. The default is usually 100 and well-used. Minimum area sets the minimum section of pixels that it will reduce the bitmap to when converting it to vector shapes. The lower the number, the more individual vector shapes will be drawn and closer your result will look to the original bitmap graphic, but most of the time you don't want that, because the true potential in vector is its smoothness and simplicity, so a number around 8 or 12 is often more desirable. You can also design the corner and curve fit for your bitmap trace. When you are satisfied with the options in the Trace Bitmap dialog box, click Preview to see what it would look like. You can do this repeatedly to narrow down the right "look" for your graphic, and when you're ready to commit, click OK.

As soon as you click OK, the resulting vector image will be selected. This means the image will appear dot-filled. You can click off the Stage to deselect and look at your work.

Using Illustrator to Convert Bitmap to Vector

There is another way to convert your bitmap graphics to vector art, and that's by using a separate program, Adobe Illustrator. Illustrator comes as part and parcel with the Adobe Creative Suite, and so if you have the full suite of Adobe tools, you can switch to Illustrator and do your vector tracing there and then drag and drop the results into Flash.

If you have Illustrator and wish to try it, open Illustrator now. Open a new print document, the size of which is irrelevant. Paste your smiley face image onto the Illustrator art board. The controls to paste the image are the same as the ones you use in Flash.

With the smiley face selected, look directly under the menu bar, about the middle of the options bar, for the Live Trace button shown in Figure 3.20. Click the drop-down list arrow beside the Live Trace button and select Tracing

Figure 3.20
The Live Trace button in Adobe Illustrator.

Options to open the Tracing Options dialog box. Here, you can play around with a wider array of settings to convert your bitmap to vector. Try using Mode set to Color, Max Colors set to 6, and Path Fitting set to 3 px.

You can put a check in the Preview checkbox here to preview your work before committing to it, but the preview option will create a lag on your computer as it struggles to keep up with your changes once this option is turned on.

Once you're satisfied with the look of your image, click Trace to store your changes.

Where the Live Trace button once was you should now see two new buttons: Expand and Live Paint, which you can see in Figure 3.21. Click Expand to reduce the image to its constituent vector shapes. These shapes will remain grouped together until such time as you right-click on them and select to Ungroup them.

Figure 3.21
The Expand and Live Paint buttons reveal themselves after you've traced your bitmap.

You can drag and drop your selected artwork directly from the Illustrator art board to the Flash Stage, once you're done.

The true power of Live Trace has some advantages over the Trace Bitmap command in Flash, especially when converting black-and-white scanned artwork. This is why I prefer using Illustrator to convert bitmaps to vector, even for Flash artwork.

WHAT'S NEXT?

Next, you will learn how to draw your own images and scan them into the computer to use them in Flash. Even if you're not an established artist, you can still make stick figures. Regardless of your level of skill, being able to draw your own images will help you later make your own Flash PSP games.

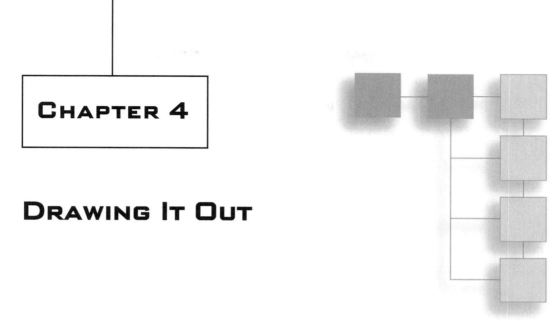

CHAPTER 4

DRAWING IT OUT

In this chapter you will learn:

- What kind of drawing tools you will need
- How to do pencil drawings
- How to make your sketches look like something
- What perspective is and how to use it
- How to scan your artwork into your computer

I started drawing when I was three years old and never stopped. Back then, I drew cartoon characters I'd seen on television and in comic strips, such as Snoopy, Charlie Brown, Garfield, and the Pink Panther. I also drew any new fantastic creature my imagination could come up with.

As I grew older, I drew people and places, experimenting with sketching real objects and ones I invented. I spent my high school years in the art room, first as a student and then as a teacher's assistant. I knew when I graduated high school that I wanted to be an artist, and I went to a fine arts college an hour away from my home. I studied perspective, composition, and figure drawing.

Yet I found I kept returning to cartoons and comics, which became my primary art focus.

People say you have to be born an artist or you'll never be an artist, that it takes a natural-born talent. This is not true. I used to have a friend, when I was a teenager, who was a really good jazz musician. He could play the guitar. After I went off to college, I met up with him again. He entered a university as an art major, because he'd decided he wanted to be an artist. He knew nothing about art, and even when I saw his first attempts to draw I admit I smirked. I didn't think he could do it.

Today, he teaches oil painting classes at a university, he lives on commissions he makes from selling his paintings, he's a member of Oil Painters of America, and he has been featured in *Art in America* magazine.

He did not start with talent. He learned it. Art is a skill, just like any other, and with enough practice and dedication, anyone can become an artist.

Art does take passion. You can't be wishy-washy about wanting to make a picture, or else your picture will come out wishy-washy, too. You have to have passion.

Almost every toddler draws pictures. Somewhere along the way from crayons to pubescence we stop drawing. There are lots of reasons we stop drawing. Maybe you had a bad art teacher who harped on you all of the time in class. Maybe other kids ridiculed your artwork. Or perhaps you simply lost the urge to draw after you saw other kids who seemed to draw so effortlessly. Whatever the reason, the ability still rests within you to draw. We just have to bring it out of you.

Usually, when someone says, "I can't draw," what they really are saying is, "I can't draw like so-and-so, so why bother?" Are you being a defeatist just because you really like someone else's artwork and think yours doesn't measure up? I'll let you in on a little secret: Every artist feels that way! There are hundreds of artists I admire and want to draw just like, but I'll never be them. But I have never let that inability hold me back, because I know my own personal style is uniquely my own, and being unique is what gets you noticed and what sells.

There are as many distinct art styles as there are artists. Just as everyone's style of handwriting is uniquely their own, every artist's drawing style is uniquely their own, too. Think how boring the world would be if every artist drew just like every other artist, and all art looked like it had popped from the same machine. Explore your differences and your own natural style.

While I was still in high school, I was accepted into a summer arts program, a camp just for artists, based on merit or work performed. There our art group called itself "drawers," and our favorite joke was "We do drawings, so we are drawers—just don't stick your socks and underwear in us!" We tromped around the woods with pads of paper and sticks of vine charcoal in our hands and did many natural drawings. We were unrefined, and therefore we saw ourselves as "drawers," not artists, because the term "artist" spoke of too much refinement for our tastes. That freedom and feeling of self-confidence followed me into my future as an adult.

There are finer books that will teach you how to be an actual artist. What this chapter will do is show you all of the ins and outs of being a drawer. Your drawings may or may not be pretty, but they will be authentically yours and they will get noticed.

GATHERING THE RIGHT SUPPLIES

Almost anything you can make a mark with can be used to draw with. The early cave painters of France and Spain produced dramatic images of hunters chasing animals with the very basic materials they found around them in their environment. There was no prehistoric art shop along the road where they could stop and buy art supplies. They had to improvise in the creation of their own drawing materials. So they used berry juice and rock dust as pigments and dyes.

Today, we are very fortunate to have a superb selection of art materials conveniently available from art shops in almost every city and town. The materials we buy today have been made based on the need, skill, and experience of artists across the globe.

All you really need to start drawing is a pencil and a sheet of paper. If you look around your home you should be able to find suitable materials for drawing, including ballpoint pens, pencils, felt-tipped and nylon-tipped pens, colored markers, and plain ruled notebook paper or blank typing paper. It is possible to draw in a wide range of other mediums as well.

Let's look at some of the most versatile tools you can find at your local art shop, as shown in Figure 4.1. Many of these should eventually find their way into your personal art studio, if you want to become an artist.

Figure 4.1
Your toolkit should include a mixture of pencils, pens, and colors.

- **Drawing table or desk.** You have to have a proper place to draw. You could draw on a sketchpad you set in your lap or draw laying stretched out on the floor, but you will quickly learn that you don't have the proper range of motion in your drawing arm when you do either of those things. Any kind of flat, sturdy surface should do, but try and find a balance between comfort and proper range of motion.

- **Pencils.** If you successfully completed kindergarten, you know what a pencil is and what it's good for. But not all pencils are made for drawing. A standard No. 2 pencil can work in a pinch, but you should use real art pencils. All pencils are made from a mixture of graphite and china clay. The more graphite there is in a pencil, the softer and darker the mark it will make. Art pencils come in varying degrees of hardness. Soft pencils are known as B, harder pencils as H. They are also numbered 2, 3, 4, 5, 6, 7, 8, and 9. You will find that the higher the number, the softer, or harder, the pencil lead. 2B and 3B are medium soft and ideal for sketching. The H pencils are too hard for most art work, being preferred tools for technical or engineering diagrams.

- **Blue color pencils.** These are used by several industry pros to make soft-tone guidelines and preliminary sketches, which they then can ink over. The reason is that blue won't show up when you make copies of your inked pages on a copying machine. Prismacolor/Col-Erase makes the best blue color pencils.

- **Graphite sticks.** These are sticks of graphite not bound by wood casing but varnished or wrapped in paper to stop the graphite from dirtying your fingers. The main advantage to using graphite sticks is that the tip can serve as a pencil, and the wide side of the sharpened end can be used for bold sweeps of pencil marks and for shading large areas.

- **Erasers.** The Pentel Clic Eraser is a refillable eraser pen that is great for detail work. You will also need larger erasers for covering larger areas. The one eraser preferred by most artists is the kneadable rubber eraser because it can be molded with your fingers into all sorts of shapes for rubbing out, modifying, or lifting out passages or work. Also, it is unique in that it does not create lots of loose pieces of paper and eraser shavings so the work does not have to be dusted off by hand, which in turn reduces the risk of smudging.

- **Pens.** The antique dip-in, sketching, or mapping pens are the most common art tool. These all have a metallic nib in a wooden or plastic holder. The pen can be dipped into ink to load the nib of the pen. You have to be careful about cleaning the nib off before storing, so the ink does not dry on it and form a crust. India ink is black and won't fade. It comes in waterproof and nonwaterproof forms but I recommend the waterproof version for sketching. Colored inks are also available, but the main problem with them is that they do fade with time in the sunlight. A regular fountain or ballpoint pen can also be used to sketch with. Some manufacturers have a whole range of fountain pens for drawing on the market, such as the Rapidograph ones.

- **Sharpie pens.** Sharpies are a standard for making thick, strong, permanent lines or filling in vast areas of a black-and-white illustration with shadow. Many black magic markers are smelly and slow-drying, or they bleed across paper, but Sharpie pens are practically quick-dry and don't fade. You can now get Sharpies in fine or fat tips and in a wide range of colors.

- **White-out.** Inking can be very messy sometimes, especially if you draw a lot, so you will want to use some corrective white-out liquid for making immediate fixes. Carefully dab it where you need to and wait for it to dry thoroughly before attempting to draw over it.

■ **Contés Carres Crayons.** These are square sticks of extra-firm pastel. The most common colors are black, gray, white, sanguine, and sepia. They offer beautiful results, especially on tinted paper.

■ **Charcoal.** Charcoal is black, burnt wood, often made in a kiln from willow wood. Charcoal can be reduced to a fine powder for fine smudging on paper. Otherwise, using charcoal is very close to using graphite sticks. However, you must use some kind of fixative spray to get the charcoal to stay on the paper.

■ **Fixative Spray.** Pencils, graphite, and especially charcoal drawings need "fixing" to prevent them from smudging. Clear fixative is widely available in spray can form. If you cannot find it in stores, most generic forms of hairspray work just as well.

■ **Paper.** Bristol board is too expensive (about $10 U.S. for 20 sheets), bond paper is too thin, and animation paper is too large. Cartridge paper is the most popular and can be obtained by the sheet or in a pad. Popular sizes are 4" × 6", 6" × 8", 9" × 12", 14" × 17", and 18" × 24". Sketching paper can be obtained in different weights and thicknesses, as well, but 50 lb. bleached white paper is ideal for most drawing work.

■ **Pencil Sharpeners, Craft Knives, and Sandpaper.** You can use any of these tools to bring your pencil point to the shape you want to use for your drawing.

■ **Drawing Boards, Pins, Clips, and Masking Tape.** You can use a clipboard for smaller works, or a sturdy piece of cardboard for larger work. Or you can buy a secure easel or other physical support for your paper. Try not to use drawing pins as they make marks in the board that can show through in other work if shading or drawing over holes. Drawing board clips hold the paper to the board just fine, but I prefer securing paper to the board with masking tape.

■ **Rulers.** An all-purpose, 12", mid-sized hypotenuse triangle will work best for most drawing needs, but it should have an inking lip or edge to prevent smearing. I also use a straight ruler composed of bendy plastic so it always lays flat to the paper, even if I get a crinkle in the paper.

■ **Computer Hardware and Software.** You should definitely get a computer, flat-bed scanner, color printer (or preferably an all-in-one printer), and image-editing software. When it comes to software, there are many options, from affordable to expensive. Most artists use the Adobe Creative Suite, which includes Photoshop, Illustrator, and Flash. Some also use Corel software or open-source software such as GIMP or Paint Dot Net. We will explore these options in more detail shortly.

If you need to pack all of your gear and be ready to take your art on the road, you will need a box or some other type of container to put your art supplies in. Most of my teen years I used a grungy tackle box that I had found in a thrift store to put my art supplies in. Tackle boxes or makeup kits work well, because they have these partitioned slots for you to put your pens, pencils, white-out, crayons, markers, erasers, and more in.

Image-Editing Software Options

The Adobe CS5, seen in Figure 4.2, the most current version of the software, is expansive (and expensive), but it is the current industry standard. The Design Premium package contains Photoshop, Illustrator, Flash, InDesign, Dreamweaver, and more. These tools can function separately, as they each do a split task in digital media production, but they are also integrated with one another. The Adobe CS5 Design Premium package costs around $1,899. You can purchase the programs separately; for instance, Photoshop CS5 costs $699 by itself. You can also try the software free for thirty days.

Besides the Adobe Creative Suite, there are many other programs you can use to edit your artwork on your computer.

Before we look at some of them, there's one very important difference to mention. Some image-editing software packages work with raster images (scanned

Figure 4.2
Adobe Photoshop CS5 is the current computer art standard in software.

photographic images, in other words), while others work with vector images (geometric precise color-fills). Some software packages do both raster and vector. For the most part, when working with your drawings, you'll want a raster program, but you'll probably want to experiment with vector, too, so the choice is up to you.

For example, in the Adobe Creative Suite, there are two image-editing programs: Photoshop and Illustrator. Photoshop is a raster image editor, although it has marginal controls for vector shapes. Illustrator is a true vector image editor, although you can bring raster images into it. Both programs look and operate similarly, but there are many differences in their tools and capabilities.

Most image-editing programs let you work in layers. This is beneficial, because you can move images on top of or under one another and blend multiple images into a single collage. Make sure your program supports layers.

It is up to you what program you choose to use.

The following are just a few samples of some image-editing software.

Corel Software

CorelDRAW Graphics Suite, currently in its X5 (version 15) edition, and displayed in Figure 4.3, is a complete graphics package that costs around

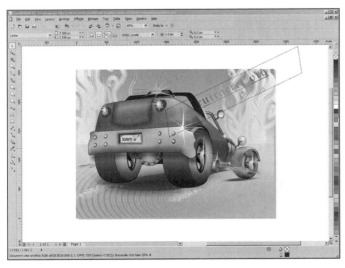

Figure 4.3
CorelDRAW Graphics Suite X5 is a decent Adobe competitor.

$499. It has two major components: CorelDRAW, which is a vector graphics editor developed and marketed by Corel Corporation, and Corel PHOTO-PAINT, which is Corel's answer to Adobe Photoshop and is a complete raster graphics editor.

You can learn more about the CorelDRAW Graphics Suite online at www.corel. com.

GIMP

GIMP—short for GNU Image Manipulation Program—is a free raster graphics editor, employed mainly as an image-editing and retouching tool. You can see a screenshot of GIMP in Figure 4.4. GIMP's current version, 2.6, was reviewed twice by Ars Technica, the PC enthusiast's resource. In the first review, Ryan Paul noted that GIMP provides "Photoshop-like capabilities and offers a broad feature set

Figure 4.4
GIMP has come a long way from its original layout, and you can't beat free software.

that has made it popular with amateur artists and open source fans. Although GIMP is generally not regarded as a sufficient replacement for high-end commercial tools, it is beginning to gain some acceptance in the pro market."

You can read more about GIMP or download the program on the GIMP Team Web site at www.gimp.org.

Paint Dot Net

Paint Dot Net, or Paint.NET, is a free raster image-editing software program for computers running Windows OS. It started development as a college undergraduate project mentored by Microsoft, originally intended to be a free replacement for Microsoft Paint, and since then has been maintained by some of the alumni who built it. It has been compared to similar programs, such as the Adobe and Corel software packages. You can see it for yourself in Figure 4.5.

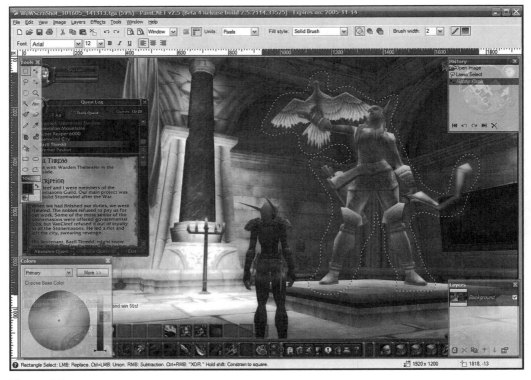

Figure 4.5
Paint Dot Net is being used here to edit a screenshot image taken from inside the *World of WarCraft* game.

You can read more about Paint Dot Net or download the program on the dotPDN Web site at www.getpaint.net.

Aviary Phoenix

Aviary, a privately held company in Long Island, New York, created the popular Web site Worth1000.com, where over 500,000 digital artists compete in daily contests. They also started making digital media more accessible to artists of all genres and backgrounds, from graphic design to audio editing, with their free online tools.

One of these tools is Phoenix, a complete raster image editor shown in Figure 4.6. Phoenix offers artists all of the same key features of a desktop

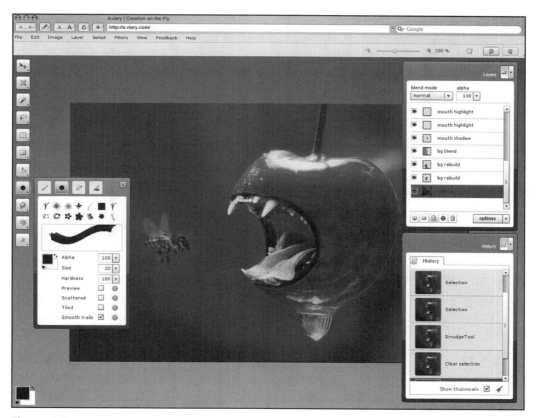

Figure 4.6
Aviary has really done something special with the release of their free web-based image editor Phoenix.

image editor but with the simplicity and access usage of a web-based application. It can be opened from aviary.com/tools/phoenix# and images made with it are saved to your desktop.

There's a great book that can teach you how to use the Aviary Phoenix web app. The book is called *More Than One Way to Skin a Cat: Create Eye-Popping Effects Using Aviary (Without Paying for Photoshop!)* by Meowza Katz and published by Course Technology PTR 2008.

To read more about Aviary Phoenix, or to use it, go online to aviary.com.

How to Hold Your Pencil or Pen

You might be thinking to yourself, "I already know how to hold a pencil or pen. I've been doing it for years!" That may be the case, but to draw takes a different holding style.

When first holding a pencil for drawing, most people adopt the writing position. They rest their hand on the paper and hold the pencil tightly in their fingers. This gives a small controlled area and allows for sketching lines and curves of very short length. It's more of a last step, or fine-detail drawing method. This is okay for writing notes, but it's not really practical for broad sketching or painting.

By lifting the hand off the page you can work from your wrist and your fingers. A single line or curve drawn from the wrist can be two to three times longer than a line drawn from the fingers when the hand is resting on the table. It will also appear more fluid.

Sit back in your chair with your hand still off the page. Try drawing a line from your elbow joint. This will give you more freedom to draw longer, free-flowing lines. You will have a much larger area for your hand and arm to sweep curved and straight lines.

Try sketching lines on your sketch pad in the ways described above, working alternately from your fingers, wrist, elbow, and shoulder. Note how each way has its advantages and disadvantages.

You also get different pencil strokes, when using pencil, from the way you hold your pencil. Hold it almost flat, with the side of the point resting against your paper, and create broad lines of value. This is an easy way to add thick shading to your work. Hold the pencil up in the air, just working from the tip of the pencil, and you will create fine thin lines. The amount of pressure applied will also vary the thickness and weight of the pencil stroke.

PENCIL DRAWING

The following exercises will teach the basics, and just the basics, behind drawing. You will start by using a pencil, preferably a 2B art pencil, but the same techniques can apply equally well with a pen or brush. Pencil is, in many ways, more forgiving, which is why it's easiest to start with. You will also need a sketchbook or unlined paper and possibly a ruler or straight edge.

Exercise 1: Outlines

Pencil and pen lend themselves best to line drawings. This means you draw the outlines of your subject, as you see them. You peer closely at what it is you are drawing and try to tell where the object's edges stop and space surrounding it starts, and you draw that terminating edge. Look at Figure 4.7 to see what I mean.

Take a look at the photograph of the church in Figure 4.8 and attempt to make your own line drawing from it. Pay careful attention to the curves and angles. Almost imagine that you are doing a connect-the-dots image as your eye travels from one point to another.

Figure 4.7
A pencil line drawing of a cartoon tank.

Figure 4.8
Trace this image with your eye and make a line drawing based off it.

Exercise 2: Shading

The easiest way to make shapes appear three-dimensional is to add values, such as highlights and shading. Try adding lights and darks to your drawings.

All you need are three values: one for the basic color of the object, one for the highlighted area, and one for the shaded area. Later, depending on your artistic style, you can add graduated tones, which will make the object appear more realistic and less like a cartoon.

To decide the placement of highlights and shadows on an object, you must determine the direction from which the light source in a given scene is coming. Most artists choose a light source off to the left or right of the scene. Highlights appear on objects on the sides and edges nearest to and facing the light source, while shade appears on the same objects on the opposite sides, facing away from the light source.

Pencils vary in degree of softness and hardness. Copy the image in Figure 4.9. Vary the strength of shading by varying the pressure of your hand on the pencil.

After you complete your tonal experimentation using your pencil, switch to your pen. You can use a variety of ink lines to create many other shading effects. These come under four headings:

- **Hatching.** Hatching is the use of parallel lines. The closer together the lines, the darker the area will look; the further apart, the lighter the area.

Figure 4.9
A lot of tonal variation can come about when pencil shading.

- **Crosshatching.** This is where one set of hatching lines are placed over another set, making an area look even darker.

- **Stippling.** Stippling uses dots. The closer the dots are, the darker the area; the further apart, the lighter the area.

- **Random Lines.** Marks, semicircles, ticks, and wiggly lines do not fall under the other three headings but can be very useful.

Draw the chart in Figure 4.10 in your sketchbook. Invent several types of hatching, crosshatching, and random lines all your own.

Return to the outline drawing you did of the cartoon tank in the last exercise. Add shading to it to make it appear more "alive," like you see in Figure 4.11.

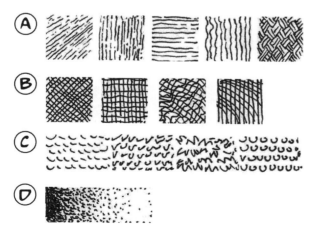

Figure 4.10
Examples of (A) hatching, (B) crosshatching, (C) random lines, and (D) stippling.

Figure 4.11
Adding shading to an ordinary line drawing can make it appear more solid.

Exercise 3: Texture

Any piece of artwork consists of three main parts: the outline of the subject, the shading or value study of it, and the ability to show, or at least suggest, the material the subject is made from. As artists, what we are trying to do is to trick the eye of the onlooker into believing that a few marks of a pencil on paper is nothing of the sort, but is wood, silk, metal, hair, fur, flesh, or whatever it is you are drawing.

Figure 4.12
Tactile values of different subjects.

You can use traditional shading, hatching, crosshatching, stippling, and random lines to gain an insight into the art of rendering textures, often referred to in the industry as texture or tactile values. You can find and sketch two very different types of materials, reflecting in your artwork the material's surface type through the use of these techniques. Or you can draw the images in Figure 4.12 as an example.

Exercise 4: Basic Shapes

All objects are made up of basic underlying shapes. A drinking glass, for instance, is a cylindrical shape. A basketball is a spherical shape. A wood crate is a cubical shape. Even people are made up of various underlying shapes: a sphere for the head, a beveled box for the torso, cylinders for the limbs, and so on. You can get rather creative, like looking for determinable features in the clouds, when looking for basic shapes in objects you're viewing. Look at some examples in Figure 4.13.

CIRCLE   CYLINDER   BOX

Figure 4.13
Basic shapes make up these art subjects.

Knowing what the basic shapes making an object up are will help you draw it. You can sketch the shapes to sketch where elements go, proportion your object better based on its shapes, and determine how light and tactile value shading will fall on an object based on the shapes making it up.

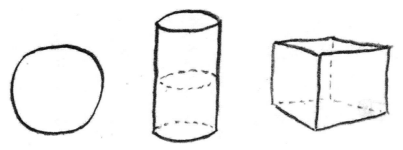

Figure 4.14
Draw an oval, cylinder, and box.

The three most-used shapes are ovals, cylinders, and boxes, although occasionally you'll see a pyramid-like or polygonal shape used. Try drawing these top-three shapes, shown in Figure 4.14, as they'll be used time and again in the following exercises.

Exercise 5: Shadows

You can also start to simulate volume for your objects by placing shadows on the ground beneath them. The placement of the light source in your picture will affect the shadow cast by the subject (see Figure 4.15). Here are several rules-of-thumb to remember when drawing shadows:

- The higher the source of light, the shorter the shadow should be.

- The lower the source of light, the longer the shadow should be.

Figure 4.15
Light casts shadow.

Figure 4.16
Add a shadow to your basic shapes like so.

- The stronger the light, the darker the shadow should be.

- The softer the light, the gentler the shadow should be.

Add a shadow to your basic shapes, the oval, cylinder, and box. Depending on where you decide to put the light source in your scene, your image can appear like the one in Figure 4.16.

Exercise 6: Perspective

Perspective is another word used to mean "point-of-view" or "view angle" and in art it is crucial to showing objects the way they should look in relation to their environment and objects next to them. To create a sense of depth or distance in your pictures you must use perspective. Applying the rules of perspective will help you in everything you draw. So when working, make it a habit to sketch guidelines lightly on your paper to make sure all of the lines in your picture are properly in perspective.

Unfortunately, perspective is the one area of drawing in which most people experience some degree of difficulty. When people hear perspective mentioned, they often go to the library, obtain a book on the subject, flip through it, see lines shooting about all over the place, and usually end up more confused than they were before they opened the book. The secret is to keep the whole business of perspective as simple as you can, to bear in mind a few basics, and to bear in mind that perspective is not something you can master in one, two, or three lessons. Learning perspective is an ongoing process.

Horizon Line

The first basic trick to perspective is this: The farther away something is, the smaller it looks. In your field-of-view, objects closer to you will look bigger and they shrink as they get closer to the horizon line. The *horizon line* is an imaginary line across your field of vision when you look straight on; not up or down, but straight ahead.

In Figure 4.17, you can see how the horizon line stays directly in front of the subject regardless if he is sitting down, standing level, or standing on a crate. To determine the horizon line when looking at a real subject you are drawing, try holding a ruler by its thin side, horizontally in front of your eyes. If you're outdoors in relatively flat terrain you might notice that the horizon line coincides to where the sky and earth meet each other in the far distance, from your viewpoint. This is where your horizon line should be in your composition.

Generally, I draw my subject lightly first, then apply the horizon line to my sketch. The horizon line is then used to apply perspective to the rest of your work and to check and corroborate your subject.

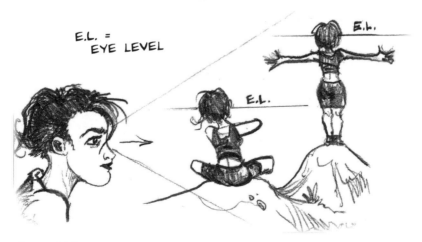

Figure 4.17
The horizon line remains at eye level to the viewer.

Figure 4.18
Parallel lines run off to apparently merge at the vanishing point.

Vanishing Point

When you have parallel lines running alongside each other, like edges of a sidewalk or rooftops, note that the parallel lines appear to get closer together the farther away they are. In fact, they will almost seem to meet on the horizon line. The point where they do meet is called the *vanishing point*. We know that the lines don't really merge, but by having them vanish on the horizon line we create the illusion that they are getting further away and that the scene has more depth. Notice this in Figure 4.18.

Putting Objects in Perspective

There are multiple points-of-view you can use that are considered very dynamic.

Draw the images in Figure 4.19 in your sketchbook. Figure 4.19 shows examples of different viewpoints. The standard view is straight-on, which is how we normally see objects. Then there's the bird's-eye view, which is from a higher elevation looking down on the subject. Lastly there's the mouse-eye view, from the elevation of the ground level looking up. These last two lead to foreshortening, which is making parts of a single object look smaller as they recede, or go

Figure 4.19
The three most-used viewpoints when studying your art subject: (A) standard view, (B) bird's-eye view, and (C) mouse-eye view.

back, from the viewer. Foreshortening uses perspective, even though the horizon line has been rotated up or down, respectively.

Look at Figure 4.18. All you see is the side view of a line of village shops. With this view there is just one vanishing point on the horizon line for the sides of the buildings to converge.

In Figure 4.20 the building is set at an angle. We now have two vanishing points, one for each side. This is known as two-point perspective.

Guidelines will often want to converge at vanishing points off the page. This is normal. When it does, lay scrap paper at the sides and tape them on from

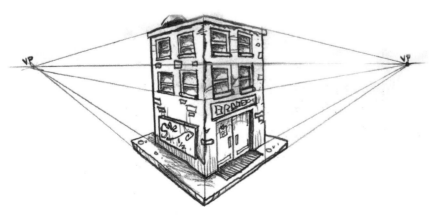

Figure 4.20
A building shown in two-point perspective.

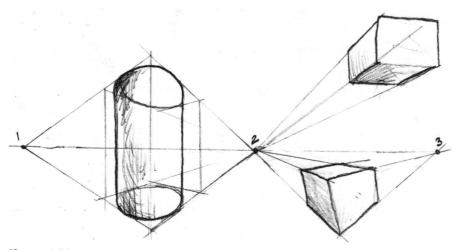

Figure 4.21
Use perspective to put basic shapes in their proper places. Cylinders can be drawn in perspective the same way you draw boxes, but with ovals filling two opposite squares, as shown here.

behind, then extend the guidelines onto it, so you can stretch your lines to the proper vanishing points. Never assume that your perspective is correct or guess at it; always try to prove it.

Most newbie artists don't realize that perspective, like I showed for drawing a building, can be used to make all of the basic shapes, including ovals, boxes, and cylinders. Practice drawing these basic shapes using one- and two-point perspective (see Figure 4.21).

Exercise 7: Drawing from Life

When starting out, many artists find it difficult to choose a subject to draw.

This is not as important if a beginner artist is attending a regular class (see Figure 4.22). Commonly, people are told to draw objects that inspire them, and respond by attempting to draw a stack of DVDs, some clothes they own, or their favorite characters from games or movies. These subjects do not present the best challenge.

There are many easily found subjects around your home to draw. Just remember, especially early on, that the aim is to choose objects to draw that will help develop your drawing skills. A selection of widely varying items for a still-life composition is suitable. For example, try drawing a pile of fruit, nuts, silk, fake fur, bottles, glasses, leaves, candles, and so on.

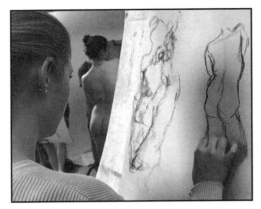

Figure 4.22
In most art schools, you are given still-life scenes and nude models to draw.

Figure 4.23
There are so many straight and curved lines and details in a single bicycle that it can really be a challenge for any artist.

Alternatively, try drawing family members (if they'll sit still long enough for you) or objects in your yard, including trees, shrubs, and plants. Outside your home, street scenes and landscapes can be drawn. These are particularly fun for drawings objects in perspective. Cars and bikes can also be very challenging, and thus make a good drawing exercise. After you've had some practice drawing, try sketching a bicycle, like the one shown in Figure 4.23, and you'll be amazed at how challenging and rewarding it can be.

Once you have drawn many scenes for the sake of exercise, you can tailor the subjects you pick to suit your taste. This way, you can make sure your pictures combine various elements of tone, line, color, and form within them while reflecting your personality.

Do this regularly. Most artists keep a sketchbook and pencil on them at all times, just in case they have to wait in line, are bored somewhere, or see a particularly engaging subject to stop and draw. Drawing on a daily basis will increase the hand-eye motor skills required to make you an artist and will give you more discipline to draw what you see.

Exercise 8: Drawing from Photographs

There are many subjects, such as people, fast-moving vehicles, or places at a given time of day, that do not sit still. Likewise, it is not always easy to get your chosen subjects to pose for you. In this case, it is easier to take a photograph (see Figure 4.24) and draw from the photograph.

It's suggested that if you decide to do your own photography, then invest in a decent digital camera. Using your cell phone camera just won't do. There are many options and availability in cameras out there, and you'll have to settle for what you know best and what your budget can afford. You can typically get a digital camera for $100 on up.

You can learn more about digital photography basics online at www.cambridgeincolour.com/tutorials.htm. There's a wealth of information there on apertures, exposures, shutter speeds, depth-of-field, and more. When you pick out the camera you want to use, go to the Web site to read more about it and how to use it more effectively.

Drawing from a photograph means you have more time with the subject, because you're not afraid of it getting up and walking off somewhere, but be forewarned that photos tend to flatten the planes of a subject and impress light contrasts that might not have been there in the original view. Your drawing will look like a photo, even if you try hard to disguise the fact you worked from a photo. It's okay, but just keep in mind that photo references shouldn't replace drawing from life.

Figure 4.24
In some cases, taking photos and using those photos to draw from can make your job as an artist easier.

Try it now. Pick out your favorite magazine, one that has color photos of people modeling clothes or cosmetics. Find one photo that draws your eye in more than the rest. Ignoring the title, captions, or other text on the page, draw the photograph to the best of your ability. Start with outlines and then add shading. Do this as a regular exercise from now on, until you develop real skill with drawing from photos.

Exercise 9: Drawing Chibis

Now let's start something different. You need to learn how to draw from your imagination, especially how to draw cartoon characters. For this reason, you'll draw a typical chibi and anime character. Both are cartoon styles that came to America from Japan.

A *chibi* is a Japanese word meaning "short person" or "small child." The word caught on amongst fans of anime, which is Japanese cartoon animation, and has come to reflect the distorted caricatures made of animated characters, especially ones with big heads and small bodies.

Study the image in Figure 4.25 and try drawing it. You can also look at the Chibi Anime Gallery for more inspiration. You can find the Gallery online at http://anime-chibis.blogspot.com.

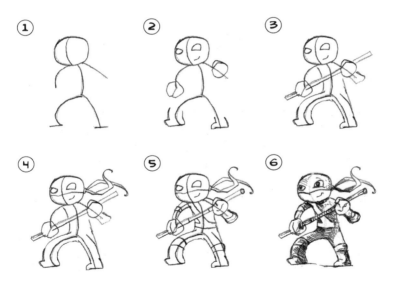

Figure 4.25
(1) First, draw a circle for the head and add one facial guideline. Draw the neck and the frame for the body. (2) Sketch out the shape of the chibi ninja's facial structure, including the line for the ninja mask. (3) Draw in the ninja's bo staff and where the hands and shoes will go. (4) Add mask ties in a fashion like they are blowing in a breeze to add action to the chibi ninja pose. (5) Add guidelines for details you will add to the ninja's costume. (6) Erase some of your guidelines to clean up your work, then add details to finish your drawing.

Exercise 10: Drawing Anime Characters

Anime is more than drawing chibis, however.

Anime started in Japan in 1917 but didn't become the style we are familiar with today until the 1960s. Anime finally crossed the water from Japan to America and became a popular art and animation style in the 1980s.

Anime is typified by bold outlines, thin bodies, outrageous clothes, moon heads, weird spiky hairdos, pointy chins, big eyes, and small mouths.

Like any other type of visual entertainment, anime has its own set of genres, demographics, and even ratings. Unlike American cartoons, which are always aimed at children, anime can be targeted toward older, even 18+ audiences, and complex plot themes, violence, horror, and even nudity are quite common. Most American anime is toned down to reflect more American values, however.

Study the image in Figure 4.26 and try drawing it. If you feel confident with your start in Figure 4.26, then draw Figure 4.27.

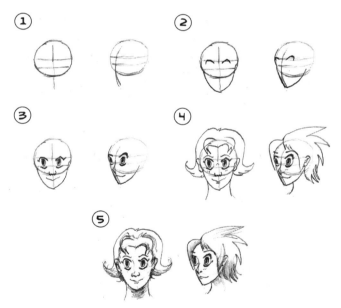

Figure 4.26
(1) Draw a circle with guidelines for the face. (2) Sketch out some more details to the face. (3) Draw the details of the eyes, nose, and mouth for the face. It's ideal to draw the eyes first and then the rest. Eyes are very important in anime. (4) Draw the hair. You can be as crazy and imaginative as you want to when it comes to anime hair. (5) Erase the guidelines you drew, clean up your piece, and then add fine details and shading.

Figure 4.27
To draw an anime magic girl: (1) Start with basic guidelines, an oval for the head, and oblong boxes for the upper torso and hips. (2) Add more guidelines for the hands and draw the eyes. Hands and eyes are two of the most expressive parts of a person, so they should be given a lot of detail. (3) Give the girl some hair and outline the limbs. (4) Erase your guidelines as you add final details. Shade when you're done.

Exercise 11: Scanning Your Artwork

To get your finished drawings off your sketchpad and into your computer, you will need to use a flatbed scanner.

How you do so is up to the model scanner you are utilizing, the computer programs you have on your computer, and your computer skills. What follows are answers to the most often queried issues with scanning pictures.

Resolution and PPI

Printer ink dots and image pixels are very different concepts, but both use the term *DPI* (*dots per inch*) in their own way. Inkjet printer DPI ratings refer to printer ink dots (the four colors of ink), which is not the same thing as image pixels.

You often hear image resolution called *PPI* (*pixels per inch*), and that is indeed what it is. Pixels are a kind of colored dot, too. For images viewed on computer screens, scan resolution determines image size. If you scan 6 inches at 100 DPI (or 1 inch at 600 DPI), you will create 600 pixels, which will display on any screen as 600 pixels in size.

You might think greater resolution means showing more detail, and while that's generally true (within reasonable limits), it's because greater resolution makes the image larger. But you are always limited by your output device, and often cannot take advantage of maximum resolution. The images are huge, and our screens are simply not large enough.

If you don't know your screen size, then go to Windows Start > Settings > Control Panel > Display icon > Settings tab to view or change it. On a Macintosh OS, you can do the same at the Apple Monitor Control Panel.

Popular video screen size settings are:

- 640×480 or 800×600 pixels for 14" monitors
- 800×600 or 1024×768 pixels for 15" monitors
- 1024×768 or 1152×864 pixels for 17" monitors
- 1152×864 or 1280×1024 pixels for 19" monitors

As a general rule-of-thumb, scan your pictures at 300 DPI if you want to print your work, but if you are making a Flash animation or game, you can settle for less detail, so 72, 96, or 100 will work fine.

Using an All-In-One Printer

The following steps are for scanning your images if you use an all-in-one printer that has a scanner built in. This is the type of scanner bed used by most professionals. An example of one is shown in Figure 4.28.

Figure 4.28
An all-in-one printer has scanning and printing capabilities, such as this Kodak ESP 5 All-In-One Printer.

1. Blow the dust from your scanner and printing area with canned air. Clean the scanner bed and the underside of the document lid with a damp, lint-free cloth before scanning. This removes dust and fingerprints.

2. Get your computer and all-in-one printer turned on and talking to each other. Open the scanning software on your computer, if needed. If not, you can use the controls on your printer to run the show.

3. Lay the picture to be scanned face-down on the glass. Square up the photo using the guides that are usually located along the edges of the scanning bed. Close the lid.

4. Go for a higher DPI count if you plan on displaying the scanned image at larger-than-life size. Otherwise, you can select a lower resolution.

5. Click the Scan button on your computer's scanning software window. Some all-in-one printers need you to press the Scan button on the printer itself, so check the manual before using.

6. Get a preview of the scanned image up on your computer monitor. This might happen automatically depending on your software settings; if not, you will have to prompt your computer to display one.

7. Accept the scan and save it to your hard drive. Remember to put your picture away.

A few last words.

Make sure your picture is clean and dry before scanning; remove any dust, hair, or fingerprints from the surface of the picture. Exercise caution when cleaning your artwork so as not to smear the image.

Use the scanner bed even if your all-in-one printer has a document feeder. The feed process can do horrible things to your picture. Trust me.

JPEG (pronounced "Jay-peg") files can compress the image to a smaller size for ease of storage, but the higher you set the compression factor, the more the picture quality will suffer. TIFF files do not significantly compress the information and preserve quality, but their file size can be 10 or more times bigger than JPEGs.

COMPOSITION

There are five major principles you should know that govern how to make an image look really cool.

Look around you. Look at the game box art that draws your eye in, or the poster on your wall that you could stare at for hours, or the desktop wallpaper that lights up your computer monitor's screen. These are all images you delight in or could enjoy looking at for a while. Why is that, though? If you had to put your finger on what it is that makes these images particularly enchanting, could you figure it out?

Usually, the reason that the images draw and hold your eye is because the artist knew about composition and the five principles that follow, and made good use of them to keep you absorbed in their artwork.

Composition means the placement or arrangement of visual elements or ingredients in a work of art, following the artist's thought process, their message, and the layout of the design.

What follows are the five principles of composition you should keep in mind when drawing scenes.

Principle 1: Simplicity in Design

It's true of most things, as it is of drawing: keep it simple! The KISS (keep it simple, stupid) principle is one to keep in mind as you draw. Remember, your viewer can take a single circle with two dots in it and a curvy line and interpret them to be a smiley face. The human mind is adept at seeing images even where there are none. So no matter how simple your image is, people will see something in it.

You can take the minimalist approach, if you wish, and restrict your drawings to short direct line drawings, counting on color values to make objects stand apart from one another. Or you can reduce the quantity of objects you show in a given scene. Reducing the number of objects in a scene also helps to refine your message, so that viewers know what you want them to really see.

However you decide to simplify your images, keep it consistent with your overall design.

Principle 2: Continuity in Design

A person has two eyes, and we tend to focus them on the same item at the same time. This focus means that we see with one eye, practically. What we see with our one eye when looking at a picture is not the whole picture, but parts of it, and how the picture is composed determines where our eye goes first, next, and last. Keeping the eye moving through a picture, never resting too long, is due to continuity in design.

Directing the viewer's eye through a composition can be a bit tricky. You have to grasp what object in the scene will catch the eye first and then look at connections between that object and others in the scene, because the eye will trail away from the first object along the easiest pathway for it to travel.

This can sometimes be directed by tangent lines, value contrasts, or energy of line strokes, all of which is heavier subject material than we have time to go over here.

The way that the eye is drawn through a picture can change the message of the picture, too. Look at Figure 4.29. In this oil painting by Albert Pinkham Ryder, *Jonah* (1885), the dark central figure in the sea is Jonah. Your eye is drawn from him to the God figure at the top of the painting, crisscrossing the turbulent

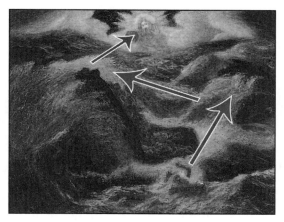

Figure 4.29
Jonah painting by Albert Pinkham Ryder, circa 1885, and the continuity of design.

waves. Because of the path your eye travels through the piece, Ryder makes you think of the terrible tribulations Jonah faces that end with salvation, making the image an uplifting and emotional one.

Principle 3: Repetition and Asymmetry in Design

Not only should a good composition be simple in execution and have continuity to lead the eye through the composition, but it should also bear repetition. Having repeated patterns, line strokes, or elements, appeals to people, because it presumes symmetry in the design and creates a more consistent and interconnected design.

The difference between *symmetry* and *asymmetry* is a vital one in composition.

Symmetry, often caused by repeated patterns, can be very appealing, but so can asymmetry. Look at the tree images in Figure 4.30. On the left is a tree that is perfectly symmetrical. The tree on the right is asymmetrical. Its sides don't match each other. Yet if given the choice between looking at the two images, people will generally gravitate toward the asymmetric one. This is because people prefer realism, and too much symmetry is unrealistic and bland.

Principle 4: Contrast in Design

Contrast is created when two parts of an image that are unlike are put beside each other, so that you are immediately taken by their differences. In art, this is

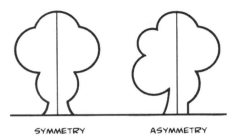

Figure 4.30
These two tree images show symmetry (left) and asymmetry (right).

most often caused by differences in value. One part of an image will be extremely dark, while the remaining part is extremely light. The distinction between light and dark will draw and capture the viewer's eye.

Frank Miller, artist on several *Batman* comics and the creator of the *Sin City* series, liked to work in pen and ink. He learned and developed many effective uses for creating contrast in his designs, to help continuity. You can see one example of his technique in Figure 4.31.

Figure 4.31
An example of Frank Miller's design techniques, this one showing contrast.

Figure 4.32
In this image by Frank Miller, radiation is created by the bars of the central figure's cell, leading the viewer's eye to the central figure inside the cell.

Principle 5: Radiation in Design

Radiation means lines, or rays, extending from one central source. In design, radiation is used to draw the eye in to a single object, to lend focus to that one object. This can be done subtly, to help the viewer find the first part of a composition to focus on, or it can be done to an extreme, as shown in Figure 4.32, to create a mood or a stylized theme.

WHAT'S NEXT?

This chapter should have prepared you for the drawing skills necessary to create digital animations in Flash so that later you can create Flash PSP games. You should now know how to draw objects, make them appear real to the viewer, and even scan your drawings into a computer. Next, we will look at making your images move by adding animation.

GET IT MOVING

CHAPTER 5

GET IT MOVING

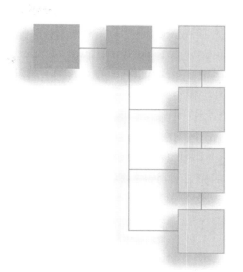

In this chapter you will learn:

- The basic principles of animation
- Traditional and Flash animation techniques
- How to make characters walk, talk, and "come alive" onscreen

Tip

"Animation is not the art of drawings that move but the art of movements that are drawn."

—Norman McLaren

Animation, as you'll quickly learn, is not all about making objects move around on the screen. There's much more to it. Animation is really about making objects look like they are coming to life on the screen, and to do so takes lots of tiny motions culminating in a realistic motion sequence.

These tiny motions are made separate but do not work separately. They converge to create ideal movement that follows the basic principles of animation, which you will learn about in this chapter.

This chapter will show you how to take your computer and make Flash movies with it.

THE BASIC PRINCIPLES OF ANIMATION

There are certain laws, similar to gravity, that do not change when you talk about animation. It doesn't matter if you're talking about 2D or 3D animation, because it's all the same. All animation abides by certain principles, and any animator worth his salt knows this.

In the 1981, Frank Thomas and Ollie Johnston wrote a book called *The Illusion of Life: Disney Animation*, which was ratified by Disney Studios. In this book, they classified 12 essential principles of animation, which are still used by industry experts today:

1. Anticipation
2. Appeal
3. Arcs
4. Exaggeration
5. Follow-through
6. Secondary motion
7. Slow-in and slow-out
8. Solid drawing (or weight)
9. Squash and stretch
10. Staging
11. Straight-ahead and pose-to-pose
12. Timing

To read more about Frank and Ollie's tips, go to http://www.frankanollie.com.

Let's look at some of the more important animation principles Frank and Ollie wrote about.

Anticipation

Anticipation is declaring to the viewer what is about to happen before it happens. It sets up the probable action and lets the viewer's eyes drink in what comes next.

Figure 5.1
By demonstrating this girl's ire in the first frame, viewers can anticipate the action in the second.

Think about it. If you were watching a show, and some guy kept purposefully irritating a girl, and suddenly you see the guy get karate-chopped, it might surprise you. You might even miss it. But if the animator started off slow, showing the girl getting more and more irritated, then the karate chop wouldn't seem to have come from nowhere. Look at Figure 5.1 to see what I mean. Anticipation is key to preparing the viewer for what is about to happen.

If a zombie apocalypse survivor uses his Louisville slugger to take off a zombie's head, his swing does not start as soon as he pulls the bat up. The action begins with the exaggerated backward swing first, as he brings the bat back over his head and builds momentum for his forward swing. If you time it just right, your viewer will have no problem imagining what is about to happen (see Figure 5.2).

This also adds drama, which a clever animator can use to manipulate his audience by getting them to anticipate one thing and then delivering them another (like in horror movies where the intrepid young girl looks in the cabinet, thoroughly expecting a monster to jump out at her, and when she does it's only her pet cat, but it makes the viewers jump anyway!).

Figure 5.2
This zombie apocalypse survivor scenario demonstrates anticipation.

Appeal

Frank and Ollie said in their book, "While a living actor has charisma, the animated character has appeal." What they were talking about was that live actors are living beings that come across mostly through their raw magnetism, but you cannot emulate raw magnetism in doodles, so you have to count on your animated characters oozing appeal.

Your audience must not mind looking at your drawings and must have a definite psychological connection to them as the action progresses. I am not suggesting that every female character has to have the curves and bust line of Lara Croft in *Tomb Raider* or that all your alien critters be cute and furry with big eyes like Ratchet from *Ratchet & Clank*, either. As you can see by the Yvette character in Figure 5.3, a character really only needs some exaggerated lines and specific visual details to become a personality. Use your best judgment when drawing to give your characters adequate appeal.

Appeal can often come out of exhibiting personality that the audience identifies with. As Irish artist J.B. Yeats once said, "Personality is born out of pain. It is the

Figure 5.3
Yvette comes across as a fumbling French vampire girl.

fire shut up in the flint." If your pen or mouse strokes can breathe that fire to life on the screen, you will have it made.

Exaggeration

Exaggeration is the process of slowing down and over-emphasizing the action you want to show in order for audiences to keep up with and understand exactly what is going on. Exaggeration also makes for more exciting animation. Indeed, it is arguably the core of truly great cartoons.

Look at the artwork of Ralph Bakshi, who designed *Wizards* and *Cool World*. His cartoon characters jump and squash all over the screen. They exist beyond the realm of realism and are more enticing because of it. Just like the character in Figure 5.4, you can stretch your characters out and exaggerate their forms to make them more enduring (though slightly less human!).

Figure 5.4
An exaggerated cartoon character.

You can also over-exaggerate motions. A backward swing you use for antici-pation can be pulled out to an extreme backward swing, or the bat, as it strikes a zombie, can almost bend in double from the impact.

Follow-Through

The survivor with the Louisville slugger won't quit swinging the bat as soon as it hits the zombie and knocks its head into orbit. The batter will follow through with his forward momentum, nearly swinging his whole body around, and the bat will continue on through where the zombie's head once stood. See Figure 5.5.

Likewise, a girl running away from zombies comes to a dead end in a city alley and stops. Yet her long hair won't stop right away. Take a look at Figure 5.6. The young lady's hair has been fanning out behind her as she runs, but when she comes to an abrupt stop, her hair will swish forward, carried by her forward momentum.

Follow-through is about not stopping everything all at once, because that would be unnatural. Related to Newton's law of physics, all things have mass and all objects with mass have momentum. If energy is applied in any given direction, the object will continue in motion until another object repels it or the object exhausts its energy.

Figure 5.5
This survivor scenario demonstrates follow-through of an action.

Figure 5.6
This runner, midst escape, shows follow-through even when she comes to a dead stop.

There should always be some obvious continuation of motion, like cause and effect; otherwise, your animation will look wooden or robotic.

Secondary Motion

Secondary motions are smaller, more detailed actions that take place during the main action to support it. They are also called overlapping actions. Secondary motions should never override or appear more important than the main action, or else they'll confuse the viewer.

Think of the anti-undead batter, again, and how his hair, clothes, and body parts react to his swing. When he approaches the swing, his feet actually leave the ground and his eyes scrunch shut to show how much force he's putting into the action. These are secondary motions, because they are subtle reinforcements of the primary motion.

Great character animation should clearly communicate to your audience what is going on onscreen.

Slow-In and Slow-Out

If you have a character's arm moving from straight up to straight out, and you want it to move at a smooth, uniform speed in the space of five frames, you will need a series of in-betweens, created in Flash by using a motion tween. You set two keyframes with five frames in-between (see Figure 5.7).

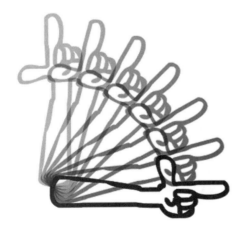

Figure 5.7
A simple motion tween showing a finger pointing.

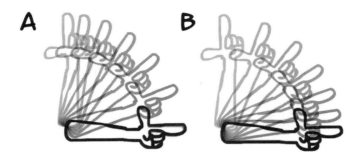

Figure 5.8
A motion tween with (A) slow-in and (B) slow-out applied.

All this works fine if you are working with a mechanical robot. But how often do people move like robots in the real world? Most often, people and other creatures have a strong tendency to speed up or slow down as we move, thanks in part to the laws of physics. This is what is referred to in animation as slow-in and slow-out.

Let's take the same number of drawings from Figure 5.7 and apply slow-in and slow-out. As you can see in section A of Figure 5.8, the arm starts out faster and slows into the stop at the bottom. Conversely, section B of that illustration shows slowing out, or speeding up as the arm gains momentum.

To do this, all you would have to do is change the motion tween's Ease property (found in the Properties panel when the motion tween is selected). The left of Figure 5.8 has an Ease value of −50 (in), and the right of that figure has an Ease value of +50 (out). Play around with each tween you create and find a better balance that looks more natural.

Solid Drawing (or Weight)

Every existing object shares space, volume, and mass. Keep this in mind, even when drawing and animating crazy characters like Wile E. Coyote. Notice that when he is riding an Acme brand rocket and runs into a boulder, his body doesn't scrunch up as skinny as he looks; instead, he flattens out like a pancake or folds up like an accordion.

When a rubber ball bounces, in the principle of squash and stretch, it flattens out when it hits the ground and stretches out when it leaps through the air. This is because of weight distribution through the object due to vertical mass.

You want to make your 2D images appear to carry definite weight because they will appear more solid to your viewer, and the world in which they reside, while never truly real, will appear more convincing a place.

Squash and Stretch

Twinkle animation studio co-founder Gary Leib says, "This isn't rocket science, folks. It's more like rubber ball science," and he's right!

When something like a rubber ball hits the ground, it squashes flat. When it bounces back up again, it stretches out. It goes back to normal, turning perfectly spherical again, before starting back toward the ground, in which case it elongates for a second time. Then it will hit the ground and go flat once more. It repeats this cycle until the rubber ball loses forward inertia or it strikes another object, like a wall. The repeated process of squash and stretch results in the flexible, fluid, and bouncy objects and characters you see in all cartoons.

It's not just rubber balls that do this, either. It's everything! Even Disney characters act like rubber balls when they walk, their shoes squashing a bit and their knees bending with each step they take, reflecting their quasi-elastic nature.

Practice the bouncing ball exercise shown for you in Figure 5.9 to get squash and stretch down pat. Each ball, in Flash, would be a separate frame of action.

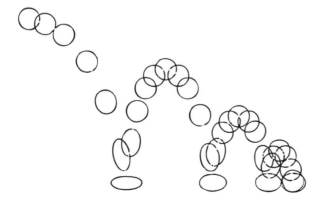

Figure 5.9
A rubber ball animation.

Timing

Traditional cartoonists of yore drew animation frames called extremes and then put a number beside them to show how many in-between frames they needed to have put between them. All this came from exposure sheets, which broke down the animation to the exact screen time each frame would be shown.

The number of frames for each pose affects the overall feel of animation, meaning you must strike the right balance between allowing the action to register with the viewer and creeping along so slowly you bore your audience.

I will take a moment to point out that timing has long been an issue of live action filmmaking, as well, and some cinematographers and directors have become well-known for their use of timing in their movies.

For example, directors M. Night Shyamalan, Roman Polanski, and Stanley Kubrick are well-known to the American public for the quirky, slow, and emotionally laden scenes. They use slower timing to lend more weight to each scene. Also, older films, especially those from the Hitchcock era, demonstrated a slower pace reflective of the time period they were filmed in.

Take a look at most anime shows. The pace will be frantic, speeding by rocket-fast during action sequences, and then slow down to a crawl during moody sequences where characters are addressing their feelings. You speed things up to increase suspense, tension, and energy, but you cannot keep a movie streaming along at that pace forever; eventually you have to let the viewer take a breather.

Find a happy medium when it comes to timing your scenes.

Other Animation Principles

What follows next are some other industry principles not specifically written in Frank and Ollie's book.

Line of Action

A line of action is an imaginary line running through the figure doing the acting. It is one of the key ingredients to producing dynamic, clear, and action-based animations. Can you spy the pirate's line of action in Figure 5.10?

Figure 5.10
The line of action is indicated, though not visible, and helps guide the viewer's eye.

Lines of action are special guidelines that show the general direction and flow of the character's movement, and they usually follow the character's spine and reaching, although this is not always the case.

A line of action gives a drawing direction, and just like rays of lines or pointing to the center of focus, a line of action can subtly lead the viewer's eye where you want it to go.

Silhouettes

The creator of *Earthworm Jim* and *Messiah* said that creating a character with a strong silhouette was important; this is imminently visible in *Earthworm Jim*, as no other character possibly shares the side profile of Earthworm Jim. The Flash games *Nevermore* and *Re-animated* take this one step further and have all of the characters drawn in silhouette, to great effect.

Take a look at Figure 5.11. Can you tell what's going on here, even without seeing all of the character details?

If you can "read" what is going on in a silhouette, chances are it's a successful animation drawing, even if you don't display the silhouette to the viewer but show the fully drawn detailed version. Silhouettes are best previewed and developed in the thumbnail stage of a drawing: When sketching the look of your characters in a scene, think about just their character outline, and their line of action, to determine how to make a successful scene animation.

Do Your Homework

There's an old saying in animation: "When in doubt, act it out." This is just as easily true for game design, as well, and in fact a lot of 3D games use mo-cap, or motion capture technology, to do just that!

Figure 5.11
This silhouette is irregular and noticeable.

If you are having trouble coming up with a character pose, then act it out yourself. And don't just act it out with your face or hands, but use your whole body. Find a full-length mirror, if you don't already own one, to pose in front of, or prepare your camcorder or web cam to record your actions. You can then use your posing as a reference guide when you are drawing.

If all else fails, don't forget the three Rs of drawing anything: research, reference, and resource. Investigate what it is you are drawing.

If you are animating some characters dancing in a Renaissance ballroom, look up waltzes and other old-fashioned dance moves, Renaissance costumes, and ballroom architecture you might want to include in your drawings. Keep a reference library of images you can use as a resource. A *morgue file* is a quick and handy collection of images you have found and can keep for reference. Every artist should keep a morgue file handy, because no one, not even Picasso, can draw in a vacuum!

The Internet can be a great place to start, but like most technology, the Web offers way too many dangerous distractions and the temptation to succumb to a tangent is too great, leading you to procrastination and not getting anything productive done.

Instead, try your local library, where the nice people working there can help you find just about any information you want for free. Just about any topic you can think of has a book written about it, often a book with pictures, and if your local library does not have a copy of that book, they can usually order it in for you for little or no fee.

Tip

"There is nothing like looking, if you want to find something. You certainly usually find something, if you look, but it is not always quite the something you were after."

—J.R.R. Tolkien

Fred Moore's 14 Points of Animation

Often regarded as having made the largest impact at the Disney animation studios, Fred Moore, shown in Figure 5.12, was posthumously honored as a Disney Legend in 1995. Moore worked as an animator at Disney during the 1930s and 1940s and is best known for creating the most endearing look of

Figure 5.12
Portrait of Fred Moore.

Mickey Mouse today and having started most of the animation precedents at the studios.

Moore's look and actions for Mickey started in 1938 with the short *Brave Little Tailor* and cemented by the acclaimed *Fantasia* shortly thereafter. Moore continued his animation tradition with *Snow White and the Seven Dwarfs*, *Pinocchio*, *Dumbo*, *Alice in Wonderland*, and *Peter Pan*. The hallmark of Fred's drawing style was his uncanny ability to give emotion, charm, and appeal to his characters, while making their actions seem very convincing.

Moore created a list of important items to check your animation against. Here is Fred's 14 Points of Animation:

1. You must have appeal in drawing.

2. Stage the characters and the scenes appropriately.

3. Is this the most interesting way [to depict the action]? Would anyone other than your mother like to see it?

4. Is it the most entertaining way?

5. Are you in character? Meaning, is your character acting out of its personality?

6. Are you advancing the character? Meaning, are you establishing the character's personality or pushing its involvement in the story forward?

7. Is this the simplest statement of the main idea of the scene?

8. Is the story point clear?

9. Are the secondary actions working with the main action?

10. Is the presentation best for the medium?

11. Does it have two-dimensional clarity?

12. Does it have three-dimensional solidity?

13. Does it have four-dimensional drawing? (This includes drag and follow through.)

14. Are you trying to do something that shouldn't be attempted? (Like trying to show the top of Mickey's head?)

ANIMATING IN FLASH

Flash has strengths and weaknesses, making Flash better for some things than it is for others. As with most software applications, if you cannot get what you want done with one tool, use another. For the animation exercises in this book, I will be using Adobe Flash CS5, which is part of Adobe's Creative Suite, but most of these principles and steps are general enough to carry over into whatever animation software you prefer using.

Symbols and Animation Sequences

Flash has unique reusable content in the form of its Library. This Library not only stores graphic images, sound effects, music files, and movie clips, it can also store symbols.

A *symbol* is any reusable object created inside Flash. A symbol can be reused throughout your movie or imported and used in other movies you make.

A copy of a symbol used within your movie is called an *instance*. Instances can have their own individual settings, such as color, size, function, and alpha transparency.

All of the symbols you can use in your movie are stored in the Flash Library, which appears as a long list from which you can drag and drop instances onto your Stage. If you decide you need to edit a symbol, all instances of that symbol within your movie are automatically edited as well, which can save you a lot of time and effort.

Using symbols correctly in your Flash movie is absolutely crucial. A movie's file size depends on the size and number of graphics and sounds used in your Flash movie. Reusing symbols rather than importing new graphics all of the time reduces the file size of your Flash movie, better enabling people to download and view it on the Web or on their Sony PSP, which is of major importance to you.

That's because a symbol's contents are taken into account and drawn only once in your movie, even if your movie contains thousands of instances of that symbol!

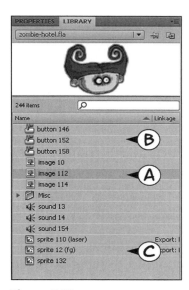

Figure 5.13
(A) Graphics symbol, (B) button symbol, and (C) movie-clip symbol.

Flash has three major types of symbols you can use (see Figure 5.13). They are:

- **Graphics:** Graphic symbols are reusable graphic images that are used mainly for drawing and animation. These symbols can be bitmap/raster images or vector art. They can be large or miniscule, and can be a combination of separate images grouped together for easy manipulation.

- **Buttons:** Button symbols are used for timeline navigation and interactivity. They respond to mouse clicks, rollovers and rollouts, and key presses. Each button has different graphic states, such as Up, Over, Down, and Hit, for which you can define different looks. Button symbols are not typically used in cartoons, except to click Play, but they are used in more interactive media, such as Web sites and video games.

- **Movie Clips:** Movie-clip symbols are reusable Flash movies with their own timelines, and can be made up of multiple images. Placing a movie clip on your Stage is like playing a movie within a movie. The great thing about movie clips is that you can also use ActionScript to control their settings.

ActionScript, by the way, lets you make Flash interactive and gives you the tools you need to make Flash games and applications. We will cover ActionScript further later on.

Tip

Make it a habit to give your symbols clever and identifiable names from the start, and use folders to group like symbols. This will help you a lot. It is easy to wind up with dozens or even hundreds of symbols in a single Flash project, which makes it next to impossible to find or edit the one you want. I typically put all of the movie clips in one set, all of the buttons in another, and all of the graphics in yet another, and I take the time to name each one so I will know what the symbol contains without having to click on it to preview it.

When working in Flash, you will find it necessary to create shorter animation sequences within the larger whole. Often, this is done by placing a blank keyframe in each of your layers on the timeline, reflecting the start of a new sequence, or by creating a new Scene in your Scene list (which you can view by going to Window > Scene in the main menu bar). The use of Scenes is largely discouraged, though, because they can sometimes cause problems with animating later on.

Evaluate the sequence you need to animate based on what is being animated, how it should look as it's animating, and what would be the most efficient animation method used.

Methods of Animation

When you come down to it, there are roughly three different methods of animation, as shown in Richard Williams' book *The Animator's Survival Kit*, which goes into the advantages and disadvantages of each method in detail.

Here are the main highlights of each method, although it would probably behoove you to purchase his book at some point in the future, if you decide to further your education in the animation field. Along with the highlights, I will discuss how you can use each method in Flash.

Straight-Ahead Animation = Frame-by-Frame Animation

This is probably the easiest way to animate, and the way that you animated when you put together your little flipbook. In straight-ahead animation, you do all your drawings consecutively from start to finish. You make drawing number one, drawing number two, and so on, illustrating each frame of animation on paper.

The primary advantage to straight-ahead animation is (a) it gets the job done, and (b) it looks good and can sometimes surprise you with its spontaneity.

The disadvantage stems from the last part. Unexpected things start occurring that get in your way. For instance, the scene may go on too long, the size or proportion of your character might change, or it might not "hit its mark" on the stage at the right time, causing lots of edits later on.

In Flash, the straight-ahead animation method is done through frame-by-frame animation, where each frame in an object layer's timeline is a keyframe with a new image on it (shown in Figure 5.14).

Each frame of animation must be drawn, edited, transformed, and prepped and can become seriously lengthy, laborious, and resource-consuming, as it takes up more room in the file's memory. Yet frame-by-frame animation can definitely look very professional.

Traditional animators call this "shooting on ones," because you are basically using each shot of motion on camera as one frame of action in Flash.

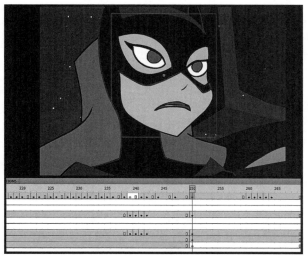

Figure 5.14
A Timeline showing frame-by-frame animation.

Pose-to-Pose = Tweened Animation

The pose-to-pose method introduces a term in Flash you are probably familiar with by now: keyframes. You do drawings that are key drawings, placed in keyframes, and then you (or somebody else on the animation team) do the in-betweens.

The key drawings are important poses the viewer needs to "read" what's going on, so they are often held on-camera for a whole second or more, allowing the audience time for the visual information to sink in before the story proceeds.

Think of a comic book. Although close to animation, a comic book is still made up of 2D still images. Each panel in a comic book, however, reveals a key pose of the characters. It's what is not shown, the frames that would come between each of the panels (indicating true animation) that make up pose-to-pose animation sequences.

In Flash, you create a keyframe for each key pose and then develop motion or shape tween animation for all of your in-betweens. Flash's tweened animation saves you a lot of long, arduous efforts drawing all of the in-betweens yourself or having someone else do it. Flash makes pose-to-pose animations much easier with tweened animation, which is shown in Figure 5.15.

The advantages to using pose-to-pose or tweened animation should be obvious: They save you a lot of time drawing each and every frame. Another advantage is that it is easier to edit the key poses or length of time for in-betweens, and less frustrating when you have to do edits.

The main disadvantage is the fact that real life is practically frame by frame, so doing frame-by-frame or straight-ahead animation looks more realistic and is therefore more interesting to watch, while pose-by-pose or tweened animation can look less real, more robotic, and therefore any animation primarily done as such will look like cheating to your audience.

Flash offers three types of tweening:

- **Motion Tweening:** The motion tweening technique involves placing a symbol somewhere on the Stage, creating a keyframe on the Timeline there, and then moving along the Timeline to a point sometime later and adding another keyframe in which the symbol's position or other setting

Figure 5.15
A Timeline showing tweened animation.

has been changed. You then apply a motion tween to the intervening frames, enabling Flash to interpolate the action that occurs between the keyframes for you.

- **Shape Tweening:** Shape tweening is similar to motion tweening, except you use separate symbols, usually vector art, in their own keyframes and add a shape tween between them. The shape tween then attempts to gradually shift the look of one symbol into the shape of the other over the course of the intervening frames. This can be a fast and ready way to animate a character's mouth or to show the character's eyes blinking.

- **Guided Motion Tweening:** Guided motion tweening uses an invisible guideline, or path, to carry the symbol from one keyframe to the next. In the intervening frames, Flash pushes the symbol a little farther along the path until it gets to the end. This is excellent if you want to animate, say, the arc of a baseball soaring through the air or the zigzag of a UFO in flight.

The Best Method

Remember that I said there are three methods for animating? Well, by this point, I am sure you have wondered to yourself, "What if we took the best of both of these methods and somehow combined the two methods into one?" Thus, you get the third animation method: the best method!

You can use straight-ahead or frame-by-frame animation where you think it calls for it, that is, where you need to show something moment by moment that would be too hard to do pose by pose or tweened. And when there are times in the animation where it would be easier to tween the animation, or carry it pose by pose, you do that instead.

Alternating between the first two methods creates a syncopated harmony that looks really good and helps tell your story.

Common Character Animations in Flash

Just as there are several common character poses you will find yourself drawing again and again, including left, right, and three-quarters view, there are also several character animations you will find yourself designing over and over as an animator, and so they are very important ones to learn.

The first is the character's walk, the second is its jump, and the third is it talking (moving the mouth in sync with the character's voice). I will show you how you can design each of these three in Flash.

Moving Your Character: Walking and Jumping

The most basic animation you will do is the walk cycle. Animated characters are expected to both walk and talk. We will get to the talking part in just a sec, but right now let's look at the walking part.

A bipedal character has two legs. That's what "biped" means: two feet. There will be times that you must animate characters with four legs, but first it is imperative to work out how to get a character walking on two legs. To do so, use the walk cycle of a normal human being from real life as a reference.

Taking a look at yourself while walking is very difficult. You can look at friends or family members as they walk, but *The Animator's Reference Book* by Les Pardew and Ross S. Wolfley will do you one better. Not only does this reference

Figure 5.16
A basic walk cycle animation shown from a side profile.

book show you still-frame images of people walking, but also bending, jumping, running, and more.

Look at Figure 5.16 for one example of a bipedal character's side profile walk cycle.

Exercise 5.1: Creating a Character Rig

This exercise will teach you how to create a Fluppet. A *Fluppet* is the shortened version of the name "Flash puppet," and is a euphemism given to characters made in Flash that are rigged with bones for easier animation.

Bones allow for inverse kinematics (IK), which is a scientific term that allows you to arrange symbols in a special collection called an armature. Basically, you use this armature, which can resemble a skeleton, to control shapes, much like a puppet.

In the following steps you will construct a Fluppet.

1. Open a new Flash document that uses ActionScript 3.0.

2. Make sure you're using the Essentials workspace. You can use whatever workspace you find fits your style and workflow later on, but to follow the exercises in this book, you will be need to use the Essentials workspace. For your benefit, each new Flash document you start, the first thing you should do is go to the workspaces button (top right on the main menu). Click the arrow to make the drop-down list appear and select Essentials, if it's not already selected, and then select Reset 'Essentials' to return the Essentials workspace to its default settings (see Figure 5.17). This will make your workspace appear identical to the one shown in the screen captures in this book.

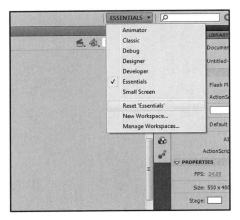

Figure 5.17
The Reset 'Essentials' option returns the current workspace, called Essentials, to its default settings.

3. Change your magnification to Fit in Window, as shown in Figure 5.18. This zooms in so that your view is eclipsed by the Stage, and the Pasteboard (gray area) outside the Stage does not show as much.

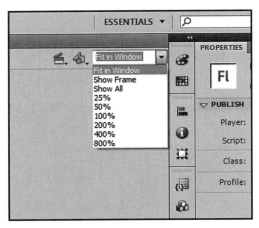

Figure 5.18
Find Fit in Window in the magnification options drop-down list.

4. Select the Brush tool from the Tool bar. This will paint whatever your currently selected Fill color is on the Stage, creating any shape you desire. In the Brush tool's options, found at the bottom of the Tool bar, click on the Brush Size and select the mid-sized

brush. Make sure your Fill color is set to black (#000000). If it is not black, click the Fill color swatch to open a swatches panel and click on black.

5. Using your Brush tool, paint the shapes you see in Figure 5.19. The blobs on the left will be your character's torso and neck. The upper-right blob is a sword, and the smaller blobs beneath it are, in order, the upper thigh, the lower leg (with foot), the upper arm, and the lower arm (with fist).

6. After quickly painting the first set of limbs here, switch to the Selection tool (hotkey V) and drag a marquee over them to select them. Go to Edit > Copy (hotkey Ctrl + C or Cmd + C) and then right-click on an empty spot on the Stage and select Paste in Place from the pop-up options list. The duplicate limbs should then be moved down a little ways from the originals. This way, you have limbs that will appear in front of and behind the character's torso.

7. You will have to change your Fill color to white (#FFFFFF) to paint a dab inside the head to represent the character's eye, as I have done in Figure 5.19.

Figure 5.19
When you get done drawing your character's bits and pieces on Layer 1, this is what the results should look like.

8. This next step is tedious, but it will save you a headache later on. With the Selection tool (hotkey V), double-click on the head shape to select it, then right-click on it and choose Convert to Symbol from the pop-up options list. In the Convert to Symbol dialog box, name your symbol charHead. Set its Type to Graphic. Compare your screen to `Figure 5.20, then click OK.

9. Do the same with the remaining pieces of our character, which should complete eleven different graphic symbols. Name them as follows.

   ■ charBody
   ■ charSword

Figure 5.20
Convert the head shape to a graphic symbol named charHead.

- charFrontUpLeg
- charFrontDnLeg
- charFrontUpArm
- charFrontDnArm
- charBackUpLeg
- charBackDnLeg
- charBackUpArm
- charBackDnArm

10. Go to File > Save As and save your Flash document as trialChar.fla.

11. Select all of the limbs that you marked "Back," because these are the limb parts that will go behind the character's torso. Go to Modify > Arrange > Send to Back. This switches their stacking order on Layer 1, so that, no matter what, they will appear behind the other limbs and the torso. This would be more important if they were colored different than what they are, but as they are silhouetted in black, they won't be as noticeable to the viewer—even if they are out of sorting order.

12. Do the same with the limbs you marked "Front," go to Modify > Arrange > Bring to Front, so that you know that they are the front-most objects.

13. Move the limbs you marked "Back" one by one to their position behind the torso. They should be slightly higher on the Stage, and shifted to the right, of the ones you placed that you marked "Front." You may need to move the charBody shape off to the side while you position the limbs, and then move it back when you're done.

14. Move the limbs you marked "Front" one by one to their position in front of the torso. They should be slightly lower on the Stage and shifted to the left of the ones you placed marked "Back." Again, you may have to move the charBody shape to one side while you work, and then move it back when you're through. Compare your work to Figure 5.21.

Figure 5.21
Your character should look like this when all of its pieces are assembled.

15. Before we add our armature, it might be easier to make the charBody shape transparent temporarily, so that we can see where to place our bones. Using the Selection tool (hotkey V), select the charBody object and look in your Properties panel. Under Color Effect, click the drop-down list arrow beside Style and pick Alpha. Click and drag the slider until you set the Alpha to 50% (as shown in Figure 5.22). Alpha basically makes your object appear transparent, with 0% being completely invisible and 100% being completely opaque. 50% gives you a semi-transparent look. Deselect charBody by clicking any empty space off the Stage before continuing.

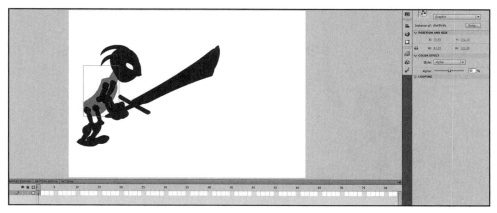

Figure 5.22
Make the charBody object transparent by adding a 50% Alpha Color Effect in the Properties panel.

16. Select the upper arm piece you sent to the back marked "Back." Rotate it until it aims out. Do the same with the lower arm and fist piece you marked "Back," so that it appears that your character is extending his arm straight out in front of him. Place the sword in his fist, like you see in Figure 5.23.

Figure 5.23
Rotate the arm pieces out in front of the character's body and put the sword object in his hand.

17. Switch to the Bone tool (hotkey M) from the Tool bar. The Bone tool's icon looks just like a bone. Click on the neck of your character's transparent torso and drag down and to the right, releasing when your cursor is on the shoulder of the back upper arm object. Where you started clicking is the fatter part of the bone, called the head, and the thinner part at the other end is called the tail.

18. Click on the end of the tail, which should have connected the neck of your body to the upper arm, and drag it down to the elbow section of the lower arm, and let go to connect the lower arm to the upper arm. Your screen should now resemble Figure 5.24.

Figure 5.24
Keep adding bones to connect the back arm segments.

19. Return to the very first bone you made. Click and drag from the head's circle to the top of your charHead object and let go, to connect the head with the body.

20. Again, from the very first bone you made, click and drag from its inner circle to the shoulder of the front upper arm. Then click and drag another bone to the elbow of the front lower arm. This connects the front arm to your character's body. You can tell when and where the bone will connect to the next segment, because a tiny image of a bone will appear next to your cursor as you're clicking and dragging the tail; otherwise, all you'll see is a circle with a line through it, meaning "no-no." If you have troubles, as I did, getting the upper arm's bone to connect to the lower arm appropriately, you will have to switch to the Selection tool (hotkey V), move the armature's upper arm up and out to the side of the body, and then select the lower arm. With the lower arm selected, switch to the Free Transform tool (hotkey Q), which is used to scale, resize, and rotate objects. You should see a pattern of black squares surround the edges of the lower arm, which should still be selected. Move your cursor just outside of the black squares until your cursor changes into a circular arrow and then click-drag to rotate that lower arm to match the position of the upper arm. Then click somewhere inside the lower arm and drag it up to meet the upper arm. Now you should be able to return to the Bone tool (hotkey M). Click on the upper arm to reveal its bone and click-drag from the bone's end point to the lower arm's elbow section. When you release, it should connect the lower arm to the upper arm correctly (see Figure 5.25).

Figure 5.25
Sometimes, to connect the segments right, you may have to move them out to the sides and away from obscuring objects.

21. Now, when you added your very first bone, a new layer was created on your Timeline, called the Armature layer. This is where all of the symbols forming your IK chain are stored. As you add new bones, the symbols from Layer 1 are "lifted" and added to your Armature layer. If you were to click the Show or Hide All Layers icon button out beside your Armature layer on your layer list (its icon looks like a human eye; to find the button

matching the Armature layer, which will appear as a dot when "off," simply scan down the row below the human eye), then you'd see the objects added to your armature vanish and only the symbols left on Layer 1 still appear visible. Keep the Armature layer's visibility on right now.

22. Even though we're nowhere near through, go ahead and test your IK chain as it exists so far. Using the Selection tool (hotkey V), select the sword shape. Move it around the Stage, noting how the other bones are pulled along with it in a ragdoll fashion. We already have some interesting animation going on. However, some things will appear out of whack real quick. For instance, your arms appear double-jointed, able to bend in physically impossible directions, and the body twists and turns, too, which it shouldn't be able to do. We need to add something called constraints to fix these problems.

23. Click on the head of your very first bone, then look in the Properties panel for Joint: Rotation. There is a checkbox called Enable beneath that. Uncheck that checkbox to turn rotation for this bone off (see Figure 5.26). This will lock the head of the bone in place, while its tail is free to move around.

Figure 5.26
Disable Joint: Rotation in the Properties panel for the first bone.

24. Click on the head of the elbow bone of the back arm. This time, leave Joint: Rotation > Enable checked, but place a check next to Constrain. This lets the joint rotate, but restricts its rotational amount to an nth degree. You can use the sliders beside Min and Max to narrow or widen the degree of constraint you place on any joint. You may also notice a small icon, similar to a bow and arrow, appear next to the elbow joint on the Stage, like in Figure 5.27. Play with the Min and Max values of this constraint. Then, when you feel comfortable with the results, add a constraint to your other elbow bone joint as well.

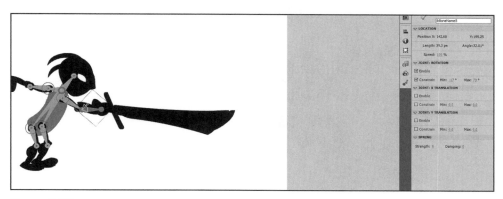

Figure 5.27
For joints like elbows and knees, you can add a rotation constraint as you see here.

25. Now, from the central bone, which is the first bone you created, use the Bone tool (hotkey M) to drag down two new bones, each of which will connect to the hip part of the upper legs. The upper legs then need to be connected to the knee sections of the lower legs. If you do your job right, the central bone should still refuse rotation (you unchecked Joint: Rotation > Enable), so when you take the Selection tool (hotkey V) and move the feet of your character around, his legs should move but his hips stay locked in place. If not, double-check to make sure that Joint: Rotation > Enable is unchecked for your first central bone. Compare your screen to Figure 5.28.

Figure 5.28
Your finished Fluppet should look similar to this screen capture.

26. You can play around with different rotation constraints or other values to fine-tune your Fluppet, if you wish, but otherwise we have the basic armature complete. Select your charBody and set its Color Effect back to None in the Properties panel.

27. Set your character's starting pose. You will want him to look like the character I've posed in Figure 5.29. This makes a decent starting pose, because he could start walking or jumping from here. Because Layer 1 is an empty layer (you can tell because its Frame 1

Figure 5.29
Arrange your armature so that your character is in a starting pose similar to this.

will appear white with an open circle inside it), you can delete it. To do so, right-click on the layer name and choose Delete Layer from the options list that comes up.

28. Be sure to save your file (trialChar.fla). The hotkey for this is Ctrl + S or Cmd + S.

Exercise 5.2: Animating a Walk Cycle

This exercise will teach you how to animate a basic Flash character walk. You will be using the IK you've already set up to do so.

1. Now it's time to add your walk animation! Nothing could be easier. With trialChar.fla still open, move your cursor over the right edge of Frame 1 on the Armature layer. When your cursor becomes a double arrow, click and drag to Frame 24. When you let go, the animation will expand to Frame 24, and you will currently be on Frame 24.

2. Simply give your character a different pose, like the one shown in Figure 5.30, and your changes will be automatically saved as a new keyframe and the frames between Frame 1 and Frame 24 will become a tween, in essence, interpolating between the two keyframes. Try to select only the hands, feet, or head, with the Selection tool when posing your figure. Some Flash developers even add invisible motion clips to use as handlers to their armature, but we don't need to get that involved.

3. Scrub through your animation to test it out. To do so, click and drag the red box playhead above the Timeline left and right across the Timeline. You will see your animation play out below. Go to Frame 1. Press Enter (or Return) and watch the

Figure 5.30
Set this as the next pose for your character.

animation play through at normal speed. Normal speed, by the way, is set by the FPS in your Properties panel.

4. Right-click on Frame 48 of the Armature layer and choose Insert Pose from the pop-up options list. On Frame 48, you need to rotate the legs to go the opposite direction and the head to bob a bit more. When you feel like your work is done, scrub through the animation again to test it out.

5. Right-click on Frame 72 of the Armature layer and choose Insert Pose from the options list. This will be our final frame of the walk cycle, so we want it to appear identical to your first frame, in order for the animation to actually cycle. Right-click on Frame 1 and choose Copy Pose from the options list, then right-click on Frame 72 and choose Paste Pose. Be careful when right-clicking and doing these commands, however, as I have noticed that occasionally, instead of my cursor selecting just the frame I want, it would select the entire animation. You can tell if all of the frames or just one are selected by how the frames are tinted. A dark green tint indicates that a frame or frames are selected, while a light green color indicates that a frame is deselected. Typically, if you deselect the frames by clicking on a blank spot below the layers in the Timeline, and then right-click on a frame, you'll select just that frame.

6. Go to Frame 1. Press Enter (or Return) and watch the animation play through at normal speed. Even at the default 24fps, which is set in the Properties panel, this is very slow. We want to speed it up. Move your cursor over the right edge of the final frame of your animation, until you see the double arrows appear, then click-drag the final frame back to Frame 20, and release. Now the animation will only be 20 frames long, but it retains the key poses we set. See the comparison of the "before" and "after" in Figure 5.31.

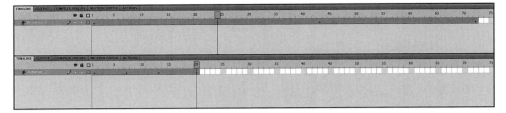

Figure 5.31
The top is the before image of the Timeline, with 72 frames, and the bottom shows you the animation's span reduced to 20 frames.

7. But wait! You're wondering why he only appears to be running in place, aren't you? This would be great if we painted a treadmill under his feet, but because we want to show him walking across the Stage, we better do something about that. All you have to do is this: First, right-click on Frame 1, where you have a keyframe, to select that frame. Select the Free Transform tool (hotkey Q). Drag your guy all the way to the left, just off the Stage. Right-click on the next frame that has a keyframe and drag your guy onto the left side of the Stage. Right-click on the next keyframe and move him to the right side of the Stage. Finally, on Frame 20, the last keyframe, move him off the Stage completely. Scrub back through your animation to see your changes.

8. You're done with your walk cycle! Go to File > Save As (hotkey Ctrl + Shift + S or Cmd + Shift + S) and save your Flash document as charAnimWalk.fla. Once saved, you can close it.

Exercise 5.3: Animating a Jump Cycle

Now that you have a Fluppet you can animate, making a character jump in place will be a piece of cake.

1. Open trialChar.fla, where you made your Fluppet and your character is in its starting position.

2. If you need to, reset your Essentials workspace (go to the Essentials button, upper right of the menu bar, click the drop-down list arrow, and select Reset 'Essentials').

3. Get the Free Transform tool (hotkey Q) from the Tool bar and press Ctrl + A or Cmd + A to select all of the objects on the Stage. They should show the black bounding box with black anchor points that comes inherent to the Free Transform tool's use. Click and drag your entire guy to the bottom center of your Stage, as you see in Figure 5.32.

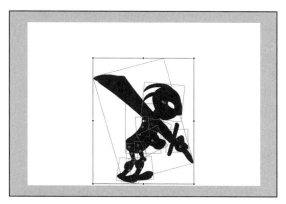

Figure 5.32
Position your character at the bottom of the Stage using the Free Transform tool.

4. Return to using the Selection tool (hotkey V). Change the pose of your guy to resemble the one shown in Figure 5.33. He is bending his knees in preparation of a jump. You should move his hands slightly and his head should rotate down, too. This is his anticipation pose.

Figure 5.33
This is the anticipation pose, where your little guy is getting ready to jump.

5. Move your cursor over the right edge of Frame 1 until it changes into double arrows, and then click and drag the end frames to Frame 20. Deselect all of the frames by clicking below the layers on the Timeline. Move your playhead back to Frame 5.

6. On Frame 5, set your character's pose to resemble Figure 5.34. Then switch to the Free Transform tool, select everything on your Stage (Ctrl + A or Cmd + A), and move your character into the air. You should also, while adjusting everything with the Free Transform tool, rotate him just ever so much counterclockwise, so that he appears to be pointing straight up.

Figure 5.34
This is pose number two on Frame 5.

7. Move your playhead to Frame 10 and, using the Selection tool again, change your character's pose to resemble that in Figure 5.35. Switch back to the Free Transform tool, select all objects, rotate him back clockwise, and move him down the Stage just a nudge.

Figure 5.35
This is pose number three at Frame 10.

8. Move your playhead to Frame 18. Go back to the Selection tool. Now change your pose to look like the one in Figure 5.36, and when you're done, use the Free Transform tool to move him all the way to the bottom of the Stage.

9. Lastly, deselect all frames. Then right-click on Frame 1 and select Copy Pose. Deselect all frames before right-clicking on Frame 20 and choosing Paste Pose. You now have a complete jump cycle! Test your animation by going to Frame 1 and pressing Enter or Return to play through your animation. To give you an indication of what your animation

Figure 5.36
This is pose number four at Frame 18.

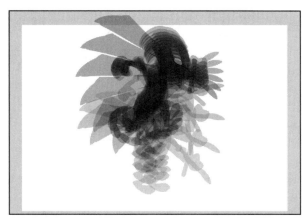

Figure 5.37
An example of the character jumping in action.

should look like when played through, take a look at Figure 5.37, where onion skin has been turned on to show multiple frames on the Stage at once.

10. Save your document as trialAnimJump.fla and close it.

Lip Syncing

Lip syncing is quite simply the act of matching up a character's mouth and lip positions with the spoken lines of dialogue. If you have ever chuckled in derision at one of those old karate movies with poor dubbing, where the mouths don't match the words you hear, then you know just how important lip syncing can be.

AY, EE, I   OH, OO   U

F, V   M, B, D   C, D, G, K, L, N
R, S, TH, Y, Z

Figure 5.38
Mouth movements in sync with consonants.

Figure 5.38 shows you that there are a number of mouth positions to make your lip syncing easier, as this is what most people generally look like when sounding out the letters. This is just a helpful suggestion, as everyone sounds out words different, which anyone who has ever tried to learn lip reading can tell you, but Figure 5.38 shows you the basic ones.

Just as nobody enunciates each and every word they speak just right, you don't have to draw each and every vowel or syllable in Flash. It would look just silly. Look for special emphasis on certain words within the dialogue, and place emphasis in the scene by having your character linger on that vowel or syllable, or show the character giving a grand facial or hand gesture, in accompaniment of the dialogue.

Also, you don't want a static face while a person talks. Their whole face should carry the weight of their words. For this reason alone, you should set the character's eyes, brows, nose, and mouth on separate layers from the head layer.

Figure 5.39
Some examples of different facial expressions a single character could show.

Then you can animate these parts of the face individually to provide a wide range of expressions. Some examples of character expressions are given in Figure 5.39.

Exercise 5.4: Animating a Lip Sync

We're going to get away from our Fluppet for a moment and work on a close-up of a character saying the word, "Hello." This is short and simple, but the execution takes some getting used to.

1. Open your Web browser. You can search for a WAV file of a person saying "Hello," or you can use the free sound effect created by Blizzard Entertainment on the web page http://simplythebest.net/sounds/WAV/events_WAV/startup_wavs.html. Optionally, you can use your computer's built-in sound recorder and a microphone to record yourself saying, "Hello," but because we have not covered sound recording yet, it is better to use a premanufactured sound bite. Save your WAV file to the same folder you are saving all of your Flash documents to.

2. In Flash, open a new Flash document that uses ActionScript 3.0. Save your new Flash file as trialAnimTalk.fla.

3. If you need to, reset your Essentials workspace so that you know you are starting with a clean slate.

4. Select the Brush tool (hotkey B). You will need to change the Brush Size to a much larger brush. Make sure your Fill color is set to black (#000000). Draw an outline of a character's head like the one shown for you in Figure 5.40. Once you have it completely outlined, and there are no gaps, switch to the Paint Bucket tool (hotkey K). Make sure your Fill color is still set to black (#000000). Click inside the outline you made to fill it in, like in Figure 5.41.

Figure 5.40
Use the Brush tool to paint an outline of the character's upper body and head. Make sure there are no gaps.

Figure 5.41
Fill in your outline using the Paint Bucket tool.

5. Rename Layer 1 by double-clicking its name in the layers list in the Timeline panel and, when you see the name highlighted, type Head.

6. Insert a new layer just above the Head layer and name it Eye 1. Change your Fill color to white (#FFFFFF) and paint an eye shape like you see in Figure 5.42. Make sure you're on the Eye 1 Layer when you paint this eye and not on the Head layer.

Figure 5.42
Paint the first eye.

7. Insert a new layer just above the Eye 1 layer and name it Eye 2. With your Fill color still set to white (#FFFFFF), paint an eye shape like you see in Figure 5.43.

Figure 5.43
Paint the second eye.

8. Now insert a new layer named Mouth above the other layers. When you get done, your Timeline should appear like the screen in Figure 5.44.

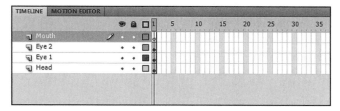

Figure 5.44
This is how your layer order should look.

9. Go to File > Import > Import to Library. In the Import to Library dialog box, search and find the "Hello" WAV file you saved to your computer. Once you find it, click Open. The WAV file will be added to your Library panel. Go to your Library panel, which is grouped behind your Properties panel, and find your sound file. When you select it, a preview of the sound, including a waveform and play buttons, will show up in the preview window of the Library panel (as seen in Figure 5.45). Test-play your sound file to see how it sounds in Flash.

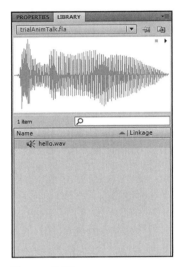

Figure 5.45
Preview the sound file in your Library panel.

10. Insert a new layer above the Mouth layer and call this new layer Hello SFX. Click and drag the sound file from your Library panel to your Stage. When you release your mouse, the sound will be dropped to the Stage. Its waveform will appear on the Hello SFX layer, and it will start playing on Frame 1 of the Hello SFX layer when you test your movie. You may not be able to see much of the waveform for now, being that the sound effect goes further than one frame. So expand Hello SFX's frames by right-clicking on a frame further down the Timeline and choosing Insert Frame from the options list. I finally expanded my Hello SFX layer's Timeline to Frame 20. This gave me the full waveform and three additional blank frames to look at.

11. However, you might not want your sound effect starting on Frame 1. Click on and drag the keyframe on Frame 1 to Frame 5. Then expand your Timeline again until you can see the complete waveform again, as shown in Figure 5.46. Your animation, if you used the same sound file I did, will be 25 frames long. Remember Frame 25, as it will be the end of the animation.

12. Expand the Head layer to the end of your animation.

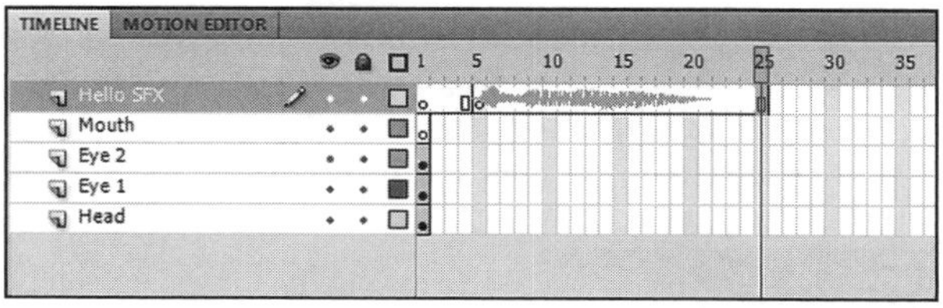

Figure 5.46
Expand your sound layer so that you can see the waveform, plus some additional blank frames.

13. On the Mouth layer, insert a blank keyframe on Frame 5. This is where the sound starts, so we want our guy's mouth to appear and start moving here. Lock your Head layer so that you won't accidentally edit it while editing the Mouth layer (to do this, click in the row under the Lock icon beside the Head layer).

14. Change your Stroke color to white (#FFFFFF), then select the Pen tool (hotkey P) from the Tool bar. Then go to the Mouth layer. Comparing your work to Figure 5.47, start drawing the outline of the guy's mouth with the Pen tool. Start at the top-left corner and work your way around the outline, clicking once to add a straight-lined corner point and click-dragging to add a smooth or rounded corner point (smooth corner points will show up with directional handles coming off from them that indicate the direction of the Bezier curve). Finally, close your shape by clicking on the original point you made.

Figure 5.47
Draw the mouth's first position with the Pen tool.

15. Switch to the Paint Bucket tool (hotkey K). Make sure your Fill color is still white (#FFFFFF), then click inside your mouth outline.

16. Enlarge the view of your Timeline so you can see your waveform better. To do so, click the drop-down options list in the upper right-hand corner of the Timeline panel and choose Preview from the available view choices.

17. Insert a blank keyframe (right-click on the frame and choose Insert Blank Keyframe) where you see a dip in the sound waveform, between where the guy says "He-" and "-llo." Use the Pen tool (hotkey P) to draw another outline, this one resembling the shape you see in Figure 5.48. Fill the shape in white with the Paint Bucket tool (hotkey K).

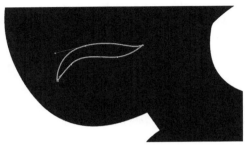

Figure 5.48
Draw the mouth's second position.

18. Insert a blank keyframe where the waveform changes from "Hell-" to "-o." Use the Pen tool to draw a wobbly oval, like you see in Figure 5.49, and then fill it in white with the Paint Bucket tool.

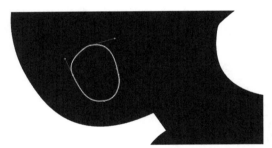

Figure 5.49
Draw the mouth's third position.

19. See where the waveform stops? You should have a few blank keyframes after it. Go to Frame 5 of the Mouth layer. Right-click on Frame 5 and choose Copy Frames, then go to the frame of the Mouth layer right before the sound waveform quits. Right-click and choose Paste Frames. Your screen should now resemble Figure 5.50.

20. You're going to add a shape tween in-between the shapes you've made. Right-click on a frame between the first two shapes and choose Create Shape Tween from the pop-up options list. The in-between frames should appear green. Do the same between the second and third shapes and the third and final shapes. Scrub through your animation to see the mouth moving. If you don't like where one shape is at, or it doesn't match your sound file, click and drag the shape's keyframe where you want it to be.

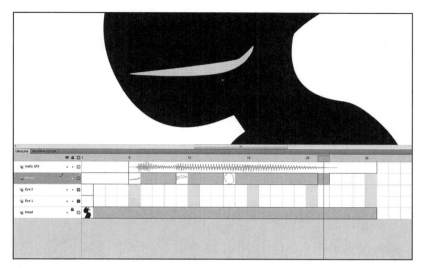

Figure 5.50
Copy the first mouth position to the final mouth position.

21. Let's add an eye blink to make the eyes do something special here. Right-click on Frame 15 of the Eye 2 layer and Insert Keyframe. Use the Free Transform tool (hotkey Q) to squash the eye. Then right-click on Frame 16 and Insert Blank Keyframe. Copy Frame 15 and paste it to Frame 17, and then copy Frame 1 and paste it to Frame 18. Expand your Eye 2 layer to match the end of the total animation.

22. Do the exact same thing to the Eye 1 layer. Except, when you're squashing the eye, you might nudge or rotate it slightly to add a subtle difference. Subtle differences in animation, after all, are what will really sell a piece to your audience; even though people may not see all of the subtle differences you put in, they will react to it as a natural effect of life.

23. Swing your playhead to Frame 1 and press Enter or Return to see (and listen to) your animation. If you see anything remiss, fix it, then test your animation again until you're satisfied.

24. That's it! Save your file (trialAnimTalk.fla) and close it.

WHAT'S NEXT?

You have learned about artwork and animation, but they cannot exist by themselves. What they need is a story to connect them. The next chapter shows you some great ways to make up stories and write a narrative.

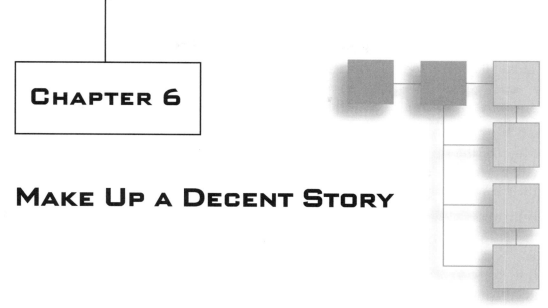

CHAPTER 6

MAKE UP A DECENT STORY

In this chapter you will learn:

- How to make up a story
- Storytelling techniques, such as the monomyth and ABDCE method
- How to create compelling characters for your stories
- How to draw your characters

Even if English and creative writing are not your best subjects, and when it comes to telling a ghost story around a camp fire you find yourself at a loss, don't feel doomed when it comes to making up stories for your animations and games! Anyone can learn to tell a good story, even if you have to do so off a formula. And trust me, most stories are developed from formulas anyhow, so it's truly tale-in-a-test-tube time.

This chapter is designed to show you how to create a good story. You will also learn how to make unforgettable characters as well.

TELLING A STORY

Humans have been telling stories since the days of cavemen, if not earlier. After hunting wild game, cave people would gather around a bonfire late at night to be regaled with stories of fearsome beasts and near death.

This still goes on today. Modern stories are more complex, of course, and may fit specific genres: Westerns, romances, fantasies, science fiction tales, mystery novels, horror yarns, and more. No matter the genre, the essence of storytelling hasn't changed; stories still entertain us and connect us on a subconscious level.

Many of the stories we partake through various direct media: books, television, and movies. Video games, quite often, will have storylines driving them, too, and their stories can be even more twisting and complex.

A lot of people make the mistaken assumption that coming up with story ideas is a talent that only a small fraction of people are born with and cannot be taught. For ages, these same people have thought the same about art. Yet you've seen how drawing is just a skill you can learn. Storytelling is a skill, too. However, coming up with ideas is not all that hard. Once you begin making up stories yourself, you will see inspiration is all around you.

So how do you get started?

"'Begin at the beginning,' the King said gravely, 'and go on till you come to the end: then stop.'" This is a quote in reaction to a question by the White Rabbit, in *Alice in Wonderland*. It is still true.

Most famous published authors advise: "Writers write." They say to just put words to paper, start somewhere, and eventually you will have something. Of course, it's not as easy as all that, and (at the same time) it is.

Here are the top ten writing tips you should follow:

1. Start writing and keep writing. Write every day. Don't edit as you write, as editing carries with it a different mindset entirely. Write "in the cracks," meaning anytime you can.

2. Writing is rewriting. Be prepared to edit and edit often. You might do it in cycles or pause to proofread as you go. Most of the written words you read have been edited at least a dozen or so times before you ever see them.

3. All writing must communicate ideas clearly. This is achieved through unity of purpose. Find out what the point is you're trying to get across, and use the right wording to convey your meaning (connotation). Also, identify and keep in mind your audience, and write on their level.

4. Choose your viewpoint, or point-of-view (POV), early on and stick with it. This includes what sentence structure you're using, past or present tense (e.g., "He says," is present tense, while "He said," is past).

5. Don't ever create stick figures to hang your plot on. Make every character (including the setting, because the setting is a character, too) as compelling and richly detailed as fits your story.

6. Outline your characters, settings, and plots/subplots on paper, so you don't lose track of where you're headed. Keep in mind that all events must have causes (storytelling is all about cause-and-effect relationships).

7. Never use a verb other than "said" to carry dialogue — and never stick on tacky adverbs. Never write something like "John admonished her gravely . . ." because it just looks silly.

8. Avoid substandard English. Keep your contractions, accentuations, and sorry sentence structure under control. Monitor your use of commas, semicolons, hyphens, exclamation points, "loaded" words, and similar-sounding words. Very rarely use the phrase "suddenly," and avoid patois or jargon like the plague.

9. Leave out any part the reader is likely to skip, including prologues, long descriptions, or other such windy items. If you hate writing it, it bores you to tears, or you'd skip past it when re-reading it, get rid of it.

10. Double-check your spelling. Modern word processors such as Microsoft Word have automatic spell-checking programs you can and should use, but these aren't as formidable as yourself. Arm yourself with a dictionary and thesaurus, and be prepared to use them.

So, without further ado, let's look at writing tackle, or the tidbits you will use to write with.

Tip

One of the greatest apparatus you have at your disposal, as a writer, is the human language. You should consider English as a viable tool. Believe it or not, a person who can put words together convincingly well will go much farther in life and achieve more than a person who does not. Spelling and grammar cannot be the last priority when you write. Get yourself a good dictionary and thesaurus and study the laws of grammar. Even if you think no one will read your movie script but you, or that only your friends will read the dialogue in your video game, don't be so sure, because you never know who will be reading these things and what it might mean for you if they do. Keep your writing neat and tidy and spelled correctly, and if you have any questions, consult your English teacher or someone with more knowledge who can help you proofread your work.

Storytelling Tackle Box

Following are some of the terms that will invariably crop up over and over again while developing a strong narrative for your animation or video game.

Characters: the Good, the Bad, and the Just So-So

Characters are the actors in your story.

The main character, also called the *protagonist*, is the hero of the story, while secondary characters, such as monsters, enemies, villains, allies, and henchmen, are supporting the story through their interactions with your main character.

Many stories feature another prominent character, the villain. The villain, also called the *antagonist*, does whatever he or she can to place obstacles in the path of the hero.

As Holly Lisle writes in her *Create a Character Clinic*, "Every fictional character, just like every human being, has a compelling need... The compelling need is the desire that gets your character out of bed in the morning, which pulls him through the day, that makes him take risks, or that drives him to challenge others." It is this need, and the pursuit of it, that moves the character.

Every character in your story has to have a motivation. To understand your character's motivation, ask yourself, "Why does the character do this and is it consistent with his or her beliefs?"

Almost all motivation boils down to Maslow's Hierarchy of Needs.

Abraham Maslow is a guy featured in almost every popular psychology textbook. He developed the now-famous Hierarchy of Needs, which is shown in Figure 6.1, as he sought the critical elements that lead to a healthy personality. His Hierarchy of Needs is deceptively simple. It says that people are motivated by five needs, in order of priority. Without one need being met, a person will have a difficult time meeting the next, and so on. What follows is Maslow's Hierarchy of Needs (in order).

Figure 6.1
Maslow's Hierarchy of Needs.

1. **Physiological Needs**—These include every human being's need for air, water, rest, sleep, food, and surcease. These are biological and animal needs.

2. **Safety Needs**—These include shelter, income, self-defense, protection, transportation, and "the good things in life."

3. **Love and Belonging Needs**—These include acceptance, love, compassion, empathy, and understanding from other people, our religion, and ourselves. It's been proven that baby chimps will die without a mother's touch, and human beings are no different.

4. **Esteem Needs**—These include gaining respect and glorification from others and respecting ourselves.

5. **Actualization Needs**—Once we have all of our other needs met, we can transcend the physical reality and start became true spirits. Maslow saw this as the true evolution of mankind, that one day we'd surpass our basic needs and become better, wiser people because of it.

Where are you at on Maslow's Hierarchy of Needs? You are probably, like the majority of people, somewhere between #1 and #3. This is normal.

Keep in mind that characters act out of their motivation every single time, even if their actions appear mysterious. It's not a mystery; the audience just doesn't understand their motivation yet.

Tip

Motivation is the past, goal is the future, and conflict is the present.

We'll study the inner workings of significant character building in the latter half of this chapter.

What's Your Story?

Story is what happens during your narrative.

You can generally sum up your whole story in a fast blurb, also called a high concept. For instance, Stephen King wrote a creepy book, later turned into a movie, called *The Shining*, and you could sum it up as, "Jack Torrance and his family go to be caretakers at a haunted resort lodge, and Jack goes crazy and tries to kill his family." That would be the high concept of Stephen King's *The Shining*.

You might've heard writing stories described as "hook, line, and sinker." The hook is the high concept, the genesis of the story, a sort of "What if. . .?" The line is the story progression, also called a plot. The sinker is the climax of the story, when it all comes to an ultimate peak ending. If you have a startling, neat-sounding hook, you can draw your audience in. If your line moves along real sweet, you can keep your audience guessing until you reach the sinker. This fishing analogy isn't far off from what writing is all about. Set your hook, reel your line, and snag your readers on the sinker.

Often, the high concept (or "hook") stems directly from your original idea for your story. You may get your ideas from anywhere at any time, which is one reason it is so important for you to keep a notebook at your side all of the time, just in case your imagination supplies you an idea when you least expect it. I, personally, have several notebooks filled with story hooks from random ideas I've received. When I get the time to create and am at a loss what to make, I can raid my private stash of story hooks.

Here is just a sampling of story hooks you might use:

Inspiration for Story Hooks (High Concept Ideas)

The protagonist suffers as a determined bride-to-be forces him closer to marriage with no way out. Can he discover why this is happening, who (or what) she is, and put a stop to the wedding in time?

A pretty ring in a pawnshop window seems to "call" to every passerby. It is a cursed ring that turns its wearer into a decomposing ghoul. The ring drops off when the ghoul has practically become a skeleton. The ring, it turns out, was found in the lonely house of a young college girl, whose family say she's gone missing without a trace.

A series of serial killings seem to have cropped up in an otherwise quiet suburban neighborhood. The murder weapon is apparently a long sword, and all of the victims are young women who all attend the same school. Police arrest an ex-convict working as a janitor at the girls' school, but the real perpetrator is a loathsome spirit that has contacted a psychic teen boy also at the school.

A number of apparent break-ins at a local greenhouse with no obvious signs of entry warrant the keeper to stay there overnight. Unfortunately, he makes the grisly discovery that the intruder is none other than an alien plant organism lured to the greenhouse by the new fertilizer he's been using, and he must fight against the creature. (See Figure 6.2.)

A traveling circus requests the protagonist's help. The circus was attacked by some nasty men, and the authorities are turning the other cheek (possible pay-offs?). The circus freaks were abducted from the circus and enslaved by the nasty men. The hero must track the men down and help the freaks escape somehow (perhaps by posing as a freak himself in order for the men to capture him, too?).

A creepy haunted house sucks up visitors, usually only trick-or-treaters, and spits them out every Halloween to run as creatures dressed up just like children to run down dark lanes, hoping to lure unfortunate souls back to the house.

Something mysterious has laid waste to once fertile ground. It was a cancerous meteorite from outer space, and the worst is yet come...

The protagonist invents a time traveling machine, which is stolen by a corporation intent on using it for their own insidious greedy plans. So the hero invents a second device to thwart them. He must go back in time to stop their meddling in the past, setting traps for them, and then finally face them on their own turf.

Set It Somewhere

The *setting* is the world the story takes place in and that the characters share as actors on a stage. A setting can be as small as a phone booth or as wide as a galaxy, depending on the scope of the story you are crafting.

Settings for most stories determine the underlying mechanics of the story; setting defines the reality, character professions and races, the physical laws, and metaphysical laws (for example, magic spells, spaceships, laser blasters, and so on).

Before determining how big to make the setting, consider the scope of your story and the impact you want to leave the audience with. Are you hoping to make a

Figure 6.2
Watch out! Behind you!

story surrounding an intergalactic war between 30 different alien species? Then your scope will be enormous, and the setting can be, too (within reason). Are you telling a cozy murder mystery involving an amateur sleuth, skillful killer, and nine unwitting suspects/victims? Then your scope will be a whole lot smaller and may never even have to leave one house. See Figure 6.3.

With your setting's description, it's best to start small and build up as you go. Lay the framework with a simple high concept for your setting, such as: "A remote winter-bound log cabin in the woods." As you start writing, you can make a map of the cabin and add more details on closer inspection.

Having trouble deciding on a setting? Here are some great starts:

Setting Inspirations

Climate or Landform	Sites of Interest
Aerial ship, habitat, or castle in the clouds	Caverns or mineshafts
Archipelago (chain of small connected isles)	Cities
Arctic/subarctic	Dungeons
Desert	Fortresses or strongholds
Forest, fairy, haunted, or otherwise	Mansions or castles
Inland sea or lake	Restaurants
Jungle	Ruins

Climate or Landform	Sites of Interest
Misty moor	Service buildings
Mountain range or redneck hills	Shelters, such as inns, cabins, or motels
Oceanic (on a cruise vessel or outpost at sea)	Shrines
Outer space (where no one can hear you belch!)	Temples
Prairies ("We're not in Kansas anymore... Are we?")	Utility companies
Subterranean, in dank tunnels or crypts	Warehouses
Swamp	Wharfs
Tropical or volcanic island	Wilderness
Uninhabited ruins or decrepit mansion	
Urban landscape or suburban residence	
Weather-beaten domicile	

Figure 6.3
Mystery and suspense stories do better in small, isolated settings.

I know it sounds contradictory, but you shouldn't overburden your audience with too much description of your setting, because that is dull and will wear them out; yet you should know as many intimate details of your setting as possible, almost as if you yourself have lived or do live there.

If the place you are using as a setting is a real place, see if you can't visit it for a time; or write about what you know, using your personal surroundings as a setting.

If the place you are using is a fantasy place out of your imagination, draw a map of it (at least a mental one) and include as many details as possible, but remember that this is just for your information, not to bore the audience with. Of course, if you're quite the artist, and your map looks impressive when you get done with it, when you're done making your project, you might showcase your map somewhere in your game or animation or include it in the supplemental or advertising material.

Digging Plots

The driving storyline of the game, or the path that the story takes, is called *plot*. Don't confuse plot with bits of land set aside to dig graves in! Plot takes on many guises in stories. Fiction stories usually have a major linear plot line, with several engaging subplots to keep the reader guessing.

A *subplot* is a minor plot that is not central to the story but has something to do with the interrelationships of the characters or the characters and the setting.

For example, your main plot in a cozy mystery set in a winter-bound cabin could be "Whodunit?" or, more literally, "Who killed Mr. Body?" A possible subplot could even be one of the red herrings: Miss Ivy is implicated in a dalliance with Mr. Body and Mr. Brown found out about her indiscretion and is mad at her; the protagonist will have to (a) prove that neither Miss Ivy nor Mr. Brown killed Mr. Body, and (b) get Mr. Brown back together with Miss Ivy by informing him that it was all a big misunderstanding.

Generally, the larger your story, the more subplots you will want to introduce.

A great parallel to this is spinning plates. There's a magic trick where an illusionist takes multiple poles and starts dinnerware spinning, precariously balanced on the ends of the poles. The real trick is keeping the plates spinning at the same rate so they don't fall off the poles. Each subplot is a dinner plate spinning at the end of a magician's pole. Get a subplot up in the air and keep it moving, then move to another and another, then back to the first before the reader forgets about it, and so on. This also keeps suspense going in a story.

Give It Meaning

Probably the most dubious term in storytelling is theme. Theme is meant to reflect the story's main idea, moral, or meaning. You can see the morals behind most of Aesop's Fables, and they, in their way, are themes, but a lot of times it is more difficult to pierce your own story's heart and bleed its meaning out in a single descriptive sentence, especially if it's an idea you just came up with.

Not all stories have to include an appropriate moral. Some stories are just for entertainment purposes. Plus, morals often go hand-in-hand with a person's religious beliefs, and if a story is not religious, it does not have to have a moral.

One of the most clichéd morals told in stories comes from teen slasher films of the 1980s (see Figure 6.4): you always know that the character who does the bad things, such as drinking, taking drugs, having sex, trespassing, or staying up past their curfew, will "get it" before too long by the horrifying ski-mask-wearing

Figure 6.4
In teen slasher films, anyone can buy it at any time, but especially if they're not being good kids.

monster. This moral is repeated over and over again to reinforce life lessons, that teens should do the "right thing" or else suffer the (habitually fatal) consequences. This moral is cloaked in the story so well that it does not come off as if the writer is preaching to the audience, but it's there nonetheless.

You can inject a theme or moral in your story, as well, and if you weave it in really well, no one will catch on.

There's Story Back There

The history of all of the events that have led up to the current action in the story is what we refer to when we say *backstory*.

The backstory can be as far-reaching as the creation myth of the world comprising the setting, or the abduction of the perilous princess the night before the handsome prince wakes up and sets off on his quest. Backstory is sometimes referred to by the characters in bits of expository dialogue or shown in flashbacks.

Flashbacks are so overused that audiences dread them. They are moments where the current narrative is put on hold while the writer takes the audience back weeks or even years, to see what happened "back when." This is supposed to make the ongoing narrative make better sense, by exposing facts the audience did not have before. Yet it also removes the audience from the action of the real story, and so it can lose people's attention if the writer's not careful.

It's best—as the writer—to know as much of the backstory as possible. However, you don't have to tell your audience any of it. Knowing the backstory, or what took place before your story starts, makes your story events more credible, but unless you feel it's absolutely vital for your audience to know it, don't tell them.

Keep 'em on the Edge of Their Seats

Suspense is the core ingredient of a good story. Allow your reader some unfulfillment, some fear or unknown element, until the very end of your story, when you're wrapping it up and tying all loose ends. Suspense calls for a deep emotional response in the reader, which compels him or her to stay engaged to see how your story will be resolved.

Remember, for suspense to work you have to use characters the audience will care for and worry about. You might have to make the characters even more identifiable for a wider target audience to do so, as long as your audience is sympathetic toward your characters' desires.

You can use plot twists and unexpected turns in the storyline to escalate suspense; you can also use life's essential weirdness (coincidences, synchronicity, déjà vu, and so on) to up the unknown element.

"Thou shalt have conflict on every page," say the Wee Gods of Storytelling.

Conflict arises out of the challenge that the hero must overcome. For instance, the princess is kidnapped by an evil warlock, and the prince must rescue her. The conflict coming out of this is that the evil warlock lives in a dark castle on the other side of a haunted forest, and the prince has obstacle after obstacle to face before he can get there. Conflicts can be internal (within us) or external (with others).

Are things becoming too complacent? If so, you run the risk of boring your audience. Invent a new crisis or bring an old one back. However, don't fall for the old "alligator in the transom" device; that is, when you have two characters talking at their office and, suddenly and out of nowhere, you drop an alligator onto them. Sudden and inexplicable crises that aren't connected to the story's action are unbelievable and negatively affect your story.

Complications add stumbling blocks and obstacles for the hero to overcome. Complications must:

- Derive from the story (no throwing whipped cream pies at a funeral!)
- Make real sense
- Be significantly challenging without appearing overwhelmingly hopeless

Allow the hero several failed attempts before overcoming conflict; this builds suspense and audience identification.

Don't delay conflict resolutions just thinking it will build more suspense; it will usually only frustrate the audience. Eventually, all those spinning plates will have to come down.

Arc, Not Ark!

The story arc is a description of the curve of action within the story, often the transformation of the main character but also of the minor changes in difficulty and danger.

A proper arc rises in tension throughout the course of the story, and finally at the end there is a major climax followed by a *denouement*, which is a series of events that take place after the climax as part of catharsis. The denouement is often accompanied by an epilogue.

Appropriate pacing is essential in capturing the arc.

Coming to a Header: the Climax

The *climax* is the final showdown, the last battle between the hero and the force of darkness, or whatever your story has in equivalence. Fiction reaches climax when the main challenge is answered and the hero reaches the conclusion of all his or her desires.

The climax is always anticipated and perceived by the audience, and if it comes too early or does not fulfill their hopes, then it becomes a bungle, or anticlimax. A proper climax thrills and surprises us.

The number one no-no in developing plots is to have a predictable story. You know your story is predictable when your audience starts figuring out plot twists before they are expected to. If these symptoms crop up, then you've just lost your audience completely. They might become so bored with your movie or game that they might never watch or play it again.

Make sure your audience is constantly on the edge of their seat, and place well-crafted twists and turns designed to surprise and delight throughout your story. Never let your story get dull.

After the climax, you need to take the spinning plates down, one at a time. This doesn't mean that you have to tie up every loose end or explain everything in your story. Leaving some plates spinning will lend mystery and leave your audience begging for more. You should take down just enough spinning plates to satisfy your audience enough that they'll brag about your story to their friends and family, spreading your story to an even wider audience.

Storytelling Formulas

As a writer, the yarns you spin through your narratives have the power to change people's moods and affect the experience they have, whether watching an animation or playing a video game.

If you are having trouble with structure or outlining your narrative, there are three main storytelling formulas you can use to construct great stories:

- Elmer Rice's Greek drama setup, called the Three-Act Method
- The ABDCE method for short-story construction
- The monomyth popularized by Joseph Campbell and used in the *Star Wars* saga

Whether you already know how to tell a story or not, take a look at these three. You never know what you might learn.

Rice's Three-Act Method

When talking about early Greek dramas, American playwright Elmer Rice, best known for winning the Pulitzer Prize for his 1929 play *Street Scene*, said there was a definitive formula behind them all.

Greek dramas were always told in three acts, and each of these acts framed a particular part of the story. Here was his break-down:

- **Act One:** Get a man up a tree
- **Act Two:** Throw rocks at him
- **Act Three:** Get him down out of the tree

This is the method that almost all Greek dramas were told throughout the ages, and it still works today.

Act One   It is in this first act that you should answer the where (setting), who (main characters), and what (plot) of your story, and introduce the whats of any subplots. You should also introduce the antagonist's main goal, or at least evidence of it. At the end of this act there's generally a twist, which alters existing conditions and forces the characters into action.

Act Two   Most of this act is composed of interconnected patterns of suspense, as the characters uncover each piece of the puzzle or overcome each hurdle one at a time. It develops the complications and builds the dramatic crisis. Halfway in, both the main and subplots should twist. At the end of Act Two, things should not look good for the characters.

Act Three   This third act is primarily composed of two things: the climax and the denouement. The characters experience increasing dilemmas, to the point at which they're not sure whether they'll succeed or survive, leading up to the climax. The climax pretty much concludes the story. From the climax, the story progresses into the denouement, which should tie up all loose ends and answer most questions. The end.

ABDCE

So you've doled your story out into three acts, like Rice said, and you still have plot problems? Can't seem to structure your story? Try using the ABDCE method, then.

This tried-and-true acronym, invented by the Greek playwright Aeschylus—who also invented the Greek tragedy—can be seen as the apparatus in many short stories and can work equally well for games or animations.

(I know, I know. Why does it always come back to the Greeks? Well, there's a very good reason for that. The Greeks were the ones who accomplished the most in story structure and the development of modern dramatizations.)

Here is what ABDCE stands for:

- **A is for action.** Begin your story with a bang. The Greeks called this starting *en medias res*, or in the middle of the thick of it. Dive right in, and don't worry about the audience getting lost or needing more information at first, because what you want to do is hook them first. Your beginning doesn't have to be Jackie Chan style, but anything with plenty of motion and emotion will do.

- **B is for background.** Now that you've gotten your audience excited and eating up the world of your story, step outside the immediate action for a moment and provide backstory information about your characters, grounding your audience further in the story.

- **D is for development.** Now that you have set the ball rolling and provided some crucial background information, your story premise has been set. You've wound up your story and it's time to let it go. Allow characters to clash, and let their complications further the story.

- **C is for climax.** Eventually it's time for the critical point, the point the story has been building toward all along. This is the instant that changes the course of all events in your story. Every story needs a central moment that carries the emotion to its peak. After all, this is what the audience has been waiting on the edge of their seat for.

- **E is for ending.** Now it's time to wind down the story. No one likes a story to linger like month-old leftovers, so let your story fade swiftly and gracefully out the door after the climax has passed.

Whenever you find yourself struggling to space out your story, give the ABDCE method a try as a series of ladder steps to hang your material on.

The Monomyth

Mythology holds a wealth of possibilities.

The film *O Brother Where Art Thou*, if you didn't already know, was based on the Greek myth of *Ulysses*. Of course, if you really watch the film, it doesn't seem anything like the original myth it was based on, and rightly so; metaphors remained the same but details were changed to quite another era. The underlying structure of the story remains a warped mirror image of *Ulysses*.

Hercules, Cinderella, Robin Hood, and Red Riding Hood have been plumbed to their depths in recent times, but thousands of other myths, fairy tales, legends, and religious stories can still be mined for ideas (see Figure 6.5).

CUT IT OUT AND JUST TELL ME WHERE I NEED TO
TAKE THE AMULET OF KINGS!!

Figure 6.5
There are lots of tales in the public domain still waiting for tribute.

The world's leading mythologist, Joseph Campbell, wrote a book called *The Hero with a Thousand Faces* that is a great resource for understanding the relationships between these stories. When considering the story you are telling, be sure to get a copy, and while you are at it, read Christopher Vogler's *The Writer's Journey*. Vogler takes an authoritative look at some mythic archetypes set forth by Joseph Campbell and how they relate to books and film. The material in *The Writer's Journey* applies to electronic games and cartoons as much as it does cinema.

Using Mythic Archetypes   There's substantial proof that mythic archetypes are powerful symbols that go directly to the audience's subconscious, meaning that the audience reacts immediately to such metaphors, without having to take a lot of time drawing conclusions why it is so.

For instance, some of the character archetypes that have the all-entrenched mythic connotation are the Hero and the Shadow, who represent the never-ending battle between good and evil. These are the five character archetypes you must remember: the Hero, the Shadow, the Mentor, the Trickster, and the Guardian.

The Hero   The Hero is the protagonist of the story, and classically he has the courage to do what he thinks is right, even against his own best judgment, the cleverness to get out of trouble time and again, and a strong code of ethics. The Hero is often resourceful and good at what he does.

The Shadow   The Shadow, also referred to as the villain, is the Hero's archenemy, the total opposite of everything the Hero is and stands for. The Shadow (shown in Figure 6.6) is a projection of the Hero's baser dark side, and therefore also has some of the same characteristics as the Hero, except for the Hero's code of ethics.

The Hero and Shadow will always stand valiantly opposed, as this is the most primal archetype.

Mentor   The Mentor comes across the Hero's Journey in the Supernatural Aid stage; ideally the Mentor is an older, wiser version of the Hero himself, but debilitated in some way so that he doesn't do any active heroism. The Mentor provides tips and help along the Hero's path, and he may even sacrifice himself to help the Hero's cause.

Figure 6.6
A lineup of classic villains.

Trickster   The Trickster is not always present in the Hero's Journey but when he does appear he is a prankster who may trick, ambush, or trap the Hero, either to get the Hero to open his eyes and see the big picture or to aid the Shadow in leading the Hero down a dead end.

The Trickster, shown in Figure 6.7, appears even more frequently in ancient myths, as the Norse god Loki, the Native American Coyote, and the African Anansi, where his actions are chaotic neutral at best: aiding and pranking humans, never forthright or predictable.

Guardian   Another mythic archetype is the Guardian. Guardians are not the Hero's allies; a Guardian shares some relationship with the Shadow (like being a henchman or evil accomplice) and stands as an obstacle or trial along the Hero's Journey. The Guardian tests the Hero's abilities, and if the Hero perseveres, the Guardian gives the Hero new items or powers to stand up to the Shadow with.

Figure 6.7
One representation of the Trickster archetype.

Hero's Journey   The *monomyth*, as described by mythologist Joseph Campbell in his *The Hero with a Thousand Faces*, is the core story behind every great myth. George Lucas got the ideas for his *Star Wars* and *Indiana Jones* film series after studying Campbell's findings, and several other movies, including *The Matrix* and *Stargate*, have used the monomyth as a story formula. The monomyth is filled with many steps, more like story suggestions, that naturally follow one another in a chain of events common to legends, fairy tales, books, and more.

These steps (also shown in Figure 6.8) are as follows, in proper sequence:

- **Ordinary Surroundings**—Most stories begin with the Hero in his normal world, so that when he is taken out of it through the course of his journey the special world into which he enters is more profound. This is the "fish out of water" concept. Think of Alice falling down the rabbit hole.

- **The Call to Adventure**—Something happens in the Hero's world to set the story in motion and draw him in. The Hero is presented with a

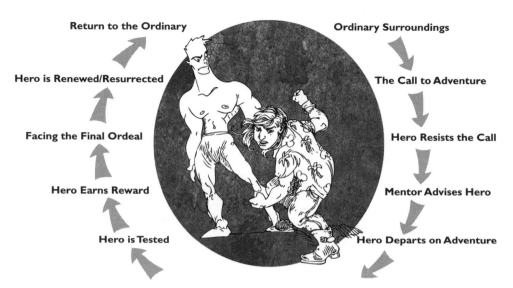

Figure 6.8
The monomyth.

problem, challenge, or quest, which will take him further away from everything ordinary he used to know.

- **Hero Resists the Call**—The Hero may have some reluctance to get involved with the story and could require additional incentive to move forward. If this happens, it is usually a self-sacrificing acceptance (not only has the Shadow taken over the kingdom, but now he's kidnapped the Hero's girlfriend, too, and the Hero isn't going to stand for that!).

- **Mentor Advises Hero**—The Hero encounters aid in the persona of an advisor (the Mentor) or a supernatural force. It is here that the Hero often finds a map, where to get a weapon that will smite the Shadow, or other useful tool to aid him in his quest.

- **Hero Departs on Adventure**—Prepared for adventure, the Hero crosses a threshold into a new and dangerous part of the imaginary world. His journey truly begins in earnest. Fraught with peril, this strange new world will test the Hero's nerve.

- **Hero is Tested**—Once our Hero has escaped the ordinary and advanced down a dangerous path on a noble goal, he will face many obstacles and tests. He also begins to learn the rules of the special world into which he has entered, which are inevitably different from the world from which he came. Along the way he will also make new friends and new enemies.

■ **Hero Earns Reward**—The Hero finds the object of his journey in a very dangerous place.

■ **Facing the Final Ordeal**—The Hero finds himself in the darkest moment of the story, where his fears become reality in a deadly confrontation. Everyone questions whether the Hero will live or die. Through this brush with death, the Hero is reborn or changed by his experience.

■ **Hero is Renewed/Resurrected**—Now changed for the better, the protagonist can take possession of the treasure he was seeking. This treasure need not be a physical object, but can be more profound than that. The journey is not yet over, though. Treasure in hand, the Hero must return to his normal world. However, the forces he's disturbed by his actions are often vengeful, pursuing him as he returns. Chase scenes are very appropriate during this stage.

■ **Return to the Ordinary**—The Hero returns to the everyday world, but is often different from when he left. Campbell likens this scene to rebirth and transformation, where the Hero—like a phoenix—dies and is resurrected an avenging angel.

CHARACTER DEVELOPMENT

Whether you're reading a comic, watching a cartoon, or playing a video game, the two things you are really paying close attention to are characters and the story line.

The story is outlined by the writer, conveyed to the audience by actions on-screen, and understood on a subliminal level by that audience, who may partake in it. Characters are outlined by writers, developed by artists, and tested by the way they relate to the story.

As a writer, your characters have to be immediately compelling and keep your audience's attention. As an artist, you must be able to draw great characters.

Elvira, Conan, Sherlock Holmes, Doctor Who, Indiana Jones, Darth Vader, Spongebob Squarepants... Their names evoke memories and feelings, don't they? All of these characters, plus many more, have become memorable in their own right. They exist beyond the stories they were originally a part of or the line drawings and color compositions they were imparted to their audiences by; they have become cultural icons.

Sometimes a character becomes a legend overnight, but in fact, it is the struggle, creative vision, and luck of its creators that lead to a character's ultimate success, on and off the page. No characters start fully formed.

First, a writer will generate a character idea, add details to that initial character concept, and top the details off with a cool-sounding name. Then, an artist will sit down and brainstorm character looks. Character concept sketches are drawn (see Figure 6.9 for one such sketch). Amid countless variations, a single sketch

Figure 6.9
An example of character concept artwork.

will be chosen and launched into a full-fledged character. Finally, a character for a comic, cartoon, or electronic game is born.

Before you draw your characters, first take some time to get to know them and create a description of them. The next section will teach you all about character generation as it pertains to writing.

"I Have a Brilliant Personality!"

Tip

"Character is what we do when we think no one is looking."

— H. Jackson Brown, Jr.

Creating a memorable character that audiences will feel for and want to know the outcome of conflicts the character might face is definitely rewarding, from a commercial standpoint and an artistic and technical one.

One of the most important elements of a character's particular appeal is personality.

There used to be this funny college-education commercial on an Oklahoma City TV channel that had would-be recruiters asking this young lady what skills she had, and she would answer (over and over again), "I have a brilliant personality!" The recruiters, needless to say, would just shake their heads. They wanted hard, concrete work-related skills, not a "brilliant personality." What the TV commercial also hit on, that's true, is that every human being—unless they're a wooden store mannequin—has a personality.

Personality is the basis of who we are. Skills are what we do.

Personality traits are important, not only because they influence the audience's reactions, but also because they can shape the character's looks, behavior, and dialogue. All of the most successful characters ever have well-defined personalities. Some may even appear as caricatures of ordinary personalities. Spongebob Squarepants, for example, is a nerdier-than-life fry cook who is *so* perky he is almost unbelievable; but then again, his environment and the circumstances he finds himself in are equally unbelievable, so he fits.

Before you make up a character, you have to make sure you know some of its primary character traits and what skills it might possess.

Writing Character Profiles: the Old-School Approach

Get yourself a piece of notebook paper, and get ready to fill in some blanks.

Using the old-school approach to character generation, much like the paraphernalia used for tabletop RPGs such as *Dungeons & Dragons,* you make up details about your character, almost as if you were interviewing that character about their most intimate particulars, or getting an ID for them at the Department of Motor Vehicles.

Details you want to know about your character include, but are not limited to:

- **Name**—See "Choosing the Perfect Name" later in this chapter for hints.
- **Age**—Characters typically range from age 6 to age 75, but this is up to you.
- **Gender**—Male or female?
- **Height/Weight**—How tall is the character and how heavy are they?
- **Eye and Hair Color**—What color (and texture, maybe?) are their eyes and hair?
- **Profession**—Do they have a job, or are they a student?
- **Income Level**—How much money do they make?
- **Education**—Where did they go to school, or are they still attending?
- **Residence**—Where do they live, and who else lives there?
- **Family/Friends**—Who are their family and closest friends?
- **Place and Date of Birth**—Where and when were they born?
- **Pets**—Do they have any animals for pets?
- **Hobbies**—Do they have any special things they like to do?
- **Pet Peeves**—Is there anything that really sets them off?
- **Likes**—What's their favorite TV shows, books, or movies? What about food or drinks? Clothing name brands or other merchandise they buy on a regular basis?

■ **Background**—Give as much background information on the character as you can. Where did they grow up? What was life like up to the point the story starts?

■ **Equipment**—What do they regularly carry with them? A cell phone? Camera? Sketchbook and pencil? What?

Next, rate the following character attributes on a scale of 1 to 6, with 1 being poor, 3 being average, and 6 being exceptional.

Rate the Following Character Attributes (1–6)		
Mental Attributes	**Physical Attributes**	**Social Attributes**
Aptitude—Ability to pick up new skills, learn operations, and blend in wherever you go.	**Agility**—Physical dexterity, grace, and finesse.	**Perception**—Awareness, observation, and sense acuity.
Common Sense—Practical knowledge, sensibility, and handiness.	**Prowess**—Physical might and athleticism.	**Presence**—Charm, beauty, force of personality, and social skill.
Intellect—Smarts, education, and the ability to learn and memorize information.	**Tenacity**—Endurance, stamina, and stubborn willpower.	**Subterfuge**—Lying, obscuring motivation, sleight-of-hand, and not getting caught.

Next, list the top five most frequently used skills the character is in possession of. If you don't have a clue what skills are, or what skills may be included, take a look at the following table.

Possible Skills to Choose From		
Acting	Animal Handling	Arts/Crafts
Auto Repair	Brawling	Buying and Selling
Carpentry	Computer Use	Criminal Science
Dance	Diplomacy	Disguise
Drivers Ed	Electronics Repair	Escape Artistry
Farming	Fast Talk	First Aid/CPR
Fishing	Forensics	Gambling
Gymnastics	Hiking	Hunting
Information Research	Interrogation	Invention
Knowledge, specific	Labor	Leadership
Lock-picking	Martial Arts	Masonry
Mathematics	Medicine	Melee Weapon Use

Music	Naturopathy	Natural Survival
Pageantry	Parachuting	Party Hosting
Partying	Pickpocket	Pilot
Public Speaking	Reading and Writing	Riding
Rock Climbing	Running	Science
Scuba Diving	Second Language	Seduction
Shooting	Singing	Sleight-of-hand
Sneaking	Sports	Stealth
Surgery	Swimming	Thrown Weapon Use
Trap Setting	Welding	

That should give you a pretty decent profile of your character. If you feel like you're still struggling to "step into their shoes," then you might want to use one or more of the next character creation methods. You can always leave some of the information blank on the character's profile and finish it later, after you've truly "found" your character.

Freeman's Trait Triangle

Giving your character three foremost traits, displayed as three sides of a triangle (Freeman calls it a Trait Triangle) as shown in Figure 6.10, you can straight away see how the traits would interrelate to shape the character's behavior and the choices they would make.

Whatever you do, don't choose dull or agreeable traits.

Figure 6.10
Trait Triangle.

Making your character strong, loyal, and stalwart is fine and dandy if you are tailoring a stereotypical Prince Valiant, but stereotypes are boring and predictable in any story. Mix it up more. Try making your character heroic, ugly, and clumsy, like Shrek, and you instantly have a winner on your hands. Trust the process.

Pop Psych: Creating Nested Personalities

There is another method, born of psychology, for creating a fictional character's personality. This method says people are complex constructions of multiple personalities and that we all have different sides we show to different people or to no one but ourselves.

Here is how it breaks down:

- **Ego**—The character's core identity, which must be protected at all costs.
- **Superego**—The character's parental inner voice or higher self. Imagine this as the angel sitting on one shoulder, telling the character what not to do.
- **Id**—The character's childlike inner voice and whimsy. Imagine this as the devil sitting on the character's other shoulder, telling the character what to do.
- **World Mask/Demeanor**—How the character appears to the rest of the world, which can change depending on the setting and circumstance just like donning an outfit.

Using Character Personality Archetypes

There are some character types that are just as conventional as the classic Hero, Shadow, Guardian, or Trickster archetypes found in mythology.

An archetype is an original model of a person, ideal example, or a prototype after which others are copied, patterned, or emulated. Personality archetypes can help make a fictional character seem more three-dimensional and thus more realistic. These archetypes are also instantly identifiable, because they appeal to your audience's subconscious and are more symbolic in nature.

Decent archetypes can help you by providing a jumping-off point to developing characters. What follows are the most often used archetypes in fiction, from the 1940s to today.

- **Best Friend** (male)—Decent regular Mister Nice Guy (think Tom Hanks).

- **Boss** (female)—A take-charge kind of woman.

- **Chief** (male)—The quintessential alpha hero, someone used to giving orders.

- **Free Spirit** (female)—Playful fun-loving hippy/artsy type.

- **Librarian** (female)—Prim and proper but repressed spirit, brainy but insightful.

- **Lost Soul** (male)—Tortured brooding loner type.

- **Nurturer** (female)—Capable and comforting caretaker or mothering type.

- **Professor** (male)—Logical introverted bookworm or genius.

- **Rebel** (male)—The bad boy image, who is a bit of an idealist.

- **Smooth Operator** (male)—Fun irresistible charmer.

- **Spunky Kid** (female)—The mousy girl with moxie or all-American girl-next-door appeal.

- **Survivor** (female)—Mysterious manipulative cynic.

- **Swashbuckler** (male)—Physically daring and daredevil explorer.

- **Waif** (female)—The typical damsel in distress.

- **Warrior** (female)—Thoroughly modern heroine, tough-as-nails fighter.

- **Warrior** (male)—The weary white knight or reluctant protector of the weak.

That may seem like a fairly comprehensive list of archetypes. Yet modern archetypes can come even closer to simulating real human attitudes.

The following are some more modern personality archetypes. The name of each is separated by parentheses. To combine two archetypes, take the word in parentheses from one archetype and add it to the second archetype's expression. For instance, a combination of (Artsy) Creator and (Dueling) Action Hero becomes an Artsy Action Hero.

Personality Archetypes to Choose From

(Expression 1) Expression 2	Description
(Artsy) Creator	Artistic and imaginative eccentric
(Babe) of the Woods	Young, naive, and innocent
(Caged) Animal	Frustrated, wild, and impulsive
(Charismatic) Mediator	Natural-born speaker or leader
(Chic) Elegant	Stylish and graceful
(Cloaked) Enigma	Mysterious and secretive
(Controlling) Critic	Cynical and judgmental
(Detached) Thinker	A serious scientific mindset
(Dueling) Action Hero	Noble, gallant, and romantic
(Fanatic) Phoenix	Visionary and prophetic believer
(Grunt) Worker	Diligent and hardworking
(Lone) Warrior	Reckless, hotheaded, and mercenary
(Mischief) Fool	Joking, witty, and playful
(Miscreant) Alienist	Antisocial, psychotic, and scary
(Mooch) Slacker	Easy-going, idle, and lazy
(Plotting) Kraken	Paradoxical, deep, and selfish
(Sensual) Hedonist	Indulgent and pleasure-seeking
(Sleeping) Dreamwalker	Mystic, all-knowing, and psychic
(Sniveling) Sycophant	Flattering hanger-on

Adding Little Idiosyncrasies

Tip

"If you want your characters to be fully fleshed-out human beings, you will not make them perfect."

—Holly Lisle

Identify at least three, preferably more, idiosyncrasies in the character's makeup. An idiosyncrasy is defined as a personal peculiarity of mind, habit, or behavior; a singular quirk. These quirks can be totally useless skills or absurd qualities that stand out.

For instance, a character might have a complex physical system where he cannot drink anything with caffeine or it may kill him, but he can, and does, imbibe in super-hot jalapenos all day long. The same character might also have a passion for picking up stray bits of metal he finds on the ground whenever he goes for a walk, and keeps them in a shoebox at home.

These sorts of things make a character different, interesting, unpredictable, and identifiable.

Here are a few suggestions if you're stuck for idiosyncrasies:

Inspiration for Character Idiosyncrasies

Afraid of doctors, medicine, or shots	Hair grows extraordinarily fast
Always getting into trouble	Happy and bubbly all of the time
Always klutzy	Has frequent nightmares
Bends into yoga pretzel positions with ease	Haunted by bad memories or a ghost
Can change outfits in a second	Immodest to the point of being vulgar
Can do higher math in their head	Lazy and mooches off others
Can find their way even in the dark or blindfolded	Likes and eats weird food concoctions
Can pick up stuff with their toes	Makes perfect paper origami
Can sleep with eyes open	One eye is a different color than the other
Carries odd smell	Picks nose in public
Color blind and clothes show it	Picks up stray kittens
Compulsively clean	Really good thumb wrestler
Cracks knuckles really loud	Speaks only in whispers
Easily angered and prone to tantrums	Suffers from mistaken identity all of the time
Extremely lucky, but only in the weirdest ways	Thin blooded (gets cold easily)
Gossips continuously	

Choosing the Perfect Name

Another element of character appeal that you should concentrate on is the character's name. Your character's name is really important, as it reflects the character, gives the audience something to identify them with, and can be oft-spoken of once the character reaches iconic status.

The choice of name should not be lightly made. It influences the audience's perceptions of that character.

If you name a character Grunt Masterson, you would automatically assume just by the name that the character is tough or surly; it's a good name for a thug, but not for a romantic hero. Whereas someone named Guybrush Threepwood sounds like, and should act like, a total dweeb.

A character's name should fit the character. It should also fit the story you are telling, and it should be short enough that the player can become instantly familiar with it.

Avoid making too many characters' names similar to one another or homonyms in a story. You run the risk of confusing the audience or causing undo frustration if the player has to remember some character based solely on name alone. For instance, you should never have two characters, one named Cindy and one named Sandy, because they run together when you hear them out loud.

If you need help picking out a really good name, your best bet is to use a baby name guide. That may sound weird, but that's exactly what most writers use. Baby name guides will even tell you the name's meaning and origin. Sometimes, when you have a specific character in mind, it's easier to find a descriptive word tag for that character and then find a name's meaning that matches the word tag.

For example, the Irish name Braon stands for "tear drop," so it would match a sad or depressed character in your story perfectly. And if you have a fighter in your tale, you might want to consider the Hebrew name Gideon, as it means "mighty warrior." Try to couple name meanings with your character's personality.

Don't have time to raid your local bookstore or library to pick up a baby name guide? You can also go online to any of these Web sites and search for names:

- Kudobaby.com
- Babynology.com
- Cool-Baby-Names.com

Allowing for Personality Growth

Tip

"Character does not form in the moments when we're happy. Character forms when things start to go wrong."

—Holly Lisle

In traditional film and literature, the worth of the plot is measured by the main character's personality growth, or how far the character has to go to get what he wants most and how much they have to change to meet the challenges they face. Characters such as Nick (*Nick and Norah's Infinite Playlist*) and Napoleon Dynamite reveal humanity's ever-present desire to rise above the contented state and reach for something better.

What are the challenges that define such characters? What approach to these challenges best exemplify their personality? How does what happens to the character change them into a different person?

Do all of your characters have to reveal personality growth or become different people? No, they don't.

On the other side of the fence are those stories where events happen, but the character doesn't seem to change or grow at all; they merely survive. Doctor Who, James Bond, Lara Croft, and Conan are all perfect examples of characters that we can count on to be just the way they are, no matter what story we watch or read with them as central figures. It is even true that considering characters like these, if they were to change dramatically, we would actually be offended beyond belief.

The Face Behind the Attitude

Now that you have a story and the written description of the character to go in it, all you need to come up with is what that character looks like.

Designers find the greatest challenge to making a character is evincing a strong reflection of the character's personality in a single visage that can be glorified through words or in art without looking like every other character that has come before.

What are some dramatic and telling features that will draw and hold your audience's attention? What if your character was portrayed in film or appeared larger than life, billboard-sized? What would attract your attention to the character then?

Take a look at some of the methods detailed previously you may have used to create your character. How would each of those character archetypes, traits, or idiosyncrasies show up or be represented in the character's physical appearance? Say, if you wrote down in your notebook that your character is "lazy," what visual cues could you use to reveal that they are lazy? Are their shoelaces always untied, hair uncombed, and shirt wrinkled? Create a crafted visual hook by selecting one or more of these specific traits about your character and accentuating them.

Many characters have a distinct costume that sets them apart. Color schemes and noticeable familiar details should remain consistent, endearing your character to your audience. Set your character apart from the rest by developing habitual stances, looks, and visual traits.

The first impression audiences have of a character is its appearance, and often this impression is formed before the audience ever starts watching the animation or picking up the game controls, likely in a trailer or demo or box art the developer has released. The character's first impression must encompass personality, voice, expression, vitality, and flair.

Drawing Thumbnails and Model Sheets

Do several thumbnails of your character before you make the final decision on what they will look like. Thumbnails are smaller sketches that cover the salient points concisely without any real details. Fill one or more pages with thumbnails; then squint at them to see which one leaps off the page at you. If squinting doesn't help, put the thumbnails away for a day or two; when you look at them again, one of the images may call to you more than the rest.

Choose the strongest most impressionable image for your character, and sit down and get busy drawing.

First do a full-featured drawing; after that, draw a model sheet. Model sheets, which are sometimes called turnarounds, depict the same character from

Figure 6.11
One character's model sheet.

multiple angles, in multiple poses, and with multiple expressions—in other words, in as many varieties as possible.

See Figure 6.11 for one example of a model sheet, or visit www.AnimationMeat. com for more.

Model sheets help you not only when you are drawing, but also when other artists work with you to complete a project.

Note

When you look at an artist's work, you are really seeing the final polished product they came up with. There is no telling how much preliminary work it took for the artist to get to that stage. So you shouldn't worry if it takes you time to get from a basic character to a fully realized character.

Drawing Bodies in Proper Proportion

Learning the proper physical proportions of human anatomy and developing a practical technique are key to sketching figures successfully. People know what people look like, so if the body you draw looks odd, chances are people will notice.

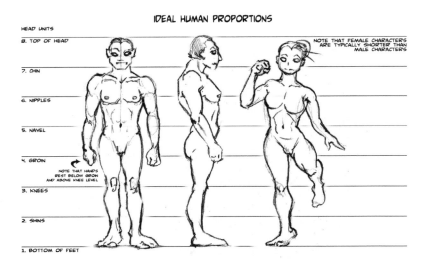

IDEAL HUMAN PROPORTIONS

HEAD UNITS

8. TOP OF HEAD

NOTE THAT FEMALE CHARACTERS
ARE TYPICALLY SHORTER THAN
MALE CHARACTERS

7. CHIN

6. NIPPLES

5. NAVEL

4. GROIN

NOTE THAT HANDS
REST BELOW GROIN
AND ABOVE KNEE LEVEL

3. KNEES

2. SHINS

1. BOTTOM OF FEET

Figure 6.12
Ideal human proportions.

Even if you're shooting to make a wild and crazy toon character, you should have knowledge of real anatomy before designing exaggerated anatomy. I was delighted when I got into college and started studying fine art, because some of the first classes I took were figure drawing classes. In figure drawing, you use a live model as reference to understand how to draw human anatomy. This is vital for anyone, even artists who later go off to draw/paint fantasy or cartoon figures.

There are between seven and eight heads in height for an adult figure and between three and four heads in a young child or chibi figure; by "head" I mean the measured length of someone's head. Look at Figure 6.12 to imprint these proportions in your mind. Notice how I call these "ideal" proportions. This is because everybody is different, and some people don't fit within these sets of parameters. That's okay.

Body shape can let a person know a lot about character, especially gender, age, strength, how much they work out, and more. Males typically have a larger rib cage and upper torso, while females typically have larger pelvises. Take a look at Figure 6.13 for a classic hero and heroine body shape.

Figure 6.13
A classic hero and heroine body shape.

You can morph this setup in many different ways to create a cast of thousands. For instance, you can elongate the torso and limbs to make a taller character and give them a square head, or you can squash the torso and make the limbs shorter. These endless variations, when placed in your other drawings, will make your characters more identifiable and compelling.

Drawing Faces

This demonstration is intended to be a quick guide. Drawing faces is a subject deserving an entire book and a lot of practice to master; however, there are a few fast rules that if followed correctly can help you to sketch faces more successfully. Study Figure 6.14 as you read on.

1. The head is roughly an egg shape with a scooped shape attached at the front for a jaw.

2. Draw halfway lines. The eyes are on a line halfway between the top of the skull and the bottom of the chin. The bottom of the nose is on a line

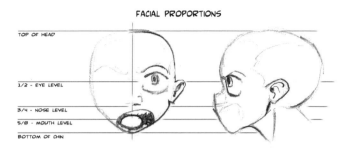

Figure 6.14
Drawing a character's head starts with an oval shape, some guidelines, and features on top of those.

halfway between the center of the eye line and the bottom of the chin. The middle of the mouth is on a line halfway between the bottom of the nose and the bottom of the chin. The top of the ears are just slightly above the center of the eye line, and the bottoms of the ears are on the bottom of the nose line.

Note

Imagine that these halfway lines aren't guidelines that remain straight across, cutting the head in half every time. If the head is rotated to the side, that would look very silly. Imagine these halfway lines are ellipses that run clear around the oval you've drawn for the head, and when the head rolls from side to side, the halfway lines turn, too. If you have problems imagining this, get a permanent marker and draw lines all of the way around a hard-boiled egg, pretending the egg is a head, and then look what happens to the ellipses you drew when the egg is rolled from side to side. The contours of the face, hair, and features can be built upon the foundation of the guidelines of the head, no matter what its incline or pose, in much the same way.

3. A vertical line down the center of the face sees the eyes, nose, mouth, and ears divided equally on either side of it. The eyes are kept one eye length apart.

4. Place the facial features on the guidelines you drew, then erase your guidelines when you're done.

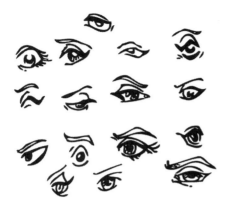

Figure 6.15
A wide assortment of cartoon eyes.

An age-old adage says that eyes are the windows to the soul. Indeed, eyes and eyebrows are among the most genuinely expressive features people have, and they can set one character's appearance apart from another's.

Eyes are just as diverse as fingerprints, and just as much so in drawings. Look at the eyes in Figure 6.15. Good guys and girls, small children, and cute fuzzy things tend to have large eyes with wide pupils and thin eyebrows, whereas bad guys and shifty characters often have much narrower eyes and big bushy eyebrows.

The size, slope, and contour of the eyes add a lot of character to people, as do the size and thickness of the brows. For instance, eyebrows that rise up in the middle, just above the bridge of the nose, could indicate confusion, surprise, shock, sadness, or interest, while if they slope down into a sharp V over the bridge of the nose they could indicate rage or disgust.

As a structure made of cartilage that can and does come in all shapes, the nose can be insufferably difficult to draw. Some artists opt to use a dot, dash, or single line to indicate a nose, while others draw long sweeping vertical lines ending in more realistic nasal depressions. Still others, using the old-school Saturday-morning-comic-strip style, use bulbous ovals for noses.

You have just as much freedom, if not more, with mouths. Keep in mind the other half of expressions, besides eyes, is found in a person's lips, from an O of fright to a sideways D of joy. You can draw mouths simply as a set of lines or more detailed and realistic; it is really up to you. Men's lips tend to be thinner than women's, and the bottom lip is generally larger than the upper lip. When the mouth is open, some teeth typically show. You can draw teeth as just a white space; you can add lines to separate individual teeth; or you can attempt some style in between these two.

People's faces stop growing as they mature, except for the nose and ears, which continue to grow for the rest of your life; the older a person, the larger the nose and ears will look in comparison to the remainder of their face. People get wrinkles, too, mostly from demonstrating the same facial expressions over and over again. Common areas for wrinkles are at the corners of the eyes, around the mouth, and along the forehead.

Little children are different-looking, too, in that they have big round heads relative to the size of their bodies, and their bodies are rounded all over by what is referred to as "baby fat," which goes away as they grow older. Kids have small unformed lips, button noses, and missing teeth, all of which helps shape their facial structure.

Look at Figure 6.16 to sketch some varieties of facial features.

Drawing Hands and Feet

Arms and legs are jointed cylinders that come off of the torso or pelvis. They appear thicker, generally, the closer they are to the body, and taper out to the end of the wrists or ankles.

You can cheat when sketching hands and feet. Feet you can make out of single flattened ovals or joined spheres. Try making hands by drawing long ovals and sticking thumbs onto them. You don't worry about individual fingers for now. If you hadn't noticed before, most cartoon drawings of hands show fewer fingers than human beings have, and this is no mistake; this convention came about because it is easier for artists to paint and animate only a few fingers, if any, and it also helps prevent drawers from making their characters' hands look like bunches of bananas.

Figure 6.16
Several different kinds of faces.

However, if you do want to draw more realistic hands, you can sketch the hand shown in Figure 6.17.

Drawing Hairstyles and Costumes

Hair and clothing are extensions of the character's personality. Just like we humans fuss with our own hair and outfits on a nearly daily basis, in part to show our individuality and to look good when we go out, you can make the best impression of your character by dressing them with the right part or fixing them with a special hairdo.

Hair and clothes are rarely plastered to the skin. Instead, they have volume and life all their own. People arrange their hair in countless ways, including cut, dyed, permed, and styled. Block in hair when sketching, and then draw hair in clumps or shapes.

Look at a beauty magazine if you have trouble imagining hairstyles.

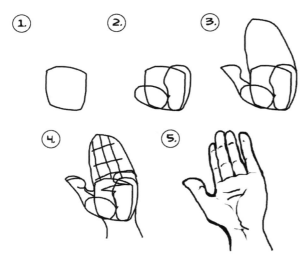

Figure 6.17
Try drawing this hand, then look at and draw your own hand.

Although clothing is worn primarily for protection, modesty, and warmth, another primary reason people wear clothes is for individual expression. Characters can show their personality in the clothes they wear and the way they wear them. Clothing can alter perceptions of a person, instantly giving away clues about their personality, tastes, socio-economic status, profession, beliefs, and whether they belong to a specific group. It can also be used to determine time period (see Figure 6.18) and convey visual interest.

Peruse costume books, fashion magazines, illustrated history books, and even your own wardrobe for inspiration. Placing different outfits on your character can be lots of fun in and of itself.

Establishing Poses

If you get stuck when trying to draw a character in a specific pose, try sketching a stick figure in that pose and build a model over that skeletal framework, like you see in Figure 6.19.

Alternatively, you could ask a friend to pose for you or use a mirror and pose yourself. What you really are after are the base proportions of shapes in the character's pose, and what body parts overlay or are in front of or behind other

Figure 6.18
Costumes can help define, for the viewer, the time period of your story, as you can tell by this Old West garb I'm wearing here.

Figure 6.19
Use a stick figure to rough in where body parts go in any pose.

body parts when the body is in that specific pose. This process can take a while to learn, and you might need to take figure-drawing classes at an art school to get really good at it.

Drawing Facial Expressions and Body Language

Drawing facial expressions can be a terrifying challenge. We look at faces every day of our lives, and faces are what we focus on when trying to understand another person's emotions or reactions. Despite this obvious familiarity, we find drawing facial expressions a challenging task. However, by making very simple changes to a basic face, you can portray a wide range of expressions.

Most expressions are universal. If you were to fly from San Diego, California, to Russia, and step off the plane there, you would still understand when a native smiled at you that they probably were being friendly. If you know the facial expression you are trying to draw, chances are good your audience will recognize it, because many expressions are universal in nature. For example, a down-turned mouth and eyebrows drawn together in a sharp V over the bridge of the nose are pretty universal indicators the character is furious.

See a range of facial expressions for just one character in Figure 6.20.

To get better at drawing expressions, set up a mirror in front of your work station and model for yourself any time you need to see how a facial expression should look.

Of course, people don't just express themselves with their faces; their bodies can convey a lot of feeling and even help them communicate without words. To see what I mean, go to a crowded place and sit and draw passersby for awhile. Notice how people carry themselves and use gestures and body movements to

Figure 6.20
A pirate demonstrating a range of different facial expressions.

Figure 6.21
Ichabod Crane spots a pumpkin. Oh! The horror!

communicate. For example, a guy with hunched shoulders, hands in his pockets, staring at his feet while he walks, is obviously not a happy camper. Also, when you do this exercise, be on the lookout for interesting or unusual physical quirks or habits you can give your characters.

As with facial expressions, you can exaggerate a character's posturing as well. One of the most notable examples of this is the cartoon *take*, where a character overreacts to something unexpected; different artists have played around with takes, but usually the character leaps off their feat, their eyes jump out of his skull, and his mouth drops to the floor.

Figure 6.21 shows one example of a character doing a take.

Depending on your art style, and the needs of the story, you can try all kinds of expressions with your characters.

Drawing Creatures

You can draw animals and other nonhumans in a similar way to drawing people, using simple shapes and guidelines and adding features on afterward.

Try drawing the creatures you see in Figure 6.22.

Figure 6.22
Creatures can be sketched just like humans.

Creatures make good characters, too, because you can use their natural physical characteristics, such as tails, ears, snouts, and claws, to great effect. Use a photograph of the original animal as reference when drawing so you get the proportions and anatomy correct.

If you are drawing a mythical or imaginary beast, you should use a combination of artist renderings of that type of creature and photographs of animals that are pretty close to the creature you are drawing; for instance, when drawing dragons, you can look at paintings by Keith Parkinson, a well-known dragon painter, and photos of crocodiles, iguanas, and bats.

WHAT'S NEXT?

Telling a story in a sequence of images is a very different way of storytelling. In the next chapter, we'll look at the tricks of the trade when it comes to framing a shot, composing images to direct the viewer's eye where you want them to look, and more.

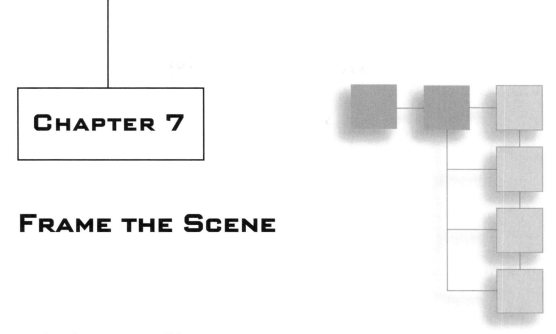

CHAPTER 7

FRAME THE SCENE

In this chapter you will learn:

- To compose scenes using composition and the Rule of Thirds
- How a storyboard helps artists plan an animation
- What the different camera shots are that you can use
- To control, or change the position of, a camera
- To create backgrounds in Flash
- To use multiple Flash layers to add depth to a scene

You can draw 2D images and animate them in Flash now, but there's a lot more to making a movie than putting objects in motion.

First, you need to learn how to plan your animation better, which is done through the use of composition, camera shots and transitions, and planning, because the manner in which you show your objects in motion will greatly affect your viewer's entertainment.

Then, you need to learn how to put backgrounds together in Flash, because your characters can't float in blank space forever!

USING COMPOSITION CORRECTLY

Tip

"Good composition is like a suspension bridge. Each line adds strength and takes none away."

—Robert Henri

Everything the audience sees in your animation or game is through a window. That window is rectangular, and its exact dimensions depend on the size you give it, although the default size for the Flash Stage is 550 × 400 pixels for a standard Web project. This rectangular window is the only way the audience can see what you want them to. This both limits what you can show them and gives you a great tool to capitalize on.

Have you not noticed that most artwork, from the days of Renaissance painters splashing oils on canvas, to today's digital artists sticking vector art on a computer screen, is done with a rectangular frame around it? This has not changed much, and indeed, there are many means to using this rectangular frame to make your audience see exactly what you want them to see, and even play tricks on their eyes, that you might not have thought possible before.

In addition to layout and visual design matters, the composition of your camera shots can convey a lot of information about the perspective and emotion of your scene.

In Chapter 4, Drawing It Out, you learned about the five primary principles of composition, which were simplicity, continuity, repetition/asymmetry, contrast, and radiation. These should be integral to every composition, every Flash scene, you create. Besides these, however, you must not overlook the Golden Rule, or Rule of Thirds.

Applying the Compositional Golden Rule

The ancient Greeks studied shapes, patterns, and proportions that they saw existing in the natural world all around them, and they found that, among them all, there persisted a "Golden Proportion" that was simple, beautiful, and perplexing. Simply stated, this Golden Rule, or as it came to be known, the Rule of Thirds, is a set of art techniques used to locate saddle points for focus within any image.

In your mind's eye, you can divide your blank canvas horizontally and vertically into three separate sections, sort of like a Tic-Tac-Toe grid. This makes three rows and three columns, or nine individual cells. There are four linear intersections that provide the best key focal areas in which you ought to place items and/or characters.

For instance, if you put your focal object in the dead center of your image, the overall feel would be dull and uncomfortable to the viewer. Tilt that focal point to one side, to one of the linear intersections, and you will have a fresher, more vibrant composition.

Also note how the upper right-hand intersection has the most dominant focal point, while the lower left-hand intersection has the weakest. You can use this to create a mood within a composition. For instance, in Figure 7.1, notice that the illustration is given a certain atmosphere just by placing the objects along the Rule of Thirds.

CAMERA PLACEMENT

You can make many comparisons between animating in Flash to live-action filming. The similarities are amazing.

Your own eyes represent the camera position. The scenes that you draw represent a single frame of the film. Your artistic sensibilities determine at what angle we see the character(s). If you keep this analogy going somewhere in the back of your mind, your drawings will appear clearer and your overall continuity will be better off.

Imagine that your Flash Stage is the camera's view lens, and that you are the director. The world you want the viewer to see can be compelling, or not, depending on your point of view. Seeing a play at a local theater company is very different depending on whether you sit in the front row or the box seats, isn't it? So, too, is the placement of your view for every shot of your Flash movie.

Charlie Chaplin used to say that comedy is best filmed in the long shot while tragedy is best in the close-up, because it's when you come in close and really see all of the details that objects and people appear more real and more dramatic by comparison.

Figure 7.1
The Rule of Thirds was used to give this frightening scene more visual interest.

Tip

By the way, although you will be learning about changing a camera's placement in this section, don't overuse it. The amateur animator will want to move the camera around more than is actually needed, just because it seems cool at first. Don't fall into this trap. The more you minimize camera movement, the easier time you will have animating, and the more your viewers will be able to "drink in" all of the artwork.

The questions you need to ask yourself with each new camera shot or angle you give are the following:

1. What is the new information you're giving the viewer?

2. Does this advance the personality of your character(s)?

3. Does this advance the plot of your narrative?

4. What is the main mood of the piece, and does this shot confirm it?

Using the Imaginary 180-Degree Line

When setting the camera's position, draw an imaginary 180-degree line connecting the focal objects on stage, as seen in Figure 7.2. You can position your camera anywhere you choose on one side of this 180-degree line, but do not cross this line to get a shot. If you do, the screen directions will reverse, and the viewer can get very confused.

If you set up a left/right relationship between two or more objects in a given scene, keep the left/right relationship consistent. This way, the landscape will always be familiar. The audience won't have to spend time getting their bearings again. Their focus can remain on the characters and the narrative.

Figure 7.2
Place an imaginary 180-degree line between focal objects in each scene. Your camera cannot cross this line.

During an action sequence, or when the actors constantly move around the set, the 180-degree line between them will move around, too. In this situation, you still have to keep the left/right relationship of the characters consistent, unless you actively show the transition across the 180-degree line in a continuous pan.

During these action shots, the camera will have to find new positions, because it must move about to access the best view of the action or emotions. Place the camera where it will produce maximum emotion from your scene and reaction in your viewer.

Choosing the Perfect Camera Angle

In Flash, the camera's eye is the Flash Stage, so anything you place on the Stage will appear in the camera shot. Camera position speaks volumes about the emotions of a scene. Actors use facial expressions and body language to convey their feelings, so place the camera where it will have maximum access to seeing those. These choices are not logical or mechanical. They are often intuitive. You have to develop a feel for it. Where you place your camera will create viewer reaction and an emotional response to your characters' dilemmas.

The most often used camera positions include the wide shot, the full shot, the medium shot, the close-up, and the extreme close-up. These have been used in film and animation for generations, and there's no reason they can't apply to your Flash cartoon or game.

The Wide Shot

Before you see the action going on onscreen, there is often some kind of shot that establishes for the viewer where the action is taking place. The *wide shot* (see Figure 7.3) is the best place to begin. As with most scene setups, your camera shot is going to be determined by the action taking place in it. In this case, what you want to do is establish the locale, so you start with a wide shot that includes the locale.

The Full Shot

We know where our characters are, but who are our characters? It is time to cut to a full shot. A *full shot* (see Figure 7.4) is pretty much what it sounds like: You show a good view of the full character or characters, from head to toe, so that the viewer can see what they look like and tell what they are doing.

Figure 7.3
A wide shot.

Figure 7.4
A full shot.

Figure 7.5
A medium shot.

The Medium Shot

Whenever showing the entire character, or the character's feet, for instance, would be pointless to carrying the action of the narrative, we use a *medium shot* (see Figure 7.5). Most medium shots show the character's upper body and head but nothing else. Medium shots are often used in movies, TV shows, and comics when two or more characters are talking. To indicate a character's personal expression, facial expressions and hand gestures are used.

The Close-Up

In the *close-up* (see Figure 7.6), we focus on a character's face, particularly in a dramatic scene to show facial expression. A close-up may even show a bit of the shoulders, but the central concentration is on the face.

The Extreme Close-Up

The most overused shot in horror film movies has to be the *extreme close-up* (see Figure 7.7). The primary difference between the close-up and the extreme close-up is that the close-up shows a character's face, but an extreme close-up usually

Figure 7.6
A close-up.

Figure 7.7
An extreme close-up.

focuses on the eyes. Eyes are the windows of the soul, as they say, and close-ups show the eyes so they can show you a character's soul.

Occasionally, an extreme close-up can focus on other body parts. It can also be used to show the viewer important details about the action in-scene they shouldn't miss, such as the broken piece of glass a character is about to step on, a car tire deflating after running over a tack, or a fist about to smash through a plate glass window.

Other Useful Camera Shots

Notice that animators who do a lot of cartoons get tired of drawing facial expressions and mouths moving in synch to the voiceovers. A lot of times, they will do these a little bit before cutting away. In this case, you don't even see a lot of animation going on, as the artist shows you the look on the fellow's face the guy is talking to, or a breeze ruffling the tree branches over the characters' heads, all while the voiceover continues, overlapping the scene. These tricks effectively conceal the fact that less animation is happening during long periods of exposition, and they also keep the audience from getting bored.

The Cutaway Shot   The *cutaway* is a shot that shows something else, it doesn't matter what, other than the main action, before returning back to the main action. Like the example given above, you could start one character giving a long-winded speech and then cutaway to something else going on in the background that has nothing to do with the current action, which has slowed to a crawl.

The Cut-In Shot   Similar to a cutaway is a *cut-in shot*, where you cutaway to another shot, but whatever the new shot is, it gives something more to the current action. For instance, you could show a woman searching produce aisles in a grocery store for oranges. You could cut-in a shot of the oranges, hidden behind some apples or melons, then go back to the woman. You effectively draw the viewer's attention to some element of the scene that has direct impact on the main action.

The Over-the-Shoulder Shot   An *over-the-shoulder*, or OTS, shot is seen exactly as the name implies. The camera we are viewing all of the action through appears to be positioned over someone's shoulder. This is often used in film and TV during dialogue scenes, as the person talking will be the shoulder the camera is mounted on and you can see the reaction on the other person's face to what the first person is saying.

The Point-of-View Shot   A *point-of-view*, or POV, shot has the camera positioned where the main character is standing, as though the viewer is looking through the eyes of that character. This is similar to the first-person view you see in shooter games like *Doom*, and, in fact, the 2005 movie adaptation of *Doom*, featuring Dwayne Johnson ("The Rock"), used a POV shot for more than three minutes, where the action switches to the main character's sight and the viewer feels like they are really there, going on a rampage and killing an array of horrifying mutants.

The Noddy Shot   A particular shot common to news story interviews is the *noddy shot*. In the noddy shot, to help break up long-winded dialogue without a

Figure 7.8
(A) On the left, a bird's-eye view. (B) On the right, a worm's-eye view.

lot of action to keep the eyes busy, the camera will sometimes switch to a medium close-up of the interviewer or a person listening, who nods or otherwise indicates they are listening. The noddy shot has been helpful in live action when you have to edit a nine-minute speech down to three minutes, because you can cut-in the noddy shot to conceal your edits.

The Bird's-Eye View or Worm's-Eye View   These two angles are used most often to make one object appear to loom over another. The *bird's-eye view* is a top-down shot that uses height to dwarf the perspective, while the *worm's-eye view* can make places appear larger and more ominous than what they really are. See examples of each in Figure 7.8.

Changes in Camera Angles

Even with all of these camera shots, the camera itself is not an immobile lump of lead, even when shooting live action. Cameras move, rotate, dip, and dance to capture just the right angle of the scene you want. In animation and video games, cameras are virtual, meaning they don't have a physical form and can literally be taken anywhere.

In Flash, the Stage is the camera's eye, so any time you want it to look like the camera is moving, you must grab and rearrange the items on the Flash stage to maintain the illusion of the camera in motion.

Zoom In/Out

The most widely heard bit of terminology in the industry, and often the most misused, is the zoom in/out.

If you zoom in on a particular scene, it does not mean the camera moves closer to the scene but that the camera lens focuses in on a particular object, making it appear dominant in the scene. When you zoom out, you are giving the impression of backing off or taking your focus off of the subject.

In Flash, you can make a zoom in/out using frame-by-frame animations, where you make an object that is being zoomed out from blurrier than one being zoomed in on.

Truck In/Out

Truck in or truck out is also referred to as pushing in or pulling out, because you are referring to physically pushing the camera closer to the subject or pulling it back, farther away from the subject.

In Flash, the easiest way to depict a truck in/out is to animate the objects with a Motion Tween, and then use the Free Transform tool (hotkey Q) to scale the objects larger for a truck in or scale the objects smaller for a truck out. You can add a very slight rotation, too, to great effect.

Tilt Up/Down

You tilt the camera up to get a better look at a subject just over your head, and you tilt down to get a better look at a subject on the ground. This is a great way to get shots of objects from dramatic angles, rather than looking at them straight on.

Pan Left/Right

You swivel the camera to your left or right when you say you are panning left or right. You can pan the camera left to right to show a car entering a scene, passing you, and leaving the scene again.

Diagonals and Foreshortening

From a graphic standpoint, it is always recommended to show diagonals in your compositions, such as in Figure 7.9. This happens naturally whenever you use a

Figure 7.9
Use of diagonal lines, given naturally in perspective views, makes for great dramatic sequences.

low- or high-angle camera for a scene, but can also be achieved by rotating the camera so that the horizon line is at a slight diagonal. When you use foreshortening, the perspective adds diagonals to the scene naturally.

Ways to Cut from Shot to Shot

Up until now I have mentioned that you can cut from one view of a scene to the next, or to a view of a different scene altogether.

A *cut* is a term taken from the old days of film making, because when the film editor came to the last frame in a scene, he would literally cut the roll of film with a pair of scissors and attach the film to the next frame from a different roll with film paste.

The way to make a cut in Flash is to overlap one scene with another, and when it comes time, establish keyframes in each of the different Flash layers, and have one scene disappear while the other appears. Or you could use separate Flash elements that are actually called Scenes, and switch between these Scenes, but Flash Scenes are not generally recommended.

Whether you think about your cuts or not, a cut is used between every new shot within a scene. You can also do special things between cuts to add dramatic impact.

Fade-In/Out

First, you can *fade-in* to a scene, meaning that you start out with a completely black or white screen and gently ease in to the shot. Doing the opposite is called a *fade-out*, where you go from an established shot and ease the picture out to completely black or white. This can be used to make a room look like the sun's going down outside, turning everything dark, or that the characters are outside becoming lost in a white blur of a blizzard.

To do a fast fade in Flash, you can create a black rectangle that is the same size as your Stage, align it to cover the stage, and give it a short Motion Tween where you change the Color Effect Alpha from 0% to 100% (for a fade-out) or from 100% to 0% (for a fade-in).

Dissolve

A *dissolve* is what happens when one scene becomes more and more transparent, slowly revealing another scene beneath it that comes into clearer and clearer focus. Dissolves are old hat in Hollywood, but they are still used on occasion to show the passing of time or if the story is going into a flashback.

To do a dissolve in Flash, you would use the same technique as a fade, but instead of tweening a black rectangle you'd take a screen capture of the first scene, and apply the tween to that screen capture, from Alpha 100% to 0%, or until you've revealed the scene underneath, in another layer.

Blur/Zip Pan

Another nice way to transition between two scenes is with a *blur* or *zip pan*. The two are separated only by their look: A blur pan shows a brief blurry motion frame, while a zip pan shows quick lines of action. They are usually horizontal, diagonal, or radial (in a swirl).

A blur or zip pan, whether in live action or animation, offers us a quick and cheap way to transition between two drastically different scenes or settings, and can be used to imply traveling.

You don't have to look any further than the old live-action TV series *Batman* with Adam West and Burt Ward, where they frequently used these types of pans to show Batman and Robin racing from one place to the next: "Quick, Robin, to the Bat Cave!" (see Figure 7.10).

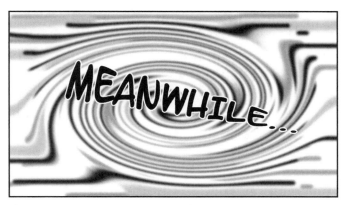

Figure 7.10
A transition pan like they used to use in the TV show *Batman*.

DRAWING STORYBOARDS

Storyboards are a series of illustrations or images displayed in sequence for the purpose of previsualizing a motion graphic media sequence. Although "motion graphic media sequence" is a long term, it can mean cartoon animations.

If you draw an animation, you should start by drawing a storyboard. Storyboards, like the ones shown in Figure 7.11 and Figure 7.12, are loosely sketched or roughed in so the artist knows what direction to take.

Figure 7.11
One example of a storyboard.

EXT. FAMILY CEMETERY - NIGHT

With the ornate ironwork of the old Collins family mausoleum in the f.g. Willie, flashlight in hand, a bag of tools over his shoulder, can be seen coming through the trees TOWARD CAMERA.

Flashing his light about, he carefully picks his way through the crumbling monuments in the overgrown, weed-choked graveyard.

CLOSE - WILLIE

As he stops in front of the mausoleum, shines his light up at it.

HIS POV - MAUSOLEUM

An aged, marble facade overgrown with brambles and vines, 'Collins' etched in the stone over the entrance.

The FLASHLIGHT BEAM ILLUMINATES three carved female figures on the pediment, locked in embrace, their eyes lifted toward heaven...

WILLIE

He grins, pulls out a crumpled piece of paper, shines his light on it.

WILLIE

...Three graces spin high above...

Figure 7.12
Another example of a storyboard.

Reviewing the Script

There's this myth that animating a poorly conceived joke or storyline will make it better, that exciting visuals can make the dull more stirring. This is so not true! Graphics only dress up your material, and your animation will only be as good as the material you hang it on. So review your original concept or script to make sure you have something that is going to get some viewers, before even attempting to storyboard it.

Coming Up with the Sketches

Once you know your material is solid, then reread it and close your eyes. Sit there, with your eyes shut, and picture the script playing through your mind's eye. Don't edit or analyze what you see right now. Just envision the flow of things, especially the characters—their costumes, their actions, and their facial expressions. Listen for their voices, the kind of music underscoring their behavior, and any significant sound effects. Don't force this imagination process, because it has to come natural or not at all.

Have a sketchpad nearby so you can jot down these ideas as they come to you. Scribble anything that your mind has inspired in you based on the material you're using. Never concentrate on drawing perfect sketches on the first pass, but place your focus instead on the emotional emphasis that has emerged from your imagination.

Don't be overly critical or concerned with the quality of art in a storyboard, because, more than likely, nobody is going to see it but you. Concentrate instead on determining the best camera shots and proper composition in each shot to help the story flow.

With each sketch, ask yourself the same questions:

1. What is it you're trying to say in this sequence?
2. What is it you want your audience to feel?

Conveying Emotion Through Your Sketches

If properly executed, your storyboard drawings should elicit immediate reaction from viewers. You should welcome feedback, because the better the reactions, the more you know you've done well making a storyboard. The finished animation will be better off for it.

Pay close attention to any criticism you get from the people you show your storyboard to, and even ask for suggestions. Don't be a brat and get defensive. Nothing in your sketches should be set in stone, and getting feedback from other people is not an attack on you personally. In contrast, it's a way of reaching for the stars rather than settling for the moon. A great sketch will sell itself, and if it's not great, you can change it, tweak it here and there, until it is. If you act stubborn, however, a bad concept could go all the way through production and you're stuck with it then.

Storyboarding, in the purest sense, is like directing, but you have to play every part, of every actor, and bring across the message of a scene by putting yourself into the emotion of that scene.

Timing Your Sequences

If you have trouble conveying an emotion, think about the beats. The human heart beats at a pretty steady rhythm, speeding up during moments of high adrenaline and intense feeling and slowing down during soft drama and introspective moods.

The same is true about music. Music is metered out in a series of notes and delivered to the listener in a beat pattern. Musicians are very particular about hitting the right beats, because the beats form the timing of a piece and can make or break a composition's success.

As with music, animation borrows on this sense of timing, and you can typically measure the pace of a piece by its beats. Each frame you draw should be a single beat, and the speed in which they progress, or in moments of slow-building tension, don't progress, tells the viewer the mood of the piece.

Timing is an ongoing process. You will be adding and taking out frames right up to the final polishing of your animation. All of this nip-and-tuck is to keep the energy driving forward in your movie. Also, timing is just one of those things that is easier to edit iteratively, because when you can play through your animation and see where you must trim the fat or add some drag to your sequence, it's much easier to pace the timing, isn't it?

Think about camera placement, transitions, composition guidelines, mood, and timing—and you shouldn't have any problem drawing a compelling storyboard.

MAKING FLASH BACKGROUNDS

Setting is just as important as character in a good story. Really, setting can be another type of character, albeit limited in the form of interactions it can provide the viewer.

Setting can heighten the emotion of a scene, making it seem unusual, interesting, or fresh. Some people like stories that are set in far-off lands and places they would like to visit if they went on vacation. Other people like stories set some

Figure 7.13
One example of an environment.

place welcoming and familiar, like their own backyard. See Figure 7.13 for an example of an environment.

What kind of mood do you think your environments create for the viewer? Before you animate a sequence, you need to plan the set for it. Location, exterior view, interior layout, props, and furniture all need to be brought into focus. Use books and old photographs related to the subject to help stoke your creative fires and to recall all of the details.

The theater set is stationary, and so the setting remains static and unchanging, while the characters move about exaggeratedly and interact with props with much bluster. In contrast, the motion-picture camera has the freedom to move all about, and so the setting can transform or become a part of the action.

Animation and video games borrow a bit of both when it comes to set design. Most of the backgrounds are stationary, so they stay in one place, while others are animated and interactive. It's up to you what your environment needs to do.

Considering Blocking

Blocking is a term you might have heard before in drama class. It's a term used by actors and means the planning for where they stand and move to while giving their lines. Just as actors have to have a mark, or place to stand, and an area to move around while conveying their emotion to the audience, so, too, must your animated characters have a space in the background.

When designing any background, consider carefully—before getting too far into production—the blocking of the scene. Where are characters going to be placed in the background? What are they doing there? Where can they move? What parts of the background will they need to interact with? These are all valuable thoughts that need solid answers before you get to work.

Designing Backgrounds

When you design a background for your Flash, you need to keep it clear in your mind that the action does not take place in a vacuum. There has to be some indication of the setting, that is, where the action is taking place, for viewers to immerse themselves in it.

Charles Schulz, creator of *Peanuts* and the lovable Snoopy, often did not draw in backgrounds to his comic strips. Instead, he added a simple horizon line or a few tufts of grass that would cement the setting conceptually and let the rest fade to white or some off-white color. He did this intentionally. Indeed, he made his characters just as simple looking as his backgrounds, with very few illuminating details about what they looked like.

On the other end of the spectrum are the artists like the ones who do the *Batman* comics, who create endless amounts of realistic detail and sweeping vistas of Gotham, and blend it all with dark impenetrable shadows. The only problem with this mode of illustration is that, if you are not careful, you can obscure or lose your characters completely by making the background seem more interesting and dominant. You will find you might have to create a hiatus around your characters or find other ways for them to "pop out" from the background in that case.

See Figure 7.14 for examples of each.

This visual choice is really the artist's decision. What do you want to convey, and how do you want to convey it? Consider this carefully before you draw backgrounds for your Flash.

Figure 7.14
(A) A simple background versus (B) a more complex background.

Using Scanned Artwork to Make a Background

You can use your own artwork that you have scanned in to your computer for backgrounds. In this method, you have total control over how the artwork will look when in the scene before you even place it there. You could draw or paint your backgrounds, use colored pencils or pastels, or any other version of traditional art media you can think of or feel comfortable using.

It also does not matter if you use an art media that you don't use with your characters, because a background shouldn't have to compete with the main action onscreen, and having a background made entirely of pastels and vector art characters on top will serve you best by making the characters "pop" out into focus.

1. When you finish scanning your background in, import it to your Flash project Library.

2. Create a new Flash layer and call it something distinctive, like "background." I usually call my background layer "BG" for short.

3. Move your new background layer to the very bottom of your layer stack, under all of your other layers.

4. Make sure the background layer is selected, then drag an instance of your background graphic from your Library to the Stage.

5. Use the Align options to help you align the background graphic correctly on the Stage. It can help to make sure the Align/Distribute to Stage button is highlighted, or active, and then click the Align to Horizontal Center and Align to Vertical Center buttons to center the background image to the center of the Flash Stage. If this looks okay to you, use Edit > Undo to remove it.

Using Traced Photos to Make a Background

You could also use photographs for your backgrounds. There are several Flash artists who use photographs as the basis for many of their outdoor backgrounds. They bring the photographs into Flash, use the Trace Bitmap function to reduce the photos to vector artwork, as seen in Figure 7.15, and arrange them to cover the background in a logical way.

Figure 7.15
You can use Trace Bitmap to reduce an image to vector art to use as a background. On the left is the before picture of a townhouse in Eureka Springs. On the right is the result after using Trace Bitmap.

Trace Bitmap basically sends a tiny robotic tracer around every line in your artwork or photograph, modifying each of these pixel-based shapes into vector-based shapes.

Nowadays, Adobe Illustrator has a built-in image vectorization program that does this, too, but back when I first experimented with Flash (it was still Macromedia-owned then), I was pleasantly shocked to find this program a natural part of Flash.

Trace Bitmap can make any bitmap image you import into a supersmooth vector art image, and like Mathers, this can be very handy for turning raw photos into vector art backgrounds.

You can do this, too.

1. When you find your photograph and have it on your computer, import it to your Flash project Library.

2. Create a new Flash layer for your background.

3. Move your background layer to the bottom of your layer stack.

4. Make sure the background layer is selected, then drag an instance of your background graphic from your Library to the stage. Arrange it how you would like it to look. You might want it to fill up the entire scene or only one part of it. You can use the Align panel (look under Window on the main menu for Align) or go to Modify > Align on the main menu.

5. With your graphic selected, go to Modify > Bitmap > Trace Bitmap on the main menu bar. You will have several options available to you, including Color Threshold, Curve Fit, and Corner Threshold. Although I rarely adjust Color Threshold, Curve Fit is something you will more than likely want to fiddle with. To prepare an image for the Web, you will probably want to set your curves to Smooth, because the more corner points you have in your image, the more memory it takes and more wieldy it will be trying to distribute over the Internet. When ready, click OK to process your changes. It will take some time for the Trace Bitmap process, so don't worry if Flash is nonresponsive for a while.

6. You should see a grid of tiny dots covering your entire image when it is done. This shows that it has been traced. Move your image to the center of the stage, and if you need to resize it (which is easier done before you use Trace Bitmap), you can use the Free Transform tool.

Using Multilayered Environments in Flash

Many backgrounds will require characters to walk behind or over objects that exist as part of the background. This is something you should think about when considering the actors' blocking.

Characters may have to walk through doorways, stoop behind boulders, or cross in front of a chair in a living room. If they do not, if they walk over the top of a chair that is obviously supposed to be out in front of them, the audience will receive a minor shock and get distracted from the narrative.

So you must pay careful attention to what parts of the background the actors will need to interact with, and which parts should come in front of the actors.

When you need to show the characters moving behind other scene items, you can either make the objects separate to start with or trace a copy of the objects. Either way, you will have to place them on a Flash layer higher than the rest in the timeline hierarchy. This makes those items part of the *foreground*, or the area that is supposed to be visually in front of the subjects of viewer focus.

A more advanced Flash user could also use layer masks, but we won't get into that in this book, as it is a slightly more complicated though equally effective technique.

Sometimes you'll want to place a few out-of-focus or blurry-looking objects in the foreground, just to give a larger impression of depth in this virtual world. For instance, you may have an outdoor park scene and want to arrange some brush or tree boughs that hang in front of the camera, not really obscuring the view of the actors, but giving the illusion of more foliage in the environment.

Layering your background in these ways breathes more depth to your settings and makes them seem more believable. It is really easy to do with Flash, so taking the time to add a few minor foreground items will pay off in the end product. Take a look at Figure 7.16 for an example.

Figure 7.16
Use a foreground layer in front of characters, and characters in front of a background layer, like the underground lab scene from James Farr's *Xombie: Chapter Two*, as seen here.

WHAT'S NEXT?

Now you can draw, make animations, and prepare camera shots and backgrounds for your scenes in Flash, plus you know the best ways to transition between your scenes in Flash and make a composite movie. But what makes a movie really engaging goes beyond graphics into the sound experience.

Before we put together a short Flash cartoon, it's vital you know how sound is used in Flash, because movies and games wouldn't be the same without it!

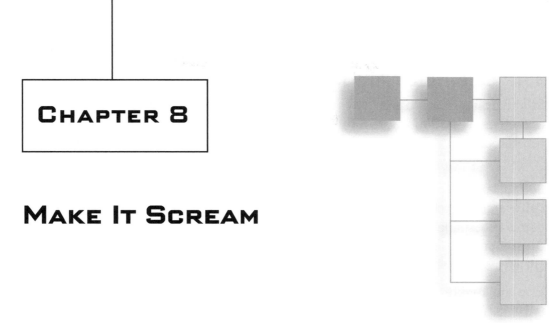

CHAPTER 8

MAKE IT SCREAM

In this chapter you will learn:

- How sound is used in cinema to support narrative
- What all that sound jargon about Hertz and decibels is about
- What influences sound effects, such as space, time, and events
- How to soundproof and set up your own recording studio
- What to remember when recording yourself
- What the differences are in compressed and uncompressed file types
- How to use Audacity or Myna to record, edit, and export audio files
- To use Flash to plug in your own custom sound effects

So far we've covered graphics, but human sight is only one of our senses, albeit an important one. People also have to *hear* things to have a complete sensory input. Although sound is an aspect of animation and games often overlooked by viewers, it is still very significant. Without sound, the visuals seen on screen just wouldn't be as complete.

In this chapter, you will learn how to make a soundtrack for your projects. You will learn how to create sound using Audacity or Myna and then incorporate it into Flash.

THE BASICS OF SOUND DESIGN

Sound design is a process by which someone specifies, acquires, and manipulates audio elements. Sound is employed in a variety of different disciplines, including theater, cinema, music recording, live music performances, and even church and school functions.

Sound makes everything come more alive. It stamps the heartbeat for our culture and provides us with an aural experience. It can support the story of a game and shape the soundtrack. Try playing a video game with the TV or the computer speakers on mute. Watch a YouTube video without headphones or a speaker and realize just how disappointing the experience quickly becomes.

You are making games for the PSP using Flash. Games use sound for several reasons, including:

- **Dialogue**—The voice-over track is used for characters talking on screen. This is so viewers can understand what it is they are saying.

- **Background Noise**—The real world is filled with real noise; for better immersion, games and animations will often incorporate recordings of real noise to emulate the real world.

- **Music**—Often prerecorded, music compositions underscore the prevalent mood or emotion of a given game level or animated scene.

- **Sound Effects**—All of the dings, whistles, bells, and so on that you hear while interacting with any application are there to reinforce commands and to give you nonverbal feedback.

You need to know what it takes for sound design to add this aural experience to your animations and video games.

First, I will show you the terminology used in conjunction with sound design. Then, you will learn what Foley sound is, the importance of a dialogue track, and where to find music to score your projects with. Lastly, we'll look at doing home sound recording, before we get to digital sound editing.

Scientific Gobbledygook Concerning Sound

Humans can perceive auditory signals coming from many different directions at once and singularly separate the sounds based on where they come from. Sound forms at least a full fifth of the way we perceive our environment, and we innately use sound as a means of survival. Being capable of telling when a noisy ambush predator like a cougar snuck up behind our ancestors helped our ancestors stay alive—and today we use sound to listen to the latest pop hits on our MP3 players.

The Greek mathematician Pythagoras not only delivered us a triangle but discovered the octave and came up with numeric ratios connected to harmony.

Galileo formed many of the scientific laws of sound.

Since the 1600s there have been numerous advances in the study of sound, some of them coming from such great individuals as Heinrich Hertz (where we get our "Hertz" from) and Alexander Graham Bell (where we get our "decibel" from).

It has been discovered that sound comes in the shape of vibration waves. Some sound waves can actually travel at frequencies so high or low that humans cannot hear them, but some animals can (such as a dog hearing a dog whistle).

Here are some of the most basic laws of sound:

- A sound wave moves in pretty much a straight-forward fashion.
- *Pitch* refers to how fast the sound wave vibrates, also known as *frequency*. Humans can discern sound frequencies by a 2:1 difference, so many of our music notes are on a scale of 2 (see Figure 8.1).
- The term *Hertz* (Hz) comes from a unit of frequency equaling one vibration per second.

Figure 8.1
In music notation like this, the different heights of notes indicate different pitches.

- *Intensity* is how loud the sound comes across, also called amplitude or volume. Intensity can be measured by decibel, or dB. The increasing intensity of a sound wave is known as *gain*.

- *Timbre* is the waveform or accuracy of the sound frequency. Timbre is different for every instrument and every voice, and it reflects a change in quality that is not dependent on intensity or frequency.

Influencing Factors on Sound Quality

The factors that influence sound quality include space, time, situation, and outside events. As with many of the other elements of media aesthetics, these factors can (and do) overlap.

Space   Location defines many sounds. Stereo sound makes it possible to hear sound relative to onscreen positioning. For instance, most of the player character's dialogue will come from the front forward-facing speaker in 5.1 Dolby surround-sound, but if you show a comrade yelling for the player to catch up and you show him slightly off-screen over on the right, you best make sure the sound comes out of the right-side speakers.

Sound perspective means that you must also match close-up video images with "near" sounds, and long shots with sounds that come from far away. Close sounds take the spotlight, often sharing more presence than the softer background noises.

The same principle takes the Doppler Effect (see Figure 8.2) from physics to media: as a loud sound source comes closer to the listener, the higher the sound gains; the further away the sound source moves from the listener, the softer the sound gets until it fades completely. Positioning themselves in a virtual world, 3D sounds take advantage of the Doppler Effect. In most 3D game engines, this is handled for you.

Figure 8.2
An illustration of the Doppler Effect.

Time   Different times of day and different climates are reflected in sound. If you are creating a summer glen, you will want to use noises such as chirping birds, breezes blowing, or tree branches rustling. On the other hand, a scene that takes place at night might have owls hooting, crickets chirping, or coyotes barking in the distance.

There are two special uses of sound that have to do with time: (a) predictive sound and (b) *leitmotiv*.

Predictive Sound   Predictive sound involves the placement of certain sounds before an event actually takes place. An example of a predictive sound would be letting the player of a game hear battle sounds coming from over a hill before showing them that there is a fight taking place or letting the player hear a rumbling noise right before an earthquake shakes the streets their character's walking down.

Leitmotiv   *Leitmotiv* is German for "leading motif." The *leitmotiv* is similar to Pavlov's bell (if you have studied psychology, you know what I mean).

Some video games play a ding noise whenever the player does something right and a "no-no" noise whenever the player does something wrong. These are examples of a *leitmotiv*.

A lot of next-generation games use soft-key music in the background and as soon as the player enters combat, tenser hard-edged music starts playing, which is another form of *leitmotiv*. The *leitmotiv* most often heard in the popular survival horror games under the *Resident Evil* title is the moaning of zombies. If the player enters a room or new area, they don't even have to see a shambling corpse; if they can hear a shuffling noise or a low moan, they know they're about to have to face off against the undead.

Situations and Outside Events   Sounds can describe a specific situation or (used cleverly) be effected by outside events that help put the listener into the scene.

Here is one example: A lonely geezer leaves the front door of his wooden shack high in the snow-capped mountains to chop wood. He crunches through snow with every step, and occasionally the forest is disturbed by the cries of hawks, but otherwise the sound stays very much muted. Why, you might ask? Snow acts as a sort of natural sound dampener, absorbing noises. So the scene would be a hushed one.

Foley Sound Effects

You may not realize it, but most film and TV sound for your entertainment pleasure does not come from original recorded sound. Sound effects you hear in cinema are rarely accurate representations of real-life sounds. They are considered "hyper real."

Engineers construct the sound in postproduction utilizing many pieces of sound they mix together in software programs to create a seamless whole. These professionals often take separate pieces from sound effects libraries and from custom recordings done in studios, what's called *Foley sound*.

Foley sounds are sounds that require the expertise of Foley artists (like the one in Figure 8.3) to record custom sound effects that emphasize sounds that should be heard in context. For instance, a Foley artist might shake a sheet of metal to record thunder or squash melons to represent a character getting squished by a falling anvil.

These sound effects are saved to a computer and digitally edited until they are exaggerated and ear-catching.

Figure 8.3
This Foley artist is recording himself banging on a metal lid to use the sound in a video game.

You can do the same, after you've learned about home sound recording. Use your imagination and your microphone to record all kinds of regular sounds, and then edit them with your sound editor to be used for great effects.

Let's Talk: A Brief Look at Dialogue

The dialogue track in any movie soundtrack is where you hear the voices of all of the characters talking. This is also called a *voiceover*, because the voices overlay the animation taking place on stage.

I started out when I was 10 years old with one of those old clunky tape recorders. I would carry that recorder around with me everywhere, taping my thoughts or sound bites off the television.

One day I got a copy of Douglas Adams' *The Hitchhiker's Guide to the Galaxy* radio screenplay. I decided to put on my own radio play, using that screenplay as the basis. Being only 10 and not having a slew of friends to help, I did all of the voices by myself by making lousy impressions of famous actors and actresses at the time. By the time I was done and showing what I had created to my mother, I had just about decided that theater was the life for me.

You, too, can do all your own voiceovers. There are plenty of animators that have done their own voices.

Walt Disney, as the story goes, was so tired of demonstrating to voice actors how they should do the voice of Mickey Mouse that one of them finally suggested, "Why don't you just do it yourself?" And he did. Walt Disney (shown in Figure 8.4) was Mickey's first voiceover, up until the late 1940s.

Figure 8.4
Walt Disney.

John Kricfalusi, creator of *Ren and Stimpy*, performed the voice of his lead character Ren Hoek, the skinny asthmatic Chihuahua. Again, nobody he interviewed could give Ren the sort of intensity John wanted, so he did the voiceover himself.

If you are at a loss for inspiration for a "voice," just look around you. There are lots of voices you can do for your recordings.

One tip is to pick an actor or actress and do your own impression of them. I remember when I was in speech and drama classes at my high school, we had a student that was fall-down funny when it came time to do humorous inter-pretations. He would pick the most outlandish clashing voices he could think to imitate and do them.

For example, he once did a classic scene from *Robin Hood* starring the voices of Peter Lorre (the creepy short guy they poked fun of a lot in *Looney Tunes*), Darkwing Duck, Darth Vader, and Barbra Streisand. He got a lot of laughs, but even if he was being serious instead of being over-the-top he would still be entertaining.

So choose voices at random that are so different from each other to sound like different people, and practice them before getting in front of the microphone.

If you feel uncomfortable doing voiceovers of the opposite gender, or if you're afraid your voice is just as bad as scratching nails on chalk boards, you might consider talking a friend into helping you. If you have the wherewithal, you could even bribe them. Tell them you will help make them a star! If you can afford to hire professional voice talent, that would be even better, but don't sweat it if you can't. Everyone has to start somewhere!

Where Do You Get the Music for a Soundtrack?

You probably already know this, but you can get in some serious trouble for using music intended for private home use in a for-profit production, even if it's a cartoon or video game.

If you pay special attention to the beginning of movies, there is usually a message warning that comes up saying, "unauthorized duplication or presenta-tion, even without monetary gain is punishable by law." That means that even though you might be legit and not intending to make a few bucks, even if you own an original copy of the product, or you are just making an unauthorized copy for your own personal use, you can still get fined or thrown in jail!

Have you ever added a song you like to a video you've uploaded to YouTube and have them send you a message telling you your video has been denied or banned, because they've detected a copyrighted song in your video? This is because YouTube doesn't want to get into trouble over copyright issues, and they don't want you to, either.

For educational or private usage, it might be fine to use an MP3 of your favorite band, be it Snoop Dogg or Paramore, but you won't be able to show it to anyone without special permission or a usage license from the artist.

Getting Permissions and Licensing

You can attempt to write to your favorite band and tell them what the music is for and if it's okay to use it, and if you get signed written permission from them, then you are in the clear.

Whether it is sound effects, music, 3D models, artwork, or anything else going into my creative pipeline, I try to keep it as clean as possible. If I ever use anything that is not my own original piece or something I have purchased to be royalty-free, I write to the piece's creator and ask them permission to use it. I don't lie; I tell them exactly what I'm using their piece for and who might see or hear it.

Gaining permissions has helped me countless times in the past, covering my rear, and I have often been amazed at how helpful other artists have been. For instance, when I started my first game, I contacted three rock bands to see if I could use their music in my game, and two out of the three eagerly agreed, sent me free CDs, and became close acquaintances! This shows it never hurts to try.

Most often, however, artists will have their lawyers draw up a single-user license and charge you a fee or percentage in royalties for using any of their creations.

Using Royalty-Free Music

On the other hand, you could use royalty-free music. *Royalty-free* means that once you pay a set price for a CD or download, you're done paying for it and can use it in any productions you want to make.

Be sure, if you go this route, to carefully read your licensing agreement with the creators of the royalty-free tunes, as there will occasionally be stipulations written into the fine print. For instance, some royalty-free places want you to advertise or credit them in your finished product, which is only fair as they are still saving you money and time having to make all that stuff yourself.

Some popular sites you might look at that have royalty-free music include:

- **Bbm.net**—http://www.bbm.net
- **DeusX.com**—http://www.deusx.com/studio.html
- **Flashsound.com**—http://www.flashsound.com
- **Flashkit.com**—http://www.flashkit.com
- **Shockwave-Sound.com**—http://www.shockwave-sound.com
- **Sound-Ideas.com**—http://www.sound-ideas.com
- **MusicBakery.com**—http://musicbakery.com (see Figure 8.5)
- **Soundrangers.com**—http://www.soundrangers.com

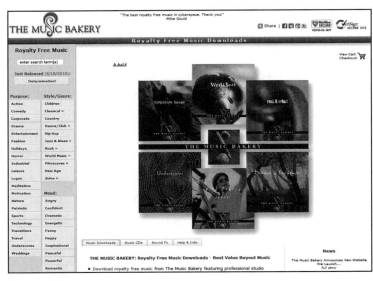

Figure 8.5
The home page of MusicBakery.com.

A number of these even have 100% free sound sources, and most incorporate directly into Flash. Check them out!

If you truly do not want to use anybody else's sound work, then you are going to have to make some of your own. To do that, you will have to learn a music-creation program or be in a band that makes the music for you.

Making It Yourself with Roc

One program you could use to make free music is from Aviary (http://www.aviary .com), the same bunch of people that made the Myna program I will show you how to use. Their music creator is called Roc. Get it? All of the Aviary programs are given bird names. Roc is said to be an enormous mythical bird of prey, able to carry off and eat whole elephants. Aviary's Roc, shown in Figure 8.6, is a free online music creator.

Roc can simulate over 50 musical instruments, including pianos, guitars, drums, and more. You generate music loops and ringtones using a simple point-and-click interface. Alternatively, you can record your own sounds through their recording program or upload MP3s from your home machine. After mixing sounds, you can download them to your machine or take them into Aviary's sound editor for further editing.

Figure 8.6
Roc, found at Aviary.com, is an online music creation tool.

SETTING UP A SOUND RECORDING STUDIO

There are some serious fundamentals to starting a recording studio space that you must bear in mind. You will probably set up your recording studio around your computer desk, in your bedroom or garage. The garage might be best, simply because of the sound isolation there.

We will discuss the two most important aspects to remember when setting up your own sound studio: soundproofing and setup—and then we'll look at what it takes to start recording.

Soundproofing Your Recording Studio

Make sure the room you use does not have serious leaks for sound to invade, such as door cracks and windows. You will want to keep noise from the outside from filtering in and you want to stop short of being a nuisance to your parents and neighbors. Sound absorption and isolation will be your primary goals.

You can drape wool blankets over the windows and door or add bookshelves filled with books to your walls. This will limit the amount of reflective sound (or echoing) while improving the sound quality when you record.

You might also make sure that your parents, siblings, or pets know you are recording before you start, so they won't walk in and disturb you in the middle of a complicated recording session. Depending on the people in your household and "house rules," you might be able to get away with hanging a DO NOT DISTURB sign on your door, like the one in Figure 8.7, as long as you tell everyone why.

Finding the Right Sound Recording Software

You will need an easy-to-use sound editing software program to do audio mixes with, and if the program you choose does not include a recording or microphone line-in system, you might have to use Microsoft's built-in sound recorder or some other inexpensive software to initially record your audio.

The following programs are the most widely used sound mixing packages available:

- Audacity
- Broadcast

Figure 8.7
As long as your parents say it's okay, you could use a DO NOT DISTURB sign to keep folks out when sound recording.

- Cool Edit Pro
- Pro-Logic
- Slab
- SONAR
- Sound Forge

Before using a sound editing program, you should check to make sure that your computer has a suitable sound card and peripheral speakers for playback.

Choosing a Microphone

Besides having the right computer software and hardware, you must also have a microphone, like the one shown in Figure 8.8.

Practice will show you whether or not you have chosen the right sound editing setup for you. Practice with your microphone to see what its sound range is like and if you pick up any background noise. If your microphone is sensitive enough to pick up the fan motor on your computer, you might have to replace

Figure 8.8
An example of a condenser microphone.

the fan motor on your computer or tone it down a notch. Practice with recording techniques until you find the right setup that works for you.

There are fundamentally two different types of microphones to choose from: dynamic and condenser.

Dynamic Microphones

Dynamic microphones use a wire coil over a magnet to catch sound waves, producing an electronic voltage in response to sound. These microphones reproduce sound pretty well, but their actual accuracy is based on voltage rather than the sound source.

Condenser Microphones

For killer vocal recording, you should consider a condenser microphone. Condenser microphones use an electronically charged stretched diaphragm over a thin plate, and fluctuations caused by sound waves passing over the diaphragm cause changes in the electronic current, producing output signals.

Condenser microphones tend to be more accurate than dynamic microphones, particularly in mid and high frequencies. Unfortunately, they are more fragile and less likely to handle abuse.

Tips on Sound Recording

If you plan on recording your own voice, you must stop and think about your voice, how you place the microphone, and how to mix digital audio files on the computer.

Listen to Yourself

Evaluate how you sound on the mic. The human voice is a complex topic in and of itself.

Don't fret if you freak out the first time you hear your own voice recorded and played back, as it probably doesn't even sound like you think you sound. This is because we hear ourselves muffled through our inner ear and can never accurately hear the timbre of our own voice unless recorded. Although you may sound different, it by no means reflects poorly on you. Your voice will do just fine for most recording efforts, unless you want to talk your friends into helping out.

Use Proper Posture

Stand or sit up straight. Let your muscles in your body relax. Don't let tension build up or it will tighten your vocal cords. Don't slump down in your chair or lean way over when talking.

Remember to Breathe

Breathing is critical to enunciation. Unless you practice breathing correctly, you can develop poor habits that make your speech pattern erratic, soft, or breathless. You should take deep breaths in, letting them out slowly, to practice proper breathing. Don't take up smoking or hollering your lungs out when you have a chest cold, because you can actually hurt your organs.

Don't Crack Up

If you talk so loud or so fast that your voice actually cracks, you are "cracking up" and it won't sound good. Breaks—or noticeable pauses or transitions in your speech—will maintain a more consistent sound. Knowing when to take breaks will increase your overall performance and if you time them well, will actually cause your listeners more pleasure listening to you.

Say It, Don't Spray It

Your unique tone, the speed with which you speak, how clearly you speak, and the interplay of your expression with the words you are reading from—these are the elements that have the most critical role in making you an effective speaker.

Part of your delivery comes from the words you are speaking, and part of your delivery comes from how you speak them. You have a unique vibe all your own. Strive to be yourself, but do so in a way that others can understand your message.

Digital Sound File Formats

It is important before we get started mixing and calling digital audio files in Flash to understand what digital sound files are called, what compression of these files is all about, and some of the most basic keywords in digital sound mixing.

Computer-based sound editing generally involves several different digital audio file formats. The file formats you will use the most with Flash are WAV and MP3 files.

WAV Files

WAV files are usually uncompressed audio files. This means that they can be quite large and sound pretty good. The quality of a WAV file is determined by how well it was originally recorded or converted. Generally, you will want to work with WAV files for your PSP game sounds; even though WAV files have larger file sizes than MP3s, they take up less memory in Flash, because they don't need to be uncompressed.

MP3s

The most popular compressed audio file on the market right now (mostly due to the popularity of iPods and other MP3 players) is the MP3.

Compression restricts the range of sound by attenuating signals exceeding a threshold. By attenuating louder signals, you limit the dynamic range of sound to existing signals.

Imagine that the audio file is a piece of paper with sheet notes on it. Compressing it is literally wadding up the piece of paper into a tiny ball. To listen to the music in its compressed state, you have to use a device like an MP3 player to unwad and smooth out the piece of paper.

MP3 stands for Moving Pictures Expert Group, Audio Layer 3. It started in the 1980s by the German Fraunhofer Institut. In 1997, the first commercially acceptable MP3 player was created, called the AMP MP3 Playback Engine, which was later cloned into the more popular Winamp software by college students Justin Frankel and Dmitry Boldyrev.

Napster and its gangbuster follow-up MP3 file-sharing services blew the lid off the MP3 boom, making it the number one most-recognized audio file on the Internet.

DIGITAL SOUND EDITING

For the purposes of this book, I will show you how to edit sounds using two different sound editing programs, both of which are easy to get your hands on, because they are free. The first one, Audacity, is free for download and takes a little bit of setup on your machine before you can work with it, but the second, Aviary's Myna, is a free application you use through your Web browser and does not require any downloading.

Exercise 8.1: Editing with Audacity

If you want to learn how to use Audacity, go ahead and follow this short tutorial. If you'd rather use Myna (or another program), you can skip this section.

1. Open your Web browser and go to http://audacity.sourceforge.net to download your own free version of Audacity. To export MP3 files from Audacity, you have to find a special plug-in called an Audacity LAME Encoder. To find out how to find and install this third-party plug-in for your machine, go to http://wiki.audacityteam.org/wiki/Lame_Installation and read the guidelines.

2. Let's record some sound. Open up Audacity and click the Record button, as shown in Figure 8.9. The program is now recording from your microphone, so you better say something. You can see the progress and the waveforms of the sounds in the Audacity window as you speak.

3. When you're done talking, click the Stop button. Play back your recording by clicking the Play button.

4. If you can't hear anything coming out, but you see a waveform in Audacity, make sure you have the volume turned up on your computer and your speakers. If everything looks good, but you still can't hear any sound, check the microphone level in the Mixer Control in Audacity, and you may need to raise it a notch.

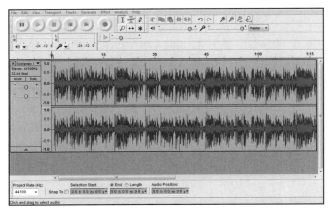

Figure 8.9
Audacity's main interface.

5. Now, if you didn't start speaking into the mic right away, you will probably have a long period of "dead air" before the sound wave you made and another chunk of "dead air" after. This is typical, but it's certainly not optimal for a sound you're recording for a cartoon or game. You have to edit your sound. Place your cursor at one side of the portion of the waveform you wish to get rid of and drag it across to the other side, highlighting the area you want eliminated. Then go to Edit > Delete. The selected portion will be removed from the waveform. Notice under the Edit menu that you also have the option to Cut and Paste, which will come in handy when you are mixing multiple sound tracks.

6. Playback the audio to make sure you didn't remove too much or not enough of the waveform. Eventually, you'll have it finished.

7. Highlight the entire waveform and experiment with the special effects that Audacity ships with. Go up to Effect on the menu and drop the list down. You can pick and play around with any of these effects, and playback the sound to hear how each effect changes the recording. When you find an effect you don't like, you can go to Edit > Undo to remove it. Some of the more useful effects are the following:

- **Amplify:** Increases or decreases the volume of your track.
- **Bass Boost:** Amplifies the lower frequencies, leaving the other frequencies untouched.
- **Change Pitch:** Changes the audio pitch without affecting the tempo.
- **Change Speed:** Resamples and changes the speed, thereby changing the pitch.
- **Change Tempo:** Changes the tempo (speed) of the audio without affecting the pitch.
- **Click Removal:** Removes clicks, pops, and other artifact noises.
- **Compressor:** Compresses the range of the audio so the louder parts are quieter.
- **Echo:** Repeats the audio again and again, softer each time, like an echo.
- **Equalization:** Amplifies or diminishes specified frequencies using curves.
- **Fade In/Out:** Fades audio in or out.
- **Invert:** Flips the audio upside down.

- **Noise Removal:** Removes constant background noise, such as the wind, fans, tape noise, or humming.
- **Normalize:** Corrects for vertical (DC) offset of the signal.
- **Nyquist Prompt:** Uses a programming language to massage the audio.
- **Phaser:** Combines phase-shifted signals with the original.
- **Repeat:** Repeats the audio a given number of times.
- **Reverse:** This makes the audio run backward, which is really cool!
- **Wahwah:** Uses a moving bandpass filter to create a "wah-wah" sound over the existing signal.

8. Lastly, you need to save the bit of dialogue or sound effect as a file so you can use it in Flash. Go to File > Export as MP3 (as long as you've installed the LAME encoder) and name your file trialTalkSnd.mp3, putting it somewhere convenient for the moment, such as your Desktop.

9. Browse to your Desktop or wherever you placed the file, and double-click (Win) or single-click (Mac) to open it in your operating system's default media player. Listen to your sound as it exists.

Exercise 8.2: Editing with Myna

This short tutorial will introduce you to editing sound digitally through the browser-based program Myna.

1. Open your Web browser and go to http://aviary.com/tools/audio-editor. Click the Sign Up button to register an account with Aviary, if you haven't done so already. You will have to make up a user name and password. Write these down, so that you'll remember them. When you're through, you should be taken to a welcome screen.

2. Click the Audio Editor (Myna) link on the far right of this welcome screen, or return to the URL listed above and click the Launch Myna button.

3. You should be in a new document named Untitled (for now). If you are not, you will more than likely be in the MynaDemo.egg file, which demonstrates how an entire song was created using Myna and multiple tracks. If you're in that file, it is probably because you did not register or sign in to Aviary first. Exit and sign back in and then launch Myna, and you should see that you're in Untitled.

4. Click the Record button at the bottom right of your screen. This will open the Audio Recorder dialog box. There will be an overlaid window that asks if you want to allow Aviary to access your webcam, microphone, or other computer components. Allow it, or you won't be able to do any recording. Once you have allowed it, you should see a screen similar to the one in Figure 8.10.

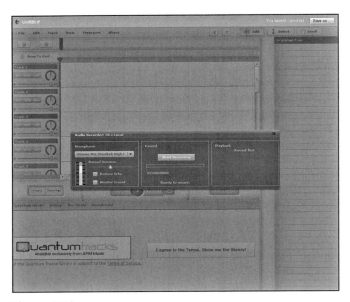

Figure 8.10
Myna's main interface.

5. On the left of the Audio Recorder dialog box, you can choose your microphone and preview the recording volume. The middle of the dialog box contains the controls, and the right side shows you playback options (after recording). Click the Start Recording button.

6. You're recording, so start speaking into your microphone. When you are through speaking your piece, click the Stop Recording button, and playback will start immediately. After listening to the playback, if you're satisfied with the way it sounds, click Import to Project. A Save Recording dialog box will appear, asking you to name your sound bite. Give it an original name, one you'll remember what the file contents are at a glance, and click Save.

7. You will be returned to the Myna interface, with a new exception: On the right, you will see a list of all imported (recorded) files, like those in Figure 8.11.

8. Find your recent recording in the list. Click and drag it from the list to Track 1 on the middle left, dropping it into the timeline.

9. Now, if you're like me, you will have a long line representing dead air between the start of your recording and when you started talking into the mic (see Figure 8.12). Myna gives you a handy editing tool to fix this. Scroll to the beginning of your recording, where it starts on the timeline, and hover over the box containing your sound recording. Two tool options will appear: Trim Start and Edit Loop Start. Trim Start looks like an arrow

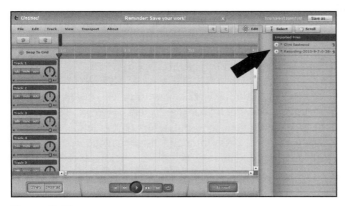

Figure 8.11
Your recorded files are shown on the right.

Figure 8.12
Notice the difference between the waveform and the "dead air" in front of it. This should be trimmed.

pointing right. Click and drag on the Trim Start tool to the frame where you see your waveform actually start, then release.

10. You have a similar tool for the end of your recording. Scroll right to the end of your recording, hover over the box, and you will see Trim End and Edit Loop End. Click and drag your Trim End to the cut-off of your waveform.

11. You may have to reposition your sound recording on Track 1's timeline, so that it starts all the way at the left, on Frame 1.

12. Save your work by clicking the Save As button at the top right of the screen. Name your creation trialTalkSnd2. You can add a description and tag words, if you would like, but this is not necessary unless you plan to share your file online with others. Click the Save As a New Creation button when finished. Wait for Aviary to save it.

13. Go to Mixdown. This allows you to share trialTalkSnd2.egg with others, if you like, but it's also the only way you'll be able to download your file. In the Mixdown window, like the one shown in Figure 8.13, preview your file's properties on the left. You can also play your file to test it. When satisfied, click on one of the download options, either MP3 or WAV. Save your file to your computer, in a place where you can find it later if you have to.

Figure 8.13
This screen allows you to distribute your creation, test it out, and also save it to your computer.

14. To make sure the file downloaded correctly, browse to where you saved your file and open it with your default media player. Listen to make sure you've saved the right file.

That's it! The sky's the limit, because you can record and edit files using Audacity or Myna. You can browse for more tutorials online, if you want to learn more about the sound editing program you prefer. But this gives you enough information to get started making sound effects and soundtracks for your PSP homebrew games made with Flash.

Importing Sounds into Flash

Now that you can make sound, let's look at how you get it into Flash, so you can use it in your PSP games. Adding sound to Flash projects is fast and easy.

Sound files are imported by choosing File > Import > Import to Library from the menu bar and browsing for the sound file.

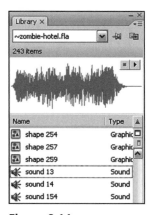

Figure 8.14
A sound file selected in the Library panel of Flash.

Selecting the file you want to use once it is located will import the file into your project's Library, and a new audio icon will appear with your other files. If you do not see your Library panel, which should be grouped behind your Properties panel, just go to Window in the menu options at the top of the screen and select Library, and it will appear. In the Library panel, selected sound files will display a waveform in the preview window, like the one you see in Figure 8.14.

Once your audio file is ready and rests within the Library for your project, it is best to add each of your sounds to a separate layer within Flash. Make sure there is a blank keyframe wherever you want the audio to start, and at least a few frames after that so that you can see the audio file once it is on a layer.

Once the audio file has been imported into the Library and a layer created to sport it, select the audio layer in your timeline, and click and drag your file from the Library panel directly onto the Stage. You should see a thin waveform appear in those few frames in the audio layer of your timeline. Now select the end frame and drag it further down the timeline. This will reveal the rest of the waveform in the audio layer. See Figure 8.15.

The waveform spikes can assist you in timing your audio to your animation, something that is also known as *synching*. If you want to move the beginning of the audio around in the layer, you can select the first frame, and drag it to the frame where you would like the audio to begin. Then just grab the last frame and drag it to where you want your audio to end.

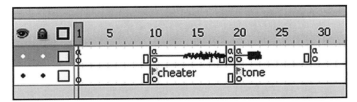

Figure 8.15
The waveform's appearance on the audio layer.

It's important to know that the audio file on the layer cannot have a keyframe anywhere between the beginning and the end of the waveform. If you insert a keyframe, it will stop the audio at that point and clear any audio after it. You can still move the frame at the end of the audio to reveal the waveform again, however. Also, it would likely make it easier if you reserve this layer only for the audio you have applied to it.

If you are importing a longer audio file that requires a fade out, you will have to do that manually. If you do not cut your audio down, your Flash file will get to the end of the animation and repeat while the previous audio continues to play. This will result in multiple layers of audio playing at once, and can distort the sound effect you're going for.

To fade the sound out, simply select it in the audio layer and you will notice the Properties panel displays the audio file name and properties. Select Fade Out from the Effect drop-down list, or click Edit to open up the waveform's Edit Envelope panel, as seen in Figure 8.16, where you can directly edit the sound's fade.

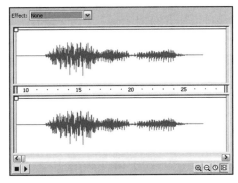

Figure 8.16
The Edit Envelope panel.

After adding audio to a project in this manner, you'd need to test your movie to see what it sounds like (by going to Control > Test Movie > In Flash Professional).

WHAT'S NEXT?

Now that you know all about adding a sound track to Flash, it is time to put together the pictures and sound and make a complete animation using everything you've learned.

YOUR FIRST ANIMATION

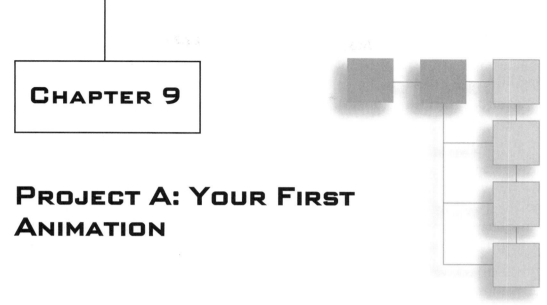

CHAPTER 9

PROJECT A: YOUR FIRST ANIMATION

In this chapter you will learn:

- The conventions for making Flash for the Sony PSP
- How to put together a complete Flash animation
- How to add sound effects and music in layers
- Why a loader might be needed

You've learned everything you've needed to, up to this point, to make a complete animation. Now you are prepared to make a short Flash movie. What you will discover in this chapter you can carry over into your video game design. In fact, the movie you make here will be added to your first game as the introductory cut-scene.

For starters, let's look at making a simple cartoon in Flash. You can then use what you learn to make more cartoons, or to apply the animation principles to your future game development efforts.

CONVENTIONS FOR MAKING FLASH FOR THE PSP

The sky's the limit, as they say, when developing Flash applications. There are so many different operations you can do, for so many different platforms. You can perform higher computational functions with ActionScript 3.0, and, using XML for a database, you can make impressive multiplayer games.

Unfortunately, you won't be able to do all of that for the Flash games you make. The PSP has many strengths, limits, and quirks that you need to know before creating content for it. In fact, to make Flash games for the PSP, you have very specific limitations you will have to operate under. This section will cover general design considerations and optimization techniques unique to making Flash for the PSP.

Ever since firmware update 2.70, the Sony PSP game console has been able to view Adobe Flash content via an Internet browser. The Flash Player must be enabled by the user from the Settings menu. For complete instructions on enabling the Flash Player on the PSP, see Chapter 15, "Spread It Around." Once enabled, any Flash content can be viewed from the built-in PSP Web browser.

The Flash Player on the PSP is version 6. This means than any Flash you want to make for the PSP must be Flash Player 6 compatible. Also, Flash Player 6 does not support Flash Video (FLV) files, so it's not possible for users to view sites such as YouTube that use FLV, nor will you be able to make use of streaming video in your Flash movies.

One of the greatest things about making Flash for the Sony PSP is that the PSP is a very powerful gaming platform, capable of rendering 3D graphics at the best frame rates for a portable device. However, you're going to learn a sad truth, and one that will severely crimp your plans for making Flash content for the PSP. Most of the graphical horsepower of the PSP is generated by low-level hardware the Flash Player won't have access to.

The Flash Player is a plug-in that runs in the PSP's Web browser. This browser, which is a software application that takes up a lot of processing power to emulate a web-browsing environment similar to one you'd see on a desktop PC, has only 2MB of RAM that it has access to, which it shares across three browser tabs. You'll have to keep your Flash beneath 1.5MB, or else performance issues will occur.

Thus, there's not a whole lot of processing power left over for your Flash movie. For a very short, simplistic animation, you can get away with 30fps, but for most Flash (especially Flash with detailed graphics, complex scripting, and more than one layer of sound), you'll need to stay between 12fps and 15fps.

Also, the screen size, or what can be seen on the PSP's viewing window, will affect your Flash performance. The average screen area you can use to make your Flash will have to be 480×272 pixels.

Most assets you use in your Flash document should be as small in file size as you can get them before importing them to Flash's library. This includes images and audio files. It's better to use small compressed bitmap images, the same kind of 8-bit pixilated images you'd see in classic video games, over vector images. Try to avoid using fancy gradients, images with lots of color information, and complex redrawing of frames, such as shape tweens. When it comes to audio, it's imperative that you edit it and compress it as much as you can before you bring it into Flash, and then be sure to use Flash's compression publishing settings when you go to publish your final SWF file.

The Sony PSP uses the directional buttons, analog control stick, and X button to navigate the browser and any Flash on the screen. The analog stick acts like a mouse to move the cursor around the screen and pressing the X button is the same as a mouse click. This hampers the use of key mapping available on a computer keyboard, which has a greater amount of input actions available to it, but this difficulty is not insurmountable. Besides, the PSP was built to play games on, and it feels comfortable in a gamer's hands.

Lastly, you'll want to keep your scripting to a bare minimum and be sure to only use the object-oriented ActionScript 2.0 scripting language for your Flash. This will run smoother and is quite a bit lighter than ActionScript 3.0, which is now available to most Flash developers.

Speaking of "light," there's a group of Flash developers who have been working with these challenges for some time now, and you can always pull information from their community sites and forums if you have to. They call the Flash they develop Flash Lite, and they have lots of guidelines, tricks, and tips for getting the most out of limited resources, especially for mobile Flash development. If you want a reference guide, you can find the complete Flash Lite Developer's Library (version 1.6) online at the following URL: http://sw.nokia.com/id/c3f23ce8-8f66-410c-87a8-b5fd850263a3/Flash_Lite_Developers_Library.zip.

As a side note with scripting issues, you will also be at a disadvantage when attempting to make a multiplayer game. For one thing, players cannot save any content to their device, so local file storage is impossible, and second, the Internet connection can't be relied on to pull information from servers. So most of the Flash games you make for the PSP will be solo games, playable by one person at a time.

So let's recap. What follows is a list of accepted conventions for making Flash that will play on the Sony PSP.

- Always make an ActionScript 2.0–ready Flash document that has publish settings set for Flash Player 6 compatibility.
- Your Flash screen size should be set to 480 × 272 pixels.
- The exported SWF file should be less than 1.5MB in file size.
- Use tiny bitmap images over complex vector art to conserve file size.
- Don't use FLV or multiple layers of sound in your document.
- Edit and compress all audio before importing it to Flash for use.
- Avoid using vector gradients, alpha colors, and shape tweens in your Flash.
- Avoid having to redraw frames as much as possible. Use as many tricks as you can to keep redraws at a minimum.
- Keep your ActionScript 2.0 scripted functions as short, trouble-free, and efficient as possible.
- Make sure user input is simple, involving mouse moves and clicks (which translates to the analog stick and X button presses) and arrow keys (which translates to directional keys).
- JavaScript, XML, and server communications are not supported, so don't use them.

The one great advantage you have in making PSP games is in the stability of the console system. Each one is the same. If you make a game that will run on your PSP, it will run on any PSP. Every PSP has the same processor, RAM, browser functionality, fonts, speakers, and screen resolution. When you create games for the PSP, you can focus on performance optimization for *just* the PSP platform.

Exercise 9.1: Creating a Short Animation

Our game, which we will make in Chapter 13, "Project B: Your First Game," will be a run-and-jump platformer featuring a strange pizza deliverer.

The main concept is that, as the gamer, you play a nematode, which is a type of round worm, and you work inside this great huge monster's body for a place called Pizza Gut. You deliver special protein pizza pies to all parts of the monster's body, for money. Along the way, you'll have to avoid leukocytes, which might mistake you for a parasite that needs to be gotten rid of.

Figure 9.1
The storyboard for our animation sequence.

What we need is a very short, comical interlude that takes place after the game has finished loading and before the game's instructions come up onscreen.

After considering and discarding many ideas, I chose a simple enough idea for the animation.

Look at Figure 9.1. First, show the nematode, who we'll call Bill, getting the pizza. Then he starts his car, which doesn't really have wheels because it flies like a rocket ship throughout the monster's body. We'll show him driving his car for a little while, and then end with him posing like a macho nematode, holding the greasy pizza box. The name of the restaurant he works for, Pizza Gut, will seem to leap off the box and zoom up to the screen, with the rest of the image fading away, just leaving the words. This will transition into the game, then.

Let's get started, shall we?

1. Open Adobe Flash and create a new ActionScript 2.0 document. In the Properties panel, set the Size to 480 x 272 pixels and the FPS to 18. Go to File > Publish Settings and in the dialog box that appears, click on the Flash tab near the top (it will appear by default, as the default Publish Settings will publish your document to SWF). Under the Flash tab, set the Player to Flash Player 6.0 (select it from the drop-down list) and make sure Script is set to ActionScript 2.0. After you are done, your screen should look like Figure 9.2. Click OK to exit the dialog box and return to the Flash workspace. Get in the habit of doing this step every time you decide to make Flash for the Sony PSP.

Figure 9.2
The Publish Settings window.

2. Save your Flash file as shortAnim.fla by going to File > Save As.

3. Once your document is saved, it's time to begin. Click the Stage color swatch in the Properties panel to open the Color Picker window and change your Stage color to #660000, a dark red color. This will help us emulate the inside of a giant monster's body without having to draw it later.

4. Change your magnification view to Fit in Window, so that you can see more of the Stage.

5. Create seven new layers in your Timeline, named the following, in descending order:

   ■ Actions

   ■ Audio

   ■ Text

   ■ Foreground

   ■ Actors

   ■ Midground

   ■ Background

6. Let's block the animation in. We know that our movie is set to 18fps, so that one second equals 18 frames of animation. Let's look at the storyboard again. Each of these six

Figure 9.3
Use the Brush tool to paint the outlines.

frames needs to have a time equivalency to pace them. #1 should last 2 seconds, #2 should last 2 seconds, #3 should last 2.5 seconds, #4 should last 3 seconds, #5 should last 3 seconds, and #6 should last 2.5 seconds. In frame talk, that means we need transitions on Frames 36, 72, 117, 171, 225, and 270. On the Timeline of your movie, insert blank keyframes on these frame numbers on the Background layer.

7. Return to Frame 1 of the Background layer. We are going to add the beginning sequence, starting here. In each sequence, we'll have to make determinations on what elements belong on which layer, and which will be animated. This is largely intuitive and will be up to you, although I'll make suggestions. For this first sequence, we need to have the hand and pizza box appear on the Background layer, and the pizza pie, which will be animated, moving in from off the left side of the Stage to the center of the empty pizza box, will be on the Actors layer.

8. On the Background layer, use the Brush tool (hotkey B) with the fill color set to black (#000000) to paint a hand holding a pizza box, as you can see in Figure 9.3. Try to make all of your Brush strokes as straightforward as possible on a single pass. You will need the top of the box and the bottom of Bill's arm to extend out past the edge of the Stage. This makes the composition more interesting.

9. Switch to the Paint Bucket tool (hotkey K) and use whatever colors you think appropriate to color Bill's arm and the pizza box. If you have difficulties, or find that the fill wants to bleed out past the drawing you made with the Brush tool, you can always change the Gap Size for the Paint Bucket tool; Gap Size is listed at the bottom of the Tool bar when you have the Paint Bucket tool selected and will increase or decrease the amount of gap the fill will ignore. When done, compare your screen to Figure 9.4.

10. Select Frame 1 on the Actors layer of the Timeline, then get the Oval tool (hotkey O). You are going to use the Oval tool to draw your pizza, starting with the crust, because it

Figure 9.4
Use the Paint Bucket tool to fill in the outlines.

would be on bottom. Set your Stroke weight to 2.0 and color to black (#000000), then set your Fill color to tan (#CC9966). Click and drag on the Stage to create an oval shape that is wider than it is tall.

11. Change your Fill color to red (#CC0000) and your Stroke color to None, and make a smaller oval inside the other one for the marinara sauce. If you don't get the second oval inside the first correctly on the first try, don't try moving it with the Selection tool! You'll only damage your artwork. Instead, undo (Ctrl + Z or Cmd + Z) and try again. One trick to getting it there is to watch where your cursor is before you start clicking and dragging. Make sure it's lower than the highest point of the tan circle and in further than the left-most edge of the tan circle. Or, you can hold Alt or Option and start click-dragging from the center of the pie, because you know then that you will be drawing the shape from the center outward. When done, compare your work to Figure 9.5.

Figure 9.5
Use the Oval tool to draw a pizza pie.

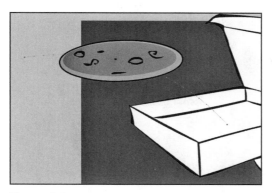

Figure 9.6
Add a bounce to the pizza pie's motion tween.

12. Use the Brush tool with Fill color set to black (#000000) to draw some squiggly lines and pepperoni shapes in the sauce. It's best to conserve the colors you use, so we don't want to add a bunch of different ones for the toppings.

13. Right-click on Frame 1 of the Actors layer and elect to Create Motion Tween. Drag the end of your tween out to Frame 35. On Frame 1, move the pie completely off the Stage to the left. On Frame 24, right-click and go to Insert Keyframe > Position. Then move the pie into the pie box. Scrub through your animation briefly to preview what this tween will look like. Adjust as you need to. For instance, I wanted to add a "hop" so I deselected all objects and then, still on the Actors layer, moved my cursor over the directional line of the tween until I saw the arc symbol appear, before clicking and dragging to reshape the directional line into a bowed shape, like in Figure 9.6.

14. Now we have a problem, because once the pie is in the box, it obscures the front-facing part of the box and Bill's hand. That's not what we want. We want it to look like it's actually in the box, don't we? This is easy to remedy. Using the Lasso tool (hotkey L), click and drag a selection area around the front-facing edge of the box and Bill's hand. When you let go, the area you "drew" a selection around will be covered in little white dots, showing that it's selected. It doesn't matter if you select too much, because we can fix it later. For now, copy it (Ctrl + C or Cmd + C).

15. Go to the Foreground layer. Insert a frame on Frame 35. Use Ctrl + Shift + V (or Cmd + Shift + V) to paste in place. Now the area you selected and copied is on your Foreground layer and will cover up your Actors, which includes the pizza pie. Scrub through your animation to see what I mean. If you selected too much of the box to copy, now would be a good time to use the Eraser tool (hotkey E) to remove the part you don't want—but don't forget to lock your Background layer first, or you might accidentally erase part of it, too!

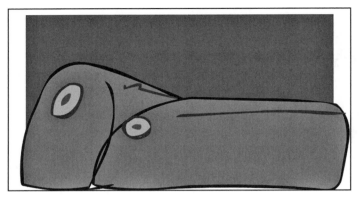

Figure 9.7
Draw the front dash of Bill's car and fill in the outlines with color.

16. Go to Frame 36 of the Background layer and verify that you have a blank keyframe there. Then use the Brush tool (hotkey B) and a black fill color to draw the outline of the car dash in Bill's car. I find that some artists prefer using a Wacom pen tablet for drawing in Flash, although you can do just as well with the computer mouse, which is what I use. Wacom pen tablets have an external screen representing a "touch pad" of sorts for the computer monitor, and a stylus shaped just like a pen, and where you draw with the stylus on the pad the input is interpreted on your computer. What works even better than pen tablets are those touch-screen computer monitors, or those that allow drawing straight on the screen.

17. Once you have an outline, use the Paint Bucket tool (hotkey K) to fill the outline in with colors of your choice. Be sure to add a place for the steering column and a keyhole for the ignition, as seen in Figure 9.7. Make sure that the console sticks out past the edges of the Stage, as we want the bottom and right-most sides to run off the Stage.

18. Lock the Background layer. On the Midground layer, draw a steering wheel coming off the steering column using the Brush tool (fill color set to black). Fill the outline of the steering column in with the Paint Bucket tool and whatever colors you see fit. Compare your work to Figure 9.8.

19. Lock the Midground layer. Go to Frame 36 of the Actors layer. Switch to the Brush tool (hotkey B) and, using a black fill color, draw Bill's hand and a car key in it, as you see in Figure 9.9. Use the Paint Bucket tool (hotkey K) to fill colors into your outlines.

20. Right-click on Frame 36 of the Actors layer and then choose Create Motion Tween. Then right-click on Frame 62 and go to Insert Keyframe > Position. On Frame 36, you want Bill's hand and car key to appear just off the Stage to the right. On Frame 62, you want his hand and car key to be up on the Stage, with the key touching the keyhole of the

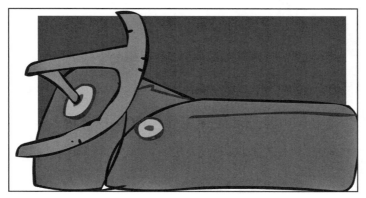

Figure 9.8
Draw and color a steering wheel for Bill's car.

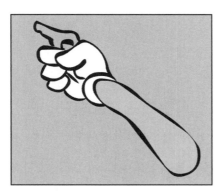

Figure 9.9
Add Bill's hand and be sure to draw a key sticking out of his hand, like so.

ignition. Once you've established the basic motion tween, go to a frame somewhere in-between those two, and, grabbing the directional line of the motion, pull it up into an arc, so that the hand seems to "bounce" on its way to the keyhole.

21. This next bit is tricky. You have to draw a frame-by-frame animation of the hand turning the key in the ignition. You can't get away with a tweened animation here, I'm afraid. Tweens decrease your Flash file size, because once you start doing frame-by-frame animations, you suffer frame redraws that add data information to your overall file, bulking up your size quicker. Unfortunately, it can't be helped. So on Frame 63, make sure you have a blank keyframe. Then draw the hand and key in the position you see in Figure 9.10. The key is already in the keyhole, and the arm is off the Stage. To get your hand and arm into the correct position and proportion to match the hand and arm that comes in the animation

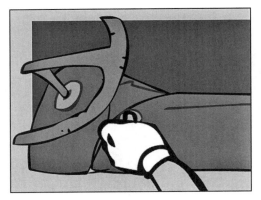

Figure 9.10
Draw the hand and key in this "crank" position here.

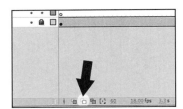

Figure 9.11
You can click this icon button to temporarily turn onion skin outlines on so as to position Bill's hand easier.

right before it, you can turn onion skin outlines on. This is the clear white double square icon button at the bottom of the Timeline, as shown in Figure 9.11. Click this icon button to turn it on, and you will see an outlined preview of the objects on the layer that come just before and after the currently selected frame. Then you can draw your hand and arm, and when you're done, turn onion skin outlines off. This is a neat trick to "trace over" images that precede current frames in the Timeline.

22. Right-click on Frame 64 and elect to Insert Keyframe. This will copy the hand you just drew to this layer, but, because it's a new keyframe, you can make all the changes to this hand you want. Use the Free Transform tool (hotkey Q) to skew the hand slightly. You can do this by moving your cursor over the right edge of your hand's bounding box, once you see the black anchor squares appear. Your cursor should change into a double set of arrows that appear to run at a slant. Click and drag on this edge, and you'll see that the edge will move up and down while the opposite edge of the bounding box, and the image, stays in place. Skew this edge up. Move the object until the key is directly over the keyhole again, if it moved from that position when you skewed the object. Move

Figure 9.12
Create a car or any other form of conveyance you can imagine a Pizza Gut employee like Bill driving inside a giant monster's body.

the transformation point to the key in this object, so that when you rotate the object, it will rotate with the key as a pivot. Then rotate the image just slightly counterclockwise.

23. Right-click on Frame 65 and the Insert Keyframe. Move the transformation point to the key, and rotate the object just a bit more counterclockwise.

24. Repeat this on Frame 66, by adding a new keyframe and rotating the object. You might also want to skew the left edge down a nudge. Repeat this again on Frame 67.

25. Right-click on Frame 66 and select Copy Frames. Right-click on Frame 68 and select Paste Frames. This duplicates everything that was going on in Frame 66 to Frame 68. Do the same thing for the remaining frames. Copy and paste Frame 65 to Frame 69, Frame 64 to Frame 70, and Frame 63 to Frame 71.

26. If you don't have one, insert a blank keyframe on Frame 72 of the Actors layer, and on that frame of that layer, draw a car using the Brush tool. Your car doesn't have to look exactly like the one I designed, which you can see in Figure 9.12. Yours can look like any car—or spaceship—you want to draw. After you draw the car, use the Paint Bucket tool to fill it in with color.

27. Right-click on Frame 72 of the Actors layer and choose Create Motion Tween. On Frame 72, use the Free Transform tool (hotkey Q) to make the car appear smaller. Remember to hold the Shift key down when clicking and dragging the corner handles to preserve the proportions of your car. On Frame 116, insert a keyframe (Position) and, again, holding down the Shift key while dragging the corner handles, resize the car until it's much bigger. Also, give it a very subtle rotation to the right. Scrub back through your animation. See how the car looks as though it is coming toward the viewer, and that it is rocking slightly? That's perfect!

Figure 9.13
Draw one of these creatures beside Bill's car, copy and paste it, and use Free Transform on the copy to make it appear opposite the original.

28. Insert a blank keyframe on Frame 72 of the Midground layer, if there's not one already. Using the Brush tool (hotkey B), create a comet-shaped cellular creature, like the ones depicted in the storyboard, and fill it in using the Paint Bucket tool (hotkey K). Switch to the Selection tool (hotkey V) and click and drag a marquee that surrounds the whole tailed creature. With it selected, copy (Ctrl + C or Cmd + C) and paste (Ctrl + V or Cmd + V). Your copy should still remain selected. Change to the Free Transform tool (hotkey Q) and click and drag the copy to the opposite side of the screen. Then, flip it across the vertical, so that it appears to be a mirror image of the first creature, and rotate it so that it is facing down if the original was facing up, or up if the original was facing down. This gives you two creatures floating to either side of the car, as you see in Figure 9.13.

29. Lock all of the other layers besides the Midground layer. You can do this pretty easily by clicking the Lock icon at the top of the Timeline panel, and then click the lock on the Midground layer to unlock it. Once you have all layers locked, excepting the Midground layer, select all (Ctrl + A or Cmd + A). Copy the selected creatures.

30. Unlock the Background layer and lock the Midground layer. On Frame 72 of the Background layer, paste a new copy of the creature pair and use the Free Transform tool (hotkey Q) to flip their images across the vertical and rotate them to appear in different spots than their originals. When you get done, your screen should slightly resemble Figure 9.14.

31. Unlock the Midground layer again. Right-click on Frame 72 of the Midground layer and choose Create Motion Tween. Insert a keyframe (Position) on Frame 116. On Frame 36 you want to use the Free Transform tool to shrink the creatures, until they appear behind the car, and on Frame 116 you want them enlarged to their regular size.

32. Do the same with the creatures on the Background layer, except that you want them to move faster than those on the Midground layer, so on Frame 116, make them so large they almost disappear off the Stage. Scrub through your animation and see if anything

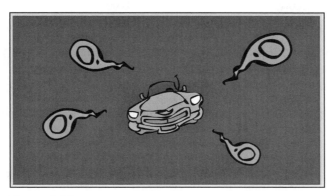

Figure 9.14
Make more of the creatures that will zoom past Bill's car.

needs tweaking. Often, the slight subtle changes you make in your animation will make it appear more believable in the end.

33. See a problem yet? I do. There's no one driving the car! It would be great to put the nematode, Bill, behind the wheel, wouldn't it? But we've already used up the Actors, Midground, and Background layers, and you can't have more than one tweened object on a single layer at the same time. So what do we do? Easy! We make a new layer. We'll put it below the Actors layer, so that it rests behind the car, but above the Midground layer, so that it's above the floating cellular creatures. Right-click on the Midground layer and elect to Insert Layer. Rename this new layer Actors 2.

34. On Frame 72 of the Actors 2 layer, insert a blank keyframe. On this frame, use the Brush tool to draw the outline of Bill's head. You don't need to draw his whole body, as it will be hidden by the car. Fill Bill's head in with color using the Paint Bucket tool (hotkey K), so that your work resembles Figure 9.15. Then, move and resize Bill behind the steering wheel of your car, or whatever you've drawn as Bill's conveyance.

Figure 9.15
Draw Bill's head to go behind the wheel of his transport.

35. Insert a blank keyframe on Frame 117 of the Actors 2 layer. Return to Frame 72, right-click on that frame, and select Create Motion Tween. On Frame 116 use the Free Transform tool (hotkey Q) to enlarge and move Bill so that he's still behind the steering wheel. On my Frame 116, I made it where Bill looks as though he's slightly shifting leftward, so that the action—though subtle—adds to the effect that he's separate from his car.

36. We're halfway there now! Save your work. After you've finished saving your Flash file, make sure you have blank keyframes on Frame 117 of the Foreground, Actors, Actors 2, Midground, and Background layers. If you don't have blank keyframes on that frame of those layers, you can right-click and add one as necessary. If you notice any gray frames filling in the Timeline in front of Frame 117 of these layers when you do so, as I had happen to me with the Foreground layer, it means that you had something on that layer that will be repeated up till Frame 117, if you're not careful. As I had to do, you can go back to the last frame you want that layer's object to be visible on and insert a blank keyframe. This will clear the intervening frames, so you have a clean slate up till Frame 117. Once you have this set up, you are free to continue.

37. On the Background layer, draw one of the cellular creatures like you did earlier at the upper part of your Stage. You'll want to be sure to color it the same as you did the ones earlier, for continuity. Draw a second and third creature on the Midground layer. Add motion tweens to the Background and Midground layers. You'll want to start the creatures off on Frame 117 in this order: the Background layer creature should start in the upper right corner of the Stage, and the Midground creatures will have one in the middle off right edge of the Stage, and one at the bottom center of the Stage, as you see in Figure 9.16. Insert ending keyframes (Position ones) on Frame 171 of both the Background and Midground layers. The easiest way to select a frame inside a motion tween to insert a keyframe in is to hold down the Ctrl or Cmd key when clicking on the frame; then, you'll select just that frame by itself, and you can right-click on it to select Insert Keyframe > Position. On these new keyframes, drag the

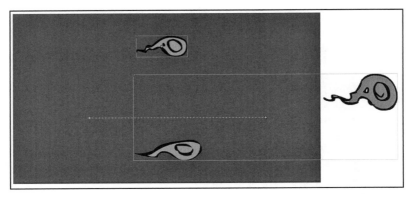

Figure 9.16
The starting position of the cellular creatures.

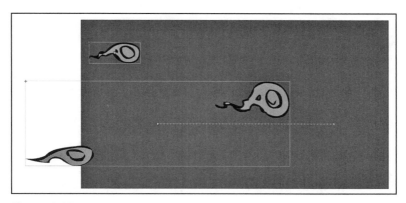

Figure 9.17
The ending position of the cellular creatures.

creatures from right to left, until the bottom left one is a ways off the Stage and the one that was off the right edge of the Stage is in the center of the Stage. See Figure 9.17.

38. On the Actors layer, draw and color Bill's ship as seen from a side profile. Be sure to use the same colors you used before for his ship, to preserve continuity. It's perfectly okay, this time, to draw Bill behind the wheel as part of the object. Right-click on Frame 117 of the Actors layer and choose Create Motion Tween. Right-click on Frame 145 and go to Insert Keyframe > Position. Move Bill's car to the center of the Stage. Right-click on Frame 170 and go to Insert Keyframe > Position, dragging Bill's car off the bottom right edge of the Stage. Somewhere between Frame 117 and Frame 145, click and drag the directional line of the tween until you have the motion arcing up. Somewhere between Frame 145 and Frame 170, click and drag the directional line of the tween until you have the motion arcing down. Your complete tween directional line, when you're finished, should resemble a sideways letter W. Compare your work to Figure 9.18.

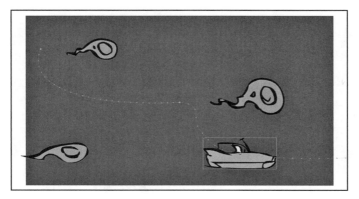

Figure 9.18
Add Bill's car and make it loop around the cellular creatures, like so. This shot was taken at random from Frame 155.

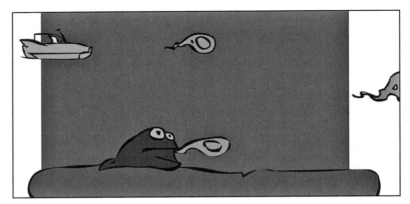

Figure 9.19
Add your Foreground image, that of a hump of ground and a creature resting on top of it.
This shot was taken on Frame 117.

39. Now it's time to add our Foreground image. Paint a large ground image and a creature resting on top of it. Both should be drawn on Frame 117 of the Foreground layer and should encompass the bottom fifth of the Stage, actually going off the bottom of the Stage and extending past the right edge of the Stage (see Figure 9.19). Create a motion tween on this layer. Insert a position keyframe on Frame 170. On Frame 170, move this object from right to left ever so slightly.

40. Insert a blank keyframe on Frame 171 of the Background layer, if there isn't one there already, and draw a large yellow star-shaped explosion.

41. Insert a blank keyframe on Frame 171 of the Actors layer, and draw and color Bill standing with a greasy pizza box in hand, as seen in Figure 9.20. You can draw him with

Figure 9.20
Draw Bill posing like so.

Figure 9.21
Make Bill come toward the camera.

his mouth open or closed. The choice is up to you. The main task is to make him look like he's doing a heroic pose, which is why I chose to put his fist on his "hip" and have him looking defiantly at the camera.

42. Create a motion tween on the Actors layer, and insert a position keyframe on Frame 224. On Frame 224, use the Free Transform tool to enlarge Bill and rotate him ever so slightly clockwise, until he looks like Figure 9.21. You will want the starburst behind him to extend to Frame 224, but remove any frames on the Background layer past Frame 224. To do so, click on Frame 225 of the Background layer, then, holding down the Shift key, click on the last visible frame of that same layer. All of the intervening frames will be selected. Right-click on them and choose Remove Frames from the pop-up options list.

43. If you want to animate the starburst image on the Background layer, that is up to you. I chose to do a small counterclockwise rotation between Frame 171 and Frame 210. Then I added a color effect style, Alpha, starting at 100% Alpha on Frame 210 and ending with 0% Alpha on Frame 224. This made it look like my starburst vanished.

44. Insert a blank keyframe on Frame 171 of the Text layer. Using the Text tool (hotkey T), click and drag anywhere on your Stage to make a text box. Type the words "Pizza Gut," then highlight all by pressing Ctrl + A or Cmd + A. In the Properties panel, change the font to one more applicable to this restaurant's logo. If you have it or want to get it, the royalty-free font Hot Pizza is available on the Internet and is closest to the parodied parlor's original font. Change the font size and align it center. Switch it from Dynamic Text to Static Text in the second drop-down list of the Properties panel. This will keep it from behaving oddly during animations. Then change the color to a bright red, to make it stand out. Lastly, right-click on your finished logo and convert it to a graphic symbol you name g_PGlogo.

Figure 9.22
Fit the Pizza Gut logo to Bill's pizza box.

45. Create a motion tween starting on Frame 171 of the Text layer. Switch to the Free Transform tool (hotkey Q) and shrink your logo, rotate it, and skew it until it looks like the logo is laying on top of the pizza box that you've drawn in Bill's hand, as you can see in Figure 9.22. On Frame 224, enlarge and rotate your logo so that it remains in place on the pizza box.

46. Insert a new position keyframe on Frame 270 of the Text layer. Enlarge and straighten up your logo, until it's almost half as big as the Stage, centered, and aligned near the top. The logo that was on the pizza box has now jumped off and is becoming the title of our video game.

47. Insert a new position keyframe on Frame 270 of the Actors layer. Enlarge Bill and the pizza box, pushing them off the Stage's left and bottom edges. Also, add a Color Effect style Alpha. Remember, to do so you have to deselect all, then click on the object you want to add it to, and look for Color Effect to pop up in the Properties panel. Start your Alpha at 100% on Frame 225 and fade it out to 0% by Frame 270. This will take Bill out of the picture.

48. Add a blank keyframe to Frame 171 of the Foreground layer. Then add another blank keyframe to Frame 225 of the Foreground layer. Draw a black outline of a word balloon and fill it with white. When you are done, you might want to select it and use the Smooth option in the Tool bar to reduce the corner edges of the word balloon. When it looks ready, resize it to fit the Pizza Gut logo as it exists on Frame 225. Next, add a motion tween to the Foreground layer for this object. Lock all other layers except for this one.

49. Insert a new position keyframe on Frame 270 of the Foreground layer. Enlarge and straighten up your word balloon to fit the logo as it swells and fills the screen, as seen in Figure 9.23. Add a Color Effect style Alpha, starting at 0% on Frame 225 and emerging to 100% by Frame 270.

50. Right-click on Frame 270 of the Actions layer and insert a blank keyframe. Go to Window > Actions (hotkey F9) to open the Actions panel. Verify that Frame 270 is selected, then type "stop();" in the window. Similarly, you can get to it by the roll-out on the left of the Actions panel, by expanding Global Functions > Timeline Control and clicking on Stop. Compare your screen to Figure 9.24. Close the Actions panel when you're done.

Figure 9.23
Grow the word balloon to fit the Pizza Gut logo as it appears on Frame 270.

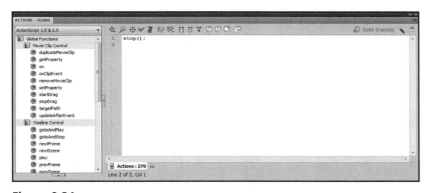

Figure 9.24
Add a stop(); action on Frame 270, so your movie will stop there.

51. You're almost done! Save your work. After you've finished saving your Flash file, it's time to add sound to your animation. The first step is to skim through your movie and see what sounds would need to be added and where. For your first animation, I'll make some suggestions of my own.

   ■ A sound effect accompanying the pizza pie going into the box, starting in Frame 20.

   ■ A sound effect of a car engine being turned over, starting in Frame 64.

   ■ A car driving or spaceship loop sound, starting in Frame 72.

   ■ A slightly different car or spaceship loop sound, starting in Frame 117.

   ■ A "ta-dah!" sound effect of some kind, starting in Frame 171.

- A voiceover saying "Pizza Gut," starting in Frame 235 or 240 (depending on how fast you say it).

- A soft-key, jazzy, or peppy musical accompaniment, starting in Frame 1 and looping the whole length of the animation.

52. You can either make these sounds yourself or look for them online. The voiceover will probably need to be done by you, using your mic to record, because there isn't a sound bite like it anywhere on the Internet.

Note

Whenever you want to record a voiceover but don't want to use your own voice or record another living person, you can still do so, thanks to the power of technology! You can experiment with computer speech synthesis, if you so decide. This is the technology that takes anything you type and spits out a human read-out of it. You can experiment with speech synthesis with AT&T Labs Natural Voices Text-to-Speech Demo online at http://www2.research.att.com/~ttsweb/tts/demo.php.

53. After you get your sounds, edit them in your chosen sound editing program and export them as the most compressed file type possible, to conserve space in your finished movie. Then, one by one, import these sounds into your Flash library (File > Import > Import to Library). After you import the sounds, listen to them in your Library preview window.

54. Following the preceding instructions for starting frames, go through your Audio layer and insert blank keyframes on Frame 20, 64, 72, 117, 171, and 235 (or 240). Drag and drop the sounds where they need to go on their start frames. Two of them, both the car or spaceship loop sounds, may need to be looped. You can do that after dropping the sounds onto the Stage by looking in the Properties panel for Repeat. Click the drop-down list arrow for Repeat, and select Loop from the choices. I did not have this problem. Instead, my problem was that the loops were too long and overlapped one another when I played it back. So I had to return to my sound editing software and trim them until I had a usable sound effect.

55. Where do you put the music, you might be asking? You can put it on Frame 1 of the Audio layer. Be sure to set it to Loop in the Properties panel. I used a jazzy bongo piece I found on Flashkit's Web site.

56. Save your animation when you're done. Then, go to Control > Test Movie > In Flash Professional. Your movie will open and play within the built-in Flash Player emulator. Also, a SWF file will be exported to the same folder where you've been saving your work. If, during play testing, you notice something that's not right, go back to Flash and fix it. There could be a step you skipped, or some tweaking to be done to the audio or image files. This is not uncommon. In fact, digital animation and video game development is an

iterative procedure. That means that you try a lot of different things, over and over, until you get it right. Your animation or game is never perfect the first time. In fact, most projects take hundreds of tries and lots of fine-tuning to get it "right."

Exercise 9.2: Adding a Loader

The last step is to add a loader. A *loader* is a very brief animation that occurs while your movie is loading into the end user's browser.

When the movie is already installed on a computer's hard drive, as yours will be, you won't see the loader actually working, but when viewers go to your movie on the Internet, the page will appear blank for a long time and they'll scratch their heads, wondering what's going on if you don't stick something on the screen to show them that your Flash movie is loading. That's why a loader is so important, especially on larger SWF files that will take longer to download. Most web surfers these days are used to seeing a loader of some kind, whether it's a whirling disc of light or the simple phrase "Loading. . ."

The main components of any loader are:

- Something that shows how much has been loaded so far.

- Something that shows how much is left still to load.

- Something that shows how fast the file is loading.

Thankfully, loaders are pretty easy to make. Adding a loader to your Flash movie will be quick and painless. Yet there are literally thousands of different ways you can make one and tailor it to your particular theme of movie. What I will show you is just one way that you can do it.

1. Open your shortAnim.fla file, if it's not already open in Adobe Flash.

2. Go to Window > Other Panels > Scene (hotkey Shift + F2) to bring the Scene panel up. Click the little Add Scene button (far bottom left of the Scene panel). Your new scene, by default, will be named Scene 2, just as your original scene was called Scene 1. Double-click the name Scene 2 in your Scene panel and rename it Loader. Move the Loader scene above Scene 1 in the stacking order, so that the movie will play the Loader scene first. You might also take the time to double-click on and rename Scene 1 to Movie, to save yourself the trouble later.

3. Click on the Loader scene in the Scene panel, if you don't already have it selected. Note that you are currently in the Loader scene in your Flash workspace window. Let's start building our loader, then! Close your Scene panel, just to get it out of our way for now.

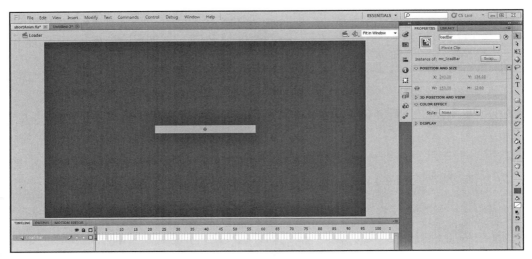

Figure 9.25
Setting up the mc_loadBar in the Properties panel.

4. The first thing we need to start with is the load bar. Name your current layer *Load Bar*. Use the Rectangle tool (hotkey R) with a Fill but no Stroke to draw a rectangle on the Stage. I made a 150 x 12 green (#33CC00) rectangle. If you forget to disable the Stroke before making your shape, you can always double-click on the outline after you make your shape and press the Delete key to remove it.

5. Select your rectangle shape and convert it to a new movie clip named mc_loadBar. Set its registration point to the left center. With your new movie clip selected, go to the Properties panel and give your movie clip the instance name loadBar. Check Figure 9.25 for a visual aid. You might also want to put your mc_loadBar somewhere on the Stage you think looks best, or use the Align options to align it horizontal and vertical center. It's up to you.

6. Create a new layer named Border. Inside this layer you will use the Rectangle tool with a Stroke but no Fill to create a colored outline. I chose a red (#990000) as my Stroke color, to match my background color and yet still remain distinct. Make sure your Border layer is above your Load Bar layer in the Timeline stacking order, so that it appears in front of the green rectangle.

7. Now that you've finished with the basic load bar, it's time to get started on your percentage text area. Create a new layer called Load Text. Use the Text tool (hotkey T) to draw a text box the size you want. It really only has to be one line long and not even that long across. Just long enough to fit a maximum of 4 characters in this case.

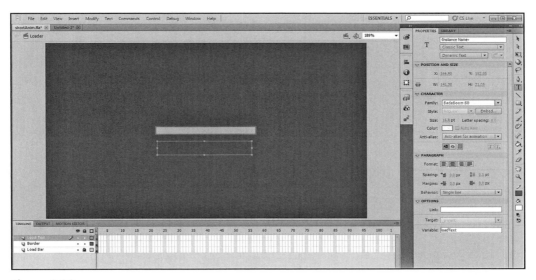

Figure 9.26
Create a dynamic text placeholder for Load Text.

I changed my font to one that's legible and a size of 16 point. At the top of your Properties panel, be sure the drop-down box is set to Dynamic Text in this instance. At the bottom of the Properties panel, in the Options section, give the text box the Variable name loadText. See Figure 9.26 to see what I mean. You can center your text field under or above the load bar, as you like.

8. Believe it or not, you're finished building your loader! Now, all you have to do is add the appropriate scripting to make it work. Create a new layer called Actions and insert a blank keyframe on Frame 2 and Frame 3. Be sure that all of your frames below span the three frames so your loader doesn't strobe. To do this, right-click on the third frame of each layer and choose Insert Frame.

9. Click on the empty keyframe in Frame 1 on the Actions layer. Go to Window > Actions (hotkey F9) to open the Actions panel. With this frame still selected, add the following code:

```
bytes_loaded = Math.round(this.getBytesLoaded());
bytes_total = Math.round(this.getBytesTotal());
getPercent = bytes_loaded/bytes_total;
this.loadBar._width = getPercent*100;
this.loadText = Math.round(getPercent*100)+"%";
```

```
if (bytes_loaded == bytes_total) {
    this.gotoAndPlay(3);
}
```

10. Add this code to Frame 2 of the Actions layer:

```
this.gotoAndPlay(1);
```

11. That's it! You're through. Save your Flash file.

Let me describe what you've just done.

The line `bytes_loaded = Math.round(this.getBytesLoaded());` declares the variable "bytes_loaded", which uses a feature in Flash called getBytesLoaded and determines how many bytes of your movie have been loaded thus far by the user's browser. The `Math.round()` in the code tells Flash to round the number off so it becomes a whole number rather than an eight-decimal-place number, because no one wants to read a percentage that goes out to the eighth decimal!

The part that starts `getPercent` takes the variables `bytes_loaded` and `bytes_total` and divides them so we can determine how much has been loaded thus far in our movie. I declared it in a variable because we will be using it twice in the script, so instead of typing it twice, a variable saves time.

The line `this.loadBar._width = getPercent*100;` takes the value produced by the `getPercent` variable and multiplies it by 100. The 100 is purely arbitrary, because you can multiply the results by whatever you like. The number you place there determines the ending width of your mc_loadBar movie clip. Because you drew the border for your clip on the stage already, I recommend using the width of your movie clip on the stage. You can select your clip and open the Properties panel to see what the width is.

What the final conditional on Frame 1 (the part that starts if (`bytes_loaded == bytes_total`)) says is that if the number produced in the variable `bytes_loaded` is finally equal to the number produced from the variable `bytes_total`, then the movie should `gotoAndPlay` the third frame on the Timeline, which is empty and has no scripting to stop it, so it will carry right on to Scene 1 of our movie.

The ActionScript you placed on Frame 2 is there because if all of the bytes are not loaded in your movie in Frame 1, it will automatically move on to Frame 2. Because we can't let it pass Frame 2 yet, because the movie isn't finished loading, we must send it back to Frame 1. This will keep looping around over and over until both the `bytes_loaded` and the `bytes_total` variables are equal in numbers. Then the conditional statement declared at the end of the actions in Frame 1 will send the movie directly to Frame 3 and your movie or game or whatever will start from there.

WHAT'S NEXT?

You've accomplished the hardest first step: completing a task set out for you. With that out of the way, the next exercises will be decidedly easier, because you'll know that you can do it! Now that you've built a short animation, it's time to focus more keenly on PSP game development with Flash.

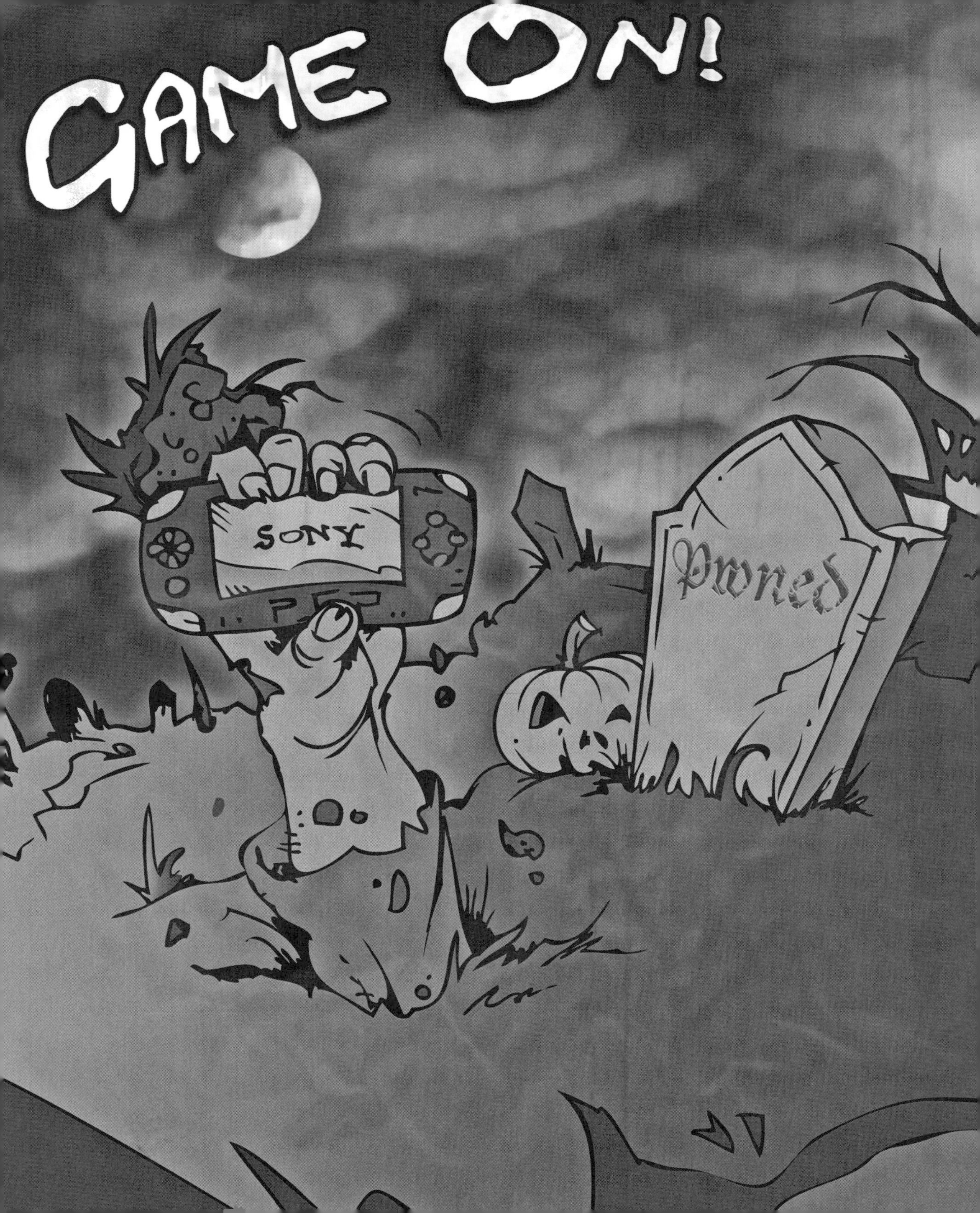
GAME ON!
SONY
Pwned

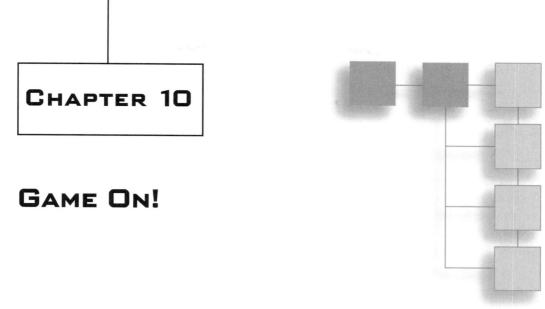

CHAPTER 10

GAME ON!

In this chapter you will learn:

- What it's like to be a game designer
- What goes into making a great game
- The terminology used in game development
- What game genres exist

This chapter will show you how video games are made, commercially and by independent developers.

This chapter does not include program code or resource files or an actual tutorial, because that comes later. This chapter shows you what goes into making a video game, the production process, the types of video games you can make, and some basic tricks of the trade that you can use in making your own video games.

In other words, this chapter shares with you the academics behind making fun PSP games.

WHAT ARE VIDEO GAMES?

A game is, by definition, any activity conducted in a pretend reality that has a core component of play. Video games are special games where the play is tied within an electronic device, whether that device is a computer screen and keyboard, TV screen and console, or handheld machine.

Danc, a game designer, pixel artist, and tool maker in the industry who runs the website www.LostGarden.com, says that a video game can be best described as an onion, with layers: "A game is built like an onion. Each layer of the game polishes an aspect of the previous structure and makes it slightly more appealing. Areas near the inner core give you the most bang for your buck. Areas near the outer edges of the game design are easier to change without unbalancing the system, but don't make as big of an impact."

Danc lists the layers as such (see Figure 10.1):

1. **Core Mechanics**—The fundamental gameplay, with its risks and rewards. Gameplay is a commonly used term meant to describe the interactive aspects of video game design. Gameplay involves the player interacting with the game.

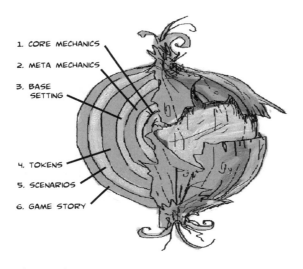

Figure 10.1
Danc's game onion layers form the important features of a modern video game in order of priority, from the center out.

2. **Meta Mechanics**—The rules that tie together the core mechanics. For instance, a role playing game (RPG) can be seen as a string of multiple battle scenes, but the meta mechanics tell a story and create an exploratory mode that pull these battles together.

3. **Base Setting**—The backstory of the game, its character description, and its setting. This is seen as a hook from a marketing perspective, because it gets the player excited to play the game.

4. **Tokens**—This includes the graphics and sound effects in the game. These are just like board game tokens, in a way. For instance, a gnarly snarling alien in the game *Prey* is a token that can hurt the character if not dealt with or avoided.

5. **Scenarios**—This includes the game levels and scripted events. The core mechanics often involve the interactions between various game tokens. Things like game levels and scripted events put the tokens into proper perspective.

6. **Story**—The narrative element of the game can provide an overall wrapper of context around the mechanics and tokens and gives the player an evocative base for gameplay.

A video game starts with at least two, sometimes three layers, and some games have all six layers. Most only have five.

Game Genres

The easiest way to create your game's core mechanics is through the use of game genre. The following are roughly the most popular game genres on the market.

Action Games

Action games are games where the player's reflexes and hand-eye coordination make a difference in whether they win or lose. The most popular action games include:

- **Shooter**—These games particularly measure a gamer's speed, precision, timing, and aim. The player moves their character through each game level, shooting at enemies and other targets, while trying to avoid being hurt. Typical tokens include enemies, ammunition, weapon upgrades, medical kits (for healing), and maze-like maps.

- **Platform Game**—These allow the player's character to explore the upper reaches of a playfield by jumping on moving platforms and climbing ropes and ladders, all the while avoiding or knocking away enemies in a fast-paced animated world where one wrong step could spell disaster. These games used to be called sidescrollers, because the background would scroll from one side to another as the player moved her character from Point A to Point B.

- **Racing Game**—Racing games feature fast vehicles moving along twisting tracks or difficult terrain in a race to the finish line. Some have mayhem and combat, with the vehicle being a weapon in and of itself.

- **Sports Game**—These feature rules and team meets just like their real-world counterparts. Great sports games have realistic motion-captured animation, moves that follow realistic physics, game rules following official athletic guidelines, referees, cheering crowds, announcers, and those little touches that make the sport more realistic.

- **Fighting Game**—These are "duke-'em-out" games that focus on competing against opponents in virtual arena combat. Some games that resemble fighting games feature an open arena, like half a city block, where the gamer must mow down countless oncoming enemies before moving on to the next area, such as the game *Gungrave*.

- **Stealth Game**—These are games that reward players for sneaking into and out of places without being seen and striking enemies silently. This is one genre that moves slower than most, because the gamer must have a bit of patience hiding in darkness and stealthily sneaking up on or past the guards. Great stealth games should have lots of contrasting light-and-dark areas the player can use strategically to hide in, sneak attacks (such as tranquilizer darts or garroting), and lots of wandering guards to avoid.

- **Survival Horror Game**—Survival horror games are those that feature horror themes, less ammunition, and fewer weapons than other action games. Combat is still a part of most survival horror games (yet some have no combat at all and force the player to hide or run away from danger), but the player must ration ammunition and avoid direct confrontations, while navigating dark maze-like environments, always on the alert for unexpected attacks from monstrous enemies.

Adventure Games

Adventure games traditionally combine puzzle-solving with storytelling. What pulls the game together is an extended, often twisting narrative, calling for the player to visit different locations and encounter many different characters. Often, the player's path is blocked and he must gather and manipulate certain items to solve some puzzle and unblock the path.

There are at least four different types of adventure games. There are completely text-based adventure games, graphic adventure games, and visual novels (which are a popular Japanese variant featuring mostly static anime-style graphics and resemble mixed-media novels).

Another type of adventure game you might have seen—and even played before—is the hunt-the-pixel or "hidden image" adventure game. This manner of adventure game, a trendy genre for amateur game developers to undertake, is a series of graphic puzzles that has the player going on a virtual scavenger hunt.

RPGs

RPGs got their start in pencil and paper in the 1970s with the late great Gary Gygax's *Dungeons and Dragons*. It exploded into the video game market with *Final Fantasy*, which was not the first electronic-based RPG but definitely won the most attention world-wide, sealing RPGs as a dominant mainstay in the game industry.

Today's more complex computer role-playing games like *Neverwinter Nights*, *World of Warcraft*, *Diablo 3*, *EverQuest*, *Torchlight* (see Figure 10.2), and *Elder Scrolls IV: Oblivion* offer players pretend worlds with an amazing level of immersion.

The main goal of most RPGs is for the player to gain enough experience or treasure for completing missions and beating monsters to make his character stronger (experience can enhance a character's prowess and treasure can be used to purchase better weapons and armor for a character).

Figure 10.2
Torchlight from Runic Games is a fantasy-themed RPG set in the fictional town of Torchlight and is one of the first games made with the free OGRE game engine software to go from indie development to pop stardom in the game industry.

Along the path to reaching this goal, players travel to many locations and meet many *non-player characters* (NPCs), which are characters not controlled by the player but are a supporting cast of characters controlled by an artificial intelligence programmed into the game itself.

Strategy Games

Strategy games envelop a great deal of mental-challenge-based games, where the player builds an empire, fortress, realm, world, or other construct, manages the resources therein, and prepares against inevitable problems like decay, hardship, economic depravity, revolution, or foreign invaders.

Construction and Management Simulations

A related type of strategy game is the *Construction and Management Simulation*, or CMS. A CMS game is very much like a sandbox with lots of neat building and management tools, where the player virtually gets to play God and design their own little world, such as in *The Sims*, *Spore*, *GhostMaster*, and *Rollercoaster Tycoon*.

Other Video Game Genres

Besides the genres already mentioned, there are several more. The following are a few not stated previously:

- **Advertainment Games**—These games advertise a particular brand or service and are generally developed as part of a public relations' campaign. The main purpose behind one of these games is to market the company's service/product to the public.

- **Artificial Life Games**—These make players care for a creature or virtual pet. Viacom's *Neopets* is one of the best-known artificial life games on the market. Although there are lots of artificial life games on the market, many (like the *Webkinz*) are tied to a merchandise/toy product line.

- **Casual Games**—These include such traditional games as Chess, Poker, Texas Hold 'em, Solitaire, mah-jongg, and trivia.

- **Consumer Games**—A newer strategy game offshoot, one pioneered by Gamelab's *Diner Dash* in 2004 (see Figure 10.3), features a customer-service core play, where the player is in charge of an eatery and must

Figure 10.3
Diner Dash from Gamelab started a whole "feed-'em-up" nonviolent game genre.

please customers to make the biggest profits. This style of strategy game teaches players money sense, management, and prioritization skills.

- **Customization Games**—These include all manner of games, from the dress-up doll games to the create-a-scene games, and are especially popular in the online Flash game department, because they're so short and simple they are not viable as commercial enterprises (unless you count fashion designer games, such as *Imagine: Fashion Designer*).

- **Puzzle Games**—Puzzle games never have much of a story but instead focus on mental challenges. Popular puzzle games include *Bejeweled* and *Tetris*. A newer puzzle game that has sought to break boundaries in the industry is *Plants vs. Zombies*, which has appealed to a huge audience because of its offbeat theme.

- **Serious Games/Edutainment Games**—These games facilitate schools by teaching subjects in the guise of having fun, or they can help companies instruct their employees.

Games are still fairly new, and, as a growing media, their genres are constantly in flux. If you don't see a game genre here that you want to use, or if you have an innovative design for a new game genre, go with it. If you do, just be consistent and clear with your core mechanics and game rules.

How Is a Video Game Made?

Video game design begins with an idea. The idea is the kernel of a game. It can be original or it can be a modification of an existing game concept. The game idea will usually fall within one of several game genres (mentioned previously), though designers enjoy experimenting with mixing the genres.

Game Developer Job Titles

Game development is a multidisciplinary process.

A single triple-A game title, like Bungie's *Halo 3*, may have from 30 to 300 talented individuals on the project team and generally costs the same as a Hollywood blockbuster to make. Because it costs so much to develop a triple-A title, most development teams are funded by a big-time publisher such as Microsoft, Nintendo, Activision, or Electronic Arts. Though this funding assists in reducing the enormous costs of building a game from scratch, the publisher often gains exclusive publishing rights to the finished game and the game must be set to make money even before its release date, often a daunting challenge for a new game developer.

Note

When we talk about a *triple-A (AAA) game title*, this description refers to an individual title's success or anticipated success if it is still under development. Triple-A titles are defined by the cost spend and the return-on-investment. Most triple-A title games cost between $10 and $12 million to make and become a smash hit, selling well over a million copies.

Game developers fall into several skill-based job classifications. The broadest categories of developers are as follows:

- **Artists**—These people create the game's graphic assets through the development of concept artwork, 2D characters, 3D polygonal models (see Figure 10.4), and more, including props, weapons, vehicles, and monsters.

Figure 10.4
An example of a 3D model created from polygons. The model is from a no-longer-active *Lone Wolf* game that was being produced by Singapore-based company Ksatria in 2008.

■ **Leaders**—These people communicate between the other team members and make sure everyone is doing what they should be doing and that development milestones are reached on time.

■ **Level Artists**—These people take the design documents and use the game technology, including game engines and map editors, to construct the individual maps, levels, and environments players will play through over the course of the game.

■ **Programmers**—These people make the most money on the development team, because they have to script the program code that lets the computer know what to do and how to react to the game's players.

■ **Sound Artists**—These people set up Foley sound effects, musical scores, ambient sounds, and voiceover narratives to make the game sound so sweet to listen to.

■ **User Interface (UI) Artists**—These people design the look and feel of the game's shell interface, including the menu screens and in-game options lists. UI artists must test usability against aesthetics to maintain thematic style and gameplay.

■ **Writers**—These people not only write the storyline for the game, but they also write the dialogue/events that take place within the game and the game's manual.

Consider the preceding categories umbrella categories, as the descriptions are vague enough that several roles follow under each one. There are few standards in the industry as of yet when it comes to proper job titles, so one game company may call the level artists world builders while another may call them terrain editors, when they are talking about the same job role.

Independent Game Developers

Music is big business, just like video games. Typically, record companies compete for listing in the Top 40 and music artists whine when they're not getting the respect they think that they ought to be getting. However, in the music industry there are still some artists that are not afraid to experiment and create really edgy tunes outside the mainstream. From garage bands and unlicensed artists comes the wild side of independent music. Indie musicians are sonic artists who aren't afraid to take risks. They settle for lesser gigs so they can play the music they want to without the heavy influence of record companies.

In precisely the same way, indie game designers are also rebels who thumb their noses at the big industry giants. If you want to see real innovation in the game industry, you have to peer at the margins, at the independent game designers.

You could become an independent game designer and, working in your bedroom or garage and on your own time, you could make the next hot game title. All you need is determination and practice and the right software. This millennium is the age of do-it-yourself. If you have an idea for a great game, or even just an idea for a game you and your friends would like to play, you could make it happen.

You could devote a little time to learning the software, talk some friends into helping you design the art and audio assets, and with the right game development software you could make your game yourself, without ever leaving home. It might take seven weeks or twelve months, but then you'd have your idea out there. You could distribute it on the Web, burn it to CD-ROM and sell copies at conferences or online, enter it into indie game contests, and generally get your video game noticed.

THE FOUR FS OF GREAT GAME DESIGN (4FOGGD)

Game industries employ thousands of testers and market researchers and spend millions of U.S. dollars a year to determine what makes a great game. I have a specific formula of what makes a great game.

There are 4FOGGD that must always be present for any game to be great. The Four Fs cannot exist without one another. They are listed here in their order of priority. When I speak of priority, I mean that if ever a conflict of interests should come up during development, you should always abide by what takes priority in the list.

FUN – FAIRNESS – FEEDBACK – FEASIBILITY

Fun

Games are intended to be fun, by definition. Fun is a word synonymous with games. Fun is a short and simple word, easy to spell, and it is innate. Even the smallest child will begin inventing their own personal game if bored, and the purpose behind this natural instinct is to escape ennui by having a little fun.

The complexity and character of people's games evolve with their age and mental understanding. A game that outreaches a participant's age or understanding will quickly tire the participant and leave them bored. A boring game is no fun at all, as boredom is the antithesis to fun.

Give your players a fun, fresh, and original experience, one that is sure to encourage replaying and word-of-mouth advertisement, and you've done your first duty as a game designer. If your game is the slightest bit offbeat, offers cathartic release, or is irreverent and funny, it will get played.

Fairness

Frustration can be a healthy motivator in games, challenging core gamers to achieve greater heights for themselves, but frustration can also lead to anger or worse, to frustration. Angry or frustrated players of electronic games are prone to throwing their game controllers or beating their computer keyboards while uttering epithets, none of which is conducive to a great game. Playing fair with your player equals better rewards in the end.

Do not force gamers to repeat complicated moves in the game or learn their lesson by seeing their character die over and over again. Don't kill their characters off suddenly or inexplicably without giving them a heads-up as to why. Avoid meaningless repetition or wrist-slapping like this. Help the gamer out without removing the challenges altogether.

As Duane Alan Hahn, game aficionado, says, "Play is supposed to be the opposite of work, but most video games are just jobs with a little bit of fun thrown in. These games can leave players feeling abused, frustrated, and overly aggressive... Your game can either irritate or alleviate. Which would you rather do?"

Look at Nintendo's *Super Mario Kart*. There is a subtle shifting of balance in that game so that it appears challenging enough to keep the player's interest. The computer-controlled racers speed up when they lag behind your racer, and they slow down when they are way out ahead of you so that you, the gamer, always think there is a way to beat the game. A designer could program those other racers to be so fast and smart they'd beat you every single time, but where would the fun in that be? So treat your gamers fairly.

Feedback

If the player does something right, give the player a reward. Give that player a Twinkie! If the gamer does something downright stupid, show him that it was wrong to try that particular action: punish him.

Video games are really all about risks versus rewards and pushing a player's buttons. A game world is little better than a Skinner Box, like the one in Figure 10.5, and if you know anything about psychology you will do just fine in the game industry.

Figure 10.5
B.F. Skinner testing a rat in a Skinner Box.

However, there are two critical rules of thumb to your punishments and rewards.

First, you should have your punishments and rewards fit the actions and environment, and always be consistent with your use of them. If the player always gets a higher score for grabbing purple jellyfish, and he grabs a purple jellyfish and his score is suddenly lowered, that gamer will become irate and wonder what sort of mean trick you're playing on him (see Fun, from earlier).

Second, you should make your punishments and rewards come immediately so the player can get the gist of causal relationships. For instance, if your gamer has his character walk on lava, the lava should immediately burn or hurt the player's character. Similarly, jumping off a precipice and falling five stories should hurt. And beating up the bully should get the player character a kiss from the beautiful damsel he was attempting to rescue.

Feasibility

Encourage player immersion whenever and wherever in your game you can. To this end, avoid inconsistencies and a little terror called feature creep. *Feature creep* comes when a game designer gets too close to his project and begins adding "neat features" that really add nothing to the game or do not fit with the original game concept. For instance, if a somber horror game about mutants suddenly introduces a switch to the gamer that, if pulled, drops a bunch of gaily colored soda pop machines out of the ceiling to squash the mutants, the game has choked (and so might the gamer!). This fun little feature has weakened the original game concept and the player's anticipations of the game being a serious horror game.

Keep your games simple. "I would say simplicity is a key factor in any good game design," Thorolfur Beck, founder of game development company CCP, comments. "Simplicity in interface, game systems, etc. . . . Simplicity does not have to mean few possibilities (just look at Chess), but creating a real good, well-balanced, simple game system is a much harder task than creating a very complex one."

Players are notorious for loading up a game and playing it. They hate to be bothered reading the game manual or having to look up a walk-through guide online. If the player consistently feels lost and frustrated, you have failed to make a great game. As Atari veteran Mark Cerny puts it, "Keep the rules of the game simple. Ideally, first-time players should understand and enjoy the game without instructions."

WHAT'S NEXT?

You have enough know-how under your belt to begin dreaming up game ideas and get started down the path to be a developer, so now let's look at making up game objectives.

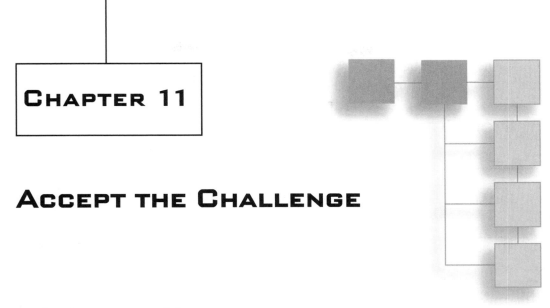

CHAPTER 11

ACCEPT THE CHALLENGE

In this chapter you will learn:

- How to entertain players through game narrative and story devices
- How to add conflict to your game
- Why you should use behavioral science to make games addictive
- What player immersion is and how to obtain it
- How to put the player in control
- What types of game objectives exist and how to employ them

A video game is not just pretty pictures and awesome sound effects. If video games were that simple, then they'd be motion pictures. Games have to involve the player. Just as a story has a central conflict that keeps the reader involved, with an invested interest in the outcome ("Will Dina find her missing boyfriend? I must keep reading to find out!"), so, too, does a video game have a central conflict that keeps the gamer playing. This central conflict in video games is what you call an objective.

A video game's objective can be a quest, a mission, or a goal. Whatever its appearance, it drives the gamer to keep playing until he achieves it.

We'll look at the use of objectives in this chapter, and, more importantly, how you can keep your gamers engrossed in your games. The more engaged you can make the gamer, the better your game is, and the better your game is, the more people will talk about it and the more it will get noticed.

WATCH THIS, NOW! ENTERTAINING THE PLAYER

Tip

"Fairy tales do not tell children the dragons exist. Children already know that dragons exist. Fairy tales tell children the dragons can be killed."

—G.K. Chesterton

A motion picture is about a decent fellow having stones thrown at him, and we, the audience, wait with baited breath to see what he will do. Video games, on the other hand, are unique, because we cannot sit on our laurels and watch the action: we *are* that guy, and we decide what the guy will do when the stones are launched at him.

Telling an Interactive Story

In literature this sort of interactive fiction has been portrayed in classic Choose-Your-Own-Adventure (see Figure 11.1) or Fighting Fantasy game books. If you don't know what one is, you should look at some of Joe Dever's game books as an example, which can be found online at http://projectaon.org. I grew up

Figure 11.1
Book covers of several Choose-Your-Own-Adventure books.

reading them, and they can be a lot of fun. In fact, several game developers make a paper prototype of their game resembling a Choose-Your-Own-Adventure game book before starting the digital version.

Basically, a game book starts each page describing what you, the reader, and the player see: "The castle gates look rusted with age and pelting acid rains, and the stones show signs of weathering and pitting. A guard mans the gates, but a little ways down the trail to your left you see what looks like a side door, hidden against the castle wall by an overgrown oak tree." Then the game book gives you your choices: "If you wish to walk up to and ask the guard to enter the castle, turn to Page 24. If you wish to go down the path to your left and see if you can get in the side door, turn to Page 31." You don't read the books cover-to-cover but follow the twists in the story based on your decisions.

Writing a game narrative is a lot like these early game book examples.

Just remember:

- Keep the gameplay and mechanics in mind at all times
- Ensure the writing relates to the gameplay
- Use narrative tools, such as setting and journals, to tell the story
- Accept that most of the actual story will have to be revealed in backstory or character dialogue

MAKING YOUR GAMES ADDICTIVE

The news media often touts that video games are addictive. This is especially true of South Korea, where suicide attempts are often linked to the amount of video game play time spent. You probably even know one or more kids addicted to games, whether they can't stop playing *Call of Duty* or *World of WarCraft*. Games *must* be addictive.

So how do you make your game truly addictive? How does anyone? The methods are simple, really. I'll show you how.

Everybody into the Skinner Box: Using Behavioral Science

Every video game is designed around a central element, and that is the participation of its audience. In other words, video games are about the players, and players are people—just like you and I. Therefore, the study of the players' minds has come up time and again with some significant findings that help you design your game. Most of these findings fall under the heading of behavioral psychology and have been printed in scientific journals, yet they are just as important to game developers as they are to scientists.

Behavioral psychology focuses on how a species learns and how minds observe and respond to their environment. What comes out of the study of behavioral psychology is not so much a formula for making great games as it is an approach to understanding why players react in certain ways. Psychology offers a framework and vocabulary for understanding what and how you teach a game to a player.

B.F. Skinner discovered you could control behavior by training subjects with simple stimulus and reward. His Skinner Box was a cage where a small animal, usually a rodent, could press a lever and in turn receive food pellets. In 2001, Nicholas Yee, a research scientist at the Palo Alto Research Center (PARC), likened the MMORPG *EverQuest* (shown in Figure 11.2) to "a virtual Skinner Box."

Game developers actually tailor a lot of their games to be virtual Skinner Boxes. Let's look at how this is accomplished.

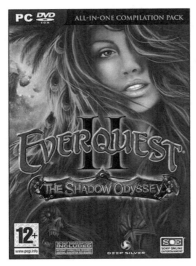

Figure 11.2
Sony Online Entertainment's *EverQuest* was lauded as addictive online gaming since its release.

Hit the Lever, Click the Mouse, Smash the Button: Making Players Work for Rewards

A *contingency* is a rule or set of rules governing when positive reinforcement is given.

For example, a role-playing game may have the player character raise to a new skill level and gain bonus character points every 1,000 experience points won in the game.

This can also be put on a schedule. Using the same example, the *fixed ratio schedule* would be that *every* time the player character reaches 1,000 experience points, he gains a new skill level and bonus character points to spend. Or you could set it up as a progressive fixed ratio, by having the first target set at 1,000 experience points, the next at 1,500 experience points, the next at 2,000 experience points, and so on.

You could take the ratio one step further, however.

Think of it this way: If your rat in a cage can hit a lever and always see two pellets drop out, he'll become complacent, knowing that food is there whenever he gets hungry. However, the rat will continue hitting the lever, obsessively even, if only one pellet drops out at random every five to ten hits. Adding a degree of uncertainty to the lever-hitting madness makes the matter more addictive.

These are called *variable ratio schedules* in Skinner vocabulary. A variable ratio schedule is indicated in many fantasy online games, where an enemy may drop valuable items totally at random when he is defeated. It's the same level of addiction you see in gambling casinos, where the players plug away at slot machines, knowing they can't quit *now*, because the very *next* one could be a winner.

A steady ratio schedule is also very important. The more certain the player is that his reward is going to be something really good really soon, he'll work at it even harder. When the player knows the reward is a ways off, such as when the player achieves one objective ("Yay! I got the fabled sword!") and has a long trek to go to the next ("Ugh! You mean I have to go all the way back to the village?"), the player's motivation will be low and the player may get bored.

This is also true about the start of a video game. Notice how, in most online role-playing games, it is easier to earn rewards (or level up) at the beginning of the game, but then the time and effort spent to earn those rewards increases exponentially. This is the way these online games ease the player in, providing lots of promises, and then delaying the gratification the player seeks.

The player is shown (or learns pretty early on in the game) what the contingencies are in the game, because these are the basic building blocks of goal reinforcement when it comes to video game design. Provide a steady ratio schedule, one where each player response produces a reward, and the player will play harder longer.

In-Game Items as Rewards

Your brain treats items and goods in the video game world the same as it would if they were real. Because, for all intents and purposes, they are.

Most gamers will tell you, if it takes time, effort, skill, and a little luck to obtain an item (especially when that item might take you five hours of game play to reach!), then that item has value, whether it's virtual or not. As Lee Sang-eun, a gamer of *Lineage*, says, "I feel a little awkward paying money for something that only exists on the computer screen. But it's a simple trade of money for someone's labor. I mean, it's real work."

This is why the highest court in South Korea ruled that virtual goods are to be officially treated the same as genuine goods. Virtual goods today are a whopping $5 billion industry worldwide! Just look at Figure 11.3.

Figure 11.3
Zynga's *Café World* had a special Labor Day sale, where you could spend real money to buy Café Cash or Café Coins at a reduced rate. Online games are making dough taking people's money to get in-game benefits in this manner.

Humans have a natural hoarding and gathering instinct. This instinct is kicked into high gear when we march our little Mario character around the game world, picking up stars and coins. It's pushed into an even higher gear with subscription-based online games, where we are sent running around endlessly collecting game items that may have nothing to do with the game itself, just for the sake of collecting.

No, You Can't Have It: Elimination and Punishment

On the other hand, what happens when you stop providing the expected reward? The B.F. Skinner studies show that an individual will continue to meet the ratio to receive the reward, so long as the reward is forthcoming. The reward stops coming, and the individual will either lose interest in performing whatever action it is, or they avoid it in frustration. This means that you could potentially harm the success of your game if you suddenly withdraw the contingency.

To avoid losing a player's interest, you could switch tactics. Instead of providing just one contingency, introduce another. This can keep a player from being turned off from your game, which could be an epic fail on your part.

Another move you can make, the real naughty move, is to provide punishments if the player quits playing. This is the main addiction element behind games like *Neopets*, *Farmville*, and *Animal Crossing*, because if the player doesn't play the game, then their pets, crops, or towns suffer or even die out—and the player can't face that, not after putting so much time and energy into growing or building them up.

This is a real coup de gras of game development, where you keep the player clicking and clicking just so they don't lose the stuff they worked so hard to get.

What to Do When Conditioning and Behavioral Science *Doesn't* Work

Not every game can be a virtual Skinner Box.

In fact, the use of behavioral science in game development has formed a controversy in the game industry. *Braid* game creator Jonathan Blow remarks that the Skinner-style of game mechanics is a blatant form of "exploitation."

These games are still fun, he admits, but they are designed in such a way to keep gamers subscribing to games even during long periods when they *aren't* having fun but constantly button mashing.

To sum up: you know the logical process that goes into making games; you know they must be fun and fair; you know you should provide feedback and make your game feasible to the player; and you know the most popular game types.

But what really separates a game from other media, such as listening to music, watching a movie, or reading an engrossing book, is an element only games have: interactivity!

IMMERSING THE PLAYER IN YOUR GAME WORLD

You've heard of immersion before. When you hear the word immersion, you might immediately think of slipping into a hot tub and letting the warm bubbly water cover you. That's one form of immersion, and the slow sinking goodness of climbing into a Jacuzzi is more similar to game immersion than you might think.

Have you ever played a game that you focused on so hard that when your friend called or your parents interrupted your concentration, you realized with shock you'd been playing for hours straight? Have you ever been playing a game so intently you didn't want to stop? If the answer to either of these was "Yes," then it's because you've discovered another key element of popular games: *immersion*.

Immersion (view Figure 11.4) makes gamers want to spend more time playing a game. It creates addictive game play by submerging players in the entertainment form. With immersion, you get so engaged in a game you forget it's a game! You lose track of the outside world.

Pulling Those Heart Strings: Emotioneering

One of the premiere ways to inspire immersion in players, to gently sink them into your game world, is by getting them to care. Once a player cares about their character, the outcome of the game, or the game's story or environment, then you can get that player to make hard decisions and manipulate them through the challenges you have set up for them.

Figure 11.4
This guy is so engrossed in his game that he might easily forget to take out the trash when his parents tell him.

You will learn that making players care about what happens in a game is not always an easy task. A radical new way game developers are approaching their trade is through *emotioneering*, whereby they use gamer emotions as buttons to press to make the experience more fraught, immersive, and riveting.

Fashion design guru Marc Eckō broke onto the video game world in 2006 with *Getting Up: Contents Under Pressure*, a game about a graffiti artist. Eckō called games "emotional entertainment products" because he considered games to be a form of entertainment unique in that it's the only form of entertainment that forces players to interact with it on a closely personal and emotional level. Emotions can be used to make players care about the games they play.

Eckō is not the only game creator out there who shares this viewpoint. Screenwriter David Freeman (see Figure 11.5) started the Freeman Group, which studies the many ways writers can put emotions into games. Freeman pioneered *emotioneering*, a cluster of techniques seeking to evoke in gamers a breadth and depth of rich emotions. These emotions not only create stronger immersion, but they also generate control points for the designer to maneuver the player through the game.

In Freeman's own words: "Emotioneering is the term I created to describe a body of over 1000 techniques for making games emotionally immersive. That is,

Figure 11.5
David Freeman.

they evoke, in a player, a wide breadth and depth of emotions. I believe that all techniques to make games emotionally engaging fall into 34 categories. These categories include: techniques to get a player to identify with the character they play; techniques to get a player to bond with an NPC; techniques to give an NPC a quality of emotional depth, even if the NPC speaks just one line of dialogue; techniques to take the player on an emotional journey; and many others. Those are just a few categories of emotioneering techniques. There are 30 others."

Here are some of Freeman's techniques in a nutshell:

- Keep the plot twists coming. Remember: "Out of the frying pan, into the fire."

- Have the other characters recognize or refer to one another as if they were real people.

- Give the player ambivalent feelings toward an ally or enemy character, like loving and hating them at the same time.

- Force the player to do something evil or otherwise violate his character's integrity.

- Have the player discover he has been tricked or betrayed by an ally.

- Set up incongruous events (like when the main character of Nintendo's *Chrono Cross* suddenly switches places with the main villain and has to gain new allies after losing all of his friends).

What are some new ways you can see that games can tug on players' emotions and affect them on a deeper, more personal level?

VIDEO GAME OBJECTIVES

A real game wouldn't be a game if it didn't offer the player a challenge. The types of objectives games offer vary widely, from the accumulation of resources to puzzles to self-preservation. Many objectives are staples of the game genres they belong in; others fit with the gameplay and are thus included.

Types of Game Objectives

Most of the time, objectives take the form of obstacles that must be overcome. Either the player's character faces hordes of hungry zombies shuffling along a grainy windswept city street, or the player's character is trapped at the base of a mountain protected by hired assassins and must get past them all to reach the top and save the princess.

These game obstacles, and the resulting types of objectives, can be classified into these categories:

- Locks
- Mazes
- Monsters
- Traps
- Quests
- Puzzles

Locks

Players are so used to locks (and the standard manner in which the locks must be unlocked) that they just roll their eyes now and say, "Another locked door, huh? Okay. I guess I'll go find the key. . ." Locks by their very nature fence the player in, preventing access to some area or reward in the game until that moment when the player beats the challenge and unlocks the next area or recovers the reward.

Figure 11.6
In *Silent Hill 4: The Room*, from Konami, Henry is stuck in his apartment thanks to a seriously locked door.

The simplest and most prosaic locks is a common lock: a locked door (see Figure 11.6), a jammed gateway, or elevator without power stands in the way of the player getting to level three or three hundred. The player knows when encountering any aperture that is locked that he must find the key to unlocking it.

Other locks are subtler. For instance, an overbearing guard standing at attention at the gate the player wants passage through might just be overcome if the player bribes him with a peanut butter and banana sandwich.

And let's not forget blood locks. *Blood locks* are where the player is locked in a single locale (usually a room or arena) with lots of foes to defeat, and the exit from the locale will not appear until the player destroys all oncoming enemies. Blood locks can be seen in most third-person fighting and shooter games, such as Midway's *Gauntlet: Dark Legacy* and SouthPeak Interactive's *X-Blades* (see Figure 11.7). An imaginative twist on this is the '80s' game from LucasArts, *Zombies Ate My Neighbors*, where the lock's goal is not to defeat all of the zombies (and other monsters) that keep popping up, but to save the neighbors, and once you've saved all of the neighbors you can, a door leaving the level will appear.

Figure 11.7
In *X-Blades*, the player must fight all attacking monsters, and once they are no more, passage from the area will open up so the player can continue.

Whatever the lock mechanism you might use, it will be a powerful and vital tool in your arsenal of gameplay devices, and it should be scripted with intelligence and creativity to work right.

Mazes

Below-average gamers can get lost in standard game levels, so making the level more difficult to get through by adding in lots of twists, turns, and dead ends might quickly make for a player headache. On the other hand, if you use an in-game map or set up a trail of bread crumbs and some clever surprises along the way, a maze can become a wonderfully entertaining way to break the monotony of locked doors (see Figure 11.8).

A maze can be one of the simplest ways to make a game more fun, as long as you don't leave the player completely in the dark on where to go. Besides, no one likes a straight-and-narrow game environment with nothing in it but blank space, so tinker with your game maps and make them thrilling to explore.

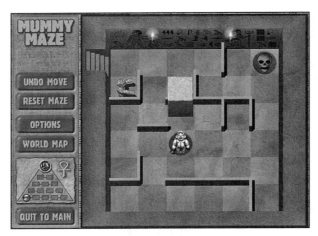

Figure 11.8
The PopCap game *Mummy Maze* features a maze challenge, where the player must avoid being "got" by a mummy while navigating a pyramid maze.

Monsters

Fighting games have progressive matches where the player must beat a tough opponent. Shooters have hordes of stinking zombies, war-time combatants, shielded androids, or other dehumanized monsters running at the player, which must now be mowed down with fire power. RPGs have dungeons littered with monsters to tackle, and tackling them wins the player treasure or experience points.

Battles with monsters typify the combat system of these game genres. There is always something to be gained by overcoming the monsters in games, no matter how unlikely it might seem. Even killer crows tend to drop boxes of gold.

Monsters should never get short shrift. They scare and titillate us on an instinctive level, and they make for fearsome foes, even if they are normal-looking humans in tanker gear. Either the monsters block the door to escape or they carry the key to the next level. Many games will ramp up the difficulty by using an evolution of ever-tougher monsters for us to fight. And the toughest of all are the "boss monsters" that guard the gates on the hero's journey (or at least the end of the level).

Traps

Traps, as shown in Figure 11.9 are a hodgepodge of suspense, scenery, and intrigue. Good traps can have whole stories behind them. Give some thought to each and every trap you place.

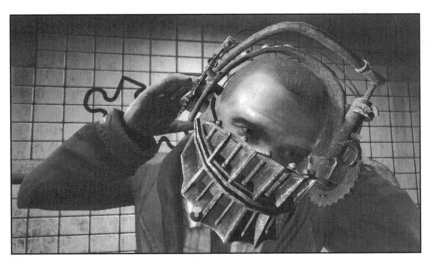

Figure 11.9
In *Saw: The Video Game*, from Zombie Studios and Konami, Detective David Tapp wakes to find himself in a reverse bear trap.

A trap in a high cleric's abbey may appear and work very differently from a trap set in a demon warlord's dungeon. Traps reflect the places and people who built them, even if they do share a common goal: to stop trespassers or thieves. Use style to cater your traps to the game's locale. Consider adjusting traps according to their immediate surroundings, including terrain, special features of the land, and weather conditions.

Traps need not be lethal. Some may be designed to wound, harm, or hold a trespasser. Others may raise an alarm, scare off, or deter would-be invaders in other ways. Some traps may not have actually been designed to be traps in the first place but through age and disuse, or negative natural conditions, accident-prone areas may have developed. A typical example of such is a rickety bridge that, over the years, has planks that have started to rot and rope that has started to fray: a once-solid bridge may end up a death trap for our hero!

Quests

Quests are special sets of challenges that take place in both stories and games, thus linking narrative and play. Quest games, including the *King's Quest* series, have quests that make up activities in which the players must overcome specific challenges to reach a goal, and when players successfully surmount the challenges of the quest and achieve the quest's main goal, the player's actions bring about or unlock a series of events comprising the game story.

Game writers often cite Joseph Campbell's monomyth or "hero's journey" as a pattern for their quest games. In the "hero's journey" there are several legendary steps, which you can imagine as a staircase, where the first step starts with the hero in his own world confronted with a terrible evil threat requiring him to go where he's never gone before or do things he's never done before. This mythic story structure forms the basis for the majority of our ancient legends and our current Hollywood story compositions. For a look at this pattern, watch *Star Wars* or *The Lord of the Rings*. You can read more about the monomyth in Chapter 6, "Make Up a Decent Story."

As Jesper Juul explained in *Half-Real: Video Games between Real Rules and Fictional Worlds*: "Quests in games can actually provide an interesting type of bridge between game rules and game fiction in that the games can contain predefined sequences of events that the player then has to actualize or affect." You don't have to write a quest game to use quests to improve your games.

Many of your standard action or shoot-'em-up games, including 2K Games' *BioShock*, have implemented quests to reveal narrative and create further depth of player experience.

Puzzles

The most noted use of puzzles in video games, aside from actual puzzle games like *Bejeweled* and *Tetris*, are the use of objects to further the story. If players do not know what key will unlock a specific lock mechanism to continue their quest in the game, they have to find it.

Sometimes this is through the obvious use of in-game objects. For instance, say that the player's character can see a key lodged in the keyhole on the other side. If the player can find something small, like an ice pick, he can push the key out, and if he has something thin and flat, like a newspaper, he can pull the key through the bottom of the door. Then he can unlock the door.

Some puzzles are cryptographic or clue-driven in nature, where the player must supply a crucial bit of info, such as a password, key code, whodunit, etc., to pass by a guard, a locked door, open a wall safe, or close the case. To figure out what the code/password/other is, the player must search for clues. These clues are often left lying around in convenient journals, computer e-mail messages, tape recordings, or found by talking to people. The player may have to figure out what something cryptic means to identify a clue, such as a *cryptogram* (a short encrypted text message) or *rebus* (a word puzzle that uses pictures or parts of pictures to represent words).

When constructing puzzles, keep in mind the maturity and intelligence of your target audience. How old are they? Would they understand or "get" what you want them to figure out? Don't let a good game bottleneck because of a tough puzzle challenge.

WHAT'S NEXT?

Now that you understand the player's motivation and psyche and know how to entertain them better, let's look at game worlds and what goes in to making them.

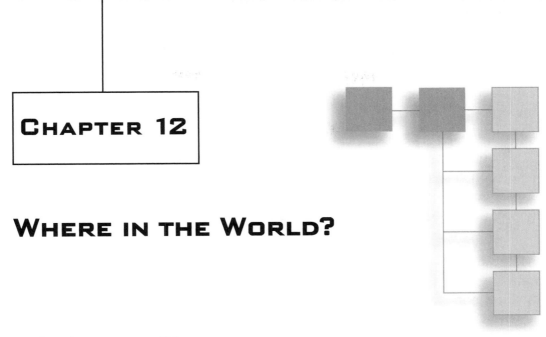

Chapter 12

Where in the World?

In this chapter you will learn:

- How to make game worlds seem real and immersive
- How to make game interface decisions
- What a HUD and other game interfaces should look like

Without an appropriate playground in virtual space, a game could never take place. Just as a sports game has to have a playing field or arena, so, too, do video games have to have a virtual world. Gameplay has to have a background for reference, a playing field for the player to explore, find resources, and beat combatants in (or whatever the game's objective may be).

One of the key features players look at when playing games is the artwork. Simply stunning vistas, crumbling mountain ruins, and rusty futuristic metal-work can always astound a gamer, but making those places explorable and interactive helps further game immersion, putting the player into the game like nothing else can. This is the connection between playing a video game and being at an amusement park, like Disney World.

Imagine Your Game as an Amusement Park

Everything you learned about setting in Chapter 6, "Make Up a Decent Story," applies here. The game world reflects the game's setting, and as such, the setting can be just as important as the characters entering it. But it's much more important than that.

Disney theme park imaginer Danny Hillis now makes computer games. He says, "Parks take you out of the every day and re-create that sense of wonder from childhood, the time when nothing made sense, when you didn't know what would happen next and didn't need to. They're wonderful, thrilling, and unpredictable—but safe. That's how I felt the first time I played *The Legend of Zelda*. It was a new thing."

I often tell my students that designing a game is a lot like being a host at a haunted house theme park (shown in Figure 12.1), or a really good travel agent. You are removing the players from their safe, predictable reality construct and plunking them down somewhere completely new and scary. This is both fun and challenging for you, the game's designer.

You are also designing for your gamers a weekend getaway, a retreat. If you don't start thinking about it that way, you will end up creating for them a sloppy awful place they'll never want to come back to. Consider the game world as a giant amusement park, vacation resort, or haunted house—and the player as a client, tourist, or visitor. Players play games, watch movies, and read books about far-off locales, pretty or scary landscapes, and places the players

Figure 12.1
The properly set up haunted house theme park is sure to scare would-be visitors.

themselves wish they could visit. This is one of the main components of escapism, and one of the leading motivations for gamers to play video games.

So mull over the visual and emotional impact of every part of your world. Put yourself in your player's shoes all of the time, and just have fun. If you're not having fun, the player won't have any fun. This will guarantee game immersion on a deeply psychological level.

If you have a game that is decent to play, has a great story, and unique characters, it might still suffer on the player market. You might not know why, but it might be because the levels are plain and uninteresting. Get it in your head quickly that, as a game designer, you are delivering a whole package: treat your players as tourists and be their tour guide, setting them up for thrills in lush and exciting game worlds!

DESIGNING GAME LEVELS

Inside this game world there are several scenes, or chapters, called *levels*. Each level is its own distinctive region with its own set of objectives that the player must reach before he can travel to the next level. To continue the analogy of the haunted house, levels are like each of the rooms visitors go into to get scared.

Being a level artist is like being part architect, part interior designer, part illusionist, and part tour guide.

What Are Levels Good For?

Levels create space and define the virtual reality. They also play an important role in gameplay because they provide a point of reference for the player and set the stage for the action.

Levels serve a multifold purpose. Here are some of the top reasons why you use level architecture:

- To set the stage
- To create game flow
- To set the mood or theme
- To fence the player in

Setting the Stage

Impressiveness and decoration are frequently the only ways that real-life architecture influences game architecture. Buildings created in virtual space do not suffer with usability concerns.

Windows and doors can look like real windows and doors, but the level artist doesn't have to worry about sizing them correctly so people can use them. Although you want to make places look like they *could* exist, they don't have weight, they don't really exist, and so you don't have to confine yourself to physical limitations when building them. Game levels can twist and wind and ignore the laws of physics or gravity.

Game environments are little better than a theatrical stage with cardboard props. A lot of times, games will have buildings that are merely "false fronts" and have no real depth to them, or tree lines with nothing beyond them but the illusion of a bigger world out there. You might have witnessed these first hand in games where your character falls outside the actual level and is floating in empty space.

Level design, therefore, is more about gameplay than it is about a perfect simulation of the real world. Compare levels to movie sets in that they both support the narrative by putting certain details in graphic context for the viewer or gamer. They do this by mimicking real-world buildings and objects, but they do so only as necessary to the story.

Creating Game Flow

The most important function of levels in games is to support the gameplay. When working off a game outline, a game can be long or short, depending on the built-in challenges and resources. It can also be based on the detail of your levels. A game where each level is the size a small dormitory will be vastly different from a game where each level is the size of Las Vegas, obviously. The pacing of the game's action can be short and sweet or long and meditative and is often dictated by the size and complexity of the game's levels and their content.

Proper pacing in a game is even more important than how the game looks. Pacing is imperative, a real sink-or-swim mark for a game creator. A balance between player resources and game objectives is one of the keys to pacing the game. Alternate between forcing the player to struggle to stay alive and reflectively exploring or solving puzzles; this increases the playability of the game.

Setting the Mood or Theme

Another function of level design is to support the mood or theme of your game. The reason that mood or theme gets a back seat to game flow is because there should be a careful balance between each, and if there is any dispute, game flow must take priority. It is far too easy to create a beautiful game level but not think to make it serviceable to the player. Kevin Saunders of Obsidian Entertainment says, "If a level plays well, you'll find a way to make it pretty, but the reverse isn't necessarily true."

People respond emotionally and reactively to familiar settings. A creepy candle-lit castle has a vastly different atmosphere than a bright cheerful glen with birds chirping in the trees. Level design, when used appropriately, sets up game atmosphere, and game atmosphere becomes the background for gameplay and reflects the mood and emotional string-pulling you, the game designer, are trying to accomplish.

Fencing the Player In

Level design also serves to hide the fact the player character is actually inside a big invisible box he cannot escape. The box must have virtual constraints as to how far, and where, a game character can explore, because virtual space is virtually infinite, but the system resources to display objects is not. Without a proper frame of reference, the player would not be able to get around in the virtual world you are creating. Without appropriate level architecture, the player character could even wander outside the bounds of the game field!

Keeping the player from wandering off the game field you have constructed or going places you don't want him to go is called *"fencing the player in."* You can see an example of this in Figure 12.2. Your fences may be frustrating for the player as a general rule of thumb, because nobody likes being told he cannot go somewhere nor do something he wants to do, so you have to make your fences patently obvious. The player has to understand that the fences are part of the level and not merely thrown in to frustrate him. Most games don't advertise their game world boundaries, but there has not been a game built yet that didn't have some kind of boundary. Essentially, the level design puts these boundaries into graphic context.

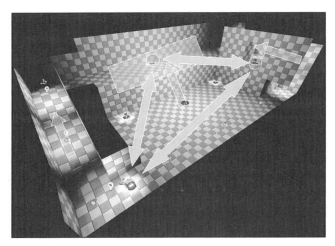

Figure 12.2
This demonstration in the Unreal level editor shows how the designer plans to fence the player in and thereby craft the flow of the level.

If I Ever Meet You, I'll Ctrl+Alt+Delete You!

Tip

"The interface is one of the least understood yet most critical elements in the game. The interface is the connection between the player and the game world."

—Richard Wainess, M.S.Ed. (Senior Lecturer, University of Southern California)

The gamer has to interact with the game through its *interface*. The interface is the way the computer program interprets what the player wants (input) and displays important information or options back to the player (output). A game-specific interface is the connection between the player and the game itself.

Common Game Interfaces

There are many different game interfaces that are becoming the standards for gaming media. They are:

- Manual interfaces or input devices
- Feedback interfaces
- Graphical user interfaces

Figure 12.3
This overview shows many of the most popular console controllers used from the 1980s to today.

Manual Interfaces

First, there are the *manual interfaces*, the hardware-based input devices like the keyboard/mouse or console controller (see Figure 12.3), which have preprogrammed options allowing the player to move their character around onscreen and execute specific actions therein. These interfaces are closely linked to the game's hardware platform.

N o t e

The motion-sensing EyeToy manual interface allows players to control actions in the game through body movement. What type of game, besides the ones you might have seen advertised for the EyeToy, might be ideal for this kind of interface?

Feedback Interfaces

There are *feedback interfaces*, such as the vibrations from rumble functions on console controllers or noises and lights coming from the game. Dedicated computer gamers prefer Dolby surround sound speakers with heavy bass and even go so far as to purchase gaming motion chairs, which have built-in subwoofers to provide bass and a rumbling sensation to enhance users' experience as they play a video game.

Graphical User Interfaces

There are also onscreen information panels that make up the visual part, the graphical user interface. A *graphical user interface*, often abbreviated GUI and pronounced "gooey," employs graphical images and widgets in addition to text messages to represent vital information and options to the player. Most of the time, but not always, the obtainable actions the player can take are performed through the manipulation of graphical elements or through keyboard commands.

In the GUI alone, there are many types of interfaces. There are menu screens, loading screens, character screens, options screens, save/load screens, and much more. Each can appear distinct and characteristic.

Perhaps the most important GUI a design team must create is the *heads-up display*, or HUD. The HUD, one example of which is in Figure 12.4, shows the player at a glance the most vital information the player must know from the game, such as health, ammunition, score, and power.

Planning the Game Interface

Creating a detailed plan for your user interface in the game graphics section of your game design documents can really help drive the design of the interface. Figuring out the little details of the game's look, such as in-game menu screens

Figure 12.4
A Western game HUD.

and the HUD, will force you to make many gameplay decisions early on. It may even settle decisions for the direction the game's construction might take.

Color Scheme and Texture

Color is a vital ingredient in video games. What color is each of the buttons and elements of your game going to be? Keep your colors consistent with the theme. Colors have a dynamic effect on people's moods and the way they react intuitively to objects. The same can be true of texture. Having bright-red rusty elements immediately cause the player to react apprehensively or be afraid of getting hurt or dirty, while having soft blue fur elements make the player feel relaxed and comforted. These intuitive effects can be manipulated by a game developer to set the mood or theme of the game.

Typeface

Planning what fonts to use in your game interface can also appeal to the player's mood and play up the theme of the game. A comic book–style font family is excellent for a superhero or funny game, but a typeface font that looks like it is dripping blood would better fit a horror game. Looking at a font list that shows you the typeface used will give you an immediate sense about the fonts you might want to use.

Flash lets you embed specific typefaces you choose to use in your application, so even if the device you're publishing to couldn't normally read it, it will if your fonts are embedded in the final published SWF file.

Putting It All Together

Once you have settled on a mock-up you like, you can finalize the piece and pick it apart to see how you will include it in your game. Some custom interface pieces are easy to make in Flash, such as buttons, and input fields can display current game scores.

WHAT'S NEXT?

Now that you are a bit better prepared for designing games for the Sony PSP using Flash, it's time to design your first game. In the next chapter we'll make a platformer using everything you've learned so far.

YOUR FIRST GAME

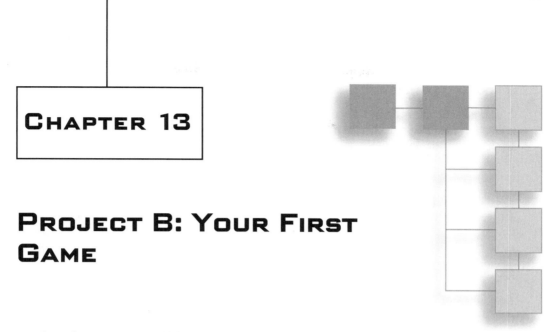

CHAPTER 13

PROJECT B: YOUR FIRST GAME

In this chapter you will learn:

- What making a Flash game requires
- To make an action platformer game in Flash

Finally, you've made it! It has taken a while to get here, I know, but understanding the Flash program and how games work had to take precedence. Now you are ready to jump in, figuratively speaking, and start designing Flash games for the PSP.

Upon embarking, we will start with some basic scripting to get you used to the computer logic that takes place in the Flash environment. The initial game I will show you how to make has some very basic scripting, and I will walk you through it every step of the way. The next chapter will give a brief overview, kind of a shotgun approach, to making lots of different games.

Do not fall for the false assumption that the bigger, more complicated a game's programming is, the better the game will be. Clunky heavy-ended games often fail on the trial floor when simpler, cleverer games outrace them in terms of player enjoyment.

Exercise 13.1: Creating a Platformer

A platformer, if you've already forgotten, is a game where the player must move his character back and forth across the stage and jump to different platforms, which sometimes, but not always, are in motion. A platformer requires hand-eye coordination, problem-solving, and the knack for timing jumps just right.

I gave you a heads-up on what this platformer would be about when we made a short animation. The player will control Bill, a nematode (roundworm) who works for Pizza Gut. Bill, Pizza Gut, and the game environments are all inside a giant monster's body. So we could see organs, blood vessels, mucus, and all kinds of nasty stuff to run and jump around on. Bill has to get pizza pies to customers without dying or being killed off by leukocytes, who mistake him for a parasite. Players will use their arrow keys to move and jump Bill around. Pressing the space bar will fire a weapon once Bill has one.

That's the gist of our game. Now get ready to build it!

1. Open the Adobe Flash program and create a new ActionScript 2.0 document. In the Properties panel, set the Size to 480 x 272 pixels and the FPS to 18. Go to File > Publish Settings and in the dialog box that appears, click on the Flash tab near the top (it will appear by default, as the default Publish Settings will publish your document to SWF). Under the Flash tab, set the Player to Flash Player 6.0 (select it from the drop-down list) and make sure Script is set to ActionScript 2.0. After you are done, your screen should look like Figure 9.2. Click OK to exit the dialog box and return to the Flash workspace. Get in the habit of doing this step every time you decide to make Flash for the Sony PSP.

2. Click the color swatch beside Stage in the Properties panel to change your Stage color to #660000, a dark red color. This will help us emulate the inside of a giant monster's body.

3. Save your Flash file as testPlatform.fla by going to File > Save As.

4. Use the Brush tool to create Bill, as you see him in Figure 13.1. I zoomed in so that I could give him lots of detail. I left off one of his arms, because it will only appear when

Figure 13.1
Bill takes shape.

he's shooting his blaster, not before. After drawing him, I used the Free Transform tool to shrink him. In the end, I made him 72.85 pixels wide and 60.75 pixels high.

Note

_____

> If you decide that you're a better programmer than you are an artist, don't give up hope! You can bribe an artist friend of yours to do this job for you, or—if you're doing this project just for fun—you can find sprite characters online to use. Simply copy or download a character image and edit it in Paint or Photoshop before bringing it into Flash. You can find lots of sprite images on The Spriters Resource (http://www.spriters-resource.com).

_____

5. Convert your drawing of Bill into a movie clip symbol that you name hero. Put his registration point at the bottom center when you do so. Also, give him the instance name hero. This is for scripting purposes.

6. With your hero movie clip selected on the Stage, open the Actions panel. First, we need to script Bill to have some lateral (that is, left and right) movement. We will also attach friction to it, for added realism. Type in the following to tell the program that when the movie loads, we want the character's speed set to 0 and his maximum movement rate set to 10.

```
onClipEvent (load) {

    speed = 0;
    maxmove = 10;


}
```

7. Now we're going to get into the guts of writing the character's behaviors. The `onClipEvent (enterFrame)` means that everything inside this bracketed section will run and refresh every frame of the movie as it plays. The first behavior we start with is if the player is dead. If the player dies, we animate Bill to look dead. All of the behaviors are shown in quotations in the script. "Left" means that Bill is moving left, and "right" means Bill is moving right. Right now, we haven't designed these animations, but we will later.

```
onClipEvent (enterFrame) {
        if (_root.dead)
        {

            this.gotoAndStop("dead");

        }
        else
```

```
{

        speed *= .85;
        if (speed > 0)
        {

                dir = "right";

        }
        else if (speed < 0)
        {

                dir = "left";

        }
        if (dir == "right")
        {

                this._x += speed;
                _root._x -= speed;

        }
        if (dir == "left")
        {

                this._x += speed;
                _root._x -= speed;

        }
```

8. Next, we need to type the code that will confirm the key binding. We are going to map the movement behaviors to the left and right arrow keys, which, on the Sony PSP, will be the directional buttons.

```
if (Key.isDown(Key.LEFT))
{

        if (speed > -maxmove)
        {
                speed-;
```

```
        }
        this.gotoAndStop("run");
        this._xscale = -100;

    }
    else if (Key.isDown(Key.RIGHT))
    {

        if (speed < maxmove)
        {

            speed++;

        }
        this._xscale = 100;
        this.gotoAndStop("run");

    }
```

9. We need to anticipate the attack state for when Bill has a gun to shoot leukocytes. When Bill is shooting, he will stop moving for a moment. We'll call this state "idle." You might wonder what the ! (exclamation point) in front of the conditional attacking means. When you see ! in front of a conditional word like this, it does not mean emphasis or excitement, like you'd usually use ! for; instead, it means a negative, so in this case, it means NOT attacking. Before Bill can shoot his weapon, you want to make sure he's not attacking already.

```
        if (speed < 1 && speed > -1 && !attacking)
        {

            speed = 0;
            this.gotoAndStop("idle");

        }

    }

}
```

10. The next bit of code we need to add to Bill's script is for jumping, because a platformer wouldn't be much if you didn't include jumping.

```
if (Key.isDown(Key.UP) && !jumping)
{

        jumping = true;

}
if (jumping)
{

        this.gotoAndStop("jump");
        this._y -= jump;
        jump -= .5;
        if (jump < 0)
        {

                falling = true;

        }
        if (jump < -15)
        {

                jump = -15;

        }

}
```

11. Now that we've added jump functionality, we need to set jump to 0 and jumping to true within the main load even for the character. The reason we do this is so that when the game starts, Bill will fall to the ground. Scroll back up to the place where you first started typing this ActionScript in the hero's scripts and edit your onClipEvent (load) to look like this:

```
onClipEvent (load) {

        jumping = true;
        jump = 0;
        speed = 0;
        maxmove = 15;

}
```

12. If you tested your game right now, Bill would simply fall right out of the screen. We'll need to add some ground for him to fall onto, but before we even do that, we need to add a hit test so that Bill will know when he touches down on the ground. We use hit tests anytime we need to see if one object collides with another in the Flash environment. Insert the following code snippet directly after the last jumping events, between the second and last closing brackets. What this will do is test to see if Bill touches an object instance called ground, its X or Y coordinates that is, while falling, and if so, then it stops him from falling any farther.

```
if (_root.ground.hitTest(this._x, this._y, true) && falling)
{
        jump = 12;
        jumping = false;
        falling = false;
}
```

13. Now Bill would land on a ground object, if you had one, but when he trotted about, he'd walk right off the edge of the object and keep going. This isn't very realistic, even for a cartoon character! We've got to make it where he responds to gravity. To do this, go back up to where you set your onClipEvent (enterFrame) and, right after the opening brackets, type in this snippet:

```
if (!_root.ground.hitTest(this._x, this._y, true) && !jumping)
{

        this._y += 6;

}
```

14. If your code is refusing to work properly, or you got lost somewhere, don't worry. It's not the end of the world. Most coders run into this trouble, and often, if you proofread your code, you'll find a comma where it's not supposed to be or a missing semicolon or a capital letter when a lowercase letter was needed. So get in the habit of proofreading all your code. Review your scripting for the hero object. So far it should read as such:

```
onClipEvent (load) {

        jumping = true;
        jump = 0;
        speed = 0;
        maxmove = 15;


}
```

```
onClipEvent (enterFrame) {
     if (!_root.ground.hitTest(this._x, this._y, true) && !jumping)
     {

          this._y += 6;

     }

     if (_root.dead)
     {

          this.gotoAndStop("dead");

     }
     else
     {

          speed *= .85;
          if (speed > 0)
          {

               dir = "right";

          }
          else if (speed < 0)
          {

               dir = "left";

          }
          if (dir == "right")
          {

               this._x += speed;
               _root._x -= speed;

          }
          if (dir == "left")
          {
```

```
        this._x += speed;
        _root._x -= speed;

    }
    if (Key.isDown(Key.LEFT))
    {

        if (speed > -maxmove)
        {

            speed-;

        }
        this.gotoAndStop("run");
        this._xscale = -100;

    }
    else if (Key.isDown(Key.RIGHT))
    {

        if (speed < maxmove)
        {

            speed++;

        }
        this._xscale = 100;
        this.gotoAndStop("run");

}

if (speed < 1 && speed > -1 && !attacking)
{
```

```
            speed = 0;
            this.gotoAndStop("idle");


      }

      if (Key.isDown(Key.UP) && !jumping)
      {

            jumping = true;

      }
      if (jumping)
      {

            this.gotoAndStop("jump");
            this._y -= jump;
            jump -= .5;
            if (jump < 0)
            {

                  falling = true;

            }
            if (jump < -15)
            {

                  jump = -15;

            }

            if (_root.ground.hitTest(this._x, this._y, true) && falling)
            {
                  jump = 12;
                  jumping = false;
```

```
                      falling = false;
                }
            }


        }


    }
```

15. Save your work before continuing. Using your imagination and Flash drawing tools (including the Rectangle, Oval, Brush, and Paint Bucket tools), draw some environment objects to start with, just enough to test our script out with. Think along the lines of the old *Super Mario Bros.* objects that you'd see, like donut hills, palm trees, and floating islands. However, you're designing the inside of a gargantuan monster's body, so you should have mushy grounds, fringed villi, ropy tendons, spongy cellular masses, and more. Use a biology book for ideas. As you can see in Figure 13.2, I drew a large purple mass and two floating platforms extending out in space, and later I'll add more to it. Whatever you design, select it and convert it into a movie clip symbol named ground. Give it the instance name of ground, too.

16. Go to Control > Test Movie > In Flash Professional. Play what you have so far. If it's not working right, or you receive any bug errors, there's probably a mistake somewhere, either in your code or in the names you gave to the objects. Double-check everything if you can't get your game (so far) to play. Otherwise, you should be able to use the left and right arrow keys to walk and the up arrow key to make Bill jump. Test out your platforms, stairs, or whatever you've added to be sure Bill can reach them. If one

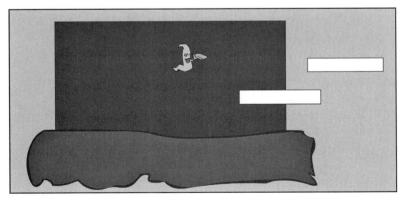

Figure 13.2
Here's a simple ground object for Bill to start crawling around on.

or more of your ground objects are out of reach when they shouldn't be, then you need to go back into Flash, double-click on your ground object, and edit them as you see fit. Once everything seems to work satisfactorily, it's time to give Bill better animation.

17. In Scene 1, double-click on your hero movie clip object. This should open up the hero object's Timeline edit mode. In the hero's Timeline, go to Frame 2 and insert a new keyframe. Go to Frame 3 and insert another one. Now you should have three keyframes for your hero movie clip. Go back to hero's Frame 1. In the Properties panel, under Label, type "idle" for the label name, as you see in Figure 13.3. This places a red flag on that frame in the Timeline, indicating that there's a label for that frame in the animation. Go to hero's Frame 2 and give it the label name run, and name hero's Frame 3 jump. These labels will be read by the script you've already written, so that the animations will be called during movement execution.

18. You can ignore the idle animation for now, but let's look at run. Go to hero's Frame 2. Switch to the Free Transform tool (hotkey Q) and skew Bill forward, so that he looks like he's leaning toward his destination a little (see Figure 13.4). You could get fancy and completely redraw him, but a little skew will work for now.

19. Go to hero's Frame 3. With the Free Transform tool, hold down the Alt or Option key while dragging in one of the vertical edges to make Bill appear slightly stretched out. Take the Eraser tool (hotkey E) and erase his bottom half. Using the Brush and Paint

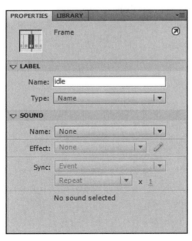

Figure 13.3
Give each of your three frames separate label names: idle, run, and jump.

Figure 13.4
Make Bill look like he's running.

Figure 13.5
Make Bill look like he's jumping.

Bucket tools, redraw his tail so that is looks as though he were jumping. You can see what I mean by comparing your work to Figure 13.5. You're done animating Bill! Exit back to Scene 1. Save your work. Test your movie to see what it looks like.

20. Let's add some incentive for Bill. As with many platformers, there have to be some pick-up items that will add to the player's score, be they stars, coins, nifty boxes, or anything else you can dream up. For now, I'll use the very mundane symbol of a dollar bill. Bill's after bills. What can I say? He's a part of the capitalist system. Go to Scene 1, Frame 1, and add the following code snippet for the main Timeline in your Actions panel (make sure you have Frame 1 selected and not one of your objects!). What this will do is add a number variable, or placeholder, for the player score. Any code added to the main

Timeline is equivalent to _root.your_code, because the main Timeline is considered the _root of your project.

```
score.text = 0;
```

21. Use the Flash drawing tools to draw a dollar bill, as I did in Figure 13.6. Optionally, you could find a piece of clip art and bring it in. After you have it, press F8 to convert it to a movie clip named cash. With your cash object selected, go to the Actions panel and input the following code. Basically, you're checking to see if the hero object (i.e., Bill) touches the cash object, and if so, you add +1 to the player's score and make the cash object disappear (that's what unloadMovie(this) means!).

```
onClipEvent (enterFrame) {

    if (this.hitTest(_root.hero))
    {

        _root.score.text ++;
        unloadMovie(this);

    }

}
```

22. But wait! We don't have any way of showing the player's score yet. So far, all we have are numbers floating around in cyberspace. We need to find a way of representing them to the player. Select the Text tool (hotkey T) and draw a text box in one corner of your Stage. Set your text box to Dynamic Text (not Static Text!). Give your text box the instance name score, to match the variable we've arranged. Also, you'll want to steer clear of using fancy fonts when it comes to this. Drop down the font list and choose

Figure 13.6
Draw a pick-up item for Bill to grab.

Figure 13.7
Setting up the score text field.

_sans, and Flash will use whatever device fonts come loaded with the end user's device, focusing on the sans serif fonts, such as Arial, Helvetica, and so on. If you really must have a special font, you can embed it in your published movie by using the Text > Font Embedding command. Make sure the point size of your text is large enough to be legible, too. I made mine 20 point. Compare your Properties panel to the one in Figure 13.7.

23. Create a second dynamic text field. Type in a single dollar sign $ and move this text field directly to the left of your score text field. Give this new text box the instance name scorekeeper. This tells the player what the numbers stand for.

24. At the moment, the text boxes would stay right where they are instead of moving with the player, so change that by editing the hero object's code. Find where it says (dir == "right") and (dir=="left"), and edit them to read as follows. You're telling the score and scorekeeper text field to move when the player character moves.

```
if (dir == "right")
{
        this._x += speed;
        _root._x -= speed;
        _root.score._x += speed;
}
if (dir == "left")
{
        this._x += speed;
        _root._x -= speed;
        _root.score._x += speed;
}
```

25. Save and test your work. If everything works the way it should, then you can duplicate the cash object as many times as you need to. Either hold down Ctrl or Option and click and drag the first cash object to drag duplicates off from it, or use copy and paste to create multiple pick-up items. In a platformer, there are usually two places you put pick-up items: along the course, where you want players to go (this helps lead them toward their goal, like so many bread crumbs), or in out-of-the-way, hard-to-reach places (encouraging players to fight to get them).

26. Let's add enemies to your level. Bill has incentives to play through the level, to reach all of the dollar bills we've spread around, but right now, besides falling off the platforms, there are no obstacles for him to overcome. So, let's add one. Then, just like the cash objects, we can duplicate the enemy as many times as we want. First, create or find an enemy picture and make it a movie clip symbol called enemy with the instance name enemy. You can see the one I'm using in Figure 13.8.

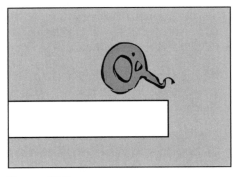

Figure 13.8
This mistaken leukocyte wants to end Bill's quest.

27. With your enemy object selected on the Stage, open the Actions panel and add the following script for it. Basically, you're setting the enemy object to move slowly back and forth in place, as if it were on patrol.

```
onClipEvent (load) {

        enemyspeed = 2;
        enemystepsright = 0;
        enemystepsleft = 0;
        enemydir = "left";


}
onClipEvent (enterFrame) {

        if (!dead)
        {

                if (enemydir == "right")
                {

                        enemystepsright += 1;
                        this._xscale = -100;
                        this._x += enemyspeed;


                }
                else if (enemydir == "left")
                {

                        enemystepsleft += 1;
                        this._xscale = 100;
                        this._x -= enemyspeed;


                }
                if (enemystepsright == 100)
                {

                        enemystepsright = 0;
```

```
                    enemydir = "left";


            }
            else if (enemystepsleft == 100)
            {

                    enemystepsleft = 0;
                    enemydir = "right";


            }


        }

}
```

28. Right now, your enemy and player character can't really see each other. In fact, they just run through one another without effect. We want them to be able to hurt one another. So, first we set up a player attack animation. Double-click on the hero object to edit it on the Stage. Insert a new blank keyframe on Frame 4 and label it attack. On mine, I copied Bill's appearance from the idle frame, Frame 1, to Frame 4. In this frame, attach to Bill an arm holding a blaster. You can see what I did in Figure 13.9. Alternatively, you can use any weapon you want. The red circle out in front of Bill is something you *must* have. This is a checker. First, it is supposed to represent the blaster's ammo and the fact that it's a short-range weapon. Second, it will be used in a hit test to see if it's touching the

Figure 13.9
Give Bill something to fight back with.

enemy, and if it is, it will kill the enemy. You must place an object out in front of Bill like this. Convert your object into a movie clip symbol and give it the instance name attack-point. I animated my attackpoint object by double-clicking on it, and, in its Timeline, adding three more keyframes, in which I rotated the ball and its electric rays in a clockwise manner.

29. Exit edit mode and return to Scene 1. With the hero object selected, go to its ActionScript and add the following code snippet under the other key bindings. I'd suggest adding it right after you're finished checking for the right arrow key being pressed. You'll use the down arrow key to fire your weapon.

```
else if (Key.isDown(Key.DOWN))
{

        this.gotoAndStop("attack");
        attacking = true;
        speed = 0;

}
```

30. How our hero code is set up now, if the character's speed is below 1 and greater than negative 1, he'll go to his idle state. We don't want that. We want him to keep firing. So we need to edit the next function in the code to read as follows, pretty much just putting an else-if instead of an if before the statement:

```
else if (speed < 1 && speed > -1 && !attacking)
{

        speed = 0;
        this.gotoAndStop("idle");

}
```

31. Select your enemy object, and in its Actions, place the following directly after the onClipEvent (enterFrame) opening brackets. What you're doing is telling the program that if the hero destroys the enemy, then remove the enemy.

```
if (this.hitTest(_root.hero.attackpoint))
{
```

```
                    enemyspeed = 0;
                    enemystepsright = 0;
                    enemystepsleft = 0;
                    dead = true;
                    unloadMovie(this);


              }
              if (this.hitTest(_root.hero) && !dead)
              {


                    _root.hero.jumping = false;
                    _root.dead = true;


              }
```

32. Return, once more, to your hero's Actions. Scroll to the very bottom. After the very last set of closing brackets, press Return or Enter to start a new line of code. Then type the following snippet. This will check to see if the player has released the down arrow key, and if so, stops firing.

```
onClipEvent (keyUp) {

        // on Key Up
        if (Key.getCode() == Key.DOWN)
        {
                attacking = false;
        }
}
```

33. Now you just need to set up a dead state for the hero object. Double-click on your hero movie clip symbol to enter its Timeline edit mode, where you placed your idle, run, and jump frames. Insert a new blank keyframe on Frame 4 and give it the label name dead. Draw Bill knocked out here, as shown in Figure 13.10.

34. Save and test your game so far. Note that when Bill walks off the edge of the game environment, he disappears off the screen but the game still keeps going. This isn't right. So let's change that. Add a large rectangular object that is longer than your level. If you add it to your level later, you can always use the Free Transform tool to stretch out this object. Convert this object to a movie clip named restart. In your restart object's Actions,

Figure 13.10
Bill's been done in!

type the following code. Where I have the numbers 72 and 140, you need to type in the numbers for your character's starting X and Y positions, respectively, wherever you want your hero object to spawn at.

```
onClipEvent (enterFrame) {

    if (this.hitTest(_root.hero))
    {
        _root._x = 0;
        _root.hero._x = 72;
//record whatever the starting X position is and record that number here
        _root.hero._y = 140;
//record whatever the starting Y position is and record that number here
        _root.hero.speed = 0;


    }


}
```

35. Lastly, we need to add player health. We'll do so in the form of a health bar, as that sort of HUD, or heads-up display, is the one most commonly found. In Scene 1, draw a rectangle to the Stage that has a bevel of 7.0, a Stroke color of red, and a Fill color that's a rainbow gradient (see Figure 13.11). Look at Figure 13.12 to see how it should look. To change the appearance of the rainbow gradient as I did, use the Gradient Transform tool (hotkey F) to stretch out the gradient fill and move it to the right, so that only the colors red, yellow, and green would be seen. Convert this bar to a movie clip symbol named healthBar with its registration point on the middle left. Give this symbol an instance name of healthbar.

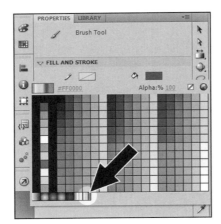

Figure 13.11
Add a rainbow gradient for the Fill color.

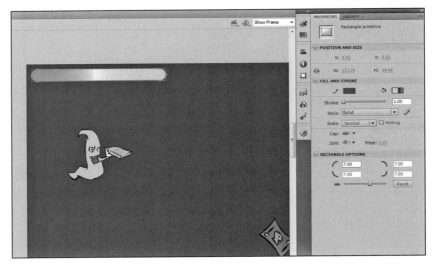

Figure 13.12
You can adjust the rainbow gradient until the health bar shape has this appearance.

36. Go back to Scene 1, Frame 1, and on its Actions, add the following.

```
playerhealth = 100;
```

37. Click on the enemy object and, in its Actions, put the following code right after the closing brackets of the attackpoint hit test function and before the if (!dead) statement.

```
if (this.hitTest(_root.hero))
{

        if (_root.playerhealth <= 0)
        {

                _root.dead = true;
                _root._x = 0;
                _root.gotoAndStop(2);

        }

        if (_root.playerhealth >= 1)
        {
                _root.playerhealth -= 5;
                _root.healthbar._xscale -= 5;
        }
}
```

38. In the preceding code, we told the program that if the player is killed by the enemy, then go to Frame 2 of Scene 1, which is our `_root`. We need to make a Frame 2. First, add a `stop();` action on Frame 1. Then, insert a blank keyframe on Frame 2. Use the Text tool (hotkey T) to add a static text field that says something along the lines of "You Died!" Place a `stop();` action on Frame 2. Go to the main menu bar and go to Window > Common Libraries > Buttons to bring up the Buttons Library. Scroll down to Classic Buttons and find the subfolder Arcade Buttons, Playback. Select the gel Right button, which is round and green. Drag and drop the gel Right button from the Library preview window to the Stage. Add the following code script to this button in the Actions panel, to let the player try the game again. Then return to Frame 1.

```
on (release) {
        gotoAndStop(1);
        _root.playerhealth += 100;
        _root.dead = false;
        _root.hero.jumping = true;
        _root.hero.speed = 0;
        _root.score.text == 0;


}
```

39. We need to get the healthbar object to move with the player. Edit the hero object's Actions so that this part reads like so.

```
if (dir == "right")
{

        this._x += speed;
        _root._x -= speed;
        _root.score._x += speed;
        _root.scorekeeper._x += speed;
        _root.healthbar._x += speed;

}
if (dir == "left")
{

        this._x += speed;
        _root._x -= speed;
        _root.score._x += speed;
        _root.scorekeeper._x += speed;
        _root.healthbar._x += speed;

}
```

40. Last but not least, we need to give Bill a way to renew himself. So we need to add a health pick-up item. This item will work the exact opposite of the bad guys, actually giving Bill more life. First, draw an object you want to use for your health pick-up. I chose a heart, because it's certainly one of the most oft-used in platformers. Convert your drawing to a movie clip symbol named healthPU and give it the instance name healthpickup. Give it the following action.

```
onClipEvent (enterFrame) {

    if (this.hitTest(_root.hero))
    {

        _root.playerhealth += 10;
        _root.healthbar._xscale += 10;
        unloadMovie(this);

    }

}
```

41. Save your work and test your game. It should run swimmingly! The only problem, though, is that it's quiet. There are no sound effects or music to accompany the action. Let's fix that. Double-click your hero object to edit Bill again. Add a new layer above Layer 1 in his Timeline. For each frame of his behaviors, insert a new blank keyframe on your new layer. Find some effects that sound like a ray gun firing and an "Ouch!" sound. Import those sounds to your Library. Drag and drop the ray gun sound to Bill's attack state frame, and the "Ouch!" to Bill's dead state frame. Exit edit mode and return to Scene 1.

42. Find a music piece that matches the short animation one you added in Chapter 9, Project A: Your First Animation. I went with a jazzy bongo score for my movie, but you can choose whatever you want. Import it to your Library, then drag it to Frame 1 of a new audio layer you place in your Timeline. Set it to loop. There! You're done for now. Save your Flash file.

Note

Did you know that an uncompressed WAV file, although larger in general file size than a compressed MP3 file, will reduce your final Flash file's size? You'd think it would be the other way around, but when you import compressed files into Flash, the application has to uncompress them for publishing to SWF, which, in turn, makes your file size larger. Try using a WAV file instead of an MP3 file next time, and you'll see the difference!

KEEP YOUR LEVEL GROWING

Now you have carte blanche to add more items to your game level, to really make it something.

What I would do, if I were you, is extend the width of the level out to the right as far as possible, keeping the restart object stretched out under the level, to cover the possibilities of the player wandering out-of-bounds, and when you get to the end, put a movie clip symbol that looks like a customer waiting for his food. The customer should have a script like the following, which propels the player to Frame 3, and on Frame 3, you'd have a "You Passed!" text box or other such win screen.

```
//Code for customer object at end-of-level
onClipEvent (enterFrame) {

    if (this.hitTest(_root.hero))
    {
```

```
        _root.playerhealth == 100;
        _root.score.text += 25;
        _root._x = 0;
        _root.gotoAndStop(3);
        unloadMovie(this);


    }


}
```

Code That Was Included in This Chapter

If you find that you're having trouble, or your game is not running the way it ought to, here I have repeated all of the final code that should be included in your game. Double-check each item to make sure there's not some minor gaff causing a glitch in your program. If you still find that your game will not run right, you can skip to the next chapter and try an easier game programming exercise.

Frames 1 and 2

For Frame 1 of Scene 1.

```
score.text = 0;
playerhealth = 100;
stop();
```

For Frame 2 of Scene 1.

```
stop();
```

Hero

For the player character that has the instance name hero.

```
onClipEvent (load) {

        jumping = true;
        jump = 0;
```

```
        speed = 0;
        maxmove = 15;

}

onClipEvent (enterFrame) {

        if (!_root.ground.hitTest(this._x, this._y, true) && !jumping)
        {

              this._y += 6;

        }



        if (_root.dead)
        {

              this.gotoAndStop("dead");
        }
        else
        {

              speed *= .85;
              if (speed > 0)
              {

                    dir = "right";

              }
              else if (speed < 0)
              {

                    dir = "left";
```

```
        }
        if (dir == "right")
        {

                this._x += speed;
                _root._x -= speed;
                _root.score._x += speed;
                _root.scorekeeper._x += speed;
                _root.healthbar._x += speed;
        }
        if (dir == "left")
        {

                this._x += speed;
                _root._x -= speed;
                _root.score._x += speed;
                _root.scorekeeper._x += speed;
                _root.healthbar._x += speed;
        }
        if (Key.isDown(Key.LEFT))
        {

                if (speed > -maxmove)
                {
                        speed--;

                }
                this.gotoAndStop("run");
                this._xscale = -100;

        }
        else if (Key.isDown(Key.RIGHT))
        {
```

```
            if (speed < maxmove)
            {
                    speed++;

            }
            this._xscale = 100;
            this.gotoAndStop("run");

}
else if (Key.isDown(Key.DOWN))
{

            this.gotoAndStop("attack");
            attacking = true;
            speed = 0;

}
else if (speed < 1 && speed > -1 && !attacking)
{

            speed = 0;
            this.gotoAndStop("idle");

}


if (Key.isDown(Key.UP) && !jumping)
{

            jumping = true;

}
if (jumping)
{

            this.gotoAndStop("jump");
```

```
            this._y -= jump;
            jump -= .5;
            if (jump < 0)
            {

                  falling = true;

            }

            if (jump < -15)
            {

                  jump = -15;

            }

            if (_root.ground.hitTest(this._x, this._y, true) && falling)
            {
                  jump = 12;
                  jumping = false;
                  falling = false;
            }

      }


}
onClipEvent (keyUp) {

      // on Key Up
      if (Key.getCode() == Key.DOWN)
      {

            attacking = false;

      }
}
```

Restart

For the item used to restart the game if the hero falls into it, given the instance name restart.

```
onClipEvent (enterFrame) {

        if (this.hitTest(_root.hero))
        {
                _root._x = 0;
                _root.hero._x = 72;
                _root.hero._y = 140;
                _root.hero.speed = 0;

        }


}
```

Enemy

For an enemy character that has the instance name enemy.

```
onClipEvent (load) {

        enemyspeed = 2;
        enemystepsright = 0;
        enemystepsleft = 0;
        enemydir = "left";


}
onClipEvent (enterFrame) {

        if (this.hitTest(_root.hero.attackpoint))
        {

                enemyspeed = 0;
                enemystepsright = 0;
                enemystepsleft = 0;
                dead = true;
```

```
            unloadMovie(this);

        }

    if (this.hitTest(_root.hero))
    {

            if (_root.playerhealth <= 0)
            {
                    _root.dead = true;
                    _root._x = 0;
                    _root.gotoAndStop(2);

            }
            if (_root.playerhealth >= 1)
            {
                    _root.playerhealth -= 5;
                    _root.healthbar._xscale -= 5;

            }
    }

    if (!dead)
    {

            if (enemydir == "right")
            {
                    enemystepsright += 1;
                    this._xscale = -100;
                    this._x += enemyspeed;

            }
            else if (enemydir == "left")
            {
```

```
                    enemystepsleft += 1;
                    this._xscale = 100;
                    this._x -= enemyspeed;

            }
            if (enemystepsright == 100)
            {

                    enemystepsright = 0;
                    enemydir = "left";

            }
            else if (enemystepsleft == 100)
            {

                    enemystepsleft = 0;
                    enemydir = "right";

            }

        }

}
```

Pick-Up Items

For the score pick-up items that have the instance name cash.

```
onClipEvent (enterFrame) {

        if (this.hitTest(_root.hero))
        {

                _root.score.text++;
                unloadMovie(this);
        }

}
```

For the health pick-up items that have the instance name healthpickup.

```
onClipEvent (enterFrame) {

    if (this.hitTest(_root.hero))
    {

        _root.playerhealth += 10;
        _root.healthbar._xscale += 10;
        unloadMovie(this);

    }

}
```

Exercise 13.2: Putting It All Together

Wait! We want to add the short animation we made in Chapter 9 as an intro sequence and add a play button somewhere. So let's do that now.

1. Open Flash. Create a new document that is 480 x 272 pixels and has a Stage color of #660000 and FPS of 18. Save your Flash file as finalPlatform.fla. Do not close this file yet.

2. Open shortAnim.fla, which you created in Chapter 9. Go to the Loader scene, if you're not already there. Right-click on Frame 1 of the topmost layer and choose Select All Frames from the pop-up options list. Then right-click on Copy Frames.

3. Return to finalPlatform.fla and right-click on Frame 1 of Layer 1 and choose Paste Frames. All of the work you did in the other scene will get dumped here. Move all of the graphical content to the center of the Stage, where it belongs. Check that your scripts in Frame 1 and 2 of the Actions layer are intact. Rename the Actions layer Load Actions.

4. Insert a new layer above the Load Actions and call it Intro MC. Insert a new blank keyframe on Frame 4 of the Intro MC layer. On this frame, draw a rectangle somewhere on the Stage. Select your rectangle and open the Align panel. Make sure the Align to Stage checkbox is checked, and then click the Match Width and Height button, the Align Left Edge button, and the Align Top Edge button, in that order. See Figure 13.13. Convert the rectangle to a movie clip symbol called mc_intro. Double-click mc_intro to go into edit mode. Select and delete the rectangle there.

5. Go back to shortAnim.fla. Go to the Movie scene. Right-click on Select All Frames somewhere on the Timeline, then copy the frames. Go back to finalPlatform.fla and the mc_intro editing screen. Right-click on Frame 1 of Layer 1 and choose Paste Frames.

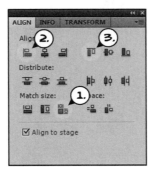

Figure 13.13
It's as easy as 1 - 2 - 3!

6. Go to the final visible frame of your mc_intro Timeline, where the Pizza Gut logo is really big. Add a new layer above all of the others and put a blank keyframe on the last visible frame, where you also have your stop(); action. In this blank keyframe, add some text that says "Play Game." Then go to Window > Common Libraries > Buttons to view your Buttons Library. Drag and drop an instance of the Arcade button (green) from the Classic Buttons > Arcade Buttons folder to your Stage. Resize this button so that it sits next to your Play Game text box. Then open its Actions and add the following script, so that when the button is pressed it takes the gamer to your game, which will start on Frame 5.

```
on (release) {
    stopAllSounds();
    _root.gotoAndStop(5);

}
```

7. Go to testPlatform.fla, where you've created your game. Right-click in the Timeline and choose Select All Frames, and then copy them. Return to finalPlatform.fla. Insert a new layer above the Intro MC layer. You don't need to name this new layer yet. Go to Frame 5 on this layer, right-click, and paste the frames there. You should see two new layers with your game starting on Frame 5. The layer with your game components is named Game, and the layer with your audio files named Music.

8. On the Game layer, you should see blank frames up to Frame 5, when the actual game will start. Right-click on Frame 4 and insert a blank keyframe. Add a stop(); action on this frame to stop the movie while the player watches your intro. When he finishes watching the intro, your player should be able to click the green button to start the game.

9. Unfortunately, you have some debugging to do. Some of your game code refers to specific frames, and now those frames will be out of whack. So we have to ferret through

the code and edit the frame numbers referenced in the script. The first one I'll point you to is in the enemy code. Select your enemy object in Frame 5 and open his actions. You will need to find and edit this statement, changing the call-out from Frame 2 to Frame 6.

```
if (this.hitTest(_root.hero))
    {

            if (_root.playerhealth <= 0)
            {

                    _root.dead = true;
                    _root._x = 0;
                    _root.gotoAndStop(6);


            }
```

10. Go to Frame 6 and select the green button. You'll need to change its actions so that it sends the player to Frame 5 if he clicks it, not Frame 1.

```
on (release) {
  gotoAndStop(5);
  _root.playerhealth += 100;
  _root.dead = false;
  _root.hero.jumping = true;
  _root.hero.speed = 0;
  _root.score.text == 0;


}
```

11. If you've added the customer object yet, then you'll need to change it, too, so that it takes the player to Frame 7.

```
onClipEvent (enterFrame) {

    if (this.hitTest(_root.hero))
    {

            _root.playerhealth == 100;
            _root.score.text += 25;
            _root._x = 0;
```

```
        _root.gotoAndStop(7);
        unloadMovie(this);


    }


}
```

12. Save your work and test it out. Voila! You should have a complete movie and game titled Pizza Gut, as shown in Figure 13.14. Be sure to gauge your final file size, too, because it has to be under 1.5MB to play in the Sony PSP.

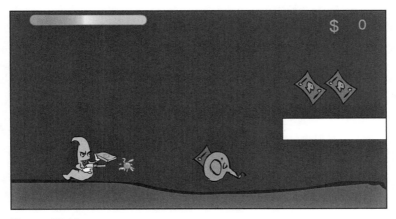

Figure 13.14
Your finished game.

WHAT'S NEXT?

Now that you have made one game, I'll show you how to make a bunch of other games. Then I'll demonstrate how to set up the Sony PSP to play Flash and how you can reveal your design abilities on the Internet.

YOUR NEXT GAME

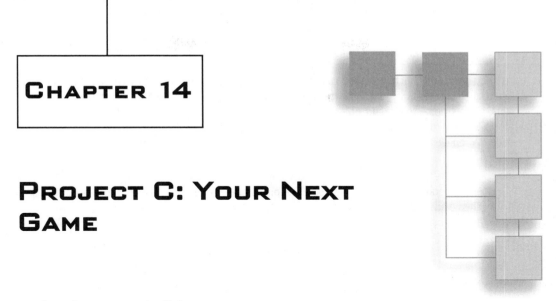

CHAPTER 14

PROJECT C: YOUR NEXT GAME

In this chapter you will learn:

- To make a tunnel maze game using Flash
- To make a dress-up doll game using Flash
- To make a shooting gallery game using Flash
- Some handy tips for making more games with Flash

You've made one game in Flash for playing on the Sony PSP. Ready to make more? This chapter will give you a bunch of very brief exercises for building diverse kinds of Flash games for the PSP. Read through the following exercises and try each of them out.

Also, remember to think outside the box when you're learning how to make these games. Although I may show you one thematic attempt or manner of Flash development, you can interpret the game mechanics however you like. There are literally dozens of Flash games on the Internet right now that use the exact same ActionScript code as their backbone but look totally different, and gamers can hardly tell they are anywhere near the same. So you might create a one kind of game and then vamp it up with your own unique dressing to make it something altogether different and unique, and that's how game design is really a form of expression in and of itself!

Exercise 14.1: Making a Tunnel Maze Game

As the title to this section makes clear, we are going to make a tunnel maze game (shown in Figure 14.1). Essentially, a tunnel maze is a twisting or turning maze the player has to navigate from a start point to an end point. Similar to any action game, the player must avoid obstacles along the way to his goal. In this case, the obstacles the player faces are the walls of the tunnel itself. Whenever the player touches the edges of the tunnel, he is forced to start the game over.

1. Open the Adobe Flash program and create a new ActionScript 2.0 document. In the Properties panel, set the Size to 480 x 272 pixels and the FPS to 18. Go to File > Publish Settings and in the dialog box that appears, click on the Flash tab near the top (it will appear by default, as the default Publish Settings will publish your document to SWF). Under the Flash tab, set the Player to Flash Player 6.0 (select it from the drop-down list) and make sure Script is set to ActionScript 2.0.

2. Save your file as mazeTunnel.fla.

3. Set your Stage color to something other than white. Select Layer 1, Frame 1 in the Timeline.

4. Go to the main menu bar and go to Window > Common Libraries > Buttons to bring up the Buttons Library. Pick a button and drag it from the Library to the Stage. Resize the button using the Free Transform tool (hotkey Q) and place it wherever you want the player to start.

5. On Frame 1, if you like, you can add text or graphics. This is kind of the start, or intro, screen to the tunnel maze game. So you can add type at the top of the screen that says,

Figure 14.1
What the finished tunnel maze game should look like.

"Tunnel Maze Game by—" and then your name, or at least add some instructions like, "Guide your way through the maze without touching the walls! Be ready, because as soon as you click the button, you'll be stuck in the maze. If you touch a wall, you'll have to start all over again." The button you've added will be the play button, which, by itself, is pretty self-explanatory, being one of those universal GUI elements, but you might want to reinforce it by adding some text beside the button saying, "Click button to play."

6. Select the button we are using for our start game button, as we want to add a script to this button. If your Actions panel (hotkey F9) is not already visible, bring it up.

7. Note that to add a script to a button, you *must* have the button selected before you start typing! If you try adding a button script to a nonselected entity, such as Frame 1 by itself, you will receive errors. You can tell if you have your button selected by looking beneath the white scripting area, where you will see a tab telling you what is currently selected. Type in the following ActionScript. This will say to the program that if the player clicks on the button, when he releases it, go to Frame 2.

```
on (release) {
    gotoAndStop(2);

}
```

8. Now right-click on Frame 2 on the Timeline and choose to Insert Blank Keyframe. A new, blank screen will accompany you as Flash takes you to Frame 2. This will be our actual game screen. Select the Rectangle tool (hotkey R) from the toolbar. You will pick one color for your Fill, and None for your Stroke (you don't want to add a Stroke here). Whatever Fill color you choose, make sure it complements but is a stark contrast to the Stage color.

9. Draw a rectangle that fills your Stage. You don't have to make the rectangle perfect because after you are done you can use the Align panel to stretch and move the rectangle. If you want to use the Align panel, and it is not already visible to you, go to the main menu and choose Window > Align (Ctrl + K or Cmd + K). Make sure your rectangle is selected and that the Adjust to Stage checkbox is checked in your Align panel. Then click the Match Width and Height button to stretch your rectangle to the stage's dimensions, and click both Align Left Edge and Align Top Edge to move your rectangle to fit exactly inside the stage.

10. Select the Eraser tool (hotkey E) from the toolbar. You can use the default Eraser shape and size, or you can change its shape and size in the options at the bottom of the toolbar. Use the Eraser to carve out the tunnels in your maze. You can make it very simple, or you can make it a long intricate maze. As you can see in Figure 14.2, I made a generic zigzagging line with a few smaller, branching tunnels. You start out with a wide area around where the player starts, which is where you placed the play button on

Figure 14.2
Your maze can literally look like anything, but this is the maze I created as part of this demonstration.

Frame 1, and end with a wide area around where the player ends, which is where we will place a finish button.

11. When you have finished with your maze, press Ctrl + A (Cmd + A) to select all. Right-click on the maze and choose Convert to Symbol from the pop-up options list. You want to make your maze into a button symbol, so choose "button" from the Type drop-down list, and name your new symbol maze_wall. See Figure 14.3.

12. Now it's time to add a script to your new button.

```
on (rollOver) {
    gotoAndStop(3);

}
```

Figure 14.3
Turn your maze into a button symbol called maze_wall.

13. If a player hits the side walls of the maze, he should be slapped on the hand to know he did something wrong. For this reason, we will create a lose screen. Right-click on Frame 3 on the Timeline and choose Insert Blank Keyframe. A new, blank screen will accompany you as Flash takes you to Frame 3. This will be the player's lose screen that he will see when he makes a mistake. Go ahead and add some text here using your Type tool. It can say anything you like, such as "Oops! You crashed." Just put something that gives the player enough feedback to show him that he messed up but not too negative that, if he comes back to this frame more than once, he won't get frustrated or mad at you.

N o t e

One way to perform this sort of positive-negative feedback successfully is the way Don Bluth did when making his game *Dragon's Lair*. If the player messed up, he showed the player a screen where the intrepid player character, Dirk the Daring, made a funny face before being reduced to a skeleton; it made players laugh as much at Dirk as they did themselves, and the player got the point that they had to try harder without feeling like their hand was slapped.

14. Add some more text that says "Try Again?" Then go to Layer 1, Frame 1, and copy the Play button. Return to Frame 3 and right-click somewhere off the Stage. Choose Paste in Place from the pop-up options list. With the button still selected, open the Actions panel to make sure that it has the same script attached to it as it did on Frame 1. This way, if the player decided he wanted to try again, he can click the button and immediately replay the game. Compare your lose screen to Figure 14.4.

Figure 14.4
The player's lose screen.

15. It's high time to add actions to your frames. We do this to stop action on each frame. Although our button scripts tell the Flash player to stop when it goes to a frame, we still should add a stop action on each frame; after all, redundancy can protect us from errors. Insert a new layer above the existing one. A new layer, called Layer 2 by default, will be added above your Layer 1.

16. Now that we have more than one layer in our stack, it's best to name our layers. Double-click on the layer title of Layer 1 and when you see it blink and become highlighted, change the name to Content simply by typing the new name and pressing Enter or Return when you're done. Do the same to Layer 2, calling it Actions, as this is the layer where we will add our frame actions.

17. Our Actions layer does not have any keyframes, besides the default one on Frame 1. We need to change that. Right-click on Frame 2 and choose to Insert Blank Keyframe from the pop-up list, and do the same with Frame 3.

18. Go to Frame 1 of the Actions layer, and with that frame selected, open the Actions panel. Add a stop(); function. Do the same to Frame 2 and 3.

19. Now is a great time to test your work so far! Save your game and then go to the main menu and choose Control > Test Movie. The shortcut for this is Ctrl + Enter or Cmd + Return. Play your game and see what it does. You should be able to click the Play button and move your cursor through the maze. If your cursor touches the walls of the maze, you should immediately go to the player lose screen, where you can click the Back button to try again.

20. After playing this for a while, you will probably wonder what the objective of the game is. You can move your cursor successfully through the maze, but there's no reward when you get to the end. We have to make that reward now, so close your Flash movie and return to the Flash program, where our game file is still open. Go to Frame 2. On the Content layer, you will want to create two text objects. First, using the Text tool (hotkey T), add some static text at the player start that says, "Start." This is superfluous, really, but it may help some players to realize that what they are looking at is a maze and they are at the start of it. Position the Start text where the player will start.

21. Holding down the Alt (Win) or Option (Mac) key while click-dragging the Start text object to the end of the maze, you create a duplicate of the Start text object. Double-click on the center of the Start text object to edit what the text says. Type "Finish" for this object, then pick the Selection tool (hotkey V) to exit the text editing phase.

22. You now have two text objects: Start and Finish. We want to turn Finish into a button, so that it will interact with the player's actions. To do so, select the Finish object, right-click somewhere on it, and choose Convert to Symbol from the pop-up options list. This will need to be a button symbol, and name this button finish.

23. The Finish button needs to take the player to a win screen when he reaches it. With the Finish button selected, go to the Actions panel. You need to add the following script to this button:

```
on (rollOver) {
    gotoAndStop(4);

}
```

24. Switch back to the Timeline panel and right-click on the Content layer on Frame 4 and choose Insert Blank Keyframe. This will be the player's win screen that he will see when he wins the game by getting to the end of your maze. Go ahead and add some text here using your Text tool. It can say anything you like, such as "Yay! You made it." You may also plan to put your credits here, telling the player who made the game and did the graphics and sound work on it. Whatever you decide, make it look fun and eye-pleasing, because this is the player's reward for surviving your maze.

25. Right-click on Frame 4 on the Actions layer and choose Insert Blank Keyframe. In the Actions panel for Frame 4, you will add another stop(); action to stop the movie here. Again, this may be redundant, but it protects you against errors later.

26. Save your Flash file and test it again. Now you should be able to navigate through the maze from Start to Finish, and when your cursor touches Finish the win screen should become visible.

Congratulations! You have just completed your first Flash game. It may be short, but it has infinite possibilities, and now you know how to design a game using Flash and ActionScript 2.0.

Tunnel Maze Game: What Else?

Your maze game only has one tunnel maze to it right now, but you can change that. You can add multiple levels, each progressively getting harder. Each one could be a different color, or contain dissimilar artwork, to give your game more variety.

To do so:

1. Add a button on the win screen that takes you to the next level, which would be on Frame 5. The button should say "Ready for the next level?"

2. On Frame 5, make another maze, just like you did on Frame 2, except name the maze button something different, such as maze_wall2.

3. The new maze button takes the player to a fresh lose screen on Frame 6, which contains a "Try again?" button that takes him back to Frame 5.

4. Your Finish button takes the player to a new win screen on Frame 7.

5. And so on...

You could also add a player score, which increases with each new level passed. This does not have to be dynamic, either. Just add a text object in the upper left- or right-hand corner of the stage, and on the first maze make it say "0." After the player has passed the first maze have it say "1." After the player beats the second maze, have it say "2," and so forth.

We also did not cover adding sound effects or music to your game. You could add more attraction and interest to your game by dropping music in for each maze level and adding appealing sound effects to your buttons. Never forget that this is an aural *and* a visual experience.

The last thing I might do to make the tunnel maze game better is to add a character that the player is moving around in the tunnel. This is the same technique used to make the crosshairs in the shooting gallery exercise demonstrated later.

1. Draw any image you like (a top-down view of an intrepid archaeologist or a side view of a submarine, for instance).

2. After importing the image to the project Library, convert it to a movie-clip symbol, named "Player." While in the Convert to Symbol dialog window, set the Registration point to the center before clicking OK.

3. Add the following code to your new Player symbol:

```
onClipEvent (enterFrame) {
     mouse.hide();
     this._x = _root._xmouse;
     this._y = _root._ymouse;
}
```

When the game starts up, your mouse cursor will be followed by your player character's image!

Exercise 14.2: Making a Dress-Up Game

In the mid-to-late 1990s, sites on the Web began creating interactive virtual dress-up games. *Dress-up games* are games in which a person can drag and drop clothes onto a paper doll–like image on the screen. As with paper dolls, these virtual dolls can be based on actual people, celebrities, or cartoon characters.

Several Web sites provide a directory of dress-up games and are updated regularly to list the new games that appear online. There are now also many online dress-up arcade sites specializing in

Figure 14.5
Tokio Miau Miau, one of the many dress-up games online.

interactive Flash-based dress-up games, such as 1dressup.com (http://www.1dressup.com). You can see a dress-up game found online in Figure 14.5.

The same game mechanic behind these dress-up games can be used to build jigsaw puzzle games, click-together Rube Goldberg invention games, or even scene creator games.

Have you ever thought of making your own dress-up game? It's not that hard to do in Flash, and it makes a great project for the Sony PSP!

First, you must have a doll to put clothes and apparel on. This doll can be anything you want it to be, from a photo of a famous celebrity to a cartoon character you have drawn yourself. Whatever it is, you must import your image into Flash and use it as the basis for your dress up game. I am going to use an image I have already created and colored (see Figure 14.6).

1. Open the Adobe Flash program and create a new ActionScript 2.0 document. In the Properties panel, set the Size to 480 x 272 pixels and the FPS to 18. Go to File > Publish Settings and in the dialog box that appears, click on the Flash tab near the top (it will appear by default, as the default Publish Settings will publish your document to SWF). Under the Flash tab, set the Player to Flash Player 6.0 (select it from the drop-down list) and make sure Script is set to ActionScript 2.0.

2. Save your file as dressUp.fla.

3. Set your Stage color to something other than white. Select Layer 1, Frame 1 in the Timeline and add a title to the Stage, such as "Dress Up Game." You might wonder how I

Figure 14.6
This is the little actress we will put in costume.

get the titles and buttons to be centered to my Stage. I'll tell you. I select an object and use the Align panel's Align Horizontal Center button to align the object to the Stage accordingly. This is a fast and professional-looking way to put objects in their place.

4. Go to the main menu bar and go to Window > Common Libraries > Buttons to bring up the Buttons Library. Scroll down to Classic Buttons and find a button you'd like to use for your play game button, then drag and drop it to the Stage. Position it in the bottom center of the screen and resize it as necessary using the Free Transform tool. The button, by itself, is sort of innocuous, so you might want to reinforce its meaning by adding some text above or to the side of the button saying, "Play." Compare your work to Figure 14.7.

5. Select the button and add a script to this button. It should read:

```
on (release) {
    gotoAndStop(2);

}
```

6. Right-click on Frame 2 of Layer 1 on the Timeline and choose Insert Blank Keyframe. Rename Layer 1 by double-clicking on its title, highlighting the previous name, then typing **contentBG**. This will be our main content layer for the background.

7. Insert a new layer above the contentBG layer, and name it Actions.

Figure 14.7
One example of a start screen.

8. Right-click on Frame 2 of the Actions layer and choose Insert Blank Keyframe. Then, on both Frame 1 and Frame 2 of the Actions layer on the Timeline, add stop(); actions so the movie freezes on those frames. Do this by selecting the frames, one at a time, and in the Actions panel, either typing "stop();" or double-clicking on stop under Global Functions > Timeline Control on the left.

9. On Frame 2 of your contentBG layer, you will Insert a Blank Keyframe and create a dressing room on the Stage. You can be simple or fancy with this, or you could import artwork and really dress it up. The easiest way to make this is to fashion a window frame out of three boxes. You can see the one I created in Figure 14.8. I used the Rectangle tool with

Figure 14.8
One example of a dressing room.

Figure 14.9
The doll in her dressing room.

Rectangle Options (in the Properties panel) set to 25.0; this gives my rectangles rounded, or beveled corners. The center box is where I'll put the dress-up doll, and the boxes on the left and right will be the areas I place clothes to put on the dress-up doll. The reason why I made this area so dark is to provide contrast, so players can pay more attention to the objects on the Stage.

10. Insert a new layer above the contentBG layer but below the Actions layer. Name your new layer Doll. Insert a Blank Keyframe on Frame 2 of the Doll layer. Here, you will want to draw the character you want to dress up, as I did in Figure 14.9. You can use the Free Transform tool to resize your doll as needed. Position the doll so that it is clearly visible and looks attractive in the dressing room you've made. When you are through arranging the dress-up doll, lock the contentBG and Doll layers by clicking on the Lock/Unlock icon beside the layer names, because we don't want to accidentally disturb any of the objects we've placed here.

11. You have a pretty neat setup for a game, and your doll is all set to be dressed. Now you have to come up with the components you can dress your doll in. I will show you how to do two outfits, and you can do the rest. Insert a new layer and name it Costumes. Make sure this layer is above all but the Actions layer in the layer stacking order. Insert a blank keyframe on Frame 2.

12. On the Costumes layer, Frame 2, draw two different outfits that would fit on your charac-ter. You can do this right on top of the dress-up doll, using the Brush and Paint Bucket tools. Whatever you design, it has to cover her completely, with no edges showing from underneath, so touch up and resize your images as needed. When you get done with each outfit, move them off the dress-up doll to the right or left of the Stage, in the spots you have designated for clothes. See Figure 14.10.

Figure 14.10
Create your costumes.

13. Right-click on one of the outfits and choose to Convert to Symbol from the pop-up options list. Make this a button symbol and name it outfit01. At the top of the Properties panel, name the instance of your button dress1.

14. With the outfit01 symbol instance on the Stage selected, go to the Actions panel. Make sure the tab below the white scripting area, signifying what object the actions will be applied to, says outfit01. If not, you do not have outfit01 selected properly. When you do, add the following code to it:

```
on (press) {
    startDrag("dress1");
    dragging = true;
}
on (release, releaseOutside) {
    stopDrag();
    dragging = false;
}
```

15. Do the same with outfit02, but change where it says "dress1" to "dress2," which is the instance name we added to outfit02.

16. Save your game file. Then test it by going to Control > Test Movie on the main menu bar. Click the Play button to enter the dressing room. Here, you should be able to click and drag your outfits on top of the dress-up doll, as exposed (or rather, covered up) in Figure 14.11. When you let go, the outfits should stay where you put it. If you have any glitches, close the Flash Player and review your code.

Figure 14.11
Test play your dress-up game.

17. As you add more and more objects, right-click on each of them onstage and choose to
    Arrange > Send to Back or Arrange > Send to Front. The reason you do this is because
    the objects you create will be made one after another. You might want one to appear in
    front or behind another, and if two or more are placed on the doll at the same time, you
    will want them to appear the way they ought to. So as you add more items to the scene,
    experiment with the Arrange options of each until you get them where you want them in
    the stacking order.

There you go! You should now be able to put a shirt and pants on your first dress-up doll. The next
thing to do is to add more clothes to dress up your doll. Go wild with designing this dress-up game
and truly express yourself.

Dress-Up Game: What Else?

Your dress-up game only has one dressing room to it right now, but you can change that. You can
add more dolls. Instead of one Play button on the start screen, have a button for each available
doll, then add more frames like Frame 2, including different dressing rooms and artwork. Use the
exact same code snippets I've shown you to build whole wardrobes and really expand your dress-
up game.

Or, as stated at the beginning of this exercise, you can use what you have learned here to make jigsaw
puzzle games, where players have to put jigsaw puzzle pieces together to "see" a whole picture.

Exercise 14.3: Making a Shooting Gallery

A shooting gallery, as opposed to a first-person shooter, does not have the player actually move his character. Instead, the player character stands in one spot while taking potshots at targets or oncoming enemies.

A *shooting gallery*, also called a gun game, is a video game genre in which the primary design element is aiming and shooting with a gun-shaped controller. Shooting galleries revolve around the protagonist shooting targets, either antagonists or inanimate objects. They generally feature action or horror themes and some may employ a humorous, parody treatment of these conventions.

1. Open the Adobe Flash program and create a new ActionScript 2.0 document. In the Properties panel, set the Size to 480 x 272 pixels and the FPS to 18. Go to File > Publish Settings and in the dialog box that appears, click on the Flash tab near the top (it will appear by default, as the default Publish Settings will publish your document to SWF). Under the Flash tab, set the Player to Flash Player 6.0 (select it from the drop-down list) and make sure Script is set to ActionScript 2.0.

2. Save your file as shootGallery.fla.

3. Set your Stage color to something other than white. Preferably, use a dark blue color to reflect the space theme. Select Frame 1 on Layer 1 in the Timeline and add a title, such as "Alien Shooting Gallery." See Figure 14.12.

4. Go to the main menu bar and go to Window > Common Libraries > Buttons to bring up the Buttons Library. Select an arcade button you like and drag and drop it on the Stage. Add some text that says "Start Shootin'!" out beside it. Set your arcade button's action to advance to the next frame, Frame 2, if the player clicks it.

Figure 14.12
Start screen for the shooting gallery game.

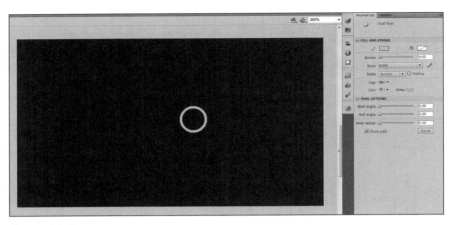

Figure 14.13
A perfect circle is the start of the crosshairs.

5. Insert a blank keyframe on Frame 2. Rename Layer 1 Player and insert a new layer above the Player layer named Actions. On the Actions layer, right-click on Frame 2 and Insert Blank Keyframe. On both Frame 1 and 2 of the Actions layer, place a stop(); function to stop the movie on those frames.

6. Go to Control > Test Movie to see it in action. So far, you should see the start screen, and when you press the red button you go to a blank screen. Now close the Flash Player and return to your project.

7. On Frame 2 of the Player layer, use your Oval tool to draw a perfect circle. Before drawing, set your Stroke color to a bright color so it will show up against the background and set your Fill color to None (the red slash mark). Set your Stroke weight to 4.0. Then draw your circle. You can draw a perfect circle by holding down the Shift key while click-dragging. You should have a yellow circular outline, as seen in Figure 14.13.

8. Use the Line tool to draw two crossing lines in the circle, as shown in Figure 14.14.

9. Select the crosshairs by dragging a marquee selection over them with the Selection tool, right-click on them, and choose Convert to Symbol. Make them a movie-clip symbol called crosshairs. Set the registration point to the center before clicking OK.

10. To make the crosshairs follow the mouse pointer, add the following script to the crosshairs symbol in the Actions panel:

Figure 14.14
Complete the crosshairs as such.

```
onClipEvent (enterFrame) {
    mouse.hide();
    this._x = _root._xmouse;
    this._y = _root._ymouse;
}
```

11. Save and test your game as you have it so far. The crosshairs should appear on the screen and move when you shift your mouse around. Close the Flash Player and return to your workspace when you're done playing.

12. Insert a new layer underneath the Player layer in the layer stacking order. Name your new layer Cover. Lock your other layers, but keep your Cover layer unlocked so you can edit it. Insert a blank keyframe on Frame 2 of the Cover layer.

13. On Frame 2 of the Cover layer, draw the front face of a brownstone building, one with several windows that can be carved away from the drawing with the Eraser tool, so that you can see past the building to the background layer beneath it, as shown in Figure 14.15. You could add any kind of cover you can think of, but I got this idea from old Halloween animations. The important thing here is to make some variety, so it's not too easy to spot an alien, and give the player a point of reference for the game level.

14. Now we need to add the targets for the player to shoot at. Insert a new layer beneath the Player and Cover layers. Rename the new layer Targets. Lock all other layers except Targets.

15. Out beside the Stage, so that you can see what you're doing, draw an almond-eyed alien creature. You can make him cute or menacing or somewhere in-between. The alien I drew is shown in Figure 14.16. Using the Selection tool (hotkey V), drag a marquee

Figure 14.15
Draw some cover here, but leave enough room for the player to snipe at aliens.

Figure 14.16
Draw an alien.

completely around the alien drawing you made. With him selected, right-click on his image and choose Convert to Symbol from the pop-up options list. Make him a movie-clip symbol called mc_alien.

16. Double-click on the mc_alien movie-clip symbol to edit it within its own Timeline. Right-click on Frame 1 of Layer 1 and select Create Motion Tween from the pop-up options list. On Frame 1, use the Free Transform tool (hotkey Q) to shrink in the side edges of the alien until he's wafer thin and really tall. On Frame 5, enlarge him to his normal shape.

Figure 14.17
This is what your alien's animation should look like. I have onion skins turned on to reveal multiple frames at once.

On Frame 18, the last frame, make him tall and skinny again. Go back to Frame 13 and make him look normal once more. Then go to Frame 1. Switch to the Selection tool (hotkey V). Deselect all and then select your alien. With him selected, add a Color Effect style Brightness of 100%. On Frame 5, make that a Brightness of 0%. On Frame 18, change the Brightness to 100%. On Frame 13, change it back to 0%. Scrub through your animation. If you did this correctly, he should look like he's teleporting out of a bright white light, standing around for several frames, and then teleporting back to nowhere again. See what I mean in Figure 14.17. Now grab the right-most edge of your tween in the Timeline, at the end of Frame 18, and drag it to 12. This will rearrange the position of your keyframes and shorten the length of mc_alien's animation. We do this to make the game more challenging.

17. Double-click anywhere off the stage to return to Scene 1 and exit the movie-clip editing mode. Your alien movie-clip will appear as it would in the first frame of its animation. Click and drag it anywhere you like. With the mc_alien symbol instance selected on stage, go to Modify > Convert to Symbol (hotkey F8) and make it a button symbol named btn_alien. Double-click the button symbol you just made to enter its edit mode. Insert a keyframe under where it says Hit in the Timeline. Because we're using a movie clip symbol for a button, the game would default to having a clickable area only where the first frame of the alien is in the movie clip. Because he's flat like a wafer, this is no good for us. In the keyframe you just made in the Hit frame, draw a rectangle where the gamer can shoot the alien to score points (see Figure 14.18). This rectangle won't show up in the final game but it will make the game go much smoother. Exit edit mode when you're done.

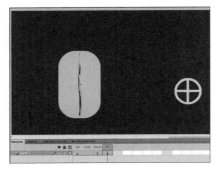

Figure 14.18
Add a hit field to tell the computer where the player can tap this button to receive his points. You could, optionally, make it smaller; for instance, place the rectangle only where the alien's head would be and then make the player attempt only head shots.

18. Using the Actions panel, attach the following ActionScript to the btn_alien symbol you have on Stage. This will count every time the player clicks on the alien and places it in a score field.

```
on (press) {
    _root.score.text++;

}
```

19. Let's add the score field now. Go to Frame 2 of the Player layer in Scene 1. Draw a text box in the upper right-hand corner of your Stage. Make it long enough for four characters to fit into. Set your font to the default device _sans, which means any sans serif font found on the platform the game is played on. Give this text box the instance name score. Also, make sure it's set to Dynamic Text. Add a second text box to the left of this one. Make this new text box a Static Text one that says, "Score." This will tell the player what the numbers beside it mean.

20. On Scene 1, Frame 2 of the Actions layer, add this code to the one that's already there, which should say stop();. This starts our score variable at 0.

```
score.text = 0;
```

21. With the btn_alien symbol selected on the Stage, right-click it and convert it to a movie clip symbol simply named Alien. Double-click the Alien symbol to go into its Timeline, and place the following lines of code on Frame 1 of the movie clip's Timeline. This sets up the Alien symbol so that it moves around the screen randomly but never leaves the screen. That way, you can put the Alien symbol anywhere on the Stage, and it doesn't matter, because he won't stay there. He'll appear behind the building's windows at completely random intervals.

```
xmin = 10;
ymin = 10;
ymax = 272;
xmax = 480;
newxy = function ()
{
  ranx = randomInBetween(xmax, xmin);
  rany = randomInBetween(ymax, ymin);
};
randomInBetween = function (max, min)
{
  return (Math.ceil(Math.random() * (max - min)) + min);
};
newxy();
this.onEnterFrame = function ()
{
  var _loc1 = this;
  _loc1._x = _loc1._x + (ranx - _loc1._x) * 1.000000E-001;
  _loc1._y = _loc1._y + (rany - _loc1._y) * 1.000000E-001;
  if (Math.round(_loc1._x) == ranx || Math.round(_loc1._y) == rany)
  {
    newxy();
  }
};
```

22. You could create more than one copy of the Alien symbol. If you wanted to up the extraterrestrial frenzy, you could copy and paste a couple of aliens on the Stage. However, the more aliens, the easier it will be for the player to shoot one of them and up his score.

23. Save your game and test it out by going to Control > Test Movie on the main menu. Click the button to start play. Whenever you shoot an alien, you'll gain points. If you find any glitches, go back through this exercise and check your code for errors, because it should work just fine.

Shooting Gallery: What Else?

Your shooting gallery only has one environment right now and only one kind of target, but you can change that.

You can add new frames after the first, and attach a script that counts the score variable. Once the variable reaches a certain number, like 100, then it could take the player to the next frame of the movie, where you'd have a new cover environment besides the brownstone.

You can also come up with creative enemies whose appearance differs from one another, such as mutant dogs, Frankenstein monsters, bloodthirsty vampires, and more. Or raise the difficulty by making the random movement of the creatures faster.

Besides adding more targets, you could tease the player by throwing in victims. You'd make victims the same way you did the alien here, but instead of them adding points to a player's score for shooting them, they'd reduce the player's score if they're accidentally shot! Make the victims look like victims, too, with wide mouths and eyes, so players can tell the difference between them and the monsters.

MORE GAMES

Of course, these are by no means the only game gems you can create using Flash. Flash is so versatile, especially when you learn to use the ActionScript better, that you can create virtually any game imaginable.

The games in this chapter are what I refer to as "beginner-level" games to design. For more tutorials, you can look online. There are several free Flash tutorials that will show you how to make brick-breaker games, *Dance Dance Revolution* clones, platformers, and more. However, many of the tutorials will stray heavier on the programming side and are thus more difficult to attempt unless you're already an adept Flash user.

Be sure, too, when you are seeking out Flash tutorials to only look for tutorials involving ActionScript 2.0. Most of them do, but some may not.

Here is a list of Flash tutorial sites you may find helpful:

- **Deziner Folio** — http://www.dezinerfolio.com/2008/02/06/20-free-tutorials-to-create-your-own-flash-game
  and
  http://www.dezinerfolio.com/2008/10/31/20-free-tutorials-to-create-your-own-flash-game-2

- **Flash Game Tuts** — http://www.flashgametuts.com

- **Flashkit** — http://www.flashkit.com

- **Tutorialized** — http://www.tutorialized.com/tutorials/Flash/Games/1

What's Next?

Now that you know all about making games in Flash for the Sony PSP, it is time to play them on the Sony PSP. In the next, and final, chapter, I will show you how to prepare your games for the PSP and how to showcase your finished games over the Internet.

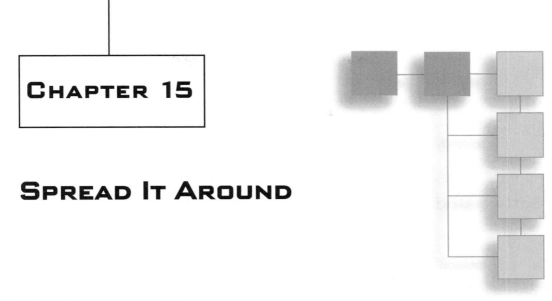

CHAPTER 15

SPREAD IT AROUND

In this chapter you will learn:

- How to set up the PSP to play Flash files
- Several of the most common sites for Flash PSP gaming
- How to build your own sites to distribute your Flash PSP games

You can make games in Flash. Now you're just uncertain how to get them to display on a Sony PSP. You know what? It's easy! And if you can get your Flash games to show up on *your* PSP, then you can get them to show up on *any* PSP, and this chapter will show you how.

SETTING UP FLASH PLAYER ON THE PSP

You don't need a hacked PSP to play Flash games. The Sony PSP firmware upgrade 2.70 or better has a built-in Flash Player plug-in for Internet Explorer. This means that homebrewed Flash games like the ones you've created can run on the PSP. To find out what version of firmware you have with your PSP, go to: http://us.playstation.com/psp.

Setting Up Flash Player on PSP Slim & Lite

If you have the newer PSP Slim & Lite, then the instructions are fairly easy.

1. First, open the PSP Internet browser. Push the triangle button on the left side to open up the browser menu options list.

2. Select the Tools menu, which has a Toolbox icon.

3. Click on Settings > View Settings. Go to On next to the Flash option and click X. Use the arrow keypad on the left side of the PSP to change the setting to On.

4. Click X and then go to OK and click X.

Now you should be able to access Flash games.

Setting Up Flash Player on the Original PSP

If you have the original PSP and your system software says 2.70 or higher, then you're ready to continue to the next section. If not, you might need to upgrade to a later version of firmware by going to: http://us.playstation.com/support/systemupdates/psp/index.htm.

You will need to enable the Flash Player plug-in on your original PSP. To enable the Flash Player, you must be connected to the Internet at least once. If you want to connect your PSP system to the Internet for online gaming or surfing of web pages, you will need to set up Infrastructure Mode.

Infrastructure Mode connects the PSP system to a network via a Wireless Access Point (WAP), such as a wireless router or modem in your home. If you don't have a Wi-Fi router, then you can try to find a public "hot spot" open near you. The best places to try and find an open Wi-Fi connection are high schools, universities, libraries, coffee shops, hotels, and so on.

If you're at home, you'll need a wireless Internet connection set up. If you're connecting to a network outside your home, you may need the network password.

The following instructions show you how to connect online with the PSP system using common connection settings.

1. Go to Settings > Network Settings. Press the X button.

2. Select Infrastructure Mode (see Figure 15.1) and press the X button. The Ad Hoc Mode lets two PSP systems communicate directly to one another.

3. Highlight New Connection to create a new connection or highlight an existing connection to edit. Press the X button. You can create and save up to 10 connections here.

4. Highlight Scan and press the right direction button. Your PSP will search for nearby access points. Once it discovers some, select the access point you want to use. The SSID, as shown in Figure 15.2, is the name assigned to an access point. If you do not recognize the SSID or the SSID is not displayed, contact the person who set up or maintains the access point and ask him or her about it.

5. Once you've selected an SSID, you can change it or press the right directional button to keep it and go on.

6. Select the type of security you will use. The type of security settings required varies depending on the access point. For details on what type

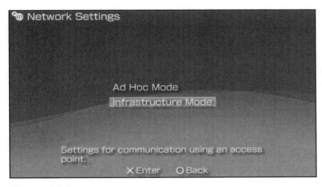

Figure 15.1
On this screen, select Infrastructure Mode.

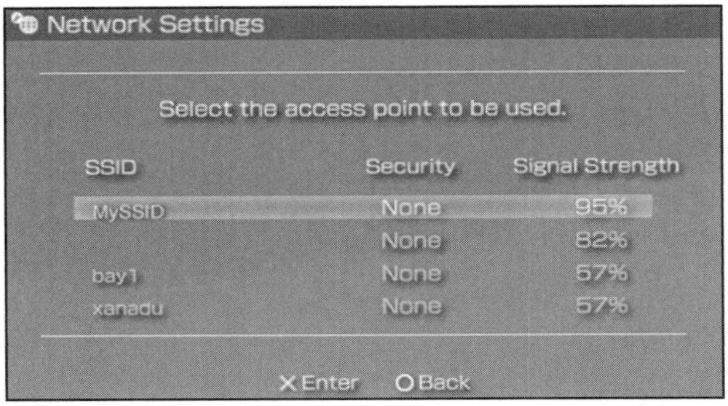

Figure 15.2
SSIDs are the names of the connection points available.

to use, contact the person who set up or maintains the access point or experiment by selecting one and trying it.

7. Press the X button to enter the encryption key using the onscreen keyboard. The key field always displays eight asterisks, even if you enter more than eight characters, so don't worry about it.

8. Select Easy. Basic Internet settings are set for you automatically. Custom is only for advanced users.

9. Enter a name for the connection. You can choose any name for the connection. Try to use one that you will remember. The default name will be the same as the SSID.

10. Check the Setting List, like the one shown in Figure 15.3, and make sure that all of the information was entered correctly. Press the X button to save your settings, then test the connection. Your PSP will attempt to connect to the access point.

11. Confirm the connection test results. If the connection is successful, information about the network connection will be displayed. Also, scroll down to the see that Internet Connection says Succeeded.

If you have some serious problems connecting with the Infrastructure mode with your PSP, you can check Sony's troubleshooting guide online at http://us. playstation.com/support/answer/index.htm?a_id=472.

Make sure the Flash Player is turned on in the settings of the Internet browser on your PSP. Consult your PSP manual on how to set this up. Flash games will

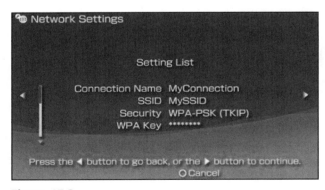

Figure 15.3
Review the Setting List carefully before continuing.

not work if the Flash Player is not activated, and only if the Flash file is made for Flash Player 6 or lower and is smaller than 2MB (preferably 1.5MB or less). This means that you will not be able to view FLVs like the ones on YouTube, until Sony Computer Entertainment America releases PSP system software with a specific Flash update included.

So now you just need to go and get some Flash games and move them over to your PSP. There are a lot of different ways to do so, which we'll go into now.

PLAYING FLASH GAMES ON YOUR PSP

Now that you have set up your PSP to run Flash games, it's practically a cinch to play Flash games on the PSP, and you don't need to have an Internet connection, either. This is a bonus, because using the Internet connection for long periods of time can cost money.

Using Your Computer and USB Cable Connector

The following instructions are for nabbing Flash games using your computer and PSP, via a USB connection.

1. Connect your PSP to your computer using the USB cable. On your PSP select Settings > USB Connection.

2. Find the Flash game on your computer that you want to play on your PSP. If you don't have one yet, you can go to step #3. If you do have one, like one of the Flash games you made earlier in this book, then skip to step #4.

3. Open your computer's Internet browser. Go to the Web site with the Flash game you want. There are two ways to get the file. One is if you have a direct link to the SWF file. If the Web site provides you a direct link, like some do, then right-click on the link and choose Save Link As (or whatever command your browser utilizes). Save the file in the format gamename.swf, replacing "gamename" with whatever name the Flash game has, but being sure to use all lowercase letters. The other way to do this is to go up to File on the browser's main menu and select Save Page

As (or whatever your browser's phrasing is) after the page has finished loading. Save the web page, including the SWF file embedded in it, on your hard drive somewhere. Then go to the folder where you saved the web page and delete all of the files except for the SWF file, which you should rename gamename.swf (or whatever the title of the Flash game you have here).

4. Open the folder containing your SWF file. Select the SWF file, which should read something like gamename.swf. If it's not all lowercase, change it now.

5. Right-click on the file and select Copy (hotkey Ctrl + C or Cmd + C).

6. Open My Computer and you will see an icon named Removable Disc. If you have any problems seeing your PSP here, you should consult the PSP manual.

7. Open Removable Disc. Go to the PSP folder and then the COMMON folder inside it.

8. In the COMMON folder, paste your SWF file (Ctrl + V or Cmd + V).

9. Safely disconnect your PSP from your computer.

10. In the address bar of your PSP Internet browser, type the following "file:/ PSP/COMMON/gamename.swf"—remembering to adjust the name to whatever you named your Flash file—and your game should load.

Using Your PSP's Wireless Internet Connection

The following instructions are for finding and playing Flash games online, without use of your computer as intermediary. This will only work when a direct link to the SWF file is given on a Web site, however.

1. You should have the Infrastructure mode already set up to surf the Web with your PSP. If you do not, go back and follow the instructions.

2. Go to the Web site with the Flash game you want.

3. Select the link to the Flash game and press the triangle button.

4. In the menu that comes up select Save Link Target.

5. Make a note of the file name.

6. Select destination and change it to /PSP/COMMON from the list. Then click Save.

7. In the PSP's Internet browser, type the following "file:/PSP/COMMON/ gamename.swf"—replacing gamename.swf with the name of the Flash file you just saved to your PSP. Your game should load.

Troubleshooting Potential Problems

The following are some of the known issues that you might run into trying to play Flash files on your PSP.

- If you get an error message that says your PSP is out of memory, your game file may be too large or have too much graphic content to load. Nothing can be done, unless you want to edit your game.

- If the game freezes up for no apparent reason, your Flash Player may have crashed. Try reloading the page.

- If the game appears jerky, or moves along at a lower frame rate than what it did on your computer, that is because the PSP has less processing power to use for the Flash Player and is one of the reasons why the Flash games you make for the PSP should run at 12fps to 15fps.

- If the Flash file simply won't run, it might be that the Flash file was set for something higher than Flash Player 6. Currently, most Web browsers use Flash Player 10, and so many Flash developers stick with that publish setting. As a PSP Flash developer, you must strive for Flash Player 6 or lower.

WHERE TO FIND AND DISTRIBUTE FLASH GAMES

If you've been on the Internet at all lately, there's a great chance you've been playing a Flash game. You probably know where all of the best Flash games are. If not, then I will list a few for you. However, it's important to note that not all

Flash games are created equally. What I mean is, most Flash games won't play on your PSP, simply because they were created at a higher frame rate, larger file size, or for a Flash Player version better than Flash Player 6. So it's like finding a needle in a haystack to uproot Flash games that meet the exact requirements to be able to play on the PSP.

On the other hand, there are exceptional Web sites that cater to Flash PSP games in particular. You can find Flash games that fit all of the necessary requirements on these sites. Plus, you can advertise your own homebrewed Flash games on these sites, to give other PSP users the chance to play your games.

PSP Flash Gaming

The main site for Flash PSP distribution is PSP Flash Gaming, which has a lot of games you can download, handy tutorials, and a place for you to distribute your finished Flash games. You can find PSP Flash Gaming (shown in Figure 15.4) on the Web at http://www.pspflashgaming.com.

If you have a Flash game you'd like to submit to PSP Flash Gaming, you can send them an e-mail at submissions@pspflashgaming.com.

Figure 15.4
A screen capture of PSP Flash Gaming's home page.

Figure 15.5
A screen capture of PSP Flash Zone's home page.

PSP Flash Zone

Another site for Flash PSP games is PSP Flash Zone, shown in Figure 15.5. PSP Flash Zone, on the Internet at http://www.pspflashzone.com, has all kinds of user-created content that has been uploaded just for PSP gamers to get their Flash on.

Plus, if you're looking to show off your Flash games, they have a quick-and-painless upload system. Simply give your name, the game name, its genre type, a short description of your game, a 50 × 50 pixel GIF thumbnail image, and your SWF file (which must be under 500Kbs). Then you're in business! See how other gamers rate your work.

PSPonme.com

The last site I'll mention, one targeted toward PSP Internet browsers specifically, is PSPonme.com. Boasting over 1,100 Flash PSP games, this site is set up for people who are accessing it through their PSP browsers to find and download direct SWF links. They also offer a selection of other PSP-related items, including MP4 videos, MP3 music, PSP demos, and YouTube video access through their sister site, PSPube.com.

Other Popular Flash Sites

Many of the sites listed here can only be accessed through your computer's Internet browser, and the majority of Flash games on these sites do not run on the PSP, although it never hurts to try. Optionally, you can advertise your Flash creation skills on many of these sites, even if your main target audience is for PSP owners, or use the SWF files you find on these sites as inspiration for your own game creations.

- **Addicting Games**—http://www.addictinggames.com
- **Andkon Arcade**—http://www.andkon.com/arcade
- **Armor Games**—http://armorgames.com
- **Flash Arcade**—http://www.flasharcade.com
- **Flash Games on Newgrounds**—http://www.newgrounds.com/game
- **Flash-Games.net**—http://www.flash-games.net
- **Kongregate**—http://www.kongregate.com
- **Online Flash Arcade**—http://www.onlineflasharcade.net

PUBLISHING YOUR FLASH TO THE WEB

These days, the easiest way to self-publish is to build a Web site and put your art on it, and get people to come to your Web site to see it, which is something that anybody can do for little or no cost.

There's no question that the Internet has profoundly changed our society. These days, people from all over the world chat over the Web, instantaneously sharing information in ways humans never considered possible before the birth of the Web. In this day and age, "I found it online," has become a household refrain.

Write Your Site

You could code all your web pages by using HTML. HTML is a simple markup language that tells the browser how to display code on the page. It's so simple, in fact, that anyone can learn to do it. There are numerous HTML tutorials online that can get you up to snuff in hand-coding in no time. To find them, search Google for "HTML tutorial."

Note, too, you don't need special software, such as Adobe Dreamweaver, to hand-code web pages in HTML. You can use a text editor such as Notepad (Windows) or BBEdit (Macintosh) to type your code and then save your resulting file with the .HTML extension. When you open it later, it will launch in your default browser to preview.

Save all your web files to a single folder with index.html as your home page.

Once you have your pages created, upload them to a Web host server by way of file transfer protocol (FTP) or other upload option. This is usually dependent on which host you go with. Whatever you do, don't lose your FTP, log-in, or password information on any of the sites or servers you decide to use. If you lose this information, you might have problems retrieving access to your site. Write them down in a notebook, so that you don't lose them.

Using Free Online Web Builders If you feel completely out-of-place trying to code your own Web site by yourself, or you would prefer whipping something together with very little effort and don't have to possess the most amazing or customized site, you can make use of one of several free online web builders.

Some of these kits create Web sites for you on a trial basis, asking you to pay money for adequate hosting or maintenance, while others are free if you agree to use their hosting service. Be sure to read the fine print of any web builder that says it's "free," because too many people have been disappointed before from using them.

- **DoodleKit**—http://doodlekit.com/home (see Figure 15.6)
- **Handzon Sitemaker**—http://www.handzon.com
- **Moonfruit**—http://www.moonfruit.com
- **Wix**—http://www.wix.com
- **Yola**—http://www.yola.com

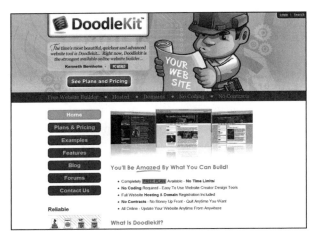

Figure 15.6
The homepage of DoodleKit's site.

Blog and Community Profiles   Do you keep a blog or community profile, such as a MySpace or Facebook page? These are other reputable ways to get your Flash noticed.

You don't have to learn anything about HTML, and the blog or community service editors are nowhere near as complicated as Dreamweaver can appear. Some of these types of sites will allow you to host Flash videos on them, but if they don't, you can always get a file sharing site like 4shared.com to put your Flash on and then link to those files on your blog or community profile.

WHAT'S NEXT?

Hopefully this book has taught you a lot. You have gone through an arduous process. If you skimmed most of this book, it is probably a good time to go back and read the chapters that have interested you the most or read about specific areas where your skills might be weak.

Overall, it is my hope that this book has shown you (a) how to draw, (b) how to animate your drawings, (c) how to make up stories and games, and (d) how to put all those skills together into Flash animations and games you can put on the Web for Sony PSP users to play through their Internet browser's built-in Flash Player plug-in.

Now it's up to you to carry what you have learned to the next level.

One way to do that is to continue the exercises where I left off. Build them into full, engaging, and appealing Flash masterpieces. Play around with the various software programs mentioned in this book and find the ones you like using. Practice and improve your skills in art, animation, and game design. This can remain a hobby for you, or you can change it into your career goal.

Whatever you do with what I have taught you, I hope you have a fun time doing it!

INDEX

Biografía

John Grisham se graduó en Derecho por la
Universidad Estatal de Mississippi y por la Ole
Miss Law School, trabajó durante dos legislaturas
en la Cámara de Representantes de Mississippi, y
en la actualidad ejerce la abogacía como *criminal
defense attorney* en este estado. Junto con su
esposa y sus dos hijos reside en una casa de
campo cerca de Oxford. Sus novelas *La tapadera*,
Tiempo de matar y *Cámara de gas*, publicadas por
Editorial Planeta, han sido grandes bestsellers
mundiales.

Legítima defensa

John Grisham

Traducción de
Enric Tremps

Planeta

Título original: *The rainmaker*

Primera edición en esta colección: septiembre de 1997
Segunda edición en esta colección: marzo de 1998
Tercera edición en esta colección: mayo de 1998
Cuarta edición en esta colección: marzo de 1999

© John Grisham, 1995
© por la traducción: Enric Tremps, 1995
© Editorial Planeta, S. A., 1999
Córcega, 273-279 - 08008 Barcelona (España)
Edición especial para Ediciones de Bolsillo, S. A.

Diseño de cubierta: Estudi Propaganda
Fotografía de cubierta: © Davis Oliver (Tony Stone) y PhotoDisc
Fotografía autor: © Marion Vance

ISBN 84-08-02237-7
Depósito legal: B. 15.430 - 1999
Fotomecánica cubierta: Nova Era
Impresor: Litografía Rosés
Impreso en España - Printed in Spain

A los abogados defensores norteamericanos

En la redacción de este libro he contado en todo momento con la ayuda de Will Denton, destacado abogado defensor de Gulfport, Mississippi. A lo largo de veinticinco años, Will ha luchado denodadamente por los derechos de los consumidores y de personas indefensas. Sus triunfos jurídicos son legendarios y cuando yo trabajaba como abogado defensor, deseaba parecerme a Will Denton. Me ha facilitado sus viejos sumarios, contestado a innumerables preguntas, e incluso corregido el manuscrito.

Jimmie Harvey es un buen amigo y excelente médico de Birmingham, Alabama, que me ha conducido cuidadosamente por el impenetrable laberinto de los procedimientos médicos. Algunas secciones de este libro son fidedignas y legibles gracias a su colaboración.

Gracias.

UNO

Mi decisión de llegar a ser abogado se convirtió en decididamente irrevocable cuando me percaté de que mi padre odiaba la profesión jurídica. Yo era un adolescente desmañado, avergonzado de mi propia torpeza, frustrado con la vida, horrorizado de la pubertad; además, mi padre estaba a punto de mandarme a una escuela militar por insubordinación. Él era un ex marine y estaba convencido de que los jóvenes debían vivir a toque de corneta. Puesto que yo me había acostumbrado a responderle y tenía aversión a la disciplina, su solución consistió en alejarme de la casa. Transcurrieron muchos años antes de que lo perdonara.

También era ingeniero industrial y trabajaba setenta horas semanales para una empresa que, entre muchas otras cosas, fabricaba escaleras. Por su propia naturaleza, las escaleras son artefactos peligrosos y su compañía era objeto frecuente de demandas judiciales. Como responsable de diseño, mi padre era el portavoz predilecto de la empresa en juicios y atestados. No puedo decir que reproche su odio por los abogados, pero yo llegué a admirarlos por lo mucho que le amargaban la vida. Después de discutir ocho horas con ellos llegaba a casa y empezaba a tomar martinis. No se molestaba en saludar, dar besos, ni cenar. Después de aproximadamente una hora sin dejar de incordiar mientras deglutía cuatro martinis, perdía el conocimiento en su desvencijado sillón. Uno de los juicios duró tres semanas y cuando concluyó, con un severo veredicto contra la empresa, mi madre llamó a un médico y lo ingresaron un mes en un hospital.

Más adelante quebró la empresa y, evidentemente, atribuyó toda la culpa a los abogados. Nunca oí mencionar que tal vez ciertos errores de dirección pudieran haber contribuido a la quiebra.

El alcohol pasó a dominar su vida y se deprimió. Pasó muchos años sin trabajo fijo, lo cual me complicó realmente la vida, porque me vi obligado a servir mesas y repartir pizzas para seguir contra viento y marea en la universidad. Creo que hablé con él dos veces durante mis primeros cuatro años de estudios. El día en que supe que había aprobado el ingreso a la Facultad de Derecho regresé a casa orgulloso con la gran noticia. Mi madre me contó más adelante que mi padre había pasado una semana en cama.

Dos semanas después de mi visita triunfal, mi padre estaba cambiando una bombilla en el desván —y juro que es verdad— cuando se le dobló la escalera y se cayó de cabeza al suelo. Permaneció un año en coma en una residencia sanitaria, hasta que alguien tuvo la misericordia de desenchufar la máquina.

Pocos días después del funeral sugerí la posibilidad de una demanda judicial, pero mi madre no se sentía con fuerzas para ello. Además, siempre he sospechado que estaba parcialmente ebrio cuando se cayó. Por otra parte, en aquellos momentos no recibía remuneración alguna, de modo que en nuestro tortuoso sistema, su vida tenía escaso valor económico.

Mi madre recibió un total de cincuenta mil dólares del seguro de vida y volvió a casarse con poco acierto. Mi padrastro es un hombre sencillo, un cartero jubilado de Toledo, y pasan la mayor parte del tiempo bailando danzas folclóricas y viajando en un Winnebago. Yo guardo las distancias. Mi madre no me dio ni un centavo del dinero, dijo que era lo único de lo que disponía para resolver su propio futuro y, puesto que yo había demostrado bastante habilidad para vivir sin nada, consideró que no lo necesitaba. Según ella, mis perspectivas de ganar dinero en el futuro eran buenas, pero no las suyas. Estoy seguro de que Hank, su nuevo marido, le llenaba la cabeza de consejos financieros. Algún día, mi camino y el de Hank volverán a cruzarse.

En mayo, dentro de un mes, acabaré mis estudios en la Facultad de Derecho y en julio me presentaré al examen de colegiatura. No me licenciaré con matrícula de honor, aunque estoy entre la primera mitad de mi promoción. Lo único inteligente que he hecho durante mis tres años en la Facultad de Derecho ha sido despachar primero las asignaturas más difíciles, para poder tumbarme a la bartola este último semestre. Esta primavera, mis clases son un chiste: Derecho deportivo, Derecho artístico, antología selecta del código napoleónico y, mi asignatura predilecta, problemas jurídicos de los ancianos.

A esta última opción se debe que esté sentado aquí, en una desvencijada silla tras una mesa plegable, en un edificio metálico, caluroso y húmedo, con una diversidad de personas de la tercera edad, como a ellas les gusta llamarse. Sobre la única puerta visible hay un letrero pintado a mano, que define majestuosamente el lugar como «Parque de los Cipreses, edificio para ciudadanos de la tercera edad», aunque aparte del nombre, no existe en el mismo el menor indicio de flores ni vegetación. Sus paredes están desnudas y parduscas, a excepción de una vieja fotografía descolorida de Ronald Reagan en un rincón, entre dos tristes banderas: la nacional y la del estado de Tennessee. Evidentemente, el edificio —pequeño, triste y sombrío— fue construido en el último momento con unos pocos dólares sobrantes de la subvención federal. Yo hago garabatos en un cuaderno, sin atreverme a mirar a la muchedumbre que avanza progresivamente en sus sillas plegables.

Deben de ser una cincuentena en total, blancos y negros a proporciones iguales, con una media de por lo menos setenta y cinco años de edad, algunos ciegos, aproximadamente una docena en sillas de ruedas y muchos con audífonos. Se nos había dicho que siempre se reunían aquí a las doce del mediodía, para disfrutar de una comida caliente, cantar un poco y recibir la visita ocasional de algún candidato político desesperado. Después de alternar un par de horas, regresan a sus casas y cuentan las horas hasta el momento de regresar. Nuestro catedrático nos había contado que para ellos aquél era el momento más emocionante del día.

Cometimos el error garrafal de llegar a la hora del almuerzo. Nos sentaron a los cuatro en un rincón junto con nuestro catedrático, el profesor Smoot, y nos observaron atentamente mientras picoteábamos un trozo de pollo que parecía de plástico y unos guisantes helados. Mi puré era amarillo, cosa que no le pasó desapercibida a un viejo chivo barbudo que llevaba sujeta al bolsillo de su sucia camisa una placa donde se leía «mi nombre es Bosco». Bosco farfulló algo relacionado con el puré amarillo y yo se lo ofrecí junto con mi trozo de pollo, pero inmediatamente intervino la señorita Birdie Birdsong y lo obligó a sentarse de nuevo en su silla a empujones. La señorita Birdsong tiene unos ochenta años, pero está muy ágil para su edad y desempeña la labor de madre, dictadora y guardia de seguridad para la organización. Dirige la comunidad como una veterana encargada de una sala hospitalaria, con abrazos y caricias, bromeando con otras ancianas de cabello azulado, riéndose en un tono agudo y de vez en cuando echándole una mala mirada a Bosco, que es, indudablemente, el niño travieso de la pandilla. Le riñó por haber admirado mi puré, pero al cabo de unos instantes apareció un plato lleno de engrudo amarillento ante su encandilada mirada y se lo comió con sus rechonchos dedos.

Transcurrió una hora. El almuerzo prosiguió como si aquellas almas hambrientas deglutieran un suculento banquete, sin la menor esperanza de volver a comer jamás. Sus temblorosas cucharas y tenedores iban y venían, subían y bajaban, entraban y salían como si transportaran metales preciosos. El tiempo carecía por completo de importancia. Se hablaban a gritos cuando algo les molestaba. Se les caía la comida al suelo y llegó el momento en que fui incapaz de seguir mirándolos. Incluso me comí el puré. Bosco, con codicia todavía en la mirada, estaba pendiente de todos mis movimientos. La señorita Birdie circulaba por la sala, hablando alegremente un poco de todo.

El profesor Smoot, un estulto intelectual con su correspondiente pajarita ladeada, una frondosa cabellera y tirantes rojos, admiraba cariñosamente el entorno como si acabara de disfrutar de una suculenta comida. Es un alma caritativa de poco más de cincuenta años, con unos modales parecidos a los de Bosco y sus amigos, consagrado desde hace veinte años a impartir misericordiosos conocimientos que los demás profesores rehúyen y por los que pocos alumnos se interesan: Derechos de los menores, Derechos de los incapacitados, la violencia doméstica, los problemas de los enfermos mentales y, evidentemente, Derechos de los vejestorios, como denominamos esta asignatura a sus espaldas. En una ocasión introdujo una asignatura llamada Derechos prenatales del feto, pero suscitó una terrible polémica y el profesor Smoot se tomó inmediatamente un período sabático.

El primer día de clase nos explicó que el propósito de su asignatura era el de hacernos entrar en contacto con los verdaderos problemas legales de personas de carne y hueso. En su opinión, todos los estudiantes ingresan en la Facultad de Derecho con cierto grado de idealismo y el deseo de servir al público, pero después de tres años de una competencia brutal sólo aspiran a un empleo en un buen bufete, donde puedan convertirse en socios en siete años y ganar un montón de dinero. Está en lo cierto.

Sus clases no son obligatorias y empezaron con once alumnos. Pero después de un mes de aburridas conferencias y exhortaciones constantes a sacrificar el dinero y trabajar gratis, el grupo había quedado reducido a cuatro estudiantes. La asignatura carece de valor y casi no exige trabajo alguno, y eso fue lo que me atrajo a la misma. Ahora bien, si durara todavía un mes más, dudo seriamente de que la aguantara. En este momento detesto la Facultad de Derecho y tengo graves reservas respecto al ejercicio de la profesión.

Éste es mi primer encuentro con verdaderos clientes y estoy aterrado. Aunque las personas que están sentadas ahí son débiles y ancianas, me miran fijamente, como si yo fuera poseedor de una gran sabiduría. Después de todo, soy casi abogado, visto traje oscuro, tengo delante un cuaderno en el que dibujo círculos y cuadrados, frunzo con inteligencia el ceño y, por consiguiente, debo ser capaz de ayudarlos. Sentado junto a mí frente a nuestra mesa plegable está Booker Kane, un negro que es mi mejor amigo en la facultad. Está tan asustado como yo. Sobre la mesa hay unas cartulinas dobladas en las que figuran nuestros nombres escritos con rotulador: Booker Kane y Rudy Baylor. Ése soy yo. Junto a Booker se encuentra el atril tras el que chilla la señorita Birdie, y al otro lado del mismo hay otra mesa con unas cartulinas que proclaman la presencia de F. Franklin Donaldson IV, un arrogante cretino que se ha pasado los tres años en la facultad agregando iniciales y cifras delante y detrás de su nombre. Junto a él está una auténtica zorra, N. Elizabeth Erickson, una chica de cuidado que viste trajes a rayas, corbatas de seda y con un enorme complejo a la espalda. Muchos sospechamos que también usa braguero.

Smoot está de pie a nuestra espalda, contra la pared. La señorita Birdie da las noticias: informes médicos y esquelas. Chilla ante un micrófono conectado a un amplificador de sonido que funciona asombrosamente bien. Cuatro grandes altavoces cuelgan de los rincones de la sala, y su penetrante voz retumba y bombardea por doquier. Los que usan audífonos los desconectan o se los quitan. De momento, nadie duerme. Hoy anuncia tres defunciones y cuando por fin deja de hablar, veo lágrimas en muchos ojos. Dios mío, no permitas que esto me ocurra a mí. Concédeme otros cincuenta años de trabajo y diversión, y luego una muerte instantánea mientras duerma.

A nuestra izquierda, junto a la pared, la pianista resucita y golpea el atril con unas partituras. La señorita Birdie, que tiene ilusiones de analista política, empieza a soltar un discurso sobre un propuesto incremento en los impuestos sobre artículos de consumo en el momento en que la pianista ataca el teclado. *Hermosa América*, creo. Martillea con gran deleite las notas de la introducción, mientras los vejestorios abren su libro de himnos a la espera de la primera estrofa. La señorita Birdie no pierde el compás. Se ha convertido ahora en la directora del coro. Levanta las manos, da una palmada para llamar la atención y empieza a agitarlas frenéticamente con la nota inicial de la primera estrofa. Los que pueden se ponen de pie.

El griterío decrece enormemente al llegar a la segunda estrofa. La letra no les resulta tan familiar y esos pobres diablos son incapaces de ver más allá de sus narices, de modo que los libros no les sirven de gran cosa. Bosco cierra de pronto la boca, pero sigue tarareando a pleno pulmón con la mirada en el techo.

El piano deja de sonar inesperadamente cuando las partituras se caen del atril y se desparraman por el suelo. Fin de la canción. Todos miran fijamente a la pianista que, bendita sea, deambula entre las partituras y da zarpazos en el aire.

—¡Gracias! —exclama la señorita Birdie frente al micrófono, y, de pronto, todos se desploman en sus sillas—. Gracias. La música es algo maravilloso. Démosle gracias a Dios por la hermosura de la música.

—¡Amén! —grita Bosco.

—Amén —repite otra reliquia desde la última fila.

—Gracias —responde la señorita Birdie antes de volver la cabeza para mirarnos a Booker y a mí con una sonrisa—. Ahora —prosigue en tono dramático, mientras mi compañero y yo nos apoyamos en los codos para mirar de nuevo al público—, para el programa del día de hoy estamos encantadísimos de que nos visite de nuevo el profesor Smoot, acompañado de algunos de sus inteligentes y apuestos estudiantes —dice al tiempo que deja caer sus lacias manos hacia nosotros y muestra sus dientes grises y amarillos para sonreír a Smoot, que se ha acercado sigilosamente a su lado—. ¿No os parecen apuestos? —agrega con un ademán—. Como bien sabéis, el profesor Smoot es catedrático de Derecho en la Universidad Estatal de Memphis, donde estudió mi hijo menor, aunque como sabéis no se licenció, y cada año el profesor Smoot nos hace una visita con algunos de sus alumnos, que escucharán vuestros problemas legales y os darán consejos, que siempre son buenos y, debo agregar, gratuitos —declara antes de volver la cabeza, para brindarle a Smoot otra empalagosa sonrisa—. Profesor Smoot, en nombre de nuestro grupo, le doy la bienvenida al Parque de los Cipreses. Agradecemos su interés por los problemas de la tercera edad. Gracias. Le queremos.

Se retira del atril y empieza a aplaudir furiosamente al tiempo que mueve entusiasmada la cabeza en dirección a sus compañeros para que la emulen, pero ni un alma levanta la mano, ni siquiera Bosco.

—Menudo éxito —farfulla Booker.

—Por lo menos le quieren —respondo en un susurro.

Hace diez minutos que están sentados ahí, inmediatamente después de su almuerzo, y me percato de que empiezan a pesarles los párpados. Estarán roncando antes de que Smoot termine.

Se acerca al atril, ajusta el micrófono, se aclara la garganta y espera a que la señorita Birdie se instale en su asiento de la primera fila.

—¡Tenías que haber aplaudido! —le susurra enojada a un pálido individuo que estaba sentado junto a ella.

Él no la oye.

—Gracias, señorita Birdie —dice Smoot—. Es siempre un placer visitar el Parque de los Cipreses.

Su tono es sincero y no me cabe la menor duda de que el profesor Howard L. Smoot se considera realmente privilegiado de estar aquí en este momento, en el centro de este deprimente edificio, ante este triste grupo de ancianos, con los únicos cuatro alumnos restantes en su asignatura. Smoot vive para esto.

Nos presenta. Yo me levanto momentáneamente con una fugaz sonrisa, luego vuelvo a sentarme y mi rostro adopta de nuevo un ceño inteligente. Smoot habla de la asistencia sanitaria, de los recortes presupuestarios, de los testamentos, de las exenciones tributarias, del abuso de los ancianos y de los pagos compartidos de las compañías de seguros. Los vejestorios caen como moscas. Los efugios de la Seguridad Social, la legislación pendiente, normas para las residencias geriátricas, la planificación estatal, medicamentos mágicos... Habla y habla al igual que en clase. Yo bostezo y me siento adormecido. Bosco empieza a consultar su reloj cada diez segundos.

Por fin, Smoot decide concluir su perorata, expresa una vez más su agradecimiento a la señorita Birdie y al resto de los presentes, promete regresar año tras año y se sienta a un extremo de la mesa. La señorita Birdie da exactamente dos palmadas y lo abandona. Todos los demás permanecen impasibles. La mitad roncan.

—Ahí los tenéis —dice la señorita Birdie en dirección a su rebaño mientras agita las manos hacia nosotros—. Son buenos y gratuitos.

Se nos acercan con lentitud y torpeza. Bosco, en primera fila, todavía me guarda rencor por el puré, porque me echa una mala mirada y se dirige al otro extremo de la mesa, para sentarse frente a la letrada N. Elizabeth Erickson. Algo me dice que no será el último en dirigirse a otro en busca de asesoramiento jurídico. Un negro anciano elige a Booker como abogado y acercan sus cabezas encima de la mesa. Yo procuro no escucharlos. Hablan de algo relacionado con una ex esposa y un divorcio de hace muchos años, que puede o no estar oficialmente cerrado. Booker toma notas como un verdadero abogado y escucha con atención, como si supiera exactamente lo que debe hacer.

Por lo menos, Booker tiene un cliente. Durante cinco minutos me siento completamente estúpido, mientras mis tres condiscípulos susurran, toman notas, escuchan compasivamente y mueven la cabeza ante los problemas que les exponen.

Mi soledad no pasa inadvertida. Por fin, la señorita Birdie

Birdsong introduce la mano en su bolso, saca un sobre y se acerca a mi extremo de la mesa.

—Usted es la persona con quien realmente deseaba hablar —susurra al tiempo que acerca su silla al ángulo de la mesa.

Ella se inclina hacia delante, yo lo hago a la izquierda, y en aquel preciso momento, cuando sólo unos centímetros separan nuestras cabezas, inicio mi primera sesión como asesor jurídico. Booker me mira de reojo con una perversa sonrisa.

Mi primera sesión. El verano pasado trabajé como pasante en un pequeño bufete del centro de la ciudad, con doce abogados, cuyos honorarios se medían exclusivamente por horas. No se valoraban las contingencias. Allí aprendí el arte de la facturación, cuya primera norma es que el abogado pasa gran parte de su tiempo celebrando conferencias. Conferencias con los clientes, conferencias telefónicas, conferencias con los abogados de la parte contraria, con jueces, socios, peritos de seguros, pasantes y administrativos, conferencias programadas, conferencias decisivas, conferencias anteriores al juicio y conferencias posteriores. No hay más que pensar en cualquier actividad y los abogados organizan una conferencia relacionada con la misma.

La señorita Birdie mira subrepticiamente un lado para otro, como indicación segura de que no debo levantar la voz ni la cabeza, porque lo que está a punto de confiarme es sumamente serio. Y esto me viene como anillo al dedo, porque no me apetece que nadie oiga mi respuesta inevitablemente ingenua e insustancial respecto al problema que va a revelarme.

—Lea esto —me dice.

Cojo el sobre y lo abro. ¡Aleluya! ¡Un testamento! El testamento de Colleen Janiece Barrow Birdsong. Smoot nos había advertido que más de la mitad de estos clientes querrían que repasáramos y tal vez actualizáramos sus testamentos, y eso no nos asusta, porque el año pasado tuvimos que estudiar una asignatura llamada Bienes y Testamentos, que nos ha convertido relativamente en expertos en la detección de problemas. Los testamentos son documentos bastante sencillos, que incluso los abogados más inexpertos pueden redactar a la perfección.

Éste está mecanografiado y tiene aspecto oficial. En sus dos primeros párrafos descubro que la señorita Birdie es viuda, tiene dos hijos y una retahíla de nietos. El tercer párrafo me deja atónito y la miro fugazmente mientras lo leo. Luego vuelvo a leerlo. Ella ríe afectadamente. El texto ordena al ejecutor del testamento que entregue a cada uno de sus hijos la suma de dos millones de dólares y a depositar un millón de dólares a nombre de cada uno de sus nietos. Cuento, lentamente, ocho nietos. Hablamos, por lo menos, de doce millones de dólares.

—Siga leyendo —susurra, como si en realidad pudiera oír los cálculos en mi mente.

El cliente de Booker, el viejo negro, está ahora llorando, debido de algún modo a un antiguo idilio que fracasó hace muchos años y a unos hijos que lo han abandonado. Procuro no escuchar, pero es imposible. Booker escribe afanosamente e intenta hacer caso omiso del llanto. Bosco se ríe a carcajadas al otro extremo de la mesa.

En el párrafo quinto del testamento se conceden tres millones de dólares a una iglesia y dos millones a una universidad. A continuación figura una lista de organizaciones benéficas, que empieza por la asociación de diabéticos y termina con el zoológico de Memphis, junto a cada una de las cuales figura una cantidad nunca inferior a cincuenta mil dólares. Sin abandonar el ceño hago unos cálculos rápidos y llego a la conclusión de que la señorita Birdie posee un capital neto de por lo menos veinte millones.

De pronto detecto una multitud de problemas en el testamento. En primer lugar, no es lo grueso que debería ser. La señorita Birdie es rica y los ricos no redactan testamentos sencillos y delgados. Sus documentos son gruesos y densos, con depósitos, usufructuarios, transferencias generacionales y toda clase de provisiones y cláusulas redactadas y ejecutadas por sofisticados abogados tributarios de los grandes bufetes.

—¿Quién ha redactado esto? —le pregunto.

El sobre no tiene membrete, ni indicación alguna del autor del documento.

—Mi antiguo abogado, ahora fallecido.

Menos mal que está muerto. Violó la ética profesional al elaborar este documento.

De modo que esa amable viejecita, de dientes grises y amarillos y voz melodiosa, es propietaria de veinte millones de dólares. Y, evidentemente, no tiene abogado. La miro antes de concentrarme de nuevo en el testamento. No viste como una persona rica, no lleva oro ni diamantes, ni dedica tiempo ni dinero a su peinado. Lleva un sencillo vestido de algodón de los que no se planchan y su gastada chaqueta rojiza podría proceder de Sears. He visto algunas viejas ricas a lo largo de mi vida y no suelen pasar desapercibidas.

Este testamento tiene por lo menos dos años de antigüedad.

—¿Cuándo falleció su abogado? —pregunto ahora con suma dulzura.

Nuestras cabezas permanecen gachas y nuestras respectivas narices a escasos centímetros entre sí.

—El año pasado. De cáncer.

—¿Y ahora no tiene abogado?

—Si lo tuviera, no estaría aquí hablando con usted, ¿no le parece, Rudy? Un testamento no tiene nada de complicado, de modo que he supuesto que podría revisarlo.

La avaricia es algo curioso. Tengo un empleo a partir del primero de julio en Brodnax & Speer, un pequeño bufete de explotadores con quince abogados, dedicado casi exclusivamente a representar a compañías de seguros ante los tribunales. No era el trabajo que quería, pero de la forma en que se desarrollaron los acontecimientos, Brodnax & Speer me ofreció empleo cuando todos los demás bufetes me lo negaron. He decidido dedicarles unos años, aprender las cosas básicas y luego buscar algo mejor.

¿No dejaría al personal de Brodnax & Speer realmente impresionado si llegara el primer día con una cliente que posee por lo menos veinte millones? Me convertiría inmediatamente en un mago, en una joven estrella con un toque milagroso. Puede que incluso solicite un despacho más amplio.

—Claro que puedo revisarlo —respondo apocado—. Lo que ocurre es que, bueno, ya sabe, aquí se trata de mucho dinero y yo...

—Silencio —susurra enérgicamente acercándose todavía más—. No mencione el dinero —agrega mientras mira furtivamente a su alrededor, como si acecharan ladrones a su espalda—. Me niego a hablar de ello —insiste.

—De acuerdo. No tengo ningún inconveniente. Pero creo que tal vez debería pensar en hablar de este asunto con un abogado tributario.

—Eso era lo que decía mi antiguo abogado, pero no quiero hacerlo. En lo que a mí concierne, un abogado es un abogado y un testamento es un testamento.

—Cierto, pero podría ahorrarse mucho dinero en impuestos si organizara sus bienes.

Mueve la cabeza como si yo fuera un perfecto idiota.

—No me ahorraré ni un centavo.

—Oiga, perdone, pero creo que tal vez se equivoque.

—Rudy, permítame que se lo explique —susurra después de colocar una mano jaspeada sobre mi muñeca—. Los impuestos no significan nada para mí porque, como usted comprenderá, estaré muerta. ¿Entiende?

—Pues, sí, claro, supongo. Pero ¿y sus herederos?

—De eso se trata. Estoy furiosa con ellos y quiero eliminar de mi testamento a mis dos hijos y a algunos de mis nietos. Fuera, fuera, fuera. No recibirán nada, ¿comprende? Cero. Ni un centavo, ni una astilla de mis muebles. Nada.

De pronto se le ha endurecido la mirada y fruncido la cara alrededor de la boca. Me estruja la muñeca sin percatarse de ello. Momentáneamente, la señorita Birdie no sólo está enojada sino ofendida.

Al otro extremo de la mesa se entabla una discusión entre Bosco y N. Elizabeth Erickson. Él critica a gritos a Medicaid, Medicare y a los republicanos en general, mientras ella señala una hoja de papel e intenta explicarle por qué no están cubiertos ciertos gastos médicos. Smoot se pone de pie lentamente y se acerca al extremo de la mesa para ofrecer su ayuda.

El cliente de Booker intenta recuperar su compostura desesperadamente, pero las lágrimas ruedan por sus mejillas y Booker empieza a ponerse nervioso. Le asegura al anciano caballero que sí, efectivamente, él, Booker Kane, investigará el asunto y pondrá las cosas en su lugar. El acondicionador de aire se pone en funcionamiento e impide oír parte de la conversación. Los platos y cubiertos se han retirado de las mesas y ahora practican toda clase de juegos: damas chinas, naipes, bridge y un juego de Milton Bradley con dados. Afortunadamente, la mayoría ha venido a comer y alternar, no en busca de asesoramiento jurídico.

—¿Por qué quiere excluirlos? —pregunto.

Me suelta la muñeca y se frota los ojos.

—Es muy personal y prefiero no hablar de ello.

—Comprendo. ¿Quién recibirá el dinero? —pregunto dejándome llevar de pronto por el poder que se me ha otorgado de escribir las palabras mágicas que convertirán a personas corrientes en millonarias.

La miro con una sonrisa tan radiante y falsa que espero no haberla ofendido.

—No estoy segura —responde pensativa mirando a su alrededor como si se tratara de un juego—. Todavía no he decidido a quién dárselo.

Bueno, ¿qué le parecería un millón para mí? Texaco está a punto de demandarme por cuatrocientos dólares. Se han roto nuestras negociaciones y me ha escrito su abogado. El propietario de mi casa quiere desahuciarme, porque le debo dos meses de alquiler. Y estoy aquí charlando con la persona más rica que he conocido en mi vida, a quien probablemente no le queda mucho tiempo de vida y que se plantea encantadoramente a quién darle su fortuna.

—Me entrega un papel con una columna de cuatro nombres escritos claramente en mayúsculas y dice:

—Éstos son los nietos que quiero proteger, los que todavía me quieren —dice. Después se lleva las manos junto a la boca y se acerca a mi oído—: Deles un millón de dólares a cada uno.

Me tiemblan las manos cuando escribo en mi cuaderno. ¡Caramba! Así de simple, acabo de crear cuatro millonarios.

—¿Y los demás? —pregunto en un apagado susurro.

Retira repentinamente la cabeza, yergue la espalda y responde:

—Ni un centavo. Nunca me llaman, ni me mandan regalos ni felicitaciones. Exclúyalos.

Si yo tuviera una abuela con veinte millones de dólares, le mandaría flores una vez por semana, felicitaciones cada día por otro, bombones cuando lloviera y champán cuando no lo hiciera. La llamaría una vez por la mañana y dos por la noche antes de acostarme. La llevaría a la iglesia todos los domingos y me quedaría con ella, sosteniéndole la mano, durante toda la ceremonia. A continuación iría con ella a almorzar y luego a alguna subasta, al teatro, a una exposición, o adonde diablos se le ocurriera a la viejecita. Yo cuidaría de mi abuela.

Y eso es lo que me proponía hacer por la señorita Birdie.

—De acuerdo —respondo solemnemente, como si hubiera hecho lo mismo muchas veces—. ¿Y nada para sus dos hijos?

—Eso he dicho. Absolutamente nada.

—¿Puedo preguntarle qué le han hecho?

Emite un profundo suspiro aparentemente de frustración y levanta la mirada al techo, como si detestara contármelo, pero luego se acerca, apoya los codos sobre la mesa y me lo cuenta de todos modos.

—El caso es que Randolph, el mayor —susurra—, que tiene casi sesenta años, acaba de casarse por tercera vez con una pequeña zorra que no hace más que interesarse por el dinero. Si le dejo algo a Randolph acabará en manos de esa cualquiera y prefiero dejárselo a usted, Rudy, que a mi propio hijo. O al profesor Smoot, o a cualquiera, antes que Randolph. ¿Me comprende?

Mi corazón deja de latir. Estoy al borde, a escasos centímetros de que me toque el gordo con mi primer cliente. Al diablo con Brodnax & Speer y sus numerosas entrevistas.

—No puede dejármelo a mí, señorita Birdie —respondo con la más radiante de mis sonrisas.

Mis ojos, así como probablemente mis labios, mi boca y mi nariz, le suplican que diga es mi dinero y se lo dejaré a quien me dé la gana. Y si quiero que sea suyo, Rudy, ¡maldita sea, suyo es!

Pero en su lugar responde:

—El resto del dinero es para el reverendo Kenneth Chandler. ¿Lo conoce? Ahora aparece siempre por televisión, desde Dallas, y hace infinidad de cosas maravillosas en todo el mundo con nuestros donativos, como construir residencias, alimentar niños y divulgar las enseñanzas de la Biblia. Quiero que se quede él con el dinero.

—¿Un evangelista televisivo?

—Es mucho más que un evangelista. Es un maestro, un estadista y un asesor. Almuerza con jefes de Estado, ¿sabe? y, además, es encantador. Tiene la cabeza cubierta de rizos prematuramente canosos, pero jamás osaría teñírselos.

—Claro que no. Sin embargo...

—La otra noche me llamó. ¿No le parece increíble? Por televisión, su voz es suave como el terciopelo, pero por teléfono es francamente seductora. ¿Me comprende?

—Sí, creo que sí. ¿Por qué la llamó?

—El mes pasado, cuando le mandé el donativo correspondiente a marzo, le escribí una pequeña nota comunicándole que, ahora que mis hijos me habían abandonado, estaba rehaciendo mi testamento y pensaba dejarle algún dinero para sus buenas obras. No habían transcurrido todavía tres días cuando me llamó, muy seguro de sí mismo, encantador y vibrante por teléfono, para preguntarme cuánto pensaba dejarle para sus obras. Le lancé una cifra al azar y no ha dejado de llamarme desde entonces. Me ha dicho que incluso vendrá en su propio Learjet para conocerme si lo deseo.

No encuentro palabras. Smoot ha cogido a Bosco del brazo para intentar tranquilizarlo y convencerlo de que vuelva a sentarse frente a N. Elizabeth Erickson, que en este momento, evidentemente avergonzada por su primer cliente, parece haberse desprendido de su complejo y sólo desea esconderse bajo la mesa. Mira fugazmente a su alrededor y yo le brindo una pequeña sonrisa, para que sepa que estoy observándola. Junto a ella, F. Franklin Donaldson IV está sumergido en una profunda consulta con una pareja de ancianos. Hablan de un documento que parece un testamento. Me siento orgulloso de pensar que el que yo tengo entre manos tiene un valor muy superior al que a él le preocupa.

Decido cambiar de tema.

—Señorita Birdie, usted ha dicho que tenía dos hijos, Randolph y...

—Sí, Delbert. Olvídese también de él. Hace tres años que no sé nada de él. Vive en Florida. Fuera, fuera, fuera.

Hago un rasgo con mi pluma y Delbert pierde sus millones.

—Debo ayudar a Bosco —dice de pronto e inmediatamente se pone de pie—. Me da mucha lástima. No tiene a ningún pariente ni amigo, a excepción de nosotros.

—No hemos terminado.

Se inclina sobre la mesa hasta que nuestras caras están de nuevo a punto de tocarse.

—Sí, Rudy, hemos terminado. Limítese a hacer lo que le he dicho. Un millón para cada uno de esos cuatro y todo lo demás para Kenneth Chandler. El resto del testamento sigue igual: ejecutor, fianza, administradores... Es muy sencillo, Rudy. Siempre hago lo mismo. El profesor Smoot dice que volverá dentro de un par de semanas con el documento perfectamente redactado y mecanografiado. ¿No es cierto?

—Supongo.

—Me alegro. Entonces, hasta pronto, Rudy.

Se acerca al otro extremo de la mesa y coloca un brazo sobre los hombros de Bosco, que se tranquiliza inmediatamente y se comporta como es debido.

Yo estudio el testamento y tomo notas. Es reconfortante saber que Smoot y los demás profesores podrán orientarme y ayudarme, y que dispongo de dos semanas para reflexionar y decidir lo que debo hacer. No tengo por qué hacerlo, me digo a mí mismo. Esa encantadora viejecita con veinte millones merece más asesoramiento del que yo puedo facilitarle. Necesita un testamento que ella misma sea incapaz de comprender, pero que sin duda inspire el respeto de Hacienda. No me siento estúpido, simplemente inadecuado. Después de tres años estudiando Derecho, soy muy consciente de lo poco que sé.

El cliente de Booker intenta ocultar sus emociones y a su abogado ya no se le ocurre qué decirle; sigue tomando notas y farfulla un sí o un no cada pocos segundos. Estoy impaciente por hablarle de la señorita Birdie y de su fortuna.

Echo una ojeada al reducido público y en la segunda fila veo a una pareja que me mira fijamente. En este momento soy el único abogado disponible y parecen indecisos sobre si probar suerte conmigo. La mujer lleva un fajo de documentos sujetos con gomas elásticas. Le susurra algo a su marido y éste mueve la cabeza, como si prefiriera esperar a otro de los jóvenes linces jurídicos.

Lentamente se levantan y se acercan a mi mesa. Me miran fijamente. Yo les sonrío. Bienvenidos a mi despacho.

Ella se instala en la silla de la señorita Birdie. Él se sienta al otro lado de la mesa y guarda las distancias.

—Hola —saludo sonriente al tiempo que les tiendo la mano. Él la estrecha lánguidamente, después se la ofrezco a ella—. Me llamo Rudy Baylor.

—Yo me llamo Dot y él Buddy —responde ella mientras ladea la cabeza en dirección a su marido y hace caso omiso de mi mano.

—Dot y Buddy —repito y empiezo a tomar notas—. ¿Cuál es su apellido? —pregunto, con el calor de un asesor consumado.

—Black. Dot y Buddy Black. En realidad nos llamamos Mar-

22

varine y Willis Black, pero todo el mundo nos conoce como Dot y Buddy.

Dot lleva el pelo rizado y plateado por encima. Parece limpio. Lleva unas zapatillas blancas baratas, calcetines castaños y unos vaqueros extragrandes. Es fuerte, delgada y en cierto aspecto dura.

—¿Cuál es su dirección? —pregunto.

—Ochenta sesenta y tres Squire, en Granger.

—¿Trabajan?

Buddy no ha abierto todavía la boca y tengo la impresión de que Dot es quien lleva la voz cantante desde hace años.

—Yo cobro una pensión de invalidez de la Seguridad Social —responde Dot—. Sólo tengo cincuenta y ocho años, pero sufro del corazón. Buddy también tiene una pequeña pensión.

Buddy se limita a mirarme. Lleva unas gruesas gafas con montura de plástico, cuyas patillas apenas llegan a sus orejas. Tiene las mejillas rojas y rollizas. Su cabello es gris y frondoso, con un toque castaño. Dudo de que se lo haya lavado desde hace por lo menos una semana. Lleva una camisa de mezclilla roja y negra, todavía más sucia que su cabello.

—¿Qué edad tiene el señor Black? —pregunto dirigiéndome a la esposa, puesto que no estoy seguro de que me responda si se lo pregunto a él.

—Llámele Buddy, ¿de acuerdo? Somos Dot y Buddy. Nada de señores, ¿comprende? Tiene sesenta y dos años. ¿Puedo aclararle algo?

Asiento inmediatamente. Buddy mira fugazmente a Booker.

—No está bien de la cabeza —susurra mientras gesticula en dirección a su marido.

Yo lo miro. Él nos mira.

—Herido de guerra —agrega—. Corea. ¿Conoce esos detectores de metal que hay en el aeropuerto?

Asiento de nuevo.

—Pues podría pasar en cueros por uno de ellos y dispararía la alarma.

La camisa de Buddy está estirada al máximo y sus botones a punto de saltar, en un intento desesperado por cubrir su protuberante barriga. Tiene por lo menos tres barbillas. Intento imaginármelo desnudo por el aeropuerto internacional de Memphis, con las alarmas sonando y los guardias de seguridad víctimas del pánico.

—Lleva una placa metálica en la cabeza —resume Dot.

—Eso es... terrible —susurro al tiempo que escribo en mi cuaderno que el señor Buddy Black lleva una placa de metal en la cabeza.

23

El señor Black vuelve la cabeza a la izquierda y mira fijamente al cliente de Booker, a un metro de distancia.

De pronto, Dot se me acerca.

—Hay algo más —dice.

—La escucho —respondo impaciente después de acercarme también ligeramente a ella.

—Tiene un problema con el alcohol.

—No me diga.

—Pero todo está relacionado con su herida de guerra —aclara.

Y así, sin más, esa mujer, a la que conozco desde hace tres minutos, acaba de reducir a su marido a un alcohólico imbécil.

—¿Le importa que fume? —pregunta Dot después de introducir la mano en su bolso.

—¿Está permitido aquí? —Miro a mi alrededor en busca de algún letrero de «prohibido fumar», pero no veo ninguno.

—Por supuesto —dice Dot al tiempo que coloca un cigarrillo entre sus labios agrietados, lo enciende, lo retira de la boca y suelta una bocanada de humo en dirección a Buddy, que permanece inmóvil.

—¿Qué puedo hacer por ustedes? —pregunto, con la mirada en el montón de papeles sujetos con gruesas gomas elásticas.

Coloco el testamento de la señorita Birdie debajo de mi cuaderno. Mi primera cliente es multimillonaria y los siguientes son pensionistas. Mi incipiente carrera me precipita de nuevo a la dura realidad.

—No tenemos mucho dinero —dice sin levantar la voz, como si se tratara de un gran secreto y le avergonzara revelarlo.

Sonrío compasivamente. Por poco que posean, son mucho más ricos que yo y dudo de que estén a punto de ser demandados.

—Y necesitamos un abogado —agrega mientras retira las gomas elásticas de los papeles.

—¿Qué sucede?

—Pues que una compañía de seguros nos está estafando de lo lindo.

—¿Qué clase de póliza es? —pregunto.

Dot empuja hacia mí los papeles y luego se frota las manos, como si acabara de librarse de una carga para transferirla a alguien capaz de obrar milagros. Encima del montón hay algún tipo de póliza manchada, arrugada y manoseada. Dot suelta otra bocanada de humo y, momentáneamente, apenas logro ver a Buddy.

—Es un seguro médico —responde—. Lo contratamos hace cinco años con la Great Benefit Life, cuando nuestros hijos tenían diecisiete años. Ahora, Donny Ray está muriéndose de leucemia y esos ladrones se niegan a pagar por su tratamiento.

—¿Great Benefit?

—Exactamente.

—Nunca he oído hablar de ellos —respondo seguro de mí mismo mientras examino la primera página de la póliza, como si me hubiera ocupado de muchos casos parecidos y conociera personalmente los detalles de todas las compañías de seguros.

Compruebo que figuran dos familiares a cargo de los beneficiarios: Donny Ray Black y Ronny Ray Black. Ambos tienen la misma fecha de nacimiento.

—Perdone mi lenguaje, pero son un puñado de cabritos.

—La mayoría de las compañías de seguros lo son —agrego pensativamente y Dot sonríe; me he ganado su confianza—. ¿De modo que contrataron esta póliza hace cinco años?

—Más o menos. Nunca hemos dejado de pagar las cuotas ni utilizado sus malditos servicios, hasta que Donny Ray se puso enfermo.

Soy un pobre estudiante, sin ningún tipo de seguro. No dispongo de ninguna póliza que me proteja a mí, ni mi vida, ni mi salud, ni mi coche. Ni siquiera puedo permitirme comprar un neumático para la rueda trasera de la izquierda de mi destartalado Toyota.

—¿Y... dice que está muriéndose?

Asiente con el cigarrillo entre los labios.

—Leucemia aguda. Enfermó hace ocho meses. Los médicos le dieron un año de vida, pero no llegará porque no ha podido someterse a un trasplante de médula. Ahora probablemente es demasiado tarde.

Pronuncia la palabra «médula» como si sólo tuviera dos sílabas: «meula».

—¿Trasplante? —pregunto confuso.

—¿No sabe nada acerca de la leucemia?

—Pues, a decir verdad, no.

Dot hace tiritar los dientes y levanta la mirada al techo, como si yo fuera un perfecto idiota, luego se lleva el cigarrillo a los labios para dar una dolorosa calada.

—Mis hijos son gemelos idénticos, ¿comprende? —dice después de liberar suficientemente los pulmones de humo—. De modo que Ron, como siempre le llamamos porque no nos gusta Ronny Ray, es el donante perfecto de *meula* para Donny Ray. Eso dicen los médicos. El problema es que el trasplante cuesta alrededor de ciento cincuenta mil dólares. Y, como comprenderá, no los tenemos. La compañía de seguros debería pagar, porque está incluido en esta póliza, pero los cabritos dicen que no. De modo que, por culpa suya, Donny Ray está muriéndose.

Tiene una habilidad asombrosa para dirigirse al meollo de la cuestión.

No le hemos prestado atención a Buddy, pero ha estado escuchando. Se quita lentamente sus gruesas gafas y se frota los ojos con el reverso velludo de su mano izquierda. Lo que faltaba. Ahora a Buddy le da por llorar. Al fondo de la mesa Bosco solloza. El cliente de Booker ha sucumbido de nuevo a la culpa, al remordimiento, o a algún otro tipo de dolor, se ha cubierto la cara con las manos y no ha logrado evitar el llanto. Smoot nos observa de pie junto a una ventana, e indudablemente se pregunta qué clase de asesoramiento les ofrecemos que evoque tanta tristeza.

—¿Dónde vive? —pregunto, con el único propósito de obtener una respuesta que me permita escribir durante unos segundos en mi cuaderno y olvidar el llanto.

—Nunca ha abandonado el hogar. Vive con nosotros. Ésa es otra de las razones por las que la compañía de seguros ha denegado nuestra petición. Según ellos, ha perdido sus derechos por el hecho de ser adulto.

Repaso los papeles y echo una ojeada a la correspondencia con Great Benefit.

—¿Consta en la póliza que pierde sus derechos al convertirse en adulto?

—No, Rudy —Dot sonríe con los labios apretados y mueve la cabeza—, no consta en la póliza. La he leído una docena de veces y no dice nada al respecto. Incluso me he leído toda la letra pequeña.

—¿Está segura? —insisto, con la mirada de nuevo en la póliza.

—Completamente segura. Vengo leyendo ese maldito documento desde hace casi un año.

—¿Quién se la vendió? ¿Quién es el agente de seguros?

—Un mequetrefe que llamó a la puerta y nos convenció. Se llamaba Ott, o algo por el estilo, y no era más que un relamido estafador que hablaba muy de prisa. He intentado localizarlo, pero evidentemente ha abandonado la ciudad.

Elijo una carta del montón y la leo. La firma un inspector decano de Cleveland, está escrita varios meses después de la primera carta que he mirado y de un modo bastante abrupto exime de toda responsabilidad a la compañía, en base a que la leucemia de Donny era una condición preexistente y, por consiguiente, ajena a la cobertura de la póliza. Si en realidad Donny padece leucemia desde hace menos de un año, el diagnóstico tuvo lugar cuando hacía cuatro años que Great Benefit extendió la póliza.

—Aquí dice que la compañía está exenta de responsabilidad, porque la condición era preexistente.

—Han utilizado todos los pretextos habidos y por haber, Rudy. Llévese todos estos papeles y léalos atentamente. Exclusiones, exenciones, condiciones preexistentes, la letra pequeña... lo han intentado todo.

—¿Hay alguna exclusión relacionada con el trasplante de médula?

—Claro que no. Incluso nuestro médico examinó la póliza y dijo que Great Benefit debería pagar, porque hoy en día los trasplantes de *meula* son puramente rutinarios.

El cliente de Booker se frota la cara con ambas manos, se levanta y pide disculpas. Le da las gracias a Booker y Booker se las da a él. Luego se instala en una silla, junto a una animada partida de damas chinas. Por fin, la señorita Birdie libra a N. Elizabeth Erickson de Bosco y sus problemas. Smoot pasea a nuestra espalda.

La próxima carta es también de Great Benefit y, a primera vista, parece como todas las demás. Es breve, desagradable y concisa. Dice así: «Estimada señora Black: en siete ocasiones anteriores, esta compañía ha denegado por escrito su petición. Ahora se la denegamos por octava y última vez. ¡Usted debe de ser sumamente estúpida!» La firma el inspector decano y yo froto el membrete repujado con incredulidad. El otoño pasado estudié una asignatura llamada Ley de los seguros y recuerdo que me produjo estupor la espantosa conducta de ciertas compañías en casos de mala fe. El profesor, un comunista que visitaba temporalmente la facultad, detestaba las compañías de seguros, en realidad odiaba todas las corporaciones, y se había deleitado en el estudio de denegaciones indebidas de peticiones legítimas por parte de los aseguradores. Estaba convencido de que existían decenas de millares de casos de mala fe en este país, de los que nunca se respondía ante los tribunales de justicia. Había escrito libros sobre la litigación de mala fe, e incluso disponía de estadísticas para demostrar que mucha gente se limita a aceptar la denegación de sus peticiones, sin una investigación a fondo.

Leo de nuevo la carta, sin dejar de acariciar el sofisticado membrete de Great Benefit Life.

—¿Y nunca han dejado de pagar una sola cuota? —pregunto.

—No señor. Ni una sola.

—Tendré que ver los informes médicos de Donny.

—Los tengo casi todos en casa. Últimamente no ha visto a muchos médicos. No nos lo podemos permitir.

—¿Conoce la fecha exacta en que se diagnosticó su leucemia?

—No, pero fue en agosto del año pasado. Estuvo en el hospital para recibir una primera sesión de quimioterapia. Luego, esos estafadores nos comunicaron que no pagarían ningún otro tratamiento y el hospital se desentendió de nosotros. Nos dijeron que no podían permitirse facilitarnos un trasplante. Era, simplemente, demasiado caro. A decir verdad, no se lo reprocho.

Buddy inspecciona al siguiente cliente de Booker, una frágil viejecita también con un montón de documentos. Dot juega con su paquete de Salem y por fin se lleva otro cigarrillo a la boca.

Si la enfermedad de Donny es realmente leucemia y la padece desde hace sólo ocho meses, no se le puede excluir en absoluto como condición preexistente. Y si la leucemia no está excluida ni exenta de la póliza, Great Benefit tiene que pagar. ¿No es cierto? Así es a mi parecer, está clarísimo en mi mente, pero puesto que la ley raramente es clara, ni suele ser tan evidente, sé que algo fatal me espera en lo más recóndito de aquel montón de rechazos.

—Realmente no lo comprendo —digo, con la mirada todavía fija en esa estúpida carta.

Dot lanza un denso nubarrón de niebla azul hacia su marido y el humo burbujea alrededor de su cabeza. Creo que sus ojos están secos, pero no estoy seguro.

—Es muy sencillo, Rudy —dice Dot después de hacer chasquear sus pegajosos labios—. Son una banda de ladrones. Nos toman por unos ignorantes pordioseros, sin dinero para enfrentarnos a ellos. Yo trabajé treinta años en una fábrica de vaqueros, me afilié al sindicato y luchamos todos los días contra la empresa. Aquí sucede lo mismo. Una gran corporación que avasalla a la gente común.

Además de detestar a los abogados, mi padre expresaba a menudo la repugnancia que le inspiraban los sindicatos. Naturalmente, me convertí en un ferviente defensor de las masas obreras.

—Esta carta es increíble —dije.

—¿Cuál? —preguntó Dot.

—La del señor Krokit, donde la trata de sumamente estúpida.

—Ese cabrón. Me gustaría verle aquí y que me llamara estúpida a la cara. Yanqui hijo de puta.

Buddy agita la mano para ahuyentar el humo de su cara y farfulla algo. Yo le miro de reojo con la esperanza de que tal vez se decida a hablar, pero opta por no hacerlo. Por primera vez me percato de que el lado izquierdo de su cabeza es ligeramente más plano que el derecho, y lo imagino de nuevo desnudo de puntillas en el aeropuerto. Doblo la estúpida carta y la coloco sobre el montón.

—Tardaré unas horas en repasar todo esto —digo.

—Bueno, tiene que darse prisa. A Donny Ray no le queda mucho tiempo. De los sesenta kilos que pesaba, ha bajado a cuarenta. Algunos días está tan enfermo que apenas puede caminar. Ojalá pudiera verlo.

No me apetece ver a Donny Ray.

—Sí, tal vez más adelante.

Revisaré la póliza, las cartas y los informes médicos de Donny, consultaré a Smoot y les escribiré a los Black una bonita carta de dos páginas rebosante de sabiduría, donde les explicaré que deben acudir a un abogado especializado en demandar a las compañías de seguros por mala fe para que revise el caso. También incluiré algunos nombres de dichos abogados, con sus correspondientes números de teléfono, y entonces habré acabado con esta inútil asignatura, con Smoot y con su pasión por los derechos de los vejestorios.

Me faltan treinta y ocho días para licenciarme.

—Tendré que quedarme con todo esto —le explico a Dot al tiempo que ordeno los papeles y las gomas—. Estaré aquí dentro de dos semanas, con una carta de asesoramiento.

—¿Por qué hay que esperar dos semanas?

—Pues... debo investigar, compréndalo. Consultar a mis profesores, buscar información... ¿Puede mandarme los informes médicos de Donny?

—Por supuesto, pero ojalá se diera prisa.

—Haré todo lo que pueda, Dot.

—¿Cree que tenemos alguna oportunidad?

A pesar de ser un mero estudiante de Derecho, he aprendido el arte de la ambigüedad en el lenguaje.

—No puedo asegurarlo en este momento. Pero el caso parece prometedor. Sin embargo, es preciso revisarlo e investigarlo cuidadosamente. Es posible.

—¿Qué diablos significa eso?

—Significa que, en mi opinión, es probable que podamos demandarlos, pero debo estudiar este material para estar seguro.

—¿Qué clase de abogado es usted?

—Soy estudiante de Derecho.

Eso parece confundirla. Frunce los labios alrededor del filtro blanco del cigarrillo y me mira fijamente. Buddy refunfuña por segunda vez. Afortunadamente, Smoot se acerca por la espalda.

—¿Cómo les va por aquí? —pregunta.

Dot mira fijamente su pajarita y luego su indómita cabellera.

—Muy bien —respondo—. Ahora terminamos.

—Estupendo —dice Smoot antes de retirarse discretamente, como si el tiempo de la consulta hubiera concluido y quedaran otros clientes por atender.

—Volveremos a vernos dentro de un par de semanas —digo amablemente, con una sonrisa forzada.

Dot apaga el cigarrillo en un cenicero y se me acerca de nuevo. De pronto le tiemblan los labios y se le han humedecido los ojos. Coloca suavemente la mano sobre mi muñeca y me mira indefensa.

—Se lo ruego, Rudy, dese prisa. Necesitamos ayuda. Mi hijo está muriéndose.

Nos miramos durante un buen rato, hasta que por fin asiento y susurro algo. Esa pobre gente acaba de confiarme la vida de su hijo, a mí, a un estudiante de tercer curso de Derecho de la Universidad Estatal de Memphis. Creen sinceramente que soy capaz de recoger ese montón de basura que me han puesto delante, levantar el teléfono, hacer unas cuantas llamadas, escribir algunas cartas, refunfuñar un poco, lanzar algunas amenazas y, ¡abracadabra!, Great Benefit se pondrá de rodillas y empezará a ofrecerle dinero a Donny Ray. Además, esperan que suceda con rapidez.

Se ponen de pie y se retiran torpemente de la mesa. Tengo casi la absoluta certeza de que en algún lugar de la póliza debe haber una pequeña cláusula de exclusión, apenas legible y ciertamente indescifrable, introducida por unos malabaristas jurídicos que a lo largo de las décadas reciben unos generosos honorarios y se deleitan en redactar cláusulas en letra menuda.

Seguida de Buddy, Dot zigzaguea entre mesas plegables y serios jugadores de naipes hasta llegar a la cafetera, donde llena una taza de plástico de café descafeinado y enciende otro cigarrillo. Acurrucados juntos al fondo de la sala tomando café, me observan a veinte metros de distancia. Yo hojeo la póliza, treinta páginas de letra menuda casi ilegible, y tomo notas. Intento no prestarles atención.

Queda poca gente, que se va marchando lentamente. Estoy cansado de ejercer como abogado, ya he tenido bastante por hoy, y espero que no acuda a mí ningún otro cliente. Mi ignorancia de las leyes me produce estupor y me estremezco de pensar que en pocos meses circularé por los juzgados de esta ciudad, discutiendo con otros abogados, con jueces y con jurados. No estoy listo para andar suelto por la sociedad, con el poder de demandar.

Los estudios de Derecho no son más que tres años de tensión inútil en la facultad. Dedicamos un número incalculable de horas a la búsqueda de información que nunca necesitaremos. Se nos bombardea con conferencias inmediatamente olvidadas. Memorizamos casos y estatutos que mañana serán anulados y enmendados. Si durante los últimos tres años hubiera pasado cincuenta horas semanales trabajando a las órdenes de un letrado competente, me habría convertido en un buen abogado. Por el contrario, soy un inseguro estudiante de tercer curso asustado por el más sencillo de los problemas legales y aterrorizado por la perspectiva de mi examen de colegiatura.

Algo se mueve delante de mí y en el momento de levantar la cabeza veo a un anciano rollizo, con un enorme audífono, que se me acerca.

DOS

Al cabo de una hora fenecen las lánguidas batallas sobre damas chinas y partidas de naipes, y el último de los vejestorios abandona el local. Un bedel espera junto a la puerta cuando Smoot nos reúne para un resumen final. Le ofrecemos breves informes sucesivos de los diversos problemas de nuestros nuevos clientes. Estamos cansados e impacientes por abandonar este lugar.

Smoot ofrece algunas sugerencias, nada original ni creativo, y se despide con la promesa de que en la clase de la próxima semana hablaremos de estos auténticos problemas legales de los ancianos. Me muero de impaciencia.

Booker y yo nos marchamos en su coche, un anticuado Pontiac excesivamente grande para ser elegante, pero en mucho mejor estado que mi destartalado Toyota. Booker tiene dos hijos menores y una esposa que trabaja como maestra a tiempo partido, de modo que nada apenas por encima del borde de la pobreza. Puesto que estudia mucho y saca buenas notas, ha llamado la atención de un próspero bufete del centro de la ciudad, un despacho bastante selecto conocido por su experiencia en la defensa de los derechos humanos. Su salario inicial es de cuarenta mil anuales, que supone seis más de lo que Brodnax & Speer me ha ofrecido.

—Odio la Facultad de Derecho —digo cuando salimos del aparcamiento del edificio Parque de los Cipreses.

—Eres una persona normal —responde Booker, que no odia nada ni a nadie, y que incluso a veces asegura que estudiar Derecho es un aliciente para él.

—¿Por qué queremos ser abogados?

—Para servir al público, luchar contra la injusticia, cambiar la sociedad, ya sabes, lo habitual. ¿No escuchas al profesor Smoot?

—Vamos a tomarnos una cerveza.

—Todavía no son las tres, Rudy.

Booker bebe poco y yo bebo todavía menos, porque es una costumbre cara y actualmente debo ahorrar para comprar comida.

—Era una broma —respondo.

Conduce vagamente en dirección a la facultad. Hoy es jueves y eso significa que mañana tendré que soportar las clases de Legislación deportiva y Código napoleónico, dos asignaturas tan inútiles como la ley de los vejestorios y para las que hay que trabajar todavía menos. Pero el examen de colegiatura asoma amenazante por el horizonte y cuando pienso en el mismo me tiemblan ligeramente las manos. Si suspendo, estoy seguro de que esos amables pero formales y rigurosos caballeros de Brodnax & Speer prescindirán de mis servicios, lo que significa que estaré de patitas en la calle, después de trabajar un solo mes. Suspender el examen de colegiatura es impensable; me conduciría al paro, la quiebra, la vergüenza y el hambre. Entonces, ¿por qué pienso en ello las veinticuatro horas del día?

—Déjame en la biblioteca —digo—. Creo que repasaré estos casos y luego estudiaré para el examen.

—Buena idea.

—Odio la biblioteca.

—Todo el mundo la odia, Rudy. Está pensada para ser odiada. Su propósito principal es el de ser odiada por los estudiantes de Derecho. Eres del todo normal.

—Gracias.

—Aquella primera viejecita, la señorita Birdie, ¿tiene dinero?

—¿Cómo lo sabes?

—Me pareció oír algo.

—Sí. Está forrada. Necesita un nuevo testamento. Sus hijos y sus nietos la han abandonado y, naturalmente, quiere excluirlos.

—¿Cuánto tiene?

—Unos veinte millones.

Booker me mira con suma desconfianza.

—Eso es lo que dice —agrego.

—¿Entonces quién recibirá el dinero?

—Un apuesto predicador que sale en la televisión y que tiene su propio Learjet.

—No.

—Te lo juro.

Booker reflexiona sobre lo dicho a lo largo de dos manzanas de intenso tráfico.

—Escúchame, Rudy, no te ofendas, eres un gran muchacho, buen estudiante, inteligente y todo lo demás, ¿pero te sientes cómodo redactando un testamento para unos bienes tan cuantiosos?

—No. ¿Y tú?

—Claro que no. ¿Qué harás entonces?

—Puede que la viejecita muera mientras duerme.

—No lo creo. Es demasiado exuberante. Nos enterrará a ambos.

—Se lo pasaré a Smoot. Puede que le pida ayuda a uno de los profesores de Derecho tributario. O tal vez me limite a decirle a la señorita Birdie que no puedo ayudarla, que debe pagarle cinco de los grandes a algún poderoso abogado tributario para que se lo redacte. Yo tengo mis propios problemas.

—¿Texaco?

—Sí. Van a por mí. Y también el propietario de mi casa.

—Ojalá pudiera ayudarte —dice Booker, y sé que lo dice sinceramente.

Si tuviera el dinero me lo prestaría muy a gusto.

—Sobreviviré hasta el primero de julio. Luego me convertiré en un importante vocero de Brodnax & Speer y mis días de penuria habrán acabado. ¿Cómo diablos, querido Booker, puedo llegar a gastar treinta y cuatro mil dólares anuales?

—Parece imposible. Serás rico.

—Maldita sea, hace siete años que vivo de propinas y limosnas. ¿Qué haré con tanto dinero?

—¿Comprarte otro traje?

—¿Por qué? Ya tengo dos.

—¿Tal vez unos zapatos?

—Eso es. Eso será lo que haré. Me compraré unos zapatos, Booker. Zapatos y corbatas, y tal vez algo de comer que no esté enlatado, e incluso puede que un nuevo juego de calzoncillos.

Por lo menos dos veces al mes, desde hace ahora tres años, Booker y su esposa me han invitado a cenar. Ella se llama Charlene, es de Memphis, y hace milagros en la cocina con un presupuesto mínimo. Somos amigos, pero estoy seguro de que les inspiro compasión. Booker sonríe y desvía la mirada. Está harto de bromear sobre cosas desagradables.

Entra en el aparcamiento de la avenida Central, frente a la Facultad de Derecho de la Universidad Estatal de Memphis.

—He de hacer unos recados —dice.

—Muy bien. Gracias por llevarme.

—Volveré a eso de las seis. Estudiaremos para el examen.

—De acuerdo. Estaré abajo.

Cierro la puerta del coche y cruzo la avenida corriendo.

En un oscuro e íntimo rincón del sótano de la biblioteca, oculto tras montones de antiguos y deteriorados textos de Derecho, encuentro a solas mi mesa de estudio predilecta, que me espera sólo a mí desde hace ahora muchos meses. Está reservada oficialmente a mi nombre. El rincón carece de ventana, y a veces es frío y húmedo, por lo cual pocos son los que se atreven a acercarse al mismo. He pasado muchas horas en esta pequeña madriguera privada, resumiendo casos y estudiando para los exámenes, y en las últimas semanas he sufrido aquí muchas horas dolorosas, preguntándome qué habría sido de ella y en qué momento la había perdido. Aquí me he atormentado. La superficie llana de la mesa está rodeada de tres pequeñas paredes de madera y he grabado en mi mente todas las vetas del entorno. Puedo llorar sin ser sorprendido, e incluso blasfemar en voz baja, sin temor a ser oído.

Muchas veces, durante nuestro glorioso idilio, Sara se reunió aquí conmigo y estudiamos juntos con nuestras sillas muy juntitas. Bromeábamos y nos reíamos, sin que a nadie le importara. Podíamos besarnos y acariciarnos, sin que nadie nos viera. Ahora, sumido en la depresión y la tristeza, casi puedo oler su perfume.

Debería buscar otro lugar en este extenso laberinto donde estudiar. Aquí, cuando contemplo las paredes a mi alrededor, veo su rostro, recuerdo el tacto de sus piernas y siento un dolor terrible en el corazón que me paraliza. ¡Ella estaba aquí hace sólo unas semanas! Y ahora otro individuo le acaricia las piernas.

Cojo el montón de documentos de los Black y subo por la escalera hacia la sección de seguros de la biblioteca. Avanzo con lentitud, pero sin dejar de escudriñar mis alrededores con la mirada. Sara ya no viene mucho por la biblioteca, pero la he visto en un par de ocasiones.

Desparramo los documentos de Dot sobre una mesa abandonada entre las estanterías y leo una vez más la estúpida carta. Es espantosa, mezquina y escrita, evidentemente, por alguien convencido de que Dot y Buddy no se la mostrarán nunca a un abogado. Vuelvo a leerla y compruebo que el dolor de mi corazón ha empezado a decrecer; va y viene, y estoy aprendiendo a controlarlo.

Sara Plankmore es también estudiante de tercero de Derecho y la única chica a la que he querido. Me abandonó hace cuatro meses por un «niño bien», un aristócrata local. Me contó que eran viejos amigos del instituto y que se habían encontrado por casualidad durante las vacaciones de Navidad. Arrancó de nuevo su idilio y detestaba intimar conmigo, pero la vida sigue. Por la facultad circulan persistentes rumores de que está embarazada. Yo vomité cuando lo oí por primera vez.

Examino la póliza de los Black con Great Benefit y tomo varias páginas de notas. Parece escrita en sánscrito. Ordeno las cartas, las declaraciones y los informes médicos. Por el momento, Sara ha desaparecido y me he sumergido en la peliaguda disputa con la compañía de seguros.

Great Benefit Life Insurance Company de Cleveland, Ohio, contrató la póliza por dieciocho dólares semanales. Consulto el talonario de pagos, una pequeña libreta donde se registran las cuotas semanales. Parece que el agente, un tal Bobby Ott, acudía personalmente a casa de los Black todas las semanas.

Mi pequeña mesa está cubierta de nítidos montones de papeles y leo todos los documentos que Dot me ha entregado. No dejo de pensar en Max Leuberg, el profesor comunista provisional, y en su odio furibundo por las compañías de seguros. No se cansaba de repetir que dirigen nuestro país, controlan el sector bancario y son dueños de la propiedad inmobiliaria. Si atrapan un virus, Wall Street tiene diarrea durante una semana. Y cuando caen los réditos y se desploman sus ingresos, acuden apresuradamente al Congreso para exigir compensaciones. Los pleitos nos arruinan, alegan. Debemos impedir que esos abogados desaprensivos presenten frívolas demandas y convenzan a jurados ignorantes para que otorguen enormes cantidades, o de lo contrario nos arruinaremos. Leuberg se ponía furioso y arrojaba libros contra la pared. Nos encantaba.

Todavía está en la facultad. Creo que regresa a Wisconsin a finales de este semestre y si logro acumular el valor necesario, tal vez le pida que revise el caso de los Black contra Great Benefit. Asegura haber colaborado en varios casos famosos de mala fe en el norte, donde los jurados pronunciaron sentencias sumamente punitivas contra las compañías de seguros.

Voy a hacer un resumen del caso. Empiezo con la fecha de expedición de la póliza, seguida de una lista cronológica de todos los sucesos significativos. Great Benefit ha denegado la petición ocho veces por escrito. La octava es, evidentemente, la estúpida carta. Ya imagino a Max Leuberg silbando y riéndose cuando la lea. Huelo sangre.

Espero que el profesor Leuberg comparta mis sentimientos. Encuentro su despacho entre dos trasteros, en el tercer piso de la facultad. La puerta, cubierta de propaganda de manifestaciones y protestas por los derechos de los homosexuales, especies en vías de extinción y otras numerosas causas de escaso interés en Memphis, está entreabierta y le oigo vociferar por teléfono. Me aguanto la respiración y llamo discretamente.

—¡Adelante! —exclama, y yo entro sigilosamente.

Me ofrece una silla con un ademán. Está todo lleno de libros, fichas y revistas. El despacho parece un campo de batalla. Una barahúnda de desechos, periódicos, botellas... El peso excesivo dobla las estanterías. Numerosos carteles cubren las paredes. Trozos de papel esparcidos por el suelo forman una especie de charcos. El tiempo y la organización no significan nada para Max Leuberg.

Es un individuo de sesenta años, bajo, delgado, con una frondosa cabellera desaliñada color paja y unas manos que no dejan de moverse. Usa vaqueros descoloridos, jersey ecológicamente provocativo y unas viejas zapatillas. Cuando hace frío, a veces se pone unos calcetines. Es tan extraordinariamente activo que me pone nervioso.

—¡Baker! —exclama después de colgar el teléfono.

—Baylor. Rudy Baylor. Seguros, el semestre pasado.

—¡Claro! ¡Claro! Ya me acuerdo. Siéntese —dice ofreciéndome de nuevo la silla.

—No, gracias.

Se retuerce y empuja un montón de papeles sobre su escritorio.

—¿Qué le trae por aquí, Baylor?

Los estudiantes adoran a Max porque siempre está dispuesto a escuchar.

—Pues... ¿dispone de unos minutos?

Normalmente hablaría con más formalidad y le llamaría «señor» o algo por el estilo, pero Leuberg detesta las formalidades e insiste en que le llamemos Max.

—Sí, por supuesto. ¿Qué le preocupa?

—El caso es que estoy estudiando una asignatura con el profesor Smoot —respondo, antes de ofrecerle un breve resumen de mi visita al hogar de ancianos, mi encuentro con Dot y Buddy, y su conflicto con Great Benefit.

Parece estar pendiente de todo lo que le cuento.

—¿Ha oído hablar de Great Benefit? —pregunto.

—Sí. Es una gran organización que vende muchos seguros baratos a blancos y negros en zonas rurales. Unos desaprensivos.

—Nunca he oído hablar de ellos.

—No me sorprende. No hacen propaganda. Sus agentes van de puerta en puerta y pasan a cobrar la cuota cada semana. Estamos hablando de lo más turbio del sector. Muéstreme la póliza.

Se la entrego y la hojea.

—¿En qué se basan para denegar la petición? —pregunta sin mirarme.

—En todo. Primero la denegaron sólo por principio. A continuación dijeron que la leucemia estaba excluida. Luego alegaron que la enfermedad era una condición preexistente. Más adelante afirmaron que el peticionario, como adulto, no estaba cubierto por la póliza de sus padres. A decir verdad, han sido bastante creativos.

—¿Se han pagado todas las cuotas?

—Eso asegura la señora Black.

—Cabrones —exclama Max encantado, con una perversa sonrisa en los labios, mientras sigue repasando los papeles—. ¿Ha examinado todos los documentos?

—Sí. He leído todo lo que me han entregado los clientes.

Arroja la póliza sobre la mesa.

—Definitivamente, merece ser investigado —declara—. Pero recuerde que raramente los clientes se lo entregan todo desde el primer momento.

Le muestro la estúpida carta. La lee y en sus labios se dibuja otra pícara sonrisa. Vuelve a leerla y por fin me mira fijamente.

—Increíble.

—Eso me ha parecido a mí —respondo, como un veterano protector de los derechos de los asegurados.

—¿Dónde está el resto de los documentos? —pregunta.

Los coloco todos sobre su escritorio.

—Esto es todo lo que me ha entregado la señora Black. Dice que su hijo está muriéndose porque no pueden permitirse pagar el tratamiento. Según ella, sólo pesa cuarenta kilos y le queda poco tiempo de vida.

—Cabrones —repite casi para sus adentros, sin mover las manos—. Malditos cabrones.

Estoy completamente de acuerdo, pero no digo nada. Veo otro par de zapatillas en un rincón, unas Nike muy viejas. En una clase nos contó que en otra época usaba ropa de la casa Converse, pero había dejado de hacerlo por su política de reciclaje. Libra su propia guerra personal contra las corporaciones norteamericanas y se niega a comprar cualquier producto de un fabricante que le haya engañado en lo más mínimo. Rehúsa asegurar su vida, su salud o sus bienes, pero se rumorea que su familia es rica y, por consiguiente, puede permitirse el lujo de circular sin ningún seguro por la vida. Yo, por razones bastante evidentes, también vivo en el mundo de los no asegurados.

La mayoría de mis profesores son rancios intelectuales que acuden a clase con corbata y no se desabrochan nunca la chaqueta. Max no usa corbata desde hace décadas. Tampoco da conferencias, sino que actúa. Me sabe muy mal que nos abandone.

Sus manos vuelven a cobrar vida.

—Me gustaría estudiarlos esta noche —dice, sin levantar la mirada de los documentos.

—Estupendo. ¿Puedo pasar por la mañana?

—Desde luego. Me encontrará aquí a cualquier hora.

Suena su teléfono y lo levanta inmediatamente. Yo le sonrío y salgo por la puerta enormemente aliviado. Lo veré por la mañana, escucharé sus consejos y luego les escribiré a los Black un informe de dos páginas en el que repetiré lo que me diga.

Ahora sólo necesito encontrar un alma inteligente que se ocupe de la investigación relacionada con la señorita Birdie. Tengo a algunos sujetos en perspectiva, un par de profesores de Derecho tributario, y puede que intente verlos mañana. Bajo por la escalera y entro en la sala de recreo de los estudiantes, junto a la biblioteca. Es el único lugar del edificio donde está permitido fumar y una niebla azulada flota permanentemente debajo de las luces. Hay un televisor y una serie de sofás y sillones maltratados. Una colección de fotografías enmarcadas de final de curso adorna las paredes, repleta de rostros estudiosos lanzados tiempo ha a las trincheras de la guerra jurídica. Cuando la sala está vacía, a menudo examino las caras de mis predecesores y me pregunto cuántos habrán sido expulsados de la profesión, cuántos preferirían no haber pisado nunca este lugar y cuántos disfrutan realmente atacando y defendiendo ante los tribunales. Una de las paredes está reservada a anuncios, circulares, una amplia variedad de ofertas y demandas, y tras la misma hay una serie de máquinas de venta de refrescos y comida. Aquí es donde como muchas veces. La comida de las máquinas está infravalorada.

Discretamente retirado veo a su señoría F. Franklin Donaldson IV hablando con tres compañeros, todos ellos unos fanfarrones que escriben en la revista de la facultad y miran con desprecio a quienes no lo hacemos. Al verme manifiesta cierto interés y sonríe, lo cual es inusual, porque su entrecejo suele estar permanentemente fruncido.

—Dime, Rudy, ¿no es cierto que vas a trabajar en Brodnax & Speer? —exclama.

El televisor está apagado. Sus compañeros me miran fijamente. Dos chicas sentadas en un sofá levantan la cabeza y me dirigen la mirada.

—Sí. ¿Por qué? —pregunto.

F. Franklin IV ha conseguido empleo en un bufete donde abundan las herencias, el dinero y la pretensión, vastamente superior a Brodnax & Speer. Sus actuales compinches son W. Harper Whittenson, un arrogante mequetrefe que, afortunadamente, abandonará Memphis para ejercer en un gigantesco bufete de Dallas, J. Townsend Gross, que ha aceptado un empleo en otra gran firma, y James Straybeck, un personaje ocasionalmente amable que ha resistido tres años en la facultad sin agregar iniciales ni números a su nombre. Con un nombre tan sucinto, su futuro como abogado en un gran bufete es sumamente dudoso. Me sorprendería que triunfara.

F. Franklin IV da un paso hacia mí.

—Bueno, cuéntanos lo que ocurre. —Sonríe radiantemente.

—¿Qué ocurre? —exclamo, sin tener ni idea de lo que me está hablando.

—Claro, respecto a la fusión.

—¿Qué fusión?

—¿No te has enterado?

—¿Enterado de qué?

F. Franklin IV mira a sus compinches y los tres dan la impresión de estar divirtiéndose. Su sonrisa crece cuando me mira.

—Vamos, Rudy, de la fusión de Brodnax & Speer y Tinley Britt.

Permanezco inmóvil e intento pensar en algo inteligente o ingenioso para responderle, pero no se me ocurre nada. Es evidente que ese cretino sabe algo acerca de la fusión y que yo no sé absolutamente nada. Brodnax & Speer es un pequeño bufete de quince abogados y yo soy el único de mi clase a quien han contratado. Cuando nos pusimos de acuerdo hace dos meses no se habló de ningún proyecto de fusión.

Tinley Britt, por otra parte, es el bufete más grande, conservador, prestigioso y opulento del estado. Según las últimas informaciones, lo constituían ciento veinte abogados, la mayoría de ellos procedentes de las escuelas de élite de la costa este y muchos con experiencia como pasantes en instituciones federales. Es un poderoso bufete que representa a pudientes corporaciones y entidades gubernamentales, que dispone además de un despacho en Washington, donde cultiva relaciones con la élite. Es un bastión de política conservadora. Uno de sus socios es ex senador federal. Sus miembros asociados trabajan ochenta horas semanales y todos visten de azul marino y negro, con camisa blanca y corbata a rayas. Llevan el cabello corto y la cara obligatoriamente afeitada. Se reconoce a un abogado de Tinley Britt por su forma de andar y vestir. Todos los componentes del bufete son varones blancos anglosajones y protestantes, que han asistido a las escuelas apropiadas y pertenecido a las asociaciones debidas, por lo que el resto de la comunidad jurídica de Memphis siempre lo ha denominado Trent & Brent.

J. Townsend Gross tiene las manos en los bolsillos y me mira con una irónica sonrisa en los labios. Es el segundo de la clase y, además de conducir un BMW, lleva el cuello de la camisa lo suficientemente almidonado para haberse sentido atraído desde el primer momento por Trent & Brent.

Me tiemblan las rodillas, porque sé que Trent & Brent no aceptaría nunca a alguien como yo. Si es cierto que Brodnax & Speer se ha unido a dicho monstruo, temo la posibilidad de haber quedado descartado en el proceso.

—No me he enterado —respondo tímidamente.

Las chicas del sofá nos miran atentamente. Se hace un silencio.

—¿Estás diciéndonos que no te lo han comunicado? —pregunta con incredulidad F. Franklin IV—. Jack se ha enterado hoy alrededor de las doce —agrega moviendo la cabeza en dirección a J. Townsend Gross.

—Es cierto —afirma J. Townsend—. Pero el nombre del bufete sigue siendo el mismo.

Aparte de Trent & Brent, el nombre del bufete es Tinley, Britt, Crawford, Mize & Saint John. Afortunadamente, hace años que alguien optó por la versión abreviada. Al afirmar que no cambia el nombre, J. Townsend le ha comunicado a su reducido público que Brodnax & Speer es un bufete tan pequeño e insignificante que puede ser absorbido por Tinley Britt sin el menor contratiempo.

—¿De modo que sigue siendo Trent & Brent? —pregunto.

J. Townsend refunfuña al oír el exagerado apodo.

—Me parece increíble que no te lo hayan comunicado —prosigue F. Franklin IV.

Me encojo de hombros como si careciera de importancia y me dirijo a la puerta.

—Tal vez te preocupas demasiado, Frankie.

Intercambian sonrisas confidenciales, como si hubieran cumplido su cometido, y yo abandono la sala. El bibliotecario me hace una seña desde el mostrador en cuanto me ve entrar.

—Hay un recado para ti —dice al tiempo que me entrega un trozo de papel en el que se me comunica que llame a Loyd Beck, el socio gerente de Brodnax & Speer que me contrató.

Las cabinas telefónicas están en la sala de recreo, pero no estoy de humor para ver de nuevo a F. Flanklin IV y a su pandilla de sicarios.

—¿Puedo usar tu teléfono? —le pregunto al bibliotecario, que es un estudiante de segundo y actúa como si fuera el dueño de la biblioteca.

—Hay cabinas en la sala de recreo —responde, como si después de tres años en la facultad no supiera dónde están los teléfonos.

—Acabo de venir de allí y están todas ocupadas.

—De acuerdo —dice con el entrecejo fruncido mientras mira a su alrededor—, pero date prisa.

Marco el número de Brodnax & Speer. Son casi las seis y las secretarias dejan de trabajar a las cinco. A la novena llamada responde escuetamente una voz masculina:

—Diga.

Me coloco de espaldas a la entrada de la biblioteca y procuro ocultarme entre las estanterías.

—Hola, soy Rudy Baylor. Estoy en la Facultad de Derecho y he recibido un recado de Loyd Beck para que le llame. Dice que es urgente.

En la nota no se menciona la urgencia, pero en este momento estoy bastante nervioso.

—¿Rudy Baylor? ¿Relacionado con qué?

—Soy el joven a quien acaban de contratar. ¿Con quién hablo?

—Ah, claro, Baylor. Soy Carson Bell. Loyd está ahora en una reunión y no se le puede molestar. Vuelva a intentarlo dentro de una hora.

Conocí brevemente a Carson Bell cuando me mostraron el bufete y le recuerdo como al típico abogado ajetreado, amable unos segundos antes de volver al trabajo.

—Perdone, señor Bell, pero necesito hablar con el señor Beck.

—Lo siento, pero ahora no puede ser, ¿de acuerdo?

—He oído cierto rumor respecto a una fusión con Trent, es decir, Tinley Britt. ¿Es cierto?

—Escúcheme, Rudy, estoy ocupado y ahora no puedo hablar con usted. Llame dentro de una hora y Loyd le atenderá.

—¿Sigue vigente la oferta de empleo? —pregunto asustado y con cierta desesperación.

—Vuelva a llamar dentro de una hora —responde irritado antes de colgar el teléfono.

Escribo una nota en un papel y se la entrego al bibliotecario.

—¿Conoces a Booker Kane? —le pregunto.

—Sí.

—Bien. Estará aquí dentro de unos minutos. Dale esta nota y dile que regresaré dentro de una hora aproximadamente.

Coge el papel y refunfuña. Salgo de la biblioteca, cruzo discretamente la sala de recreo, con la esperanza de que nadie me vea, abandono el edificio y me acerco corriendo al aparcamiento, donde me espera mi Toyota. Espero que el motor arranque. Uno de mis más oscuros secretos es que todavía le debo casi trescientos dólares a una financiera por este triste cacharro. Incluso Booker cree que ya lo he pagado.

TRES

No es ningún secreto que hay demasiados abogados en Memphis. Cuando ingresamos en la facultad nos advirtieron que la profesión estaba terriblemente saturada en todas partes, que algunos de nosotros nos mataríamos a trabajar durante tres años, lucharíamos para aprobar el examen de colegiatura y no lograríamos encontrar empleo. De modo que, para hacernos un favor, nos dijeron desde el primer momento que suspenderían por lo menos a un tercio de nuestro curso. Han cumplido su palabra.

Puedo nombrar como mínimo a diez personas que se licenciarán conmigo dentro de un mes y luego dispondrán de muchísimo tiempo para preparar el examen de colegiatura, porque todavía no han encontrado trabajo. Siete años de universidad y sin empleo. También conozco a varias docenas de condiscípulos que trabajarán como ayudantes de fiscales, defensores públicos y como auxiliares administrativos de jueces mal pagados, es decir, los trabajos de los que no nos hablaron cuando ingresamos en la facultad.

De modo que en muchos sentidos me he sentido bastante orgulloso de mi empleo en Brodnax & Speer, un auténtico bufete de abogados. Sí, a veces me he sentido muy importante junto a otros de menos talento, que todavía buscan trabajo y solicitan entrevistas. Pero ahora, cuando me dirijo en mi coche al centro de la ciudad, me doy cuenta de que mi arrogancia ha desaparecido. No hay lugar para mí en un bufete como Trent & Brent. Mi Toyota tose y escupe, como de costumbre, pero por lo menos avanza.

Intento analizar la fusión. Hace un par de años, Trent & Brent absorbió un bufete de treinta abogados y fue una gran noticia en la ciudad. Pero no recuerdo si alguien perdió el empleo en dicho proceso. ¿Qué interés pueden tener en un bufete de quince abogados como Brodnax & Speer? De pronto me percato de lo poco que sé acerca de mis futuros jefes. El viejo Brodnax murió hace varios años y su rollizo rostro ha quedado inmortalizado en un horrendo busto de bronce, junto a la entrada principal del bufete. Speer es su yerno, aunque divorciado desde hace mucho tiempo de su hija. Hablé brevemente con él y me resultó bastante agradable. Durante la segunda o tercera entrevista me contaron que sus clientes más importantes eran un par de compañías de seguros, y que el ochenta por ciento de su trabajo eran los siniestros automovilísticos.

Puede que Trent & Brent necesitara cierto apoyo en su sección de accidentes de tráfico. Quién sabe.

Circulan muchos vehículos por Poplar, pero la mayoría en dirección contraria. Veo los grandes edificios del centro de la ciudad. No puedo creer que Loyd Beck, Carson Bell y todos los demás estuvieran de acuerdo en contratarme, elaboraran planes y adquirieran compromisos, y luego prescindieran de mí por una cuestión económica. No se unirían a Trent & Brent sin proteger a su propia gente. ¿O lo harían?

Durante todo el año, aquellos compañeros que iban a licenciarse conmigo el mes próximo habían recorrido toda la ciudad en busca de trabajo. Es imposible que quede una sola vacante. Ni siquiera el más insignificante empleo puede habérseles escapado.

A pesar de que los aparcamientos están quedándose vacíos y hay sitio de sobra para estacionar el coche, aparco en zona prohibida al otro lado de la calle donde se encuentra el edificio de ocho plantas en el que están situadas las oficinas de Brodnax & Speer. A dos manzanas está el edificio más alto del centro de la ciudad, cuya mitad superior está alquilada naturalmente por Trent & Brent. Desde su encumbrado pedestal pueden contemplar con desdén al resto de la ciudad. Los detesto.

Cruzo corriendo la calle y entro en el mugriento vestíbulo del edificio Powers. A la izquierda hay dos ascensores, pero a la derecha veo un rostro conocido. Es Richard Spain, miembro asociado de Brodnax & Speer, un individuo realmente agradable que me invitó a almorzar el día de mi primera visita. Está sentado en un estrecho banco de mármol, con la mirada perdida en el suelo.

—Richard —exclamo mientras me acerco a él—, soy yo, Rudy Baylor.

Permanece inmóvil, sin alterar la mirada. Me siento junto a él. Los ascensores están exactamente frente a nosotros, a diez metros de distancia.

Richard sigue embelesado.

—¿Qué ocurre, Richard? ¿Estás bien?

En este momento, el pequeño vestíbulo está desierto y reina la tranquilidad.

Vuelve lentamente la cabeza para mirarme y abre ligeramente la boca.

—Me han despedido —dice en voz baja, con unos ojos irritados de llorar o beber.

—¿Quién? —pregunto en tono grave, aunque estoy convencido de que ya conozco la respuesta.

—Me han despedido —repite.

—Por favor, Richard, cuéntamelo. ¿Qué ocurre? ¿A quién han despedido?

—Han despedido a todos los miembros asociados —responde lentamente—. Beck nos ha reunido en la sala de conferencias, nos ha comunicado que los socios habían acordado vender el negocio a Tinley Britt y que no había cabida para los miembros asociados. Así de simple. Nos ha dado una hora para vaciar el despacho y abandonar el edificio —agrega mientras bambolea de un modo extraño la cabeza, con la mirada fija en los ascensores.

—Así de simple —repito yo.

—Supongo que te preguntarás por tu empleo —dice Richard sin dejar de mirar hacia los ascensores.

—Se me ha ocurrido.

—A esos cabrones no les importas en absoluto.

Evidentemente, ya estaba convencido de ello.

—¿Por qué os han despedido? —pregunto con una voz apenas audible.

A decir verdad, no me importa que hayan despedido a los miembros asociados del bufete, pero procuro parecer sincero.

—Trent & Brent quería nuestros clientes —responde—. Y para conseguirlos, tenían que comprar a los socios. Nosotros, los miembros asociados, no éramos más que un estorbo.

—Lo siento.

—Yo también. Tu nombre se ha mencionado durante la reunión. Alguien preguntó por ti, porque eres el único a quien acaban de contratar. Beck ha respondido que intentaba ponerse en contacto contigo para darte la mala noticia. También te han despedido, Rudy. Lo siento.

Mi cabeza desciende unos centímetros. Me sudan las manos.

—¿Sabes cuánto gané el año pasado? —pregunta Richard.

—¿Cuánto?

—Ochenta mil. He trabajado setenta horas semanales como un esclavo desde hace seis años, apenas me he ocupado de mi familia, he sudado sangre para el respetable bufete de Brodnax & Speer, y ahora esos cabrones me dan una hora para recoger mis efectos personales y abandonar el edificio. Incluso han mandado a un guardia de seguridad para que me vigilara mientras guardaba mis pertenencias. Ochenta mil pavos es lo que me han pagado y yo facturé dos mil quinientas horas a ciento cincuenta, lo cual significa que el total bruto que ingresé para ellos el año pasado fue de trescientos setenta y cinco mil. Me recompensan con ochenta, me regalan un reloj de oro, me dan una palmada en la espalda y me dicen que tal vez me convierta en socio dentro de un par de años, como una gran familia feliz. Pero de pronto aparece Trent & Brent con sus millones y me ponen de patitas en la calle. Y tú también te has quedado sin trabajo, amigo. ¿No lo sabías? ¿Te das cuenta de que has perdido tu primer empleo incluso antes de empezar a trabajar?

No sé qué responderle.

Apoya lentamente la cabeza sobre su hombro izquierdo sin prestarme atención.

—Ochenta mil —repite—. Una buena tajada, ¿no te parece, Rudy?

—Sí —respondo, ante lo que para mí es una pequeña fortuna.

—¿Sabes que no hay forma de encontrar otro empleo para ganar tanto dinero? En esta ciudad resulta imposible. Nadie contrata. Hay demasiados abogados.

¿En serio?

Se frota los ojos con los dedos y se pone de pie lentamente.

—Debo contárselo a mi esposa —susurra, y empieza a andar con los hombros caídos en dirección a la puerta, la cruza y se aleja por la acera.

Subo en el ascensor hasta el cuarto piso y atravieso un pequeño vestíbulo. A través de una doble puerta de cristal veo a un robusto guardia de seguridad uniformado junto a la recepción. Me mira con una mueca al verme entrar en las dependencias de Brodnax & Speer.

—¿En qué puedo servirle? —refunfuña.

—Estoy buscando a Loyd Beck —respondo mientras intento mirar por el pasillo que queda a su espalda.

Él se mueve ligeramente para ocultar mi campo de visión.

—¿Quién es usted?

—Rudy Baylor.

Se agacha para coger un sobre de la mesa.

—Esto es para usted —responde.

Mi nombre está escrito con tinta roja. Abro la pequeña carta. Me tiemblan las manos cuando la leo.

Suena una voz por su radio y retrocede lentamente.

—Lea la carta y márchese —dice, y se retira por el pasillo.

La carta consta de un solo párrafo en el que Loyd Beck me comunica amablemente la noticia y me desea suerte. La fusión ha sido «rápida e inesperada».

Dejo caer la carta al suelo y miro a mi alrededor en busca de algo que arrojar. No se oye nada a lo largo del pasillo. Estoy seguro de que se han parapetado tras sus puertas cerradas a cal y canto, a la espera de que yo y los demás marginados desaparezcamos. Junto a la puerta hay un busto sobre una peana de hormigón, una horrible escultura en bronce del rollizo rostro del viejo Brodnax, y le escupo en la cara al pasar junto a la misma. No se inmuta. Al abrir la puerta le doy un empujón, el pedestal se tambalea y el busto se cae.

—¡Oiga! —exclama una voz a mi espalda en el momento en que la estatua se precipita contra la puerta de cristal, me giro y veo al guardia que se me acerca apresuradamente.

Durante una fracción de segundo pienso en detenerme para disculparme, pero decido cruzar rápidamente el vestíbulo y bajar corriendo por la escalera. El vigilante es demasiado viejo y corpulento para alcanzarme.

El vestíbulo principal está vacío, lo cruzo tranquilamente y abandono el edificio.

Son casi las siete, está oscureciendo y me detengo frente a una tienda de ultramarinos que se encuentra a seis manzanas. Un cartel escrito a mano anuncia latas de seis cervezas suaves por sólo tres pavos, justo lo que necesito en estos momentos.

Loyd Beck me había contratado hace dos meses, me había dicho que mis notas eran adecuadas, mi escritura correcta, mis entrevistas satisfactorias y la opinión de todos sus colaboradores unánime, en cuanto a que encajaría en la organización. Todo era maravilloso. Tenía un brillante futuro en el antiguo bufete de Brodnax & Speer.

Pero de pronto Trent & Brent les muestra un poco de dinero y los socios salen corriendo por la puerta de servicio. Esos cabrones avariciosos ganan trescientos mil al año y todavía quieren más.

Entro en la tienda y compro la cerveza. Después de pagar los impuestos me quedan cuatro dólares y algunas monedas en el bolsillo. Mi cuenta bancaria no está mucho mejor.

Sentado en mi coche, junto a una cabina telefónica, vacío mi primera lata de cerveza. No he comido nada desde el delicioso almuerzo hace unas horas con Dot, Buddy, Bosco y la señorita Birdie. Tal vez debí haber comido un poco más de puré, como Bosco. La cerveza fría llega a mi estómago vacío y se me sube inmediatamente a la cabeza.

No tardo mucho rato en beberme las demás latas. Pasan las horas mientras circulo por las calles de Memphis.

CUATRO

Mi piso es un cuchitril de dos habitaciones situado en el segundo piso de un ruinoso edificio de ladrillo llamado The Hampton,
por el que pago setenta y cinco dólares mensuales, raramente a
su debido tiempo. Está a una manzana de una ajetreada calle, a
un kilómetro y medio del campus. Es mi casa desde hace casi
tres años. Últimamente he pensado muchas veces en limitarme
a desaparecer en plena noche y luego intentar negociar alguna
forma de pagos mensuales, durante los próximos doce meses.
Hasta ahora dichos planes incluían la seguridad de un trabajo y
un cheque mensual de Brodnax & Speer. The Hampton está lleno de estudiantes, míseros como yo, y el administrador está
acostumbrado a luchar para cobrar los alquileres vencidos.

El aparcamiento está oscuro y silencioso cuando llego, poco
antes de las dos de la madrugada. Aparco cerca del contenedor
de basura, salgo, cierro la puerta y cuando me dispongo a alejarme de allí, algo se mueve de pronto relativamente cerca. Un
individuo se apea rápidamente de su coche, lo cierra de un portazo y viene directamente hacia mí. Quedo paralizado en la acera. Está todo oscuro y silencioso.

—¿Es usted Rudy Baylor? —pregunta, a escasos centímetros
de mi cara.

Es un perfecto vaquero: botas puntiagudas, Levi's ceñidos,
camisa de algodón azul, un corte de pelo impecable y barba.
Masca chicle y no parece adverso a usar los puños.

—¿Quién es usted? —pregunto yo.

—¿Es usted Rudy Baylor? ¿Sí o no?

—Sí.

Se saca unos papeles del bolsillo trasero y los agita ante mis
narices.

—Lo siento —dice sinceramente.

—¿De qué se trata? —pregunto.

—Citaciones.

Cojo lentamente los papeles. Está demasiado oscuro para leerlos, pero comprendo el mensaje.

—Usted es un funcionario del juzgado —digo derrotado.

—Sí.

—¿Texaco?

—Sí. Y The Hampton. Van a desahuciarlo.

Si estuviera sobrio, probablemente me asustaría tener una orden de desahucio en las manos. Pero ya he tenido bastantes sustos por un día. Contemplo en la oscuridad el lúgubre edificio con escombros en los parterres y hierbajos en la acera, y me pregunto cómo ese inmundo lugar ha podido conmigo.

—Está todo ahí —dice, y retrocede un paso—. Fecha del juicio, nombre de los abogados, etcétera. Es probable que pueda resolverlo con unas llamadas telefónicas. En todo caso, no es de mi incumbencia. Me limito a cumplir con mi obligación.

Menuda obligación. Acechar entre las tinieblas, asustar inesperadamente a la gente, agitar documentos ante sus narices, darles algún consejo legal gratuito y escabullirse para aterrorizar a otros.

—Por cierto —dice cuando ya se alejaba—. Soy ex policía y llevo un receptor oficial en el coche. Hace unas horas he oído una llamada curiosa. Cierto individuo llamado Rudy Baylor ha provocado desperfectos en un bufete del centro de la ciudad. Su descripción coincide con la suya. La misma marca y modelo de coche. Supongo que no tendrá nada que ver con usted.

—¿Y si lo tuviera?

—No es de mi incumbencia, ¿sabe? Pero le busca la policía. Destrucción de propiedad privada.

—¿Quiere decir que me detendrán?

—Sí. Yo en su lugar buscaría otro lugar donde dormir esta noche.

Entra en su BMW y veo cómo se aleja.

Booker me recibe en el portal de su pulcra casita de doble planta. Lleva una bata a cuadros sobre el pijama y va descalzo. Aunque no sea más que otro pobre estudiante de derecho que cuenta los días hasta que empiece su primer empleo, se preocupa de la moda. No hay mucho en su armario, pero sus prendas han sido cuidadosamente seleccionadas.

—¿Qué diablos ocurre? —pregunta nervioso, con los ojos todavía hinchados.

Lo he llamado por teléfono desde una cabina de teléfono que hay a la vuelta de la esquina.

—Lo siento —digo al entrar en su sala de estar.

Veo a Charlene en su diminuta cocina, también con una bata a cuadros, el cabello recogido en la nuca y los ojos hinchados, que prepara café o algo por el estilo. Oigo a un chiquillo que chilla desde algún lugar de la casa. Son casi las tres de la madrugada y he despertado a toda la familia.

—Siéntate —dice Booker cogiéndome del brazo para conducirme amablemente al sofá—. Has estado bebiendo.

—Estoy borracho, Booker.

—¿Alguna razón en particular? —pregunta de pie delante de mí, como un padre enojado.

—Es una larga historia.

—Has mencionado a la policía.

Charlene coloca una taza de café sobre la mesa frente a mí.

—¿Estás bien, Rudy? —pregunta con suma dulzura.

—Estupendo —respondo como un auténtico imbécil.

—Comprueba cómo están los niños —dice Booker y ella desaparece.

—Lo siento —repito.

Booker se sienta al borde de la mesilla, muy cerca de mí, y espera.

No presto atención al café. Me palpita la cabeza. Le cuento mi versión de lo sucedido desde que nos separamos ayer por la tarde. Se me traba la lengua y procuro concentrarme en lo que digo. Charlene se sienta en un sillón cercano y escucha con mucha preocupación.

—Lo siento —susurro en dirección a ella.

—No te preocupes, Rudy. No te preocupes.

El padre de Charlene es predicador en algún lugar rural de Tennessee y no tolera a los borrachos ni la conducta disoluta. Las pocas veces que Booker y yo hemos tomado alguna copa en la facultad, lo hemos hecho a escondidas.

—¿Te has tomado doce latas de cerveza? —pregunta Booker con incredulidad.

Charlene nos deja para ir a ver al niño, que ha vuelto a quejarse. Yo cuento lo de la citación, el pleito y el desahucio para concluir mi relato. Menudo día el de hoy.

—He de encontrar trabajo, Booker —digo y tomo un sorbo de café.

—En este momento tienes otros problemas más importantes. Dentro de tres meses nos presentamos al examen de colegiatura y luego ante la junta de selección. Una detención y una condena por esa gamberrada podrían arruinar tu carrera.

No se me había ocurrido. Ahora tengo una jaqueca terrible, parece que la cabeza me va a estallar.

—¿Podrías darme un bocadillo? Me siento mal. He comido

una bolsa de galletas saladas con mi segundo lote de cerveza, pero eso es todo desde el almuerzo con Bosco y la señorita Birdie.

—¿Te apetecen unos huevos con tocino? —pregunta Charlene, que me ha oído desde la cocina.

—Estupendo Charlene, gracias.

Booker está meditabundo.

—Dentro de unas horas llamaré a Marvin Shankle. Tal vez su hermano pueda utilizar su influencia con la policía. Debemos impedir que te detengan.

—Me parece una buena idea —respondo, consciente de que Marvin Shankle es el abogado negro más destacado de Memphis y futuro jefe de Booker—. De paso, pregúntale si tiene algún trabajo para mí.

—De acuerdo. Ahora quieres trabajar en un bufete negro que lucha por los derechos humanos.

—En estos momentos aceptaría un empleo en un bufete coreano especializado en divorcios. Sin ánimo de ofenderte, Booker. Debo encontrar trabajo. Van a declararme insolvente, amigo. También es posible que haya otros acreedores al acecho. No puedo más.

Me acuesto lentamente sobre el sofá. El olor a tocino que Charlene fríe en la cocina impregna el ambiente de la diminuta sala.

—¿Dónde están los papeles? —pregunta Booker.

—En el coche.

Abandona la sala y regresa al cabo de un momento. Se sienta en una silla cercana y examina la citación de Texaco y la orden de desahucio. Charlene deambula por la cocina, me trae más café y una aspirina. Son las tres y media de la madrugada. Por fin, los niños guardan silencio. Me siento seguro y protegido, incluso querido.

Todo gira lentamente a mi alrededor cuando cierro los ojos y me quedo dormido.

CINCO

Como una serpiente arrastrándose entre la maleza, entro sigilosamente en la facultad bastante después de las doce del mediodía, horas después de que hayan terminado las clases a las que debí haber asistido: Derecho deportivo y lecturas selectas del Código napoleónico; vaya chiste. Me oculto en mi rincón remoto del sótano de la biblioteca.

Booker me ha despertado en el sofá con la alentadora noticia de que había hablado con Marvin Shankle y las ruedas se movían en el centro de la ciudad. Intentaban ponerse en contacto con cierto capitán, o algo por el estilo, y el señor Shankle tenía la esperanza de poder llegar a un acuerdo. El hermano del señor Shankle es juez en uno de los tribunales de delitos penales y si no se logra anular la denuncia, quedan otros recursos. Pero todavía no se sabe con seguridad si la policía está buscándome. Booker haría unas llamadas y me mantendría informado.

Booker dispone ya de un despacho en el bufete de Shankle. Desde hace dos años trabaja allí a horas como pasante y ha aprendido más que cinco de nosotros. Llama a una secretaria entre clases, organiza diligentemente sus citas con los clientes y me habla de sus diversos casos. Será un gran abogado.

Es imposible organizar las ideas con resaca. Escarabajeo importantes notas en mi cuaderno, como por ejemplo, ¿qué voy a hacer ahora, después de llegar a este edificio sin ser detectado? Esperaré un par de horas, hasta que se vacíe la facultad. Es viernes por la tarde, el momento más tranquilo de la semana. Luego bajaré a la oficina de empleo, acorralaré a la directora y se lo contaré todo. Con un poco de suerte puede que todavía quede algún lúgubre empleo en la administración gubernamental rechazado por todos los licenciados, con un salario de veinte mil anuales para una brillante mente jurídica. O puede que algún pequeño bufete haya descubierto de pronto la necesidad de otro abogado en sus oficinas. A estas alturas, las posibilidades son escasas.

En Memphis hay un personaje legendario llamado Jonathan Lake, que se licenció en esta facultad y no pudo encontrar empleo en los grandes bufetes del centro de la ciudad. Ocurrió hace unos veinte años. Después de ser rechazado por todos los bufetes establecidos, alquiló un despacho, colgó un letrero y se declaró listo a demandar. Pasó hambre durante varios meses, hasta que una noche tuvo un accidente con su motocicleta y despertó con una pierna rota en el hospital de beneficencia de Saint Peter. Poco después, un individuo que también había tenido un accidente de moto ocupaba la cama de al lado. Dicho individuo sufría fracturas múltiples y quemaduras. Su novia estaba peor todavía y falleció a los pocos días. Se hicieron amigos, y Lake se responsabilizó de ambos casos. Resultó que el conductor del Jaguar que no había respetado la señal de stop y había embestido la moto en la que viajaban los nuevos clientes de Lake era el socio decano del tercer bufete de mayor envergadura de la ciudad. También era el mismo que, seis meses antes, había entrevistado a Lake. Además, conducía borracho cuando tuvo el accidente.

Lake lo demandó con saña. El socio decano borracho tenía un seguro muy completo y la compañía empezó a ofrecerle inmediatamente a Lake grandes cantidades de dinero. Todo el mundo deseaba zanjar el asunto cuanto antes. Seis meses después de colegiarse, Jonathan Lake aceptó una compensación de dos millones seiscientos mil dólares por ambos casos. Todo al contado, sin pagos atrasados.

Según reza la leyenda, cuando ambos estaban en el hospital, y puesto que Lake era tan joven y recién salido de la facultad, el motorista le ofreció la mitad de lo que recuperara. Lake no lo olvidó. El motorista cumplió su palabra. Se dice que Lake se llevó un millón trescientos mil.

Con un millón trescientos mil, yo me iría al Caribe, navegaría en mi propio queche y me dedicaría a saborear combinados de ron.

Pero Lake organizó un bufete, lo llenó de secretarias, pasantes e investigadores, y se dedicó seriamente a los pleitos. Trabajaba dieciocho horas diarias y estaba dispuesto a demandar a quien fuera por cualquier fechoría. Estudió mucho, perfeccionó su formación y pronto se convirtió en el abogado penalista más célebre de Tennessee.

Transcurridos veinte años, Jonathan Lake trabaja todavía dieciocho horas diarias, es propietario de un bufete con once miembros asociados, ningún socio, se ocupa de más pleitos importantes que cualquier otro abogado de la región y, según se dice, gana alrededor de tres millones anuales.

Y le gusta derrochar. Tres millones de pavos son difíciles de disimular en Memphis y Jonathan Lake es siempre noticia. Además, crece su leyenda. Cada año, un número indeterminado de estudiantes ingresa en esta facultad debido a Jonathan Lake. Tienen un sueño. Y unos cuantos licenciados dejan la facultad sin buscar empleo, porque lo único que desean es un pequeño despacho en la ciudad, con una placa en la puerta. Quieren sufrir y pasar hambre, al igual que Lake.

Sospecho que también circulan en moto. Puede que ése sea mi destino. Tal vez todavía quede esperanza. Yo y Lake.

Sorprendo a Leuberg en un mal momento. Está hablando por teléfono, expresándose con las manos y blasfemando como un marino borracho. Algo relacionado con un pleito en Saint Paul, en el que se supone que debe declarar. Finjo tomar notas, con la mirada en el suelo y procurando no escuchar, mientras él da grandes zancadas tras su escritorio sin soltar el teléfono.

—Los tiene agarrados por el cuello —dice rápidamente después de colgar mientras busca algo entre los montones de papeles de su escritorio.

—¿A quién?

—A Great Benefit. Anoche leí todos los documentos. Es un típico fraude de seguro a plazos —dice al tiempo que levanta una carpeta plegable y se deja caer en su silla con ella en las manos—. ¿Sabe qué es un seguro a plazos?

Creo saberlo, pero temo que me pregunte por los detalles.

—No exactamente —respondo.

—Los negros lo llaman «seguro callejero». Son pólizas baratas vendidas puerta a puerta, a personas de pocos ingresos. El agente que ha vendido la póliza suele pasar todas las semanas para cobrar la cuota y lo anota en el talonario de pagos que conserva el asegurado. Sus presas son personas de escasa educación y cuando hacen alguna reclamación basada en dichas pólizas, las compañías la deniegan sistemáticamente. Lo siento, por tal o cual razón, esto no está cubierto. Son sumamente imaginativos a la hora de buscar razones para no pagar.

—¿No se les denuncia?

—No muy a menudo. Los estudios demuestran que sólo un tercio de las denegaciones de mala fe acaban ante los tribunales. Las compañías, evidentemente, lo saben y es un factor que tienen en cuenta. No olvide que tratan con las clases sociales más bajas, con personas que tienen miedo de los abogados y del sistema jurídico.

—¿Qué ocurre cuando se les denuncia? —pregunto.

Agita las manos en dirección a una mosca o algún insecto volador, y dos papeles salen despedidos de su escritorio para aterrizar en el suelo.

Hace crujir violentamente las articulaciones de sus dedos.

—Por regla general, poca cosa. A lo largo y ancho del país, se han dado algunos casos de grandes compensaciones. Yo he participado personalmente en dos o tres de los mismos. Pero los jurados se resisten a convertir en millonarias a personas sencillas que compran seguros baratos. Reflexione. Aquí tenemos el caso de un demandante con facturas médicas legítimas por un total de unos cinco mil dólares, claramente cubiertos por la póliza. Pero la compañía de seguros, que dispone de un capital de unos doscientos millones, se niega a pagar. En el juicio, el abogado del demandante le pide al jurado los cinco mil dólares y también unos millones para castigar a la empresa fraudulenta. Raramente funciona. Otorgan los cinco mil, agregan unos diez mil como castigo, y la compañía vuelve a ganar.

—Pero Donny Ray Black está muriéndose porque no recibe el trasplante de médula al que tiene derecho según la póliza. ¿Estoy en lo cierto?

Leuberg me brinda una perversa sonrisa.

—Indudablemente la tiene, en el supuesto de que sus padres se lo hayan contado todo. Un supuesto siempre arriesgado.

—¿Pero si todo está aquí? —pregunto al tiempo que señalo la carpeta.

—Entonces, el caso es bastante sólido —asiente con una sonrisa y se encoge de hombros—. No es maravilloso, pero sí razonable.

—No lo comprendo.

—Es sencillo, Rudy. Esto es Tennessee. La tierra de los veredictos de cinco cifras. Aquí nadie recibe compensaciones punitivas. Los jurados son sumamente conservadores. Los ingresos per cápita son bastante bajos y los jurados tienen gran dificultad en convertir en ricos a sus vecinos. Memphis es un lugar particularmente difícil para obtener un veredicto razonable.

Apuesto a que Jonathan Lake lo lograría. Y tal vez me daría una pequeña comisión si le ofreciera el caso. A pesar de la resaca, las ruedas no dejan de girar en mi mente.

—¿Entonces qué hago? —pregunto.

—Demandar a esos cabrones.

—No estoy exactamente titulado.

—Usted no. Mande a esa gente a algún abogado famoso de la ciudad. Haga algunas llamadas en su nombre, hable con el abogado. Escriba un informe de un par de páginas para Smoot y lávese las manos —dice. El teléfono suena, él se incorpora de un brinco y empuja hacia mí la carpeta de los documentos—. Ahí hay una lista de tres docenas de casos de mala fe para que se los lea si le interesa.

—Gracias —respondo.

Agita la mano para que me marche. Cuando abandono el despacho, Max Leuberg está chillando por teléfono.

La Facultad de Derecho me ha enseñado a odiar la investigación. Hace ahora tres años que vivo aquí y he pasado por lo menos la mitad del tiempo hurgando viejos libros desgastados, en busca de antiguos casos para apoyar teorías jurídicas primitivas, en las que ningún abogado en su sano juicio ha pensado desde hace décadas. Aquí les encanta mandarle a uno en busca de tesoros perdidos. Los profesores, la mayoría de los cuales se dedican a la enseñanza porque son incapaces de funcionar en el mundo real, opinan que es útil para nuestra formación encontrar casos recónditos e incluirlos en vanos informes, a fin de obtener las buenas notas que nos permitirán incorporarnos a la profesión jurídica, como jóvenes abogados bien educados.

Esto fue particularmente cierto durante los dos primeros años en la facultad. Ahora no está tan mal. Incluso puede que el método no sea completamente descabellado. He oído millares de relatos de los grandes bufetes y de su costumbre de esclavizar a los novatos en la biblioteca durante dos años, escribiendo informes y testimonios de los juicios.

Todos los relojes se paran cuando uno se dedica a la investigación jurídica con resaca. La jaqueca empeora, las manos no dejan de temblar. Booker me encuentra el viernes por la noche en mi pequeño escondrijo, con una docena de libros abiertos sobre la mesa. La lista de casos que según Leuberg debo leer.

—¿Cómo estás? —pregunta.

Lleva traje y corbata, lo cual significa, indudablemente, que ha estado en el despacho recibiendo llamadas y dictando cartas, como un verdadero abogado.

—Bien.

Se agacha junto a mí y contempla el montón de libros.

—¿Qué es eso? —pregunta.

—Nada que ver con el examen de colegiatura. Sólo un poco de investigación para la clase de Smoot.

—Nunca habías investigado para la clase de Smoot.

—Lo sé. Me siento culpable.

Booker se pone de pie y se apoya en mi mesa.

—Dos cosas —dice, casi en un susurro—. El señor Shankle cree que el pequeño incidente en Brodnax & Speer ya está resuelto. Ha hecho algunas llamadas y le han asegurado que las presuntas víctimas han retirado la denuncia.

—Estupendo —respondo—. Gracias, Booker.

—No hay de qué. Creo que ahora ya puedes mostrarte en público. Siempre y cuando, claro está, seas capaz de abandonar tu investigación.

—Lo intentaré.

—En segundo lugar, he mantenido una larga charla con el señor Shankle. Acabo de salir de su despacho. Y el caso es que de momento no hay ninguna vacante. Ha contratado a tres nuevos miembros asociados, yo y otros dos de Washington, y no está seguro de que quepamos todos. Actualmente busca espacio para más despachos.

—No tenías por qué hacerlo, Booker.

—No era obligación, sino deseo. No tiene importancia. El señor Shankle ha prometido mantener los ojos y oídos abiertos, ya sabes, observar el campo. Conoce a mucha gente.

Estoy tan conmovido que me ha dejado casi sin habla. Hace veinticuatro horas contaba con la promesa de un buen empleo, con una bonita paga. Ahora, personas a las que ni siquiera conozco me hacen favores e intentan encontrarme algún tipo de trabajo.

—Gracias —respondo, y me muerdo el labio, con la mirada fija en mis dedos.

—Tengo prisa —dice consultando su reloj—. ¿Te apetece estudiar para el examen de colegiatura por la mañana?

—Por supuesto.

—Te llamaré.

Me da una palmada en el hombro y desaparece.

A las cinco menos diez subo por la escalera hasta la planta baja y abandono la biblioteca. Ahora ya no intento esconderme de la policía, ni temo encontrarme con Sara Plankmore, ni siquiera me preocupan las citaciones judiciales. Tampoco procuro evitar confrontaciones desagradables con algunos de mis condiscípulos. Todos se han marchado. Es viernes y la facultad está desierta.

La oficina de empleo está en la planta baja, cerca de la puerta principal, en la sección administrativa del edificio. Echo una ojeada al tablón de anuncios que hay en el vestíbulo, pero sigo andando. Normalmente está lleno de docenas de ofertas potenciales de trabajo: bufetes grandes, pequeños, despachos privados, empresas, agencias gubernamentales... Un vistazo me basta para confirmar lo que ya sabía. No hay un solo anuncio en el tablón. El mercado laboral está saturado en esta época del año.

Madeline Skinner dirige la oficina de colocación desde hace décadas. Se rumorea que está a punto de jubilarse, pero otro rumor afirma que amenaza con jubilarse todos los años para sacarle más dinero al decano. Tiene sesenta años y aparenta setenta. Es delgada, su cabello, corto y canoso, tiene multitud de arrugas alrededor de los ojos y un cigarrillo permanentemente encendido en el cenicero de su escritorio. Muchos aseguran que fuma cuatro cajetillas diarias, lo cual no deja de ser curioso, puesto que está oficialmente prohibido fumar en sus dependencias, aunque hasta ahora nadie ha tenido el valor de comunicárselo a Madeline. Goza de mucho poder, porque es ella quien atrae a los que ofrecen empleo. Sin trabajo, no habría Facultad de Derecho.

Además, desempeña muy bien su labor. Conoce a las personas adecuadas en los bufetes apropiados. En su momento encontró trabajo para muchos de los abogados que actualmente lo ofrecen y carece de escrúpulos. Si un licenciado de la Universidad Estatal de Memphis es responsable de la contratación de personal en un gran bufete y en el mismo predominan los licenciados de universidades elitistas del este, respecto a nuestra universidad, Madeline es perfectamente capaz de llamar al rector y formular una queja oficial. El rector ha llegado a visitar los grandes bufetes de la ciudad, almorzar con los socios y rectificar el desequilibrio. Madeline está al corriente de todos los empleos que aparecen en Memphis y conoce a las personas adecuadas para cada caso.

Pero su trabajo se pone difícil. Demasiada gente con título de abogado. Y ésta no es una universidad de élite.

Está de pie junto a la nevera, con la mirada en la puerta, como si estuviera esperándome.

—Hola, Rudy —dice con una voz grave.

Está sola, todos los demás se han marchado. Tiene un vaso de agua en una mano y un cigarrillo muy fino en la otra.

—Hola —respondo con una sonrisa, como si fuera la persona más feliz del mundo.

—Hablemos aquí —dice al tiempo que señala con el vaso la puerta de su despacho.

—Claro —respondo y la sigo.

Cierra la puerta y me ofrece una silla. Me siento donde me ordena y ella se instala al borde de su silla, al otro lado de la mesa.

—Menudo día, ¿no es cierto? —exclama, como si supiera todo lo que me ha ocurrido en las últimas veinticuatro horas.

—Los he tenido mejores.

—He hablado con Loyd Beck esta mañana —dice lentamente.

Esperaba que estuviera muerto.

—¿Y qué cuenta? —pregunto con presunta arrogancia.

—El caso es que anoche oí hablar de la fusión y me preocupé por usted. Es el único estudiante al que hemos colocado en Brodnax & Speer y estaba ansiosa por saber lo que le había sucedido.

—¿Y bien?

—Dice que la fusión se ha producido con mucha rapidez, una gran oportunidad, etcétera.

—Lo mismo que me han dicho a mí.

—Entonces le he preguntado cuándo le habían comunicado lo de la fusión, y me ha contestado de un modo confuso que un socio u otro había intentado llamarle un par de veces, pero el teléfono estaba desconectado.

—Ha estado desconectado cuatro días.

—Luego le he pedido que me mandara por fax la copia de cualquier correspondencia entre Brodnax & Speer y usted, Rudy Baylor, relacionada con la fusión y su función después de producirse.

—No hay ninguna.

—Lo sé. Él mismo me lo ha confesado. Lo cierto es que no hicieron nada hasta que la fusión ya se había efectuado.

—Exactamente. Nada.

Es reconfortante tener a Madeline de mi parte.

—Entonces le he explicado con sumo detalle cómo habían fastidiado a uno de nuestros licenciados y hemos mantenido una animada disputa telefónica.

No puedo evitar sonreírme. Sé quién ganó la disputa.

—Beck jura que no pensaban prescindir de usted —prosigue Madeline—. No estoy segura de creerle, pero le he explicado que debían haberlo hablado con usted hace mucho tiempo. Ahora es todavía un estudiante, casi licenciado, y a punto de convertirse en miembro asociado de un bufete, pero no un objeto. Le he dicho que sabía cómo explotaban al personal, pero también le he explicado que la esclavitud había sido abolida. No puede tomarlo o dejarlo, transferirlo o conservarlo, protegerlo o desecharlo a su antojo.

Ésa es mi chica. Exactamente lo que yo pienso.

—Después de nuestra discusión he hablado con el decano. El decano ha llamado a Donald Hucek, socio gerente de Tinley Britt. Han intercambiado varias llamadas y por fin Hucek le ha ofrecido la misma versión: Beck deseaba conservarlo, pero usted no reúne las condiciones que Tinley Britt exige a sus nuevos miembros asociados. El decano ha manifestado sus dudas y Hucek se ha comprometido a examinar su currículum y referencias.

—No hay lugar para mí en Trent & Brent —digo como si tuviera muchas opciones.

—Hucek piensa lo mismo que usted. Dice que Tinley Britt preferiría abstenerse.

—Estupendo —respondo, porque no se me ocurre nada más ingenioso que decir.

Madeline me conoce mejor. Sabe que estoy sufriendo.

—Tenemos muy poca influencia en Tinley Britt. Sólo han contratado a cinco de nuestros licenciados en los tres últimos años. Han crecido tanto que no se les puede presionar. Francamente, yo no querría trabajar con ellos.

Madeline intenta consolarme, hacerme sentir como si me hubiera ocurrido algo positivo. ¿Quién necesita a Trent & Brent y su salario inicial de cincuenta mil pavos anuales?

—¿Qué queda? —pregunto.

—No mucho —responde inmediatamente—. A decir verdad, nada —agrega después de consultar unas notas—. He llamado a todo el mundo que conozco. Había una vacante como ayudante de defensor público, a tiempo partido, doce mil anuales, pero se ocupó hace dos días. Se la ofrecí a Hall Pasterini. ¿Lo conoce? Bendito sea. Por fin ha encontrado trabajo.

Supongo que ahora la gente me bendice a mí.

—Y hay un par de perspectivas bastante buenas como asesor jurídico en pequeñas empresas, pero ambas exigen el examen de colegiatura aprobado.

El examen se celebra en julio. Por regla general, todos los bufetes contratan a sus nuevos miembros asociados inmediatamente después de la licenciatura, les pagan, los preparan para el examen y cuando lo aprueban están ya en plena carrera.

—Seguiré buscando, ¿de acuerdo? —dice después de dejar sus notas sobre el escritorio—. Puede que aparezca algo.

—¿Qué puedo hacer yo?

—Empezar a llamar de puerta en puerta. Hay tres mil abogados en esta ciudad, la mayoría de los cuales trabajan solos, o en despachos de dos o tres letrados. Éstos no tratan con nuestro servicio de colocación, de modo que no los conocemos. Vaya a su encuentro. Yo empezaría por los pequeños bufetes, de dos, tres o cuatro abogados, e intentaría convencerlos. Ofrézcase para trabajar en sus sumarios de pescado, ocuparse de sus cobros atrasados...

—¿Sumarios de pescado? —pregunto.

—Por supuesto. Todos los abogados tienen un montón de sumarios de pescado. Los guardan en un rincón y cuanto más tiempo pasa, peor huelen. Son los casos que los abogados desearían no haber aceptado.

Las cosas que no le enseñan a uno en la facultad.

—¿Puedo hacerle una pregunta?

—Claro. ¿De qué se trata?

—Ese consejo que acaba de darme sobre llamar de puerta en puerta, ¿cuántas veces lo ha repetido en los últimos tres meses?

Sonríe brevemente, después consulta un papel impreso.

—Tenemos unos quince estudiantes que todavía no han encontrado trabajo.

—Y que en estos momentos están recorriendo las calles.

—Probablemente. En realidad es difícil saberlo. Algunos tienen otros planes, que no siempre comparten conmigo.

Son más de las cinco y Madeline quiere marcharse.

—Gracias, señora Skinner. Gracias por todo. Es agradable saber que alguien se interesa.

—Seguiré buscando, se lo prometo. Venga a verme la semana próxima.

—Lo haré. Gracias.

Regreso sin ser visto a mi mesa en la biblioteca.

SEIS

La casa Birdsong está relativamente cerca del centro de la ciudad, en una zona antigua y adinerada, a sólo unos tres kilómetros de la Facultad de Derecho. Sus viejos robles a lo largo de las aceras le brindan un aspecto recluido. Algunas de sus casas son hermosas, con jardines impecables y lujosos coches que brillan frente a sus puertas. Otras parecen casi abandonadas y asoman fantasmagóricamente entre una tupida jungla de árboles descuidados y silvestres matorrales. También las hay entre lo uno y lo otro. La de la señorita Birdie es una casa victoriana de piedra blanca, de principios de siglo, con un extenso pórtico que se extiende más allá de la fachada. Necesita pintura, un nuevo tejado y cierto trabajo en el jardín. Las ventanas están mugrientas y las alcantarillas llenas de hojas, pero es evidente que alguien vive en ella e intenta cuidarla. El camino de entrada está marcado por unos setos desiguales. Aparco mi coche tras un sucio Cadillac, que tiene probablemente unos diez años.

Los tablones del pórtico crujen cuando me acerco a la puerta principal, sin dejar de mirar a mi alrededor por si aparece un perro enorme de dientes afilados. Es tarde, ya casi ha oscurecido, y no hay luces en la entrada. La gruesa puerta de madera está abierta de par en par y a través de la tela mosquitera vislumbro las formas de un pequeño vestíbulo. Puesto que no encuentro ningún timbre, llamo a la puerta mosquitera, que baila ruidosamente. Me aguanto la respiración; no oigo el ladrido de ningún perro.

Ningún ruido, ningún movimiento. Golpeo un poco más fuerte la puerta.

—¿Quién es? —pregunta una voz familiar.

—¿Señorita Birdie?

Aparece una silueta en el vestíbulo, se enciende una luz y ahí está, con el mismo vestido de algodón que llevaba ayer en el Parque de los Cipreses. Mira a través de la tela mosquitera.

—Soy yo. Rudy Baylor. El estudiante de Derecho con el que habló ayer.

—¡Rudy! —exclama, encantada de verme.

Después de sentirme momentáneamente avergonzado, me embarga de pronto la tristeza. Vive sola en esa monstruosa mansión, convencida de que su familia la ha abandonado. Lo más emocionante en su vida es cuidar de esos ancianos desamparados, que se reúnen para almorzar y cantar un par de canciones. La señorita Birdie Birdsong es una persona solitaria.

Abre apresuradamente la tela mosquitera.

—Pase, pase —repite, sin la menor curiosidad.

Me coge del brazo y me conduce por el vestíbulo y el pasillo, pulsando interruptores a su paso. Las paredes están cubiertas de docenas de retratos familiares. Las alfombras, polvorientas y desgastadas. Es una casa antigua, de aire rancio y enmohecido, que pide a gritos una buena limpieza.

—Me alegro de que haya venido —dice con dulzura, sin dejar de estrujarme el brazo—. ¿No se divirtió ayer con nosotros?

—Sí, señora.

—¿Volverá otro día?

—Me muero de impaciencia.

Me instala junto a la mesa de la cocina.

—¿Té o café? —pregunta mientras se acerca a los armarios de la cocina, sin dejar de pulsar interruptores.

—Café —respondo, al tiempo que miro a mi alrededor.

—¿Le parece bien instantáneo?

—Perfecto.

Después de tres años en la Facultad de Derecho, soy incapaz de distinguir el café real del instantáneo.

—¿Nata o azúcar? —pregunta con la mano en la nevera.

—Solo.

Pone a calentar el agua, prepara las tazas y se sienta al otro lado de la mesa. Sonríe de oreja a oreja. Le he alegrado el día.

—Me alegro mucho de verlo —dice por tercera o cuarta vez.

—Tiene una casa hermosa, señorita Birdie —digo mientras respiro el aire enmohecido.

—Muchas gracias. Thomas y yo la compramos hace cincuenta años.

Las ollas y las sartenes, el fregadero y los grifos, el fogón y la tostadora tienen, por lo menos, cuarenta años. El frigorífico es probablemente de principios de los años sesenta.

—Thomas falleció hace once años. Aquí se criaron nuestros dos hijos, pero prefiero no hablar de ellos.

Su alegre rostro adquiere momentáneamente un aspecto sombrío, pero no tarda en volver a sonreír.

—Claro. Por supuesto.

—Hablemos de usted —dice.

Es un tema que preferiría evitar.

—Desde luego. ¿Por qué no? —respondo, mientras me pongo en guardia para sus preguntas.

—¿De dónde es?

—Nací aquí, pero me crié en Knoxville.

—Estupendo. ¿Y dónde estudió?

—En Austin Peay.

—¿Austin qué?

—Austin Peay. Es una pequeña escuela de Clarksville, subvencionada por el estado.

—Muy interesante. ¿Por qué eligió la Facultad de Derecho de la Universidad Estatal de Memphis?

—Es una buena facultad y, además, me gusta Memphis.

A decir verdad, hay otras dos razones: en la Universidad de Memphis me aceptaron y podía permitírmelo.

—Estupendo. ¿Cuándo se licencia?

—Dentro de unas pocas semanas.

—Entonces será un verdadero abogado, estupendo. ¿Dónde va a trabajar?

—Todavía no estoy demasiado seguro. Últimamente he pensado bastante en colocar mi propia placa, ya sabe, trabajar por mi cuenta. Soy una persona bastante independiente y no estoy seguro de poder trabajar con otra gente. Me gusta la idea de tener mi propio despacho.

Me mira fijamente. Su sonrisa ha desaparecido. Sus ojos no se separan de los míos. Está confusa.

—Es maravilloso —dice por fin, y se levanta para preparar el café.

Si esa encantadora viejecita es multimillonaria, lo disimula a la perfección. Examino la sala. La mesa bajo mis codos tiene patas de aluminio y una superficie desgastada de formica. Todos los muebles, utensilios y aparatos fueron adquiridos hace varias décadas. Vive en una casa relativamente abandonada y conduce un viejo coche. No parece tener sirvientas ni criados. Ni ningún elegante perrito de compañía.

—Estupendo —repite mientras coloca las tazas sobre la mesa.

No emana vapor de las mismas. La mía está ligeramente caliente. El café es flojo, insípido y pasado.

—Buen café —digo al tiempo que hago chasquear los labios.

—Gracias. ¿De modo que piensa abrir su propio pequeño bufete?

—Estoy pensándolo. Sé que al principio será difícil. Pero si trabajo mucho y trato debidamente a la gente, luego no tendré que preocuparme de buscar clientes.

Sonríe con sinceridad y mueve lentamente la cabeza.

—Eso es maravilloso, Rudy. Tiene mucho valor. Creo que la profesión necesita más jóvenes como usted.

Yo soy lo último que necesita la profesión: otro buitre hambriento merodeando por las calles, buscando basura para los tribunales, intentando forzar algún acontecimiento para extraerles algún dinero a clientes destituidos.

—Puede que se pregunte por qué estoy aquí —digo entre sorbos de café.

—Me alegro de que haya venido.

—Yo también me alegro de volver a verla. Pero quería hablar con usted de su testamento. Estaba tan preocupado que anoche no pude conciliar el sueño pensando en sus bienes.

Se le humedecen los ojos. Está emocionada.

—Hay algunas cosas que me preocupan particularmente —declaro, con el ceño propio de un buen abogado, al tiempo que me saco la pluma del bolsillo para entrar en acción—. En primer lugar, y le ruego que no se lo tome a mal, me inquieta realmente que usted, o cualquier cliente, tome unas medidas tan duras con su propia familia.

La señorita Birdie aprieta los labios, pero no responde.

—En segundo lugar, y de nuevo le ruego que me disculpe, no podría vivir conmigo mismo como abogado si no le mencionara mi profunda aversión a redactar un testamento, o cualquier otro documento, mediante el cual le otorgue la mayor parte de una fortuna a un personaje de la televisión.

—Es un hombre de Dios —responde enfáticamente la señorita Birdie para defender la integridad del reverendo Kenneth Chandler.

—Lo sé. De acuerdo. ¿Pero por qué dejárselo todo, señorita Birdie? ¿Por qué no el veinticinco por ciento, por ejemplo, que sería perfectamente razonable?

—Tiene muchos gastos. Y su reactor está haciéndose viejo. Me lo ha contado todo.

—De acuerdo, pero el Señor no espera que le financie usted todos los gastos al reverendo, ¿no es cierto?

—Lo que me diga el Señor es privado, gracias.

—Por supuesto. Lo que intento decirle, y estoy seguro de que usted lo sabe, es que muchos de esos personajes han tenido grandes tropiezos, señorita Birdie. Se ha descubierto que muchos de ellos despilfarran millones dándose la gran vida: casas, coches, vacaciones, vestuario... Muchos son estafadores.

—No es un estafador.

—No he dicho que lo fuera.

—¿Qué pretende insinuar?

—Nada —respondo, tomo un largo trago de café y compruebo que no está enojada, pero poco le falta—. Estoy aquí como abogado, señorita Birdie, eso es todo. Usted me pidió que le redactara un testamento, y mi obligación es la de interesarme por todo su contenido. Tomo seriamente mi responsabilidad.

Desaparece la multitud de surcos alrededor de su boca y se suaviza de nuevo su mirada.

—Es usted amable —dice.

Supongo que muchos ancianos ricos como la señorita Birdie, especialmente los que sufrieron durante la gran depresión y han amasado su propia fortuna, protegen celosamente su dinero con la ayuda de contables, abogados y desagradables banqueros. Pero la señorita Birdie es tan ingenua y confiada como una pobre viuda jubilada.

—Necesita el dinero —dice, después toma un sorbo de café y me mira con cierta desconfianza.

—¿Podemos hablar del dinero?

—¿Por qué quieren los abogados hablar siempre del dinero?

—Hay muy buenas razones para ello, señorita Birdie. Si no toma ciertas precauciones, el gobierno se quedará con gran parte de sus bienes. Ahora pueden aplicarse algunas medidas, una cuidadosa organización del capital, que permitan ahorrar muchos impuestos.

—Tanto galimatías jurídico —exclama frustrada.

—Para eso estoy aquí, señorita Birdie.

—Supongo que quiere que incluya su nombre en algún lugar del testamento —dice, preocupada todavía por los tecnicismos de la ley.

—Claro que no —respondo, procurando aparentar asombro, pero también intentando ocultar la sorpresa de haber sido descubierto.

—Los abogados siempre intentan que incluya su nombre en mi testamento.

—Lo siento, señorita Birdie. Hay muchos abogados deshonestos.

—Eso dice el reverendo Chandler.

—No me cabe la menor duda. Escúcheme, no necesito saber todos los detalles, ¿pero puede decirme si el dinero está invertido en propiedades inmobiliarias, acciones, bonos, fondos u otros tipos de inversión? Es muy importante saber dónde está el dinero para la organización de los bienes.

—Todo está en el mismo lugar.

—Muy bien. ¿Dónde?

—En Atlanta.

—¿Atlanta?

—Sí. Es una larga historia, Rudy.

—¿Por qué no me la cuenta?

Al contrario de ayer en el Parque de los Cipreses, hoy la señorita Birdie no tiene ninguna prisa, ninguna responsabilidad. Bosco no merodea por los alrededores. No hay que ocuparse de la limpieza de las mesas, ni arbitrar ningún juego.

De modo que hace girar lentamente la taza y reflexiona con la mirada fija en la mesa.

—Realmente nadie lo sabe —dice con la voz muy baja al tiempo que suenan un par de golpes secos de su dentadura postiza—. Por lo menos nadie en Memphis.

—¿Por qué no? —pregunto, tal vez con excesivo entusiasmo.

—Mis hijos no lo saben.

—¿Lo del dinero? —pregunto con incredulidad.

—Bueno, conocen la existencia de una parte. Thomas trabajó muchísimo y ahorramos bastante. Cuando murió, hace once años, me dejó casi cien mil dólares. Mis hijos, y especialmente sus esposas, están convencidos de que el capital se ha multiplicado ahora por cinco. Pero no saben nada de Atlanta. ¿Le apetece otro café? —pregunta mientras se pone de pie.

—Por supuesto.

Coge mi taza, vierte en la misma algo más de media cucharadita de café en polvo, agrega agua tibia y la coloca de nuevo sobre la mesa. Remuevo el líquido como si anticipara un exótico capuchino.

Nuestras miradas se encuentran y expreso sólo compasión.

—Escúcheme, señorita Birdie. Si esto le resulta demasiado penoso, podemos ahorrárnoslo. Ya sabe, nos ocuparemos sólo de los detalles más importantes.

—Se trata de una fortuna. ¿Por qué tendría que ser penoso? Exactamente lo que yo pensaba.

—Muy bien. Cuénteme sólo, en términos generales, cómo está invertido el dinero. Estoy particularmente interesado en la propiedad inmobiliaria.

Es cierto. El dinero al contado y otras inversiones líquidas suelen saldarse en primer lugar para pagar impuestos. La propiedad inmobiliaria se utiliza como último recurso. De modo que no sólo la mera curiosidad motiva mis preguntas.

—Nunca le he hablado a nadie del dinero —responde, con la voz todavía muy suave.

—Sin embargo, usted me dijo ayer que se lo había contado a Kenneth Chandler.

Se hace una larga pausa mientras hace girar la taza sobre la formica.

—Sí, supongo que lo he hecho. Pero no estoy segura de habérselo contado todo. Puede que le mintiera sólo un poco. Y estoy segura de que no le revelé sus orígenes.

—De acuerdo. ¿De dónde procede?

—De mi segundo marido.

—¿Segundo marido?

—Sí, Tony.

—¿Thomas y Tony?

—Sí. Unos dos años después de la muerte de Thomas, me casé con Tony. Era de Atlanta y estaba más o menos de paso por Memphis cuando nos conocimos. Vivimos juntos, a temporadas, durante cinco años. Peleábamos continuamente. Luego me abandonó y regresó a Atlanta. Era un desgraciado que se interesaba sólo por mi dinero.

—Estoy confuso. ¿No me había dicho que el dinero procedía de Tony?

—Así es. Lo que ocurre es que él no lo sabía. Es una larga historia. Había ciertas herencias y propiedades que tanto Tony como yo desconocíamos. Tenía un hermano rico que estaba loco, en realidad todos los miembros de su familia estaban locos, y poco antes de morir, Tony heredó una fortuna de él. Exactamente dos días antes de que Tony estirara la pata, su hermano falleció en Florida. Tony murió sin testamento, su única posesión era una esposa: yo. Entonces, un importante bufete de abogados de Atlanta se puso en contacto conmigo para comunicarme que según la ley de Georgia había heredado un montón de dinero.

—¿Cuánto dinero?

—Muchísimo más de lo que Tony me había dejado. El caso es que no se lo he contado nunca a nadie. Hasta ahora. ¿Usted tampoco lo contará, verdad, Rudy?

—Señorita Birdie, como abogado suyo no puedo revelarlo. Mi juramento me obliga a guardar silencio. Se denomina secreto profesional.

—Estupendo.

—¿Por qué no le contó lo del dinero a su último abogado?

—En realidad no me inspiraba confianza. Me limité a dictarle las cantidades necesarias para los donativos, sin revelarle la cuantía del capital. Cuando dedujo que estaba forrada, quería a toda costa que incluyera su nombre en el testamento.

—¿Pero nunca se lo contó todo?

—Nunca.

—¿No le dijo de cuánto disponía?

—No.

Si mis cálculos son correctos, su antiguo testamento contenía donativos por un total de veinte millones como mínimo. De modo que el abogado conocía la existencia de por lo menos dicho capital, puesto que redactó el testamento. La pregunta evidente es: ¿de cuánto dinero dispone exactamente esta encantadora viejecita?

—¿Piensa decirme de cuánto dispone?

—Tal vez mañana, Rudy. Tal vez mañana.

Salimos de la cocina y nos dirigimos al jardín posterior. Tiene una fuente nueva junto a los rosales y desea mostrármela. La admiro atentamente.

Ahora lo veo claro. La señorita Birdie es una viejecita rica, pero no quiere que nadie lo sepa, especialmente su familia. Siempre ha gozado de comodidades en la vida y ahora, como viuda de ochenta años, no despierta sospechas al vivir de sus ahorros sobradamente adecuados.

Nos sentamos en unos bancos con ornamentos de hierro forjado y tomamos café frío en la oscuridad, hasta que por fin se me ocurren suficientes pretextos para huir.

Para financiar mi lujoso estilo de vida, durante los últimos tres años he trabajado como barman y camarero en Yogi's, un tugurio estudiantil junto al campus. Es conocido por sus suculentas hamburguesas con cebolla y por su cerveza verde el día de San Patricio. Es un lugar bullicioso, donde no cesa la animación desde la hora del almuerzo hasta la de cerrar por la noche. Las jarras de cerveza suave y aguada cuestan un dólar durante la «hora del fútbol del lunes por la noche» y dos dólares en cualquier otra ocasión.

Su propietario es Prince Thomas, un adicto al ron, con cola de caballo, un cuerpo enorme y un ego todavía mayor. Prince es uno de los personajes más pintorescos de la ciudad, un gran emprendedor a quien le encanta ver su fotografía en el periódico y aparecer en las noticias de la noche. Organiza peregrinaciones por los bares y concursos de camisetas mojadas. Ha solicitado permiso municipal para que locales como el suyo puedan permanecer abiertos toda la noche. El municipio, por su parte, le ha demandado por varios de sus pecados. Está encantado. Basta sugerirle un vicio para que organice un grupo e intente legalizarlo.

Prince dirige Yogi's con un gran margen de autonomía. Nosotros, los empleados, organizamos nuestro propio horario, administramos las propinas y trabajamos con escasa supervisión.

Tampoco tiene nada de complicado. Con suficiente cerveza tras el mostrador y abundante carne picada en la cocina, el local funciona con una precisión asombrosa. Prince prefiere ocuparse del público. Le encanta recibir a las atractivas estudiantes y acompañarlas a sus mesas. Coquetea con ellas y, en general, se pone en ridículo. Le gusta sentarse a una mesa junto a la gran pantalla y apostar en los partidos. Es un individuo corpulento con brazos musculosos, que de vez en cuando para alguna pelea.

Hay un lado oscuro de Prince. Se rumorea que está involucrado en juegos de apuestas fraudulentos. Los locales *topless* constituyen un comercio floreciente en esta ciudad y sus presuntos socios tienen antecedentes penales. Lo han publicado los periódicos. Le han juzgado dos veces por administrar apuestas ilegales, pero en ambos casos el jurado no logró llegar a conclusión alguna. Después de trabajar para él durante tres años, estoy convencido de dos cosas: en primer lugar, Prince se embolsa casi todo el dinero de la caja de Yogi's, y en segundo lugar, Prince utiliza Yogi's como tapadera de su pequeño imperio de corrupción. Lo usa para blanquear dinero y todos los años declara pérdidas, por razones de impuestos. Tiene un despacho en el sótano, un cuarto bastante seguro desprovisto de ventanas, donde se reúne con sus compinches.

A mí me da exactamente lo mismo. Se ha portado bien conmigo. Gano cinco pavos por hora y trabajo veinte horas semanales. Nuestros clientes son estudiantes y, por consiguiente, las propinas son pequeñas. Puedo cambiar de horario en época de exámenes. Todos los días vienen por lo menos cinco estudiantes en busca de trabajo, de modo que me siento afortunado de tener un empleo.

Y, a pesar de todo lo demás que pueda ocultar, Yogi's es un lugar muy agradable para los estudiantes. Prince lo pintó hace años de azul y gris, los colores de la Universidad de Memphis, y las paredes están cubiertas de banderines del equipo y fotografías deportivas. Hay tigres por todas partes. Está a un corto paseo del campus y acuden muchos estudiantes, que pasan horas charlando, riéndose y coqueteando.

Esta noche está mirando un partido. La temporada de béisbol acaba de empezar, pero Prince ya está convencido de que los Braves se clasificarán para las finales de la serie. Apuesta por cualquier cosa, pero su sujeto predilecto son los Braves. Poco importa dónde o contra quién jueguen, quién lance o quién esté lesionado, Prince apuesta siempre por los Braves.

Esta noche me ocupo del bar principal, donde mi función primordial consiste en asegurarme de que su vaso de ron con agua tónica no esté nunca vacío. Grita de alegría cuando Dave Justice gana una espectacular carrera y a continuación recauda el dinero de sus compadres. La apuesta consistía en adivinar si sería Dave Justice o Barry Bonds quien ganaría la primera carrera. Lo he visto apostar sobre si el segundo bateador en la tercera entrada acertaría o no el primer lanzamiento.

Menos mal que no sirvo a las mesas esta noche. Todavía me duele la cabeza y necesito moverme lo menos posible. Además, así puedo tomarme de vez en cuando una cerveza fresca de buena calidad, las de la botella de color verde, Heineken y Moosehead. Prince espera que su camarero beba un poco.

Echaré de menos este trabajo. ¿En serio?

Una de las primeras mesas se llena de estudiantes de derecho, caras familiares que prefiero evitar. Son mis condiscípulos, alumnos de tercero, probablemente todos ellos con trabajo.

No tiene nada de malo ser barman o camarero cuando uno es estudiante, en realidad da cierto prestigio trabajar en Yogi's. Pero el prestigio desaparecerá de repente en menos de un mes, cuando me licencie. Entonces me convertiré en algo mucho peor que un estudiante en apuros. Me convertiré en un siniestro, una estadística, otro estudiante de derecho caído por la borda de la profesión jurídica.

SIETE

Sinceramente no recuerdo el criterio que formulé y luego utilicé para elegir el bufete de Aubrey H. Long & Associates como primera alternativa, pero creo que tuvo algo que ver con su atractivo y, en cierto modo, respetable anuncio en las páginas amarillas, que iba acompañado de una sobria fotografía en blanco y negro del señor Long. El afán de los abogados por mostrar su rostro en todas partes empieza a parecerse al de los quiroterapeutas. Parecía un individuo sincero, de unos cuarenta años y con una agradable sonrisa, que contrastaba con la mayoría de los retratos en la sección de abogados. En su bufete, que está especializado en accidentes automovilísticos, hay cuatro abogados que siempre procuran que se haga justicia. Se ocupan primordialmente de lesiones y reclamaciones a compañías de seguros, luchan por sus clientes y no les cobran un centavo hasta que algo se recupera.

Qué diablos. Por algún lugar hay que empezar. Busco la dirección en el centro de la ciudad y encuentro un pequeño edificio cuadrado, realmente feo, junto a un aparcamiento gratuito, que se mencionaba también en las páginas amarillas. Empujo la puerta y suena una campanilla. Una mujer rolliza, tras un abarrotado escritorio, me recibe con una mirada displicente. La he obligado a dejar de mecanografiar.

—¿Puedo hacer algo por usted? —pregunta, con sus rollizos dedos a escasos centímetros del teclado.

Maldita sea, esto no es fácil. Fuerzo una sonrisa.

—Sí, me preguntaba si sería posible ver al señor Long.

—Está en el tribunal federal —responde, e inmediatamente dos de sus dedos golpean el teclado y generan una pequeña palabra.

¡No en cualquier tribunal, sino en el federal! El tribunal federal es para los casos importantes, de modo que cuando un picapleitos como Aubrey Long comparece ante el mismo, quiere asegurarse de que todo el mundo lo sepa. Le ordena a su secretaria que lo divulgue.

—¿Puedo hacer algo por usted? —repite.

He decidido ser sincero. El fraude y el engaño pueden esperar, aunque no mucho.

—Sí, me llamo Rudy Baylor. Soy estudiante de tercer curso de derecho en la Universidad Estatal de Memphis, estoy a punto de licenciarme y, bueno, lo que yo busco es trabajo.

Su mueca se convierte en una enorme sonrisa burlona. Separa las manos del teclado, hace girar la silla para mirarme y empieza a mover lentamente la cabeza.

—No contratamos —declara con cierto deleite.

—De acuerdo. ¿Le importaría que dejara mi currículum junto con una carta para el señor Long?

Coge escrupulosamente los papeles, como si estuvieran empapados de orina, y los deja caer sobre su escritorio.

—Los pondré con los demás —dice.

Logro obligarme a soltar una carcajada y brindarle una sonrisa.

—¿Entonces somos muchos los que venimos a solicitar empleo?

—Uno por día, diría yo.

—Qué le vamos a hacer. Siento haberla molestado.

—No tiene importancia —refunfuña, y regresa sobre su máquina de escribir.

Cuando doy media vuelta para abandonar el edificio empieza a teclear furiosamente.

Tengo un montón de cartas y copias de mi currículum. He pasado el fin de semana preparando el papeleo y organizando el ataque. En estos momentos, me sobra estrategia y me falta optimismo. He previsto seguir así durante un mes, visitar dos o tres pequeños bufetes todos los días, cinco días por semana, hasta mi licenciatura, y luego quién sabe. Booker ha convencido a Marvin Shankle para que escudriñe el mundo judicial en busca de un empleo y en estos momentos Madeline Skinner probablemente está hablando por teléfono para exigir que alguien me contrate.

Puede que algo funcione.

El segundo de la lista es un bufete de tres abogados, a dos manzanas del primero. En realidad he organizado mi estrategia para poder pasar con rapidez de un rechazo a otro sin perder tiempo.

Según el anuario jurídico, Nunley, Ross & Perry es un bufete de abogacía general, constituido por tres letrados de poco más de cuarenta años, sin miembros asociados ni pasantes.

Gran parte de su trabajo parecen ser las transacciones inmobiliarias, que me resultan insoportables, aunque éste no es el momento de dejarme llevar por mis escrúpulos. Están en el tercer piso de un moderno edificio de hormigón. El ascensor es lento y dentro hace calor.

La zona de recepción es muy agradable, con una alfombra oriental sobre un suelo de madera noble sintética. Sobre una mesilla de cristal veo ejemplares de *People* y *Us*. La secretaria cuelga el teléfono y sonríe.

—Buenos días. ¿Puedo hacer algo por usted?

—Sí. Deseo ver al señor Nunley.

Sin dejar de sonreír, dirige la mirada a una gruesa agenda sobre su impecable escritorio.

—¿Tiene usted una cita? —pregunta, perfectamente consciente de que no la tengo.

—No.

—Comprendo. El señor Nunley está muy ocupado en este momento.

Puesto que trabajé en un bufete el año pasado, tenía la absoluta seguridad de que el señor Nunley estaría muy ocupado. Es lo habitual. Ningún abogado del mundo admitiría, ni permitiría que lo hiciera su secretaria, que no estaba agobiado de trabajo.

Podría ser peor. Esta mañana podía haber estado en el tribunal federal.

Roderick Nunley es el socio decano de este bufete y, según el anuario jurídico, licenciado de la Universidad Estatal de Memphis. He procurado incluir en mi plan de ataque tantos ex alumnos de mi facultad como he podido.

—No me importa esperar —digo, y le dirijo una sonrisa.

Ella también sonríe. Todos sonreímos. Se abre una puerta del corto pasillo y se nos acerca un individuo en mangas de camisa. Levanta la cabeza, me ve y de pronto estamos cerca el uno del otro. Le entrega una carpeta a la sonriente secretaria.

—Buenos días —dice—. ¿Qué puedo hacer por usted? —pregunta, con una voz clara y realmente agradable.

La secretaria intenta responder, pero yo me anticipo.

—Tengo que hablar con el señor Nunley —digo.

—Soy yo —responde al tiempo que me tiende la mano derecha—. Rod Nunley.

—Me llamo Rudy Baylor —contesto mientras estrecho fuertemente su mano—. Soy estudiante de tercer curso en la Universidad Estatal de Memphis, estoy a punto de licenciarme, y quería hablar con usted de trabajo.

Estamos estrechándonos todavía la mano y no percibo ningún relajamiento cuando menciono el empleo.

—Claro —dice—. ¿De modo que busca trabajo? —agrega al tiempo que mira a la secretaria, como para preguntarle «¿cómo ha podido permitir que sucediera esto?».

—Sí, señor. Si pudiera concederme sólo diez minutos. Sé que está muy ocupado.

—Bueno, el caso es que dentro de unos minutos debo tomar una declaración jurada y luego me esperan en la audiencia —responde después de dar media vuelta, mirarme, echarle una ojeada a su secretaria y consultar su reloj.

Pero en el fondo es una buena persona, con una faceta amable. Puede que un día no muy lejano estuviera en mi lugar. Le suplico con la mirada, al tiempo que le ofrezco una delgada carpeta con mi currículum y una carta.

—De acuerdo, pase, pero sólo un momento.

—Le llamaré dentro de diez minutos —dice inmediatamente la secretaria para congraciarse con su jefe.

—Bien, diez minutos máximo —dice en un tono grave después de contemplar varios segundos su reloj, como todo buen abogado—. Y llame a Blanche. Dígale que llegaré unos minutos tarde.

Se han recuperado los dos de maravilla. Me atenderán, pero no antes de organizar conjuntamente mi pronta partida.

—Sígame, Rudy —agrega con una sonrisa.

Le piso los talones por el pasillo.

Su despacho es una sala cuadrada, con una pared cubierta de libros tras el escritorio y una impresionante selección de diplomas en la pared frente a la puerta. Examino los documentos enmarcados: un certificado de asistencia al Rotary Club, Boy Scout voluntario, abogado del mes, por lo menos dos licenciaturas, una fotografía de Rod con un político de rostro encarnado, afiliación a la Cámara de Comercio... Ese individuo enmarca cualquier cosa.

Sentado frente a su enorme escritorio puedo oír el tictac del reloj.

—Discúlpeme por irrumpir sin previo aviso en su despacho —empiezo a decir—, pero realmente necesito un trabajo.

—¿Cuándo se licencia? —pregunta, con los codos apoyados sobre la mesa.

—El mes próximo. Sé que es tarde para buscar trabajo, pero tengo una buena razón.

A continuación le hablo de mi empleo en Brodnax & Speer. Cuando llego a la parte de Tinley Britt, hago hincapié en lo que espero que sea su repulsión por los grandes bufetes. Es una rivalidad natural, los abogados independientes, como mi compañero Rod aquí presente, los que tienen pequeños despachos en la ciudad, frente a los de calcetines de seda de los grandes edificios. Miento un poco cuando le cuento que Tinley Britt había intentado convencerme para que trabajara para ellos, hasta llegar convenientemente a la conclusión de que no podría en modo alguno trabajar para un gran bufete. Simplemente no lo llevo en la sangre. Soy demasiado independiente. Quiero representar a la gente, no a las grandes corporaciones.

Esto dura menos de cinco minutos.

Es un buen oyente, un poco nervioso con el ruido de fondo de los teléfonos. Sabe que no va a contratarme, de modo que se dedica a pasar el tiempo, a la espera de que transcurran los diez minutos.

—Qué mala jugada —exclama compasivamente cuando concluyo el relato.

—Probablemente me han hecho un favor —respondo como buen chivo expiatorio—. Pero estoy dispuesto a trabajar. Terminaré entre los mejores treinta por ciento de mi curso. Me encanta la administración de la propiedad inmobiliaria y he hecho dos cursos de especialización en dicho campo, ambos con buenas notas.

—Gran parte de nuestro trabajo consiste en la administración de la propiedad inmobiliaria —dice afectadamente, como si se tratara del trabajo más rentable del mundo—. Y litigación —agrega en un tono todavía más afectado.

Es poco más que un oficinista, un chupatintas, probablemente muy eficaz y capaz de ganarse muy bien la vida. Pero quiere convencerme de que también es un aguerrido luchador en la sala, un picapleitos. Lo dice porque eso es sencillamente lo que hacen los abogados, parte de su rutina. No he conocido a muchos letrados, pero todavía no he encontrado a ninguno que no pretendiera convencerme de su capacidad bélica en la sala.

Se me agota el tiempo.

—Durante los siete años que he estado en la universidad me he costeado los estudios trabajando. No he tenido que pedirle ni un centavo a mi familia.

—¿Qué clase de trabajo?

—Lo que se tercie. Actualmente trabajo en Yogi's, sirviendo a las mesas y en la barra.

—¿Es barman?

—Sí, señor. Entre otras cosas.

—Es soltero —dice lentamente, con mi currículum en la mano, donde se lee con toda claridad en blanco y negro.

—Sí, señor.

—¿Alguna relación seria?

En realidad no le incumbe en absoluto, pero no estoy en condiciones de decírselo.

—No, señor —respondo.

—¿No será marica?

—No, claro que no —exclamo inmediatamente.

Compartimos unos momentos de humor heterosexual, entre dos individuos perfectamente normales.

Se echa atrás y de pronto se pone serio, como si acabara de surgir algo importante.

—Hace varios años que no contratamos a un nuevo miembro asociado. Sólo por curiosidad, ¿cuánto les pagan los grandes bufetes del centro a los recién contratados?

La pregunta tiene miga. Independientemente de lo que responda, fingirá estupor e incredulidad ante los exorbitantes salarios en los grandes bufetes. Eso, evidentemente, sentará las bases para cualquier discusión que podamos tener acerca del dinero.

Sería inútil mentir. Es probable que esté perfectamente al corriente de la gama de salarios. A los abogados les encanta chismorrear.

—Tinley Britt se empeña en pagar los mejores sueldos, como usted sabe. Creo que en estos momentos llegan a cincuenta mil.

Antes de que termine, empieza a mover la cabeza.

—No me diga —exclama atónito—. No me diga —repite.

—No pretendo ganar tanto dinero —agrego inmediatamente.

He decidido venderme barato a cualquiera que esté dispuesto a hacerme una oferta por mis servicios. Mis gastos son escasos y si logro introducir un pie en la empresa y trabajar duro un par de años, puede que aparezca algo mejor.

—¿En qué cifra ha pensado? —pregunta, como si su diminuto bufete pudiera competir con los poderosos y lo contrario fuera denigrante.

—La mitad. Veinticinco mil. Trabajaré ochenta horas semanales, me ocuparé de todos los sumarios de pescado y haré todos los trabajos indeseables. Usted, el señor Ross y el señor Perry podrán dejar en mis manos todos los casos que preferirían no haber aceptado y en seis meses estarán todos resueltos. Se lo prometo. Ganaré mi salario durante los primeros doce meses y, de no ser así, me marcharé.

Rod llega a separar los labios y veo su dentadura. Se le ha iluminado la mirada ante la perspectiva de sacar toda la basura de su despacho y ofrecérsela a otro. El timbre de su teléfono suena con fuerza e inmediatamente se oye la voz de su secretaria.

—Señor Nunley, le esperan para la declaración.

Consulto mi reloj. Ocho minutos.

Me mira y frunce el entrecejo antes de hablar.

—Interesante propuesta. Deje que lo piense. Tendré que ha-

blarlo con mis socios. Nos reunimos todos los jueves por la mañana —dice mientras se pone de pie—. Se lo propondré. A decir
verdad, no estaba previsto —agrega dispuesto ya a acompañarme a la puerta.

—No lo lamentará, señor Nunley. Veinticinco mil es una
ganga —insisto mientras retrocedo hacia la puerta.

Parece momentáneamente aturdido.

—No es por el dinero —declara, como si para él y sus socios
fuera inconcebible pagar *menos* que Tinley Britt—. La cuestión
es que actualmente nos desenvolvemos bastante bien. Ganamos
mucho dinero, ¿sabe? Todo el mundo está contento. No hemos
pensado en ampliar el negocio —agrega después de abrir la
puerta, a la espera de que me marche—. Nos mantendremos en
contacto.

Me acompaña al vestíbulo y le ordena a la secretaria que se
asegure de anotar mi número de teléfono. Me estrecha vigoro-
samente la mano, me desea suerte, promete llamarme pronto y
a los pocos segundos estoy en la acera.

Tardo unos segundos en recopilar mis ideas. Acabo de ofrecerme para prostituir mi educación y mi formación por mucho
menos de lo deseable, y en escasos minutos he acabado en la
calle.

Tal como se desenvolverían los acontecimientos, mi breve
entrevista con Roderick Nunley sería una de mis tentativas más
productivas.

Son casi las diez. Dentro de treinta minutos tengo una clase
de lecturas selectas del Código napoleónico, a la que debo asistir porque no me he presentado desde hace siete días. Podría olvidar la asignatura durante las próximas tres semanas y a nadie
le importaría, ya que no hay examen de fin de curso.

Ahora circulo libremente por la facultad, sin avergonzarme
de mostrar la cara. Cuando ya sólo faltan pocos días para el fin
de curso, la mayoría de los estudiantes de tercero abandonan el
lugar. La carrera de derecho empieza con un aluvión de intenso
trabajo y complejos exámenes, pero acaba con simples colo-
quios e insignificantes proyectos. Todos dedicamos mucho más
tiempo al examen de colegiatura que a preocuparnos por nuestras últimas clases.

La mayoría nos preparamos para ingresar en el campo laboral.

Madeline Skinner se ha hecho cargo de mi caso como si fuera el suyo propio, y sufre casi tanto como yo, porque la suerte
no nos acompaña. Puede que un senador de Memphis, que tiene

un bufete en Nashville, necesite un abogado para redactar legislación por treinta mil más beneficios, pero debe estar colegiado y tener dos años de experiencia. Una pequeña empresa busca a un abogado licenciado en economía; yo estudié historia.

—Puede que en agosto aparezca una vacante para un abogado en el departamento de Bienestar Social del condado de Shelby —dice mientras mueve los papeles de su escritorio, procurando desesperadamente encontrar algún trabajo.

—¿Abogado del Bienestar Social? —repito.

—Interesante, ¿no cree?

—¿Cuánto pagan?

—Dieciocho mil.

—¿En qué consiste el trabajo?

—Localizar a padres que no pagan la pensión asignada, recuperar el dinero, casos de paternidad... Lo habitual.

—Parece peligroso.

—Es un trabajo.

—¿Y qué puedo hacer hasta agosto?

—Prepararse para el examen.

—Y si estudio mucho y apruebo, podré trabajar para el departamento de Bienestar Social por un sueldo mínimo.

—Escúcheme, Rudy...

—Lo siento. Ha sido un día muy duro.

Prometo volver mañana para mantener una conversación que será, indudablemente, una repetición de ésta.

OCHO

Booker encontró los formularios en algún lugar recóndito del bufete Shankle. Dijo que había un miembro asociado con un despacho en el sótano que de vez en cuando se ocupaba de casos de insolvencia y disponía del papeleo necesario.

Es bastante sencillo. La lista de bienes en una página, muy fácil y rápida de rellenar en mi caso. La lista de obligaciones en otra. Espacios para información laboral, denuncias pendientes, etcétera. Es lo que se conoce como capítulo siete, o insolvencia simple, donde se confiscan los bienes para cubrir las deudas, que también desaparecen.

Ya no consto como empleado de Yogi's. Sigo trabajando allí, pero ahora cobro al contado, sin documento alguno y, por lo tanto, sin nada que controlar ni confiscar. No me veré obligado a compartir mis depauperados ingresos con Texaco. Le hablé de mi problema a Prince, le conté lo mal que estaban las cosas, lo atribuí al coste de los estudios y a las tarjetas de crédito, y le encantó la idea de pagarme al contado y engañar al gobierno. Es un ferviente entusiasta de la economía al contado y sin impuestos.

Prince me ha ofrecido un préstamo para saldar mis deudas, pero no funcionaría. Cree que pronto ganaré una fortuna como joven abogado de éxito, y no he tenido el valor de confesarle que probablemente seguiré con él algún tiempo.

Tampoco le he revelado lo cuantioso que debería ser el préstamo. Texaco me reclama seiscientos doce dólares con ochenta y ocho centavos, incluidos los costes jurídicos y los honorarios de los abogados. El propietario de mi casa me ha denunciado por ochocientos nueve dólares, incluidos también costes y honorarios. Pero los verdaderos buitres esperan entre bastidores. Me escriben cartas abusivas, con la amenaza de poner el caso en manos de sus abogados.

Tengo una tarjeta MasterCard y otra Visa, expedidas por diferentes bancos de Memphis. Entre el día de Acción de Gracias y la Navidad del año pasado, durante un breve período de felicidad después de haberme asegurado que tendría un buen trabajo al cabo de unos meses y cuando estaba vanamente enamorado de Sara, decidí hacerle un par de encantadores regalos para las vacaciones. Con la tarjeta MasterCard le compré un brazalete de oro y diamantes por mil setecientos dólares y con la Visa unos antiguos pendientes de plata, que me costaron mil cien dólares. El día que me comunicó que no deseaba volver a verme jamás, fui a una tienda de exquisiteces y compré una botella de Dom Pérignon, un cuarto de kilo de *foie gras*, un poco de caviar, unos excelentes quesos y otras chucherías para nuestra celebración navideña. Me costó trescientos dólares, pero qué diablos, la vida es breve.

Los insidiosos bancos que me habían expedido las tarjetas habían elevado inexplicablemente el límite de mi crédito pocas semanas antes de las vacaciones. De pronto podía gastar a mi antojo, y con la licenciatura y el empleo a pocos meses vista sabía que me las arreglaría para pagar las pequeñas cantidades mensuales exigidas hasta el verano. De modo que no dejé de gastar, arrastrado por el sueño de una vida de felicidad con Sara.

Ahora me siento como un imbécil, pero con un papel y un lápiz en la mano lo he calculado todo. No ha sido difícil.

El *foie gras* se pudrió cuando lo dejé una noche encima del frigorífico, después de una desagradable velada con cerveza barata. El día de Navidad comí queso y tomé champán a solas en mi piso con las cortinas cerradas. El caviar permaneció intacto. Sentado en mi sofá torcido, contemplé las joyas sobre el suelo. Mientras comía grandes trozos de Brie y saboreaba una copa de Dom, contemplé los regalos de Navidad para mi amada y lloré.

En algún momento entre Navidad y Año Nuevo, reflexioné y decidí devolver las joyas a las tiendas donde las había comprado. Pensé en la posibilidad de arrojarlas desde el puente, como Billy Joe, o hacer algo igualmente dramático. Pero dado mi estado de ánimo, sabía que era preferible mantenerme alejado de los puentes.

El día después de Año Nuevo, cuando regresé a mi casa después de correr y dar un largo paseo, me percaté de que me habían robado. Habían forzado la puerta. Los ladrones se llevaron mi viejo televisor, mi equipo estereofónico, un bote lleno de cuartos de dólar de la cómoda y, evidentemente, las joyas que había comprado para Sara.

Llamé a la policía y formalicé la denuncia. Les mostré los recibos de mis tarjetas de crédito. El sargento se limitó a mover la cabeza y me aconsejó que hablara con mi compañía de seguros.

Derroché más de tres mil dólares comprando con plástico. Ahora ha llegado el momento de saldar la cuenta.

Mi desahucio está previsto para mañana. En el código de insolvencia hay una provisión maravillosa que concede un aplazamiento automático de toda acción jurídica contra el deudor. De ahí que veamos a las opulentas corporaciones, incluidos mis amigos de Texaco, acudir al tribunal de insolvencia cuando necesitan protección temporal. El dueño de mi casa no puede hacer nada contra mí mañana, ni siquiera atosigarme por teléfono.

Salgo del ascensor y respiro hondo. El vestíbulo está lleno de abogados. Hay tres jueces dedicados exclusivamente a casos de insolvencia y sus salas están en este piso. Oyen docenas de casos todos los días y en cada uno de ellos interviene un grupo de abogados, uno para el deudor y varios para los acreedores. Parece un parque zoológico. Oigo numerosas conferencias importantes cuando circulo, abogados que discuten sobre cuentas médicas impagadas, o el valor de una furgoneta. Entro en la secretaría y espero diez minutos, mientras los abogados que están delante de mí entregan sus peticiones. Conocen muy bien a las secretarias, con las que coquetean y charlan amigablemente. Cómo me gustaría ser un importante abogado especializado en insolvencias, para que esas chicas me llamaran Fred o Sonny.

Un profesor nos dijo el año pasado que, en esta época de incertidumbre económica, reducción de empleo, empequeñecimiento de las corporaciones y todo lo demás que había calculado, la insolvencia sería el sector de mayor crecimiento en el futuro. Lo afirmaba un individuo que nunca había facturado una sola hora en un bufete privado.

Pero hoy parece indudablemente lucrativo. Se presentan solicitudes de insolvencia a diestro y siniestro. Todo el mundo está en quiebra.

Le entrego mis papeles a una apresurada secretaria, una chica atractiva con la boca llena de chicle. Examina la solicitud y me mira atentamente. Llevo una camisa de algodón azul y pantalón caqui.

—¿Es usted abogado?

Su voz es fuerte y me percato de que la gente vuelve la cabeza para mirarme.

—No.

—¿Es usted el deudor? —pregunta, levantando todavía la voz, al tiempo que hace chasquear su chicle.

—Sí —respondo apresuradamente.

El deudor puede presentar su propia petición sin necesidad de ser abogado, aunque esta información no se divulga en ninguna parte.

La secretaria asiente y sella mi solicitud.

—La tarifa de registro son ochenta dólares, por favor.

Le entrego cuatro billetes de veinte. La chica coge el dinero y lo mira con desconfianza. En mi petición no figura ninguna cuenta bancaria, porque la cerré ayer, eliminando así uno de mis bienes por un valor de once dólares y ochenta y cuatro centavos. Mis demás bienes son los siguientes: un Toyota muy usado, quinientos dólares; muebles y utensilios varios, ciento cincuenta; colección de discos láser, doscientos; textos jurídicos, ciento veinticinco; ropa, ciento cincuenta. Todas estas pertenencias se consideran de uso personal y por consiguiente exentas del proceso que acabo de iniciar. Puedo quedármelo todo, pero debo seguir pagando los plazos del Toyota.

—¿Al contado, eh? —exclama, mientras me extiende un recibo.

—No tengo cuenta bancaria —respondo casi a gritos para que se enteren los que han estado escuchando.

Me mira fijamente y le aguanto la mirada. Vuelve a su ajetreado trabajo y, al cabo de unos minutos, me entrega una copia de la solicitud y el recibo. Tomo nota mental de la fecha, la hora y la sala de mi primera vista.

Casi logro llegar a la puerta antes de que alguien me pare. Un joven robusto de barba negra y rostro sudado me toca ligeramente el brazo.

—Discúlpeme, caballero —dice. Me paro para mirarlo y me coloca una tarjeta de visita en la mano—. Me llamo Robbie Molk y soy abogado. No he podido evitar oírle. He pensado que tal vez necesite un poco de ayuda con su DI.

DI son las siglas de declaración de insolvencia, en la jerga de moda de los abogados.

Examino la tarjeta y luego su cara picada de viruelas. He oído hablar de él. También le he visto su anuncio en los periódicos. Anuncia el «capítulo siete» por ciento cincuenta dólares de anticipo y aquí está ahora, en la secretaría del juzgado como un buitre, con la esperanza de cazar a algún incauto que disponga de los ciento cincuenta dólares.

Acepto educadamente su tarjeta.

—No, gracias —respondo procurando ser amable—. Me ocuparé de ello personalmente.

—Hay muchas formas de meter la pata —replica inmediatamente, como con toda probabilidad lo ha hecho un millar de veces—. Un siete puede ser delicado. Yo resuelvo mil por año. Doscientos por anticipado y me ocupo absolutamente de todo. Dispongo de un bufete completo y todo el personal necesario.

Ahora son doscientos dólares. Supongo que al conocerlo personalmente agrega otros cincuenta. Sería muy fácil censurarlo ahora, pero algo me dice que Molk no es susceptible de ser humillado.

—No, gracias —respondo y sigo mi camino.

El descenso es lento y penoso. El ascensor está lleno de abogados, todos mal vestidos, con maletines desvencijados y zapatos mugrientos. No dejan de hablar de exenciones y bienes embargables. Una jerga jurídica insufrible. Discusiones terriblemente importantes. Parecen incapaces de abandonarlas.

Se me ocurre cuando estamos a punto de llegar a la planta baja. No tengo ni idea de lo que estaré haciendo dentro de un año y no es improbable, sino todo lo contrario, que me dedique a subir y bajar en este ascensor, discutiendo trivialidades con estas mismas personas. Con toda probabilidad seré exactamente como ellos, suelto por las calles, intentando sacarles dinero a quienes no pueden pagar y acechando en los juzgados en busca de trabajo.

Esa terrible idea me produce náuseas. En el ascensor hace calor y falta aire. Creo que voy a vomitar. Se detiene, desembocan todos apresuradamente en el vestíbulo y se dispersan, sin dejar de hablar y negociar.

El aire fresco me aclara la cabeza cuando paseo por Mid-America Mall, una avenida peatonal con un ingenioso coche para trasladar a los borrachos de un lado para otro. Solía llamarse calle Mayor y es todavía la sede de muchos abogados. Los juzgados están a pocas manzanas. Paso frente a los altos edificios del centro de la ciudad y me pregunto qué ocurrirá en sus incontables bufetes: asociados ajetreados, trabajando dieciocho horas diarias porque el compañero trabaja veinte, jóvenes socios hablando entre sí para elaborar la estrategia del bufete, y socios decanos atrincherados en sus opulentos despachos de las esquinas, mientras centurias de jóvenes abogados esperan sus instrucciones.

Eso era sinceramente lo que yo deseaba cuando ingresé en la Facultad de Derecho. Anhelaba la presión y el poder que genera trabajar con personas listas y altamente motivadas, todas ellas sometidas a tensiones, presiones y fechas límite. El bufete en el que trabajé como pasante el año pasado es pequeño, sólo había doce abogados, pero con muchos pasantes, administrativos y secretarias, y a veces el caos me resultaba estimulante. Yo era un miembro insignificante del equipo, pero soñaba con ser algún día su capitán.

Compro un helado en la calle y me siento en un banco de Court Square. Las palomas me contemplan. Tengo delante el imponente First Federal Building, el edificio más alto de Memphis, donde se encuentra el bufete de Trent & Brent. Me gustaría trabajar aquí. Es fácil para mí y mis amigos hablar mal de Trent & Brent. Lo hacemos porque no tenemos el nivel necesario para ellos. Los odiamos porque no les importamos, no están dispuestos a tomarse la molestia de concedernos una entrevista.

Supongo que existe un Trent & Brent en todas las ciudades, en todos los campos. Yo no he alcanzado su nivel, no pertenezco a su mundo, de modo que me limitaré a odiarlos toda la vida.

Hablando de bufetes, y puesto que estoy en el centro de la ciudad, he decidido pasar unas horas llamando a sus puertas. Tengo una lista de abogados que trabajan solos, o que han formado sociedad con otros dos o tres letrados. El único factor alentador al entrar en un campo tan horriblemente saturado es la enorme cantidad de puertas a las que uno puede llamar. Cabe la esperanza, no dejo de repetirme a mí mismo, de que en el momento oportuno encuentre el bufete que nadie ha hallado todavía y conozca a un abogado ajetreado que necesite desesperadamente a un novato que se ocupe de la parte más monótona de su trabajo. También puede tratarse de una mujer. No me importa.

Camino unas manzanas hasta el edificio Sterick, el primer rascacielos de Memphis, donde actualmente tienen sus bufetes centenares de abogados. Charlo con algunas secretarias y les entrego copias de mi currículum. Me asombra la cantidad de bufetes donde trabajan recepcionistas temperamentales, e incluso mal educadas. Mucho antes de que se mencione el tema del empleo me tratan a menudo como a un pordiosero. Un par de ellas me han arrebatado el currículum de las manos y lo han arrojado a un cajón. Siento la tentación de presentarme como cliente potencial, el apenado marido de una joven que acaba de ser arrollada por un enorme camión, con una póliza de seguros muy completa. Y el conductor iba borracho. Tal vez un camión Exxon. Sería divertido ver a esas zorras incorporarse de un brinco, sonreír de oreja a oreja y salir corriendo para ofrecerme un café.

Voy de despacho en despacho, sonriendo cuando me apetecería blasfemar, repitiendo las mismas palabras a las mismas mujeres:

—Sí, me llamo Ruby Baylor y estoy en el último curso de la Facultad de Derecho de la Universidad Estatal de Memphis. Desearía hablar con el señor mengano o zutano acerca de un posible trabajo.

—¿Un qué? —preguntan a menudo.

Sigo sonriendo cuando les entrego mi currículum y pregunto de nuevo por el jefazo, que siempre está demasiado ocupado, y ellas se deshacen de mí con la promesa de que alguien se pondrá en contacto conmigo.

La zona Granger de Memphis está al norte de la ciudad. Sus abigarradas hileras de casas de ladrillo en calles arboladas son prueba irrefutable de un barrio nacido durante el auge de la construcción, inmediatamente después de la segunda guerra mundial. Sus habitantes trabajaban en fábricas cercanas, plantaron árboles delante de las casas y construyeron jardines en la parte trasera. Con el transcurso del tiempo, sus habitantes originales se trasladaron al este, donde construyeron casas más bonitas, y Granger se convirtió lentamente en un barrio de jubilados y blancos y negros de clase baja.

La casa de Dot y Buddy Black tiene el mismo aspecto que otras muchas. Está en una parcela llana, de setecientos cincuenta metros cuadrados a lo sumo. Los indispensables árboles frente a la casa han sufrido algún percance. En un garaje para un solo coche descansa un viejo Chevrolet. El césped y los arbustos están muy pulcros.

Aparco detrás del Chevrolet y los doberman, a escasos metros, gruñen.

Estamos a media tarde y la temperatura es de más de treinta grados. Las puertas y las ventanas están abiertas. Miro por la tela mosquitera de la puerta principal y llamo suavemente.

No me alegra estar aquí, porque no deseo ver a Donny Ray Black. Lo imagino tan enfermo y depauperado como lo describió su madre, y mi estómago es débil.

La señora Black se acerca a la puerta, cigarrillo en mano, y me mira fijamente a través de la tela mosquitera.

—Soy yo, señora Black, Rudy Baylor. Nos conocimos la semana pasada en el Parque de los Cipreses.

Los vendedores puerta a puerta deben ser una molestia en Granger, porque me contempla sin reconocerme. Se acerca otro paso a la puerta y se lleva el cigarrillo a la boca.

—¿Se acuerda de mí? Me ocupo de su caso contra Great Benefit.

—Lo había tomado por un testigo de Jehová.

—Pues no lo soy, señora Black.

—Mi nombre es Dot. Creí que ya se lo había dicho.

—De acuerdo, Dot.

—Esos malditos nos vuelven locos. Ellos y los mormones. Y los sábados por la mañana, antes del amanecer, aparecen los boy scouts vendiendo buñuelos. ¿Qué desea?

—Pues, si dispone de un minuto, me gustaría hablar de su caso.

—¿Qué hay que hablar?

—Me gustaría repasar algunos datos.

—Me parecía que ya lo había hecho.

—Tenemos que hablar un poco más.

Suelta una bocanada de humo a través de la tela mosquitera y abre lentamente la puerta. Entro en una diminuta sala de estar y la sigo a la cocina. El ambiente de la casa es húmedo y pegajoso, con olor a tabaco rancio en todas partes.

—¿Quiere tomar algo? —pregunta.

—No, gracias.

Me siento junto a la mesa de la cocina. Dot se sirve una cola *light* y se sienta con la espalda apoyada en los armarios de la cocina. No se ve a Buddy por ninguna parte. Supongo que Donny Ray está en su habitación.

—¿Dónde está Buddy? —pregunto alegremente, como si se tratara de un viejo amigo al que echo mucho de menos.

—¿Ve ese viejo coche? —responde al tiempo que mueve la cabeza en dirección al jardín trasero.

En un rincón lleno de arbustos y hierbajos, junto a un dilapidado cobertizo y bajo un arce, veo un viejo Ford Fairlane. Es blanco, con dos puertas, ambas están abiertas. Un gato descansa sobre el capó.

—Está sentado en el coche —aclara.

El vehículo está rodeado de maleza y parece carecer de neumáticos. Nada se ha tocado a su alrededor desde hace décadas.

—¿Adónde va? —pregunto, y ella incluso sonríe.

—Buddy no va a ninguna parte —responde después de sorber ruidosamente su cola—. Compramos el coche nuevo en 1964. Se sienta ahí todos los días, desde que se levanta hasta que se acuesta, a solas con los gatos.

Tiene cierta lógica. Está solo, sin que el humo de los cigarrillos le contamine el cuerpo y sin preocuparse de Donny Ray.

—¿Por qué? —pregunto, evidentemente convencido de que no le importa hablar de ello.

—Buddy no está bien de la cabeza. Ya se lo dije la semana pasada.

Cómo podía haberlo olvidado.

—¿Cómo está Donny Ray?

Se encoge de hombros y se instala en una silla, al otro lado de la endeble mesa de la cocina.

—Tiene días buenos y días malos. ¿Quiere conocerlo?

—Tal vez luego.

—Está en cama la mayor parte del tiempo, pero puede andar un poco. A lo mejor le digo que se levante antes de que usted se marche.

—Sí. Quizá. Lo que quería decirle es que he trabajado mucho

en su caso. Me refiero a que he pasado muchas horas estudiando todos sus documentos. Además de varios días en la biblioteca consultando las leyes y, francamente, creo que deben presentar una soberana demanda contra Great Benefit.

—Creía que eso ya estaba decidido —responde y me dirige una dura mirada.

Dot tiene cara de pocos amigos, indudablemente como consecuencia de una ardua vida con ese chiflado del Fairlane.

—Puede que sí, pero tenía que estudiarlo. Mi consejo es que prosigan con la demanda y que lo hagan cuanto antes.

—¿A qué espera?

—Pero no confíe en una solución rápida. Se enfrentan a una gran corporación. Disponen de muchos abogados, capaces de demorar y postergar el proceso. Así se ganan la vida.

—¿Cuánto puede tardar?

—Meses, tal vez años. Puede que los obliguemos a liquidar inmediatamente cuando presentemos la demanda. O que ellos nos obliguen a ir a juicio y presenten luego un recurso de apelación. Es imprevisible.

—Habrá fallecido en unos meses.

—¿Puedo hacerle una pregunta?

Resopla y asiente en perfecta armonía.

—Cuando Great Benefit denegó por primera vez esta solicitud, los médicos acababan de diagnosticar la enfermedad de Donny Ray. ¿Por qué han esperado hasta ahora para consultar a un abogado? —pregunto, utilizando el término «abogado» en un sentido muy amplio.

—¿Cree que me hace sentir orgullosa? Estaba convencida de que la compañía de seguros honraría su compromiso y acabaría por pagar, ya sabe, se responsabilizaría de sus gastos y tratamiento. Les escribía y me contestaban. No lo sé. Supongo que fui una imbécil. Habíamos pagado las cuotas con absoluta regularidad a lo largo de los años, sin retrasarnos una sola vez. Suponía que harían honor a la póliza. Además, tenga en cuenta que nunca había recurrido a un abogado. Ningún divorcio, ni nada por el estilo. Dios sabe que debí haberlo hecho —dice mientras vuelve tristemente la cabeza hacia la ventana, con una mirada melancólica al Fairlane y a la pesadumbre que contiene—. Bebe medio litro de ginebra por la mañana y otro medio litro por la tarde. Y la verdad es que no me importa. Hace que se sienta feliz, le mantiene alejado de la casa y no es como si le impidiera realizar un trabajo productivo, ¿comprende a lo que me refiero?

Ambos contemplamos la silueta desplomada en el asiento delantero. La maleza y el arce sumen al vehículo en la sombra.

—¿Se la compra usted? —pregunto, como si importara.

—Claro que no. Paga al chiquillo de los vecinos para que se la traiga a escondidas. Cree que no lo sé.

Se oye un movimiento en el fondo de la casa. No hay aire acondicionado que ahogue los sonidos. Alguien tose.

—Escúcheme, Dot, me gustaría ocuparme de este caso. Sé que no soy más que un novato, un chiquillo a punto de terminar la carrera, pero lo he estudiado ya durante muchas horas y conozco el caso mejor que nadie.

Su mirada es inexpresiva, desprovista casi de toda esperanza. Cualquier abogado es tan bueno como el siguiente. Confiará tanto en mí como en cualquier otro, lo cual no significa gran cosa. Es curioso. A pesar de todo el dinero que gastan los abogados en propaganda provocativa, publicidad barata por televisión, agresivos carteles y precios de rebajas en los anuncios, todavía existen personas como Dot Black, incapaces de distinguir a un guerrero de los juzgados de un estudiante de tercer curso de Derecho.

—Probablemente tendré que asociarme con otro abogado —digo, contando con su ingenuidad—, sólo para utilizar su nombre hasta que apruebe el examen de colegiatura, ¿comprende?

No parece haberlo asimilado.

—¿Cuánto costará? —pregunta con no poca desconfianza.

Le brindo una radiante sonrisa.

—Ni un centavo. Lo aceptaré como contingencia. Me quedaré con un tercio de lo que se recupere. Si no se recupera nada, mis servicios serán gratuitos. Nada por adelantado.

Sin duda ha visto este sistema de propuesta anunciado en algún lugar, pero parece no tener ni idea.

—¿Cuánto?

—Los demandaremos por varios millones —respondo dramáticamente y ella queda atrapada.

No creo que en el cuerpo derrumbado de esa mujer persista una sola pizca de codicia. Todo sueño que pudiera haber tenido de una buena vida se desintegró hace tanto tiempo que ni siquiera puede recordarlo. Sin embargo, le encanta la idea de atacar a Great Benefit y provocarles sufrimiento.

—¿Y usted se queda con un tercio?

—No confío en sacarles millones, pero me quedaré sólo con la tercera parte de lo que les obliguemos a pagar. Y me refiero al tercio de lo que quede después de saldar los gastos médicos de Donny Ray. Usted no tiene nada que perder.

Dot da una palmada en la mesa con la mano izquierda.

—Adelante. No me importa lo que se quede, hágalo. Inmediatamente, ¿de acuerdo? Mañana mismo.

Cuidadosamente doblado en el bolsillo llevo un contrato por servicios jurídicos, que he encontrado en un libro de formularios en la biblioteca. En este momento debería sacarlo y obligarla a firmar, pero no me atrevo a hacerlo. Desde un punto de vista ético no puedo firmar un contrato para representar a alguien hasta que esté colegiado y disponga de una licencia que me autorice a ejercer la profesión. Creo que Dot hará honor a su palabra.

Consulto mi reloj como un auténtico abogado.

—Voy a ponerme a trabajar —digo.

—¿No quiere conocer a Donny Ray?

—Quizá la próxima vez.

—No se lo reprocho. No es más que piel y huesos.

—Volveré dentro de unos días, cuando disponga de más tiempo. Tenemos mucho de que hablar y tendré que hacerle a Donny Ray unas preguntas.

—Dese prisa, ¿de acuerdo?

Charlamos unos minutos sobre el Parque de los Cipreses y todo lo que allí se celebra. Ella y Buddy van una vez por semana, si logra mantenerlo sobrio hasta el mediodía. Es la única ocasión en que salen juntos de la casa.

Ella quiere charlar y yo deseo marcharme. Me acompaña a la puerta, examina mi sucio y abollado Toyota, hace algunos comentarios despectivos respecto a los productos importados, particularmente los japoneses, y les chilla a los doberman.

Se queda junto al buzón, con un cigarrillo en la mano, observando cómo me alejo.

A pesar de que acabo de declararme insolvente, todavía puedo derrochar el dinero. Gasto ocho dólares en una maceta con un geranio y se la llevo a la señorita Birdie. Asegura que le encantan las flores, está completamente sola y creo que es un detalle por mi parte. Sólo un poco de alegría en la vida de una anciana.

Llego en el momento oportuno. Está a gatas en un parterre junto a la casa, al lado del camino que conduce al garaje que hay en el jardín trasero. A lo largo del hormigón hay flores, matorrales, hiedra y setos decorativos. El jardín trasero está poblado de árboles tan viejos como ella. Hay también un patio de ladrillo, con macetas llenas de pintorescas flores.

Me da incluso un abrazo cuando le ofrezco mi pequeño regalo. Se quita los guantes de jardinero, los deja caer entre las flores y me acompaña a la parte posterior de la casa. Tiene el lugar preciso para el geranio. Lo plantará mañana. ¿Me apetece un café?

—Sólo agua —respondo.

El gusto de su café instantáneo diluido está todavía fresco en mi mente. Me obliga a sentarme en una ornamentada silla mientras se sacude el barro y el polvo del delantal.

—¿Agua fría? —pregunta, claramente encantada con la perspectiva de servirme algo de beber.

—Estupendo —respondo, e inmediatamente desaparece por la puerta de la cocina.

La excesiva vegetación del jardín guarda una extraña simetría. Se extiende a lo largo de por lo menos cincuenta metros, hasta llegar a un espeso cerco de setos. Más allá, entre los árboles, se vislumbra un tejado. Hay una serie de pintorescos parterres de pequeño tamaño, con gran variedad de flores, a los que ella o alguien dedica bastante tiempo. Junto a la verja veo una fuente sobre una gruesa plataforma de ladrillo, pero por la que no circula el agua. Entre dos árboles cuelga una vieja hamaca, cuyas cuerdas y tela deshilachadas se mecen en la brisa. El césped está desprovisto de hierbajos, pero demasiado crecido.

El garaje me llama la atención. Tiene dos puertas plegables, cerradas. Junto al mismo hay un pequeño almacén, con la ventana cubierta. Sobre el mismo parece haber un pequeño piso, con una escalera de madera que da la vuelta a la esquina y sube aparentemente por detrás. Hay dos grandes ventanas frente a la casa, una de ellas con un cristal roto. La hiedra consume las paredes exteriores y parece introducirse por la ventana quebrada.

El lugar tiene cierto encanto.

La señorita Birdie emerge alegremente por la doble puerta de cristal, con dos vasos de agua fría, y se sienta muy cerca de mí.

—¿Qué le parece mi jardín? —pregunta.

—Es hermoso, señorita Birdie. Muy tranquilo.

—Es mi vida —exclama al tiempo que abre los brazos y derrama el agua sobre mis pies, sin percatarse de ello—. Así es como paso el tiempo. Me encanta.

—Es muy bonito. ¿Lo cuida usted sola?

—Casi. Pago a un chiquillo para que corte el césped una vez por semana. Treinta dólares. ¿No le parece increíble? Solía costar cinco.

Sorbe ruidosamente el agua y hace chasquear los labios.

—¿Es eso un pequeño piso? —pregunto señalando a la estructura que hay encima del garaje.

—Solía serlo. Uno de mis nietos vivió aquí durante algún tiempo. Lo arreglé, instalé un baño, una pequeña cocina y quedó muy bonito. Estudiaba en la Universidad de Memphis.

—¿Cuánto tiempo vivió aquí?

—No mucho. En realidad prefiero no hablar de él.

Debe tratarse de uno de los que hay que eliminar del testamento.

Después de pasar mucho tiempo llamando a la puerta de los bufetes, mendigando trabajo y recibiendo el trato abusivo de las prepotentes secretarias, uno pierde las inhibiciones. Se le endurece la piel. El rechazo es fácil, porque se aprende rápidamente que lo peor que puede ocurrir es oír la palabra «no».

—¿Supongo que no habrá pensado en alquilarlo ahora? —pregunto sin titubear, ni miedo alguno a ser rechazado.

Su vaso queda paralizado en el aire y contempla el piso como si acabara de descubrirlo.

—¿A quién?

—Me encantaría vivir aquí. Es encantador y parece ser muy tranquilo.

—Como una tumba.

—Pero sólo durante algún tiempo. Ya sabe, hasta que empiece a trabajar y pueda arreglármelas.

—¿Usted, Rudy? —pregunta con incredulidad.

—Me gusta mucho —respondo con una sonrisa semiforzada—. Es perfecto para mí. Soy soltero, llevo una vida muy tranquila y no puedo pagar mucho alquiler. Es maravilloso.

—¿Cuánto puede pagar? —pregunta inmediatamente, como un abogado con un cliente destituido.

Me coge de improviso.

—Pues... no lo sé. Usted es la dueña de la casa. ¿Cuánto pide?

Mueve la cabeza y contempla las copas de los árboles.

—¿Qué le parece cuatrocientos dólares mensuales, o mejor dicho, trescientos?

Es evidente que la señorita Birdie no ha administrado nunca ninguna finca. Se saca cualquier número de la cabeza. Menos mal que no se le ha ocurrido empezar por ochocientos.

—Creo que antes deberíamos echarle una ojeada —respondo cautelosamente.

Se pone inmediatamente de pie.

—Está muy descuidado, ¿sabe? En los últimos diez años lo he utilizado para guardar trastos. Pero podemos limpiarlo. Creo que el agua funciona —dice, me coge de la mano y me conduce hacia el garaje—. Habrá que conectarla. No estoy segura acerca de la calefacción y el aire acondicionado. Hay algunos muebles, no muchos, cosas viejas que no me servían —agrega mientras empieza a subir por la crujiente escalera—. ¿Necesita muebles?

—No muchos.

La barandilla tiembla y todo el edificio parece estremecerse.

NUEVE

Se crean enemigos en la Facultad de Derecho. La competencia puede ser atroz. Se aprende a engañar y traicionar, en preparación para la vida real. Durante mi primer año en la facultad tuvo lugar una pelea a puñetazos entre dos estudiantes de tercero, que empezaron a insultarse en una competición de juicios simulados. Los expulsaron y luego volvieron a admitirlos. La universidad necesita el dinero de las matrículas.

Aquí hay unas cuantas personas que realmente me desagradan, y dos o tres a las que detesto. Procuro no odiar a la gente.

Pero en este momento odio al cretino que me ha hecho esto. Aquí se publica una crónica de diversas transacciones jurídicas y financieras en la ciudad. Se titula *The Daily Report* e incluye, además de las peticiones de divorcio y otra docena de categorías esenciales, una lista de los trámites de insolvencia del día anterior. Mi amigo, o grupo de amigos, decidieron que sería interesante destacar mi nombre de la lista de penalidades, ampliar un fragmento de las peticiones del capítulo siete y divulgar la noticia por la Facultad de Derecho. Dice lo siguiente: «Baylor, Rudy L., estudiante; bienes: mil ciento veinticinco dólares (exentos); deudas garantizadas: doscientos ochenta y cinco dólares a la compañía financiera Wheels & Deals; deudas no garantizadas: cinco mil ciento treinta y seis dólares y ochenta y ocho centavos; acciones pendientes: a) recuperación de una cuenta deudora por parte de Texaco, b) desahucio de The Hampton; lugar de trabajo: ninguno; representante legal: *pro se.*»

Pro se significa que no puedo permitirme contratar a un abogado y me represento a mí mismo. El estudiante que trabaja como recepcionista en la biblioteca me ha entregado un ejemplar cuando he llegado esta mañana y me ha dicho que estaban distribuidos por toda la facultad, e incluso pegados a los tablones de anuncios.

—Me pregunto a quién puede parecerle gracioso —ha dicho.

Le he dado las gracias y me he dirigido rápidamente a mi rincón del sótano, oculto una vez más entre montones de libros y alejado de rostros conocidos. Pronto terminarán las clases y me marcharé de aquí, lejos de esa insoportable gentuza.

Esta mañana tengo una cita con el profesor Smoot y llego diez minutos tarde. A él no le importa. En su despacho reina el desorden obligatorio de un intelectual con demasiado talento para estar organizado. Su pajarita está torcida, su sonrisa es sincera.

Hablamos en primer lugar de los Black y de su disputa con Great Benefit. Le entrego un resumen de tres páginas del caso, junto a mis ingeniosas conclusiones y procedimientos sugeridos. Mientras lo lee atentamente, yo me dedico a contemplar los papeles arrugados que hay debajo de su escritorio. Repite una y otra vez que está muy impresionado. Aconsejo a los Black que se pongan en contacto con un abogado y presenten una alegación de mala fe contra Great Benefit. Smoot está completamente de acuerdo. Si lo supiera.

Sólo aspiro a su aprobación, eso es todo. A continuación hablamos de la señorita Birdie Birdsong. Le digo que está bastante bien y quiere un nuevo testamento. Me reservo los detalles. Le muestro un documento de cinco páginas, el testamento revisado de la señorita Birdie, y le echa una rápida ojeada. Dice que le parece bien y que no ve ningún problema. En la asignatura de los problemas jurídicos de los ancianos no hay examen de fin de curso, ni obligación de presentar trabajo alguno. Uno se limita a asistir a clase, visitar a los vejestorios y redactar el resumen de los casos. Smoot te concede un sobresaliente.

Hace varios años que Smoot conoce a la señorita Birdie. Evidentemente es la reina del Parque de los Cipreses desde hace bastante tiempo y él la ve dos veces todos los años, cuando va de visita con los estudiantes. Hasta ahora nunca había indicado que deseara aprovecharse de los consejos jurídicos gratuitos, reflexiona, mientras tira de su pajarita. Dice que le sorprende descubrir que sea rica.

Más le sorprendería descubrir que estoy a punto de convertirme en su inquilino.

El despacho de Max Leuberg está a pocos metros del de Smoot. Me ha dejado un recado en la recepción de la biblioteca para decirme que quería verme. Max deja la facultad a fin de curso. Wisconsin le ha concedido dos años para estar con nosotros y ha llegado el momento de regresar. Probablemente le echaré un poco de menos cuando los dos nos hayamos marchado, pero en este momento es difícil imaginar cualquier afecto por algo o alguien relacionado con esta facultad.

El despacho de Max está lleno de cajas de cartón. Le sorprendo empaquetando para marcharse y nunca he visto mayor desorden. Dedicamos unos momentos difíciles a reminiscencias, en un intento vano por recordar la facultad como algo provocativo. Hasta ahora nunca le había visto tan sumiso. Parece sinceramente apenado de marcharse. Me muestra un montón de papeles que ha metido en una caja.

—Esto es para usted. Son un puñado de documentos recientes que he utilizado en casos de mala fe. Guárdeselos. Puede que le sean útiles.

Todavía no he acabado de leer el último montón de material que me entregó.

—Gracias, Max —respondo, con la mirada fija en la caja.

—¿Ha presentado ya la demanda? —pregunta.

—Pues... no. Todavía no.

—Debe hacerlo. Busque a un abogado en la ciudad con un buen historial de condenas. Alguien que tenga experiencia en casos de mala fe. He pensado mucho en este caso y cada vez me resulta más apasionante. Tiene mucho atractivo para el jurado. Imagino a los miembros del jurado enojados, con el deseo de castigar a la compañía de seguros. Alguien tiene que hacerse cargo de este caso y darse toda la prisa posible.

Corro tanto como puedo.

Se incorpora de un brinco y estira los brazos.

—¿En qué clase de bufete va a trabajar? —pregunta. Está de puntillas, haciendo algún tipo de ejercicio de yoga para tonificar las pantorrillas—. Porque éste es un caso maravilloso para que lo lleve personalmente. Se me ha ocurrido que tal vez debería llevárselo a su bufete y ocuparse usted mismo de todo el trabajo básico. Indudablemente habrá alguien con experiencia judicial en el bufete. Llámeme si lo desea. Estaré en Detroit todo el verano trabajando en un caso importantísimo contra Allstate, pero esto me interesa. Creo que puede convertirse en un gran caso, que hará época. Me encantaría ver cómo los machaca.

—¿Qué ha hecho Allstate? —pregunto intentando desviar la atención de mi bufete.

En su boca se dibuja una radiante sonrisa y cruza insólitamente las manos sobre la cabeza.

—Increíble —responde, y empieza a relatarme con pelos y señales lo maravilloso del caso.

Lamento habérselo preguntado. En mi limitada experiencia con abogados he descubierto que todos cojean del mismo pie.

Una de sus costumbres más desagradables es la de contar batallitas. Si han participado en un juicio importante, quieren que lo sepas. Si tienen entre manos un caso espectacular con el que van a enriquecerse, necesitan compartirlo con otras mentes parecidas. A Max le quita el sueño la perspectiva de dejar a Allstate en la bancarrota.

—De todos modos —dice, volviendo a la realidad—, tal vez pueda ayudarle en este caso. No voy a regresar el próximo otoño, pero mi número de teléfono y mi dirección están en la caja. Llámeme si me necesita.

Levanto la caja de Wild Turkey. Es pesada y el fondo se hunde parcialmente.

—Gracias —digo mirándole a la cara—. Le estoy muy agradecido.

—Quiero ayudarle, Rudy. No hay nada más emocionante que vencer a una compañía de seguros. Créame.

—Haré todo lo posible. Gracias.

Suena el teléfono y lo agarra inmediatamente. Abandono sigilosamente el despacho con mi pesado cargamento.

La señorita Birdie y yo llegamos a un peculiar acuerdo. No es una gran negociadora y, evidentemente, no necesita el dinero. Logro que rebaje el alquiler a ciento cincuenta dólares mensuales, servicios incluidos. También suministra los muebles necesarios para cuatro habitaciones.

Además de pagar el alquiler, me comprometo a realizar varios trabajos en la finca, principalmente ocuparme de cortar el césped y cuidar el jardín. De ese modo se ahorrará treinta dólares semanales. Podaré los setos, barreré las hojas, etcétera. Se ha hablado vagamente de eliminar los hierbajos, pero no hemos concretado nada ni me lo he tomado en serio.

Para mí es un buen trato y me siento orgulloso de mi experto enfoque. El piso merece un alquiler de trescientos cincuenta mensuales como mínimo, de modo que me ahorro doscientos dólares. Calculo que podré desenvolverme trabajando cinco horas semanales, veinte mensuales. No está mal, dadas las circunstancias. Después de vivir tres años en la biblioteca, necesito el aire fresco y el ejercicio. Nadie sabrá que hago de jardinero. Además, estaré cerca de la señorita Birdie, mi cliente.

Nuestro trato es verbal, de mes a mes, de modo que si no funciona me trasladaré.

No hace mucho vi unos pisos muy bonitos, ideales para un abogado joven y prometedor. No llegaban a los noventa metros cuadrados, tenían dos habitaciones, costaban setecientos dóla res mensuales y yo estaba dispuesto a pagarlos. Las cosas han cambiado mucho desde entonces.

Ahora voy a instalarme en una reflexión tardía bastante espartana, concebida por la señorita Birdie y luego olvidada durante diez años. Dispone de una modesta sala de estar, con una moqueta afelpada color naranja y paredes verde pálido. Hay un dormitorio, una pequeña cocina funcional y un comedor aparte. Los techos inclinados, en todas las habitaciones, proporcionan un efecto bastante claustrofóbico a mi pequeño ático.

Es perfecto para mí. Siempre y cuando la señorita Birdie guarde las distancias, todo funcionará a pedir de boca. Me ha hecho prometer que no habría fiestas escandalosas, música fuerte, mujeres fáciles, bebida, drogas, perros ni gatos. Lo ha limpiado ella misma, ha fregado los suelos y las paredes, y ha retirado toda la basura que ha podido. Se ha pegado literalmente a mi lado cuando subía por la escalera con mis escasas pertenencias. Estoy seguro de que le daba pena.

Cuando acababa de subir la última caja y antes de poder empezar a desempaquetar, ha insistido en que tomáramos un café en el jardín.

Hemos permanecido sentados unos diez minutos, el tiempo necesario para que yo dejara de sudar, y entonces ha declarado que había llegado el momento de ocuparse de los parterres. He arrancado hierbajos hasta tener agujetas en la espalda. Durante unos minutos ha trabajado conmigo, pero luego se ha situado a mi espalda para darme órdenes.

Sólo logro huir del trabajo del jardín refugiándome al amparo de Yogi's. Hoy me toca atender la barra hasta la hora de cerrar, poco después de la una de la madrugada.

Esta noche el local está lleno y me cae el alma a los pies al comprobar que en dos largas mesas de un rincón delantero hay un montón de condiscípulos. Es la última reunión de una de las diversas sociedades de la facultad, a la que nadie me invitó a pertenecer. Se denomina Los letrados y la constituyen un grupo de importantes estudiantes, de los que participan en la revista de la facultad, que se toman a sí mismos demasiado en serio. Procuran darle un cariz secreto y exclusivo, con arcanos ritos de iniciación cantados en latín y otras idioteces por el estilo. Casi todos van a trabajar en grandes bufetes, o en la administración jurídica federal. Dos de ellos van a seguir sus estudios en la Facultad de Impuestos y Tributos de la Universidad de Nueva York. Son una pandilla de ostentosos.

Les sirvo una jarra tras otra de cerveza y no tardan en emborracharse. El más escandaloso es un renacuajo llamado Jacob Staples, un abogado joven y prometedor que ya había dominado el arte del juego sucio, cuando ingresó hace tres años en la Facultad de Derecho. Staples ha descubierto más formas de engaño que cualquier otra persona en la historia de esta facultad. Ha robado exámenes, escondido libros de consulta, plagiado ideas de todos los demás, y mentido a los profesores para retrasar trabajos e informes. No tardará en ganar un millón de dólares. Sospecho que fue él quien copió mi informe del *The Daily Report* y lo distribuyó por toda la facultad. Es típico de él.

Aunque procuro no prestarles atención, de vez en cuando les sorprendo mirándome fijamente. Oigo varias veces la palabra «insolvencia».

Pero estoy ocupado y voy tomando algún sorbo de cerveza, disimulada en un tazón de café. Prince está en el rincón opuesto, mirando la televisión y vigilando con cautela a Los letrados. Hoy está pendiente de las carreras de galgos en un campo de Florida, y ha apostado en todas. Esta noche, su compañero de apuestas y copas es su abogado, Bruiser Stone, un individuo enormemente gordo y robusto, con una exuberante y frondosa cabellera canosa, y una larga perilla. Pesa por lo menos ciento cincuenta kilos y juntos parecen un par de osos sentados en las rocas comiendo cacahuetes.

Bruiser Stone es un abogado de moralidad sumamente cuestionable. Se conocen desde hace mucho tiempo, eran condiscípulos en un instituto del sur de Memphis, y juntos han hecho muchos negocios turbios. Cuentan su dinero cuando nadie los observa. Sobornan a los políticos y a la policía. Prince da la cara, Bruiser cavila. Y cuando atrapan a Prince cometiendo algún delito, Bruiser aparece en primera página alegando que se trata de una injusticia. Es muy eficaz en los juzgados, primordialmente porque se sabe que ofrece importantes cantidades de dinero a los miembros del jurado. Prince no teme los veredictos de culpabilidad.

Bruiser tiene cuatro o cinco abogados en su bufete. No puedo imaginar lo desesperado que tendría que estar para pedirle trabajo. No se me ocurre nada peor en el mundo que confesarle a la gente que trabajo para Bruiser Stone.

Prince podría organizármelo. Le encantaría hacerme ese favor y demostrar su enorme influencia.

No puedo creer que esté pensando algo así.

DIEZ

Presionado por los cuatro, Smoot acaba por ceder y nos autoriza a regresar al Parque de los Cipreses por nuestra cuenta, sin ir en grupo ni tener que soportar otro almuerzo. Booker y yo entramos sigilosamente durante la interpretación de *Hermosa América* y nos sentamos en el fondo de la sala, mientras la señorita Birdie les habla de las ventajas de las vitaminas y de un buen ejercicio. Por fin se percata de nuestra presencia, e insiste en que nos acerquemos al atril para presentarnos formalmente.

Concluido el programa, Booker se instala en un rincón, donde se reúne con sus clientes y les ofrece asesoramiento que no quiere que oigan los demás. Puesto que yo ya he hablado con Dot y he pasado horas charlando con la señorita Birdie de su testamento, no me queda mucho que hacer. El señor DeWayne Deweese, mi tercer cliente de la visita anterior, está en el hospital y le he mandado por correo un resumen perfectamente inútil de mis sugerencias para ayudarle en su pequeña guerra privada contra la Administración de Veteranos.

El testamento de la señorita Birdie está incompleto y sin firmar. En los últimos días se ha vuelto muy susceptible respecto al mismo. Cabe la posibilidad de que quiera cambiarlo. Dice que no ha tenido noticias del reverendo Kenneth Chandler y puede que no le deje su fortuna. Yo procuro alentarla en dicho sentido.

Hemos mantenido varias conversaciones sobre el dinero. Le gusta esperar a verme hasta el cogote de tierra y estiércol, cubierto de turba y empapado de sudor, para acercarse y preguntarme inesperadamente:

—¿Podría la esposa de Delbert reclamar ante los tribunales si no les dejo nada? —o—, ¿qué me impide regalar el dinero ahora?

Paro, emerjo entre las plantas, me seco la cara y procuro pensar en una respuesta inteligente. Normalmente para entonces ha cambiado de tema y desea saber por qué no crecen aquellas azaleas.

He abordado el tema varias veces mientras tomamos café en el jardín, pero se pone nerviosa y agitada. Los abogados le inspiran un sano recelo.

He logrado comprobar algunos datos. Es cierto que estuvo casada en segundas nupcias con Anthony Murdine. Su matrimonio duró casi cinco años, hasta que él falleció en Atlanta hace cuatro años. Al parecer, el señor Murdine dejó a su muerte una cantidad considerable de bienes, que provocaron aparentemente una gran polémica, porque el tribunal del condado de De Kalb, en Georgia, ordenó el secreto del sumario. Hasta ahí he llegado. Tengo el propósito de hablar con alguno de los abogados relacionados con dichos bienes.

La señorita Birdie quiere hablar, celebrar una entrevista. Eso hace que se sienta importante ante su gente. Nos sentamos junto a una mesa cerca del piano, alejados de los demás, y acercamos nuestras cabezas a escasos centímetros la una de la otra. Se diría que no nos hemos visto desde hace un mes.

—Necesito saber lo que debo hacer con su testamento, señorita Birdie —digo—. Y antes de redactarlo debidamente, debo saber algo más acerca del dinero.

Mira subrepticiamente a su alrededor, como si todo el mundo estuviera escuchándola. A decir verdad, la mayoría de esas pobres almas serían incapaces de oírnos aunque nos habláramos a gritos.

—No hay nada invertido en propiedad inmobiliaria —dice con la mano junto a la boca y bajando el tono de su voz—. Acciones y obligaciones, fondos mutuos, bonos municipales.

Me sorprende oírle mencionar esas formas de inversión con evidente familiaridad. El dinero debe existir realmente.

—¿Quién lo administra? —pregunto innecesariamente.

No es un dato necesario para el testamento o para los bienes, pero me muero de curiosidad.

—Una firma de Atlanta.

—¿Un bufete de abogados? —pregunto asustado.

—Claro que no. No se lo confiaría a unos abogados. Un banco de depósito. Todo el dinero está invertido. Recibo los réditos hasta mi muerte y luego lo regalo. Así lo ha organizado el juez.

—¿Cuál es la cuantía de los réditos? —pregunto con absoluto desatino.

—¿No le parece, Rudy, que eso no es de su incumbencia?

Efectivamente, no lo es. He sido objeto de una merecida reprimenda, pero al mejor estilo jurídico procuro enmendar el entuerto.

—Compréndalo, podría ser importante, por razones tributarias.

—No le he pedido que se ocupe de mis impuestos. Para eso ya tengo a un gestor. Lo único que le he pedido ha sido que redacte un nuevo testamento y, cielos, parece que es demasiado para usted.

Bosco se acerca al otro extremo de la mesa y nos sonríe. Le faltan la mayoría de los dientes. La señorita Birdie le pide educadamente que vaya a jugar unos minutos al parchís. Es extraordinariamente amable y afectuosa con esa gente.

—Redactaré su testamento como usted lo desee, señorita Birdie —afirmo seriamente—. Pero debe decidirse.

Yergue la espalda, lanza un dramático suspiro y aprieta la dentadura postiza.

—Déjeme reflexionar.

—De acuerdo. Pero no lo olvide, hay muchas cosas en su testamento actual que no le gustan. Si le ocurriera algo...

—Lo sé, lo sé —responde sin dejar de agitar las manos—. No me sermonee. He hecho veinte testamentos en los últimos veinte años. Lo sé todo al respecto.

Bosco está llorando junto a la cocina y ella acude rápidamente para consolarlo. Por suerte, Booker acaba su consulta. Su último cliente es el anciano con quien pasó tanto tiempo durante nuestra primera visita. Evidentemente, el viejo no está demasiado satisfecho con el planteamiento de Booker y, en un momento dado, oigo que mi compañero le dice:

—Oiga, es gratuito. ¿Qué quiere que le diga?

Salimos apresuradamente después de despedirnos de la señorita Birdie. Los problemas jurídicos de los ancianos acaban de pasar a la historia. Dentro de unos días terminan las clases.

Después de odiar durante tres años la Facultad de Derecho, de pronto estamos a punto de ser liberados. En una ocasión oí que un abogado decía que han de transcurrir varios años antes de que desaparezcan el dolor y el sufrimiento de la facultad, hasta que, como con casi todo en la vida, nos queden sólo los buenos recuerdos. Parecía ponerse realmente melancólico cuando acudían a su mente reminiscencias de sus días de gloria como estudiante de Derecho.

Yo soy incapaz de imaginar un solo momento de mi vida en que al pensar retrospectivamente en los últimos tres años considere que fueron agradables después de todo. Puede que algún día logre evocar momentos felices con mis amigos, en compañía de Booker, en el bar de Yogi's, u otras situaciones que ahora no se me ocurren. Y estoy seguro de que Booker y yo acabaremos por reírnos al pensar en estos queridos viejecitos del Parque de los Cipreses, que tanta confianza han depositado en nosotros.

Puede que un día tenga gracia.

Sugiero que nos tomemos una cerveza en Yogi's. Yo invito. Son las dos de la tarde y está lloviendo, qué mejor forma de pasar la tarde que en la mesa de un bar. Puede que sea nuestra última oportunidad.

A Booker realmente le apetece, pero le esperan en su despacho dentro de una hora. Marvin Shankle le ha encargado que trabaje en un sumario que debe presentarse el lunes en el juzgado. Pasará todo el fin de semana sumergido en la biblioteca.

Shankle trabaja siete días por semana. Su bufete ha sido el pionero en gran parte de la litigación relacionada con los derechos civiles en Memphis y ahora cosecha vastas recompensas. Son veintidós abogados, todos negros, la mitad mujeres, y todos procuran sujetarse al horario brutal que impone Marvin Shankle. Las secretarias hacen turnos, de modo que siempre hay por lo menos tres disponibles, a cualquier hora del día o de la noche. Booker idolatra a Shankle y sé que en pocas semanas él trabajará también los domingos.

Me siento como un atracador circulando por los barrios periféricos en busca de la sucursal bancaria donde robar con mayor facilidad. Encuentro el bufete que estaba buscando, en un edificio moderno de piedra y cristal de cuatro pisos. Está en el este de Memphis, en una transitada calle que conduce en dirección oeste al centro de la ciudad y al río. Aquí fue donde aterrizaron los blancos.

En el bufete hay cuatro abogados, todos de unos treinta y cinco años, ex alumnos de la Universidad de Memphis. He oído decir que eran amigos en la facultad, fueron a trabajar en grandes bufetes en la ciudad, se hartaron de la presión y se reunieron aquí, en un lugar más tranquilo. He visto su anuncio en las páginas amarillas, una página entera, que según los rumores cuesta cuatro mil dólares mensuales. Se ocupan de todo, desde divorcios hasta transacciones inmobiliarias o parcelación, pero, evidentemente, su anuncio hace hincapié en su experiencia con víctimas de siniestros automovilísticos.

Independientemente de lo que haga un abogado, suele declararse experto en el campo de las lesiones personales, porque para la inmensa mayoría de los abogados que no tienen clientes a los que puedan facturar por horas eternamente su única esperanza de ganar una cantidad respetable de dinero consiste en representar a personas lesionadas o muertas en accidentes automovilísticos. El caso por ejemplo de la víctima de una colisión, en la que el otro conductor sea culpable y esté asegurado. Pasa una semana en el hospital, con una pierna rota y la consiguien-

103

te pérdida de salario. Si el abogado logra ponerse en contacto con él, antes de que lo haga el tasador de la compañía, puede sacarle cincuenta mil dólares al seguro. El abogado dedica un tiempo considerable al papeleo, pero probablemente no tenga necesidad de recurrir al juzgado. Invierte un máximo de treinta horas en el caso y recibe unos honorarios de unos quince mil. Eso equivale a quinientos dólares la hora.

Magnífico trabajo si uno puede conseguirlo. De ahí que casi todos los abogados en las páginas amarillas de Memphis apelen a las víctimas de accidentes automovilísticos. No es preciso tener experiencia en los juzgados; el noventa y nueve por ciento de los casos se resuelven sin acudir al juez. El quid consiste en conseguir el caso.

No me importa su anuncio. Lo único que me interesa es convencerles de que me ofrezcan un empleo. Permanezco unos momentos sentado en mi coche mientras la lluvia cae sobre el parabrisas. Preferiría que me azotaran antes de entrar en esa oficina, sonreírle amablemente a la recepcionista, charlar como un vendedor a domicilio y poner en práctica mi última estratagema, para poder saltar la valla y hablar con uno de sus jefes.

No puedo creer que esté haciéndolo.

ONCE

Mi pretexto para no asistir a la ceremonia de licenciatura es que tengo entrevistas en ciertos bufetes. Entrevistas prometedoras, le aseguro a Booker, aunque él sabe que no es cierto. Es perfectamente consciente de que lo único que hago es llamar de puerta en puerta y distribuir mi currículum como quien arroja confeti por toda la ciudad.

Booker es la única persona a quien le importa que me ponga una toga y un birrete, y participe en la celebración. Le decepciona que no asista. Mi madre y Hank están de viaje por algún lugar de Maine, observando la aparición de nuevas hojas verdes en los árboles. Hablé con ella hace un mes y no tiene ni la más remota idea de cuándo termina el curso.

He oído decir que la ceremonia es sumamente aburrida, con largos discursos pronunciados por viejos y ampulosos jueces, exhortando a los licenciados a amar la ley, a tratarla como una profesión honorable, respetarla como a una amante celosa y reconstruir su imagen tan mancillada por nuestros predecesores. *Ad nauseam.* Prefiero sentarme en Yogi's y ver cómo Prince apuesta en las carreras de chivos.

Booker estará allí con su familia: Charlene y sus hijos, sus padres, sus suegros, sus abuelos, tías, tíos y primos. El clan Kane constituirá un grupo formidable. Abundarán las lágrimas y las fotografías. Ha sido el primero de su familia en acabar una carrera universitaria y el hecho de licenciarse en Derecho es motivo de gran orgullo para ellos. Siento la tentación de ocultarme entre el público sólo para ver a sus padres cuando reciba el diploma. Probablemente lloraría con ellos.

No sé si la familia de Sara Plankmore estará presente en la celebración, pero no pienso arriesgarme. Me resulta insoportable la idea de verla sonreír ante la cámara acompañada de su prometido, S. Todd Wilcox. Con su holgada toga sería imposible ver si tenía la barriga abultada. Pero tendría que mirarla fijamente. Por mucho que me esforzara, sería incapaz de alejar la mirada de su cintura.

Es preferible no asistir a la ceremonia. Madeline Skinner me confesó hace un par de días que todos los demás licenciados habían encontrado algún tipo de trabajo. Muchos se contentaron con menos de lo que esperaban. Por lo menos quince de ellos se lanzan a la calle por cuenta propia, con un pequeño bufete y dispuestos a entrar en acción. Han conseguido dinero prestado de sus padres y tíos, y han alquilado pequeños despachos con muebles baratos. Madeline tiene los datos. Conoce el destino de todo el mundo. No estoy dispuesto en modo alguno a sentarme ahí con una toga y un birrete rodeado de ciento veinte condiscípulos, todos ellos conscientes de que yo, Rudy Baylor, soy el único imbécil que no ha conseguido empleo. Más me valdría ponerme una toga fluorescente y un birrete de neón. Ni pensarlo. Preferí recoger ayer mi diploma.

La ceremonia empieza a las dos de la tarde y exactamente a esa misma hora entro en el bufete de Jonathan Lake. Por primera vez, ésta será una segunda visita. Estuve aquí hace un mes para entregarle tímidamente mi currículum a la secretaria. Esta visita es diferente. Ahora tengo un plan.

He investigado un poco el bufete Lake, como es comúnmente conocido. Puesto que el señor Lake no es muy partidario de compartir su riqueza, es el único socio. Tiene doce abogados que trabajan para él, siete de ellos conocidos como juristas asociados y otros cinco más jóvenes que hacen un poco de todo. Los siete juristas asociados son expertos en juicios. Cada uno dispone de una secretaria, un pasante, e incluso el pasante tiene secretaria. En conjunto forman una denominada unidad ejecutiva, y cada una de ellas trabaja independientemente de las demás y sólo Jonathan Lake interviene en alguna ocasión para prestar apoyo. Él se reserva los casos que le interesan, habitualmente los que ofrecen un mayor potencial de un consistente veredicto. Le encanta demandar a los ginecólogos en casos de partos problemáticos y últimamente ha ganado una fortuna en un pleito por intoxicación con amianto.

Cada jurista asociado es responsable de su propio personal, puede contratar y despedir a su antojo, y se ocupa también de generar nuevos casos. He oído que casi el ochenta por ciento del negocio del bufete llega en forma de casos recomendados por otros abogados, picapleitos callejeros y letrados especializados en transacciones inmobiliarias, que de vez en cuando se encuentran con un cliente que ha sufrido lesiones. La remuneración de un jurista asociado viene determinada por varios factores, incluido el volumen de negocio que genera.

Barry X. Lancaster es la joven estrella floreciente del bufete, recientemente ascendido a jurista asociado, que en Navidad le sacó dos millones a un médico de Arkansas. Tiene treinta y dos años, está divorciado, vive en el despacho, y estudió Derecho en la Universidad de Memphis. He hecho mis deberes. También ha puesto un anuncio pidiendo un pasante. Lo he visto en *The Daily Record*. Si no puedo empezar como abogado, ¿qué tiene de malo hacerlo como pasante? Algún día se convertirá en una divertida anécdota, cuando tenga éxito y dirija mi propio gran bufete: el joven Rudy no pudo encontrar empleo como abogado y empezó pegando sellos en el despacho de Jonathan Lake; quién lo diría ahora.

Tengo una cita a las dos con Barry X. La recepcionista parece pensárselo dos veces, pero no insiste. Dudo que me reconozca de mi visita anterior. Desde entonces debe haber visto un millar de rostros. Me oculto tras una revista en un sofá de cuero y admiro las alfombras persas, los suelos de roble y las enormes vigas del techo. Este edificio era un antiguo almacén, situado cerca del distrito médico de Memphis. Se dice que Lake gastó tres millones de dólares para renovarlo y decorarlo como monumento a sí mismo. Lo he visto descrito en dos revistas diferentes.

A los pocos minutos, una secretaria me conduce por un laberinto de pasillos y vestíbulos a un despacho del piso superior. En el piso de abajo hay una biblioteca abierta, desprovista de paredes, sólo un sinfín de estanterías repletas de libros. Hay un único estudioso junto a una larga mesa, rodeado de textos, inmerso en una marea de teorías contradictorias.

El despacho de Barry X. es largo y estrecho, con paredes de ladrillo visto y un suelo que cruje al andar. Está adornado con antigüedades y accesorios. Nos estrechamos la mano y nos sentamos. Es fuerte y delgado, y recuerdo haber visto en las ilustraciones de la revista que el señor Lake había instalado un gimnasio para los empleados, que incluía una sauna y unos baños turcos.

Barry está bastante ocupado. Necesita indudablemente reunirse con su equipo para organizar la estrategia de algún caso importante. Su teléfono está situado de tal forma que veo parpadear las luces constantemente. Sus manos permanecen tranquilas y relajadas, pero no puede evitar consultar su reloj.

—Hábleme de su caso —dice después de unos breves comentarios preliminares—. Algo relacionado con una reclamación denegada por una compañía de seguros.

Ya está receloso, porque no visto como un cliente habitual, sino con chaqueta y corbata.

—La verdad es que estoy aquí en busca de trabajo —confieso sin tapujos.

¿Qué puedo perder? Lo único que puede hacer es pedirme que me marche.

Hace una mueca y agarra un trozo de papel. Esa maldita secretaria ha vuelto a meter la pata.

—He visto su anuncio para un pasante en *The Daily Record*.

—¿Es usted pasante? —pregunta inmediatamente.

—Podría serlo.

—¿Qué diablos quiere decir?

—He estudiado tres años en la Facultad de Derecho.

Me observa momentáneamente, mueve la cabeza y consulta su reloj.

—Estoy muy ocupado. Entréguele la solicitud a mi secretaria.

De pronto me pongo de pie y me apoyo en el escritorio.

—Voy a proponerle un trato —exclamo con dramatismo, y él levanta la cabeza sobresaltado.

Entonces le suelto mi discurso habitual sobre el hecho de que soy un estudiante listo y voluntarioso, entre el primer treinta por ciento de mi promoción, y le hablo de mi empleo con Brodnax & Speer y de lo mal que se han portado conmigo. Disparo todos mis cañones. Tinley Britt; mi odio por los grandes bufetes. Me vendo barato. Cualquier cosa para empezar. Necesito desesperadamente un trabajo.

Después de hablar sin interrupción durante un par de minutos, vuelvo a sentarme en mi silla.

Reflexiona unos instantes mientras se muerde una uña. No sé si está furioso o encantado.

—¿Sabe lo que me molesta? —dice por fin, evidentemente lejos de estar encantado.

—Sí, las personas como yo que mienten en la recepción para poder llegar hasta aquí y pedirle trabajo. Eso es exactamente lo que le molesta. No se lo reprocho. Yo también estaría molesto, pero lo superaría, y me diría: ese muchacho está a punto de ser abogado, pero en lugar de pagarle cuarenta mil, puedo contratarle para hacer el trabajo más duro por, digamos, veinticuatro mil.

—Veintiún mil.

—Acepto —respondo—. Empezaré a trabajar mañana por veintiún mil. Y trabajaré el año entero por el mismo salario. Prometo quedarme los doce meses, aunque apruebe el examen de colegiatura. Trabajaré sesenta o setenta horas semanales. Sin vacaciones. Le doy mi palabra. Firmaré un contrato.

—A nuestros pasantes les exigimos cinco años de experiencia. Nuestro trabajo es complejo.

—Lo aprenderé rápidamente. El verano pasado trabajé como auxiliar en un bufete del centro de la ciudad, me ocupaba exclusivamente de pleitos.

Aquí ocurre algo injusto y acaba de percatarse de ello. He entrado empuñando la espada y le he tendido una emboscada. Es evidente que lo he hecho otras veces, a juzgar por la rapidez de mis respuestas.

No lo compadezco. Puede echarme cuando se le antoje.

—Se lo mencionaré al señor Lake —dice, cediendo un poco—. Tiene unas normas bastante rígidas en lo concerniente al personal. No estoy autorizado a contratar un pasante que no se ajuste a nuestras especificaciones.

—Por supuesto —respondo con tristeza.

Otra patada en el trasero. En realidad, ya empiezo a acostumbrarme. He descubierto que los abogados, aunque estén muy ocupados, sienten cierta compasión por un recién licenciado que no encuentra trabajo. Una compasión muy limitada.

—Puede que dé su aprobación, en cuyo caso el trabajo es suyo —dice para suavizar el golpe.

—Hay algo más —insisto—. Tengo un caso. Un caso muy bueno.

Eso le provoca un gran recelo.

—¿Qué clase de caso? —pregunta.

—De mala fe, por parte de una compañía de seguros.

—¿Es usted el cliente?

—No. Soy el abogado. Me he tropezado casualmente con él.

—¿Cuánto hay en juego?

Le entrego un resumen de dos páginas del caso de los Black, abundantemente modificado y más sensacionalista. Desde hace algún tiempo, cada vez que algún abogado lee la sinopsis y me rechaza, la perfecciono gradualmente.

Barry X. la lee atentamente, con mayor concentración que todos los que la han visto hasta ahora. Mientras la lee por segunda vez, yo admiro las paredes de ladrillo envejecido y sueño con un despacho parecido.

—No está mal —dice cuando termina, con un destello en la mirada que parece delatar que está más emocionado de lo que aparenta—. Deje que lo adivine. Usted quiere el empleo y una participación en el negocio.

—No. Sólo el empleo. El caso es suyo. Me gustaría trabajar en el mismo y es imprescindible que trate con el cliente. Pero los honorarios son suyos.

—Una porción de los honorarios. El señor Lake se queda con la mayor parte —afirma con una torcida sonrisa.

En todo caso y con toda franqueza, no me importa cómo se

repartan el dinero. Lo único que quiero es un empleo. Sólo de pensar en la perspectiva de trabajar para Jonathan Lake, en un entorno tan suntuoso, me da vueltas la cabeza.

He decidido reservar para mí a la señorita Birdie. Como cliente no tiene tanto atractivo, porque no gasta nada en abogados. Además, probablemente llegará a los ciento veinte, de modo que carece de utilidad como comodín. Estoy seguro de que existen abogados expertos que le mostrarían las diversas formas de darles dinero, pero eso no interesaría al bufete de Lake. Su especialidad son los pleitos. Lo suyo no es redactar testamentos y valorar bienes.

Vuelvo a ponerme de pie. Ya he abusado bastante del tiempo de Barry.

—Sé que está muy ocupado —digo con toda la franqueza posible—. Le he hablado con absoluta sinceridad. Puede pedir referencias en la Facultad de Derecho. Llame a Madeline Skinner si le parece bien.

—La loca de Madeline. ¿Sigue todavía ahí?

—Sí, y en este momento es mi mejor amiga. Ella responderá por mí.

—Claro. Me pondré en contacto con usted lo antes posible.

Estoy seguro de que lo hará.

Me pierdo dos veces cuando intento encontrar la puerta principal. Puesto que nadie me observa, admiro tranquilamente los despachos desparramados por el edificio. En un momento dado me detengo al borde de la biblioteca y contemplo los tres niveles de pasillos y corredores. No existen dos despachos que se parezcan en lo más mínimo. Las salas de conferencias están repartidas irregularmente. Secretarias, administrativos y auxiliares se desplazan silenciosamente sobre suelos de madera.

Trabajaría aquí por mucho menos de veintiún mil.

Aparco silenciosamente detrás del largo Cadillac y me apeo sin hacer ruido alguno. No estoy de humor para trasplantar crisantemos. Rodeo sigilosamente la casa y me encuentro con un gran montón de enormes sacos de plástico blanco. Docenas y docenas. Toneladas de estiércol. Cada saco contiene cincuenta kilos. Ahora recuerdo que hace unos días la señorita Birdie mencionó algo relacionado con la fertilización de los parterres, pero no tenía ni idea.

Me apresuro a alcanzar la escalera que conduce a mi piso y cuando ya casi estoy arriba oigo que me llama.

—Rudy. Rudy querido, vamos a tomar un café —dice junto

al monumento de estiércol, con una sonrisa que exhibe sus dientes grises y amarillos.

Se siente realmente feliz de verme. Está a punto de oscurecer y le encanta tomar café en el jardín durante la puesta del sol.

—Claro —respondo, al tiempo que dejo la chaqueta doblada sobre la barandilla y me quito la corbata.

—¿Cómo estás, querido? —canturrea con la cabeza levantada.

Hace aproximadamente una semana que ha empezado a llamarme «querido». Querido eso y querido lo otro.

—Muy bien. Cansado. Me duele la espalda.

Hace varios días que me quejo de la espalda, pero todavía no ha captado la indirecta.

Me instalo en mi silla habitual mientras ella prepara su horrenda infusión en la cocina. Es casi la hora del crepúsculo y el jardín empieza a quedar sumido en la sombra. Cuento los sacos de estiércol. Ocho de anchura, cuatro de profundidad y ocho de altura. Eso son doscientos cincuenta y seis sacos, a cincuenta kilos por saco, supone un total de doce mil ochocientos kilos de estiércol, que alguien debe esparcir. Yo.

Tomamos café, a diminutos sorbos en mi caso, y me pregunta por todo lo que he hecho hoy. Miento y le cuento que he hablado con unos abogados sobre unos pleitos, antes de dedicarme a estudiar para el examen de colegiatura. Lo mismo que mañana. Siempre muy ocupado, como es habitual entre los abogados. Evidentemente no dispongo de tiempo para acarrear una tonelada de estiércol.

Ambos tenemos los sacos blancos delante, pero ninguno de nosotros quiere mirarlos. Evito que se crucen nuestras miradas.

—¿Cuándo empezarás a trabajar como abogado? —pregunta.

—No estoy seguro —respondo, antes de explicarle por enésima vez que debo estudiar mucho durante las próximas semanas, sumergirme plenamente en los libros, con la esperanza de aprobar el examen.

No podré ejercer hasta que lo haya aprobado.

—Estupendo —dice antes de perderse momentáneamente en la lejanía—. Nos conviene empezar cuanto antes con ese estiércol —agrega moviendo la cabeza y levantando la mirada al cielo.

En este momento no sé qué responder.

—Hay un buen montón —digo al cabo de unos instantes.

—No será tan difícil. Yo también ayudaré.

Eso significa que señalará con la pala y charlará incesantemente.

—Bueno, tal vez mañana. Ahora es tarde y hoy he tenido un día muy duro.

Reflexiona unos instantes.

—Esperaba que pudiéramos empezar esta tarde —insiste—. Yo también ayudaré.

—El caso es que todavía no he comido —respondo.

—Te prepararé un bocadillo —dice inmediatamente.

Para la señorita Birdie, un bocadillo es una lonja transparente de embutido de pavo, entre dos finas rebanadas de pan blanco sin grasa. Ni una gota de mostaza o mayonesa. Jamás se le ocurriría agregar lechuga ni queso. Necesitaría por lo menos cuatro para saciar el más mínimo vestigio de hambre.

Suena el teléfono y se levanta para dirigirse a la cocina. Todavía no dispongo de una línea independiente en mi piso, aunque hace dos semanas que me la ha prometido. Actualmente tengo un supletorio, lo cual significa que no puedo hablar en privado por teléfono. Me ha pedido que limite mis llamadas para que ella pueda disponer de acceso a la línea. Raramente llama.

—Es para ti, Rudy —dice desde la cocina—. Un abogado.

Es Barry X. Dice que ha hablado con Jonathan Lake y que podemos mantener otra conversación. Me pregunta si puedo acudir a su despacho ahora, en este mismo momento, donde estará trabajando toda la noche. Y quiere que le lleve el sumario. Desea ver todos los documentos relacionados con el caso de mala fe.

Mientras hablamos, observo cómo la señorita Birdie prepara cuidadosamente un bocadillo de pavo. En el momento en que lo corta por la mitad, cuelgo el teléfono.

—Debo salir corriendo, señorita Birdie —exclamo sin aliento—. Ha surgido un contratiempo. He de hablar inmediatamente con este abogado de un caso importante.

—Pero tu...

—Lo siento. Me lo comeré mañana.

La dejo con medio bocadillo en cada mano y aspecto deprimido, como si le pareciera realmente increíble que no comiera con ella.

Barry me recibe en la puerta principal, que está cerrada con llave, aunque dentro hay todavía mucha gente trabajando. Le sigo a su despacho, con un paso ligeramente más rápido que en los últimos días. No puedo evitar mi admiración por las alfombras, los estantes de libros y las obras de arte, y pienso que no tardaré en formar parte de aquel entorno. Yo, uno de los componentes del bufete Lake, los abogados más destacados en los juzgados de la zona.

Me ofrece una empanada de huevo, los restos de su cena. Dice que come tres veces al día en su despacho. Recuerdo que está divorciado y ahora comprendo por qué. No tengo hambre.

Pulsa un botón de su dictáfono y coloca el micrófono al borde de la mesa, cerca de mí.

—Grabaremos la conversación. Mañana la transcribirá mi secretaria. ¿De acuerdo?

—Por supuesto —respondo, lo que se le antoje.

—Le contrataré como pasante por un período de doce meses. Su salario será de veintiún mil dólares anuales, pagaderos en doce partes iguales el día quince de cada mes. No tendrá derecho a seguro médico ni a ningún otro beneficio adicional hasta que haya cumplido un año en la empresa. Transcurridos los primeros doce meses, evaluaremos nuestra relación y exploraremos la posibilidad de renovar su contrato, no como pasante, sino como abogado.

—De acuerdo. Me parece bien.

—Tendrá un despacho y vamos a contratar a una secretaria para que le ayude. Su horario mínimo serán sesenta horas semanales, a partir de las ocho de la mañana y hasta cuando sea. Ningún abogado de este bufete trabaja menos de sesenta horas semanales.

—No tengo ningún inconveniente.

Trabajaré noventa horas. Eso me mantendrá alejado de la señorita Birdie y de su estiércol.

Estudia cuidadosamente sus notas.

—Y nosotros nos convertiremos en los abogados de... ¿cómo se llama su caso?

—Black. *Black contra Great Benefit*.

—De acuerdo. Representaremos a los Black contra Great Benefit Insurance Company. Usted trabajará en el caso, pero no tendrá derecho a ningún beneficio del mismo si lo hubiera.

—Eso es.

Se acerca al micrófono y pregunta:

—¿Se le ocurre algo más?

—¿Cuándo empiezo?

—Ahora. Me gustaría revisar el caso esta noche, si tiene tiempo.

—Por supuesto.

—¿Algo más?

Respiro hondo.

—A principios de este mes presenté una petición de insolvencia. Es una larga historia.

113

—¿No lo son siempre? ¿Siete o trece?

—Un simple siete.

—Entonces no afectará sus ingresos. Por otra parte, estudiará para su examen de colegiatura en sus horas libres, ¿de acuerdo?

—Desde luego.

Para el dictáfono y vuelve a ofrecerme una empanada de huevo. La rechazo. A continuación le sigo por una escalera de caracol hasta una pequeña biblioteca.

—Aquí es fácil perderse —dice.

—Es increíble —respondo admirado por el laberinto de salas y pasadizos.

Nos sentamos junto a una mesa y empezamos a examinar los documentos de los Black. Le impresiona mi organización. Pide ciertos papeles. Los tengo a mano. Quiere fechas y nombres. Los conozco de memoria. Hago copias de todos los documentos, una para su ficha y otra para la mía.

Lo tengo todo menos un contrato firmado para representar legalmente a los Black. Eso parece sorprenderle y le cuento cómo se ha establecido nuestra relación.

Necesitamos un contrato, repite varias veces.

Abandono el edificio después de las diez y me sorprendo sonriendo por el retrovisor cuando cruzo la ciudad. Llamaré a Booker a primera hora de la mañana para darle la buena noticia. Luego le llevaré unas flores a Madeline Skinner y le daré las gracias.

Puede que sea un trabajo humilde, pero a partir de ahí puedo ascender. Dentro de un año estaré ganando más dinero que Sara Plankmore, S. Todd, N. Elizabeth, F. Franklin y un centenar de imbéciles de los que me he ocultado durante el último mes. Es sólo cuestión de tiempo.

Paro en Yogi's y tomo una copa con Prince. Le comunico la maravillosa noticia y me da un fuerte abrazo. Dice que lamenta que me vaya. Le respondo que me gustaría seguir trabajando aproximadamente un mes, tal vez los fines de semana, hasta después del examen de colegiatura. A Prince todo le parece bien.

Me siento solo a una mesa del fondo, con una cerveza fresca y contemplo la escasa clientela. Ya no estoy avergonzado. Por primera vez en varias semanas, no me agobia la humillación. Ahora estoy listo para entrar en acción, listo para emprender mi carrera. Sueño con enfrentarme algún día a Loyd Beck ante un tribunal.

DOCE

Al repasar los casos y documentos que me entregó Max Leuberg, no ha dejado de asombrarme el extremo al que han llegado las opulentas compañías de seguros para estafar a personas indefensas. Ni un solo dólar es demasiado insignificante para sus arcas. Ninguna estratagema excesivamente compleja para obtenerlo. También me ha sorprendido el pequeño número de asegurados que presentan denuncias. La mayoría no consultan siquiera a un abogado. Les muestran una retahíla de cláusulas y apéndices, y los convencen de que sólo creían estar asegurados. Cierto estudio señala que no llegan al cinco por ciento las denegaciones de mala fe que llega a ver algún abogado. Las personas que contratan dichas pólizas no son gente educada. La mera idea de comparecer en un juzgado y declarar ante un juez y un jurado basta para que no hablen.

Barry Lancaster y yo dedicamos la mayor parte de dos días a estudiar los documentos de los Black. Barry se ha ocupado de varios casos de mala fe a lo largo de los años, con diferentes grados de éxito. No se cansa de repetir que los jurados de Memphis son tan conservadores que es difícil obtener un veredicto justo. Hace tres años que oigo lo mismo. Para una ciudad meridional, Memphis es un poderoso centro sindicalista, y las ciudades con fuerza sindical suelen producir buenos veredictos para los demandantes. Pero por alguna razón incomprensible, aquí raramente se da el caso. Jonathan Lake ha obtenido un puñado de veredictos de millones de dólares, pero ahora prefiere celebrar juicios en otros estados.

Todavía no he conocido al señor Lake. Asiste a un juicio importante en algún lugar y no parece preocuparle conocer a su nuevo empleado.

Mi despacho temporal está al borde de una pequeña biblioteca, con vista al segundo piso. En la misma hay tres mesas redondas y ocho estantes de libros, todos ellos relacionados con trata-

115

miento médico equívoco, nocivo o ilegal. Durante mi primer día en el bufete, Barry me mostró una bonita sala cerca de su despacho y me contó que sería mía dentro de un par de semanas. Necesita pintura y hay que reparar la instalación eléctrica. ¿Qué se puede esperar de un almacén?, ha repetido varias veces.

No he conocido a nadie más en el bufete y estoy seguro de que ello se debe a que trabajo como simple pasante, y no como abogado. No soy nada nuevo ni especial. Los pasantes van y vienen.

Las personas que trabajan aquí están muy ocupadas y no se caracterizan por su camaradería. Barry apenas habla de los demás abogados del bufete y me da la impresión de que cada equipo de juristas actúa bastante por su cuenta. También tengo la sensación de que dirigir un pleito bajo la supervisión de Jonathan Lake es un asunto delicado.

Barry llega al despacho todas las mañanas antes de las ocho y he decidido esperarlo junto a la puerta, hasta que me entreguen una llave del edificio. Evidentemente, el señor Lake es muy cauteloso en cuanto a permitir acceso al bufete. Se debe a una larga historia relacionada con la intervención de los teléfonos, hace muchos años, durante un ensañado pleito contra una compañía de seguros. Barry me lo contó cuando le mencioné por primera vez la llave. Tal vez deberá esperar varias semanas, me respondió. Y pasar por el detector de mentiras.

Me instaló al borde de la biblioteca, me dio instrucciones y se retiró a su despacho. Durante los dos primeros días comprobaba lo que hacía cada dos horas aproximadamente. Copié todos los documentos de los Black. Sin su conocimiento hice una segunda copia de todos los papeles para mi archivo personal, que me llevé a mi casa al final del segundo día, en el elegante maletín que me ha regalado Prince.

Según las indicaciones de Barry, redacté una carta bastante implacable dirigida a Great Benefit, señalando todos los hechos importantes e irregularidades por su parte. Cuando su secretaria acabó de mecanografiarla tenía cuatro páginas. Entonces, Barry la recortó severamente y me ordenó regresar a mi rincón. Es sumamente concienzudo y está muy orgulloso de su capacidad de síntesis.

Durante mi tercer día en el bufete acumulé por fin el valor necesario para preguntarle a su secretaria por los papeles relativos a mi empleo. Estaba ocupada, pero me respondió que se ocuparía de ello.

Aquel día, Barry y yo salimos de su despacho poco después de las nueve. Había finalizado la carta dirigida a Great Benefit, una obra maestra de tres páginas que se remitiría por correo certificado, con acuse de recibo. Nunca menciona su vida ajena al despacho. Le sugerí que tomáramos juntos una cerveza y nos comiéramos un bocadillo, pero rechazó inmediatamente mi propuesta.

Me dirigí a Yogi's en busca de algo de comer. El local estaba lleno de condiscípulos borrachos y el propio Prince servía a contrapelo las bebidas. Le sustituí para que pudiera regresar a sus quehaceres habituales. Estaba encantado.

Volvió a su mesa predilecta, donde su abogado, Bruiser Stone, fumaba un Camel tras otro y aceptaba apuestas sobre un combate de boxeo. Bruiser ha aparecido de nuevo en el periódico esta mañana negando que tuviera información alguna. Hace un par de años, la policía encontró un cadáver en un contenedor de basura, detrás de un local *topless*. El difunto era un maleante local, propietario de parte del negocio de la pornografía en la ciudad, que evidentemente quería introducirse en el negocio de las tetas al aire. Cometió el error de pisar un terreno equivocado sin la propuesta adecuada y fue decapitado. Bruiser no haría algo semejante, pero la policía parece estar bastante convencida de que sabe exactamente quién lo hizo.

Últimamente ha venido mucho por aquí, donde no deja de beber y hablar secretamente con Prince.

Menos mal que tengo un trabajo como Dios manda. Estaba casi decidido a pedirle un empleo a Bruiser.

Hoy es viernes, mi cuarto día como empleado del bufete Lake. Se lo he contado a un puñado de personas y me gusta cómo suena cuando lo pronuncio. Tiene un tono muy agradable. El bufete Lake. Todo el mundo lo conoce. Basta mencionar el nombre para que todo el mundo recuerde el magnífico edificio y sepa que es la sede del gran Jonathan Lake y de su equipo de provocativos letrados.

Booker estuvo a punto de echar a llorar. Compró chuletas y una botella de vino sin alcohol. Charlene preparó la comida y lo celebramos hasta la medianoche.

No tenía previsto levantarme antes de las siete de la mañana, pero alguien llama ruidosamente a la puerta de mi piso. Es la señorita Birdie.

—¡Rudy! ¡Rudy!

Quito el cerrojo e irrumpe en mi casa.

—Rudy. ¿Estás despierto?

Me contempla en mi pequeña cocina. Llevo calzoncillos y camiseta, nada indecente. Mis ojos apenas están abiertos y mi cabello completamente revuelto. Estoy casi despierto.

Está saliendo el sol, pero su delantal ya esta manchado de tierra y sus zapatos cubiertos de barro.

—Buenos días —digo esforzándome por no parecer enojado.

—¿Te he despertado? —pregunta alegremente mientras me sonríe con sus dientes grises y amarillos.

—No, estaba levantándome.

—Estupendo. Tenemos trabajo que hacer.

—¿Trabajo? Pero...

—Sí, Rudy. Hace demasiado tiempo que te has despreocupado del estiércol, ha llegado el momento de trabajar. Se pudrirá si no lo utilizamos.

Parpadeo y procuro enfocar la mirada.

—Hoy es viernes —farfullo con cierta inseguridad.

—No. Es sábado —replica.

Nos miramos mutuamente unos segundos y consulto mi reloj, algo a lo que ya me he acostumbrado después de sólo tres días de trabajo.

—Es viernes, señorita Birdie. Viernes. Hoy he de trabajar.

—Es sábado —repite obstinadamente.

Seguimos mirándonos unos instantes. Ella observa mis calzoncillos y yo sus zapatos enfangados.

—Escúcheme, señorita Birdie —digo amablemente—. Sé que hoy es viernes y me esperan en el despacho dentro de una hora y media. Nos ocuparemos del estiércol este fin de semana.

Evidentemente sólo intento tranquilizarla. Mañana por la mañana había previsto quedarme en el despacho.

—Se pudrirá.

—No antes de mañana.

¿Se pudre realmente el estiércol en los sacos? No lo creo.

—Mañana quería ocuparme de las rosas.

—Por qué no se ocupa hoy de las rosas mientras estoy en el despacho y mañana esparcimos el estiércol.

Reflexiona unos instantes y de pronto se entristece. Baja los hombros y pone cara de pesar. Es difícil saber si se siente avergonzada.

—¿Me lo prometes? —pregunta sumisamente.

—Se lo prometo.

—Me dijiste que te ocuparías del jardín si te rebajaba el alquiler.

—Sí, lo sé.

¿Cómo podía haberlo olvidado? Me lo ha recordado ya una docena de veces.

—Bien, de acuerdo —dice, como si hubiera conseguido exactamente lo que se proponía.

Luego sale y baja por la escalera, sin dejar de musitar consigo misma. Cierro sigilosamente la puerta y me pregunto a qué hora me llamará mañana.

Me visto y voy en mi coche al despacho, donde hay ya media docena de coches aparcados y el edificio parcialmente iluminado. Todavía no son las siete. Espero en mi coche hasta que veo llegar otro vehículo al aparcamiento y me acerco a la puerta para coincidir con un hombre de edad madura. En una mano lleva un maletín y una taza de café, mientras con la otra busca las llaves en el bolsillo.

Parece sobresaltado por mi presencia. Ésta no es una zona particularmente peligrosa, pero está cerca del centro de Memphis y la gente desconfía.

—Buenos días —digo amablemente.

—Buenos días —refunfuña—. ¿Qué se le ofrece?

—Soy el nuevo pasante de Barry Lancaster, vengo a trabajar.

—¿Cómo se llama?

—Rudy Baylor.

Deja de mover momentáneamente la mano y me mira con ceño. Su labio inferior se levanta, se dobla hacia fuera y mueve la cabeza.

—No me suena. Yo soy el administrador general. Nadie me ha dicho nada.

—Me ha contratado hace cuatro días, se lo juro.

Introduce la llave en la cerradura mientras mira temerosamente por encima del hombro. Me toma por un ladrón o un asesino. Llevo chaqueta y corbata, y mi aspecto es bastante respetable.

—Lo siento. El señor Lake tiene unas normas de seguridad muy rigurosas. Nadie entra en el edificio antes de la hora de apertura, a no ser que esté en nómina —dice antes de saltar al interior—. Dígale a Barry que me llame esta mañana —agrega y me cierra la puerta en las narices.

Decido no esperar en la puerta a que llegue la próxima persona que esté en nómina. Voy en mi coche hasta una cafetería a pocas manzanas, donde compro un periódico, una empanada y un café. Después de una hora respirando humo de cigarrillo y escuchando chismes, regreso al aparcamiento, donde encuentro más coches que antes: vehículos elegantes, modelos alemanes y otras lujosas marcas importadas. Aparco cuidadosamente junto a un Chevrolet.

La recepcionista me ha visto ir y venir varias veces, pero me trata como a un perfecto desconocido. No pienso comunicarle que ahora soy un empleado, como ella. Llama a Barry y éste autoriza mi entrada en el laberinto.

Lo esperan en el juzgado a las nueve para comparecer en un

caso de responsabilidad de productos defectuosos, y está ajetreado. Estoy decidido a hablar con él de mi inclusión en la nómina de la empresa, pero es un mal momento. Puede esperar un día o dos. Momentáneamente, mientras introduce los sumarios en un grueso maletín, me ilusiono con la idea de acompañarlo esta mañana al juzgado.

Pero él tiene otros planes.

—Quiero que vea a los Black y regrese con un contrato firmado. Es preciso hacerlo ahora —dice con verdadero hincapié en la palabra «ahora», de modo que no me quepa la menor duda sobre lo que debo hacer, antes de entregarme una fina carpeta—. Aquí está el contrato. Lo preparé anoche. Examínelo. Deben firmarlo los tres: Dot, Buddy y Donny Ray, puesto que es adulto.

Asiento confiadamente, pero preferiría que me azotaran antes de pasar la mañana con los Black. Por fin conoceré a Donny Ray, justo cuando ya creía poder postergar eternamente nuestro encuentro.

—¿Y luego? —pregunto.

—Estaré en el juzgado todo el día. Venga a reunirse conmigo en la sala del juez Anderson.

Suena su teléfono y agita la mano para despedirme, como si hubiera concluido nuestra entrevista.

La idea de reunir a los Black alrededor de la mesa de la cocina para una firma colectiva no me apetece. Me veré obligado a ver cómo Dot cruza el jardín para acercarse al destartalado Fairlane, refunfuñando a cada paso y luego convenciendo a Buddy con alguna estratagema, para que abandone sus gatos y su ginebra. Probablemente tirará de su oreja para sacarle del coche. Podría ser desagradable. Y luego deberé esperar nervioso mientras se dirige al fondo de la casa para preparar a Donny Ray, y aguantarme la respiración cuando venga para conocerme a mí, su abogado.

Para evitarlo en la medida de lo posible, paro junto a una cabina telefónica y llamo a Dot. Es lamentable. En el bufete Lake disponen de la tecnología electrónica más avanzada y me veo obligado a utilizar un teléfono público. Afortunadamente responde Dot. No puedo imaginar una conversación con Buddy. Dudo que su Fairlane tenga teléfono.

Contesta con su recelo habitual, pero accede a verme unos minutos. No le pido exactamente que reúna a la familia, pero subrayo que necesito la firma de todos ellos. Además, y para no perder la costumbre, le digo que tengo muchísima prisa, que debo presentarme en el juzgado, que los jueces me esperan.

Los mismos perros gruñen tras la verja metálica de la casa adjunta cuando aparco frente a la casa de los Black. Dot está en su abarrotado pórtico, con un cigarrillo a escasos centímetros de los labios y una nube azulada que asciende por el jardín desde su cabeza. Hace un rato que fuma y espera.

Le brindo una forzada sonrisa y la saludo efusivamente. Las arrugas alrededor de su boca apenas se alteran. La sigo a través de la abigarrada y mugrienta sala de estar, frente al sofá rasgado situado bajo una colección de viejos retratos de los Black en sus tiempos felices, caminando sobre una vieja moqueta sucia salpicada de pequeñas alfombras para ocultar los agujeros, hasta llegar a la cocina donde nadie nos espera.

—¿Café? —pregunta al tiempo que me ofrece mi silla habitual.

—No, gracias. Sólo un vaso de agua.

Llena un vaso de plástico con agua del grifo, sin hielo, y lo coloca delante de mí sobre la mesa. Ambos miramos lentamente por la ventana.

—No logro convencerlo para que venga —dice sin la menor frustración.

Supongo que hay días en los que Buddy está dispuesto a venir y otros no.

—¿Por qué no? —pregunto, como si su conducta pudiera racionalizarse.

Se limita a encogerse de hombros.

—También necesita a Donny Ray, ¿no es cierto?

—Sí.

Abandona la cocina y me deja con mi agua tibia y la vista de Buddy. En realidad no es fácil verlo, porque el parabrisas no se ha limpiado desde hace décadas y el capó está cubierto de gatos sarnosos. Lleva puesta algún tipo de gorra, probablemente con orejeras de lana, y levanta lentamente la botella. Parece estar envuelta en una bolsa de papel castaño. Toma un sosegado trago.

Oigo a Dot, que habla suavemente con su hijo. Cruzan lentamente la sala de estar y entran en la cocina. Me pongo de pie para saludar a Donny Ray Black.

Sea cual fuere la causa, está definitivamente a punto de morir. Tiene un aspecto terriblemente desvaído y demacrado, con las mejillas hundidas y pálido como la cera. Ya no era corpulento antes de la enfermedad, pero ahora, doblado por la cintura, no es más alto que su madre. Su cabello y sus cejas, de color negro azabache, contrastan con la palidez de su piel. Pero sonríe y me tiende una cadavérica mano, que estrecho fuertemente.

Dot, que no ha dejado de sostenerlo por la cintura, lo ayuda a sentarse suavemente en una silla. Lleva unos vaqueros holgados y una sencilla camiseta blanca, que cuelga torpemente de su esqueleto.

—Encantado de conocerte —digo, procurando evitar sus ojos hundidos.

—Mi mamá ha hablado muy bien de ti —responde con una voz débil y carrasposa, pero pronunciando con claridad.

Nunca supuse que Dot dijera cosas agradables de mí.

Donny Ray apoya la barbilla en ambas manos, como si su cabeza fuera incapaz de sostenerse sola.

—Dice que vas a demandar a esos cabrones de Great Benefit y los obligarás a pagar —agrega, con más desesperación que enojo.

—Así es —respondo al tiempo que abro mi carpeta, saco una copia de la carta que Barry X. ha mandado a Great Benefit y se la entrego a Dot, que está de pie a la espalda de Donny Ray—. Hemos presentado esto —explico como un diligente abogado, utilizando el término «presentar», en lugar de «mandar», que suena mejor y da la impresión de que estamos actuando realmente—. No confiamos en una respuesta satisfactoria por su parte, de modo que dentro de unos días iniciaremos los trámites de la demanda. Probablemente les pediremos un millón como mínimo.

Dot echa una ojeada a la carta y la deja sobre la mesa. Me esperaba una retahíla de preguntas sobre la razón por la que no los hemos demandado todavía. Temía que se enojara. Pero se limita a frotarle suavemente la espalda a Donny Ray y a mirar melancólicamente por la ventana. Se expresará con cautela, porque no desea disgustar a su hijo.

—¿Va a venir papá? —pregunta Donny Ray, con la mirada fija en la ventana.

—Dice que no —responde Dot.

Saco el contrato de la carpeta y se lo entrego a Dot.

—Antes de demandarlos hay que firmar esto. Es un contrato entre ustedes, los clientes, y mi bufete. Un contrato de representación legal.

Son sólo dos páginas.

—¿Qué contiene? —pregunta Dot con cierta desconfianza.

—Bueno, lo habitual. El texto es muy comprensible. Ustedes nos contratan como abogados, nosotros nos ocupamos del caso, saldamos todos los gastos y nos quedamos con un tercio de lo que se recupere.

—¿Entonces para qué se necesitan dos páginas de letra menuda? —pregunta al tiempo que coge un cigarrillo de una cajetilla que está sobre la mesa.

—¡No lo enciendas! —exclama Donny por encima del hombro, después se gira para mirarme—. No me sorprende que esté muriéndome.

Se coloca el cigarrillo entre los labios sin titubear, pero no lo enciende, y sigue examinando el documento.

—¿Y los tres debemos firmarlo?

—Efectivamente.

—Pues ha dicho que no pensaba entrar en la casa —declara Dot.

—Entonces llévaselo al coche —replica Donny Ray enojado—. Llévale el documento y una pluma, y oblígale a firmar este maldito contrato.

—No se me había ocurrido —dice Dot.

—Lo hemos hecho otras veces —comenta Donny Ray antes de agachar la cabeza y rascarse el cráneo.

La exclamación le ha dejado sin aliento.

—Supongo que podría hacerlo —agrega Dot, todavía indecisa.

—¡Hazlo, maldita sea! —exclama Donny Ray.

Dot hurga en un cajón, hasta encontrar una pluma. Donny Ray levanta la cabeza y la apoya sobre sus manos. Sus muñecas son tan delgadas como el palo de una escoba.

—Volveré en seguida —dice Dot, como si fuera a hacer un recado a la vuelta de la esquina y estuviera preocupada por su hijo.

Cruza lentamente el jardín para dirigirse a la zona de hierbajos. Uno de los gatos del capó ve que se aproxima y se esconde debajo del coche.

—Hace unos meses... —empieza a decir Donny Ray con la respiración entrecortada y bamboleando ligeramente la cabeza—. Hace unos meses —repite después de hacer una prolongada pausa—, necesitábamos que un notario certificara su firma y tampoco quiso moverse. Mi madre localizó a una notaria que acudía a domicilio por veinte dólares, pero cuando llegó, mi padre se negó a salir del coche. Entonces mi madre y la notaria se le acercaron entre los hierbajos. ¿Ves ese gran gato color naranja sobre el coche?

—Sí.

—Es una gata a la que llamamos *Garras*. Es una especie de gato de vigilancia. El caso es que cuando la notaria introdujo las manos en el coche para recuperar los documentos de Buddy, que por supuesto estaba como una cuba y apenas consciente, *Garras* saltó del techo del vehículo y la atacó. Nos costó sesenta dólares de asistencia médica y unas nuevas medias. ¿Habías visto alguna vez a alguien con leucemia aguda?

—No. Nunca hasta ahora.

—Ahora peso cincuenta kilos. Hace once meses pesaba setenta y dos. La leucemia fue detectada a tiempo para ser tratada. Tengo la suerte de tener un hermano gemelo idéntico, con una médula ósea exactamente igual a la mía. Un trasplante me habría salvado la vida, pero no podíamos permitírnoslo. Estábamos asegurados, pero ya conoces el resto. Supongo que estás al corriente de todo, ¿no es cierto?

—Sí. Estoy muy familiarizado con tu caso, Donny Ray.

—Me alegro —responde aliviado.

Vemos cómo Dot ahuyenta a los gatos. *Garras* se finge dormida sobre el techo del vehículo. No quiere saber nada de Dot Black. Las puertas del coche están abiertas y Dot introduce el contrato. Oímos su penetrante voz.

—Ya sé que crees que están locos —dice Donny Ray, como si me leyera el pensamiento—. Pero son buenas personas que han tenido algunos tropiezos en la vida. Ten paciencia con ellos.

—Son agradables.

—Estoy aniquilado en un ochenta por ciento. Si hubiera recibido un trasplante, maldita sea, aunque fuera hace sólo seis meses, habría tenido el noventa por ciento de probabilidades de curarme. Es curioso cómo los médicos utilizan cifras para comunicarnos si vamos a vivir o a morir. Ahora es demasiado tarde.

De pronto se queda sin aliento, cierra los puños y se estremece de pies a cabeza. Su rostro adquiere un tono ligeramente rosado conforme jadea y, durante unos instantes, me parece que debo ayudarlo. Se golpea el pecho con ambos puños y temo que su cuerpo entero se desmorone.

Por fin recupera el aliento y aspira rápidamente por la nariz. Es en este preciso momento cuando empiezo a odiar a Great Benefit Life Insurance Company.

Ya no me avergüenzo de mirarlo. Es mi cliente y cuenta conmigo. Estoy a su entera disposición, a pesar de sus deficiencias.

Su respiración ha recuperado la normalidad, en la medida de lo posible, y sus ojos están rojos y húmedos. No sé si está llorando o simplemente recuperándose del ataque.

—Lo siento —susurra.

Garras maúlla con tanta fuerza como para que la oigamos y cuando miramos la vemos volar por los aires, hasta aterrizar entre los hierbajos. Evidentemente, la gata se había interesado demasiado por mi contrato y Dot le ha dado un buen guantazo. Ahora le chilla a su marido, que está todavía más hundido tras el volante. Introduce la mano en el vehículo, coge los papeles y regresa hacia nosotros a grandes zancadas, al tiempo que todos los gatos se ponen a cubierto.

—Ochenta por ciento, ¿comprendes? —dice Donny Ray con la voz ronca—. Por consiguiente, ya no aguantaré mucho tiempo. Con lo que obtengas de este caso, te ruego que cuides de ellos. Han tenido muchas dificultades en la vida.

Estoy tan conmovido que soy incapaz de responder.

Dot abre la puerta y deja caer el contrato sobre la mesa. La parte inferior de la primera página está ligeramente rasgada y la segunda está manchada. Espero que no sean excrementos de gato.

—Ahí está —dice.

Misión cumplida. Buddy ha firmado el contrato, aunque su firma es completamente ilegible.

Señalo los lugares apropiados. Donny Ray y su madre lo firman, y el trato está cerrado. Charlamos unos minutos y empiezo a consultar mi reloj.

Cuando me marcho, Dot está sentada junto a Donny Ray, le acaricia suavemente el brazo y le dice que todo se resolverá.

TRECE

Estaba dispuesto a explicarle a Barry X. que no podría trabajar el sábado, debido, entre otras cosas, a las exigencias de la dueña de mi casa. También estaba preparado para sugerirle que trabajaría unas horas el domingo por la tarde si me necesitaba. Pero no tenía por qué preocuparme. Barry se ausenta durante el fin de semana y puesto que no osaría intentar entrar en el edificio sin su ayuda, el asunto queda inmediatamente zanjado.

Por alguna razón, la señorita Birdie no llama a mi puerta antes del amanecer, en lugar de lo cual se mantiene ocupada frente al garaje, debajo de mi ventana, preparando toda clase de herramientas. Deja caer los rastrillos y las palas, limpia la porquería seca del interior de la carretilla con un pico, afila un par de azadas, y todo sin dejar de cantar y hacer gorgoritos. Por fin bajo poco después de las siete y finge sorprenderse de verme.

—Caramba, buenos días, Rudy. ¿Cómo estás?

—Muy bien, señorita Birdie. ¿Y usted?

—De maravilla, simplemente de maravilla. Hermoso día, ¿no te parece?

El día acaba apenas de empezar y es demasiado temprano para evaluar su hermosura. En todo caso, parece bastante bochornoso para ser tan temprano. El insufrible calor veraniego de Memphis no puede estar muy lejano.

Me permite tomar una taza de café instantáneo y comer una tostada antes de empezar a hablar del estiércol. Le encanta comprobar que pongo manos a la obra. Bajo su dirección, cargo el primer saco de cincuenta kilos en la carretilla y la sigo alrededor de la casa, por el jardín delantero, hasta llegar a un pequeño parterre cerca de la calle. Con su taza de café en la mano, sin quitarse los guantes, me indica el destino preciso del estiércol. El desplazamiento me ha dejado casi sin aliento, especialmente el último tramo por la hierba húmeda, pero abro gustoso el saco y empiezo a repartir el estiércol con una horca.

Mi camiseta está empapada cuando termino con el primer saco, al cabo de quince minutos. Nos acompaña a mí y a la carretilla hasta el borde del jardín, donde volvemos a cargar. En realidad me indica exactamente el saco que quiere y lo transportamos a un lugar cerca del buzón.

Esparcimos cinco sacos durante la primera hora. Doscientos cincuenta kilos de estiércol. Y estoy sufriendo. La temperatura alcanza los veintisiete grados a las nueve de la mañana. La convenzo para que me permita tomar un vaso de agua a las nueve y media, y me resulta difícil ponerme de pie después de permanecer diez minutos sentado. Poco después me duele realmente la espalda, pero me muerdo la lengua y procuro no hacer demasiadas muecas. Le pasa inadvertido.

No soy perezoso y cuando estaba en la universidad, no hace mucho, mi forma física era excelente. Corría y practicaba varios deportes, pero en la Facultad de Derecho no he tenido mucho tiempo para dichas actividades en los últimos tres años. Me siento como un enclenque mequetrefe después de pocas horas de trabajo duro.

Para almorzar me da dos de sus insulsos bocadillos de pavo y una manzana. Como muy despacio en el jardín, bajo el ventilador. Me duele la espalda, mis piernas están entumecidas, e incluso me tiemblan las manos cuando roo el pan como un conejo.

Mientras espero a que termine en la cocina, contemplo mi pequeño piso situado sobre el garaje, a través de un pequeño espacio verde más allá del monumento de estiércol. Me sentí muy orgulloso de mí mismo cuando negocié el alquiler mensual por la ínfima suma de ciento cincuenta dólares mensuales, ¿pero fue realmente un acierto? ¿Quién se beneficia verdaderamente del trato? Recuerdo haberme sentido ligeramente avergonzado por aprovecharme de esa encantadora viejecita. Ahora la metería en un saco vacío de estiércol.

Según un viejo termómetro que cuelga de un clavo en la pared del garaje, la temperatura a la una del mediodía es de treinta y cuatro grados. A las dos por fin me entra calambre en la espalda y le explico a la señorita Birdie que debo descansar. Me mira con tristeza y contempla lentamente el montón de sacos blancos, en el que no parecemos haber hecho mella.

—Qué le vamos a hacer. Si no hay otra alternativa...

—Sólo una hora —suplico.

Accede, pero a las tres y media estoy empujando de nuevo la carretilla, con la señorita Birdie pisándome los talones.

Después de ocho horas de intenso trabajo he dispersado exactamente setenta y nueve sacos de estiércol, menos de un tercio del cargamento.

Poco después del almuerzo había insinuado por primera vez que me esperaban en Yogi's a las seis. Por supuesto es mentira. Me he comprometido a trabajar en la barra desde las ocho hasta la hora de cerrar. Pero ella no puede saberlo y estoy decidido a librarme del estiércol antes de que anochezca. A las cinco dejo simplemente de trabajar. Le digo que estoy cansado, que me duele la espalda, que debo ir a trabajar y subo por la escalera mientras ella me contempla desde el jardín con tristeza. No me importa que me eche de la casa si se le antoja.

El majestuoso sonido de los truenos me despierta tarde el domingo por la mañana y permanezco entumecido entre las sábanas, con el son de la copiosa lluvia en el tejado. Mi cabeza está perfectamente, anoche dejé de beber cuando trabajaba. Pero el resto de mi cuerpo parece inmerso en hormigón, incapaz de moverse. El más mínimo movimiento me produce un dolor insoportable. Duele incluso cuando respiro.

Ayer, en algún momento de la epopeya, la señorita Birdie me preguntó si esta mañana me gustaría rezar con ella. Asistir a la iglesia no es una de las condiciones de mi alquiler, pero por qué no hacerlo, pensé. Si esa solitaria anciana desea que la acompañe a la iglesia, es lo mínimo que puedo hacer por ella. Ciertamente no puede perjudicarme.

Entonces le pregunté a qué iglesia asistía. Al Tabernáculo de la Abundancia, en Dallas, me respondió. Participa en directo, vía satélite, a la ceremonia del reverendo Kenneth Chandler, sin moverse de su propia casa.

Me disculpé. Parecía disgustada, pero no tardó en reponerse.

De niño, mucho antes de que mi padre sucumbiera al alcohol y me mandara a una escuela militar, iba de vez en cuando a la iglesia con mi madre. Mi padre nos acompañó un par de veces, pero no hizo más que refunfuñar y tanto mi madre como yo preferíamos que se quedara en casa leyendo el periódico. Era una pequeña iglesia metodista con un simpático pastor, el reverendo Howie, que contaba historias divertidas y hacía que todo el mundo se sintiera querido. Recuerdo la satisfacción de mi madre cuando oía sus sermones. Había muchos chiquillos en las clases de catecismo, y no me importaba que me lavaran y almidonaran los domingos por la mañana para asistir a la iglesia.

En una ocasión le practicaron a mi madre una pequeña operación y permaneció tres días en el hospital. Como es de suponer, las señoras de la parroquia conocían hasta los más íntimos detalles de la operación y, durante tres días, nuestra casa se llenó de cacerolas, pasteles, tartas, panes y numerosos recipientes con más comida de la que mi padre y yo podíamos consumir en un año. Organizaron también un sistema de vigilia. Se turnaron para supervisar la comida, limpiar la cocina y recibir a otras damas que traían más comida. Durante los tres días que mi madre permaneció en el hospital, y los tres primeros días a partir de su regreso a casa, en todo momento estuvo con nosotros por lo menos una de dichas damas, a mi parecer custodiando la comida.

A mi padre le resultó odioso. Por una parte, con la casa llena de señoras beatas, no podía circular a sus anchas ni tomar una copa. Creo que sabían que le gustaba empinar el codo y puesto que habían logrado ocupar la casa, estaban decididas a sorprenderlo. Además, esperaban de él que se comportara como un amable anfitrión, cosa que mi padre era incapaz de hacer. Después de las primeras veinticuatro horas, pasó la mayor parte del tiempo en el hospital, pero no exactamente cuidando de su indispuesta esposa. Estaba en la sala de espera, viendo la televisión y tomando colas sazonadas con alcohol.

Lo recuerdo con cariño. Nunca había habido tanto calor en nuestra casa, ni comida tan deliciosa. Las señoras cuidaban de mí como si mi madre hubiera fallecido y me encantaba ser el centro de atención. Eran las tías y abuelas que nunca había conocido.

Poco después de la recuperación de mamá, el reverendo Howie se vio obligado a huir debido a una indiscreción que nunca comprendí plenamente, y desapareció la congregación. Alguien insultó a mi madre y a partir de entonces dejamos de frecuentar la iglesia. Creo que mi madre y Hank, su nuevo marido, asisten de vez en cuando a alguna ceremonia.

Al principio eché de menos la iglesia, pero luego me acostumbré a no acudir a la misma. A veces, mis amigos me instigaban a que volviera, pero no tardé en considerarme demasiado sofisticado para asistir. Una novia que tuve en la universidad me llevó a misa varias veces, precisamente los sábados por la noche, pero yo soy demasiado protestante para comprender esos ritos.

La señorita Birdie ha mencionado tímidamente la posibilidad de trabajar en el jardín esta tarde. Pero le he explicado que hoy es el día del Señor, consagrado al descanso, y que mis creencias me impiden trabajar los domingos.

No ha sabido qué responder.

CATORCE

Tres días seguidos de lluvia intermitente han obligado a interrumpir mi trabajo de jardinero. El martes por la noche me he escondido en mi piso para preparar el examen de colegiatura. De pronto suena el teléfono, es Dot Black y en seguida me percato de que algo anda mal, de lo contrario no me llamaría.

—Acabo de recibir una llamada del señor Barry Lancaster —dice—. Asegura que es mi abogado.

—Así es, Dot. Es un abogado muy experto de mi bufete. Trabaja conmigo.

Supongo que Barry sólo ha querido comprobar algunos detalles.

—Pues eso no ha sido lo que me ha dicho. Ha llamado para preguntarme si Donny Ray y yo podemos pasar mañana por su despacho, dice que necesita que firmemos unos documentos. He preguntado por usted y me ha contestado que no trabaja allí. Quiero saber qué ocurre.

Yo también. Farfullo unos segundos y sugiero que hay alguna confusión. Se me forma un enorme nudo en el estómago.

—Es un gran bufete, Dot, y yo soy nuevo, compréndalo. Probablemente se ha olvidado de mí.

—No. Sabe exactamente quién es. Dice que antes trabajaba allí, pero ahora ya no. Es todo muy confuso, ¿sabe?

Lo sé. Me desplomo en una silla y procuro pensar con claridad. Son casi las nueve.

—Tranquilícese, Dot. Permítame que llame al señor Lancaster para enterarme de lo que ocurre. Volveré a llamarla dentro de un minuto.

—Quiero saber qué sucede. ¿Ha demandado ya a esos cabrones?

—La llamaré dentro de un minuto, ¿de acuerdo? Hasta luego.

Cuelgo el teléfono y marco inmediatamente el número del

bufete Lake. Tengo la desagradable sensación de que eso ya me ha sucedido.

La recepcionista de guardia me conecta con Barry X. Decido ser cordial, seguirle la corriente, esperar a ver qué dice.

—Barry, soy yo, Rudy. ¿Ha visto los resultados de mi investigación?

—Sí, tiene muy buen aspecto —responde, aparentemente cansado—. Escúcheme, Rudy, puede que tengamos un pequeño problema con su empleo.

El nudo avanza a zarpazos hasta mi garganta. Me da un vuelco el corazón. Se me paraliza la respiración.

—¿Ah, sí? —logro exclamar.

—Sí. No pinta bien. Esta noche he hablado con Jonathan Lake y no está dispuesto a autorizar su empleo.

—¿Por qué no?

—No le gusta la idea de que un abogado ocupe el puesto de un pasante. Y pensándolo bien, a mí tampoco me parece una buena idea después de todo. El caso es que el señor Lake cree, y coincido con él, que la tendencia natural de un abogado en dicha posición sería la de intentar ocupar la próxima vacante que emergiera como miembro asociado. Y ésa no es nuestra forma de funcionar. Es un mal negocio.

Cierro los ojos y me entran ganas de llorar.

—No lo comprendo —digo.

—Lo siento. He hecho todo lo posible, pero no he logrado convencerlo. Dirige el bufete con mano férrea y tiene cierta forma de hacer las cosas. Para serle sincero, me ha metido un buen rapapolvo por el mero hecho de pensar en contratarlo.

—Quiero hablar con Jonathan Lake —declaro con toda la firmeza posible.

—Imposible. Está demasiado ocupado y, además, él no desea hablar con usted. Por otra parte, no cambiará de opinión.

—Es usted un hijo de puta.

—Oiga, Rudy, nosotros...

—¡Hijo de puta! —chillo por teléfono y me siento bien.

—Cálmese, Rudy.

—¿Está Lake ahora en su despacho?

—Probablemente. Pero no le...

—Estaré ahí en cinco minutos —exclamo e inmediatamente cuelgo el teléfono.

Al cabo de diez minutos doy un frenazo, chirrían los neumáticos y paro el coche frente al almacén. Hay tres coches en el aparcamiento y las luces del edificio están encendidas. Barry no está esperándome.

Llamo a la puerta, pero no aparece nadie. Sé que pueden oírme, pero son demasiado cobardes para acudir. Probablemente llamarán a la policía si no desisto.

Pero no puedo desistir. Me dirijo a la fachada norte y llamo a otra puerta, para repetir luego la misma operación en una salida de emergencia de la parte trasera. Me acerco a la ventana del despacho de Barry y lo llamo a voces. Tiene las luces encendidas, pero no me hace caso. Vuelvo a la puerta principal y sigo llamando.

Emerge de las tinieblas un guardia de seguridad uniformado y me agarra por el hombro. Me tiemblan las rodillas del susto. Levanto la cabeza para mirarlo. Mide por lo menos metro noventa, es negro y lleva una gorra negra.

—Debes marcharte, hijo —dice amablemente con una voz grave—. Retírate antes de que llame a la policía.

Sacudo su mano de mi hombro y me alejo.

Permanezco mucho tiempo sentado a oscuras en el destartalado sofá que la señorita Birdie me ha prestado e intento poner las cosas en cierta perspectiva. No tengo mucho éxito. Me tomo un par de cervezas calientes. Blasfemo y lloro. Me propongo vengarme. Pienso incluso en matar a Jonathan Lake y a Barry X. Esos perversos cabrones se han confabulado para robarme el caso. ¿Qué les cuento ahora a los Black? ¿Cómo les explico lo sucedido?

Camino por el piso a la espera del alba. Anoche llegué incluso a reírme cuando pensé en sacar de nuevo mi lista de bufetes y volver a llamar de puerta en puerta. Siento escalofríos ante la perspectiva de llamar a Madeline Skinner.

—Soy yo, Madeline. Aquí estoy de nuevo.

Por fin me quedo dormido en el sofá y alguien me despierta poco después de las nueve. No es la señorita Birdie, sino dos policías de paisano. Me muestran sus placas en la puerta y los invito a que entren. Llevo un pantalón corto deportivo y una camiseta. Me escuecen los ojos, me los froto, e intento descubrir por qué he atraído de pronto a la policía.

Podrían ser gemelos, ambos de unos treinta años, no mucho mayores que yo. Visten vaqueros, zapatillas, los dos tienen un bigote negro y actúan como un par de actores secundarios por televisión.

—¿Podemos sentarnos? —pregunta uno de ellos al tiempo que agarra una silla y se sienta.

Su compañero hace lo mismo y ambos se acomodan.

—Por supuesto —respondo como un listillo—. No se queden de pie.

—Siéntese usted también —dice uno de ellos.

—¿Por qué no? —respondo antes de instalarme entre ellos, que se inclinan hacia delante, sin dejar de actuar—. ¿Qué diablos ocurre? —pregunto.

—¿Conoce usted a Jonathan Lake?

—Sí.

—¿Sabe dónde está su bufete?

—Sí.

—¿Estuvo usted allí anoche?

—Sí.

—¿A qué hora?

—Entre las nueve y las diez.

—¿Cuál fue la razón de su visita?

—Es una larga historia.

—Disponemos de todo el tiempo necesario.

—Quería hablar con Jonathan Lake.

—¿Lo hizo?

—No.

—¿Por qué no?

—Las puertas estaban cerradas y no pude entrar en el edificio.

—¿Intentó forzar alguna puerta?

—No.

—¿Está seguro?

—Sí.

—¿Volvió al edificio después de la medianoche?

—No.

—¿Está seguro?

—Sí. Pregúntenselo al guardia de seguridad.

Se miran entre sí. Algo ha dado en el blanco.

—¿Vio al guardia de seguridad?

—Sí. Me pidió que me marchara y lo hice.

—¿Puede describirlo?

—Sí.

—Hágalo.

—Un negro robusto, probablemente de metro noventa, uniformado, gorra, pistola, etcétera. Pregúntenselo, él les dirá que me marché cuando me lo ordenó.

—No podemos preguntárselo —responden mientras intercambian nuevamente miradas.

—¿Por qué no? —pregunto, con el presentimiento de que van a responderme algo terrible.

—Porque está muerto.

Ambos me miran atentamente para ver cómo reacciono. Estoy tan estupefacto como lo estaría cualquiera. Siento que me perforan con la mirada.

—¿Cómo... cómo murió?

—Quemado en el incendio.

—¿Qué incendio?

Asienten desconfiados, sin apartar la mirada de la mesa, y cierran unánimemente la boca. Uno de ellos se saca un cuaderno del bolsillo, como un periodista novato.

—Ese pequeño coche que está ahí, el Toyota, ¿es suyo?

—Saben que lo es. Tienen ordenadores.

—¿Lo condujo anoche al bufete?

—No. Lo empujé. ¿Qué incendio?

—No se haga el listillo, ¿vale?

—De acuerdo. Trato hecho. Yo no me haré el listillo, a condición de que tampoco se lo hagan ustedes.

—Es posible que alguien haya visto su coche en la vecindad del bufete a las dos de la madrugada —dice su compañero.

—No es verdad. No puede tratarse de mi coche —respondo, sin poder saber si mienten—. ¿Qué incendio? —insisto.

—El bufete Lake se incendió anoche. Ha quedado completamente destruido.

—Arrasado —agrega su compañero.

—Y ustedes son de la brigada antiincendios —digo todavía estupefacto, pero al mismo tiempo enojado de que me consideren implicado en el siniestro—. Y Barry Lancaster les ha contado que yo soy un excelente sospechoso de haber incendiado el local, ¿no es cierto?

—Nos ocupamos de incendios y también de homicidios.

—¿Cuántas personas han fallecido?

—Sólo el guardia. La primera llamada se recibió a las tres de la madrugada, de modo que el lugar estaba desierto. Evidentemente, el guardia quedó de algún modo atrapado cuando se derrumbó el tejado.

Casi deseo que Jonathan Lake hubiera estado con el guardia, y luego pienso en los hermosos despachos, con sus cuadros y sus alfombras.

—Están perdiendo el tiempo —exclamo, ahora más enojado de que sospechen de mí.

—El señor Lancaster dice que estaba bastante furioso cuando fue anoche al bufete.

—Cierto. Pero no lo suficiente como para incendiar el local. Están perdiendo el tiempo. Se lo prometo.

—Dice que acababan de despedirlo y quería enfrentarse al señor Lake.

—Cierto. Todo eso es verdad, pero no demuestra que tuviera motivos para incendiar su despacho. Abran los ojos.

—Un asesinato cometido durante un incendio puede acarrear la pena de muerte.

134

—¡No me diga! Estoy con ustedes. Encuentren al asesino y ásenlo. Pero déjenme tranquilo.

Supongo que mi ira es bastante convincente, porque ambos se arredran simultáneamente. Uno de ellos se saca un papel doblado del bolsillo de la camisa.

—Aquí tengo un informe —dice—, de hace un par de meses, según el cual se le buscaba por destrucción de propiedad privada. Algo relacionado con la rotura de un cristal, en un bufete de la ciudad.

—Sabía que sus ordenadores funcionaban.

—Una conducta un poco extraña para un abogado.

—He visto cosas peores. Además, no soy abogado. Soy un pasante, o algo por el estilo. Acabo de terminar la carrera. Por otra parte, se retiró la denuncia, y estoy seguro de que este dato figura claramente en algún lugar de su papel. Y si realmente creen que el haber roto un cristal en abril está de algún modo relacionado con el incendio de anoche, el verdadero pirómano puede quedarse tranquilo. Está a salvo. Nunca lo atraparán.

En este momento uno de ellos se incorpora de un brinco y su compañero le emula inmediatamente.

—Le conviene hablar con un abogado —dice uno de ellos señalándome con el dedo—. En este momento, usted es el principal sospechoso.

—Claro, claro. Como ya les he dicho, si yo soy el principal sospechoso, el verdadero asesino está de suerte. Van muy desencaminados.

Cierran de un portazo y desaparecen. Espero media hora y me subo al coche. Conduzco unas cuantas manzanas y me sitúo cuidadosamente cerca del almacén. Aparco, ando otra manzana y me oculto en una tienda de ultramarinos. Veo los restos humeantes del edificio a dos manzanas. Sólo uno de sus muros sigue en pie. Docenas de personas circulan de un lado para otro: abogados y secretarias que señalan en todas direcciones, y bomberos que deambulan con sus pesadas botas. La policía aísla la zona con cinta amarilla. El aire está impregnado de un penetrante olor a madera quemada y una nube grisácea cubre el barrio entero.

Los suelos y los techos del edificio eran de madera y, con muy pocas excepciones, también las paredes. Si pensamos además en la enorme cantidad de libros repartidos por el edificio, así como el inevitable volumen de papel archivado, es fácil comprender que ardiera con tanta virulencia. Lo desconcertante es el hecho de que había una extensa red de rociadores antiincendios repartidos por el edificio, cuyos tubos pintados estaban por todas partes, a menudo incorporados en la decoración del local.

Por razones evidentes, Prince no es madrugador. Suelen ser alrededor de las dos cuando cierra Yogi's y se desploma en el asiento trasero de su Cadillac. Firestone, su chófer de toda la vida y presunto guardaespaldas, lo conduce a casa. En un par de ocasiones, cuando los dos estaban demasiado borrachos para conducir, los he llevado a ambos a su casa.

Prince suele estar en su despacho a las once, porque en Yogi's hay una actividad momentánea a la hora del almuerzo. Lo encuentro tras su escritorio a las doce, hojeando papeles y cuidando la resaca. Toma analgésicos y bebe agua mineral hasta la hora mágica de las cinco de la tarde, cuando penetra en su mundo tranquilizador del ron con agua tónica.

El despacho de Prince está en un cuarto desprovisto de ventanas, debajo de la cocina, muy escondido y accesible sólo a través de tres puertas sin indicación alguna y por una escalera oculta. Es un cuadrado perfecto, con las paredes completamente cubiertas de fotografías de Prince estrechando la mano de políticos locales y otros personajes fotogénicos. También hay numerosos recortes de periódico enmarcados en los que se menciona a Prince como sospechoso, acusado, detenido, juzgado y declarado siempre inocente. Le encanta ver su nombre en los periódicos.

Está de un humor de perros, como de costumbre. A lo largo de los años he aprendido a no cruzarme en su camino hasta después de la tercera copa, generalmente a las seis de la tarde. De modo que llego con seis horas de antelación. Me hace una seña para que entre y cierro la puerta a mi espalda.

—¿Qué ocurre? —refunfuña.

Tiene los ojos irritados. Con su largo cabello negro, su frondosa barba, camisa abierta y cuello velludo, me ha recordado siempre a Wolfman Jack.

—Estoy metido en un pequeño lío —respondo.

—¿Qué tiene eso de nuevo?

Le cuento lo sucedido anoche: que me he quedado sin empleo, el incendio y la policía. Hago especial hincapié en el hecho de que hay un cadáver, que le preocupa particularmente a la policía. Como es perfectamente lógico. Me resulta difícil pensar que yo pueda ser el principal sospechoso, pero sin duda así lo cree la policía.

—De modo que Lake ha sido asado —comenta, al parecer encantado, puesto que un buen incendio intencionado como éste es lo que a Prince le hace feliz y le alegra la mañana—. Nunca me había gustado.

—Él no está muerto. Su negocio ha quedado temporalmente paralizado. Volverá.

Y eso es lo que más me preocupa. Jonathan Lake distribuye mucho dinero entre muchos políticos. Cultiva relaciones para comprar favores. Si está convencido de mi participación en el incendio, o aunque sólo busque temporalmente un chivo expiatorio, la policía me acosará despiadadamente.

—¿Me juras que no lo hiciste?

—Por favor, Prince.

Reflexiona, se acaricia la barba y me percato inmediatamente de que, de pronto, le encanta hallarse en el centro de la acción. Crimen, muerte, intriga, política... un fragmento habitual de la vida en la cloaca. Si además estuvieran involucradas algunas bailarinas semidesnudas y algún soborno a la policía, habría sacado ya una botella para celebrar la ocasión.

—Creo que debes hablar con un abogado —dice sin dejar de acariciarse la barba.

Ésa, tristemente, es la verdadera razón por la que estoy aquí. Había pensado en llamar a Booker, pero ya le he molestado demasiado. Además, en este momento padece la misma limitación que yo, es decir, no hemos pasado el examen de colegiatura y no podemos ejercer como abogados.

—No puedo permitírmelo —respondo, a la espera de las próximas palabras en su guión.

Si en este momento tuviera cualquier otra alternativa, me lanzaría encantado a por ella.

—Déjalo en mis manos —dice—. Llamaré a Bruiser.

—Gracias —asiento—. ¿Crees que me ayudará?

Prince sonríe y extiende los brazos.

—Bruiser hará lo que le pida, ¿comprendes?

—Por supuesto —respondo sumisamente.

Levanta el teléfono y marca un número. Lo oigo refunfuñar con un par de personas, hasta que logra hablar con Bruiser. Se expresa con rapidez y frases entrecortadas, propias de alguien que sabe que sus teléfonos están intervenidos.

—Bruiser, soy Prince. Sí, sí. Debo verte cuanto antes... Un pequeño asunto con uno de mis empleados... Sí, sí. No, en tu despacho. Treinta minutos. De acuerdo.

Cuelga.

Compadezco al pobre técnico del FBI que intente extraer pruebas incriminatorias de aquella conversación.

Firestone acerca el Cadillac a la puerta trasera, y Prince y yo nos instalamos en el asiento posterior. El coche es negro y las ventanas intensamente ahumadas. Vive en la oscuridad. En tres años, nunca he visto que participara en actividad alguna al aire libre. Va de vacaciones a Las Vegas, donde no sale nunca de los casinos.

Escucho lo que no tarda en convertirse en un abrumador relato de los mayores triunfos jurídicos de Bruiser, en casi todos los cuales está involucrado Prince. Curiosamente, empiezo a relajarme. Estoy en buenas manos.

Bruiser estudió derecho por las noches y acabó la carrera a los veintidós años, lo cual, según Prince, constituye una hazaña. Son amigos de la infancia y en el instituto apostaron un poco, bebieron mucho, persiguieron a las chicas y se pelearon con los chicos. Vivían en un barrio conflictivo del sur de Memphis. Podrían escribir un libro. Al otro lado de la calle hay una cafetería que permanece abierta día y noche, y junto a la misma está el club Amber, un llamativo garito de alterne con chicas *topless* y un letrero de neón al estilo de Las Vegas. Es un barrio industrial de la ciudad, cerca del aeropuerto.

A excepción de la palabra «abogado» pintada en negro sobre una puerta de cristal en el centro de la manzana, nada indica la profesión que se ejerce en el edificio. Una secretaria con vaqueros ceñidos y labios embadurnados de carmín nos recibe con una radiante sonrisa, pero no nos detenemos. Sigo a Prince por el vestíbulo.

—Solía trabajar al otro lado de la calle —susurra Prince.

Espero que fuera en la cafetería, aunque lo dudo.

El despacho de Bruiser es extraordinariamente parecido al de Prince: sin ventanas ni oportunidad alguna de que penetre la luz del sol, grande, cuadrado y chabacano, y cubierto de fotografías de personajes importantes aunque desconocidos estrechando sonrientes la mano de Bruiser. Una de las paredes está reservada a armas de fuego: toda clase de rifles, mosquetones y galardones de tiro. Tras la enorme butaca de cuero giratoria de Bruiser hay un acuario elevado con lo que parecen tiburones en miniatura deslizándose por sus turbias aguas.

Está hablando por teléfono y nos indica con la mano que nos sentemos frente a su largo y ancho escritorio.

—Son auténticos tiburones —me comunica inmediatamente Prince después de sentarnos.

Auténticos tiburones en el bufete de un abogado. Menuda broma. Prince se ríe.

Miro fugazmente a Bruiser, pero procuro que no se crucen nuestras miradas. El teléfono parece diminuto junto a su enorme cabeza. Los mechones desaliñados de su larga cabellera canosa le llegan a los hombros. El teléfono casi desaparece en su larga y espesa perilla, completamente gris. Sus ojos, rodeados de múltiples ojeras trigueñas, son oscuros y se mueven con rapidez. A menudo he pensado que debe de tener antepasados mediterráneos.

Aunque le he servido a Bruiser millares de copas, nunca he mantenido una conversación con él. Jamás lo he deseado. Ni tampoco me apetece ahora aunque, evidentemente, mis opciones son limitadas.

Refunfuña algunos comentarios breves y cuelga el teléfono. Prince hace las presentaciones y Bruiser asegura que me conoce bien.

—Claro, hace mucho que conozco a Rudy —dice—. ¿Qué ocurre?

Prince me mira y yo cuento todo lo sucedido.

—Lo he visto en las noticias de esta mañana —agrega Bruiser cuando llego a la parte del incendio—. He recibido ya cinco llamadas relacionadas con el tema. No se necesita gran cosa para que los abogados empiecen a chismorrear.

Sonrío y asiento, porque creo que es lo que se supone que debo hacer, y paso a hablar de la policía. Termino sin otra interrupción, y quedo a la espera del consejo y asesoramiento de mi abogado.

—¿Pasante? —pregunta evidentemente perplejo.

—Estaba desesperado.

—¿Y dónde trabajas ahora?

—No lo sé. En este momento lo único que me preocupa es que no me detenga la policía.

Bruiser sonríe.

—Yo me ocuparé de eso —afirma en tono afectado—. Tendré que hacer unas llamadas.

Prince me ha asegurado repetidamente que Bruiser conoce a más policías que el propio alcalde.

—Conviene que se oculte, ¿no es cierto? —pregunta Prince, como si yo fuera un criminal fugado de la justicia.

—Sí. Ocúltate.

Por alguna razón, estoy convencido de que se ha ofrecido muchas veces ese mismo consejo en este despacho.

—¿Qué sabes sobre incendios intencionados? —pregunta entonces Bruiser.

—Nada. No nos han hablado de ello en la facultad.

—Pues yo me he ocupado de varios casos de incendios intencionados. Pueden transcurrir varios días antes de que determinen si el incendio ha sido intencionado. En un viejo edificio como ése puede haber ocurrido cualquier cosa. Si ha sido intencionado, tardarán algunos días en detener a alguien.

—No quiero que me detengan. Especialmente teniendo en cuenta que soy inocente. No me apetece aparecer en los periódicos —declaro mientras contemplo la pared cubierta de recortes y artículos.

—No te lo reprocho —dice, con la cara muy seria—. ¿Cuándo te presentas al examen de colegiatura?

—En julio.

—¿Y luego?

—No lo sé. Buscaré algo.

De pronto, mi amigo Prince interviene en la conversación.

—¿No puedes encontrarle algo aquí, Bruiser? Maldita sea, tienes un montón de abogados. ¿Qué importa uno más? Es un estudiante ejemplar, trabaja mucho y es inteligente. Respondo por él. El muchacho necesita un trabajo.

Vuelvo lentamente la cabeza para mirar a Prince, que me sonríe como si fuera Papá Noël.

—Éste es un lugar fantástico para trabajar —agrega alegremente—. Aquí aprenderás lo que hacen los verdaderos abogados.

Se ríe y me da una palmada en la rodilla.

Ambos miramos a Bruiser, cuyos ojos se mueven rápidamente de un lado para otro, mientras busca desesperadamente pretextos en su mente.

—Claro, por supuesto. Siempre me gusta encontrar a alguien con un buen talento jurídico.

—¿Te das cuenta? —exclama Prince.

—Por cierto, dos de mis asociados acaban de marcharse para abrir su propio bufete. De modo que tengo dos despachos vacíos.

—¿Te das cuenta? —repite Prince—. Ya te he dicho que todo se resolvería.

—Pero no se trata exactamente de un empleo asalariado —agrega Bruiser, cada vez más entusiasmado con la idea—. No señor. No es así como yo trabajo. Espero que mis asociados se ganen su propia remuneración, generen sus propios honorarios.

Estoy demasiado aturdido para hablar. Prince y yo no habíamos hablado del empleo, ni deseaba su ayuda en dicho sentido. En realidad no quiero que Bruiser Stone sea mi jefe. Pero tampoco puedo ofenderle, con la policía al acecho y referencias concretas a la pena de muerte. Soy incapaz de acumular la valentía necesaria para decirle a Bruiser que es lo suficientemente artero para representarme, pero demasiado para ser mi jefe.

—¿Cómo funciona el sistema? —pregunto.

—Es muy sencillo y eficaz, por lo menos en lo que a mí respecta. Y ten en cuenta que a lo largo de veinte años lo he probado todo. He tenido un montón de socios y docenas de asociados. El único sistema que funciona es aquel en el que el miembro asociado está obligado a generar suficientes honorarios para cubrir su salario. ¿Puedes hacerlo tú?

—Puedo intentarlo —respondo encogiéndome de hombros.

—Claro que puedes —agrega Prince para darme ánimos.

—Tú consigues mil dólares mensuales en honorarios y te guardas un tercio de lo que generas. Tu tercio se aplica al promedio. Otro tercio se ingresa en el fondo del bufete, para cubrir los gastos generales como la administración y cosas por el estilo. El último tercio me lo guardo yo. Si no alcanzas el promedio mensual, me debes lo que falte. Yo voy sumando la deuda, hasta que tengas un buen mes. ¿Comprendes?

Durante unos segundos reflexiono sobre ese absurdo sistema. Lo único peor a estar sin empleo es tener un trabajo en el que se pierda dinero y en el que las deudas mensuales sean acumulativas. Se me ocurren una serie de preguntas específicas y carentes de respuesta, pero Prince interrumpe cuando estaba a punto de formular la primera.

—Me parece justo. Excelente propuesta —exclama al tiempo que me da otra palmada en la rodilla—. Podrás ganar una fortuna.

—Es mi única forma de trabajar —dice Bruiser por tercera o cuarta vez.

—¿Cuánto ganan tus asociados? —pregunto, sin esperar que me diga la verdad.

Frunce los largos surcos de su frente. Está meditabundo.

—Varía. Depende de lo que te esfuerces. Uno ganó cerca de los ochenta el año pasado, otro sólo veinte.

—Y tú ganaste trescientos mil —exclama Prince con una sonora carcajada.

—Ojalá.

Bruiser me observa atentamente. Está ofreciéndome el único trabajo posible en la ciudad de Memphis y parece saber que no estoy ansioso por aceptarlo.

—¿Cuándo puedo empezar? —pregunto en un torpe intento por parecer entusiasmado.

—Ahora mismo.

—Pero el examen de colegiatura...

—No te preocupes por eso. Hoy mismo puedes empezar a generar honorarios. Te mostraré cómo hacerlo.

—Vas a aprender mucho —declara Prince casi arrobado de satisfacción.

—Hoy te pagaré mil pavos para que te inicies —dice Bruiser, como el último de los grandes derrochadores—. Te mostraré las dependencias y pondremos, por así decirlo, las ruedas en movimiento.

—Estupendo —respondo con una sonrisa forzada.

Es absolutamente imposible en este momento seguir otro rumbo. No debería siquiera estar aquí, pero estoy asustado y necesito ayuda. En este momento no se menciona lo que le deberé a Bruiser por sus servicios. Pero no es una de esas personas compasivas que de vez en cuando le hacen un favor a un pobre.

Me siento ligeramente indispuesto. Puede que sea la falta de sueño, el susto de que me haya despertado la policía, o tal vez el hecho de estar sentado en este despacho, viendo cómo nadan los tiburones, acechado por dos de los peores granujas de la ciudad.

Hasta hace relativamente poco, yo era un estudiante de tercer curso de Derecho, listo y alegre, ansioso por ejercer la profesión, trabajar duro, convertirme en un miembro activo del colegio de abogados, iniciar mi carrera profesional y en general hacer lo mismo que mis compañeros. Sin embargo, ahora estoy sentado aquí, tan débil y vulnerable que acepto prostituirme por mil dudosos dólares mensuales.

Bruiser recibe una llamada telefónica urgente, probablemente de alguna bailarina *topless* acusada de lenocinio, y nos levantamos discretamente. Cubre el auricular y susurra que quiere verme esta tarde.

Prince se siente tan orgulloso que está a punto de estallar de alegría. Así, sin más, acaba de salvarme del cadalso y encontrarme trabajo. Mientras Firestone sortea velozmente el tráfico de regreso a Yogi's, no hago más que pensar en que no logro alegrarme por más que me lo proponga.

QUINCE

Decido ocultarme en la facultad. Paso un par de horas escondido entre estantes de libros en el sótano, buscando y examinando numerosos casos de mala fe por parte de compañías de seguros. Me dedico a matar el tiempo.

Conduzco lentamente en la dirección general del aeropuerto y llego al edificio de Bruiser a las tres y media. El barrio es peor de lo que parecía hace unas horas. A ambos lados de la calle, que tiene cinco carriles para el tráfico, hay numerosas industrias ligeras, almacenes de mercancías y pequeños bares y clubes oscuros donde los obreros se relajan. Está cerca de la pista del aeropuerto y los escandalosos reactores pasan a escasa altura.

La manzana de Bruiser se denomina Greenway Plaza, y sentado en mi coche, en el aparcamiento lleno de escombros, me percato de que además de la lavandería y del videoclub, hay una bodega y un pequeño café. Aunque es difícil de determinar debido a las ventanas ahumadas y puertas selladas, parece que el bufete ocupa seis o siete pisos contiguos en el centro de la manzana. Aprieto los dientes y abro la puerta.

Veo a la secretaria de vaqueros tras un tabique que llega a la altura del pecho. Va teñida de rubio y tiene un cuerpo excepcional, con sus curvas y hendiduras magníficamente destacadas.

Le explico el motivo de mi presencia. Temo una mala reacción por su parte y que me eche a la calle, pero me trata con cortesía. En un tono inteligente y sensual, que nada tiene que ver con el de una cualquiera, me pide que rellene los formularios de empleo necesarios. Me deja atónito descubrir que este bufete, el despacho de abogados de J. Lyman Stone, ofrece un seguro médico a todo riesgo a sus empleados. Leo atentamente la letra menuda, medio a la expectativa de que Bruiser haya incluido pequeñas cláusulas que hinquen todavía más hondo sus garras en mi carne.

Pero no encuentro ninguna sorpresa. Le pregunto si puedo

ver a Bruiser y me dice que espere. Me siento en una de las sillas de plástico junto a la pared. La sala de espera tiene el mismo aspecto que las de la Seguridad Social: suelo de baldosas debidamente desgastadas, con su correspondiente capa de mugre, sillas baratas, endebles tabiques y una asombrosa selección de revistas rasgadas. Dru, la secretaria, contesta el teléfono sin dejar de mecanografiar. Llama con mucha frecuencia y hace gala de su extraordinaria eficacia, a menudo charlando con los clientes mientras escribe a toda velocidad.

Por fin me manda a ver a mi nuevo jefe. Bruiser está tras su escritorio, examinando mis formularios con la minuciosidad de un contable. Me sorprende su interés por los detalles. Me recibe atentamente, repite las condiciones económicas de nuestro acuerdo y coloca delante de mí un contrato, en el que se han rellenado con mi nombre los espacios en blanco. Lo leo y lo firmo. Hay una cláusula que nos compromete a ambos a anunciar con treinta días de antelación la rescisión del empleo. Me alegra comprobar su existencia, aunque sospecho que tiene sus buenas razones para incluirla.

Le hablo de mi reciente declaración de insolvencia. Mañana debo comparecer en el juzgado para un primer encuentro con los acreedores. El trámite se denomina examen del deudor y durante el mismo los abogados de mis acreedores tienen derecho a sacar a relucir mis trapos sucios. Pueden preguntar prácticamente lo que se les antoje acerca de mis finanzas y de mi vida en general. Pero será un asunto discreto. En realidad, es probable que no acuda nadie a interrogarme.

Debido a la vista pendiente, es preferible que permanezca unos días sin empleo. Le propongo a Bruiser que guarde los formularios y aplace mi primer salario hasta después de la vista. La propuesta tiene un aire fraudulento y a Bruiser le gusta. No tiene ningún inconveniente.

Me ofrece una visita rápida de las dependencias. Es exactamente lo que imaginaba: un antro de esclavos con salas dispersas aquí y allá, recuperadas de los pisos contiguos conforme se ampliaba el bufete y se derribaban tabiques, convirtiéndolo en un laberinto. Me presenta a dos mujeres ajetreadas en una pequeña sala repleta de ordenadores e impresoras. Dudo que hayan bailado sobre las mesas de los clubes.

—Creo que ahora tenemos seis chicas —dice conforme avanzamos.

Las secretarias son simplemente chicas.

Me presenta a un par de abogados, unos individuos bastante agradables y mal vestidos, que trabajan en despachos abigarrados.

—Ahora tenemos sólo cinco abogados —explica cuando entramos en la biblioteca—. Solíamos tener siete, pero eso supone demasiados quebraderos de cabeza. Prefiero cuatro o cinco. Cuanto más personal contrato, más tengo que arbitrar. Ocurre lo mismo con las chicas.

La biblioteca es una sala larga y estrecha, con libros desde el suelo hasta el techo sin ningún orden aparente. En el centro hay una larga mesa cubierta de libros abiertos y montones de cuartillas.

—Algunos de esos individuos son unos puercos —farfulla para sí—. Bien, ¿qué te parecen mis pequeñas dependencias?

—Estupendas —respondo.

Y no miento. Me alivia comprobar que aquí se ejerce realmente la abogacía. Puede que Bruiser sea un maleante con contactos en los bajos fondos, negocios turbios e inversiones fraudulentas, pero no deja de ser abogado. En sus oficinas suena el ruido del trabajo legítimo.

—No tan espectacular como los magnates del centro de la ciudad —declara, sin complejo alguno—. Pero está todo pagado. Lo compré hace quince años. Aquí está tu despacho —agrega, cuando salimos de la biblioteca.

Dos puertas más allá, junto a una máquina de venta de refrescos, hay un viejo cuarto con un escritorio, unas sillas, archivos y cuadros de caballos en las paredes. Sobre la mesa hay un teléfono, un dictáfono y un montón de cuadernos. Todo está pulcro. Huele a desinfectante, como si lo hubieran limpiado hace menos de una hora.

Me entrega un llavero con dos llaves.

—Ésta es para la puerta principal y la otra para tu despacho. Puedes entrar y salir libremente cuando se te antoje. Pero ten cuidado por la noche. Ésta no es la mejor zona de la ciudad.

—Tenemos que hablar —digo después de recibir las llaves.

Consulta su reloj.

—¿Cuánto tiempo?

—Dame treinta minutos. Es urgente.

Se encoge de hombros y le sigo a su despacho, donde acomoda su voluminoso trasero en su butaca de cuero.

—¿Qué sucede? —pregunta, en un tono muy profesional, al tiempo que se saca una pluma de diseño del bolsillo y se coloca delante el cuaderno obligatorio.

Empieza a escribir antes de que yo diga la primera palabra.

Le hago un rápido resumen del caso de los Black, que dura diez minutos. Al mismo tiempo relleno los baches de la terminación de mi empleo en el bufete Lake. Le explico cómo Barry Lancaster me ha utilizado para robar el caso y eso conduce a mi estratagema.

—Tenemos que presentar hoy mismo la denuncia —declaro gravemente—. Porque técnicamente el caso pertenece a Lancaster y no creo que tarde en acudir al juzgado.

Bruiser me mira fijamente con sus ojos negros. Creo que he despertado su interés. Le atrae la idea de ganarle la carrera al bufete Lake.

—¿Y los clientes? —pregunta—. Han firmado con Lake.

—Sí, pero voy a hacerles una visita ahora mismo. Me escucharán.

Saco de mi maletín el borrador de una denuncia contra Great Benefit en la que Barry y yo trabajamos varias horas. Bruiser lo lee atentamente.

A continuación le muestro una carta de rescisión de contrato dirigida a Barry X. Lancaster, que yo mismo he mecanografiado, para que la firmen los tres miembros de la familia Black. La examina lentamente.

—Buen trabajo, Rudy —dice, y me siento como un tahúr consagrado—. Deja que lo adivine. Presentas la denuncia esta tarde y luego les llevas una copia a los Black. Se la muestras y les haces firmar la carta sólo de rescisión de contrato.

—Exactamente. Sólo necesito tu nombre y tu firma en la denuncia. Me ocuparé de todo y te mantendré informado.

—Eso dejará al bufete Lake con un palmo de narices, ¿no es cierto? —reflexiona mientras tira de un pelo rebelde—. Me gusta. ¿Cuánto puede reportar esta demanda?

—Probablemente lo que decida el jurado. Dudo que haya pacto extrajudicial.

—¿Y te ocuparás del juicio?

—Puede que necesite un poco de ayuda. Calculo que no se celebrará hasta dentro de uno o dos años.

—Te presentaré a Deck Shifflet, uno de mis asociados. Antes trabajaba para una gran compañía de seguros y examina muchas pólizas para mí.

—Estupendo.

—Su despacho está cerca del tuyo. Vuelve a escribir esto, ponle mi nombre y lo presentaremos hoy. Pero sobre todo asegúrate de que los clientes estén con nosotros.

—Los clientes están con nosotros —afirmo rotundamente, mientras imagino a Buddy acariciando sus gatos y ahuyentando moscas en su Fairlane, a Dot fumando junto a la puerta y vigilando el buzón, como si esperara la llegada inminente de un cheque de Great Benefit, y a Donny Ray sosteniéndose la cabeza con las manos—. Cambiando ligeramente de tema —agrego después de aclararme la garganta—, ¿se sabe algo de la policía?

—No hay de qué preocuparse —responde en tono afectado,

cual jorguín que ha hecho otra hechicería—. He hablado con algunos conocidos y ni siquiera están seguros de que el incendio haya sido intencionado. Podrían transcurrir varios días.

—De modo que no van a detenerme en plena noche.

—No. Han prometido llamarme antes de detenerte. Yo les he asegurado que te entregarías, depositarías la fianza, etcétera. Pero no llegará a tanto. Tranquilízate.

En efecto, me tranquilizo. Confío en la capacidad de Bruiser Stone para extraerle promesas a la policía.

—Gracias.

Cuando sólo faltan cinco minutos para la hora de cerrar entro en la secretaría del juzgado y presento mi denuncia de cuatro páginas contra Great Benefit Life Insurance Company y Bobby Ott, el agente desaparecido que vendió la póliza. Mis clientes, los señores Black, reclaman doscientos mil dólares de gastos y una compensación por perjuicios causados de diez millones. Desconozco por completo la cuantía del capital social de Great Benefit y tardaré mucho tiempo en averiguarlo. Elijo al azar la suma de diez millones, simplemente porque suena bien. Los abogados lo hacen constantemente.

Evidentemente, mi nombre no aparece en ningún lugar. J. Lyman Stone consta como abogado del demandante y su exuberante rúbrica, que adorna la última página, le confiere a la demanda el peso de la autoridad. Le entrego al funcionario un cheque de la empresa para cubrir el coste de la demanda y el proceso queda iniciado.

¡La compañía Great Benefit ha sido oficialmente demandada!

Me apresuro a cruzar la ciudad hasta la zona de Granger en el norte de Memphis, donde encuentro a mis clientes prácticamente como cuando los dejé hace unos días. Buddy está en el jardín. Dot va en busca de Donny Ray a su habitación. Nos sentamos los tres alrededor de la mesa, donde ellos admiran su copia de la demanda. Están muy impresionados con la cuantía de la suma. Dot no deja de repetir la cifra de diez millones, como si poseyera el número que ha ganado la lotería.

Llega el momento en que me veo obligado a contarles lo ocurrido con esos horribles personajes del bufete Lake. Un conflicto de estrategia. No actuaban con la rapidez que a mí me parecía necesaria. No les gustaba el ímpetu con que yo enfocaba el caso. Etcétera, etcétera.

En realidad, no les importa. La demanda ha sido presentada y disponen de un documento que lo demuestra. Quieren saber qué ocurrirá ahora, cuándo tendrán alguna noticia. ¿Cuáles son las probabilidades de que se resuelva con rapidez? Sus preguntas me desalientan. Sé que durará mucho más de lo debido y me parece una crueldad ocultárselo.

Los convenzo para que firmen la carta dirigida a Barry X. Lancaster, su ex abogado, por la que se prescinde de sus servicios. Hay también un nuevo contrato con el bufete de J. Lyman Stone. Hablo con suma rapidez cuando les explico la necesidad de este nuevo conjunto de documentos. Desde las mismas sillas junto a la mesa de la cocina, Donny Ray y yo vemos cómo Dot se abre nuevamente paso entre los hierbajos y discute con su marido para que firme los papeles.

Les dejo más animados que a mi llegada. Les produce una satisfacción considerable el hecho de haber demandado a la compañía, que odiaban desde hace tanto. Por fin toman represalias; han sido pisoteados y me han convencido de que los habían maltratado. Ahora han pasado a formar parte de los millones de norteamericanos que todos los años demandan a alguien. Ello hace que de algún modo se sientan patrióticos.

Sentado en mi cálido y pequeño coche en hora punta pienso en la locura de las últimas veinticuatro horas. Acabo de firmar un aventurado contrato. Mil dólares mensuales son una suma insignificante, pero me asusta. Más que un salario es un préstamo y no tengo ni idea de cómo espera Bruiser que empiece a generar ingresos inmediatamente. Aunque llegue a cobrar del caso Black, tendrán que transcurrir muchos meses.

Seguiré trabajando en Yogi's durante algún tiempo. Prince me paga todavía al contado: cinco dólares por hora, más la comida y unas cuantas cervezas.

Hay bufetes en esta ciudad donde se espera que los miembros asociados vistan todos los días con elegancia, tengan un vehículo presentable, vivan en una casa respetable, y frecuenten incluso los clubes de moda. Claro que les pagan mucho más de lo que me paga Bruiser, pero también les crean una serie de obligaciones sociales innecesarias.

No en mi caso. No en mi bufete. Puedo vestir como quiera, conducir lo que desee, frecuentar los lugares que se me antojen y nadie dirá nunca nada al respecto. En realidad, me pregunto cómo reaccionaré cuando alguno de los chicos del bufete me invite a tomar un par de copas en el *topless* de enfrente.

De pronto soy mi propio amo. Experimento una maravillosa sensación de independencia conforme el tráfico avanza centímetro a centímetro. ¡Puedo sobrevivir! Trabajaré duro con Bruiser y probablemente aprenderé mucho más derecho que en los bufetes del centro de la ciudad. Soportaré las injurias, el sarcasmo y el desprecio de los demás por trabajar en un lugar tan despreciable. Me dará fuerzas. No hace mucho pecaba un poco de soberbia, cuando me sentía seguro con Brodnax & Speer, y luego con Lake; no me vendrá mal este ejercicio de humildad.

Ya ha oscurecido cuando aparco en Greenway Plaza. La mayoría de los coches han desaparecido. Al otro lado de la calle, las llamativas luces del club Amber han atraído el conjunto habitual de camionetas y coches alquilados por las grandes empresas. El neón rodea la totalidad del tejado del edificio e ilumina toda la zona.

El comercio carnal, sin que sea fácil explicar por qué, está en auge en Memphis. Ésta es una ciudad muy conservadora y con muchas iglesias, en pleno corazón del cinturón bíblico. Aquí, los aspirantes a cargos públicos se adhieren rápidamente a un riguroso código moral, que los electores suelen recompensar con sus votos. No puedo imaginar que elijan a un candidato que sea tolerante con el comercio carnal.

Veo a un grupo de negociantes que se apean de un coche y entran en el club Amber. Se trata de un norteamericano acompañado de cuatro japoneses que van a culminar indudablemente un día de negociaciones con unas copas y una agradable inspección de los últimos adelantos en silicona norteamericana.

La música está ya muy fuerte. El aparcamiento se llena con rapidez.

Me dirijo apresuradamente a la puerta principal del bufete y la abro. Los despachos están vacíos. Maldita sea, probablemente se han trasladado todos al otro lado de la calle. Esta tarde he tenido la clara impresión de que el bufete de J. Lyman Stone no es un lugar para fanáticos del trabajo.

Todas las puertas están cerradas, supongo que con llave. Aquí nadie confía en los demás. Sin duda pienso cerrar también la mía.

Me quedaré unas horas. Debo llamar a Booker y ponerle al corriente de mis últimas aventuras. Hemos descuidado nuestros estudios para el examen de colegiatura. A lo largo de tres años hemos logrado estimularnos y motivarnos mutuamente. La fecha del examen asoma amenazante por el horizonte, como una cita con el pelotón de ejecución.

DIECISÉIS

Sobrevivo durante la noche sin que me detengan, pero duermo poco. Entre las cinco y las seis de la madrugada, impulsado por los pensamientos confusos que invaden atropelladamente mi cerebro, me levanto de la cama. He dormido menos de cuatro horas en los dos últimos días.

Su número está en la guía y llamo a las seis menos cinco. Estoy tomando mi segunda taza de café. Llama diez veces antes de que responda una voz adormecida.

—Diga.

—Con Barry Lancaster, por favor —digo.

—Soy yo.

—Hola Barry, soy Rudy Baylor.

Se aclara la garganta y le imagino incorporándose en la cama.

—¿Qué ocurre? —pregunta en un tono mucho más decidido.

—Lamento llamarle tan temprano, pero sólo quería mencionarle un par de cosas.

—¿A saber?

—A saber, que los Black presentaron ayer una demanda contra Great Benefit. Le mandaré una copia cuando dispongan de unas nuevas dependencias. También firmaron un documento de rescisión, de modo que han prescindido de sus servicios. Ya no tiene por qué preocuparse de ellos.

—¿Cómo se las ha arreglado para presentar una demanda?

—A decir verdad, eso no es en absoluto de su incumbencia.

—Maldita sea, claro que lo es.

—Le mandaré una copia de la demanda y lo comprenderá. No tiene un pelo de tonto. ¿Tienen ya una nueva dirección, o funciona todavía la antigua?

—Nuestro apartado de correos no ha sufrido daño alguno.

—Claro. Por cierto, le agradecería que no me involucrara en ese asunto del incendio intencionado. No tuve nada que ver con el incendio y si insiste en implicarme, me veré obligado a llevarle ante los tribunales.

—Tiemblo de miedo.

—Se le nota. Limítese a dejar mi nombre tranquilo.

Cuelgo antes de que pueda responder. Observo el teléfono durante cinco minutos, pero no me llama. Menudo cobarde.

Siento una enorme curiosidad por ver cómo hablan del incendio los periódicos de la mañana, y decido tomar una ducha, vestirme y salir rápidamente al amparo de la oscuridad. El tráfico es escaso cuando conduzco hacia el sur en dirección al aeropuerto, hasta Greenway Plaza, donde empiezo a sentirme como en mi casa. Aparco en el mismo lugar que abandoné hace siete horas. El club Amber, en cuyo aparcamiento hay montones de basura y latas de cerveza, está oscuro y silencioso.

El pequeño local de la planta baja, junto a donde creo que se encuentra mi despacho, está alquilado por una corpulenta alemana llamada Trudy que dirige un café barato. La conocí anoche, cuando entré en su local para comprar un bocadillo, y me dijo que abría a las seis para servir cafés y buñuelos.

Cuando entro está sirviendo. Charlamos unos momentos mientras me tuesta un bollo y me sirve un café. Ya hay una docena de clientes apretujados alrededor de las pequeñas mesas y Trudy está preocupada. El repartidor de buñuelos lleva retraso.

Compro un periódico y me instalo en una mesa junto a la ventana, está empezando a salir el sol. En primera plana de la sección metropolitana hay una gran fotografía del almacén del señor Lake en llamas. Un breve artículo describe la historia del edificio, dice que ha quedado completamente arrasado y que el señor Lake calcula las pérdidas en unos tres millones de dólares. Se le cita diciendo: «Su renovación ha sido como un idilio que ha durado cinco años. Estoy desolado.»

Llora, muchacho, llora. Echo una rápida ojeada al artículo y no veo que se mencionen en ningún lugar las palabras «incendio intencionado». Luego lo leo detenidamente. La policía no hace declaraciones: el asunto está todavía bajo investigación, demasiado pronto para especular, sin comentario. Las evasivas habituales de los polis.

No esperaba que mencionaran mi nombre como el de un posible sospechoso, pero de todos modos me siento aliviado.

Estoy en mi despacho procurando dar la impresión de que estoy ocupado y preguntándome cómo generar unos honorarios de mil dólares durante los próximos treinta días, cuando Bruiser irrumpe en la estancia y me entrega un papel.

—Es la copia de un informe de la policía —refunfuña, ya de camino a la puerta.

—¿Sobre mí? —pregunto horrorizado.

—¡Claro que no! Es el informe de un accidente de tráfico. Ocurrió anoche en la esquina de Airways y Shelby, a pocas manzanas de aquí. Puede que uno de los conductores estuviera borracho. Parece que se saltó un semáforo en rojo —dice y se queda mirándome fijamente.

—Representamos a uno de los...

—¡Todavía no! Para eso estás tú aquí. Ve y consigue el caso. Averigua lo sucedido. Hazles firmar un contrato. Investígalo. Parece que las lesiones pueden ser importantes.

Estoy sumamente perplejo cuando abandona mi despacho. Da un portazo y le oigo refunfuñar mientras se aleja por el pasillo.

El informe del accidente está repleto de información: nombres de los conductores y pasajeros, direcciones, números de teléfono, lesiones, desperfectos de los vehículos y declaraciones de testigos presenciales. Hay un croquis de cómo cree la policía que se produjo el accidente y otro que muestra cómo encontraron los vehículos. Ambos conductores sufrieron lesiones e ingresaron en el hospital, y al parecer el que se saltó el semáforo en rojo había bebido.

Muy interesante, ¿pero qué hago ahora? El accidente tuvo lugar a las diez y diez de la noche, y de algún modo la información ha caído en las sucias manos de Bruiser a primera hora de la mañana. Vuelvo a leerlo y luego lo contemplo fijamente un buen rato.

Una llamada a la puerta me sacude de mi estado de confusión.

—Adelante —respondo.

Se entreabre la puerta y un individuo bajo y delgado asoma la cabeza.

—¿Rudy? —pregunta en un tono agudo y nervioso.

—Sí, adelante.

Se desliza por la estrecha abertura y avanza sigilosamente hasta instalarse en la silla frente a mi escritorio.

—Soy Deck Shifflet —declara sin ofrecerme la mano ni una sonrisa—. Bruiser me ha dicho que tenías un caso del que querías hablar —agrega mientras mira por encima del hombro, como si alguien hubiera entrado tras él en el despacho y estuviera ahora escuchándolo.

—Encantado de conocerte —respondo.

Es difícil saber si Deck tiene cuarenta o cincuenta años. La mayor parte de su pelo ha desaparecido y los escasos mechones supervivientes están impregnados de brillantina y aplastados a su generosa calva. El poco cabello alrededor de sus orejas es ralo y predominantemente canoso. Usa unas gafas cuadradas de montura metálica, bastante gruesas y sucias. También es muy difícil determinar si su cabeza es demasiado grande o su cuerpo excesivamente pequeño, pero no armonizan. Su frente está compuesta por dos mitades redondeadas, unidas en una hendidura más o menos central que desciende de pronto hacia la nariz.

El pobre Deck es una de las personas menos agraciadas que he visto en mi vida. Su rostro exhibe las secuelas de un devastador acné juvenil. Su barbilla es prácticamente inexistente. Cuando habla se le arruga la nariz y levanta el labio superior, mostrando cuatro grandes dientes, todos del mismo tamaño.

El cuello de su camisa blanca con dos bolsillos está sucio y desgastado. El nudo de su sencilla corbata de lana roja es tan grande como mi puño.

—Es un caso contra una compañía de seguros —aclaro, procurando eludir la mirada de unos enormes ojos que me observan parapetados tras sus gafas—. ¿Eres uno de los miembros asociados del bufete?

Frunce la nariz y el labio, y exhibe la dentadura.

—Más o menos. No exactamente. El caso es que no soy abogado todavía. He estudiado Derecho y estoy licenciado, pero no he aprobado el examen de colegiatura.

Ah, una alma gemela.

—Vaya, hombre —exclamo—. ¿Cuándo terminaste los estudios?

—Hace cinco años. Lo cierto es que tengo algunos problemas con el examen. Lo he intentado seis veces.

Ésa no es noticia de mi agrado. Sinceramente, no sabía que una misma persona pudiera presentarse tantas veces al examen de colegiatura.

—Caramba —susurro—, cuánto lo siento.

—¿Cuándo te presentas? —pregunta nervioso, sin dejar de mirar a su alrededor.

Está sentado al borde de la silla, como si tuviera que salir corriendo inesperadamente. Con el índice y el pulgar de su mano derecha se pellizca el reverso de su mano izquierda.

—En julio. Vaya palo, ¿no te parece?

—Sí, un buen palo. Y que lo digas. Hace un año que no lo intento. No sé si volveré a presentarme jamás.

—¿En qué universidad estudiaste?

Se lo pregunto porque me pone muy nervioso. No estoy seguro de querer comentar con él el caso de los Black. ¿Cómo encaja en este asunto? ¿Cuál será su parte de los beneficios?

—En California —responde, con el rostro más contorsionado que he visto en mi vida: ojos que se abren y se cierran, cejas que vibran y labios que tiemblan—. Estudiaba por las noches. En aquella época estaba casado y trabajaba cincuenta horas semanales. No me quedaba mucho tiempo para los libros. Tardé cinco años en terminar la carrera. Mi esposa me abandonó y yo me trasladé aquí.

Sus oraciones se hacen progresivamente cortas, hasta que sus palabras se pierden en la lejanía y me deja momentáneamente en vilo.

—Sí, bueno, ¿cuánto hace que trabajas para Bruiser?

—Casi tres años. Me trata como a cualquier otro asociado. Busco los casos, me ocupo de ellos y le doy su parte. Todo el mundo está contento. Suele pedirme que examine los casos de seguros cuando llegan. Durante dieciocho años trabajé para la Pacific Mutual, hasta que me harté e ingresé en la Facultad de Derecho...

Una vez más, sus palabras se pierden en la lejanía.

—¿Cómo te las arreglas cuando has de comparecer en el juzgado? —pregunto después de observar y esperar.

Se ríe como si fuera muy gracioso.

—En realidad, he comparecido varias veces personalmente. Hasta ahora nunca me han descubierto. Circulan tantos abogados por el juzgado que es imposible tenernos a todos controlados. Cuando se trata de un juicio llamo a Bruiser. O tal vez a otro de los miembros asociados.

—Bruiser me ha dicho que había cinco abogados en el bufete.

—Sí. Yo, Bruiser, Nicklass, Toxer y Ridge. Pero yo no lo llamaría bufete. Cada uno funciona por cuenta propia. Ya lo descubrirás. Buscas tus propios casos y clientes, y te quedas con un tercio de los ingresos brutos.

Impresionado por su franqueza, decido proseguir.

—¿Es un buen negocio para los asociados?

—Depende de tus aspiraciones —responde sin dejar de volver la cabeza, como si Bruiser pudiera escucharle—. En otras partes hay mucha competencia. A mí me viene como anillo al dedo, porque puedo ganar cuarenta mil anuales ejerciendo la profesión sin estar colegiado. Pero no se lo digas a nadie.

Ni soñarlo.

—¿Cuál es tu función en mi caso contra la compañía de seguros? —pregunto.

—Ah, eso. Bruiser me pagará si se recibe alguna compensación. Le ayudo con sus sumarios, pero soy el único en quien confía. A ninguno de los demás se le permite tocar sus sumarios.

Ha despedido a varios abogados que intentaron entrometerse. Yo soy inofensivo. No puedo ir a otra parte, por lo menos hasta que apruebe el examen de colegiatura.

—¿Cómo son los demás abogados?

—Personas normales. Vienen y van. No elige a los más listos, ¿sabes? Contrata a jóvenes que circulan por las calles. Trabajan aquí uno o dos años, consiguen algunos clientes, hacen contactos y luego abren su propio despacho. El personal se renueva constantemente.

Aumenta mi curiosidad.

—¿Puedo hacerte una pregunta? —digo, contra mis mejores instintos.

—Por supuesto.

Le entrego el informe del accidente y lo examina velozmente.

—Bruiser te lo ha entregado, ¿no es cierto?

—Sí, hace unos minutos. ¿Qué espera que haga?

—Conseguir el caso. Encuentra a la víctima, hazle firmar un contrato con el bufete de J. Lyman Stone y ocúpate del caso.

—¿Cómo puedo encontrarlo?

—Por lo que parece está en el hospital. Ése suele ser el mejor lugar donde encontrarlos.

—¿Vas a los hospitales?

—Por supuesto. Con mucha frecuencia. El caso es que Bruiser tiene ciertos contactos en la comisaría central. Muy buenos contactos, amigos de su infancia. Le facilitan estos informes casi todas las mañanas. Los distribuye por la oficina y espera que consigamos los casos. No hay que ser físico nuclear.

—¿Qué hospital?

Levanta la mirada de sus enormes ojos al techo y mueve con asco la cabeza.

—¿Qué te han enseñado en la facultad?

—Poca cosa, pero ciertamente no a perseguir ambulancias.

—Entonces te conviene aprender con rapidez. De lo contrario, te morirás de hambre. Fíjate en este número de teléfono del conductor lesionado. Simplemente llama, dile a quien conteste que perteneces al cuerpo de bomberos de Memphis, o algo por el estilo, y que necesitas hablar con el conductor lesionado, como quiera que se llame. Evidentemente, no podrá ponerse al teléfono porque está en el hospital. ¿Qué hospital? Necesitas la información para tu ordenador. Te lo dirán. Siempre funciona. Utiliza tu imaginación. La gente es crédula.

Siento náuseas.

—¿Y luego?

—Luego vas al hospital y hablas con la persona en cuestión.

155

Claro, no eres más que un novato. Lo siento. Te diré lo que vamos a hacer. Compremos un par de bocadillos, nos los comeremos en el coche de camino al hospital y le haremos firmar un contrato a ese muchacho.

En realidad no me apetece. Preferiría abandonar este lugar y no volver jamás. Pero de momento no tengo otra cosa que hacer.

—De acuerdo —respondo con mucha reticencia.

—Reúnete conmigo en la puerta principal —dice después de ponerse de pie—. Yo me ocuparé de llamar y averiguar en qué hospital está.

El hospital es el de beneficencia de Saint Peter, un centro municipal sumamente ajetreado donde reciben a la mayoría de los accidentados. Entre sus numerosos servicios figura el de atención a incontables indigentes.

Deck lo conoce bien. Cruzamos la ciudad en su destartalada y pequeña furgoneta, su única pertenencia después del divorcio provocado por cinco años de abuso alcohólico. Ahora está rehabilitado, es un miembro orgulloso de Alcohólicos Anónimos y ha dejado incluso de fumar. Sin embargo confiesa que le gusta apostar y los nuevos casinos que aparecen junto a la línea estatal en Mississippi le tienen preocupado.

Su ex esposa y sus dos hijos siguen en California.

Me informa de todos estos detalles en menos de diez minutos, mientras mastico un perrito caliente. Deck conduce con una mano, come con la otra, y hace muecas y contorsiones sin dejar de hablar con la boca llena de ensalada de pollo, mientras cruzamos medio Memphis. Soy incapaz de mirarlo.

Aparcamos en el lugar reservado para médicos, porque Deck tiene una tarjeta que le identifica como doctor. El vigilante parece conocerlo y nos autoriza a entrar.

Deck me conduce entonces directamente al mostrador de información en el vestíbulo principal, abarrotado de gente. A los pocos segundos ha conseguido el número de la habitación de Dan Van Landel, nuestro objetivo. Deck tiene los dedos de los pies deformados y cojea ligeramente, pero me resulta difícil seguirle cuando se dirige a los ascensores.

—No actúes como un abogado —susurra entre dientes, mientras esperamos rodeados de enfermeras.

¿Cómo podría alguien tomar a Deck por abogado? Subimos en silencio hasta el octavo piso y salimos del ascensor con un tropel de gente. Deck, lamentablemente, lo ha hecho ya muchas veces.

A pesar de la curiosa forma de su cabeza, su renquera y sus

demás idiosincrasias, pasamos inadvertidos. Avanzamos por un abigarrado pasillo, hasta que se cruza con otro en una ajetreada sala de enfermeras. Deck sabe exactamente cómo encontrar la habitación ochocientos ochenta y seis. Giramos a la izquierda y nos cruzamos con enfermeras, técnicos y un médico que examina un diagrama. Junto a la pared hay una colección de camillas desprovistas de sábanas. Las baldosas del suelo están gastadas y necesitan una buena limpieza. Entramos por la cuarta puerta a la izquierda, sin llamar, en una habitación semiprivada. Está casi a oscuras. En la primera cama hay un individuo con las sábanas hasta la barbilla pendiente de un culebrón en un pequeño televisor suspendido sobre la cama.

Nos mira horrorizado, como si hubiéramos venido a extraerle un riñón, y me odio a mí mismo por estar aquí. Es injusto que vulneremos la intimidad de esas personas de un modo tan despiadado.

Deck, por otra parte, está en todo. Resulta difícil creer que ese intrépido impostor sea el mismo ratonzuelo acobardado que entró en mi despacho hace menos de una hora. Entonces estaba asustado de su propia sombra. Ahora parece poseer un valor ilimitado.

Avanzamos unos pasos hasta un biombo. Deck titubea unos instantes, hasta comprobar que Dan Van Landel está solo, y se acerca.

—Buenas tardes, señor Van Landel —dice en un tono sincero.

Van Landel tiene cerca de treinta años, aunque es difícil determinar su edad porque lleva vendajes en la cara. Uno de sus ojos está hinchado, casi cerrado, y tiene una laceración debajo del otro. Tiene un brazo fracturado y una de sus piernas en tracción.

Afortunadamente está despierto y no nos vemos obligados a tocarlo ni chillarle. Yo me quedo al pie de la cama, cerca de la puerta, con la esperanza de que no nos sorprenda ningún médico, enfermera, o miembro de su familia.

—¿Puede usted oírme, señor Van Landel? —pregunta Deck con la compasión de un sacerdote después de acercarse todavía más al paciente.

Van Landel está perfectamente sujeto a la cama y no puede moverse. Estoy seguro de que le gustaría sentarse o incorporarse, pero está completamente inmovilizado. No puedo imaginar su espanto. Hasta ahora yacía con la mirada en el techo, probablemente todavía aturdido y dolorido, y de pronto tiene ante sí uno de los rostros más extraños que ha visto en su vida.

Parpadea rápidamente para enfocar la mirada.

—¿Quién es usted? —refunfuña sin separar los dientes, sujetos por una prótesis metálica.

Esto es injusto.

Deck sonríe y muestra sus cuatro dientes relucientes.

—Deck Shifflet, bufete de abogados de Lyman Stone —responde con extraordinario aplomo, como si se supusiera que debía estar aquí—. ¿No habrá hablado con alguna compañía de seguros?

Así de simple, Deck establece quiénes son los malos. Evidentemente, no somos nosotros, sino los muchachos de los seguros. Da un paso de gigante para ganarse su confianza. Somos nosotros contra ellos.

—No —farfulla Van Landel.

—Estupendo. No lo haga. Lo único que pretenden es estafarle —le aconseja Deck, que se ha acercado todavía un poco más—. Hemos examinado el informe del accidente. Un caso claro en el que no se respetó un semáforo en rojo. Dentro de una hora aproximadamente iremos a examinar los coches —agrega al tiempo que consulta su reloj, para darse importancia—, tomaremos fotografías, hablaremos con testigos y, bueno, ya sabe, haremos todo lo necesario. Debemos actuar con rapidez, antes de que los peritos de la compañía de seguros presionen a los testigos. No sería la primera vez que los sobornan para que declaren en falso, ¿comprende? Tenemos que darnos prisa, pero necesitamos su autorización. ¿Tiene abogado?

Me aguanto la respiración. Si Van Landel responde que su hermano es abogado, me encontraré de patitas en la calle.

—No —responde.

Deck entra a matar.

—Bueno, como ya le he dicho, debemos actuar con rapidez. Nosotros nos ocupamos de más siniestros que cualquier otro bufete de Memphis y obtenemos compensaciones astronómicas. Las compañías de seguros nos temen. No cobramos un centavo. Nos quedamos con el tercio habitual de la compensación —dice mientras saca un contrato de las páginas centrales de un cuaderno.

Es un contrato breve, de tres párrafos en una sola página, cuyo único propósito es el de atrapar al cliente. Deck lo agita frente a la cara de Van Landel, de forma que éste se ve obligado a cogerlo. Lo sujeta con la mano de su brazo sano e intenta leerlo.

Alabado sea. Acaba de pasar la peor noche de su vida, tiene suerte de seguir vivo, y ahora, con la mirada turbia y la mente confusa, se supone que debe examinar un documento legal y tomar una decisión inteligente.

—¿No puede esperar a que venga mi esposa? —casi suplica.

¿Estamos a punto de ser sorprendidos? Me agarro al pie de la cama y toco inadvertidamente un cable que sacude una polea, que levanta su pierna un par de centímetros.

—¡Ay! —gime.

—Lo siento —digo retirando inmediatamente las manos.

A juzgar por su forma de mirarme, Deck sería capaz de estrangularme.

—¿Dónde está su esposa? —pregunta después de recuperar el control.

—¡Ay! —gime de nuevo el pobre hombre.

—Lo siento —repito instintivamente.

Tengo los nervios destrozados. Van Landel me mira aterrado y meto las manos firmemente en mis bolsillos.

—Volverá en seguida —responde con dolor evidente en cada sílaba.

Deck tiene una respuesta para todo.

—Hablaré con ella más tarde en mi despacho. Necesito que me facilite un montón de información —dice al tiempo que coloca el cuaderno bajo el contrato, para facilitar la firma, y destapa la pluma.

Van Landel farfulla algo, luego agarra la pluma y firma. Deck guarda el contrato en el cuaderno y le entrega una tarjeta de visita al nuevo cliente, que le identifica como pasante del bufete de J. Lyman Stone.

—Sólo un par de advertencias —agrega Deck en tono autoritario—. No hable con nadie a excepción de su médico. Acudirán los representantes de la compañía de seguros, con toda probabilidad hoy mismo, e intentarán hacerle firmar formularios y documentos. Incluso puede que le ofrezcan una suma de dinero. No les diga absolutamente nada bajo ninguna circunstancia. Tiene mi número de teléfono. Llámeme a cualquier hora del día o de la noche. En el reverso está el número de mi compañero aquí presente, Rudy Baylor, a quien también puede llamar a cualquier hora. Nos ocuparemos juntos de su caso. ¿Alguna pregunta? Bien —prosigue antes de darle a su interlocutor la oportunidad de gemir o refunfuñar—, Rudy volverá por la mañana con unos documentos. Dígale a su esposa que nos llame esta tarde. Es muy importante que hablemos con ella —añade al tiempo que le da unos golpecitos en la pierna sana, decidido a marcharse antes de que cambie de opinión—. Le conseguiremos un montón de dinero —asegura.

Nos despedimos antes de desaparecer rápidamente.

—Y así es como se hace, Rudy —dice Deck cargado de orgullo cuando llegamos al vestíbulo—. Coser y cantar.

Nos apartamos para cederle el paso a una mujer en una silla

de ruedas y a un paciente que trasladan en una camilla. El vestíbulo está abarrotado de gente.

—¿Y si ya hubiera tenido un abogado? —pregunto cuando empiezo a recuperar el aliento.

—No tenemos nada que perder, Rudy. Eso es lo que debes recordar. Hemos llegado con las manos vacías. Si por cualquier razón nos hubiera echado de la habitación, ¿qué habríamos perdido?

Cierta dignidad, un poco de autorespeto. Su razonamiento es perfectamente lógico. No respondo. Camino con paso firme y decidido, procurando no mirar cómo avanza a trompicones.

—Lo cierto, Rudy, es que en la facultad no te enseñan lo que necesitas saber. Son todo libros, teorías y nobles conceptos sobre el ejercicio de la abogacía como profesión, entre caballeros, ya sabes. Una vocación honorable, regida por un extenso código ético.

—¿Qué tiene la ética de malo?

—Nada, supongo. Es decir, creo que un abogado debe atenerse a lo básico: luchar por su cliente, abstenerse de robar y procurar no mentir.

La ética según Deck. Hemos pasado horas y horas explorando los dilemas éticos y morales, y de pronto llega Deck y reduce el código ético a tres conceptos básicos: luchar por el cliente, no robar y procurar no mentir.

Giramos inesperadamente a la izquierda y entramos en un pasillo más nuevo. Saint Peter es un laberinto de extensiones y anexos.

—Pero lo que no te enseñan en la facultad puede perjudicarte —prosigue Deck, que está de humor para dar una conferencia—. Piensa en ese individuo, Van Landel. Tengo la sensación de que estabas nervioso en su habitación.

—Sí, tienes razón.

—No deberías estarlo.

—Pero es inmoral acosar a un cliente potencial. Equivale a perseguir ambulancias.

—Exactamente. ¿Pero a quién le importa? Es preferible que lo consigamos nosotros que el que nos vendrá pisando los talones. Puedes estar seguro de que en las próximas veinticuatro horas, algún otro abogado se pondrá en contacto con Van Landel e intentará hacerle firmar un contrato. Así es como se hace, Rudy. Es el mercado, la competencia. Hay mucho abogado suelto.

Como si no lo supiera.

—¿Seguirá con nosotros? —pregunto.

—Probablemente. Hasta ahora hemos tenido suerte. Hemos llegado en el momento oportuno. Suele haber un cincuenta por ciento de probabilidades cuando llegas, pero se convierte en un ochenta cuando firman el contrato. Es preciso que le llames dentro de un par de horas, habla con su esposa, dile que puedes pasar por aquí esta noche y hablar del caso con ellos.

—¿Yo?

—Por supuesto. Es fácil. Tengo algunas fichas que puedes examinar. No es preciso ser un genio.

—Pero no estoy seguro...

—Escúchame, Rudy, tranquilízate. No te dejes impresionar por este lugar. Ahora es nuestro cliente, ¿de acuerdo? Tienes derecho a visitarle y nadie puede impedírtelo. No pueden echarte. Relájate.

Tomamos café en tazas de plástico en una cafetería del tercer piso. Deck prefiere esta pequeña cafetería porque está cerca de la sala ortopédica, y porque es de construcción relativamente reciente y pocos abogados la conocen. Se sabe que los abogados merodean por las cafeterías de los hospitales a la caza de pacientes lesionados, me cuenta en voz baja sin percatarse de que él está haciendo lo mismo. Lo dice con cierto desdén por dicha conducta. La ironía le pasa a Deck inadvertida.

Parte de mi trabajo, como joven asociado del bufete de J. Lyman Stone, consistirá en deambular por estos parajes y explorar sus pastos. Hay también una gran cafetería en la planta principal del hospital Cumberland, a dos manzanas de aquí. Y en el hospital VA hay tres cafeterías. Deck sabe evidentemente dónde están y comparte dicha información conmigo.

Me aconseja que empiece por Saint Peter, porque es donde se encuentra la mayor unidad de traumatología. Me dibuja un mapa en una servilleta con el emplazamiento de otros lugares de captación potencial: la cafetería principal, un pequeño restaurante cerca de la sala de maternidad, en el segundo piso, y un café junto al vestíbulo principal. La noche es un buen momento, asegura, sin dejar de estudiar las presas, porque los pacientes suelen aburrirse en sus habitaciones y, si su condición se lo permite, van a tomar algo a la cafetería. No hace muchos años, cuando uno de los abogados de Bruiser merodeaba por la cafetería principal a la una de la madrugada, captó a un joven que padecía quemaduras. El caso se saldó al cabo de un año por dos millones. Lamentablemente, dicho joven había prescindido de los servicios de Bruiser y contratado a otro abogado.

—Se nos escapó —dice Deck como un pescador desilusionado.

DIECISIETE

La señorita Birdie se acuesta después de la repetición de MASH, a las once de la noche. Me ha invitado varias veces a ver la televisión con ella después de la cena, pero hasta ahora he encontrado siempre un buen pretexto.

Sentado en los peldaños junto a la puerta de mi piso, espero a que su casa se quede a oscuras. Veo su silueta de puerta en puerta, comprobando los cerrojos y cerrando las persianas.

Supongo que los ancianos se acostumbran a la soledad, aunque nadie haya previsto pasar los últimos años de su vida a solas, sin la compañía de sus seres queridos. Cuando era joven, estoy seguro de que debía confiar en pasar esta etapa rodeada de nietos. Sus propios hijos estarían cerca, comprobando a diario cómo estaba su mamá, trayéndole flores, galletas y regalos. La señorita Birdie no se proponía pasar sus últimos años completamente sola, en una antigua casa impregnada de viejos recuerdos fenecientes.

Raramente habla de sus hijos o de sus nietos. Hay unas cuantas fotografías repartidas por la casa, pero a juzgar por el aspecto de su atuendo, son bastante antiguas. Hace varias semanas que estoy aquí y no soy consciente de que haya tenido un solo contacto con su familia.

Me siento culpable de no sentarme con ella por la noche, pero tengo mis razones. Mira un culebrón tras otro por televisión y no puedo soportarlos. Lo sé porque habla constantemente de ello. Además, debo estudiar para mi examen.

Hay otra razón por la que guardo las distancias. La señorita Birdie ha insinuado varias veces que la casa necesita una mano de pintura y que si algún día logra acabar con el estiércol, dispondrá de tiempo para el nuevo proyecto.

Hoy he escrito y mandado una carta a un abogado de Atlanta, que he firmado como pasante del bufete de J. Lyman Stone, interesándome por los bienes de Anthony L. Murdine, difunto marido de la señorita Birdie. Indago lentamente, con escaso éxito.

Cuando se apaga la luz de su dormitorio desciendo sigilosamente por la desvencijada escalera y cruzo de puntillas el húmedo césped con los pies descalzos, hasta una hamaca hecha trizas que cuelga precariamente entre dos pequeños árboles. Hace unos días pasé una hora acostado en la misma y no sufrí ningún percance. Entre los árboles, la hamaca ofrece una espléndida vista de la luna llena. Me mezo suavemente. La noche es cálida.

He estado deprimido desde la visita de esta mañana a Van Landel en el hospital. Cuando ingresé en la Facultad de Derecho, hace algo menos de tres años, lo hice con la noble aspiración de utilizar algún día mi título para contribuir a una pequeña mejora de la sociedad y ejercer una honorable profesión gobernada por cánones éticos, que en mi opinión todos los abogados luchaban por defender. Estaba realmente convencido de ello. Sabía que no podía cambiar el mundo, pero soñaba con trabajar en un ambiente intenso, rodeado de personas ingeniosas, fieles a ilustres valores. Deseaba trabajar intensamente y crecer en mi profesión, para atraer a los clientes por mi reputación y no mediante una publicidad engañosa. Y conforme aumentaran mi pericia y mis honorarios, podría aceptar casos y clientes de escasa popularidad sin preocuparme del dinero. Estos sueños no son inusuales entre los neófitos en la Facultad de Derecho.

Un mérito innegable de la facultad fueron las horas dedicadas al estudio y comentarios de la ética. Se hizo tanto hincapié en el tema que supusimos que nuestro colectivo pretendía celosamente imponer un riguroso código de conducta. Ahora me deprime la realidad. Durante el último mes, un auténtico abogado tras otro han mutilado progresivamente mi ilusión. He quedado reducido a cazador furtivo en las cafeterías de los hospitales por mil dólares mensuales. Me produce náuseas y tristeza comprobar en lo que me he convertido, y me azora la velocidad de mi caída.

Mi mejor amigo en la universidad era Craig Balter. Compartimos piso durante dos años. El año pasado asistí a su boda. Craig tenía un objetivo cuando ingresó en la universidad, que era el de convertirse en profesor de historia en una escuela secundaria. Era muy inteligente y la universidad demasiado fácil para él. Charlamos largo y tendido sobre cómo enfocar nuestras vidas en el futuro. Me daba la impresión de que la enseñanza era un objetivo demasiado humilde para él y se enojaba conmigo cuando comparaba mi futura profesión con la suya. Yo aspiraba a obtener un alto nivel de éxito y fortuna. Él iba encaminado a trabajar en las aulas, donde su salario dependería de factores ajenos a su control.

Craig consiguió un master y se casó con una maestra. Ahora da clases de historia y ciencias sociales en un instituto. Su esposa está embarazada y trabaja en un parvulario. Viven en una bonita casa de campo con un par de hectáreas de terreno y jardín, y son las personas más felices que conozco. Entre ambos ganan probablemente alrededor de cincuenta mil anuales.

Pero a Craig no le importa el dinero. Hace exactamente lo que siempre ha deseado. Sin embargo, yo no tengo ni idea de lo que estoy haciendo. El trabajo de Craig es enormemente gratificante, porque afecta la mente de los jóvenes. Puede prever los resultados de sus esfuerzos. Yo, por otra parte, iré mañana al despacho con la esperanza de atrapar, a tuertas o a derechas, a algún cliente desorientado, inmerso en algún grado de sufrimiento. Si los abogados ganaran lo mismo que los maestros se cerrarían inmediatamente el noventa por ciento de las Facultades de Derecho.

Las cosas deben mejorar. Pero antes de que eso suceda, hay por lo menos otros dos desastres en perspectiva. En primer lugar, podrían detenerme o crearme otros problemas por lo del incendio del bufete Lake, y en segundo lugar, podría suspender el examen de colegiatura.

Ambas perspectivas me mantienen inquieto en la hamaca hasta altas horas de la madrugada.

Bruiser llega temprano a su despacho, con los ojos irritados y resaca, pero impecablemente ataviado: elegante traje de lana, camisa blanca de algodón perfectamente almidonada y una distinguida corbata de seda. Incluso su frondosa melena parece haber recibido un trato especial esta mañana, está limpia y reluciente.

Debe presentarse en el juzgado para participar en la discusión preliminar de un caso de tráfico de drogas, y está nervioso y ajetreado. Me ha llamado a su despacho para recibir instrucciones.

—Buen trabajo con Van Landel —dice, rodeado de sumarios y documentos, mientras Dru circula atareada por el despacho, bajo la mirada iracunda de los tiburones—. He hablado hace unos minutos con la compañía de seguros. Amplia cobertura. La culpabilidad parece clara. ¿Cómo está la víctima?

Anoche pasé una hora angustiosa con Dan Van Landel y su esposa en el hospital. Me formularon un sinfín de preguntas, primordialmente en torno a la cuantía de la compensación. No pude responderles nada concreto, pero hice una admirable exhibición de jerga jurídica. De momento siguen con nosotros.

—Fracturas múltiples de pierna, brazo y costillas, además de abundantes laceraciones. Su médico dice que permanecerá diez días en el hospital.

Bruiser sonríe.

—Sigue trabajando en el caso. Ocúpate de investigar. Escucha a Deck. Existe la perspectiva de una buena compensación.

Muy interesante para Bruiser, pero yo no participaré de los beneficios. Este caso no cuenta como generador de honorarios para mí.

—La policía quiere tomarte declaración sobre el incendio —menciona mientras levanta un sumario—. Hablé con ellos anoche. Lo harán aquí, en este despacho, en mi presencia.

Lo dice como si ya estuviera organizado y yo no tuviera otra alternativa.

—¿Y si me niego? —pregunto.

—Probablemente te llevarán a la comisaría para interrogarte. Si no tienes nada que ocultar, sugiero que declares. Yo estaré aquí. Puedes consultarme lo que desees. Habla con ellos y luego te dejarán tranquilo.

—¿De modo que consideran el incendio intencionado?

—Están bastante convencidos.

—¿Qué quieren de mí?

—Saber dónde estabas, qué hacías, horas, lugares, coartadas, cosas por el estilo.

—No puedo responder a todo, pero puedo decir la verdad.

—Entonces por la verdad alcanzarás la libertad —sonríe Bruiser.

—Permíteme que tome nota.

—Lo haremos a las dos de esta tarde.

Asiento sin decir palabra. Es extraño que en este estado de vulnerabilidad confíe plenamente en Bruiser Stone, cuando no lo haría en ninguna otra circunstancia.

—Necesito tiempo libre, Bruiser —digo.

Sus manos quedan paralizadas en el aire y me mira fijamente. Dru, desde un rincón donde examina un fichero, para y me mira. Uno de los tiburones parece haberme oído.

—Acabas de empezar —responde Bruiser.

—Sí, lo sé. Pero falta muy poco para el examen de colegiatura y voy retrasado con mis estudios.

Ladea la cabeza y se acaricia la perilla. Su mirada es dura cuando bebe y se divierte. Ahora, sus ojos parecen rayos láser.

—¿Cuánto tiempo?

—Me gustaría venir por las mañanas y trabajar hasta eso de las doce del mediodía. Luego, si me lo permiten mis compromisos en los juzgados y citas con los clientes, querría retirarme a estudiar en la biblioteca.

Mi supuesto chiste pasa completamente inadvertido.

—Podrías estudiar con Deck —sonríe Bruiser y yo suelto una sonora carcajada—. Te diré lo que vamos a hacer —prosigue con seriedad—. Trabajarás hasta el mediodía, recogerás tus libros y te instalarás en la cafetería de Saint Peter. Estudiarás como un condenado, pero también mantendrás los ojos abiertos. Quiero que apruebes el examen, pero en este momento me preocupa mucho más conseguir nuevos casos. Llévate un teléfono móvil para que pueda ponerme en contacto contigo en cualquier momento. ¿Te parece bien?

¿Por qué lo habré hecho? Podía haberme mordido la lengua en lugar de mencionar el examen.

—Por supuesto —respondo con el entrecejo fruncido.

Anoche en la hamaca pensé que tal vez, con un poco de suerte, podría olvidarme de Saint Peter. Ahora va a convertirse en mi segunda morada.

Los dos mismos agentes que vinieron a mi casa se presentan a Bruiser para que les conceda permiso para interrogarme. Nos sentamos los cuatro alrededor de una mesilla redonda, en un rincón de su despacho. En el centro de la misma se colocan dos magnetófonos, ambos conectados.

Pronto empieza a ser aburrido. Les repito a esos payasos lo mismo que les conté cuando nos conocimos y pierden una enorme cantidad de tiempo reconstruyendo cada pequeño detalle. Intentan obligarme a que me contradiga en algún aspecto perfectamente insignificante («me parecía haber entendido que su camisa era azul marino, ahora dice que era simplemente azul»), pero me limito a contarles la pura verdad. No hay ninguna mentira que ocultar y, al cabo de una hora, parecen percatarse de que no soy su hombre.

Bruiser se enoja con ellos y en varias ocasiones les ordena que prosigan. Durante algún tiempo le obedecen. Sinceramente, creo que le temen.

Por fin se marchan y Bruiser me asegura que ya no volverán a molestarme. He dejado de ser sospechoso y no hacen más que cubrir el expediente. Por la mañana hablará con su teniente y se olvidarán de mí.

Le doy las gracias. Me entrega un diminuto teléfono, que cabe en la palma de mi mano.

—Llévalo siempre contigo —dice—. Especialmente cuando estés estudiando. Puede que te necesite con urgencia.

El minúsculo artilugio crece de pronto. A través del mismo estaré sujeto a su voluntad día y noche.

Me manda a mi despacho.

Regreso a la cafetería próxima a la sala ortopédica, firmemente decidido a ocultarme en un rincón, dedicarme a estudiar, tener ese maldito teléfono móvil a mano, pero hacer caso omiso de la gente a mi alrededor.

La comida no está mal. Después de comer siete años en cantinas universitarias, cualquier cosa sabe bien. Como un bocadillo de pimiento con queso y patatas fritas para cenar, y distribuyo mi material de estudio para el examen sobre la mesa del rincón, de espaldas a la pared.

Primero devoro mi bocadillo mientras veo comer a los demás. Casi todos los presentes llevan algún tipo de indumentaria médica: médicos con mono blanco, enfermeras de uniforme y técnicos con bata de laboratorio. Se sientan en pequeños grupos y hablan de enfermedades y tratamientos que nunca he oído. Para personas supuestamente interesadas por la salud y la nutrición, comen la peor basura imaginable: patatas fritas, hamburguesas, nachos, pizza... Observo a un grupo de médicos concentrados en su comida y me pregunto qué pensarían si supieran que entre ellos se encontraba un abogado que estudiaba para su examen de colegiatura a fin de poderlos demandar algún día.

Dudo que les importe. De vez en cuando aparece algún paciente con muletas, o en una silla de ruedas empujada por un auxiliar. No detecto a ningún otro abogado al acecho.

Pago mi primer café a las seis de la tarde y me sumerjo en un doloroso repaso de contratos y transacciones inmobiliarias, que me recuerdan el horror de mi primer curso en la facultad. Persisto. Lo he postergado hasta ahora y ya no dispongo de un mañana. Transcurre una hora antes de ir a por otro café. La clientela es ahora escasa y detecto a dos pacientes accidentados al otro lado de la sala. Ambos llevan bastantes vendas y escayola. Deck ya les habría acosado, pero yo no.

Al cabo de un rato me sorprende descubrir que me siento a gusto. El lugar es tranquilo y nadie me conoce. Es ideal para estudiar. El café no está mal y a partir de la segunda taza va a mitad de precio. Estoy lejos de la señorita Birdie y, por consiguiente, sin tener que pensar en trabajos físicos. Mi jefe quiere que esté aquí y aunque se supone que debo estar al acecho, nunca sabrá la diferencia. Afortunadamente no tengo ningún cupo. No estoy comprometido a contratar un número determinado de casos semanales.

167

El teléfono emite un triste gemido. Es Bruiser haciendo una comprobación. ¿Ha habido suerte? No, respondo, mientras observo cómo esos dos desgraciados en sus sillas de ruedas comparan sus lesiones. Dice que ha hablado con el teniente y que las cosas pintan bien. Está convencido de que se concentrarán en otras pistas, otros sospechosos. ¡Buena pesca!, exclama con una carcajada antes de colgar, para dirigirse indudablemente a Yogi's y tomar unas copas con Prince.

Después de estudiar otra hora dejo la mesa para subir al octavo piso y visitar a Dan Van Landel. Está dolorido, pero dispuesto a hablar. Le comunico la buena noticia de que hemos hablado con la compañía de seguros del otro conductor y dispone de una buena póliza. Le explico que su caso lo tiene todo, repitiendo lo que hace un rato me ha contado Deck: clara culpabilidad (¡el conductor borracho por si faltaba poco!), una póliza de seguros muy completa y unas buenas lesiones. Buenas en el sentido de que sus huesos fracturados podrán convertirse fácilmente en esa condición mágica de la invalidez permanente.

Dan logra sonreír amablemente. Está contando ya su dinero. Claro que todavía no ha llegado el momento de repartir el pastel con Bruiser.

Me despido y prometo visitarle mañana. Puesto que me han destinado al hospital, podré visitar a todos mis clientes. ¡Vaya servicio!

La cafetería vuelve a estar llena de gente cuando regreso y recupero mi posición en el rincón. He dejado los libros desparramados sobre la mesa y en uno de ellos se lee claramente *Texto de colegiatura Elton*. El título ha llamado la atención de un grupo de jóvenes médicos en la mesa contigua y me miran con recelo cuando me instalo en mi silla. Se hace un mutis instantáneo y comprendo que han estado hablando de mi material. No tardan en marcharse. Voy a por otro café y me sumerjo en las maravillas de los procesos federales.

La clientela se reduce a un puñado de personas. Ahora tomo café descafeinado y me asombra lo que he llegado a repasar en las últimas cuatro horas. Bruiser llama de nuevo a las nueve y cuarenta y cinco. Parece que está en algún bar. Quiere que esté en su despacho a las nueve de la mañana para comentar algún aspecto jurídico de su actual juicio de narcotráfico. Le aseguro que allí estaré.

Detestaría que mi abogado se inspirara en teorías jurídicas para utilizar en mi defensa, mientras tomaba copas en un bar de alterne.

Pero Bruiser es mi abogado.

A las diez estoy solo en la cafetería. Permanece abierta toda la noche, de modo que la cajera no me presta ninguna atención. Estoy profundamente sumergido en el lenguaje de las negociaciones preliminares cuando de repente oigo el estornudo delicado de una joven. Levanto la cabeza y, dos mesas más allá, veo a una paciente en una silla de ruedas, la única persona, aparte de mí, que hay en la cafetería. Lleva la pierna derecha escayolada a partir de la rodilla y la tiene extendida, ofreciendo una vista de la parte inferior de la escayola. A juzgar por mis conocimientos médicos a esta altura de mi carrera parece reciente.

Es muy joven y extraordinariamente atractiva. No puedo evitar contemplarla unos segundos antes de concentrarme de nuevo en mis notas. Luego vuelvo a mirarla. Tiene el cabello oscuro, parcialmente recogido en la nuca. Sus ojos son castaños y parecen húmedos. Sus marcadas facciones son hermosas, a pesar de una contusión en el lado izquierdo de la mandíbula. Una desagradable contusión, como las que suelen dejar los puñetazos. Lleva la bata blanca habitual del hospital y bajo la misma parece casi frágil.

Un anciano con una chaqueta rosada, una de las innumerables almas caritativas que trabajan como voluntarios en Saint Peter, coloca suavemente un vaso de zumo de naranja sobre la mesa, frente a ella.

—Toma, Kelly —dice como un perfecto abuelo.

—Gracias —responde ella con una leve sonrisa.

—¿Te parecen bien treinta minutos? —pregunta.

—Treinta minutos —asiente al tiempo que se muerde el labio inferior.

—¿Puedo hacer algo más por ti?

—No, gracias.

Le da unos golpecitos en el hombro y abandona la cafetería.

Estamos solos. Procuro no mirarla, pero es imposible. Me concentro todo el tiempo que puedo en mis papeles y luego levanto lentamente la cabeza hasta verla. No está directamente enfrente de mí, sino a un ángulo de casi noventa grados. Levanta el vaso y veo los vendajes de sus muñecas. Todavía no se ha percatado de mi presencia. En realidad, me doy cuenta de que no veía a nadie aunque la sala estuviera llena de gente. Kelly está en su propio mundo.

Parece tener el tobillo fracturado. La contusión del rostro cumpliría los requisitos de Deck de lesiones múltiples, aunque no parece haber laceración. Las heridas de las muñecas son desconcertantes. A pesar de su atractivo, no siento la tentación de acosarla. Parece muy triste y no deseo empeorar su estado de ánimo. Lleva una fina alianza en el anular de la mano izquierda. No debe de tener más de dieciocho años.

Procuro concentrarme en mi lectura por lo menos durante cinco minutos consecutivos, pero veo que se seca los ojos con una servilleta de papel. Ladea ligeramente la cabeza a la izquierda conforme fluyen las lágrimas de sus ojos. Solloza discretamente.

Comprendo rápidamente que el llanto no tiene nada que ver con el dolor de su tobillo fracturado. Su causa no son las lesiones físicas.

Mi perversa imaginación de jurista se desata. Puede que estuviera involucrada en un accidente automovilístico en el que haya fallecido su marido y ella haya resultado herida. Es demasiado joven para tener hijos, sus padres viven lejos y llora la muerte de su esposo. Podría ser un caso extraordinario.

Alejo esos terribles pensamientos de mi mente y procuro concentrarme en el libro que tengo delante. Ella no deja de sollozar en silencio. Varios clientes vienen y van, pero ninguno de ellos se sienta a su mesa ni a la mía. Vacío mi taza de café, me levanto sigilosamente y paso exactamente por delante de ella en dirección a la barra. La miro, ella me mira, nuestras miradas permanecen enlazadas un prolongado segundo y casi tropiezo con una silla metálica. Me tiemblan ligeramente las manos cuando pago el café. Respiro hondo y me detengo junto a su mesa.

Levanta lentamente sus hermosos ojos húmedos.

—No me gusta entrometerme —digo—, pero ¿puedo ayudarte en algo? ¿Te duele? —pregunto al tiempo que muevo la cabeza en dirección a la escayola.

—No —responde con una voz apenas audible—. Gracias de todos modos —agrega con una pequeña sonrisa arrebatadora.

—De acuerdo —respondo mirando hacia mi mesa, a menos de seis metros de distancia—. Si necesitas algo, estoy ahí estudiando para mi examen de colegiatura.

Me encojo de hombros como si no supiera qué hacer, pero manifestándole que soy atento, estoy a su disposición y suplicándole que me disculpe si me he propasado. Pero mi interés es sincero y estoy a su disposición.

—Gracias —repite.

Después de haber aclarado que soy una persona casi legítima, que estudia voluminosos textos con la esperanza de incorporarse pronto a una noble profesión, me acomodo en mi silla. Seguro que debe estar impresionada. Me sumerjo en mis estudios, ajeno a su sufrimiento.

Transcurren varios minutos. Paso una página y aprovecho

para mirarla. Ella está mirándome y me da un vuelco el corazón. Hago caso omiso de ella tanto tiempo como puedo y levanto la cabeza para mirarla. Se ha sumido de nuevo en su sufrimiento. Retuerce la servilleta. Las lágrimas ruedan por sus mejillas.

Me duele el corazón de verla sufrir de ese modo. Me encantaría sentarme junto a ella, tal vez rodearla con mi brazo y charlar. Si está casada, ¿dónde diablos está su marido? Mira hacia mí, pero creo que no me ve.

Su acompañante de chaqueta rosa llega exactamente a las diez y media, e intenta recuperar rápidamente su compostura. Él le acaricia suavemente la cabeza y le ofrece unas palabras de consuelo que no logro oír antes de empujar con ternura su silla de ruedas. Al marcharse me mira deliberadamente y me brinda una radiante y prolongada sonrisa.

Siento la tentación de seguirla a lo lejos y averiguar el número de su habitación, pero me controlo. Luego pienso en buscar al hombre de la chaqueta rosa y pedirle los detalles, pero no lo hago. Intento olvidarla. No es más que una chiquilla.

La noche siguiente llego a la cafetería y me instalo en la misma mesa. Oigo a la misma gente hablando apresuradamente de los mismos temas. Visito a los Van Landel y eludo sus interminables preguntas. Intento detectar a otros tiburones al acecho en estas aguas turbias y hago caso omiso de varios clientes potenciales a la espera de ser acosados. Estudio durante varias horas. Mi concentración es excelente y nunca he estado tan intensamente motivado.

También estoy pendiente del reloj. Cerca de las diez me pongo nervioso y empiezo a mirar a mi alrededor. Intento conservar la calma y seguir estudiando, pero no puedo evitar sobresaltarme cada vez que alguien entra en la cafetería. Dos enfermeras comen en una mesa y un técnico lee un libro a solas en otra.

Aparece a las diez y cinco, con el mismo anciano que empuja su silla de ruedas hasta la misma mesa de la noche anterior, y me sonríe cuando se acomoda.

—Zumo de naranja —dice.

Lleva todavía el cabello recogido en la nuca, pero si no me equivoco se ha puesto un poco de rímel y maquillaje en los ojos. También lleva un poco de carmín pálido en los labios y el efecto es espectacular. No me había percatado anoche de que no llevaba maquillaje. Hoy, con sólo unos ligeros toques, está excepcionalmente hermosa. Su mirada es clara, radiante, desprovista de tristeza.

Su acompañante coloca el vaso de zumo sobre la mesa y dice exactamente lo mismo que anoche:

—Aquí lo tienes, Kelly. ¿Te parece bien treinta minutos?

—Digamos cuarenta y cinco.

—Como quieras —responde antes de retirarse.

Saborea el zumo con la mirada perdida en la superficie de la mesa. Hoy he pasado mucho tiempo pensando en Kelly y hace mucho que he decidido cómo proceder. Espero unos minutos, finjo que ella no está presente mientras me concentro en mis libros y luego me levanto lentamente, como si hubiera llegado el momento de tomar otro café.

—Tienes mejor aspecto esta noche —digo después de detenerme junto a su mesa.

Esperaba que le dijera algo parecido.

—Me siento mucho mejor —responde con una radiante sonrisa que muestra una impecable dentadura.

Su rostro es encantador, a pesar de esa terrible contusión.

—¿Te apetece algo?

—Una Coca-cola. Este zumo es amargo.

—Por supuesto —respondo antes de dirigirme a la barra, sin palabras para expresar mi emoción.

Me sirvo yo mismo dos refrescos de la máquina automática, pago y coloco los vasos sobre su mesa. Dirijo la mirada a la silla vacía al otro lado de la mesa, como si estuviera completamente confundido.

—Por favor, siéntate.

—¿Estás segura?

—Te lo ruego. Estoy harta de hablar con enfermeras.

Me instalo en la silla y apoyo los codos sobre la mesa.

—Me llamo Rudy Baylor —digo—. Y tú eres Kelly...

—Kelly Riker. Encantada de conocerte.

—El gusto es mío.

Es una chica muy atractiva, pero ahora que puedo mirarla sin disimulo a menos de un metro, estoy ineludiblemente boquiabierto. Sus ojos son de un castaño suave con un destello de picardía. Es exquisita.

—Lo siento si te molesté anoche —digo ansioso por proseguir la conversación, puesto que hay muchas cosas que deseo saber.

—No me molestaste. Lamento haberte ofrecido un espectáculo tan lamentable.

—¿Por qué vienes a la cafetería? —pregunto, como si yo perteneciera al lugar y ella fuera una intrusa.

—Para no estar siempre en mi habitación. ¿Y tú?

—Estoy preparando mi examen de colegiatura y éste es un sitio tranquilo.

172

—¿Entonces vas a ser abogado?

—Eso es. He acabado la carrera hace unas semanas y ahora trabajo en un bufete. Cuando haya aprobado el examen estaré listo para actuar.

Bebe con una paja y hace una ligera mueca al cambiar de posición.

—Una fractura muy molesta, ¿no es cierto? —pregunto moviendo la cabeza en dirección a su pierna.

—Es el tobillo. Me han insertado un clavo.

—¿Cómo ocurrió?

Ésta era la próxima pregunta más evidente y espero que me la responda con toda facilidad.

Pero no es así. Titubea y se le humedecen inmediatamente los ojos.

—Un accidente doméstico —responde, como si hubiera ensayado esa vaga explicación.

¿Qué diablos significa eso? ¿Se cayó por la escalera?

—Claro —digo, como si fuera perfectamente comprensible.

Me preocupan sus muñecas, porque no están escayoladas sino sólo vendadas. No parecen rotas ni dislocadas. Tal vez laceradas.

—Es una larga historia —farfulla entre sorbos, y desvía la mirada.

—¿Cuánto hace que estás aquí? —pregunto.

—Un par de días. Esperan a comprobar si el clavo está recto. De lo contrario, volverán a operarme. —Hace una pausa mientras juega con la paja—. ¿No es éste un lugar un poco extraño para estudiar?

—En realidad, no. Es tranquilo, hay café en abundancia y está abierto toda la noche. Llevas una alianza matrimonial.

Eso me ha preocupado más que cualquier otra cosa.

Se contempla el anillo, como si no estuviera segura de que seguía en su dedo.

—Sí —responde antes de fijar la mirada en la paja.

La alianza está sola, sin un diamante que la acompañe.

—¿Entonces dónde está tu marido?

—Haces muchas preguntas.

—Soy abogado, o casi. Es la formación que recibimos.

—¿Por qué quieres saberlo?

—Porque es extraño que estés sola aquí en el hospital, evidentemente herida, y él no te acompañe.

—Ha estado aquí hace un rato.

—¿Ha regresado a casa para cuidar de los niños?

—No tenemos hijos. ¿Y tú?

—Tampoco. Ni hijos, ni esposa.

—¿Qué edad tienes?

—Haces muchas preguntas —respondo con una sonrisa y la mirada fija en el destello de sus ojos—. Veinticinco. ¿Y tú?

—Diecinueve —responde después de reflexionar unos instantes.

—Eres jovencísima para estar casada.

—No fue por elección.

—Lo siento.

—No es culpa tuya. Quedé embarazada cuando apenas había cumplido los dieciocho, me casé poco después, tuve un aborto a la semana de la boda y desde entonces las cosas han ido de mal en peor. ¿Satisface eso tu curiosidad?

—No. Sí. Lo siento. ¿De qué te apetece hablar?

—De la universidad. ¿Dónde estudiaste?

—En Austin Peay y luego en la Facultad de Derecho de la Universidad de Memphis.

—Siempre había querido ir a la universidad, pero no salieron así las cosas. ¿Eres de Memphis?

—Nací aquí, pero me crié en Knoxville. ¿Y tú?

—De una pequeña ciudad a una hora de aquí. Nos marchamos cuando quedé embarazada. Mi familia se sentía humillada. Los padres de mi marido son unos indeseables. Era el momento de marcharse.

Aquí hay asuntos familiares sumamente desagradables casi a flor de piel de los que prefiero mantenerme alejado. Ha mencionado ya dos veces su embarazo, cuando era totalmente innecesario. Pero se siente sola y le apetece hablar.

—¿De modo que os trasladasteis a Memphis?

—Huimos a Memphis, nos casamos ante un juez de paz, una ceremonia realmente elegante, y luego tuve el aborto.

—¿A qué se dedica tu marido?

—Conduce una excavadora. Bebe como un condenado. Es un ex jugador que todavía sueña con el béisbol de primera división.

No le había preguntado tanto. Supongo que él debía de ser un admirado atleta en el instituto, ella la animadora más atractiva, y formaron la perfecta pareja norteamericana, el señor y la señora del instituto de Podunk, la más hermosa, la más apuesta, la más atlética, la que más probabilidades tiene de éxito, hasta que una noche olvidan el preservativo y llega la catástrofe. Por alguna razón deciden no abortar. Puede que terminen sus estudios en el instituto y puede que no. Avergonzados, huyen de Podunk para refugiarse en el anonimato de la gran ciudad. Después del aborto involuntario, el idilio toca a su fin y al despertar descubren que ha llegado la vida real.

Él todavía sueña con la fama y la fortuna del deporte de élite. Ella siente nostalgia de la vida sin preocupaciones que apenas acaba de pasar y sueña con una universidad que nunca verá.

—Lo siento —dice—. No debí haberlo mencionado.

—Eres lo bastante joven para ir a la universidad —respondo.

Se ríe de mi optimismo, como si dicho sueño estuviera muerto y sepultado desde hace mucho.

—No terminé mis estudios secundarios.

¿Qué puedo responderle? Soltarle un ridículo discurso de aliento, decirle que puede terminar sus estudios en la escuela nocturna, que está a su alcance si realmente lo desea.

—¿Trabajas? —pregunto en su lugar.

—De vez en cuando. ¿Qué clase de abogado quieres ser?

—Me gustan los juicios. Me gustaría ejercer mi carrera en los juzgados.

—¿Representando delincuentes?

—Tal vez. Tienen derecho a ser oídos en la sala y a una buena defensa.

—¿Asesinos?

—Sí, pero la mayoría no pueden pagar a un abogado particular.

—¿Violadores y personas que abusan de los menores?

—No —respondo con el entrecejo fruncido después de reflexionar unos instantes.

—¿Hombres que maltratan a sus esposas?

—No, nunca.

Lo digo con toda sinceridad y, además, tengo ciertas sospechas respecto a sus heridas. Considera mis preferencias aceptables.

—La defensa penal es una especialidad inusual —aclaro—. Es probable que me concentre primordialmente en casos civiles.

—Pleitos y demandas.

—Sí, eso es. Derecho civil.

—¿Divorcios?

—Prefiero evitarlos. Es un trabajo muy desagradable.

Hace esfuerzos considerables para mantener la conversación de mi lado, alejada de su pasado y ciertamente de su presente. No me importa. Las lágrimas pueden aparecer inesperadamente y no deseo estropear la conversación. Quiero que perdure.

Se interesa por mis experiencias en la universidad: los estudios, las fiestas, las sociedades, la vida en las residencias, los exámenes, los profesores y los viajes. Ha visto muchas películas y tiene una idea romántica de cuatro años perfectos en un bonito campus, con las hojas de los árboles amarillas y luego rojas en otoño, estudiantes con jersey que compiten para formar parte del equipo y nuevas amistades que duran toda una vida. Esta pobre chica, que no llegó a terminar sus estudios secundarios, tiene sueños maravillosos. Su lenguaje es perfecto y su vocabulario más amplio que el mío. Me confiesa con reticencia que se habría graduado en el primer o segundo lugar de su promoción de no haber sido por su idilio juvenil con Cliff, el señor Riker.

Con poco esfuerzo realzo los días de gloria de mis estudios universitarios, pasando por alto hechos tan esenciales como el de haber trabajado cuarenta horas semanales repartiendo pizzas para pagarme los estudios.

Quiere que le hable de mi bufete y estoy en plena reelaboración fantástica de J. Lyman y sus dependencias cuando suena el teléfono a dos mesas de distancia. Le digo que me llaman del despacho y me disculpo.

Bruiser me llama desde Yogi's, borracho, acompañado de Prince. Les divierte que esté donde estoy mientras ellos se emborrachan y apuestan por cualquier cosa que transmita el canal deportivo. El ruido de fondo parece el de una manifestación.

—¿Cómo va la pesca? —exclama Bruiser por teléfono.

Le sonrío a Kelly, indudablemente impresionada por la llamada, y le explico lo más discretamente posible que, en este mismo momento, estoy hablando con un cliente potencial. Bruiser se troncha de risa y le pasa el teléfono a Prince, que está todavía más borracho. Me cuenta un chiste de abogados que no tiene ninguna gracia relacionado con la persecución de ambulancias. A continuación me suelta un discurso autopanegírico por haberme colocado con Bruiser, que me enseñará más sobre leyes que cincuenta catedráticos. Esto dura bastante y al poco rato aparece el acompañante voluntario de Kelly para conducirla a su habitación.

Doy unos pasos en dirección a la mesa, cubro el auricular con la mano y digo:

—Me siento feliz de haberte conocido.

—Gracias por la bebida y la conversación —sonríe.

—¿Mañana por la noche? —pregunto sin que Prince deje de chillarme al oído.

—Tal vez —responde al tiempo que me guiña intencionadamente un ojo.

Me tiemblan las rodillas.

Es evidente que su acompañante de chaqueta rosa ha circulado por este lugar el tiempo suficiente para reconocer a un impertinente. Me mira con ceño y se la lleva rápidamente. Volverá.

Pulso un botón del teléfono y dejo a Prince con la palabra en la boca. Si lo recuerdan más adelante, lo cual me parece sumamente dudoso, le echaré la culpa a Sony.

DIECIOCHO

A Deck le encantan los retos, especialmente cuando incluyen la acumulación de basura mediante discretas conversaciones telefónicas con chivatos anónimos. Le facilito los datos básicos, relacionados con Kelly y Cliff Riker, y en menos de una hora entra orgulloso en mi despacho con una radiante sonrisa.

—Kelly Riker ingresó en Saint Peter hace tres días, a medianoche para ser exactos, con lesiones múltiples —lee en sus notas—. La policía había acudido a su casa respondiendo a una llamada anónima, donde tenía lugar una pelea doméstica bastante violenta. La encontraron en el sofá de la sala de estar, gravemente apaleada. Cliff Riker estaba evidentemente intoxicado, muy agitado, e inicialmente quiso dispensarles a los agentes la misma medicina que le había administrado a su esposa. Tenía un bate de aluminio en las manos, evidentemente su arma predilecta. No tardaron en someterlo, detenerlo, acusarlo de agresión física y llevárselo. Ella fue trasladada en una ambulancia al hospital. Hizo una breve declaración ante la policía, según la cual, su marido había regresado a casa borracho después de un partido de béisbol, estalló una discusión estúpida, se pelearon y él ganó. Dijo que le había golpeado dos veces con el bate en el tobillo y le había dado dos puñetazos en la cara.

Anoche no pude conciliar el sueño pensando en Kelly Riker, en sus ojos castaños y piernas morenas, y la idea de que haya sido víctima de tal agresión me produce náuseas. Deck observa mi reacción, de modo que mi rostro permanece impasible.

—Lleva las muñecas vendadas —digo y Deck gira con orgullo la página.

Tiene otro informe de otra fuente, obtenido de la brigada de rescate del departamento de Bomberos de Memphis.

—Lo de las muñecas no está muy bien documentado. En algún momento de la pelea le sujetó las muñecas contra el suelo e intentó hacer el amor con ella. Su estado no era el que suponía, probablemente demasiada cerveza. Ella estaba desnuda cuando la encontró la policía, envuelta en una manta. No podía escapar, debido a su tobillo fracturado.

—¿Qué ocurrió con él?

—Pasó la noche en el calabozo. Su familia pagó la fianza. Debe presentarse ante el juez dentro de una semana, pero no ocurrirá nada.

—¿Por qué no?

—Lo más probable es que ella retire la denuncia, se besen y hagan las paces. Luego aguantará hasta que se repita.

—¿Cómo lo sabes?

—Porque no es la primera vez. Hace ocho meses, la policía recibió la misma llamada, la misma pelea, todo idéntico, a excepción de que ella tuvo más suerte. Sólo unas contusiones. Evidentemente, el bate no estaba a mano. Los policías los separaron, les dieron unos consejos, después de todo no son más que chiquillos recién casados, se besaron e hicieron las paces. Hace tres meses intervino el bate en la pelea y ella pasó una semana en Saint Peter con costillas fracturadas. Se transfirió el caso a la sección de abusos familiares de la policía de Memphis, e hicieron todo lo posible para infringir un severo castigo. Pero ella le quiere y se niega a declarar contra él. Se retira la denuncia. Ocurre permanentemente.

Tardo unos momentos en asimilarlo. Sospechaba de algún conflicto familiar, pero no tan horrible. ¿Cómo puede un hombre apalear a su esposa con un bate de aluminio? ¿Cómo puede Cliff Riker golpear con sus puños un rostro tan hermoso?

—Ocurre constantemente —repite Deck, leyendo a la perfección mi pensamiento.

—¿Algo más?

—No. Sólo que no te acerques demasiado.

—Gracias —respondo, débil y mareado—. Gracias.

—No hay de qué —dice después de levantarse.

No es sorprendente que Booker haya estudiado para el examen mucho más que yo. Y, como de costumbre, está preocupado por mí. Ha programado una sesión de repaso maratoniana para esta tarde en una sala de conferencias del bufete Shankle.

Fiel a sus instrucciones, llego a las doce en punto. Las oficinas son modernas y ajetreadas, y lo más curioso del lugar es que todos son negros. He visto numerosos bufetes durante el último mes, y sólo recuerdo a una secretaria negra y a ningún abogado negro. Aquí no hay una sola cara blanca.

Booker me muestra rápidamente las dependencias. A pesar

de ser la hora del almuerzo, hay mucha actividad. Los pasillos bullen con el ruido de ordenadores, fotocopiadoras, faxes, teléfonos y voces. Las secretarias comen apresuradamente en sus escritorios, inevitablemente cubiertos de montones de documentos pendientes. Los abogados y los pasantes son bastante amables, pero no pueden perder el tiempo. Y las normas del vestir son rigurosas: traje oscuro y camisa blanca para los hombres, vestido formal para las mujeres; nada de colores llamativos ni pantalones.

Comparaciones con el bufete de J. Lyman Stone acuden a mi mente, pero las evito.

Booker me explica que Marvin Shankle dirige el bufete con mano dura. Viste impecablemente, es sumamente profesional en todos los aspectos y mantiene un horario inhumano. Espera otro tanto de sus socios y empleados.

La sala de conferencias está en un rincón tranquilo. Yo estoy encargado del almuerzo y desenvuelvo los bocadillos que he traído de Yogi's. Bocadillos gratuitos. Charlamos cinco minutos sobre la familia y los amigos de la facultad. Me hace algunas preguntas sobre mi trabajo, pero sabe guardar las distancias. Ya se lo he contado todo, o casi todo. Prefiero no revelarle mi nuevo destino en Saint Peter, ni la naturaleza de mi actividad en el hospital.

¡Booker se ha convertido en un auténtico abogado! Consulta su reloj después del tiempo destinado a cumplidos y emprende la espléndida tarea que ha programado para esta tarde. Trabajaremos incesantemente durante seis horas, descansando sólo para tomar café y acudir al servicio, y a las seis en punto debemos abandonar el local porque otras personas lo han reservado.

Desde las doce y cuarto hasta la una y media repasamos los impuestos directos federales. Booker es quien más habla, porque siempre ha comprendido mejor el tema tributario. Trabajamos con apuntes y los impuestos son tan confusos para mí ahora como en otoño del año pasado.

A la una y media me permite ir al servicio y tomar un poco de café, y desde entonces hasta las dos y media tomo la iniciativa con las normas federales referentes a pruebas admisibles. Es emocionante. La extraordinaria energía de Booker es contagiosa y cubrimos con suma rapidez un montón de material tedioso.

Suspender el examen de colegiatura es una pesadilla para cualquier joven asociado, pero intuyo que sería particularmente desastroso para Booker. Para mí, francamente, no sería el fin del mundo. Destruiría mi orgullo, pero me repondría. Estudiaría más a fondo y me presentaría de nuevo dentro de seis meses. A Bruiser no le importaría, a condición de que captara unos cuantos clientes cada mes. Un buen caso de quemaduras y no esperaría que volviera a presentarme al examen.

Pero puede que Booker tuviera problemas. Sospecho que el señor Marvin Shankle le amargaría la vida si no aprobara al primer intento. Y si lo suspendiera dos veces, probablemente lo pondría de patitas en la calle.

A las dos y media en punto, Marvin Shankle entra en la sala de conferencias y Booker me presenta. Tiene unos cincuenta años, es apuesto y está en buena forma. Su cabello es ligeramente canoso alrededor de las orejas. Habla con una voz suave, pero su mirada es intensa. Da la impresión de poder ver a través de las paredes. Es un personaje legendario en los círculos jurídicos del sur y supone un honor conocerlo.

Booker ha organizado una conferencia. Durante casi una hora escuchamos atentamente a Shankle, que nos habla de los conflictos jurídicos relativos a los derechos civiles y a la discriminación en el trabajo. Tomamos apuntes, formulamos algunas preguntas, pero sobre todo escuchamos.

Luego se marcha para asistir a una reunión y dedicamos la próxima media hora a repasar la legislación antimonopolios. A las cuatro otra conferencia.

Nuestro próximo conferenciante es Tyrone Kipler, uno de los socios formado en Harvard, especializado en Derecho constitucional. Empieza lentamente y sólo acelera cuando Booker lo acribilla a preguntas. Me sorprendo a mí mismo imaginando que me oculto de noche entre los matorrales con un descomunal bate de béisbol y le propino una soberana paliza a Cliff Riker. Para no quedarme dormido, doy vueltas a la mesa, tomo café y procuro concentrarme.

Al final de la hora, Kipler está alegre y animado, y le formulamos un sinfín de preguntas. De pronto se queda con la palabra en la boca, consulta su reloj y dice que debe marcharse. Le espera un juez en algún lugar. Le damos las gracias y desaparece a toda prisa.

—Nos queda una hora —dice Booker a las cinco y cinco—. ¿Qué vamos a hacer?

—Tomémonos una cerveza.

—Lo siento. Las alternativas son el derecho de la propiedad o ética.

Necesito la ética, pero estoy cansado y no me apetece que me recuerden la gravedad de mis pecados.

—Repasemos el derecho de la propiedad.

Booker cruza rápidamente la sala y trae los libros pertinentes.

Son casi las ocho cuando avanzo penosamente por el laberinto de corredores en el corazón de Saint Peter y descubro a un médico y una enfermera que ocupan mi mesa predilecta. Compro un café y me siento cerca. La enfermera, que es muy atractiva, parece bastante apenada y, a juzgar por sus susurros, zozobra su idilio. Él tiene sesenta años, con cabello trasplantado y una nueva mandíbula. Ella tiene treinta y evidentemente no será promocionada al rango de esposa. Sólo amante por ahora. Musitan con mucha seriedad.

No estoy de humor para estudiar. He estudiado bastante para un solo día, pero me motiva el hecho de que Booker esté todavía en su despacho, trabajando y preparándose para el examen.

Los amantes se retiran al cabo de unos minutos. Ella está llorando. Él es frío y despiadado. Me instalo en mi silla, desparramo mis notas sobre la mesa y procuro estudiar.

Y espero.

Kelly llega poco después de las diez, pero es otro individuo quien empuja hoy su silla de ruedas. Me mira fríamente y señala una mesa del centro de la sala. La conduce al lugar de su elección. Le miro. Él me mira.

Supongo que se trata de Cliff. Es aproximadamente de mi altura, no más de metro ochenta y tres, robusto y con una incipiente barriga de tomar cerveza. Pero sus hombros son anchos y se le marcan los bíceps a través de una camiseta excesivamente ceñida, cuya función es la de exhibir sus músculos. Lleva vaqueros ajustados y el cabello castaño y ondulado, demasiado largo para ser elegante. Tiene abundante vello en su cara y antebrazos. Cliff es uno de esos que empiezan a afeitarse a los trece años.

Tiene los ojos verdosos y un rostro atractivo, que le hacen parecer mayor de diecinueve. Da la vuelta al tobillo que fracturó con un bate de béisbol y se dirige a la barra en busca de bebidas. Ella sabe que estoy mirándola. Escudriña deliberadamente sus entornos y, en el último momento, me guiña un ojo. Casi derramo el café.

No se precisa una gran imaginación para deducir lo que ha mediado entre ellos últimamente. Amenazas, disculpas, súplicas y más amenazas. Esta noche parecen pasárselo mal. Ambos están enfurruñados. Sorben sus refrescos en silencio. Intercambian de vez en cuando un par de palabras, pero su actitud es la de unos amantes juveniles en pleno enfado semanal. Uno dice algo breve y el otro responde todavía con mayor brevedad. Sólo

se miran cuando es estrictamente necesario, contemplan fijamente el suelo y las paredes. Yo me oculto tras un libro.

Ella se ha colocado de modo que pueda verme sin ser sor-
prendida. Él está casi completamente de espaldas a mí. Vuelve
de vez en cuando la cabeza, pero sus movimientos se anuncian
con mucha antelación. Me sobra tiempo para rascarme la cabeza y enfrascarme en mis estudios antes de que pose su mirada
en mí.

Después de diez minutos de silencio casi absoluto, ella dice
algo que provoca una reacción agitada. Ojalá pudiera oírlos. De
pronto, él está excitado y le chilla. Ella responde por un igual. Aumenta el volumen de sus voces y pronto logro discernir que discuten sobre si ella declarará o no contra él ante un juez. Parece no
haberlo decidido todavía. Eso preocupa realmente a Cliff. Pierde
con facilidad los estribos, lo cual no es sorprendente en un fanático sureño pagado de sí mismo, y ella le dice que baje la voz. Mira
a su alrededor y deja de chillar. No oigo lo que dice.

Después de provocarlo, lo tranquiliza, aunque todavía parece muy enojado. Con los nervios a flor de piel, durante un rato
se ignoran mutuamente.

Entonces ella vuelve al ataque. Farfulla algo y a él se le yergue la espalda. Le tiemblan las manos y su lenguaje se llena de
blasfemias. Discuten un minuto, antes de que ella deje de hablar
y de prestarle atención. A Cliff no le gusta ser ignorado y levanta la voz. Ella le dice que se calle, que están en público. Él levanta aún más la voz para expresar lo que hará si ella no retira
la denuncia, decirle que tal vez acabe en la cárcel, etcétera.

Ella responde algo que no logro oír y de pronto él le da un
guantazo a su vaso de plástico y se incorpora de un brinco. La bebida se esparce por media sala, salpicando el suelo y otras mesas.
Ella está empapada. Suspira, cierra los ojos y echa a llorar. Se le
oye blasfemando y pataleando mientras se aleja por el pasillo.

Me levanto instintivamente, pero ella mueve de inmediato la
cabeza y vuelvo a sentarme. La cajera ha presenciado el espectáculo y se le acerca con una toalla. Se la entrega a Kelly y ella se
seca la Coca-cola de la cara y de los brazos.

—Lo siento —le dice a la cajera.

Su bata está empapada. Hace un esfuerzo para no llorar
mientras se seca las piernas y la escayola. Yo estoy cerca, pero
no puedo ayudarla. Supongo que teme que regrese y nos sorprenda hablando.

Hay muchos lugares en este hospital donde uno puede sentarse a tomar una Coca-cola o un café, pero le ha traído aquí
porque quería que lo viera. Estoy seguro de que lo ha provocado
para que presenciara su genio.

Nos miramos prolongadamente mientras se seca la cara y los brazos. Le ruedan las lágrimas por las mejillas y se las seca. Posee la inexplicable habilidad femenina de producir lágrimas, sin dar la impresión de que esté llorando. No solloza ni se convulsiona, no le tiemblan los labios. Está simplemente ahí, en otro mundo, mirándome con los ojos empañados y acariciándose la piel con la toalla blanca.

Pasan los minutos, pero pierdo la noción del tiempo. Aparece un auxiliar lisiado y friega el suelo a su alrededor. Entran tres enfermeras charlando alegremente y riéndose, pero al verla bajan inmediatamente el tono de sus voces. La miran, susurran y de vez en cuando me echan una fugaz ojeada.

Hace el tiempo suficiente que se ha marchado para suponer que no vuelve y me emociona la idea de actuar como un caballero. Las enfermeras se retiran y Kelly mueve lentamente su dedo índice para llamarme. Ahora puedo acercarme.

—Lo siento —dice cuando me agacho cerca de ella.

—No te preocupes.

Y luego dice algo que nunca olvidaré:

—¿Puedes acompañarme a mi habitación?

En otras circunstancias, esas palabras podrían tener amplias consecuencias, y mi mente se traslada momentáneamente a una playa exótica, donde dos jóvenes amantes deciden por fin lanzarse a la aventura.

Su habitación, evidentemente, es un cubículo semiprivado cuya puerta puede abrir multitud de gente. Incluso algún abogado.

Empujo cuidadosamente su silla de ruedas entre las mesas hasta el pasillo.

—Quinto piso —dice por encima del hombro.

No tengo ninguna prisa. Me siento muy orgulloso de mi caballerosidad. Me encanta que los hombres vuelvan la cabeza para mirarla cuando avanzamos por el pasillo.

Pasamos unos momentos a solas en el ascensor y me agacho junto a ella.

—¿Estás bien? —pregunto.

Ha dejado de llorar. Sus ojos están todavía húmedos y ligeramente irritados, pero ha recuperado la compostura.

—Sí, gracias —asiente inmediatamente antes de agarrarme la mano y apretarla—. Muchas gracias.

El ascensor da una sacudida y se detiene. Entra un médico y Kelly me suelta rápidamente la mano. Me coloco detrás de la silla de ruedas, como un fiel marido. Quiero que nos cojamos de nuevo de la mano.

Son casi las once, según el reloj de pared del quinto piso. A excepción de algunas enfermeras y auxiliares, el pasillo está silencioso y desierto. Una enfermera en su puesto de guardia me mira dos veces al verme pasar. La señora Riker ha salido con un hombre y ahora regresa con otro.

Giramos a la izquierda y ella señala una puerta. Me llevo una agradable sorpresa al descubrir que dispone de una habitación privada, con su propia ventana y cuarto de baño. Las luces están encendidas.

No estoy seguro de saber hasta qué punto puede realmente moverse, pero en este momento está completamente desvalida.

—Tienes que ayudarme —dice.

Sin necesidad de que lo repita me agacho cuidadosamente y ella me rodea el cuello con los brazos. Aprieta y estruja más de lo necesario, pero no me quejo. Su bata está manchada de Cocacola, pero no me importa. Está pegada a mi cuerpo y me percato inmediatamente de que no lleva sujetador. La aprieto contra mí.

La levanto suavemente de la silla con mucha facilidad, puesto que no pesa más de cincuenta kilos, incluida la escayola. La traslado con la mayor lentitud posible, cuidando en todo momento de su frágil pierna y ajustando su posición mientras la deposito parsimoniosamente sobre la cama. Nos soltamos con reticencia. Nuestras caras están a pocos centímetros de distancia cuando irrumpe en la habitación la enfermera, con el crujido de sus suelas de goma en las baldosas del suelo.

—¿Qué ha ocurrido? —pregunta al tiempo que señala la bata manchada.

Todavía estamos desatando nuestros brazos e intentando separarnos.

—Ah, eso. Un pequeño accidente —responde Kelly.

La enfermera se detiene. Abre un cajón debajo del televisor y saca un camisón doblado.

—Tendrás que cambiarte —dice después de arrojar el camisón sobre la cama, junto a Kelly—. Y hay que darte un baño de esponja —agrega, y mueve la cabeza hacia mí—. Dile que te ayude.

Respiro hondo y me siento mareado.

—Puedo arreglármelas sola —responde Kelly, al tiempo que coloca el camisón sobre la mesilla de noche.

—La hora de visita ha terminado, amigo —dice la enfermera y antes de abandonar la habitación agrega—: Ahora tenéis que despediros.

Cierro la puerta y vuelvo junto a su cama, donde nos observamos mutuamente.

—¿Dónde está la esponja? —pregunto, y ambos nos reímos.

Al sonreír se le forman unos hermosos hoyuelos en las mejillas.

—Siéntate aquí —dice dando unos golpecitos al borde de la cama.

Me siento junto a ella, con las piernas colgando. No nos tocamos. Se cubre con la sábana hasta los sobacos, como para ocultar las manchas.

Soy perfectamente consciente de las apariencias. Una esposa maltratada sigue estando casada hasta que se divorcia, o hasta que asesina al cabrón de su marido.

—¿Qué te ha parecido Cliff? —pregunta.

—Tú querías que lo viera, ¿no es cierto?

—Supongo.

—Merece que le peguen un tiro.

—Parece un castigo muy severo para un pequeño enfado, ¿no crees?

Hago una pausa y desvío la mirada. He decidido no fingir con ella. Puesto que estamos hablando, hagámoslo sinceramente.

¿Qué estoy haciendo aquí?

—No, Kelly, no es severo. Cualquier hombre que apalee a su esposa con un bate de aluminio merece que le peguen un tiro —respondo sin dejar me mirarla atentamente y compruebo que no se altera.

—¿Cómo lo sabes? —pregunta.

—Las huellas del papeleo. Informes de la policía, de la ambulancia y del hospital. ¿Cuánto vas a esperar hasta que decida golpearte en la cabeza con su bate? ¿Te das cuenta de que podría matarte? Un par de golpes certeros en el cráneo...

—¡Cállate! No me recuerdes cómo se siente una —dice después de volver la cara hacia la pared y, cuando me mira de nuevo, se le han llenado los ojos de lágrimas—. No sabes de qué estás hablando.

—Entonces, cuéntamelo.

—Si hubiera querido hablar de ello, lo habría hecho. No tienes derecho a hurgar en mi vida.

—Presenta una petición de divorcio. Mañana te traeré los papeles. Hazlo ahora, mientras estás en el hospital recibiendo tratamiento por la última agresión. ¿Qué mejor prueba? Será cosa de coser y cantar. En tres meses, serás una mujer libre.

Mueve la cabeza, como si yo fuera un perfecto imbécil. Probablemente lo soy.

—Tú no lo comprendes.

—Por supuesto que no. Pero veo el cuadro. Si no te deshaces de ese cretino, puedes estar muerta en menos de un mes. Tengo los nombres y números de teléfono de tres grupos de apoyo a mujeres maltratadas.

—¿Maltratadas?

—Efectivamente, maltratadas. Tú eres una mujer maltratada, Kelly. ¿No te has dado cuenta? Ese clavo en tu tobillo significa que te maltratan. Esa contusión en tu mejilla es una prueba evidente de que tu marido te apalea. Hay gente que puede ayudarte. Solicita el divorcio y deja que te ayuden.

Reflexiona unos instantes. La habitación está silenciosa.

—El divorcio no funcionará. Ya lo he intentado.

—¿Cuándo?

—Hace unos meses. ¿No lo sabes? Estoy segura de que consta en el juzgado. ¿Qué ha ocurrido con las huellas del papeleo?

—¿Qué ocurrió con el divorcio?

—Retiré la petición.

—¿Por qué?

—Porque me cansé de recibir golpes. Iba a matarme si no la retiraba. Dice que me quiere.

—Eso está muy claro. ¿Puedo hacerte una pregunta? ¿Vive tu padre, o tienes algún hermano?

—¿Por qué?

—Porque si tuviera una hija y su marido la maltratara, le rompería la crisma.

—Mi padre no lo sabe. Tanto él como mi madre siguen disgustados por el embarazo. Nunca lo superarán. Detestaron a Cliff desde el momento en que puso pie en casa y cuando estalló el escándalo, no quisieron saber nada de nosotros. No he hablado con ellos desde que abandoné la casa.

—¿Ningún hermano?

—No. Nadie que me proteja. Hasta ahora.

Sus palabras me producen un fuerte impacto y tardo unos instantes en asimilarlas.

—Haré cuanto esté en mi mano —respondo—. Pero debes solicitar el divorcio.

Se seca las lágrimas con los dedos y le ofrezco un pañuelo de papel de la mesilla.

—No puedo hacerlo.

—¿Por qué no?

—Me matará. Me lo repite constantemente. Cuando lo intenté por primera vez, tenía un abogado desastroso, que encontré en las páginas amarillas o en algún lugar parecido. Imaginé que eran todos iguales. Y a él se le ocurrió la ingeniosa idea de entregarle a Cliff los papeles del divorcio en su lugar de trabajo, en presencia de su pandilla, sus compañeros de copas, con quienes juega al béisbol. Evidentemente, Cliff se sintió humillado. Fue entonces cuando ingresé por primera vez en el hospital. Al cabo de una semana retiré la petición de divorcio y desde entonces no ha dejado de amenazarme permanentemente. Me matará.

El miedo y el terror son palpables en su mirada. Cambia ligeramente de posición y hace una mueca, como si hubiera sentido un pinchazo en el tobillo.

—¿Puedes colocarme una almohada debajo de la pierna? —pregunta con un gemido.

—Por supuesto —respondo al tiempo que salto inmediatamente de la cama y cojo unas almohadas que ella señala sobre la silla.

—Dame también el camisón —agrega al cabo de unos segundos, después de mirar a su alrededor.

Me acerco con indecisión a la mesilla y le entrego el camisón limpio.

—¿Quieres que te ayude? —pregunto.

—No, pero date la vuelta —responde cuando ya está quitándose la bata.

Me vuelvo con mucha lentitud.

No se apresura. Sin motivo alguno arroja la bata manchada a mis pies. Ahí está, a un metro escaso, completamente desnuda a excepción de unas braguitas y la escayola. Estoy convencido de que podría volver la cabeza, mirarla y no le importaría. Me mareo sólo de pensar en ello.

Cierro los ojos y me pregunto: ¿qué estoy haciendo aquí?

—Rudy, ¿te importaría traerme la esponja? —susurra—. Está en el cuarto de baño. Mójala con agua caliente. Y dame también una toalla, por favor.

Vuelvo la cabeza y la veo sentada en medio de la cama, cubierta hasta el pecho con una fina sábana. No ha tocado el camisón.

La contemplo embaucado.

—Allí —dice, e indica la puerta del cuarto de baño con la cabeza.

Entro, cojo la esponja y mientras la mojo en el lavabo, la miro por el espejo. A través de la rendija de la puerta veo su espalda desnuda. Su piel es suave y morena, pero tiene un cardenal entre los hombros.

Decido que me ocuparé yo del baño. Estoy seguro de que ella lo desea. Está dolida y vulnerable. Le gusta coquetear y quiere que vea su cuerpo. Siento escalofríos.

Luego oigo voces. La enfermera ha regresado y circula por la habitación cuando salgo del baño. Se detiene y me sonríe, como si casi nos hubiera sorprendido.

—Ha llegado la hora de marcharse —dice—. Son casi las

once y media. Esto no es un hotel —agrega, y me quita la esponja de la mano—. Yo la lavaré. Ahora debes marcharte —concluye, fingiéndose enfadada.

A las tres de la madrugada bajo sigilosamente a la hamaca para mecerme sin pensar en nada en la tranquilidad de la noche, contemplar el parpadeo de las estrellas a través de las ramas de los árboles, y recordar con deleite cada uno de sus movimientos, oigo su voz torturada y admiro sus piernas en mis sueños.

Me ha tocado protegerla, no tiene quien lo haga. Espera que la rescate y la ayude a recomponerse. Es evidente para ambos lo que ocurrirá entonces.

Siento cómo me agarra el cuello y se aprieta contra mí durante unos segundos maravillosos. Siento el peso de su liviano cuerpo que descansa con naturalidad en mis brazos.

Desea que la vea y frote su piel con la esponja caliente. Sé que lo desea. Y esta noche me propongo hacerlo.

Veo salir el sol entre los árboles y me quedo dormido contando las horas hasta volver a verla.

DIECINUEVE

Estoy en mi despacho estudiando para el examen porque no tengo otra cosa que hacer. Y no puedo hacer nada porque todavía no soy abogado, ni lo seré hasta que apruebe el examen de colegiatura.

Me resulta difícil concentrarme. ¿Por qué estaré enamorándome de una mujer casada pocos días antes de mi examen? Mi mente debería estar lo más clara posible, libre de embarazos y distracciones, perfectamente sintonizada y canalizada a un solo propósito.

Ella es una perdedora, estoy convencido de ello. Es una chica destrozada con cicatrices, muchas de las cuales podrían ser permanentes. Y él es peligroso. La idea de que cualquier otro hombre acariciara a esa encantadora animadora le pondría indudablemente furioso.

Reflexiono con los pies sobre la mesa, las manos cruzadas en la nuca y la mirada perdida en la lejanía cuando de pronto se abre la puerta y Bruiser irrumpe en el despacho.

—¿Qué estás haciendo? —exclama.

—Estudiando —respondo al tiempo que recupero inmediatamente una posición correcta.

—Tenía entendido que ibas a estudiar por la tarde.

Ahora son las diez y media, y él pasea de un lado para otro frente a mi escritorio.

—Compréndelo, Bruiser, hoy es viernes. El examen empieza el próximo miércoles. Estoy asustado.

—Entonces vete a estudiar al hospital. Y consigue algún caso. No he visto nada nuevo en tres días.

—No es fácil estudiar y acosar al mismo tiempo.

—Deck lo hace.

—Claro, Deck es el estudiante perpetuo.

—Acabo de recibir una llamada de Leo F. Drummond. ¿Te suena el nombre?

—No. ¿Debería hacerlo?

—Es socio decano de Tinley Britt. Excelente jurista, experto en toda clase de pleitos comerciales. Raramente pierde. Un abogado realmente extraordinario, un gran bufete.

—Estoy bien informado acerca de Trent & Brent.

—Pues vas a conocerlos todavía mejor. Representan a Great Benefit. Drummond está encargado del caso.

Debe haber por lo menos un centenar de bufetes que representen al millar de compañías de seguros que debe existir en esta ciudad. ¿Y cuál es el índice de probabilidades de que la compañía que más detesto, Great Benefit, contrate al bufete que maldigo todos los días de mi vida, Trent & Brent?

Curiosamente me lo tomo bien. A decir verdad, no me sorprende.

De pronto comprendo por qué Bruiser camina de un lado para otro y habla con tanta rapidez. Está preocupado. Por mi culpa ha presentado una demanda de diez millones de dólares contra una gran compañía, representada por un abogado que lo intimida. Es divertido. Nunca imaginé que Bruiser Stone tuviera miedo de nada.

—¿Qué ha dicho?

—Sólo ha querido ponerse en contacto. Dice que le han asignado el caso al juez Harvey Hale con quien, maldita sea, compartía un piso en Yale hace treinta años, cuando ambos estudiaban derecho, y que, dicho sea de paso por si no lo sabes, era un excelente defensor de compañías de seguros antes de su infarto, a raíz del cual el médico le ordenó que cambiara de actividad. Entonces logró que le nombraran juez, en cuya capacidad no ha abandonado el concepto propio de un defensor de que un veredicto justo debe ser inferior a los diez mil dólares.

—Lamento habértelo preguntado.

—De modo que nos enfrentamos a Leo F. Drummond y a su considerable personal, que cuentan con su juez predilecto. Tienes en perspectiva una tarea bastante ardua.

—¿Yo? ¿No piensas participar?

—Yo estaré ahí, pero el caso es tuyo. Te agobiarán con papeleo —dice de camino a la puerta—. No olvides que ellos cobran por hora. Cuanto más papeleo, más horas pueden facturar.

Suelta una carcajada antes de dar un portazo, aparentemente encantado de que los poderosos estén a punto de machacarme.

Me han abandonado. Hay más de un centenar de abogados en Trent & Brent y de pronto me siento terriblemente solo.

Deck y yo nos tomamos un tazón de sopa en la pequeña cafetería de Trudy. Su reducida clientela a la hora del almuerzo está constituida exclusivamente por obreros. El local huele a grasa, sudor y carne frita. Es el lugar donde Deck prefiere almorzar, porque aquí le han salido varios casos, relacionados sobre todo con accidentes laborales. Uno de ellos se resolvió con una compensación de treinta mil dólares. Le correspondió un tercio del veinticinco por ciento, es decir, dos mil quinientos dólares.

Frecuenta también algunos bares de la zona, me confiesa en voz baja con la boca cerca de la sopa. Se quita la corbata, procura parecerse a uno de los muchachos, y toma un refresco. Escucha las conversaciones de los obreros, cuando se refrescan el gaznate después del trabajo. Puede que los aconseje sobre los mejores bares, donde se encuentran lo que él denomina los mejores pastos. Deck es generoso con los consejos cuando persigue casos y acecha clientes.

Y sí, efectivamente, en algunas ocasiones ha frecuentado incluso clubes de comercio carnal, pero sólo para acompañar a sus clientes. Hay que circular, repite en más de una ocasión. Le gustan los casinos de Mississippi y comparte la noble opinión de que son lugares indeseables, porque atraen a personas pobres que dedican al juego el dinero de la compra. Pero podrían tener un aspecto positivo. Crecerá la delincuencia. Es de esperar que con el crecimiento del juego aumente el número de divorcios e insolvencias. Necesitarán abogados. Albergan mucho sufrimiento potencial y él lo sabe. Tiene algo en perspectiva.

Me mantendrá informado.

Consumo otra excelente comida en el restaurante de Saint Peter, como oigo que un grupo de internos lo denominan: ensalada de pasta en un tazón de plástico. Estudio esporádicamente y vigilo el reloj.

A las diez aparece el anciano de la chaqueta rosa, pero llega solo. Se detiene, mira a su alrededor, me ve y se me acerca con la cara muy seria, evidentemente disgustado con su misión.

—¿Es usted el señor Baylor? —pregunta con mucha corrección.

Asiento y deja sobre la mesa un sobre que lleva en la mano.

—Es de la señora Riker —dice antes de retirarse.

Es un sobre blanco, de tamaño normal. Lo abro y en su interior encuentro una postal que dice así:

Querido Rudy:

Mi médico me ha dado de alta esta mañana, de modo que ahora estoy en casa. Gracias por todo. Reza por nosotros. Eres maravilloso.

Después de la firma agrega una posdata: «Te ruego que no me llames, ni me escribas, ni intentes verme. Sólo causaría problemas. Gracias de nuevo.»

Sabía que estaría aquí, esperándola fielmente. Con todos los pensamientos lujuriosos que han pululado por mi mente durante las últimas veinticuatro horas, nunca se me había ocurrido que pudiera marcharse. Estaba seguro de que nos veíamos esta noche.

Camino sin rumbo fijo por los interminables pasillos del hospital, procurando serenarme. Estoy decidido a volver a verla. Me necesita, porque soy la única persona que puede ayudarla.

En la guía de una cabina encuentro el nombre de Cliff Riker y marco el número. Un mensaje grabado me informa de que el teléfono ha sido desconectado.

VEINTE

Llegamos a la planta principal del hotel a primera hora del miércoles por la mañana y nos conducen eficientemente, como a un rebaño, a un salón mayor que un campo de fútbol. Estamos todos registrados y catalogados, después de haber pagado hace tiempo la matrícula. También estamos muertos de miedo.

De los aproximadamente doscientos candidatos que nos presentamos a esta convocatoria del examen de colegiatura, por lo menos la mitad terminamos la carrera el mes pasado en la Universidad Estatal de Memphis. Son mis amigos y enemigos. Booker se instala en una mesa lejos de mí. Hemos decidido no sentarnos juntos. Sara Plankmore y S. Todd están en un rincón, al otro extremo de la sala. Se casaron el sábado pasado. Una agradable luna de miel. Él es apuesto, con los modales y la arrogancia de un aristócrata. Ojalá suspenda. Y Sara también.

Aquí se siente la competencia, al igual que durante las primeras semanas en la facultad, cuando a todos nos preocupaba enormemente el progreso inicial de los demás. Saludo con la cabeza a algunos conocidos, al tiempo que les deseo silenciosamente que suspendan, como ellos me lo desean a mí. He ahí la naturaleza de la profesión.

Cuando estamos todos debidamente sentados junto a mesas plegables generosamente dispersas, recibimos diez minutos de instrucciones. A las ocho en punto nos entregan los papeles.

El examen comienza con una sección denominada multiestado, que consiste en una serie interminable de preguntas donde sólo hay que marcar la respuesta, y trata de la legislación general común a todos los estados. Es absolutamente imposible saber si estoy bien preparado. La mañana se prolonga. Para almorzar como un bocadillo con Booker en el hotel, sin mencionar el examen.

La cena es un bocadillo de pavo con la señorita Birdie en el jardín. A las nueve estoy en la cama.

El examen acaba por agotamiento a las cinco de la tarde del viernes. Estamos demasiado cansados para celebrarlo. Recogen por última vez nuestros papeles y nos dicen que podemos retirarnos. Se dice algo de tomar una copa para recordar los viejos tiempos y seis de nosotros nos reunimos en Yogi's a beber unas cervezas. Prince ha salido esta noche y Bruiser brilla por su ausencia, de lo cual me alegro, porque detestaría que mis amigos me vieran en presencia de mi jefe. Concededme un año y tendré un trabajo mejor.

Después de nuestro primer semestre en la facultad, descubrimos que era preferible no comentar nunca los exámenes. Cuando se comparan las respuestas, uno pasa a ser dolorosamente consciente de lo que ha olvidado.

Comemos pizza y tomamos unas cervezas, pero estamos demasiado agotados para hacer juerga. Booker me comunica de regreso a casa que el examen le ha puesto físicamente enfermo. Está seguro de haberlo suspendido.

Duermo doce horas. Le he prometido a la señorita Birdie que hoy me ocuparé de mis labores en la finca, en el supuesto de que no llueva, y la luz del sol inunda mi piso cuando por fin despierto. El tiempo es cálido, húmedo y pegajoso, como es habitual en Memphis durante el mes de julio. Después de tres días forzando la vista, la imaginación y la memoria en una sala desprovista de ventanas, estoy listo para un poco de sudor y suciedad. Abandono la casa sin ser visto y, al cabo de veinte minutos, aparco frente al domicilio de los Black.

Donny Ray está delante de la puerta, con unos vaqueros, zapatillas, calcetines oscuros, camiseta blanca y una gorra típica de béisbol, que sobre su demacrado rostro parece excesivamente grande. Camina con un bastón, pero necesita que una mano firme sujete su frágil brazo para conservar el equilibrio. Dot y yo lo conducimos por el camino frente a la casa, y lo acomodamos en el asiento delantero de mi coche. Para Dot supone un alivio que salga unas horas de la casa por primera vez desde hace varios meses. Ahora se queda a solas con Buddy y los gatos.

Donny Ray se sienta con el bastón entre las piernas y apoya la barbilla sobre el mismo cuando cruzamos la ciudad. Después de darme las gracias, apenas dice palabra.

Terminó el bachillerato hace tres años, a los diecinueve, y su hermano gemelo, Ron, lo hizo un año antes. No intentó ingresar en la universidad. Durante dos años trabajó de dependiente en una tienda de ultramarinos, pero dejó el empleo después de un atraco. Su historial laboral es irregular, pero nunca ha abandonado el domicilio paterno. A juzgar por los informes que he examinado hasta ahora, nunca ha percibido unos ingresos superiores al salario mínimo.

Ron, sin embargo, logró licenciarse en la Universidad de Texas, en El Paso, y ahora prepara un doctorado en Houston. Él también sigue soltero y raramente regresa a Memphis. Nunca estuvieron muy unidos, dice Dot. A Donny Ray le gustaba quedarse en casa, leer libros y construir modelos de aeroplanos. Ron salía en moto y cuando tenía doce años formó parte de una pandilla de chiquillos. Eran buenos chicos, afirma Dot. El historial está perfectamente documentado con pruebas claras y abundantes de que la médula ósea de Ron cumple los requisitos necesarios para efectuarle un trasplante a Donny Ray.

Avanzamos en mi pequeño coche destartalado. Donny Ray mira fijamente hacia delante, con la visera de la gorra a media frente, y sólo abre la boca cuando le formulo alguna pregunta. Aparcamos junto al Cadillac de la señorita Birdie y le explico que este antiguo caserío en este barrio señorial de la ciudad es donde vivo. No sé si está impresionado, pero lo dudo. Le ayudo a rodear la montaña de estiércol hasta un lugar sombrío del jardín.

La señorita Birdie sabe que voy a traerlo y espera ansiosa con limonada fresca. Después de las presentaciones, se apodera inmediatamente del control de la situación. ¿Galletas? ¿Pastelitos? ¿Algo para leer? Coloca cojines en el banco a su alrededor, sin dejar de charlar alegremente. Tiene un corazón de oro. Le cuento que conocí a los padres de Donny Ray en el Parque de los Cipreses y se siente particularmente unida a él. Un miembro de su rebaño.

Cuando está debidamente instalado en un lugar fresco, sin que le toque directamente el sol, que podría dañar su delicada piel, la señorita Birdie declara que ha llegado el momento de empezar a trabajar. Escudriña dramáticamente el jardín, se rasca la mandíbula en actitud meditabunda y luego posa lentamente la mirada en el estiércol. Da unas cuantas órdenes para impresionar a Donny Ray y entro en acción.

No tardo en empaparme de sudor, pero en esta ocasión lo disfruto plenamente. La señorita Birdie se queja durante la primera hora de la humedad y luego decide ocuparse de las flores, que están en lugares más frescos. Oigo que habla incesantemente con Donny Ray, que no dice gran cosa, pero disfruta del aire libre. En una de las ocasiones, cuando paso con la carretilla, veo que están jugando a las damas. En otro momento la veo sentada muy cerca de él, mostrándole un álbum de fotografías.

He pensado muchas veces en preguntarle a la señorita Birdie si estaría dispuesta a ayudar a Donny Ray. Estoy convencido de que esa encantadora mujer extendería un cheque para el trasplante, si dispone realmente del dinero. Pero no lo he hecho por dos razones. En primer lugar, es demasiado tarde para un trasplante. Y en segundo lugar, se sentiría humillada si no dispone del dinero. Ya le incomoda bastante mi actual interés por su capital. No puedo pedirle dinero.

Cuando le diagnosticaron la leucemia, se hizo un pequeño esfuerzo encaminado a recaudar fondos para su tratamiento. Se organizó un grupo de amigos, que colocaron el retrato de Donny Ray en los recipientes de leche distribuidos por los cafés y tiendas de ultramarinos del norte de Memphis. Según ella fue poco lo que recaudaron. Alquilaron un local y celebraron una gran fiesta con comida y música regional, para la que contrataron incluso a un disc-jockey de música country. Les faltaron veintiocho dólares para cubrir los gastos.

La primera sesión de quimioterapia costó cuatro mil dólares, de los cuales dos tercios fueron absorbidos por Saint Peter. Lograron reunir el resto del dinero. Al cabo de cinco meses, la leucemia estaba de nuevo en auge.

Mientras manipulo la pala y sudo, canalizo mi energía mental y la transformo en odio por Great Benefit. El trabajo no es excesivo, pero necesitaré mucha fortaleza moral para sustentarme cuando empiece la guerra contra Tinley Britt.

El almuerzo es una agradable sorpresa. La señorita Birdie ha preparado sopa de pollo, no exactamente lo que yo elegiría en un día como hoy, pero un cambio agradable para descansar de los bocadillos de pavo. Donny Ray come medio plato y dice que necesita hacer una siesta. Le apetece probar la hamaca. Le ayudamos a cruzar el jardín y a acomodarse en la misma. Aunque la temperatura es superior a los treinta y dos grados, pide una manta.

Nos sentamos a la sombra, tomamos limonada y hablamos de lo triste que está Donny Ray. Le cuento por encima lo del pleito contra Great Benefit y hago hincapié en mi demanda por diez millones de dólares. Me hace algunas preguntas generales sobre el examen y luego entra en la casa.

Cuando regresa lleva un sobre en la mano de un abogado de Atlanta y reconozco el nombre del bufete.

—¿Puedes explicarme esto? —pregunta delante de mí, con las manos en las caderas.

Dicho abogado le ha escrito una carta a la señorita Birdie y ha adjuntado una copia de la que yo le había mandado a él. En la mía le explicaba que yo representaba ahora a la señorita Birdie Birdsong, que me había pedido que redactara un nuevo testamento y que para ello necesitaba información acerca de los bienes de su difunto marido. En la carta dirigida a ella se limita a preguntarle si le autoriza a facilitarme dicha información. Su tono parece bastante indiferente, como si se limitara a obedecer órdenes.

—Todo está por escrito —respondo—. Yo soy su abogado, sólo intento obtener información.

—No me dijiste que te proponías indagar en Atlanta.

—¿Qué tiene eso de malo? ¿Qué oculta, señorita Birdie? ¿Por qué tanto secreto?

—El juez decretó secreto de sumario —responde encogiéndose de hombros, como si de ese modo se zanjara el asunto.

—¿Qué contiene el sumario?

—Un montón de basura.

—¿Relacionada con usted?

—¡Cielos, claro que no!

—De acuerdo. ¿Con quién entonces?

—La familia de Tony. Su hermano, que vivía en Florida y estaba forrado de dinero, tuvo varias esposas y un montón de hijos. Están todos como un cencerro. Hubo una gran pelea sobre sus testamentos, cuatro en total según tengo entendido. No sé gran cosa al respecto, pero oí decir que cuando todo terminó, los abogados recibieron seis millones de dólares en honorarios. Parte del dinero fue a parar a Tony, que vivió lo suficiente para heredarlo según la ley de Florida. Él ni siquiera llegó a saberlo, porque falleció casi inmediatamente. Lo único que dejó fue a una esposa. Yo. Eso es todo lo que sé.

No tiene importancia cómo obtuvo el dinero, pero sería interesante conocer la cantidad heredada.

—¿Quiere hablar de su testamento? —pregunto.

—No. Luego —responde al tiempo que extiende el brazo para coger los guantes de jardinería—. Ahora pongámonos a trabajar.

Al cabo de unas horas estoy sentado con Dot y Donny Ray en el jardín lleno de hierbajos, junto a la cocina de su casa. Buddy, afortunadamente, se ha acostado. Donny Ray está agotado después de pasar el día con la señorita Birdie.

Es sábado noche y en los barrios residenciales el olor a carbón y carne asada impregna el bochornoso ambiente. Las voces de los cocineros de jardín y sus invitados se filtran a través de las verjas de madera e impecables setos.

Es más cómodo permanecer sentado y escuchar que hablar. Dot prefiere fumar, tomarse una taza de café instantáneo descafeinado y de vez en cuando comentar algún chisme relacionado con los vecinos, o con algún perro del vecindario. El jubilado de la casa de al lado se cortó un dedo la semana pasada con una sierra, y lo menciona por lo menos tres veces.

No me importa. Puedo permanecer muchas horas sentado escuchando. Mi cerebro está todavía aturdido del examen. Necesito poco para entretenerme. Y cuando logro olvidarme de las leyes, mis pensamientos se centran en Kelly. Debo descubrir una forma inofensiva para ponerme en contacto con ella. Lo haré, es sólo cuestión de tiempo.

VEINTIUNO

El palacio de Justicia del condado de Shelby es un edificio moderno de doce plantas situado en el centro de la ciudad. La idea es la de resolver cualquier problema jurídico en un solo centro. Dispone de numerosas salas y despachos para secretarios y funcionarios. También alberga las dependencias del fiscal del distrito y del sheriff. Tiene incluso calabozos.

El tribunal penal está dividido en diez secciones, diez jueces con sus correspondientes listas de casos. Los pisos intermedios están abarrotados de abogados, policías, acusados y parientes. Es una jungla impenetrable para un abogado novato, pero Deck sabe cómo desenvolverse en la misma. Ha hecho algunas llamadas.

Señala la puerta de la cuarta sección y dice que se reunirá allí conmigo dentro de una hora. Entro por la doble puerta y me siento en el banco de la última fila. El suelo está enmoquetado y los muebles son depresivamente modernos. Los abogados están apretujados como hormigas al frente de la sala. A la derecha hay una zona reservada a los acusados, donde una docena de detenidos vestidos de naranja esperan para presentarse por primera vez ante el juez. Una versátil fiscal con un montón de sumarios busca el correspondiente a cada acusado.

En la segunda fila veo a Cliff Riker. Está muy cerca de su abogado consultando unos documentos. Su esposa no está en la sala.

Entra el juez por una puerta trasera y todo el mundo se levanta. Se despachan varios casos, se reducen o anulan fianzas y se fijan fechas futuras. Los abogados se consultan brevemente entre sí, asienten y susurran a su señoría.

Llaman a Cliff y éste sube con aire de fanfarrón al estrado. Su abogado lo acompaña con los documentos. La fiscal comunica a la sala que la acusación contra Cliff Riker se ha retirado por falta de pruebas.

—¿Dónde está la víctima? —interrumpe el juez.

—Ha optado por no comparecer —responde la fiscal.

—¿Por qué? —pregunta el juez.

Porque está en una silla de ruedas, quiero exclamar.

La fiscal se encoge de hombros, como si no lo supiera y, además, como si realmente no le importara. El abogado de Cliff también se encoge de hombros, como si le sorprendiera que la mujer no estuviera presente para mostrar sus lesiones.

La fiscal es una persona muy ocupada, con docenas de casos para presentar antes del mediodía. Relata brevemente un resumen de los hechos, la detención y la falta de pruebas, debido a que la víctima no está dispuesta a declarar.

—Ésta es la segunda vez —declara el juez con la mirada fija en Cliff—. ¿Por qué no se divorcia de ella antes de que la mate?

—Estamos buscando ayuda, su señoría —responde Cliff en un tono plañidero, claramente fingido.

—Pues dense prisa. Si vuelve a comparecer con una acusación semejante, no sobreseeré el caso. ¿Me ha comprendido?

—Sí, señor —responde Cliff, como si lamentara enormemente la molestia.

Se le entregan los documentos al juez y éste los firma, sin dejar de mover la cabeza. Caso sobreseído.

Una vez más no se ha oído la voz de la víctima. Está en casa con un tobillo fracturado, pero no ha sido eso lo que le ha impedido comparecer. Está escondida porque prefiere no recibir otra paliza. Me pregunto el precio que habrá pagado por retirar la denuncia.

Cliff estrecha la mano de su abogado, avanza con arrogancia por el pasillo, pasa junto a mi banco y sale por la puerta libre para hacer lo que se le antoje con toda inmunidad, porque ella no tiene quien la ayude.

Hay una lógica frustrante en esta administración de justicia. A poca distancia, con sus monos anaranjados y debidamente esposados, hay un grupo de violadores, asesinos y narcotraficantes. La administración apenas dispone de tiempo para ocuparse de esos maleantes, e implementar algún nivel de justicia. ¿Cómo cabe esperar que se interese por los derechos de una mujer maltratada?

Mientras yo me examinaba la semana pasada, Deck hacía llamadas telefónicas. Encontró la nueva dirección y número de teléfono de los Riker. Acababan de trasladarse a un gran complejo de pisos, al sudeste de Memphis. Un dormitorio, cuatrocientos dólares mensuales. Cliff trabaja en una compañía naviera, no lejos de nuestras oficinas, en un muelle no sindicado. Deck sospecha que gana unos siete dólares por hora. Su abogado no es más que otro picapleitos del millón que hay en esta ciudad.

Le he contado a Deck la verdad acerca de Kelly. Me dijo que le parecía importante saberlo, porque de ese modo, cuando Cliff me vuele la cabeza con una escopeta, podrá contarle a todo el mundo por qué lo hizo.

También me ha aconsejado que la olvide. Sólo puede traerme problemas.

Hay una nota sobre mi escritorio diciéndome que acuda inmediatamente al despacho de Bruiser. Está solo tras su mesa descomunal, hablando por teléfono, el de su derecha. Hay otro a su izquierda y otros tres dispersos por la sala. Uno en su coche, otro en su maletín y el que me entregó para poder estar en contacto conmigo veinticuatro horas al día.

Hace una seña para que me siente, levanta sus ojos negros y rojos al techo, como si estuviera hablando con algún chiflado, y emite un gruñido de afirmación en dirección al teléfono. Los tiburones están dormidos u ocultos tras alguna roca. El filtro del acuario zumba y burbujea.

Deck me ha susurrado confidencialmente que Bruiser gana entre trescientos y quinientos mil dólares anuales en el bufete. Resulta difícil creerlo al contemplar su abigarrado despacho. Tiene a cuatro asociados acechando en la maleza, a la caza de víctimas de accidentes. (Y ahora me tiene a mí.) Deck logró hacerse con cinco casos el año pasado, que le aportaron a Bruiser ciento cincuenta mil. Tiene un montón de casos de drogas, y se ha ganado la reputación en el campo del narcotráfico de que es un abogado en quien se puede confiar. Pero, según Deck, los verdaderos ingresos de Bruiser Stone proceden de sus inversiones. Está involucrado, pero nadie sabe hasta qué punto, y el gobierno federal intenta averiguarlo desesperadamente, en los negocios *topless* de Memphis y Nashville. Es un sector en el que se mueve mucho dinero al contado, de modo que no hay forma de saber cuánto le reporta.

Se ha divorciado tres veces, según me cuenta Deck mientras se come un grasiento bocadillo en el local de Trudy, tiene tres hijos adolescentes que, comprensiblemente, viven con sus respectivas madres, le gusta la compañía de las jóvenes animadoras de los clubes, bebe y apuesta demasiado, y por mucho dinero que tenga en sus manos, nunca es el suficiente para sentirse satisfecho.

La policía federal lo detuvo hace siete años y lo acusó de practicar negocios ilegales, pero el gobierno no tuvo la más mínima oportunidad. Al cabo de un año se retiraron los cargos. Deck me ha confesado que le preocupa la investigación actual del FBI de los bajos fondos de Memphis, en la que aparecen constantemente los nombres de Bruiser Stone y Prince Thomas, su mejor amigo. Deck asegura también que la conducta de Bruiser es ligeramente inusual: bebe demasiado, se enoja con mayor facilidad y chilla y protesta más de lo habitual en el despacho.

Hablando de teléfonos. Deck está convencido de que el FBI ha intervenido todos los teléfonos de nuestro bufete, incluido el mío. También cree que han instalado micrófonos en las paredes. No sería la primera vez, afirma con absoluta seriedad. Y ten cuidado también en Yogi's.

Ayer por la tarde me dejó con esta reconfortante idea. Si apruebo el examen de colegiatura, me largo en cuanto tenga un poco de dinero en el bolsillo.

Por fin, Bruiser cuelga el teléfono y se frota sus irritados ojos.

—Fíjate en eso —dice al tiempo que me entrega un grueso fajo de papeles.

—¿De qué se trata?

—La respuesta de Great Benefit. Estás a punto de descubrir por qué resulta penoso demandar a las grandes corporaciones. Disponen de montones de dinero para contratar a innumerables abogados, que redactan incontables documentos. Es probable que Leo F. Drummond les cobre doscientos cincuenta por hora a Great Benefit.

Se trata de una petición para que la demanda de los Black sea sobreseída, acompañada de un informe de sesenta y tres páginas. Hay una citación adjunta para debatir dicha petición ante el juez Harvey Hale.

—Bienvenido al campo de batalla —dice Bruiser, que me observa sosegadamente.

Tengo un buen nudo en la garganta. Tardaré varios días para elaborar una respuesta adecuada.

—Es impresionante —respondo con la boca seca, sin saber por dónde empezar.

—Lee atentamente las normas. Responde a la petición. Escribe tu informe. Apresúrate. No es tan difícil como parece.

—¿Ah, no?

—No, Rudy. Es papeleo. Aprenderás. Esos cabrones presentarán todas las peticiones conocidas y muchas que se inventarán, siempre acompañadas de sendos informes. Y en todos los casos querrán comparecer ante el juez para debatir su petición predilecta. En realidad no les importa ganar o perder, ganan dinero independientemente de lo que ocurra. Además, logran retrasar el juicio. Lo tienen calculado al dedillo y sus clientes pagan la cuenta. El problema es que en dicho proceso te dejarán completamente agotado.

—Ya estoy cansado.

—Es un hueso duro de roer. A Drummond le basta chasquear los dedos y decir «quiero una petición para que el caso sea sobreseído», para que tres asociados se sumerjan en la biblioteca y dos pasantes se pongan a estudiar viejos informes en sus ordenadores. ¡Dicho y hecho! En poco tiempo disponen de un grueso informe concienzudamente investigado. Luego Drummond tiene que leerlo varias veces, estudiárselo a doscientos cincuenta por hora y tal vez pedirle a uno de sus veteranos colegas que se lo lea también. Luego tiene que editarlo, resumirlo y modificarlo, de modo que los asociados regresan a la biblioteca y los pasantes a sus ordenadores. Es una estafa, pero Great Benefit dispone de muchísimo dinero y no le importa pagar a gente como Tinley Britt.

Me siento como si hubiera retado a un ejército. Suenan dos teléfonos y Bruiser levanta el más cercano.

—A trabajar —dice antes de contestar la llamada.

Traslado el fajo a mi despacho con ambas manos y cierro la puerta. Leo la petición, así como el informe de presentación impecable y perfectamente mecanografiado, y no tardo en descubrir que está repleto de argumentos persuasivos contra casi todo lo que he alegado en la demanda. Su lenguaje, rico y claro, está desprovisto de tecnicismos innecesarios, y está extraordinariamente bien redactado. Los puntos que plantea están reforzados por multitud de autoridades, que parecen dar perfectamente en el blanco. La mayoría de las páginas están adornadas con hermosas notas a pie de página. Hay incluso un índice del contenido, otro alfabético y una bibliografía.

Lo único que falta es una orden ya redactada para que la firme el juez otorgando a Great Benefit lo que solicita.

Después de la tercera lectura me concentro y empiezo a tomar notas. Puede que haya un par de lagunas en las que cabe hurgar. El miedo y el sobresalto desaparecen. Pienso en la inmensa repugnancia que me inspira Great Benefit y lo que le ha hecho a mi cliente, y me subo las mangas de la camisa.

Puede que el señor Leo F. Drummond sea un genio de la litigación y disponga de innumerables esbirros a su servicio, pero yo, Rudy Baylor, no tengo otra cosa que hacer. Soy listo y puedo trabajar. Quiere entablar una guerra de papeleo conmigo, pues adelante. Seré yo quien le apabulle.

Deck se ha presentado seis veces al examen de colegiatura. Estuvo a punto de aprobarlo la tercera vez, en California, pero a su nota global le faltaron dos décimas. Se ha presentado tres veces en Tennessee, pero según me ha contado con extraordinaria ingenuidad, le ha faltado siempre mucho para la nota exigida. No estoy seguro de que quiera aprobarlo. Gana cuarenta mil anuales buscando casos para Bruiser, sin tener que preocuparse de las limitaciones éticas. (Aunque tampoco le importan a Bruiser.) No tiene que pagar la subscripción del colegio, ni preocuparse de actualizar su formación jurídica, ni asistir a conferencias, ni comparecer ante ningún juez, ni sentirse culpable respecto al trabajo de beneficencia, por no mencionar los gastos generales.

Deck es una sanguijuela. Mientras disponga de un abogado cuyo nombre pueda utilizar y un despacho donde trabajar, se siente feliz.

Sabe que no estoy demasiado ocupado y se ha acostumbrado a dejarse caer por mi despacho alrededor de las once. Pasamos media hora chismorreando y luego vamos a por un almuerzo barato al local de Trudy. Me he acostumbrado a él. Es simplemente Deck, un hombrecillo sin pretensiones que desea ser mi amigo.

Estamos almorzando en un rincón, rodeados de cargadores de muelle, y Deck habla tan bajo que me resulta difícil oírle. En algunos momentos, particularmente en las salas de espera de los hospitales, puede ser tan intrépido que resulta incómodo estar con él, y en otras ocasiones es tímido como un ratón. Susurra algo que quiere a toda costa que yo oiga, sin dejar de mirar constantemente por encima de ambos hombros, como si alguien estuviera a punto de atacarle.

—En el bufete solía trabajar un individuo llamado David Roy, que trabó mucha amistad con Bruiser. Contaban juntos el dinero, parecían hermanos. Roy fue expulsado del Colegio de Abogados por la manipulación fraudulenta de fondos y no pudo seguir ejerciendo como abogado —dice Deck, al tiempo que se limpia con los dedos la ensalada de atún de los labios—. Pero no le importó. Roy abandonó el bufete, cruzó la calle y abrió un club de comercio carnal. Se incendió. Abrió otro club y también se incendió. Luego otro. Se desencadenó una guerra en el negocio de las tetas al aire. Bruiser es demasiado inteligente para inmiscuirse directamente, pero siempre está en la periferia. Al igual que tu amigo Prince Thomas. La guerra dura desde hace un par de años. De vez en cuando aparece un cadáver. Más in-

cendios. Roy y Bruiser discuten por alguna razón y se enemis-
tan. El año pasado los federales acorralaron a Roy y se rumorea
que cantará. ¿Comprendes a lo que me refiero?

Asiento con la cabeza tan gacha como la de Deck. Nadie puede oírnos, pero nos echan algunas miradas por lo doblados que
estamos sobre la mesa.

—El caso es que ayer David Roy declaró ante el gran jurado.
Parece que ha hecho un trato.

Dicho esto, Deck yergue la espalda y entorna los párpados,
como si de pronto todo quedara explicado.

—¿Y bien? —pregunto, sin levantar todavía la voz.

Frunce el entrecejo, mira subrepticiamente a su alrededor y
vuelve a agacharse.

—Es bastante probable que delate a Bruiser. Puede que también a Prince Thomas. Incluso he oído que han puesto precio a
su cabeza.

—¡Un contrato!

—Sí. No levante la voz.

—¿Por parte de quién?

No será mi jefe.

—Intenta adivinarlo.

—No será Bruiser.

—No sería la primera vez —responde con una tímida sonrisa antes de darle un descomunal mordisco a su bocadillo y empezar a masticar lentamente, sin dejar de asentir.

Espero a que se haya tragado lo que tiene en la boca.

—¿Entonces qué me aconsejas? —pregunto.

—No cierres tus alternativas.

—No tengo ninguna alternativa.

—Puede que tengas que abandonar el bufete.

—Acabo de llegar.

—Tal vez la situación se ponga difícil.

—¿Qué piensas hacer tú?

—Puede que también me marche.

—¿Y los demás?

—No te preocupes por los demás, porque ellos tampoco se
preocupan por ti. Yo soy tu único amigo.

Esas palabras se me quedan grabadas durante horas. Deck
sabe más de lo que cuenta, pero después de unos cuantos almuerzos me lo habrá revelado todo. Tengo la impresión de que
busca dónde aterrizar si ocurre una catástrofe. He conocido a
los otros abogados del bufete, Nicklass, Toxer y Ridge, pero se
ocupan de sus asuntos y hablan poco. Sus puertas están siempre
cerradas con llave. A Deck no le gustan y sólo puedo especular
en cuanto a la reciprocidad de sus sentimientos. Según Deck,

Toxer y Ridge son amigos, y puede que tengan el propósito de abrir pronto su propio bufete. Nicklass es un alcohólico que está en las últimas.

Lo peor que podría ocurrir sería que acusaran oficialmente a Bruiser, lo detuvieran y lo juzgaran. El proceso duraría por lo menos un año y, entretanto, podría seguir ejerciendo en su bufete. Según tengo entendido. No se le podría expulsar del Colegio hasta que lo condenaran.

Tranquilízate, me repito a mí mismo.

Y si me echan a la calle, no será la primera vez. Hasta ahora he logrado sobrevivir.

Conduzco en la dirección de la casa de la señorita Birdie y cruzo un parque, donde se juegan por lo menos tres partidos de béisbol a la luz de unos focos.

Paro al lado de una cabina, junto a un servicio de lavado de coches, y marco el número.

—Diga —responde una voz a la tercera llamada, que me produce un escalofrío.

—¿Está Cliff en casa? —pregunto, después de bajar una octava el tono de mi voz.

Si responde que sí, me limitaré a colgar.

—No. ¿Quién llama?

—Rudy —respondo en mi tono habitual.

Me aguanto la respiración, con el temor de oír un clic seguido de un pitido, y también la esperanza de escuchar su suave y tranquilizadora voz. Maldita sea, no sé lo que espero.

Se hace un silencio, pero no cuelga.

—Te pedí que no llamaras —dice sin el menor vestigio de enojo ni frustración.

—Lo siento. No he podido evitarlo. Estoy preocupado por ti.

—No podemos hacerlo.

—¿Hacer qué?

—Adiós.

Ahora oigo un clic, seguido de un pitido.

He necesitado mucho valor para llamar y ahora me arrepiento de haberlo hecho. Hay personas con más valor que cerebro. Sé que su marido es un loco impulsivo, pero no sé hasta dónde es capaz de llegar. Si es celoso, y estoy seguro de que debe serlo, porque es un fanático sureño de diecinueve años casado con una chica hermosa, es probable que sospeche de todos y cada uno de sus movimientos. ¿Pero llegaría al extremo de intervenir su propio teléfono?

Parece improbable, pero me quita el sueño.

Hace menos de una hora que me había quedado dormido cuando suena el teléfono. Son casi las cuatro de la madrugada, según mi despertador digital. Busco el teléfono en la oscuridad.

Es Deck, que me habla excitado y con mucha rapidez desde su coche. Se acerca a mi casa, está a menos de tres manzanas. Ha ocurrido algo enorme, urgente, un maravilloso siniestro. ¡Date prisa! ¡Vístete! Me ordena que me reúna con él en menos de un minuto en la acera.

Está esperándome en su destartalada minifurgoneta. Subo, aprieta el acelerador y salimos disparados. No he tenido tiempo de cepillarme los dientes.

—¿Qué diablos estamos haciendo? —pregunto.

—Ha habido un terrible accidente en el río —responde con solemnidad, como si estuviera profundamente apenado—. Anoche, poco después de las doce, una barcaza de las utilizadas para transportar petróleo se soltó de su amarre y se desplazó con la corriente, hasta chocar con un buque de ruedas donde celebraban la fiesta de fin de curso los alumnos de un instituto. Había tal vez unos trescientos chiquillos a bordo. El buque se hundió junto a la isla de Mud, cerca de la orilla derecha.

—Eso es terrible, Deck, ¿pero qué diablos se supone que podemos hacer nosotros?

—Comprobarlo. Bruiser ha recibido una llamada. Me ha llamado a mí. Y aquí estamos. Es un descomunal siniestro, potencialmente el mayor en la historia de Memphis.

—¿Y es eso como para sentirse orgulloso?

—Tú no lo entiendes. Bruiser va a perdérselo.

—Entonces que venga, se ponga el traje de bucear y se sumerja en busca de cadáveres.

—Podría ser una mina de oro.

Deck cruza la ciudad a toda velocidad. Guardamos silencio cuando nos acercamos al centro. Nos adelanta velozmente una ambulancia y se me acelera el pulso. Después pasa otra.

Docenas de coches de policía, con sus luces parpadeantes que iluminan la noche, impiden que circule el tráfico por Riverside Drive. Los coches de bomberos y las ambulancias están casi uno encima de otro. Un helicóptero sobrevuela el río. Algunas personas forman grupos inmóviles y otras circulan apresuradas, dando voces e instrucciones. Cerca de la orilla se vislumbra el aguilón de una grúa.

Avanzamos rápidamente alrededor de la cinta amarilla de la policía y nos unimos a un grupo de curiosos junto a la ribera. La catástrofe ha sucedido hace varias horas y ha desaparecido la sensación de urgencia. Ahora esperan. Muchos de los presentes forman pequeños grupos horrorizados, sentados sobre los adoquines del muelle, observando con lágrimas en los ojos a los buceadores y personal médico en busca de cuerpos en el agua. Hay sacerdotes arrodillados que rezan con las familias. Docenas de jóvenes con su esmoquin empapado y vestidos de noche rasgados miran fijamente la superficie del agua cogidos de la mano. Un costado del buque emerge tres metros sobre la superficie del agua y los buceadores que participan en la operación de rescate, muchos de ellos con trajes negros y azules y equipo de submarinismo, se agarran al mismo. Otros trabajan desde pontones amarrados.

Está celebrándose un rito, aunque se precisa algún tiempo para comprenderlo. Un teniente de la policía avanza lentamente por una pasarela que conduce a un dique flotante y luego al muelle adoquinado. La muchedumbre, ya sosegada, se sume en una quietud absoluta. El agente se sitúa frente a un coche patrulla y se forma un corro de periodistas a su alrededor. La mayoría de los presentes permanecen sentados, envueltos en mantas y sumidos en ferviente plegaria. Son los padres, parientes y amigos.

—Lamento comunicarles que hemos identificado el cadáver de Melanie Dobbins.

Sus palabras retumban en el silencio, que rompen casi inmediatamente el llanto y los lamentos de los familiares de la niña. Se abrazan y consuelan mutuamente. Sus amigos se agachan junto a ellos y los abrazan. Entonces se oye el gemido de una mujer.

Los demás vuelven la cabeza para mirarla, pero también respiran con alivio. Sus malas noticias son inevitables, pero por lo menos han sido postergadas. Todavía cabe la esperanza. Más adelante me enteraría de que veintiún chiquillos habían sobrevivido, absorbidos en una bolsa de aire.

El teniente de la policía regresa al dique, donde están sacando otro cuerpo del agua.

Luego, lentamente, emerge otro rito no tan trágico, pero mucho más repugnante. Unos individuos de rostro sombrío se acercan con discreción, o incluso sigilo, a los afligidos. Llevan tarjetas de visita en la mano, que intentan entregar a los parientes o amigos de la fallecida. Se acercan todavía más en la oscuridad, sin dejar de mirarse con recelo. Asesinarían para conseguir el caso. Sólo aspiran al treinta por ciento.

Deck se percata de todo mucho antes de que yo comprenda lo que sucede. Me indica un lugar cerca de las familias, pero me niego a moverme. Penetra inmediatamente entre la muchedumbre y desaparece en la oscuridad, en busca de oro.

Vuelvo la espalda al río y al poco rato corro por las calles del centro de Memphis.

VEINTIDÓS

El tribunal del examen de colegiatura manda los resultados del examen por correo certificado. En la facultad se contaban anécdotas de candidatos que se habían desmayado junto al buzón al recibir la notificación. O de otros que corrían alocadamente por la calle, agitando la carta como unos imbéciles. Infinidad de anécdotas que entonces parecían divertidas, pero que ahora han perdido todo su humor.

Han transcurrido treinta días y la carta todavía no ha llegado. He dado la dirección de mi casa, para no arriesgarme a que alguien la abriera en el bufete de Bruiser.

El treinta y uno cae en sábado, día de la semana en que se me permite dormir hasta las nueve, antes de que mi capataz llame a mi puerta con una brocha en la mano. De pronto ha decidido que el garaje debajo de mi piso necesita una capa de pintura, aunque a mí no me lo parece. Me tienta a que abandone la cama con la noticia de que ha preparado unos huevos con tocino, que se enfriarán si no me doy prisa.

El trabajo progresa satisfactoriamente. La pintura produce unos resultados inmediatos, que son bastante gratificantes. La mejoría es palpable. El sol se oculta tras unas altas nubes y mi ritmo de trabajo es relajado en el mejor de los casos.

A las seis de la tarde da la jornada laboral por concluida, dice que ya he trabajado bastante, y anuncia una noticia maravillosa para la cena: ¡va a preparar una pizza vegetariana!

He trabajado en Yogi's hasta la una de la madrugada y de momento no me apetece volver allí. Por consiguiente y como de costumbre, no tengo nada que hacer en este sábado por la noche. Y lo peor es que tampoco he pensado en ello. Lamentablemente, me apetece la idea de compartir una pizza vegetariana con una anciana de ochenta años.

Después de ducharme, me pongo un pantalón deportivo y unas zapatillas. Un extraño olor emana de la cocina cuando entro en la casa. La señorita Birdie anda ajetreada de un lado para otro. Hasta ahora nunca había preparado una pizza, me comunica, como si la noticia debiera alegrarme.

No está mal. El calabacín y los pimientos amarillos están un poco duros, pero la ha condimentado con abundantes setas y queso de cabra. Además, estoy muerto de hambre. Comemos en la sala de estar, mientras vemos una película de Cary Grant y Audrey Hepburn. La señorita Birdie llora casi constantemente a lo largo de la cinta.

La segunda película es de Bogart y Bacall, y se me empiezan a entumecer los músculos. Tengo sueño. Sin embargo, la señorita Birdie se sienta al borde del sofá, pendiente de cada una de los palabras de aquella película, que ha visto repetidamente a lo largo de cincuenta años.

De pronto se incorpora de un brinco.

—¡He olvidado algo! —exclama, y se dirige apresuradamente a la cocina, donde oigo que hurga entre papeles.

Regresa a la sala de estar con uno en la mano, se detiene dramáticamente delante de mí y proclama:

—¡Rudy! ¡Has aprobado el examen de colegiatura!

Sostiene una sola hoja de papel blanco que yo le quito de la mano. Procede del tribunal de exámenes de Derecho de Tennessee, dirigida naturalmente a mí, y en el centro de la página destacan en negrita las majestuosas palabras: «Felicidades. Ha aprobado usted el examen de colegiatura.»

Vuelvo la cabeza para mirar a la señorita Birdie y, momentáneamente, siento el deseo de abofetearla por una invasión tan flagrante de mi intimidad. Debió habérmela entregado antes y no tenía derecho alguno a abrir la carta. Pero todos sus dientes grises y amarillos están a la vista. Tiene los ojos llenos de lágrimas, las manos en la cara, y está casi tan emocionada como yo. Mi enojo no tarda en transformarse en júbilo.

—¿Cuándo ha llegado? —pregunto.

—Hoy, cuando estabas pintando. El cartero ha llamado a la puerta y ha preguntado por ti, pero le he dicho que estabas ocupado y he firmado yo el recibo.

Firmar es una cosa, abrirla otra.

—No debió haberla abierto —digo, pero sin malicia, porque es imposible estar enojado en un momento como éste.

—Lo siento. He pensado que desearías que lo hiciera. ¿Pero no es emocionante?

Realmente lo es. Me traslado a la cocina sonriendo como un idiota y llenándome los pulmones de aire puro. Todo es maravilloso. ¡El mundo es estupendo!

—Celebrémoslo —dice con una pícara sonrisa.

—Desde luego —respondo.

Siento el deseo de correr por el jardín, hablando a voces con las estrellas.

Abre la puerta de un armario, hurga en su interior, sonríe y saca lentamente una curiosa botella.

—La guardo para ocasiones especiales.

—¿Qué es? —pregunto después de examinar la botella, nunca había visto nada parecido en Yogi's.

—Coñac de melón. Es bastante fuerte —responde con una risita.

En este momento bebería cualquier cosa. Encuentra dos tazas de café iguales, ya que en esta casa nunca se sirven bebidas, y vierte en las mismas un líquido espeso y pegajoso. El aroma me recuerda la consulta del dentista.

Brindamos por mi buena fortuna, juntamos nuestras tazas del Banco por Tennessee y tomamos un sorbo. Sabe a jarabe infantil para la tos y arde como el vodka puro. La señorita Birdie hace chasquear los labios.

—Será mejor que nos sentemos —dice.

Después de unos cuantos sorbos, ronca en el sofá. Apago el volumen de la película y sirvo otra taza. Es un licor potente y después del impacto inicial, las papilas gustativas se sienten menos agredidas. Me lo tomo en el jardín, a la luz de la luna, todavía con una sonrisa de agradecimiento al cielo por la divina noticia.

Los efectos del coñac de melón se prolongan hasta bastante después de la salida del sol. Me ducho, salgo sigilosamente del piso, me subo al coche y me alejo velozmente en retroceso de la casa, hasta llegar a la calle.

Voy a una cafetería elegante, donde sirven panecillos frescos y mermeladas del día. Compro un periódico dominguero con todos sus suplementos y los desparramo sobre una mesa del fondo. Varios artículos me resultan familiares.

Por cuarto día consecutivo, la primera plana está llena de artículos sobre la tragedia del buque de ruedas. Cuarenta y un jóvenes fallecieron. Los abogados han empezado ya a presentar demandas.

El segundo tema, en la sección metropolitana, es el último episodio de la serie sobre la investigación de la corrupción policial, y más específicamente la relación entre los negocios *topless* y la fuerza pública. El nombre de Bruiser aparece varias veces como abogado de Willie McSwane, uno de los paladines locales. Se le menciona también como abogado de Bennie Thomas, conocido también como Prince, propietario de un bar de la ciudad y en otra ocasión acusado oficialmente por el gobierno federal. Además, se cita también el nombre de Bruiser como probable objetivo de los investigadores federales.

Intuyo que se acerca el tren. El gran jurado federal está en sesión permanente desde hace un mes. Aparecen artículos en los periódicos casi a diario. Deck está cada día más nervioso.

El tercer artículo me coge completamente por sorpresa. En la última página de la sección de economía, bajo un pequeño titular que dice CIENTO SESENTA Y UNO APRUEBAN EL EXAMEN DE COLEGIATURA, aparece un comunicado de tres líneas del tribunal examinador, seguido de una lista en letra menuda de los aprobados por orden alfabético.

Acerco el periódico y leo apresuradamente. ¡Ahí estoy! Es cierto. No ha habido ningún error administrativo. ¡He aprobado el examen! Repaso velozmente los nombres de las personas, a muchas de las cuales he conocido bien durante los tres últimos años.

Busco a Booker Kane, pero no lo encuentro. Repaso varias veces la lista y se me caen los hombros. Coloco el periódico sobre la mesa y leo en voz alta los nombres, uno por uno. No hay ningún Booker Kane.

Estuve a punto de llamarlo anoche, cuando la señorita Birdie recuperó la memoria y me dio la maravillosa noticia, pero no pude hacerlo. Puesto que yo había aprobado, decidí esperar a que me llamara él. Calculé que si no lo había hecho dentro de unos días, eso significaría que había suspendido.

Ahora no estoy seguro de lo que debo hacer. Puedo verlo en este momento, ayudando a Charlene a vestir a sus hijos para ir a la iglesia, procurando sonreír con el rostro sereno, e intentando convencerla y convencerse de que el tropiezo es sólo temporal y que aprobará en la próxima convocatoria.

Pero sé que está desolado. Está apenado y enojado consigo mismo por haber fracasado. Está preocupado por la reacción de Marvin Shankle y detesta la perspectiva de acudir mañana al despacho.

Booker es un hombre sumamente orgulloso, que siempre se ha creído capaz de conseguir lo que se propusiera. Me gustaría ir a su casa y compadecerle, pero no funcionaría.

Mañana llamará para felicitarme. Superficialmente actuará como un buen perdedor, dispuesto a mejorar en la próxima ocasión.

Leo nuevamente la lista y de pronto me percato de que el nombre de Sara Plankmore no aparece. Tampoco aparece el de Sara Plankmore Wilcox. El señor S. Todd Wilcox ha aprobado, pero su joven esposa no.

Río para mis adentros. Eso es mezquino, sórdido, rencoroso, pueril, vengativo, e incluso odioso. Pero no puedo remediarlo. Decidió quedarse embarazada para poder casarse y apuesto a que la presión fue excesiva. Durante los últimos tres meses se ha dedicado a organizar la boda y elegir colores para la habitación de su futuro hijo. No se ha aplicado lo suficiente a sus estudios.

¡Ja! Soy el último en reírme después de todo.

El seguro del borracho que chocó contra Dan Van Landel tenía un límite de cien mil dólares. Deck ha convencido a la compañía del borracho de que la cuantía de la demanda de Van Landel es superior a dicho límite y está en lo cierto. La compañía está dispuesta a exceder el límite. Bruiser ha intervenido sólo en el último momento, para amenazar con la iniciación de un pleito. Deck ha efectuado el ochenta por ciento del trabajo. Yo me he ocupado de un quince por ciento. Le concedemos a Bruiser discretamente el mérito de lo restante. Pero de acuerdo con el sistema operativo del bufete de Bruiser, ni Deck ni yo participaremos en los beneficios del caso. Eso se debe a que Bruiser tiene una definición muy clara de generación de honorarios. El caso de Van Landel es suyo, porque él fue quien lo descubrió primero. Deck y yo fuimos al hospital para conseguir la firma del cliente, pero eso es lo que se supone que debemos hacer como empleados de Bruiser. Si hubiéramos descubierto el caso primero y conseguido la firma del cliente, tendríamos derecho a una parte de los honorarios.

Bruiser nos llama a ambos a su despacho y cierra la puerta. Me felicita por haber aprobado el examen. Él también lo aprobó al primer intento y estoy seguro de que eso hace que Deck se sienta todavía más estúpido. Pero Deck permanece impasible, ahí sentado lamiéndose los dientes, con la cabeza ladeada. Bruiser habla unos momentos de la compensación de Van Landel. Ha recibido el cheque de trescientos mil dólares esta mañana y los Van Landel pasarán esta tarde para recoger lo que les corresponde. Además, considera que tal vez nosotros deberíamos recibir también algo.

Deck y yo intercambiamos nerviosas miradas.

Bruiser dice que ha tenido ya un buen año, ha ganado más que en la totalidad del año anterior, y desea que su personal sea feliz. Además, el caso se ha resuelto con mucha rapidez. Él, personalmente, ha trabajado en el mismo menos de seis horas.

Tanto Deck como yo nos preguntamos qué hizo durante ese tiempo.

Por consiguiente, gracias a su bondadoso corazón, quiere recompensarnos. Le corresponde la tercera parte, es decir, treinta y tres mil dólares, pero no piensa guardárselos todos. Los compartirá con nosotros.

—Os voy a dar un tercio de mi parte, la mitad para cada uno.

Deck y yo calculamos en silencio. Un tercio de treinta y tres mil dólares son once mil, y la mitad son cinco mil quinientos.

—Gracias, Bruiser. Eres muy generoso —respondo, con un esfuerzo para conservar una expresión impasible.

—No hay de qué —dice Bruiser, como si eso formara parte de su estilo de vida—. Considéralo un regalo por aprobar el examen.

—Gracias.

—Sí, muchas gracias —agrega Deck.

Ambos estamos aturdidos, pero también pensamos en que Bruiser se queda con veintidós mil dólares por seis horas de trabajo. Eso equivale aproximadamente a tres mil quinientos dólares por hora.

Sin embargo, yo no esperaba un centavo y de pronto me siento rico.

—Buen trabajo, muchachos. Y ahora a por más casos.

Asentimos simultáneamente. Yo cuento y gasto mi fortuna. Deck indudablemente hace lo mismo.

—¿Estamos listos para mañana? —pregunta Bruiser.

A las nueve de la mañana se debate la propuesta de Great Benefit de sobreseer el caso ante su señoría Harvey Hale. Bruiser ha mantenido una desagradable conversación con el juez respecto a dicha propuesta y no anticipamos con alegría la perspectiva de dicha vista.

—Creo que sí —respondo un poco nervioso.

Redacté y presenté una respuesta de treinta páginas, y luego Drummond y sus muchachos contraatacaron con otro informe. Bruiser llamó a Hale para protestar y la conversación anduvo por malos derroteros.

—Puede que deje parte del debate en tus manos, de modo que prepárate —dice Bruiser.

Se me forma un nudo en la garganta. Mi nerviosismo se transforma en pánico.

—Manos a la obra —agrega—. Sería vergonzoso cerrar el caso con una propuesta de sobreseimiento.

—Yo también colaboro —añade cooperativamente Deck.

—Estupendo. Iremos los tres al juzgado. Dios sabe que ellos serán veinte.

La inesperada riqueza estimula el deseo de mejores cosas en la vida. Deck y yo prescindimos de nuestra sopa y bocadillo habituales en el local de Trudy para almorzar en un restaurante cercano. Pedimos solomillo.

—Nunca había repartido así el dinero —dice Deck, que aunque estamos en una mesa del fondo y nadie puede oírnos no deja de hacer muecas y mirar por encima del hombro—. Algo está a punto de ocurrir, Rudy, estoy seguro. Toxer y Ridge van a independizarse. Los federales tienen cercado a Bruiser. Está regalando dinero. Me pone nervioso, muy nervioso.

—Pero, ¿por qué? No pueden detenernos.

—No temo que me detengan. Me preocupa el empleo.

—No lo comprendo. Si acusan y detienen a Bruiser saldrá bajo fianza antes de que vuelvan la espalda. El bufete seguirá funcionando.

—Escúchame —exclama irritado—, puede que lleguen con una orden judicial y sierras de mano. Pueden hacerlo, ¿sabes? No sería la primera vez en un caso de negocios fraudulentos. A los federales les encanta tomar al asalto los bufetes de abogados, apoderarse de los ficheros y llevarse los ordenadores. Tú y yo les tenemos sin cuidado.

Sinceramente, nunca lo había pensado y supongo que parezco sorprendido.

—Claro que pueden clausurarle el bufete —prosigue con suma intensidad—. Y les encantaría hacerlo. A ti y a mí nos alcanzaría el fuego cruzado y a nadie, absolutamente a nadie, le importaría un comino.

—¿Entonces qué sugieres?

—¡Larguémonos!

Estoy a punto de preguntarle qué quiere decir, pero está perfectamente claro. Ahora Deck es mi amigo, pero quiere ir más lejos. Ahora que he aprobado el examen de colegiatura, puedo servirle de paraguas. ¡Deck quiere un socio! Antes de que le responda se lanza al ataque.

—¿De cuánto dinero dispones?

—Pues, de cinco mil quinientos dólares.

—Yo también. Suman once mil. Si aportamos dos mil cada uno dispondremos de cuatro mil. Podemos alquilar un pequeño despacho por quinientos mensuales, el teléfono y los servicios costarán otros quinientos. Podemos conseguir algunos muebles, nada especial. Trabajaremos con un presupuesto muy limitado los primeros seis meses y veremos cómo funciona. Yo me ocuparé de conseguir los casos, tú haces acto de presencia en los juzgados y nos repartimos los beneficios por un igual. Todo a medias: gastos, honorarios, beneficios, trabajo y horario.

Estoy anonadado, pero pienso con rapidez.

—¿Y una secretaria?

—No la necesitamos —responde inmediatamente, puesto que ya lo ha pensado—. Por lo menos para empezar. Entre los dos podemos ocuparnos del teléfono, e instalar un contestador automático. Tanto tú como yo sabemos mecanografiar. Funcionará. Cuando ganemos un poco de dinero, contrataremos a una chica.

—¿Cuánto costarán los gastos globales?

—Menos de dos mil. Alquiler, teléfono, servicios, suministros, copias y múltiples gastos menores. Pero podemos buscar atajos y operar de forma barata. Si reducimos los gastos nos llevamos más dinero a fin de mes. Es muy simple —dice, al tiempo que me observa mientras sorbe su té helado, antes de inclinarse de nuevo sobre la mesa—. Escúchame, Rudy, tal como yo lo entiendo, acabamos de dejar veintidós mil dólares sobre la mesa. Debíamos habernos llevado la cantidad global, con lo cual cubriríamos los gastos de un año entero. Abramos nuestro propio negocio y quedémonos con todo el dinero.

Las normas éticas prohíben que un abogado forme sociedad con alguien que no lo sea. Empiezo a mencionarlo, pero me percato de su futilidad. A Deck se le ocurrirán una docena de formas de rebatirlo.

—El alquiler parece barato —declaro, por decir algo y también para averiguar cuánto ha investigado.

Entorna los párpados y sonríe con sus relucientes dientes de castor.

—Ya he encontrado el lugar. Está en un antiguo edificio de Madison, sobre una tienda de antigüedades. Cuatro salas y unos lavabos, exactamente a medio camino entre la cárcel y Saint Peter.

¡El emplazamiento perfecto! Un lugar de ensueño para cualquier abogado.

—Es una parte conflictiva de la ciudad —comento.

—¿Por qué crees que el alquiler es tan barato?

—¿Está en buenas condiciones?

—No está mal. Tendremos que pintarlo.

—Soy un experto.

Llegan las ensaladas y me lleno la boca de lechuga. Deck mueve la comida en el plato, pero come poco. Su mente está demasiado activa para concentrarse en la comida.

—Debo marcharme, Rudy. Sé cosas que no puedo contar, ¿comprendes? Créeme, Bruiser está a punto de desplomarse. Se le ha acabado su buena racha —dice antes de hacer una pausa para coger una nuez—. Si no quieres venir conmigo hablaré con Nicklass esta tarde.

Nicklass es el único que queda aparte de Toxer y Ridge, y sé que a Deck no le gusta. También tengo la fuerte sospecha de que es cierto lo que Deck cuenta acerca de Bruiser. Basta hojear el periódico un par de veces por semana para percatarse de que tiene graves problemas. Deck ha sido su más fiel empleado en los últimos años y me asusta el hecho de que esté dispuesto a huir.

Comemos despacio y en silencio pensando en nuestros próximos pasos. Hace cuatro meses, la idea de ejercer la abogacía con alguien como Deck habría sido impensable, incluso irrisoria, sin embargo ahora soy incapaz de encontrar pretextos para impedir que se convierta en mi socio.

—¿No quieres que sea tu socio? —pregunta con tristeza.

—Estoy reflexionando, Deck. Concédeme unos minutos. Con lo que me has contado, acabas de asestarme un duro golpe en la cabeza.

—Lo siento. Pero debemos actuar con rapidez.

—¿Cuánto sabes?

—Lo suficiente para estar convencido. No me hagas más preguntas.

—Dame unas horas. Deja que lo piense.

—De acuerdo. Mañana vamos los dos al juzgado, reunámonos temprano. En el café de Trudy. No podemos hablar en el despacho. Piénsatelo y dame una respuesta por la mañana.

—Trato hecho.

—¿Cuántos sumarios tienes?

Reflexiono unos instantes. Tengo un sumario considerablemente extenso sobre el caso Black, otro bastante ralo sobre la señorita Birdie y otro sobre una inútil compensación laboral, que Bruiser me cedió la semana pasada.

—Tres.

—Sácalos de tu despacho. Llévatelos a tu casa.

—¿Ahora?

—Ahora. Esta tarde. Y cualquier otra cosa que te interese de tu despacho, te conviene sacarla cuanto antes. Pero asegúrate de que no te descubran, ¿comprendes?

—¿Nos vigila alguien?

Se contorsiona, mira a su alrededor y luego asiente cautelosamente sin que sus ojos dejen de moverse alocadamente tras sus torcidas gafas.

—¿Quién?

—Los federales, creo. El bufete está vigilado.

VEINTITRÉS

El pequeño comentario de Bruiser, sobre el hecho de que tal vez me permita participar en el debate de la vista del caso Black, me mantiene despierto casi toda la noche. Puede que no fuera más que una simple estratagema del sabio mentor, pero me tiene más preocupado que la perspectiva de formar sociedad con Deck.

Está todavía oscuro cuando llego al local de Trudy. Soy su primer cliente. El café es fresco y los buñuelos están calientes. Charlamos unos instantes, pero Trudy tiene mucho que hacer.

Yo también. Hago caso omiso de los periódicos y me concentro en mis notas. De vez en cuando miro por la ventana al aparcamiento vacío e intento detectar la presencia de agentes en vehículos sin distintivos, fumando cigarrillos sin filtro y tomando café pasado, como en las películas. En algunas ocasiones Deck es perfectamente verosímil y en otras está tan loco como parece.

También llega temprano. Le sirven su café pocos minutos después de las siete y se sienta frente a mí. El local está ahora medio lleno.

—¿Y bien? —son sus primeras palabras.

—Intentémoslo durante un año —respondo.

He decidido que firmaremos un contrato válido por un año, que incluirá además una cláusula de rescisión a treinta días, en caso de que él o yo no estemos satisfechos.

Aparecen inmediatamente sus relucientes dientes y no puede ocultar su emoción. Extiende su mano sobre la mesa, para que se la estreche. Éste es un gran momento para Deck. Ojalá sintiera yo lo mismo que él.

También he decidido que intentaré canalizarlo, procurar que la vergüenza le impida acudir a todos los siniestros. Trabajando duro y sirviendo a nuestros clientes podremos ganarnos la vida cómodamente y probablemente progresar. Estimularé a Deck

219

para que prepare su examen de colegiatura, apruebe y enfoquemos con mayor respeto la profesión.

Eso, por supuesto, habrá que hacerlo gradualmente.

Además, esperar que Deck se mantuviera alejado de los hospitales sería tan ingenuo como suponer que un borracho no acudiría a los bares. Pero como mínimo lo intentaré.

—¿Has retirado tus sumarios? —susurra mientras mira hacia la puerta, por la que acaban de entrar dos camioneros.

—Sí. ¿Y tú?

—Hace una semana que empecé a llevarme cosas.

Prefiero no hablar más del asunto. Cambio de tema para comentar la vista de los Black, pero Deck vuelve a nuestra aventura. Cuando a las ocho nos dirigimos a nuestros despachos, Deck escudriña todos los coches del aparcamiento como si estuvieran cargados de agentes especiales.

A las ocho y cuarto Bruiser todavía no ha llegado. Deck y yo hablamos de los argumentos en los informes de Drummond. Aquí, donde los teléfonos están intervenidos y hay micrófonos en las paredes, hablamos exclusivamente de asuntos jurídicos.

A las ocho y media, Bruiser brilla por su ausencia. Había dicho claramente que estaría aquí a las ocho para repasar el sumario. La sala del juez Hale está en el palacio de Justicia del condado de Shelby, en el centro de la ciudad, a unos veinte minutos. Deck llama con reticencia a casa de Bruiser, pero no obtiene respuesta alguna. Dru afirma que le esperaba a las ocho. Intenta en vano llamarle a su coche. Puede que se reúna con nosotros en el juzgado, dice la secretaria.

Deck y yo guardamos el sumario en mi maletín y salimos del despacho a las nueve menos cuarto. Asegura conocer la mejor ruta, de modo que él conduce mientras yo sudo. Tengo las manos pegajosas y la garganta seca. Si Bruiser me deja colgado para esta vista nunca se lo perdonaré. Es más, le odiaré eternamente.

—Tranquilízate —dice Deck, agachado sobre el volante, sorteando coches y cruzando semáforos en rojo, y consciente de lo asustado que estoy—. Estoy seguro de que Bruiser estará ahí —agrega sin el menor vestigio de convicción—. Y si no está, tú lo harás de maravilla. Es sólo una petición. Me refiero a que no habrá jurado en la sala.

—Cierra la boca y conduce, ¿de acuerdo, Deck? Y procura no matarnos.

—No seas tan susceptible.

Estamos en el centro de la ciudad, en pleno tráfico, cuando consulto horrorizado mi reloj. Son las nueve en punto. Deck obliga a dos peatones a cederle el paso y cruza un pequeño aparcamiento.

—¿Ves esa puerta? —pregunta al tiempo que señala una esquina del palacio de Justicia del condado de Shelby, que es un edificio masivo que ocupa toda la manzana.

—Sí.

—Entra por ella, sube un piso, y la sala es la tercera puerta a tu derecha.

—¿Crees que Bruiser estará ahí? —pregunto con una voz bastante débil.

—Por supuesto —miente, e inmediatamente da un frenazo junto a la acera y yo salto del vehículo—. Me reuniré contigo en cuanto aparque —exclama.

Subo un tramo de escaleras de hormigón, cruzo una puerta, otro tramo y me encuentro de pronto en pleno juzgado.

El palacio de Justicia del condado de Shelby es antiguo, regio y muy bien conservado. Sus suelos y paredes son de mármol, y sus dobles puertas de reluciente caoba. El vestíbulo es ancho, oscuro, silencioso y está rodeado de bancos de madera, bajo retratos de distinguidos juristas.

Dejo de correr hasta detenerme frente a la sala de su señoría Harvey Hale, tribunal del circuito división ocho, según indica la placa de bronce que hay junto a la puerta.

No hay señal de Bruiser en el vestíbulo y cuando empujo lentamente la puerta y miro hacia el interior de la sala, lo primero que no veo es su corpulenta figura. No está aquí.

Pero la sala no está vacía. Miro a lo largo de la alfombra roja del pasillo, más allá de las hileras de bancos pulidos y acolchados y de una pequeña puerta basculante, y veo a un grupo de personas que me esperan. En las alturas, con una toga negra, en un enorme sillón de cuero color borgoña y mirando con ceño hacia mí, hay un desagradable personaje que supongo que debe de ser el juez Harvey Hale. Un reloj a su espalda indica que pasan doce minutos de las nueve. Con una de sus manos se sostiene la barbilla, mientras que con los dedos de la otra tamborilea impacientemente.

A mi izquierda, tras la barrera que separa la galería pública del estrado, el palco del jurado y las mesas de los letrados, distingo a un grupo de individuos que se esfuerzan por verme. Todos tienen el mismo aspecto y visten por un igual: cabello corto, traje oscuro, camisa blanca, corbata a rayas, ceño y sonrisa de desdén.

La sala está silenciosa. Me siento como un intruso. Incluso la relatora y el alguacil parecen mirarme con desaire.

Me pesan los pies, siento un temblor en las rodillas y me encuentro desprovisto por completo de seguridad en mí mismo. Me acerco al estrado. Mi garganta parece de pergamino, mi voz seca y débil.

—Discúlpeme, señor, estoy aquí para asistir a la vista del caso Black.

La expresión del juez permanece inmutable. Sigue tamborileando con los dedos.

—¿Y quién es usted?

—Mi nombre es Rudy Baylor. Trabajo para Bruiser Stone.

—¿Dónde está el señor Stone? —pregunta.

—No estoy seguro. Se suponía que debía reunirse aquí conmigo.

Oigo voces y actividad entre los abogados que están a mi izquierda, pero no miro. El juez Hale deja de golpear con los dedos, separa la mano de su barbilla y mueve con frustración la cabeza.

—¿Por qué no me sorprende? —declara frente al micrófono.

Puesto que Deck y yo nos independizamos, estoy decidido a llevarme el caso de los Black. ¡Es mío! Nadie puede arrebatármelo. El juez Hale no tiene forma de saber en este momento que yo seré el abogado acusador en este caso, y no Bruiser. A pesar de lo asustado que estoy, decido que éste es el momento de establecerme.

—Supongo que quiere una prórroga —dice el juez.

—No, señor. Estoy preparado para el debate de la petición —respondo con todas mis fuerzas.

Cruzo la puerta y coloco el sumario sobre la mesa a mi derecha.

—¿Es usted abogado? —pregunta.

—Acabo de aprobar el examen de colegiatura.

—¿Pero no ha recibido todavía su licencia?

No sé por qué dicha distinción no se me había ocurrido hasta ahora. Supongo que me sentí tan orgulloso de mí mismo que lo había olvidado. Además, Bruiser era quien iba a hablar hoy, puede que con alguna pequeña intervención por mi parte para practicar un poco.

—No, señor. Tomamos juramento la semana próxima.

Uno de mis enemigos se aclara ruidosamente la garganta para llamar la atención del juez. Vuelvo la cabeza y veo a un distinguido caballero con un traje azul marino que se levanta parsimoniosamente de su silla.

—Con la venia de la sala —dice, como si lo hubiera repetido un millón de veces—. Para que conste en acta, mi nombre es Leo F. Drummond, de Tinley Britt, abogado defensor de Great Benefit Life.

Habla en un tono sobrio, dirigiéndose a su amigo de toda la vida y compañero de piso en Yale. La relatora ha vuelto a concentrarse en sus uñas.

—Y nos oponemos a que este joven esté presente en este asunto —agrega en un tono lento y grave, al tiempo que hace un ademán hacia mí y despierta inmediatamente mi odio—. Cielos, ni siquiera está colegiado.

Lo detesto por su tono paternalista y su absurda minuciosidad. Esto es sólo una vista, no un juicio.

—Con la venia de su señoría, la semana próxima estaré colegiado —replico, con mi voz reforzada enormemente por la ira.

—Eso no basta, su señoría —exclama Drummond, con los brazos abiertos, como si la idea fuera completamente absurda.

¡Menuda osadía!

—He aprobado el examen, su señoría.

—¿Hemos de suponer que es una gran hazaña? —exclama Drummond mirándome.

Yo lo miro a los ojos. Lo acompañan otras cuatro personas, tres sentadas a la mesa con cuadernos delante y la cuarta a su espalda. Todos están pendientes de mí.

—Es una gran hazaña, señor Drummond. Pregúnteselo a Shell Boykin —respondo.

Drummond frunce sus facciones y hace una detectable mueca. En realidad, todos sus compañeros han fruncido también sus facciones.

Ha sido un golpe bajo, pero no he podido resistirlo. Shell Boykin es uno de los dos estudiantes de mi curso, lo suficientemente privilegiados para haber sido contratados por Trent & Brent. Nos hemos odiado durante tres años y el mes pasado hicimos juntos el examen. Su nombre no aparecía en el periódico del domingo. Estoy seguro de que el prestigioso bufete debe sentirse avergonzado de que uno de sus brillantes novicios haya suspendido el examen.

Drummond frunce aún más el entrecejo y le respondo con una sonrisa. En los breves momentos en que nos observamos mutuamente aprendo una valiosa lección. No es más que un hombre. Puede ser legendario en los juzgados, con muchas muescas en su cinturón, pero es simplemente otro ser humano. No va a cruzar el pasillo y abofetearme, porque le daría una paliza. No puede lastimarme, ni tampoco pueden hacerlo su pequeña banda de corchetes.

Ambos lados de la sala están al mismo nivel. Mi mesa es tan grande como la suya.

—¡Siéntense! —exclama su señoría cerca del micrófono—. Los dos —agrega, mientras yo encuentro una silla y me instalo—. Una pregunta, señor Baylor. ¿Quién se ocupará de este caso en su bufete?

—Lo haré yo, su señoría.

—¿Y qué me dice del señor Stone?

—No lo sé. Pero este caso es mío, son mis clientes. El señor Stone se ha limitado a firmar en mi nombre hasta que aprobara el examen.

—Muy bien. Prosigamos. Conste en acta —dice al tiempo que mira a la relatora, que ya ha empezado a teclear—. Ésta es una petición del acusado para sobreseer el caso, de modo que hablará primero el señor Drummond. Les concederé quince minutos a cada uno para presentar sus argumentos y luego deliberaré. No quiero pasar aquí toda la mañana. ¿Me han comprendido?

Todo el mundo asiente. Los defensores parecen patos de madera en una caseta de tiro en la feria, con todas sus cabezas moviéndose simultáneamente. Leo Drummond se acerca a un atril portátil en el centro del estrado y empieza su discurso. Es lento, meticuloso y al cabo de cinco minutos aburrido. Resume los puntos principales ya expresados en su prolongado informe, cuya esencia es la de que el pleito contra Great Benefit es injusto porque la póliza no cubre el trasplante de médula. Luego está la cuestión de si Donny Ray Black es beneficiario de la póliza, teniendo en cuenta que es adulto y ha dejado de formar parte del núcleo familiar.

Francamente, esperaba más de ellos. Creí que el gran Leo Drummond nos obsequiaría con algo casi mágico. Hasta ayer, descubrí que estaba emocionado ante la perspectiva de esa escaramuza inicial. Esperaba presenciar una buena pelea entre Drummond, el sofisticado letrado, y Bruiser, el vocinglero de los juzgados.

Pero si no estuviera tan nervioso, me quedaría dormido. Pasa de los quince minutos sin una sola pausa. El juez Hale tiene la cabeza baja, está leyendo algo, probablemente una revista. Veinte minutos. Deck dice que Drummond cobra doscientos cincuenta dólares por hora en su despacho y trescientos cincuenta en el juzgado. Eso es bastante inferior a las tarifas de Nueva York y Washington, pero muy elevado para Memphis. Tiene buenas razones para hablar lentamente y repetirse con frecuencia. Compensa ser meticuloso, e incluso tedioso, cuando la minuta es de dicha cuantía.

Sus tres asociados toman incesantemente notas en sus cuadernos con el evidente propósito de registrar palabra por palabra el discurso de su líder. Es casi cómico y, en otras circunstancias, soltaría una carcajada. Primero se han ocupado de la investigación, luego han redactado el informe, a continuación lo han reescrito varias veces, acto seguido han respondido a mi informe y ahora escriben los argumentos de Drummond, extraídos directamente de sus informes. Pero cobran por hacer eso. Deck calcula que los honorarios de los asociados son de unos ciento cincuenta en el despacho y algo más en las vistas y juicios. Si está en lo cierto, cada uno de esos personajes clónicos se embolsa unos doscientos dólares en una hora por hacer garabatos. Seiscientos dólares. Más trescientos cincuenta para Drummond. Eso suponen casi mil dólares por hora, por lo que estoy viendo.

El cuarto hombre, sentado tras los asociados, es de edad más avanzada, aproximadamente la misma que Drummond. No toma notas, por consiguiente no puede ser abogado. Probablemente está aquí en representación de Great Benefit, puede que sea uno de los abogados de la compañía.

Me olvido de Deck hasta que me golpea en el hombro con un cuaderno. Está a mi espalda y extiende la mano por encima de la barrera. Quiere mandarme un mensaje. En su cuaderno ha escrito una nota: «Este individuo es más pesado que el plomo. Ajústate a tu informe. No hables más de diez minutos. ¿Se sabe algo de Bruiser?»

Muevo la cabeza sin volverla. Como si Bruiser pudiera estar en la sala sin ser visto.

Después de treinta y un minutos, Drummond concluye su monólogo. Lleva las gafas colgadas en la punta de la nariz. Es el catedrático que pronuncia una conferencia ante sus alumnos. Regresa a su mesa inmensamente satisfecho de su lógica aplastante y su asombrosa capacidad de síntesis. Sus clónicos agachan simultáneamente la cabeza y susurran cumplidos por su maravillosa presentación. ¡Menudo puñado de lameculos! A quién puede sorprenderle que sea tan engreído.

Coloco mi cuaderno en el atril y levanto la cabeza para mirar al juez Hale, que en este momento parece interesarse enormemente por lo que diga. Estoy muerto de miedo, pero sólo cabe seguir adelante.

Esto no es más que un pleito. La negativa de Great Benefit le ha impedido a mi cliente recibir el único tratamiento que podía haberle salvado la vida. La actuación de la compañía acabará por matar a Donny Ray Black. Nosotros tenemos razón y ellos no la tienen. Me alienta la imagen de su rostro demacrado y su cuerpo marchito. Me pone furioso.

Los abogados de Great Benefit recibirán un montón de dinero para generar confusión, embrollar los hechos, con la esperanza de embaucar al juez y luego al jurado con artimañas. Ésa es su misión y la razón por la que Drummond ha divagado durante treinta y un minutos sin decir nada.

Mi versión de los hechos y de la ley será siempre más breve. Mis informes y argumentos serán siempre claros y precisos. Espero que alguien, en algún momento, lo reconozca.

Empiezo por mencionar con nerviosismo algunos puntos básicos sobre las peticiones de sobreseimiento en general, y el juez Hale me mira con incredulidad, como si yo fuera el imbécil más supino que ha oído en su vida. Su rostro muestra incredulidad, pero por lo menos mantiene la boca cerrada. Procuro eludir su mirada.

Las peticiones de sobreseimiento raramente se conceden cuando existe una clara disputa entre ambas partes. Puede que esté nervioso y hable con torpeza, pero tengo la seguridad de que proseguirá el proceso.

Sigo mis notas sin revelar nada nuevo. Su señoría no tarda en cansarse de mi discurso, como lo hizo con el de Drummond, y vuelve a su lectura. Cuando termino, Drummond solicita cinco minutos para rebatir mis palabras y su amigo hace un ademán en dirección al atril.

Drummond habla durante otros once valiosos y costosos minutos, aclara lo que le preocupaba, aunque nos deja a los demás sumidos en las tinieblas, y vuelve a sentarse.

—Quiero ver a los letrados en mi despacho —dice Hale antes de levantarse y desaparecer inmediatamente por una puerta a su espalda.

Puesto que no sé dónde se encuentra su despacho, me pongo de pie y espero a que Drummond me muestre el camino. Es sumamente cortés cuando nos reunimos cerca del atril, e incluso me coloca el brazo sobre el hombro y dice que he hecho un trabajo excelente.

El juez ya se ha quitado la toga cuando entramos en su despacho. Está de pie tras su escritorio y nos indica con un ademán que nos sentemos.

—Adelante. Siéntense.

La sala está discretamente oscura. Unas gruesas cortinas cubren la ventana, moqueta color borgoña y estantes de densos libros desde el suelo hasta el techo.

Nos sentamos. Reflexiona.

—Este pleito me preocupa, señor Baylor —dice por fin—. No me atrevería a calificarlo de frívolo, pero, francamente, no me impresionan sus méritos. Estoy realmente harto de esta clase de pleitos. —Hace una pausa y me mira como si esperara que respondiera, pero estoy completamente perdido—. Me inclino a conceder la petición de sobreseimiento —agrega mientras abre un cajón para sacar varios frascos de píldoras, que coloca cuidadosamente sobre su escritorio, se detiene y me mira—. Puede que admitan su demanda en el tribunal federal. Preséntela en otro lugar. Simplemente prefiero no incluirla en mi saturada lista de casos —añade mientras cuenta por lo menos una docena de píldoras, que extrae de cuatro cilindros de plástico—. Discúlpenme, voy al lavabo —concluye antes de salir por una pequeña puerta a su derecha, que cierra ruidosamente.

Contemplo inmóvil y aturdido los frascos de píldoras, con la esperanza de que se atragante. Drummond no ha dicho palabra, pero como si le hubiera llegado el momento de entrar en escena, se pone de pie y apoya el trasero sobre el borde del escritorio. Me mira con una cálida sonrisa.

—Escúcheme, Rudy, soy un abogado muy caro de un bufete muy prestigioso —dice en un tono grave y confidencial, como si divulgara información secreta—. Cuando se nos encarga un caso como éste, lo primero que hacemos es calcular el coste de la defensa. Antes de mover un solo dedo, le presentamos el presupuesto a nuestro cliente. Me he ocupado de muchos casos y suelo acercarme bastante al centro de la diana —agrega antes de moverse un poco, en preparación para el golpe de gracia—. Les he comunicado a Great Benefit que el coste de defender este caso, incluido el juicio, oscilará entre cincuenta y setenta y cinco mil dólares. —Hace una pausa, a la espera de que manifieste lo mucho que me impresiona dicha cifra, pero me limito a contemplar su corbata mientras a lo lejos se oye la cisterna del retrete—. Por consiguiente, Great Benefit me ha autorizado a ofrecerles a usted y a sus clientes una compensación de setenta y cinco mil dólares para zanjar el caso.

Respiro hondo. Un sinfín de ideas descabelladas pulula por mi mente, la principal de las cuales es la cifra de veinticinco mil dólares. ¡Mis honorarios! Los veo ya sobre la mesa.

Un momento. Si su amigo Harvey está a punto de sobreseer el caso, ¿por qué me ofrece ese dinero?

De pronto lo comprendo: la jugada de los policías, uno bueno y uno malo. Harvey levanta el hacha y me aterroriza, a continuación interviene Leo con un toque de terciopelo. No puedo evitar preguntarme cuántas veces habrán jugado al «tira y afloja» en este despacho.

—Comprenda que esto no implica admisión de responsabilidades —declara—. Se trata de una oferta única, valedera sólo durante cuarenta y ocho horas, para que la tome o la deje mientras siga sobre la mesa. Si dice que no, será la tercera guerra mundial.

—¿Pero por qué?

—Simple economía. Great Benefit se ahorra dinero, sin exponerse a la posibilidad de un veredicto absurdo. No les apetece que los demanden, ¿comprende? A sus ejecutivos no les gusta perder el tiempo con declaraciones y comparecencias en los juzgados. Son gente discreta. Prefieren evitar este tipo de publicidad. Los seguros son un negocio muy competitivo y no quieren que esto llegue a oídos de sus rivales. Hay muchas razones para resolver este asunto con discreción. Muchos motivos para que sus clientes acepten el dinero y se den por satisfechos. Tenga también en cuenta que, en su mayoría, está libre de impuestos.

Es muy convincente. Podría discutir los méritos del caso y hablarle de lo malvados que son sus clientes, pero se limitaría a asentir con una sonrisa. Le entraría por una oreja y le saldría por la otra. En este momento a Leo Drummond le interesa que acepte su dinero y no se alteraría aunque hablara mal de su esposa.

Se abre la puerta y su señoría sale de su pequeño lavabo privado. Ahora es Leo quien necesita satisfacer sus necesidades biológicas. La pelota está en juego. El dúo se coordina.

—La presión alta —dice Hale como si hablara consigo mismo, cuando se sienta tras su escritorio y recoge los frascos.

No lo suficiente, querría decirle.

—Me temo, muchacho, que esta demanda no es muy consistente. Tal vez pueda presionar a Leo para que haga una oferta de compensación. Eso forma parte de mi trabajo, ¿comprende? Otros jueces lo enfocan de otro modo, pero yo no. Prefiero involucrarme en los acuerdos desde el primer momento. Agiliza los procesos. Puede que esa gente le ofrezca cierta cantidad para ahorrarse los mil dólares por minuto que le pagan a Leo. —Se ríe como si tuviera mucha gracia, se le pone el rostro colorado y tose.

Casi puedo ver a Leo en el retrete, escuchando con la oreja pegada a la puerta. No me sorprendería que tuvieran un micrófono en el mismo.

Observo al juez hasta que se le humedecen los ojos.

—Acaba de ofrecerme el coste de la defensa —digo cuando deja de toser.

Es un pésimo actor y finge sorprenderse.

—¿Cuánto? —pregunta.

—Setenta y cinco mil.

—¡Diantre! —exclama boquiabierto—. Escúcheme, hijo, sería un error no aceptarlo.

—¿Usted cree? —pregunto para seguirle el juego.

—Setenta y cinco. Caramba, eso es mucho dinero. No parece propio de Leo.

—Es una gran persona.

—Coja el dinero, hijo. Hace mucho tiempo que me dedico a esto y le aseguro que le conviene seguir mi consejo.

Se abre la puerta y Leo se reúne con nosotros. Su señoría lo mira y exclama:

—¡Setenta y cinco mil!

Se diría que el dinero sale del presupuesto de Hale.

—Eso ha sido lo que ha dicho mi cliente —aclara Leo.

Sus manos están atadas. Carece de poder de decisión.

Insisten un poco más. Yo no razono con claridad y apenas hablo. Salgo del despacho con el brazo de Leo sobre mis hombros.

Veo a Deck en el vestíbulo hablando por teléfono, y me siento en un banco para ordenar mis pensamientos. Esperaban a Bruiser. ¿Habrían intentado convencerlo a dúo del mismo modo? No, no lo creo. ¿Cómo se las han arreglado para elaborar con tanta rapidez la emboscada que me han tendido? Probablemente tenían otra estratagema preparada para él.

Hay dos cosas de las que estoy convencido. En primer lugar, Hale está realmente dispuesto a sobreseer el caso. Es un viejo enfermizo que ejerce desde hace mucho tiempo, e inmune a la presión. No le importa en lo más mínimo tener o no razón. Y puede resultar muy difícil que otro tribunal admita el caso. Las perspectivas del pleito son sumamente precarias. En segundo lugar, Drummond está demasiado ansioso por llegar a un acuerdo. Tiene miedo porque su cliente ha sido sorprendido con las manos en la masa haciendo algo muy perverso.

Deck ha hecho once llamadas telefónicas en los últimos veinte minutos y no hay rastro de Bruiser. De regreso al bufete le cuento la peculiar escena en el despacho de Hale. Deck, que se adapta inmediatamente a las circunstancias, es partidario de coger el dinero y darse por satisfecho. Señala con toda la razón que, a estas alturas, ninguna suma de dinero logrará salvarle la vida a Donny Ray, y que nos conviene aceptar lo que ofrezcan, facilitándoles un poco la vida a Dot y Buddy.

Asegura haber oído muchas sórdidas historias de pleitos mal conducidos en la sala de Hale. Para ser un juez en activo, es inusual el apoyo que manifiesta pro reforma de la ley de los agravios. Detesta a los demandantes, repite Deck en más de una ocasión. No será fácil obtener un juicio justo. Insiste en que agarremos el dinero y zanjemos el caso.

Cuando llegamos, Dru está llorando en el vestíbulo. Está histérica porque todo el mundo busca a Bruiser. Se le ha corrido el rímel por las mejillas, y no deja de gemir y sollozar. No es propio de él, repite una y otra vez. Algo malo debe haberle ocurrido.

Como maleante que es, Bruiser frecuenta la compañía de personas peligrosas de dudosa reputación. No me sorprendería que se descubriera su voluminoso cuerpo en el maletero de un coche en el aeropuerto, ni tampoco a Deck. Los maleantes lo persiguen.

Yo también lo busco. Llamo a Yogi's para hablar con Prince. Él sabrá dónde encontrar a Bruiser. Hablo con Billy, el director del local, con quien tengo una buena amistad, y a los pocos minutos descubro que Prince también ha desaparecido. Han llamado en vano a todas partes. Billy está nervioso y preocupado. Los federales acaban de marcharse. ¿Qué ocurre?

Deck va de despacho en despacho organizando la tropa. Nos reunimos en la sala de conferencias: yo, Deck, Toxer y Ridge, cuatro secretarias y dos subalternos a los que nunca había visto. Nicklass, el otro abogado, ha salido de la ciudad. Todos comparamos notas de nuestro último encuentro con Bruiser: ¿Algo sospechoso? ¿Qué se suponía que debía hacer hoy? ¿Quién habló con él por última vez? Hay una sensación de pánico en el ambiente, un aire de confusión que no mitiga el incesante llanto de Dru. Sabe que algo nefasto ha sucedido.

Se levanta la sesión, regresamos en silencio a nuestros despachos y cerramos las puertas con llave. Deck, evidentemente, me sigue. Charlamos un rato de temas superficiales, cuidando de no decir nada que no queramos que oigan por si realmente hay micrófonos en las dependencias. A las once y media nos escabullimos por una puerta trasera y vamos a almorzar.

Nunca volveremos a pisar el lugar.

VEINTICUATRO

Dudo que nunca llegue a saber si Deck estaba realmente al corriente de lo que se avecinaba, o si se limitó a ser asombrosamente profético. Es una persona sencilla y la mayoría de sus pensamientos están cerca de la superficie. Pero hay en él algo insólito, aparte de su aspecto, oculto en lo más recóndito de su ser. Tengo fundadas sospechas de que entre él y Bruiser había mucha más intimidad de lo que daban a entender, que su generosidad en el caso Van Landel era el resultado de ciertas presiones por parte de Deck, y que Bruiser anunciaba discretamente su inminente desaparición.

En todo caso, cuando mi teléfono suena a las tres y veinte de la madrugada, no me sorprende demasiado. Es Deck, con la doble noticia de que los federales han hecho una redada en nuestro bufete poco después de la medianoche y que Bruiser ha huido de la ciudad. Eso no es todo. Nuestros antiguos despachos han sido precintados por orden judicial y es probable que los federales quieran hablar con todos los empleados del bufete. Y, lo más sorprendente, Prince Thomas parece haber huido con su amigo y abogado.

Imagínate a esos dos gorilas, dice Deck por teléfono con una risita, con sus barbas y su largo pelo canoso, intentando pasar de incógnito por los aeropuertos.

Se supone que hoy, a primera hora, se dictarán las acusaciones oficiales. Deck sugiere que nos reunamos en nuestro nuevo bufete alrededor de las doce del mediodía y, puesto que no tengo nada mejor que hacer, acepto.

Contemplo el techo oscuro durante media hora, hasta que me harto. Salgo a caminar descalzo por el césped fresco y húmedo, y me tumbo en la hamaca. Un personaje como Prince inspira rumores variopintos. Adoraba el dinero y en mi primer día de trabajo en Yogi's, una camarera me contó que el ochenta por ciento no se declaraba. A los empleados nos encantaba chismorrear y especular sobre las cantidades que lograba ocultar.

Tenía también otros negocios. El testigo de un juicio sobre negocios fraudulentos declaró hace un par de años que el noventa por ciento de los ingresos de cierto bar *topless* era en dinero al contado, y que el sesenta por ciento del mismo no se declaraba. Si Bruiser y Prince eran realmente propietarios de uno o varios clubes de comercio carnal, tenían una mina de oro.

Se rumoreaba que Prince tenía una casa en México, cuentas bancarias en el Caribe, una amante negra en Jamaica, un cortijo en Argentina y otras cosas que no recuerdo. Había una puerta misteriosa en su despacho, tras la que se suponía la existencia de un pequeño cuarto lleno de cajas de billetes de veinte y cien dólares.

Si ha huido, espero que esté a salvo, que haya logrado llevarse una buena parte de su preciado dinero y que nunca lo atrapen. No me importa lo que presuntamente haya hecho, es mi amigo.

Dot me ofrece una silla junto a la mesa de la cocina, la misma silla, y me sirve un café instantáneo, en la misma taza. Es temprano y el olor a grasa de tocino impregna el aire de la abigarrada cocina. Buddy está ahí, declara con un ademán. No me molesto en mirar.

Donny Ray está muy deteriorado, dice, y hace dos días que no se levanta de la cama.

—Ayer se celebró la primera vista en el juzgado —le comunico.

—¿Ya?

—No fue un juicio ni nada por el estilo. Sólo una vista preliminar. La compañía de seguros intenta que se desestime el caso y estamos librando una gran batalla.

Procuro expresarme con claridad, pero no estoy seguro de que me entienda. Dot mira hacia el jardín a través de las sucias ventanas, aunque no en dirección al Fairlane. No parece importarle.

Eso me resulta curiosamente reconfortante. Si el juez Hale hace lo que creo que se propone y no logramos que otro juzgado admita la demanda, este caso habrá terminado. Puede que toda la familia se haya dado por vencida. Tal vez no les importe que fracasemos.

Cuando venía en mi coche he decidido que no mencionaría al juez Hale y sus amenazas. Sólo complicaría nuestra discusión. Sobrará tiempo para mencionarlo más adelante, cuando no tengamos otra cosa de que hablar.

—La compañía de seguros ha hecho una oferta para zanjar el caso.

—¿Qué clase de oferta?

—Cierta suma de dinero.

—¿Cuánto?

—Setenta y cinco mil dólares. Calculan que eso será lo que les pagarán a sus abogados por defender el caso y nos lo ofrecen ahora para saldarlo definitivamente.

Se le suben claramente los colores a las mejillas y aprieta la mandíbula.

—Esos hijos de perra ahora creen que pueden comprarnos, ¿no es cierto?

—Sí, eso es lo que creen.

—Donny Ray no necesita el dinero. Lo que necesitaba era un trasplante de *meula* el año pasado. Ahora es demasiado tarde.

—Estoy de acuerdo.

Levanta su paquete de cigarrillos de la mesa y enciende uno. Tiene los ojos húmedos e irritados. Estaba equivocado. Esta madre no se ha dado por vencida. Quiere sangre.

—¿Qué se supone que debemos hacer con setenta y cinco mil dólares? Donny Ray estará muerto, y sólo quedaremos él y yo —dice moviendo la cabeza en dirección al Fairlane—. Son unos hijos de perra.

—Estoy de acuerdo.

—Supongo que les ha dicho que aceptaríamos el dinero, ¿no es cierto?

—Claro que no. No puedo cerrar el caso sin su aprobación. Tenemos hasta mañana por la mañana para tomar una decisión.

Sale a relucir de nuevo la cuestión de la desestimación. Tendremos derecho a apelar ante cualquier veredicto adverso por parte del juez Hale. Podría tardar aproximadamente un año, pero contamos con buenas posibilidades para luchar. Eso, sin embargo, es algo de lo que prefiero no hablar ahora.

Permanecemos un largo rato en silencio, ambos perfectamente contentos de pensar y esperar. Intento organizar mis pensamientos. Sólo Dios sabe lo que pulula por su cerebro. Pobre mujer.

—Creo que debemos hablar con Donny Ray —dice después de apagar su cigarrillo en el cenicero.

La sigo a través de la oscura sala de estar y por un corto pasillo. La puerta de Donny Ray está cerrada y en la misma hay un cartel de PROHIBIDO FUMAR. Golpea suavemente y entramos. La habitación está limpia y ordenada. Desde un rincón sopla un ventilador. La ventana, con tela mosquitera, está abierta. Elevado al pie de la cama hay un televisor y junto al mismo, cerca de sus almohadas, una mesilla llena de frascos de líquidos y pastillas.

Donny Ray yace tieso como una tabla, con una sábana recogida bajo su frágil cuerpo. Me brinda una radiante sonrisa al verme, e indica el lugar junto a él donde quiere que me siente. Obedezco. Dot se coloca al otro lado.

Intenta seguir sonriendo cuando se esfuerza por convencerme de que hoy se siente bien, todo ha mejorado. Sólo está un poco cansado, eso es todo. Su voz es grave y laboriosa, sus palabras apenas audibles. Escucha atentamente cuando relato de nuevo lo sucedido en la vista de ayer y explico lo de la oferta. Dot sostiene su mano derecha.

—¿Aumentarán la cantidad? —pregunta.

Es una cuestión sobre la que Deck y yo hablamos ayer durante el almuerzo. Great Benefit ha dado un salto asombroso de cero a setenta y cinco mil. Ambos sospechamos que quizá suban a cien mil, pero no me atrevería a ser tan optimista ante mis clientes.

—Lo dudo —respondo—. Pero podemos intentarlo. Lo único que pueden hacer es negarse.

—¿Tú cuánto te llevas? —pregunta.

Le explico que según nuestro contrato me corresponde un tercio del total.

—Eso significa que cincuenta mil dólares son para ti y papá —dice mirando a su madre.

—¿Qué vamos a hacer con cincuenta mil dólares? —pregunta Dot.

—Acabar de pagar la casa, comprar un nuevo coche y guardar un poco para cuando seáis viejos.

—No quiero su maldito dinero.

Donny Ray cierra los ojos y se queda momentáneamente dormido. Yo contemplo los frascos de medicamentos. Cuando despierta me toca el brazo, intenta apretarlo y dice:

—¿Tú quieres aceptar la oferta, Rudy? Parte del dinero es tuyo.

—No. No quiero aceptarla —respondo con plena convicción, mirándole primero a él y luego a su madre, que escucha atentamente—. No ofrecerían ese dinero si no estuvieran preocupados. Quiero desenmascarar a esa gentuza.

Un abogado tiene la obligación de ofrecerles siempre a sus clientes el mejor consejo posible, independientemente de sus propias circunstancias económicas. No me cabe la menor duda de que podría persuadir a los Black para que aceptaran la oferta. Con poco esfuerzo, lograría convencerlos de que el juez Hale está a punto de desestimar el caso y el dinero que está ahora sobre la mesa desaparecerá para siempre. Podría pintarles un cuadro apocalíptico y esas personas a quien tanto han pisoteado no tendrían dificultad en creérselo.

Sería fácil. Y yo me embolsaría unos honorarios de veinticinco mil dólares, cantidad que en estos momentos me resulta incluso difícil comprender. Pero he superado la tentación. Lo he reflexionado a primera hora de esta mañana en la hamaca y he hecho la paz conmigo mismo.

No sería difícil alejarme en este momento de la profesión jurídica. Daré el próximo paso y me retiraré antes de vender a mis clientes.

Dejo a madre e hijo en la habitación, con la firme esperanza de no volver mañana para comunicarles que el caso ha sido sobreseído.

Hay por lo menos cuatro hospitales a poca distancia de Saint Peter. Hay también una Facultad de Medicina, una Facultad de Odontología, e incontables consultorios médicos. La comunidad médica de Memphis se ha concentrado en una zona de seis manzanas, entre Union y Madison. En el propio Madison hay un edificio de ocho plantas, exactamente frente a Saint Peter, conocido como Peabody Medical Arts Building. Un túnel elevado para peatones cruza la calle, a fin de que los médicos puedan ir y venir de sus consultorios al hospital. El edificio está consagrado exclusivamente a la medicina y uno de sus consultorios es el del doctor Eric Craggdale, cirujano ortopédico, que se encuentra en el tercer piso.

Ayer le hice una serie de llamadas anónimas y averigüé lo que deseaba. Espero en el enorme vestíbulo de Saint Peter, un piso por encima del nivel de la calle, y observo el aparcamiento alrededor del Peabody Medical Arts Building. A las once menos veinte veo un Volkswagen Rabbit que sale de Madison y entra en el abarrotado aparcamiento. Kelly se apea del vehículo.

Está sola, como era de esperar. Hace una hora he llamado a su marido a su lugar de trabajo, he preguntado por él y he colgado cuando se ha puesto al teléfono. Apenas veo la parte superior de la cabeza de Kelly cuando se esfuerza por salir del coche. Camina con muletas, sortea numerosas hileras de coches aparcados y se dirige hacia el edificio.

Subo al siguiente piso por una escalera automática y cruzo Madison por el túnel de cristal para peatones. Estoy nervioso, pero no tengo prisa.

La sala de espera está llena de gente. Ella está sentada de espaldas a la pared, hojeando una revista, con una escayola en su tobillo fracturado que ahora le permite andar. La silla contigua está vacía y me instalo en la misma antes de que se percate de mi presencia.

Al verme parece sobresaltada, pero me brinda inmediatamente una radiante sonrisa de bienvenida. Mira nerviosa a su alrededor. Nadie nos observa.

—Sigue leyendo tu revista —susurro al tiempo que abro un ejemplar del *National Geographic*.

—¿Qué estás haciendo aquí? —pregunta levantando la revista *Vogue* casi a la altura de los ojos.

—Tengo molestias en la espalda.

Mueve la cabeza y mira a su alrededor. La mujer que está sentada a su lado intenta mirarnos, pero un collarín le impide mover la cabeza. ¿Por qué preocuparnos, si ninguno de los presentes nos conoce?

—¿Quién es tu médico? —pregunta.

—Craggdale —respondo.

—Muy gracioso.

Kelly Riker era hermosa cuando estaba en el hospital con una simple bata, una contusión en la mejilla y sin maquillar. Ahora me resulta imposible dejar de mirarla. Lleva una camisa blanca ligeramente almidonada, como la que una joven universitaria le pediría prestada a su novio, y un pantalón corto color caqui arremangado. Su cabellera oscura desciende más allá de los hombros.

—¿Es bueno? —pregunto.

—Como cualquier otro.

—¿Te había visitado antes?

—No empieces, Rudy. No quiero hablar de ello. Creo que deberías marcharte —dice con firmeza, pero sin levantar la voz.

—Es curioso, ¿sabes? He estado pensándolo. A decir verdad, he pasado mucho tiempo pensando en ti y en lo que debería hacer.

Hago una pausa en el momento en que pasa un hombre en una silla de ruedas.

—¿Y bien? —pregunta.

—Todavía no lo sé.

—Creo que deberías marcharte.

—No lo dices en serio.

—Sí.

—No puedo creerlo. Tú quieres que no me aleje, que me mantenga en contacto, que te llame de vez en cuando, de modo que la próxima vez que te rompas algún hueso tengas a alguien que se preocupe por ti. Eso es lo que deseas.

—No habrá una próxima vez.

—¿Por qué no?

—Porque ahora ha cambiado. Intenta dejar de beber. Ha prometido no volver a ponerme la mano encima.

—¿Y te lo crees?

—Sí.

—No es la primera vez que te lo promete.

—¿Por qué no te marchas? Y no me llames, ¿vale? Sólo sirve para empeorar la situación.

—¿Por qué? ¿Por qué empeora la situación?

Titubea unos instantes, deja la revista sobre las rodillas y me mira.

—Porque conforme pasan los días pienso menos en ti.

Es ciertamente agradable saber que ha pensado en mí. Saco una tarjeta de visita del bolsillo con mi antigua dirección, la del local actualmente precintado por diversas autoridades gubernamentales, escribo mi número de teléfono en el reverso de la misma y se la entrego.

—De acuerdo. No volveré a llamarte. Si me necesitas, éste es el número de mi casa. Si te lastima, quiero saberlo.

Coge la tarjeta. Le doy un fugaz beso en la mejilla y abandono la sala de espera.

En el sexto piso del mismo edificio hay una extensa unidad de oncología. El doctor Walter Kord es el médico de Donny Ray, que actualmente se limita a recetarle píldoras y otros medicamentos a la espera de la muerte. Kord fue quien prescribió la primera sesión de quimioterapia y realizó las pruebas necesarias para determinar que Ron Black era el donante ideal para el trasplante de médula ósea a su hermano gemelo. Será un testigo fundamental para el juicio, en el supuesto de que llegue a celebrarse.

Dejo una carta de tres páginas a su recepcionista. Deseo hablar con él cuando le parezca oportuno, preferiblemente sin que me cobre la visita. Por regla general, los médicos detestan a los abogados y exigen cantidades exorbitantes de dinero para hablar con nosotros. Pero Kord y yo estamos en el mismo bando, y no tengo nada que perder al intentar establecer un diálogo con él.

Estoy sumamente nervioso cuando avanzo por esta calle, en este conflictivo barrio de la ciudad, sin prestar atención al tráfico, e intentando en vano leer los números descoloridos de las casas. La zona da la sensación de haber sido abandonada, con buena razón, pero ahora está en proceso de rehabilitación. Todos los edificios son de dos o tres pisos de altura, con media manzana de profundidad y fachadas de ladrillo y cristal. La mayoría están adosados y sólo de vez en cuando los separa un callejón. Muchos siguen tapiados y algunos se incendiaron tiempo atrás. Paso frente a un par de restaurantes, uno de ellos con mesas en la acera bajo una marquesina, pero sin clientes, una tintorería y una floristería.

La tienda de antigüedades Buried Treasures está en una esquina, en un edificio bastante pulcro de ladrillo gris oscuro, con toldos rojos sobre las ventanas. Tiene dos plantas y cuando levanto la cabeza para mirar el primer piso, tengo la sensación de haber encontrado mi nuevo domicilio.

Puesto que no veo otra puerta, entro en la tienda de antigüedades. En su diminuto vestíbulo veo una escalera, con una tenue luz arriba.

Deck me espera cargado de orgullo, con una radiante sonrisa.

—¿Qué te parece? —pregunta, a pesar de que todavía no he tenido oportunidad de ver nada—. Cuatro habitaciones, unos noventa metros, más los servicios. No está mal —dice dándome unos golpecitos en el hombro. Avanza, se vuelve y abre los brazos de par en par—. He pensado que ésta podría ser la sala de recepción y tal vez el despacho de una secretaria, cuando la tengamos. Sólo necesita una capa de pintura. Todos los suelos son de madera noble —agrega, y da un taconazo, como si no pudiera verlo—. El techo está a tres metros y medio de altura. Las planchas de yeso que recubren las paredes facilitan su pintura —añade con un gesto para que lo siga y salimos por una puerta a un pequeño pasillo—. Un cuarto a cada lado. Éste es el mayor y creo que es el que tú necesitas.

Entro en mi nuevo despacho y me llevo una agradable sorpresa. Mide aproximadamente cuatro y medio por cuatro y medio, con una ventana que da a la calle. Está vacío, limpio y con un bonito suelo.

—Y aquí está el tercer cuarto. He pensado que podríamos utilizarlo como sala de conferencias. Yo trabajaré aquí, pero lo mantendré ordenado.

Se esfuerza por complacerme y casi me da pena. Tranquilízate, Deck, me gustan las dependencias. Buen trabajo.

—Aquí está el retrete. Hay que limpiarlo, pintarlo y tal vez llamar a un fontanero —dice ya de regreso hacia la entrada—. ¿Qué te parece?

—Nos servirá, Deck. ¿Quién es el propietario?

—El comerciante de trastos de la planta baja. Un viejo y su mujer. Por cierto, tienen algunas cosas que pueden interesarnos: mesas, sillas, lámparas, e incluso algunos viejos archivos. Es barato, no tiene mal aspecto y de algún modo encaja con la decoración del piso. Además, nos lo venderá a plazos. Les encanta la perspectiva de tener a alguien más en la casa. Creo que les han robado un par de veces.

—Muy reconfortante.

—Sí. Aquí hay que tener cuidado —responde al tiempo que me entrega un muestrario cromático—. Me parece que lo más indicado es un blanco partido. Es lo menos costoso y más fácil de aplicar. La compañía telefónica estará aquí mañana. La electricidad ya funciona. Fíjate en esto.

Junto a la ventana hay una mesilla, sobre la cual hay algunos papeles y un televisor en blanco y negro.

Deck ha pasado ya por la imprenta y me muestra varios formatos de logotipos para nuestro nuevo bufete, todos ellos con mi nombre en grandes letras y el suyo, más discreto, en una esquina como pasante.

—Los he conseguido en una imprenta muy bien de precio. Tardan un par de días en servir el pedido. Yo diría unas quinientas hojas y sobres. ¿Hay alguno que te guste?

—Me los estudiaré esta noche.

—¿Cuándo quieres pintar?

—Bueno, supongo que podríamos...

—Creo que podríamos hacerlo en un día si nos aplicamos a fondo, en el supuesto, claro está, de que baste con una capa. Compraré la pintura y demás utensilios esta tarde, y procuraré empezar los preparativos. ¿Estarás disponible mañana?

—Desde luego.

—Debemos tomar algunas decisiones. ¿Adquirimos un fax ahora o esperamos? No olvides que los de la compañía telefónica vendrán mañana. ¿Y una fotocopiadora? Yo diría que no en este momento, podemos reunir todos los originales y pasaré por la copistería una vez al día. Necesitaremos un contestador automático. Uno de buena calidad cuesta ochenta pavos. Yo lo compraré, si te parece. Y debemos abrir una cuenta bancaria. Conozco al director de una sucursal del First Trust que dice que nos dará treinta cheques mensuales gratuitos y el dos por ciento de interés de nuestro dinero. Unas condiciones inmejorables. Debemos pedir los cheques, porque habrá que pagar algunas facturas —dice antes de consultar de pronto su reloj—. Caramba, casi lo había olvidado. Hace una hora se han dado a conocer las acusaciones oficiales —agrega después de pulsar un botón del televisor—, más de un centenar de cargos contra Bruiser, Bennie «Prince» Thomas, Willie McSwane y los demás.

Ya han empezado las noticias de las doce y lo primero que

vemos es una imagen en directo de nuestro antiguo bufete. Unos agentes custodian la puerta principal, de la que en este momento han retirado la cadena. El presentador explica que los empleados del bufete están autorizados a entrar y salir, pero no se les permite retirar nada. La próxima imagen es de la fachada de Vixens, un club *topless* que los federales también han precintado.

—Las acusaciones alegan que Bruiser y Thomas estaban involucrados en tres clubes —dice Deck.

El presentador lo confirma. A continuación muestran unas escenas de nuestro ex jefe refunfuñando en el pasillo de un juzgado durante un viejo juicio. Se han expedido órdenes de detención, pero no hay rastro del señor Stone ni del señor Thomas. Entrevistan al agente encargado del caso y, en su opinión, los mencionados caballeros han abandonado la región. Se efectúa una extensa búsqueda.

—Corre, Bruiser, corre —dice Deck.

El suceso es sensacional porque implica a maleantes locales, a un ostentoso abogado, a varios policías de Memphis y el negocio de la prostitución. Pero le agrega una considerable emoción el hecho de que hayan huido. Prince y Bruiser evidentemente han desaparecido y eso supera la capacidad de comprensión de los periodistas. Muestran imágenes de la detención de unos policías, de otro club *topless*, en esta ocasión con bailarinas desnudas, que las cámaras enfocan de muslos para abajo, y del fiscal federal anunciando las acusaciones a los periodistas.

Luego aparece una imagen que me rompe el corazón. Han clausurado Yogi's, han sujetado las puertas con cadenas y han colocado guardias a su alrededor. Lo denominan el cuartel general de Prince Thomas, el adalid, y a los federales parece sorprenderles no haber encontrado dinero durante la redada de anoche.

—Corre, Prince, corre —digo para mis adentros.

Esta noticia ocupa la mayor parte del telediario del mediodía.

—Me pregunto dónde estarán —dice Deck después de apagar el televisor.

Reflexionamos en silencio unos instantes.

—¿Qué hay ahí? —pregunto, refiriéndome a una caja situada junto a la mesilla.

—Mis sumarios.

—¿Algo que valga la pena?

—Suficiente para pagar las cuentas un par de meses. Algunos pequeños accidentes de tráfico, compensaciones laborales. También hay un caso de una víctima mortal que le quité a Bruiser. A decir verdad, no se lo quité. Me lo entregó la semana pasada y me pidió que revisara unas pólizas de seguro relacionadas con el mismo. De algún modo permaneció en mi despacho y ahora está aquí.

Sospecho que hay otros sumarios en la caja que Deck ha sustraído del despacho de Bruiser, pero no se lo voy a preguntar.

—¿Crees que los federales querrán hablar con nosotros? —pregunto.

—He estado preguntándomelo. No sabemos nada, ni nos hemos llevado ningún sumario que pudiera interesarles. No tenemos por qué preocuparnos.

—Yo lo estoy.

—Yo también.

VEINTICINCO

Sé que en estos días a Deck le cuesta disimular lo emocionado que está. La idea de disponer de su propio despacho y quedarse con la mitad de los beneficios, sin la debida licencia para ejercer como abogado, es terriblemente excitante. Si no me interpongo en su camino, dejará el bufete en condiciones inmejorables en menos de una semana. Nunca había visto tanta energía. Puede que esté excesivamente eufórico, pero no pienso meterme con él.

Sin embargo, cuando el teléfono llama por segunda madrugada consecutiva antes del amanecer y oigo su voz, es difícil ser amable.

—¿Has visto el periódico? —pregunta con alegría, pero sin levantar la voz.

—Estaba durmiendo.

—Lo siento. No te lo vas a creer. Bruiser y Prince aparecen en primera plana.

—¿No podías haber esperado una hora, Deck? —pregunto, decidido a poner fin inmediatamente a esa conducta antisocial—. Si te apetece levantarte a las cuatro, me parece bien. Pero no me llames hasta las siete, o preferiblemente a las ocho.

—Lo siento. Pero hay algo más.

—¿Qué?

—Adivina quién murió anoche.

Con tantos habitantes como tiene Memphis, ¿cómo diablos se supone que puedo saber quién falleció anoche?

—Me rindo —exclamo junto al auricular.

—Harvey Hale.

—¡Harvey Hale!

—Sí. Falleció de un infarto. Cayó muerto junto a su piscina.

—¿El juez Hale?

—Exactamente. Tu amiguete.

Me siento al borde de la cama e intento despejar la niebla de mi cerebro.

—Resulta difícil creerlo.

—Sí, detecto lo afligido que estás. Hay un bonito artículo sobre él en la primera plana de la sección metropolitana, con una gran foto, ataviado con su toga negra, realmente distinguido. Menudo mequetrefe.

—¿Qué edad tenía? —pregunto, como si importara.

—Sesenta y dos. Ejercía como juez desde hace once años. Impresionante historial. Está todo en el periódico. Debes leerlo.

—Sí, lo haré, Deck. Hasta luego.

Esta mañana el periódico parece un poco más pesado y estoy seguro que se debe a que casi la mitad del mismo está dedicado a la hazañas de Bruiser Stone y Prince Thomas. A un artículo le sigue otro sobre el mismo tema. No se les ha visto.

Hojeo la primera sección y paso a la metropolitana, donde me encuentro con una foto bastante antigua de su señoría Harvey Hale. Leo las afligidas reflexiones de sus colegas, incluido su amigo y antiguo compañero de piso Leo F. Drummond.

Es particularmente importante la especulación sobre quién le sustituirá. El gobernador nombrará a un sucesor, que ocupará el cargo hasta las próximas elecciones. El condado es mitad blanco y mitad negro, pero sólo siete de los diecinueve jueces de circuito son negros. Algunos están descontentos con esas cifras. El año pasado, cuando se jubiló un viejo juez blanco, se hicieron grandes esfuerzos para que lo remplazara un juez negro. No sucedió.

Curiosamente, el principal candidato para la vacante del año pasado era mi nuevo amigo Tyrone Kipler, el socio del bufete de Booker educado en Harvard, que nos dio una conferencia sobre Derecho Constitucional cuando nos preparábamos para el examen de colegiatura. Aunque todavía no han transcurrido doce horas desde la muerte del juez Hale, la sabiduría tradicional indica que Kipler será con toda probabilidad su sustituto. El alcalde de Memphis, que es negro y activo, ha declarado que tanto él como otros dirigentes insistirán en el nombramiento de Kipler.

El gobernador había salido de la ciudad y no había manifestado ninguna opinión, pero es demócrata y debe presentarse a la reelección el año próximo. En esta ocasión se verá obligado a seguir la corriente.

A las nueve en punto estoy en la secretaría del juzgado del circuito examinando el sumario de *Black contra Great Benefit*. Antes de su inoportuna muerte, el juez Hale no firmó ninguna orden de sobreseimiento de nuestro caso. Seguimos en el juego.

Hay una corona funeraria en la puerta de su sala. Es muy conmovedor.

Llamo a Tinley Britt desde una cabina, pregunto por Leo F. Drummond y me sorprende oír su voz a los pocos minutos. Le doy mi pésame por el fallecimiento de su amigo y le comunico que mis clientes no aceptan la oferta. Parece sorprendido, pero no dice gran cosa. Pobre hombre, en estos momentos tiene mucho en que pensar.

—Creo que es un error, Rudy —responde pacientemente, como si estuviera de mi lado.

—Puede ser, pero no he sido yo quien ha tomado la decisión, sino mis clientes.

—En tal caso, será la guerra —dice con una voz monótona, sin ofrecer más dinero.

Booker y yo hemos hablado dos veces desde que recibimos los resultados del examen. Como era de suponer, le quita importancia calificándolo de tropiezo temporal e insignificante. Y como también era de esperar, se alegra sinceramente de que yo haya aprobado.

Está ya sentado al fondo de un pequeño restaurante cuando llego y nos saludamos como si no nos hubiéramos visto desde hacía meses. Pedimos té y sopa de abelmosco sin consultar la carta. Sus hijos están bien. Charlene maravillosa.

Está contento ante la perspectiva de que tal vez todavía apruebe el examen de colegiatura. No sabía lo justo que había sido, pero a su nota global sólo le faltaba un punto para aprobar. Ha presentado un recurso de apelación y el tribunal revisa su examen.

Fue un duro golpe para Marvin Shankle que suspendiera. Si no lo aprueba en la próxima convocatoria, el bufete tendrá que reemplazarlo. Booker no puede ocultar su nerviosismo cuando habla de Shankle.

—¿Cómo está Tyrone Kipler? —pregunto.

Booker considera que el nombramiento es cosa hecha. Kipler ha hablado con el gobernador esta mañana y todo encaja perfectamente. El único problema podría ser económico. Como socio del bufete Shankle, gana entre ciento veinticinco y ciento cincuenta anuales. El salario de un juez son sólo noventa mil. Kipler tiene esposa e hijos, pero Marvin Shankle quiere que acepte el nombramiento.

Booker recuerda el caso de los Black. En realidad, recuerda a Dot y a Buddy de nuestro primer encuentro en la residencia del Parque de los Cipreses para ciudadanos de la tercera edad. Le cuento los últimos detalles del caso. Suelta una sonora carcajada cuando le cuento que el sumario está ahora en la sección ocho del juzgado del circuito, a la espera de que un nuevo juez se responsabilice del mismo. Le relato también mi experiencia en el despacho del difunto juez Hale, hace sólo tres días, y la forma en que los antiguos compañeros de Yale, Drummond y Hale, me acechaban alternativamente. Booker me escucha atentamente cuando le hablo de Donny Ray, de su hermano gemelo, y del trasplante que no tuvo lugar por culpa de Great Benefit.

—No te preocupes —sonríe en varias ocasiones—. Si Tyrone ocupa el cargo, lo sabrá todo acerca del caso Black.

—¿Hablarás con él?

—¿Que si hablaré con él? Le soltaré un discurso. No puede soportar a Trent & Brent y detesta las compañías de seguros, las acusa constantemente ante los tribunales. ¿Quién crees que son sus presas? ¿Los blancos de clase media?

—Todo el mundo.

—Tienes razón. Tendré mucho gusto en hablar con Tyrone. Y me escuchará.

Llega la sopa de abelmosco y le agregamos tabasco, Booker más que yo. Le hablo de mi nuevo despacho, pero no de mi nuevo socio. Me formula un sinfín de preguntas sobre mi anterior bufete. Todo el mundo en la ciudad habla de Bruiser y Prince.

Le cuento todo lo que sé, con algunos embellecimientos.

VEINTISÉIS

En esta época de juzgados saturados y jueces con exceso de trabajo, el difunto Harvey Hale dejó los casos pendientes muy bien organizados y sin demoras. Ello se debe a ciertas buenas razones. En primer lugar, era perezoso y prefería jugar al golf. En segundo lugar, sobreseía con mucha facilidad los casos que agraviaban su sentimiento de protección de las compañías de seguros y grandes empresas. Por ello, la mayoría de los abogados de los demandantes lo eludían.

Hay formas de eludir a ciertos jueces, pequeños trucos utilizados por los abogados veteranos que mantienen buenas relaciones con el personal administrativo de los juzgados. Nunca comprenderé por qué Bruiser, con veinte años de experiencia como abogado, me permitió que presentara el caso Black sin tomar medidas para eludir a Harvey Hale. Ése es otro de los asuntos que quiero discutir con él, si algún día regresa.

Pero Hale ha desaparecido y la vida es nuevamente ecuánime. Tyrone Kipler heredará pronto una lista de casos pendientes, que clama acción.

En respuesta a años de crítica tanto por parte de legos como de abogados, hace poco se reformaron las normas de procedimiento con el propósito de acelerar los procesos judiciales. Se han establecido límites de tiempo obligatorios para todos los trámites preliminares. Se ha concedido a los jueces más autoridad para condensar la litigación y se les estimula a que participen más activamente en las negociaciones. Han entrado en vigor numerosos decretos y normativas, destinados a simplificar el sistema jurídico civil.

Uno de los numerosos procedimientos de la nueva reglamentación es el denominado comúnmente de «vía rápida», destinado a acelerar el proceso de ciertos casos con relación a otros. El término «vía rápida» quedó incorporado inmediatamente a nuestra jerga jurídica. Las partes involucradas pueden solicitar que su caso siga el proceso de la vía rápida, aunque raramente ocurre. Es sumamente inusual que un acusado tenga prisa por comparecer ante un tribunal. Por consiguiente, el juez tiene autoridad para utilizarlo a su albedrío. Suele hacerse cuando los hechos son evidentes, las circunstancias claramente definidas, aunque virulentamente disputadas, y lo único que se necesita es un veredicto del jurado.

Puesto que *Black contra Great Benefit* es mi único verdadero caso, quiero que siga el procedimiento de vía rápida, y se lo cuento a Booker por la mañana mientras tomamos café. Luego Booker se lo cuenta a Kipler. El sistema jurídico en funcionamiento.

Al día siguiente de su nombramiento, Tyrone Kipler me llama a su despacho, el mismo en el que había estado no hace mucho cuando lo ocupaba Harvey Hale. Ahora es diferente. Los libros y efectos personales de Hale están siendo empaquetados. Los polvorientos estantes están vacíos. Las cortinas están abiertas. El escritorio de Hale ha sido retirado y para charlar nos sentamos en unas sillas plegables.

Kipler tiene menos de cuarenta años, habla en un tono suave y mira sin parpadear. Es increíblemente inteligente y se le pronostica una brillante carrera como juez federal algún día. Le doy las gracias por haberme ayudado a aprobar el examen de colegiatura.

Charlamos de todo un poco. Hace amables comentarios sobre Harvey Hale, pero le sorprende la escasez de casos pendientes en lista de espera. Ha revisado ya todos los sumarios abiertos y señalado algunos para acelerar su proceso. Está listo para entrar en acción.

—¿Entonces considera que el caso Black debería proceder por vía rápida? —pregunta en un tono lento y mesurado.

—Sí, señor. El asunto es simple. No habrá muchos testigos.

—¿Cuántas pruebas documentales?

Todavía no he presentado la primera.

—No estoy realmente seguro. Menos de diez.

—Tendrá problemas con los documentos —responde—. Siempre ocurre con las compañías de seguros. He demandado a muchas de ellas y nunca entregan todos los papeles. Tardaremos algún tiempo en conseguir todos los documentos a los que tiene derecho.

Me gusta que diga «tardaremos». Y no tiene nada de malo. El papel del juez, entre otros, es el de instructor. Su obligación es la de ayudar a ambas partes a conseguir las pruebas a las que tienen derecho. Aunque Kipler parece manifestar cierta parcialidad hacia nosotros. Pero tampoco creo que eso tenga nada de malo, Drummond dominó a Harvey Hale durante muchos años.

—Presente una petición para que el caso proceda por vía rápida —dice, mientras toma notas en un cuaderno—. La defensa se opondrá. Celebraremos una vista. A no ser que oiga algo sumamente persuasivo por parte del demandado, otorgaré la petición. Concederé cuatro meses para cerrar el sumario, eso debería bastar para presentar todas las pruebas documentales, intercambiar documentos, declaraciones escritas, etcétera. Cuando el sumario esté completo, fijaré la fecha del juicio.

Respiro hondo. Me parece terriblemente rápido. La idea de enfrentarme tan pronto a Leo F. Drummond y compañía en la sala, frente a un jurado, es aterradora.

—Estaremos listos —respondo, sin saber lo que debo hacer a continuación y con la esperanza de parecer más seguro de lo que me siento.

Charlamos un poco más y luego me marcho. Me dice que lo llame si tengo alguna duda.

Una hora después estoy a punto de llamarle. Al regresar a mi despacho me encuentro con un grueso sobre de Tinley Britt. Leo F. Drummond, además de afligido por su amigo, ha estado muy ocupado. La máquina de las peticiones funciona a todo vapor.

Ha presentado una petición para asegurar los costes, un delicado bofetón en mi cara y la de mis clientes. Puesto que todos somos pobres, Drummond alega estar preocupado por nuestras posibilidades para pagar los costes. Esto podría llegar a ocurrir si perdiéramos el juicio y el juez nos ordenara pagar los gastos de ambas partes. Ha presentado también una petición solicitando que el juez nos imponga sanciones económicas a mí y a mis clientes por iniciar un pleito que califica de sumamente frívolo.

La primera petición es puro exhibicionismo. La segunda es claramente malintencionada. Ambas van acompañadas de sendos informes, elegantes, con sus correspondientes notas a pie de página, índice y bibliografía.

Después de leerlas atentamente por segunda vez, llego a la conclusión de que Drummond las ha presentado para demostrarme algo. Sería sumamente inusual obtener satisfacción alguna de dichas peticiones y creo que su propósito ha sido simplemente el de mostrarme la cantidad de documentos que las tropas de Trent & Brent son capaces de producir en breve tiempo, y sobre temas insignificantes. Puesto que ambas partes deben responder a las peticiones de la parte contraria, y que yo me he negado a aceptar su oferta, Drummond me comunica que va a asfixiarme con papeleo.

Los teléfonos todavía no han empezado a llamar. Deck está en algún lugar del centro de la ciudad. No quiero adivinar por dónde puede estar deambulando. Dispongo de mucho tiempo para consagrarlo al juego de las peticiones. Me motiva el recuerdo de mi triste cliente y la estafa de la que ha sido objeto. Yo soy el único abogado de Donny Ray y se necesitará mucho más que papeleo para arredrarme.

Me he acostumbrado a llamar a Donny Ray todas las tardes, generalmente alrededor de las cinco. Cuando lo llamé por primera vez hace unas semanas, Dot mencionó lo mucho que significaba para él, y he procurado llamarlo todos los días desde entonces. Hablamos de diversas cosas, pero nunca de su enfermedad ni del pleito. Procuro recordar algo gracioso durante el transcurso del día y lo reservo para él. Sé que las llamadas se han convertido en una parte importante de su vida menguante.

Hoy da la sensación de sentirse fuerte, me cuenta que se ha levantado para sentarse en la terraza y que le encantaría salir unas horas, lejos de la casa y de sus padres.

Paso a recogerlo a las siete. Cenamos en un restaurante del barrio, especializado en carne asada. Recibe algunas miradas, pero no parece importarle. Hablamos de su infancia y comentamos anécdotas de antaño, cuando pandillas de chiquillos corrían por las calles. Nos reímos, probablemente en su caso por primera vez desde hace meses. Pero la conversación le fatiga. Apenas toca la comida.

Cuando acaba de oscurecer, llegamos a un prado cerca del parque de atracciones, donde se juegan dos partidos de béisbol en campos adjuntos. Observo atentamente ambos juegos cuando entramos en el aparcamiento. Busco un equipo con camiseta amarilla.

Dejamos el coche bajo un árbol, a lo largo de la línea derecha del campo. No hay nadie cerca de nosotros. Saco dos sillas de jardín plegables del maletero, que me he llevado prestadas del garaje de la señorita Birdie, y ayudo a Donny Ray a sentarse en una de ellas. Puede caminar solo y se empeña en hacerlo con la menor ayuda posible.

Estamos a finales de verano y la temperatura cuando oscurece oscila todavía alrededor de los treinta grados. La humedad es literalmente palpable. Se me pega la camisa en medio de la espalda. La desgastada bandera del mástil a medio campo permanece perfectamente inmóvil.

El campo es bonito y bien nivelado, con espeso césped recién cortado en la periferia. En el terreno de juego no hay césped, sino arena. Hay vestuarios, gradas, árbitros, marcador iluminado y tribuna. Esto es la primera división, la alta competición de aficionados al béisbol, con equipos formados por excelentes jugadores. O por lo menos eso creen ellos.

Los contendientes son PFX Freight, el equipo con camiseta amarilla, y Army Surplus, el equipo con camiseta verde y el apodo «artilleros» estampado sobre la misma. Y se lo toman en serio. Charlan y discuten animadamente, se alientan mutuamente y de vez en cuando les chillan a los contrincantes. Se lanzan de cabeza, discuten con los árbitros y arrojan el bate cuando la pelota sale del campo.

Yo jugué al béisbol como aficionado en la universidad, pero nunca llegó a entusiasmarme. Aquí parece que el objetivo es lanzar la pelota más allá de la verja, lo demás no importa. Eso ocurre de vez en cuando y entonces el pavoneo del bateador hace que Babe Ruth parezca un monaguillo. Casi todos los jugadores tienen poco más de veinte años, están en buena forma física, son sumamente engreídos y van mejor equipados que los profesionales: guantes en ambas manos, anchas muñequeras, líneas negras en las mejillas y otro tipo de guantes para *fielding*.

A la mayoría todavía no les ha descubierto nadie. Aún conservan la esperanza.

Hay algunos jugadores de edad más avanzada, con barrigas más grandes y pies más lentos. Es cómico verlos correr entre bases y perseguir la pelota cuando se desplaza por el aire. Casi se oye el ruido de los músculos que bambolean. Pero se aplican con mayor intensidad al juego que los jóvenes. Tienen algo que demostrar.

Donny Ray y yo hablamos un poco. Le compro palomitas de maíz y un refresco. Me da las gracias por el refrigerio y una vez más por haberle traído.

Presto particular atención al jugador de la tercera base del PFX, un joven musculoso de gran agilidad en los pies y las manos. Es veloz, concentrado, y discute bastante con los jugadores del equipo contrario. A media parte veo que se acerca a la valla junto a los vestuarios y le dice algo a su chica. Kelly sonríe y desde donde estoy veo los hoyuelos de sus mejillas y su dentadura. Cliff se ríe. Le da un fugaz beso en los labios y se reúne con los demás miembros de su equipo, que se preparan para batear.

Parecen un par de tórtolas enamoradas. Él la adora y quiere que sus compañeros vean cómo la besa. Son incapaces de saciarse uno de otro.

Ella se apoya en la verja, con las muletas a su lado y una pequeña escayola en el tobillo. Está sola, lejos de las gradas y de los demás espectadores. No puede verme al otro lado del campo. Pero, por si acaso, llevo puesta una gorra.

Me pregunto qué haría si me reconociera. Probablemente nada, a excepción de ignorarme.

Debería alegrarme de que parezca feliz, en buen estado de salud y se lleve bien con su marido. Al parecer ha dejado de maltratarla, de lo cual me alegro. La idea de que la golpeara con un bate me pone enfermo. Sin embargo es paradójico que la única forma en que conseguiré a Kelly es si sigue maltratándola.

Siento asco de mí mismo por pensarlo.

Ahora es el turno de Cliff como bateador. Acierta la tercera pelota y la manda por encima de los focos de la izquierda, hasta perderla de vista. Ha sido un golpe asombroso y mientras recorre las bases pavoneándose, le chilla algo a Kelly al llegar a la tercera. Es un gran atleta, mucho mejor que todos los demás en el campo. No puedo imaginar lo horrible que sería que me atacara con un bate.

Puede que haya dejado de beber y tal vez, al mantenerse sobrio, deje de maltratarla. Quizá ha llegado el momento de retirarme.

Al cabo de una hora, Donny Ray quiere acostarse. En el coche hablamos de su declaración. Hoy he presentado una petición para solicitarle al tribunal que me permita tomar cuanto antes su declaración escrita, la que será válida durante el juicio. Mi cliente estará pronto demasiado débil para soportar dos horas de preguntas y respuestas ante un montón de abogados, y debemos apresurarnos.

—Es preferible que lo hagamos pronto —dice en un tono suave, cuando paramos frente a su casa.

VEINTISIETE

La situación sería cómica, si no estuviera tan nervioso. Estoy seguro de que a un observador externo le parecería divertido, pero en la sala nadie sonríe. Especialmente yo.

Estoy solo en la mesa de la acusación, cubierta de peticiones e informes meticulosamente ordenados. Tengo dos cuadernos con notas y referencias, estratégicamente organizadas. Deck está a mi espalda, no junto a la mesa donde podría serme útil, sino en una silla pegada a la barra, por lo menos a un par de metros de distancia, y tengo la sensación de estar solo.

Me siento muy aislado.

Al otro lado del pasillo, la mesa de la defensa está densamente poblada. Leo F. Drummond está en el centro, frente al juez, rodeado de asociados. Dos a cada lado. Drummond, que es una lumbrera jurídica de Yale, tiene sesenta años y treinta y seis de experiencia en los juzgados. T. Pierce Morehouse tiene treinta y nueve, se licenció en Yale, es uno de los socios de Trent & Brent y tiene catorce años de experiencia en toda clase de juzgados. B. Dewey Clay Hill III tiene treinta y un años, licenciado en Columbia, no ha alcanzado todavía el rango de socio y tiene seis años de experiencia. M. Alec Plunk hijo tiene veintiocho años, dos años de experiencia, y toma la iniciativa en esta vista, porque estoy seguro de que estudió en Harvard. Su señoría Tyrone Kipler, que preside ahora la sala, estudió también en Harvard. Kipler es negro. Plunk también. No abundan en Memphis los abogados negros educados en Harvard. Se da la casualidad de que tienen uno en Trent & Brent y aquí está, con el indudable propósito de intentar establecer un vínculo con su señoría. Y si los acontecimientos se desenvuelven como es de esperar, un buen día tendremos ahí un jurado. La mitad de los electores registrados en este condado son negros, lo cual hace suponer que el jurado será mitad y mitad. M. Alec Plunk hijo será utilizado, es de suponer, para establecer una armonía y una confianza silenciosas con ciertos miembros del jurado.

Si entre los miembros del jurado hubiera una mujer camboyana, no me cabe la menor duda que Trent & Brent se limitaría a hurgar en su sentina, encontraría otra y la traería a la sala.

El quinto miembro del equipo jurídico de Great Benefit es Brandon Fuller Grone, triste e inexplicablemente carente de números e iniciales. No comprendo por qué no se autodenomina B. Fuller Grone, como correspondería a un auténtico abogado de un gran bufete. Tiene veintisiete años y hace dos que se licenció en la Universidad de Memphis, con el número uno de su promoción y una asombrosa reputación a su espalda. Era un personaje legendario cuando ingresé en la facultad y emulé su ejemplo cuando me preparaba para los exámenes de primer curso.

Excluidos los dos años que M. Alec Plunk hijo trabajó como secretario de un juez federal, hay un total de cincuenta y ocho años de experiencia apretujados alrededor de la mesa de la defensa.

Yo, hace menos de un mes que me he colegiado. Y mi ayudante ha suspendido seis veces el examen.

Hice estos cálculos ayer a altas horas de la noche, cuando circulaba por la biblioteca de la universidad, de la que no acabo de desvincularme. El bufete de Rudy Baylor posee un total de diecisiete libros, todos ellos textos sobrantes de la universidad y prácticamente inútiles.

Sentados detrás de los abogados hay dos individuos, con el inconfundible aspecto de hombres de negocios. Sospecho que son ejecutivos de Great Benefit. Uno de ellos me resulta familiar. Creo que estaba presente en la vista de la petición de sobreseimiento. No le presté mucha atención entonces, ni me preocupan particularmente ahora. Tengo ya bastante en que pensar.

Estoy bastante nervioso, pero si Harvey Hale presidiera la sala, estaría hecho cisco. A decir verdad, probablemente no estaría aquí.

Pero es su señoría Tyrone Kipler quien la preside. Me contó anoche por teléfono, durante una de las numerosas conversaciones que hemos mantenido últimamente, que hoy sería su primer día como presidente de la sala. Ha firmado algunas órdenes y desempeñado pequeñas funciones rutinarias, pero ésta es su primera vista.

Al día siguiente de que Kipler jurara el cargo, Drummond presentó una petición para transferir el caso a un tribunal federal. Alega que Bobby Ott, el agente que les vendió la póliza a los Black, ha sido incluido como acusado por razones completamente erróneas. Ott, según tenemos entendido, está todavía domiciliado en Tennessee. Es un acusado. Los Black, domiciliados también en Tennessee, son los acusadores. Es condición indispensable que acusado y acusador estén domiciliados en diferentes estados, para que sea aplicable la jurisdicción federal. Ott, según nuestra alegación, vive en este estado y ésta es razón suficiente para que el caso no pueda ser federal. Drummond presentó un extenso informe, para apoyar su tesis de que Ott no podía ser acusado.

Cuando Harvey Hale presidía la sala, el tribunal del circuito era un lugar perfecto donde apelar a la justicia. Pero en el momento en que Kipler se responsabilizó del caso, sólo se podía esperar ecuanimidad y justicia de un tribunal federal. Kipler se lo tomó como una afrenta personal. Yo coincidí con él, para lo que pudiera servirle mi opinión.

Estamos todos listos para debatir las peticiones pendientes. Además de su solicitud para transferir el caso, Drummond ha presentado también una para garantizar los costes y otra para imponer sanciones. Consideré ofensiva su petición de sanciones y presenté a mi vez otra petición también de sanciones, alegando que la suya era frívola y malintencionada. Según Deck, la batalla de las sanciones se convierte en un tema aparte en la mayoría de los pleitos, que es preferible no iniciar.

Todo el mundo es capaz de freír una trucha, le gusta repetir. El verdadero arte consiste en pescarla.

Drummond se acerca decididamente al atril. Seguimos un orden cronológico, de modo que habla de su petición para garantizar los costes, que es un asunto de menor importancia. Calcula que los costes pueden ser astronómicos si llega a celebrarse el juicio y, bueno, el caso es que le preocupa mi capacidad y la de mis clientes para hacer frente a los mismos, en el supuesto de que perdamos y el tribunal nos ordene pagarlos.

—Permítame que le interrumpa un momento, señor Drummond —dice parsimoniosamente el juez Kipler, con una voz potente y mesurada—. Aquí tengo su petición y el informe que la acompaña —agrega después de levantar dichos documentos y agitarlos en dirección a Drummond—. Ha hablado durante cuatro minutos y ha dicho exactamente lo mismo que tengo aquí por escrito. ¿Tiene algo nuevo que agregar?

—El caso es, su señoría, que tengo derecho...

—¿Sí o no, señor Drummond? Soy perfectamente capaz de leer y comprender y, dicho sea de paso, usted redacta muy bien. Pero si no tiene nada que agregar, ¿qué estamos haciendo aquí?

Estoy seguro de que esto nunca le había ocurrido al gran Leo Drummond, pero reacciona como si se tratara de algo perfectamente cotidiano.

—Sólo me propongo facilitar la labor del tribunal, su señoría.

—Denegado —dice categóricamente Kipler—. Prosiga.

Drummond sigue sin inmutarse.

—Muy bien. Nuestra próxima petición hace referencia a sanciones. A nuestro parecer...

—Denegado —dice Kipler.

—Con la venia de su señoría.

—Denegado.

Oigo la risita de Deck a mi espalda. Las cuatro cabezas de la mesa de la acusación se agachan simultáneamente para registrar el suceso. Supongo que todos escriben en mayúsculas la palabra «denegado».

—Ambas partes han solicitado sanciones y ambas peticiones quedan denegadas —dice Kipler mirando fijamente a Drummond, pero dándome al mismo tiempo una ligera bofetada.

Es cosa grave interrumpir el discurso de un abogado que habla por trescientos cincuenta dólares por hora. Drummond mira fijamente a Kipler, que está divirtiéndose de lo lindo.

Pero Drummond es un profesional curtido. Nunca delataría que le irritaba un simple juez de circuito.

—Muy bien. Paso a nuestra petición para transferir el caso a un tribunal federal.

—Adelante —dice Kipler—. Pero antes, dígame, ¿por qué no intentó transferirlo cuando el caso estaba en manos del juez Hale?

Drummond tiene la respuesta preparada.

—Entonces el caso era nuevo, su señoría, y todavía investigábamos la participación del acusado Bobby Ott. Ahora que hemos tenido tiempo para analizarlo, somos del parecer de que Ott ha sido incluido con el único propósito de eludir la jurisdicción federal.

—¿De modo que siempre ha deseado presentar el caso ante un tribunal federal?

—Sí, señor.

—¿Incluso cuando Harvey Hale era responsable del mismo?

—Exactamente, su señoría —responde sinceramente Drummond.

La expresión de Kipler refleja claramente que no se lo cree. No hay una sola persona en la sala que se lo crea. Pero es un detalle sin importancia y Kipler ha expresado claramente su opinión.

Drummond prosigue impertérrito con su argumento. Ha presenciado el ir y venir de un centenar de jueces, y no siente el más mínimo miedo ante ninguno de ellos. Tendrán que transcurrir muchos años, y muchos juicios en muchas salas, para que yo deje de sentirme intimidado por esos individuos de toga negra.

Habla durante unos diez minutos y está insistiendo en los mismos puntos señalados en su informe cuando Kipler le interrumpe:

—Discúlpeme, señor Drummond, ¿recuerda usted que hace unos minutos le he preguntado si tenía algo nuevo para presentar ante este tribunal?

Drummond queda paralizado, con la palabra en la boca, y mira fijamente a su señoría.

—¿Lo recuerda usted? —insiste Kipler—. Ha sucedido hace menos de quince minutos.

—Creía que habíamos venido a debatir estas peticiones —responde Drummond con un vestigio de nerviosismo en el tono de su voz.

—Eso es precisamente de lo que se trata. Si tiene algo nuevo que añadir, o tal vez algún punto confuso que desee aclarar, me encantaría oírlo. Pero usted se está limitando a repetir lo que ya tengo en mis manos.

Miro de reojo a mi izquierda y veo unos rostros terriblemente compungidos. Su héroe está siendo humillado. Es un triste espectáculo.

De pronto me percato de que esos muchachos se lo toman más a pecho de lo normal. El verano pasado estuve rodeado de muchos abogados cuando trabajé como pasante en un bufete, y para ellos todos los casos eran por un igual. Se trataba de trabajar duro, acumular unos buenos honorarios y aceptar serenamente los resultados. Siempre hay una docena de casos a la espera.

Percibo una sensación de pánico en su campo y estoy seguro de que no se debe a mi presencia. Es habitual, en los pleitos contra compañías de seguros, que nombren a dos abogados para su defensa. Se presentan siempre por parejas. Independientemente del caso, los hechos, las circunstancias y el trabajo necesario, siempre son dos.

¿Pero cinco? Parece una exageración. Algo sucede en su campo. Esos individuos están asustados.

—Su petición para transferir el caso a un tribunal federal queda denegada, señor Drummond. Seguirá en esta sala —afirma categóricamente Kipler al tiempo que firma la orden.

La decisión no es bien recibida al otro lado del pasillo, aunque procuran no manifestarlo.

—¿Algo más? —pregunta Kipler.

—No, su señoría —responde Drummond, mientras recoge sus papeles y se retira del atril.

Lo observo de reojo. Cuando regresa a la mesa de la defensa, mira fugazmente a los dos ejecutivos y veo que en su mirada se refleja un miedo inconfundible. Se me ponen los pelos de punta en las piernas y los antebrazos.

Ahora Kipler cambia de tema.

—El demandante ha presentado también dos peticiones —dice—. En la primera solicita que se acelere el caso y en la segunda que se tome cuanto antes declaración a Donny Ray Black. Puesto que ambas están en cierto modo relacionadas, señor Baylor, ¿por qué no nos ocupamos de ambas al mismo tiempo?

—Por supuesto, su señoría —respondo ya de pie.

¡Como si se me pudiera ocurrir sugerir lo contrario!

—¿Puede hacer su presentación en diez minutos?

Después de la devastación que acabo de presenciar, cambio inmediatamente de estrategia.

—Con la venia de su señoría, mis informes hablan por sí mismos. En realidad no tengo nada nuevo que agregar.

Qué brillante ese joven abogado. Kipler me brinda una cálida sonrisa y ataca inmediatamente a la defensa.

—Señor Drummond, usted se ha opuesto a que este caso siga la vía rápida. ¿Cuál es el inconveniente?

Hay agitación en la mesa de la defensa, y por fin T. Pierce Morehouse se levanta lentamente y se ajusta la corbata.

—Con la venia de su señoría, si me permite que me dirija a la sala, consideramos que este caso necesita cierto tiempo de preparación para el juicio. En nuestra opinión, acelerar el caso sólo servirá para sobrecargar innecesariamente ambas partes —responde Morehouse en un tono lento y comedido, con palabras cuidadosamente elegidas.

—Bobadas —exclama Kipler, mirándolo fijamente.

—¿Cómo dice?

—Que eso son bobadas. Permítame que le haga una pregunta, señor Morehouse. Como abogado defensor, ¿ha accedido usted alguna vez a que se acelerara un proceso?

Morehouse hace una mueca y mueve ligeramente los pies.

—Pues... desde luego, su señoría.

—Muy bien. Dígame el nombre del caso y la sala donde se presentó.

T. Pierce mira con desesperación a B. Dewey Clay Hill III, quien a su vez mira ansiosamente a M. Alec Plunk hijo. El señor Drummond se niega a levantar la cabeza; prefiere mantener la mirada fija en un sumario terriblemente importante.

—Lo siento, su señoría, tendré que responderle en otro momento.

—Llámeme esta tarde antes de las tres, y si a las tres no lo ha hecho, le llamaré yo. Estoy realmente ansioso por saber cuál es el caso que usted accedió a acelerar.

T. Pierce se dobla por la cintura y espira, como si acabara de recibir una patada en la barriga. Casi puedo oír el zumbido de los ordenadores de Trent & Brent a medianoche, buscando en vano dicho caso.

—Sí, su señoría —responde débilmente.

—Como usted sabe, acelerar un caso depende exclusivamente de mi discreción. Por la presente se concede la petición del demandante. La defensa presentará su respuesta dentro de siete días. Entonces se iniciará el período de presentación de pruebas, que concluirá dentro de ciento veinte días a partir de hoy.

Eso vuelve a agitar a la mesa de la defensa. Los abogados empiezan a intercambiarse papeles y documentos. Drummond y compañía susurran entre sí con el entrecejo fruncido. Los representantes de la gran empresa agachan la cabeza. Es casi divertido.

T. Pierce Morehouse permanece semisentado, con su trasero a escasos centímetros del cuero del asiento y con los brazos y codos preparados para levantarse.

—La última petición solicita que se agilice la declaración de Donny Ray Black —dice su señoría con la mirada fija en la mesa de la defensa—. Estoy seguro de que no querrán oponerse a esto —agrega—. ¿Quién de ustedes, caballeros, desea responder?

Junto con dicha petición presenté una declaración jurada de dos páginas del doctor Walter Kord, donde afirma sin ninguna ambigüedad que a Donny Ray le queda poco tiempo de vida. La respuesta de Drummond estaba repleta de divagaciones y vaguedades; parecía estar demasiado ocupado para molestarse.

T. Pierce se incorpora lentamente, abre las manos, extiende los brazos y empieza a decir algo cuando Kipler le interrumpe.

—No, me dirá que usted conoce mejor el estado de salud del paciente que su propio médico.

—No, señor —responde T. Pierce.

—Y no me dirá tampoco que ustedes se oponen seriamente a esta petición.

Es perfectamente evidente que su señoría está a punto de pronunciar una orden y T. Pierce se sitúa con suma habilidad en terreno neutral.

—Es sólo una cuestión de programación, su señoría. Todavía no hemos presentado nuestra respuesta.

—Sé exactamente cuál será su respuesta. No van a sorprenderme. Y les ha sobrado tiempo para presentar todo lo demás —dice el juez antes de dirigirse de pronto a mí—. ¿Señor Baylor? Deme una fecha.

—Cualquier día, su señoría. A cualquier hora —respondo con una sonrisa.

He ahí la ventaja de no tener otra cosa que hacer.

Los cinco abogados de la mesa de la defensa consultan apresurados sus pequeñas agendas negras, como si les pareciera remotamente posible hallar una fecha en la que estuvieran todos libres.

—Mi agenda está repleta, su señoría —responde Drummond sin levantarse.

La vida de un abogado importante gira en torno a una cosa: su agenda. Drummond nos está diciendo, con mucha soberbia, tanto a Kipler como a mí, que en un futuro próximo estará demasiado ocupado para perder el tiempo con una declaración.

Sus cuatro lacayos asienten y se frotan la barbilla simultáneamente; para mayor asombro, sus agendas están también repletas.

—¿Tiene usted una copia de la declaración jurada del doctor Kord? —pregunta Kipler.

—Sí, señor —responde Drummond.

—¿La ha leído?

—Sí, señor.

—¿Cuestiona su validez?

—Pues...

—Basta con un sí o un no, señor Drummond. ¿Cuestiona usted su validez?

—No.

—En tal caso, ese joven está a punto de morir. ¿Está usted de acuerdo en que debemos tener constancia de su testimonio para que, en su momento, el jurado sepa lo que tiene que decir?

—Por supuesto, su señoría. El caso en que, en estos momentos, mi agenda....

—¿Qué les parece el próximo jueves? —interrumpe Kipler.

La mesa de la defensa se sume en un profundo silencio.

—Me parece bien, su señoría —respondo en voz alta, sin que nadie me preste la menor atención.

—Una semana a partir de hoy —declara Kipler, sin dejar de mirarlos con gran recelo.

Drummond encuentra lo que buscaba y examina el documento en cuestión.

—Tengo un juicio en el tribunal federal a partir del lunes, su señoría. Aquí tengo la orden, si desea examinarla. Su duración estimada será de dos semanas.

—¿Dónde?

—Aquí. En Memphis.

—¿Probabilidades de llegar a un acuerdo?

—Escasas.

Kipler examina durante unos instantes su agenda.

—¿Qué les parece el próximo sábado?

—Me parece bien —repito, sin que una vez más nadie me preste atención.

—¿Sábado?

—Sí, el día veintinueve.

Drummond mira a T. Pierce. Es evidente que el próximo pretexto le corresponde a él. Se levanta lentamente, con su agenda negra en la mano como si fuera de oro.

—Lo siento, su señoría, tengo previsto pasar el fin de semana fuera de la ciudad.

—¿Con qué propósito?

—Asistir a una boda.

—¿La suya?

—No. La de mi hermana.

Estratégicamente les conviene aplazar la declaración hasta que Donny Ray haya fallecido, evitando así que el jurado vea su rostro demacrado y oiga su voz torturada. Y no cabe la menor duda de que, entre los cinco, son capaces de encontrar suficientes excusas para postergar la declaración hasta que yo muera de viejo. Pero el juez Kipler lo sabe.

—Se tomará la declaración el sábado, día veintinueve —declara—. Lamento que dicha fecha pueda resultar inconveniente para la defensa, pero Dios sabe que son bastantes para ocuparse de ello. A uno o dos no se les echará de menos —concluye mientras cierra su agenda. Se apoya sobre los codos y mira con una sonrisa a los abogados de Great Benefit—. ¿Algo más?

Es casi cruel el desprecio con que los trata, pero no alberga rencor. Ha denegado cinco de las seis peticiones, aunque con buen criterio. En mi opinión es perfecto. Además, sé que habrá otras sesiones en esta sala, otras peticiones y vistas preliminares, y sé que también recibiré mis azotainas.

Drummond se pone de pie, se encoge de hombros y examina los numerosos documentos desparramados delante de él sobre la mesa. Estoy seguro de que le apetece decir algo como «gracias por nada, juez», o «¿por qué no corta por lo sano y le entrega al demandante un millón de dólares?». Pero, como de costumbre, actúa como un letrado consumado.

—No, su señoría, esto es todo por ahora —responde, como si Kipler le hubiera ayudado inmensamente.

—¿Señor Baylor? —pregunta su señoría.

—No, señor —respondo con una sonrisa.

Basta por un día. He derrotado a los poderosos en mi primera escaramuza jurídica y no hay que abusar de la buena suerte. Entre yo y el bueno de Tyrone, hemos hecho un buen trabajo.

—Muy bien —concluye con unos suaves golpecitos sobre la mesa—. Se levanta la sesión. Y, señor Morehouse, no olvide llamarme con el nombre de aquel caso que accedió a acelerar.

T. Pierce emite un gemido de dolor.

VEINTIOCHO

El primer mes de negocios con Deck ha producido unos resultados paupérrimos. Hemos ingresado un total de mil doscientos dólares en honorarios: cuatrocientos de Jimmy Monk, un ladronzuelo de tiendas que Deck captó en el juzgado de primera instancia, doscientos de un caso de oficio que Deck consiguió de algún modo extraño y todavía incomprensible, y quinientos de un caso de compensación laboral que Deck le robó a Bruiser antes de abandonar su bufete. Los cien dólares restantes proceden de una pareja de edad madura que entró casualmente en nuestro bufete. Buscaban antigüedades, subieron equivocadamente por la escalera y me sorprendieron echando una siesta en mi despacho. Charlamos amigablemente, una cosa condujo a otra y esperaron mientras mecanografiaba sus testamentos. Me pagaron al contado y se lo comuniqué debidamente a Deck, nuestro contable. De este modo tan ético gané mis primeros honorarios.

Hemos gastado quinientos dólares en el alquiler, cuatrocientos en papel y tarjetas, unos quinientos cincuenta en conexiones y depósitos, ochocientos para el alquiler de equipos telefónicos, incluido el primer mes, trescientos del primer plazo de mesas y otros muebles suministrados por el propietario de la planta baja, doscientos del Colegio de Abogados, trescientos de gastos varios de difícil definición, setecientos cincuenta de un fax, cuatrocientos por la instalación y el primer mes de alquiler de un ordenador barato, y cincuenta de un anuncio en una guía local de restaurantes.

Hemos gastado un total de cuatro mil doscientos cincuenta dólares, en su mayoría, afortunadamente, en gastos iniciales que no se repetirán. Deck lo ha calculado al dedillo. Saldados éstos estima que el bufete nos costará mil novecientos dólares mensuales. Finge estar encantado con nuestro progreso.

Es difícil ignorar su entusiasmo. Vive en el despacho. Está solo, lejos de sus hijos y en una ciudad que no es la suya. No creo que pase mucho rato divirtiéndose por la ciudad. El único interés que ha mencionado tener es por los casinos de Mississippi.

Suele llegar al bufete alrededor de una hora después de llegar yo. Pasa la mayor parte de la mañana en su despacho, hablando por teléfono con Dios sabe quién. Estoy seguro de que atosiga a alguien, o comprueba informes sobre accidentes, o simplemente se relaciona con sus contactos. Todas las mañanas me pregunta si tengo algo para mecanografiar. Hemos comprobado que él mecanografía mucho mejor que yo, y siempre está dispuesto a escribir mis cartas y documentos. Se esfuerza como un endiablado para contestar el teléfono, corre a por café, barre la oficina y se ocupa de todas las fotocopias. No se le caen los anillos y quiere que yo sea feliz.

No se prepara para el examen. Hablamos de ello en una ocasión y cambió rápidamente de tema.

Hacia el mediodía, suele hacer planes para ir a algún lugar indeterminado y ocuparse de algún asunto misterioso. Tengo la certeza de que en algún lugar hay mucha actividad jurídica, tal vez en el tribunal municipal o en el de insolvencias, por donde circulan muchas personas que necesitan abogados. Pero no hablamos de ello. Por la noche visita los hospitales.

En los primeros días dividimos nuestras pequeñas dependencias y definimos nuestros territorios. Deck opina que yo debería pasar la mayor parte del día deambulando por los numerosos juzgados en busca de clientes. Detecto su frustración por mi escasa agresividad. Está harto de mis consideraciones éticas y tácticas. El mundo real es muy agresivo y está lleno de abogados hambrientos que saben pelear sin cuartel, y si uno se queda sentado aquí todo el día, acaba por morirse de hambre. Los buenos casos no llegarán solos ni por casualidad.

Por otra parte, Deck me necesita porque estoy legalmente autorizado a ejercer. Puede que nos repartamos el dinero, pero no es una sociedad igualitaria. Se considera prescindible y por ello se ofrece voluntario para los trabajos más duros. Está perfectamente dispuesto a perseguir ambulancias, deambular por los vestíbulos de edificios federales y acechar en las salas de urgencias de los hospitales porque está satisfecho con el convenio que le concede el cincuenta por ciento. No encontraría mejores condiciones en ningún otro lugar.

Basta con uno, repite una y otra vez. Uno oye eso permanentemente en este negocio. Un caso importante y puedes jubilarte. Ésa es una de las razones por las que los abogados cometen tantas vilezas, como la de poner anuncios a todo color en las páginas amarillas, carteles y pancartas en los autobuses, o la de acechar clientes potenciales por teléfono. Te tapas la nariz, haces caso omiso del hedor de tus actos, e ignoras el desdén de los abogados de los grandes bufetes, porque con uno basta.

Deck está decidido a encontrarlo para nuestro pequeño bufete. Mientras él deambula por la ciudad, yo logro mantenerme ocupado. Hay cinco pequeñas municipalidades incorporadas, adosadas a los límites de la ciudad de Memphis. Cada una de ellas dispone de su propio juzgado municipal, con su correspondiente cupo de jóvenes abogados de oficio para representar a acusados indigentes que han cometido delitos menores. Los jueces y los fiscales son jóvenes que trabajan a tiempo partido, en su mayoría ex alumnos de la Universidad de Memphis que suelen cobrar menos de quinientos dólares mensuales. Tienen bufetes que prosperan en los suburbios y dedican unas horas semanales a la administración de justicia penal. He ido a visitarlos, les he brindado sonrisas y cumplidos, les he expresado mi necesidad de trabajar en sus juzgados, y los resultados han sido variados. Actualmente me han nombrado para representar a seis indigentes, acusados de diversos delitos, desde posesión de drogas, pasando por hurto, hasta escándalo público. Cobraré, a lo sumo, cien dólares por caso y deben cerrarse en menos de dos meses. Después de haberme reunido con mis clientes, discutido con ellos su declaración de culpabilidad, negociado con la acusación y acudido a los suburbios para su comparecencia ante el juez, habré dedicado, como mínimo, cuatro horas a cada caso. Eso supone veinticinco dólares por hora, sin deducir gastos ni impuestos.

Pero, por lo menos, sirve para mantenerme ocupado e ingresar un poco de dinero. Conozco gente, distribuyo tarjetas y les digo a mis nuevos clientes que hablen de mí con sus amigos, que les expliquen que puedo resolver todos sus problemas legales. Pero sólo puede tratarse de otras miserias: divorcios, insolvencias y delitos en general. Es la vida de un abogado.

Deck quiere hacer publicidad cuando podamos permitírnoslo; cree que deberíamos declararnos especialistas en lesiones personales y anunciarnos en la televisión por cable, asegurarnos de que nuestros anuncios aparecen a primera hora de la mañana, a fin de poder llegar a los obreros cuando desayunan, antes de que salgan a sufrir algún percance. También se ha dedicado a escuchar una emisora de *rap* negro, no porque le guste la música, sino por su elevado índice de audiencia y porque, asombrosamente, a ningún abogado se le ha ocurrido todavía anunciarse en la misma. Ha descubierto un enclave. ¡Los abogados del *rap*!

Que Dios se apiade de nosotros.

Me gusta circular por la secretaría del juzgado, coquetear con las secretarias y familiarizarme con el lugar. Los archivos del juzgado son públicos y sus índices están informatizados. Después de descubrir el funcionamiento del ordenador, descubro varios antiguos casos de Leo F. Drummond. El más reciente es de hace dieciocho meses, y el más antiguo de hace ocho años. En ninguno de ellos estaba involucrada Great Benefit, pero en todos defendía a alguna compañía de seguros. Todos acabaron en juicio y el veredicto fue siempre favorable a sus defendidos.

He pasado muchas horas durante las últimas tres semanas estudiando dichos sumarios, tomando muchas páginas de notas y realizando centenares de copias. A continuación he elaborado un extenso interrogatorio, preguntas que una parte le manda a la otra por escrito y bajo juramento. Hay un sinfín de formas de redactar las preguntas y me dedico a imitar las suyas. Estudio los sumarios y elaboro una prolongada lista de documentos que me propongo solicitar a Great Benefit. En algunos casos los rivales de Drummond eran bastante buenos pero en otros eran lastimosos. Sin embargo Drummond parecía llevar siempre la voz cantante.

Analizo sus declaraciones, informes, peticiones, sus conclusiones escritas y sus respuestas a las conclusiones de los demandantes. Leo sus documentos en la cama, por la noche. Memorizo sus órdenes preliminares y leo incluso sus cartas al tribunal.

Después de un mes de delicadas indirectas y sutiles presiones he logrado persuadir a Deck para que haga un viaje relámpago por carretera a Atlanta. Ha pasado un par de días investigando y sus correspondientes noches en moteles baratos. Los gastos corren por cuenta del bufete.

Hoy ha regresado con las noticias que esperaba. La fortuna de la señorita Birdie es escasamente superior a los cuarenta y dos mil dólares. Su segundo marido recibió, efectivamente, una herencia de un hermano perdido en Florida, pero su parte de los bienes era inferior al millón de dólares. Antes de casarse con la señorita Birdie, Anthony Murdine había tenido otras dos esposas, que entrambas habían producido un total de seis hijos. Los hijos, los abogados y Hacienda devoraron casi la totalidad de los bienes. La señorita Birdie recibió cuarenta mil, que por alguna razón dejó en un fondo de inversión de un gran banco de Georgia. Después de cinco años de intrépidas inversiones, el capital había aumentado en unos dos mil dólares.

Sólo parte del sumario había sido declarado secreto, y Deck logró hurgar e importunar a suficientes personas para averiguar lo que deseaba.

—Lo siento —dice después de resumirme lo averiguado y entregarme copias de algunas de las órdenes judiciales.

Estoy decepcionado, pero no sorprendido.

La declaración de Donny Ray Black se había programado inicialmente en nuestro bufete, lo cual me producía cierta angustia. No es que el lugar sea mugriento, pero los despachos son pequeños y casi desprovistos de muebles. En las ventanas no hay cortinas y la cisterna del retrete, situado en unos diminutos servicios, funciona esporádicamente.

No me avergüenzo de nuestras dependencias que, en realidad, tienen cierto encanto. Es el primer bufete de un joven y futuro halcón de la jurisprudencia. Pero está destinado a provocar la burla de los muchachos de Trent & Brent, quienes están acostumbrados a lo más sofisticado. Detesto la idea de tener que soportar su arrogancia al desplazarse a este páramo. Además, no disponemos de bastantes sillas para acomodar a todo el mundo alrededor de nuestra pequeña mesa de conferencias.

El viernes, un día antes de la declaración, Dot me comunica que Donny Ray se ve obligado a guardar cama y no puede abandonar la casa. La preocupación le ha debilitado. Si Donny Ray no puede abandonar su casa, hay sólo un lugar donde se le puede tomar declaración. Llamo a Drummond y me responde que no puede aceptar que no se efectúe en mi despacho. Según él las reglas son las reglas, y no me queda más remedio que aplazarla y notificar de nuevo a todo el mundo. Lo siente muchísimo. Él, evidentemente, desearía aplazarla hasta después del funeral. Cuelgo y llamo al juez Kipler. A los pocos minutos el juez llama a Drummond y, después de unos breves comentarios, se decide tomar la declaración en la casa de Dot y Buddy Black. Curiosamente, Kipler se propone asistir a la misma. Esto es sumamente inusual, pero tiene sus razones. Donny Ray está gravemente enfermo y puede que ésta sea nuestra única oportunidad de tomarle declaración. El tiempo, por consiguiente, es de vital importancia. No es inusual que al tomar declaración estallen grandes conflictos entre los abogados de ambas partes. Entonces suele ser necesario llamar con urgencia al juez, que se ve obligado a resolver la disputa por teléfono. Si el juez es ilocalizable y los abogados son incapaces de ponerse de acuerdo, se anula la declaración y se fija una nueva fecha. Kipler sospecha que Drummond y compañía intentarán malograr el proceso con alguna pelea insignificante, que les sirva de pretexto para retirarse ofendidos.

Pero si Kipler está presente, la declaración se efectuará sin contratiempos. Intervendrá cuando sea preciso y obligará a Drummond a mantener el rumbo. Además es sábado y asegura que no tiene otra cosa que hacer.

Creo que también está preocupado, y con razón, por mi capacidad de ejecución en mi primera declaración.

Anoche no podía conciliar el sueño, pensando en la forma exacta de tomar la declaración en la casa de los Black. Es un lugar oscuro, húmedo y con una pésima iluminación, lo cual es de una gran importancia porque la declaración de Donny Ray se grabará en vídeo. El jurado debe ver su lamentable aspecto. En la casa apenas hay aire acondicionado y la temperatura suele ser de más de treinta grados. Es difícil imaginar a cinco o seis abogados, además del juez, el relator del juzgado, un cámara y Donny Ray en cualquier lugar de la casa en condiciones medianamente cómodas.

En mis pesadillas he imaginado a Dot asfixiándonos con nubes de humo azulado y a Buddy en el jardín, arrojando botellas de ginebra vacías por la ventana. He dormido menos de tres horas.

Llego a la casa de los Black una hora antes de la declaración. Parece más pequeña y calurosa que nunca. Donny Ray está sentado en la cama, mucho más animado, y me asegura que está listo para el desafío. Hemos pasado horas hablando de ello y hace una semana le entregué una lista detallada de mis preguntas y de las que previsiblemente le formularía Drummond. Dice que está en condiciones y detecto en él cierta excitación. Dot prepara café y limpia las paredes. Están a punto de llegar un juez y un grupo de abogados, y según Donny Ray, se ha pasado la noche limpiando. Buddy cruza la sala de estar cuando yo muevo un sofá. Va limpio y aseado. Lleva una camisa blanca, debidamente recogida en la cintura. Me resulta difícil imaginar el esfuerzo de Dot para lograr dicho efecto.

Mis clientes procuran siempre estar presentables, y yo me siento orgulloso de ellos.

Llega Deck cargado de aparatos. Trae una antigua cámara de vídeo, que le ha pedido prestada a un amigo, por lo menos tres veces mayor que cualquier modelo actual. Asegura, sin embargo, que funcionará correctamente. Conoce entonces a los Black. Ellos lo miran con recelo, particularmente Buddy, que ha quedado relegado a quitar el polvo de la mesilla. Deck inspecciona la sala de estar, el comedor y la cocina, y me comunica discretamente que no hay espacio suficiente. Abre un trípode en la sala de estar, derriba un estante de revistas y Buddy le lanza una mala mirada.

La casa está abarrotada de mesillas, taburetes y otros muebles de principios de los sesenta, cubiertos de recuerdos baratos. El calor aumenta minuto a minuto.

Llega el juez Kipler, saluda a todo el mundo, empieza a sudar y a los pocos minutos dice:

—Echemos una ojeada al jardín.

Me sigue por la puerta de la cocina y salimos. A lo largo del muro del fondo, en el extremo opuesto al Fairlane de Buddy, hay un roble, plantado probablemente cuando se construyó la casa, que proporciona una agradable sombra. Deck y yo seguimos a Kipler por la hierba recién cortada, aunque no rastrillada. El juez observa el Fairlane cubierto de gatos al pasar junto al mismo.

—¿Qué tiene esto de malo? —pregunta bajo el árbol.

A lo largo de la verja del fondo se extienden unos densos setos que aíslan el jardín de la parcela vecina. Entre la espesa vegetación crecen cuatro grandes pinos, que impiden el paso de los rayos del sol matutino procedentes del este y convierten la zona bajo el roble en un lugar medianamente tolerable, por lo menos de momento. La luz es abundante.

—Me parece estupendo —respondo, aunque en mi limitadísima experiencia nunca he oído hablar de una declaración al aire libre, y doy gracias a Dios por la presencia de Tyrone Kipler.

—¿Disponemos de un alargo? —pregunta el juez.

—Yo he traído uno —responde Deck, alejándose ya por el césped—. De treinta metros.

La parcela mide, a lo sumo, seis metros y medio de anchura por unos treinta de longitud. El jardín delantero es mayor que el posterior y, por consiguiente, no está lejos. Ni tampoco el Fairlane. En realidad está ahí, casi al alcance de la mano. *Garras*, el gato vigía, aposentado majestuosamente sobre el vehículo, nos observa con recelo.

—Busquemos unas sillas —dice Kipler, controlando perfectamente la situación.

El juez se sube las mangas de la camisa. Entre Dot, Kipler y yo sacamos las cuatro sillas de la cocina, mientras Deck lucha con el cable y los aparatos. Buddy ha desaparecido. Dot nos autoriza a utilizar los muebles del jardín y luego encuentra otras tres sillas manchadas y enmohecidas en un trastero.

Después de pocos minutos levantando y trasladando muebles, Kipler y yo estamos empapados de sudor. También hemos llamado la atención. Algunos de los vecinos han salido de sus escondrijos y nos observan con gran curiosidad. ¿Un negro con vaqueros colocando sillas bajo el roble de los Black? ¿Un extraño personaje, con la cabeza desproporcionadamente voluminosa, extendiendo un cable eléctrico que se le ha enredado en los tobillos? ¿Qué ocurre ahí?

Dos relatoras del juzgado llegan poco antes de las nueve y, lamentablemente, Buddy abre la puerta. Casi huyen, pero Dot las rescata y las conduce a través de la casa hasta el jardín posterior. Por suerte se han puesto pantalón en lugar de falda. Charlan con Deck respecto a los aparatos y el suministro eléctrico.

Drummond y su equipo llegan a las nueve en punto, ni un minuto antes. Lo acompañan sólo dos abogados, B. Dewey Clay Hill III y Brandon Fuller Grone, vestidos como gemelos, con chaqueta azul, camisa blanca de algodón, pantalón caqui almidonado y mocasines. Sólo se diferencian sus corbatas. Drummond no lleva corbata.

Se reúnen con nosotros en el jardín y el entorno parece dejarlos estupefactos. A estas alturas, Kipler, Deck y yo estamos sudorosos y acalorados, y no nos importa lo que piensen.

—¿Sólo tres? —pregunto después de contar los componentes de la defensa.

No les parece gracioso.

—Ustedes se sentarán ahí —dice su señoría, al tiempo que señala tres sillas de cocina—. Cuidado con esos cables.

Deck ha colocado hilos y cables alrededor del árbol, y a Grone parece preocuparle particularmente la posibilidad de electrocutarse.

Dot y yo ayudamos a Donny Ray a levantarse de la cama y a cruzar la casa hasta el jardín. Está muy débil e intenta valerosamente caminar sin ayuda. Cuando nos acercamos al roble, observo atentamente a Drummond cuando ve a Donny Ray por primera vez. Su arrogante rostro permanece impasible y me apetecería decirle: «Fíjate bien, Drummond. Observa lo que ha hecho tu cliente.» Pero no es culpa suya. La decisión de denegar la reclamación fue tomada por alguna persona todavía indeterminada de Great Benefit, mucho antes de que Drummond estuviera al corriente de ello. Sin embargo, es la persona más próxima en quien descargar el odio.

Acomodamos a Donny Ray en una mecedora acolchada. Dot coloca y ordena los cojines a su alrededor, para asegurarse de que esté lo más cómodo posible. Respira con dificultad y su rostro está húmedo. Tiene peor aspecto.

Le presento educadamente al juez Kipler, las dos relatoras del juzgado, Deck, Drummond y los otros dos componentes de Trent & Brent. Está demasiado débil para estrechar la mano y se limita a asentir e intenta sonreír.

Colocamos la cámara exactamente delante de él, con el objetivo a poco más de un metro de su cara. Deck intenta enfocar. Una de las relatoras es videógrafa titulada e intenta que Deck se quite de en medio. En el vídeo aparecerá exclusivamente Donny Ray. Se oirán otras voces, pero la suya será la única cara que verá el jurado.

Kipler me coloca a la derecha de Donny Ray y a Drummond a su izquierda. Su señoría se sienta junto a mí. Ocupamos todos nuestros lugares y acercamos las sillas al testigo. Dot está a pocos pasos detrás de la cámara, observando atentamente todos los movimientos de su hijo.

Los vecinos, muertos de curiosidad, miran por encima de la verja metálica a menos de seis metros y medio. Por una radio a alto volumen, a lo largo de la calle, se oye a Conway Twitty, pero todavía no molesta. Es sábado por la mañana y a lo lejos se oye el zumbido de segadoras de césped y cortadoras de setos.

Donny Ray toma un sorbo de agua y procura prescindir de los cuatro abogados y el juez que lo observan. El propósito de la declaración es evidente: el jurado debe oír ya su testimonio, porque ya habrá muerto cuando se inicie el juicio. Tiene que inspirar compasión. Hasta hace unos pocos años se le habría tomado declaración de la forma convencional: un relator del juzgado registraría las preguntas y respuestas, mecanografiaría la declaración y durante el juicio se la leeríamos al jurado. Pero ha llegado la tecnología. Actualmente muchas declaraciones, especialmente las de testigos moribundos, se graban en vídeo y se muestra la grabación al jurado. Ésta se registrará también según el método convencional, de acuerdo con las instrucciones de Kipler. De ese modo ambas partes y el propio juez podrán consultarla sin tener que mirar todo el vídeo.

El coste de la declaración dependerá de su duración. Las relatoras cobran por página y Deck me ha aconsejado que resuma mis preguntas. Es nuestra declaración, nosotros debemos pagarla, y calcula que costará unos cuatrocientos dólares. Los pleitos son caros.

Kipler le pregunta a Donny Ray si está listo para proceder y luego le ordena a la relatora que le tome juramento. Promete decir la verdad. Puesto que es mi testigo y el propósito de la declaración no es el de indagar, sino el de contar con una prueba suplementaria, mi interrogatorio directo debe ajustarse a las normas de aportación de pruebas. Estoy muy nervioso, pero enormemente aliviado por la presencia de Kipler.

Le pregunto a Donny Ray su nombre, dirección, lugar de nacimiento y algunos datos relacionados con sus padres y demás familia. Cosas básicas, tan fáciles para él como para mí. Responde lentamente y frente a la cámara, como se lo he indicado. Conoce todas las preguntas que le haré y la mayoría de las que Drummond, probablemente, le formulará. Está de espaldas al tronco del roble, un bonito fondo. De vez en cuando se seca la frente con un pañuelo, sin prestar atención a las miradas curiosas de nuestro pequeño grupo.

Aunque no le he pedido que aparente estar lo más enfermo y débil posible, ciertamente parece hacerlo. O puede que sólo le queden unos días de vida.

Frente a mí, Drummond, Grone y Hill con cuadernos sobre las rodillas, intentan escribir palabra por palabra las respuestas de Donny Ray. Me pregunto a cuánto ascenderán sus honorarios por asistir un sábado a una declaración. A los pocos minutos, se quitan las chaquetas azules y aflojan las corbatas.

Durante una prolongada pausa, se oye de pronto un portazo y aparece Buddy en el jardín. Se ha cambiado de camisa: ahora lleva un jersey rojo con manchas negras y una misteriosa bolsa de papel en la mano. Procuro concentrarme en mi testigo, pero no puedo evitar mirar a Buddy de reojo mientras cruza el jardín, sin dejar de observarnos con recelo. Sé exactamente adónde se dirige.

La puerta del conductor del Fairlane está abierta y salen gatos por todas las ventanas cuando se instala en el vehículo. Dot frunce el entrecejo y me mira nerviosa. Yo muevo rápidamente la cabeza, como para decirle: «Déjelo tranquilo. Es inofensivo.» Si ella pudiera lo mataría.

Hablo con Donny Ray de su educación, experiencia laboral, el hecho de que nunca ha abandonado el domicilio paterno, nunca se ha registrado como votante, ni ha tenido nunca problemas legales. Está resultando mucho más fácil de lo que imaginé anoche tumbado en la hamaca. Parezco un verdadero abogado.

Le hago una serie de preguntas muy estudiadas sobre su enfermedad y el tratamiento que ha recibido. Lo hago con suma cautela, porque Donny Ray no puede repetir nada de lo que le haya contado su médico, especular, ni expresar opiniones técnicas. Eso equivaldría a hablar de oídas. Otros testigos cubrirán dichos aspectos en el juicio, o al menos eso espero. A Drummond se le ilumina la mirada. Absorbe todas las respuestas, las analiza inmediatamente y espera la siguiente. Está perfectamente sereno.

Hay un límite en cuanto a lo que Donny Ray es capaz de resistir, tanto física como mentalmente, y también lo hay en cuanto a lo que el jurado desea presenciar. Concluyo en veinte minutos, sin haber provocado una sola protesta de la defensa. Deck me guiña un ojo, como si yo fuera genial.

Leo Drummond se presenta, para que conste, a Donny Ray y luego explica a quién representa y lo mucho que lamenta estar aquí. No se dirige a Donny Ray, sino al jurado. Habla en un tono suave y condescendiente, como si rebosara compasión.

Sólo unas pocas preguntas. Indaga discretamente si Donny Ray ha abandonado en algún momento esta casa, aunque sólo fuera una semana o un mes, para vivir en otro lugar. Puesto que pasa de los dieciocho, les encantaría establecer que había abandonado el domicilio paterno y, por consiguiente, no debería estar incluido en la póliza de sus padres.

—No, señor —responde repetidamente Donny Ray, de un modo educado y enfermizo.

A continuación Drummond se concentra brevemente en la posibilidad de otra cobertura. ¿Ha contratado Donny Ray alguna vez su propia póliza médica? ¿Ha trabajado alguna vez para alguna empresa, con su propio seguro médico?

—No, señor —responde suavemente a todas sus preguntas.

Aunque el entorno es un poco extraño, a Drummond no le es desconocido. Ha tomado probablemente millares de declaraciones y sabe cómo ser cauteloso. Al jurado le molestaría que tratara con agresividad a ese joven. En realidad, le brinda a Drummond una oportunidad maravillosa para congraciarse con el jurado, mostrando cierta compasión por el pobre Donny Ray. Además, sabe que no se puede obtener mucha información fehaciente de este testigo. ¿Para qué interrogarlo a fondo?

Drummond termina en menos de diez minutos. No me corresponde un segundo turno de preguntas. La declaración ha concluido. Así lo determina Kipler. Dot le pasa inmediatamente un paño húmedo por la cara a su hijo. Me mira en busca de aprobación y levanto el pulgar afirmativamente. Los abogados de la defensa recogen discretamente sus chaquetas y maletines, y se disculpan. Se mueren de ganas de retirarse. Yo también.

El juez Kipler empieza a entrar sillas en la casa y observa a Buddy cuando pasa frente al Fairlane. Garras está en medio del capó, listo para el ataque. Espero que no haya sangre. Dot y yo ayudamos a Donny Ray a entrar en la casa. Antes de cruzar la puerta, miro a mi izquierda y veo que Deck está junto a la muchedumbre de la verja, distribuyendo mis tarjetas. Un compañero como Dios manda.

VEINTINUEVE

La mujer está realmente dentro de mi piso, de pie en la sala de estar con una de mis revistas en la mano cuando abro la puerta. Se sobresalta y deja caer la revista al verme. Su boca se abre de par en par.

—¿Quién es usted? —pregunta casi a gritos.

No parece una ladrona.

—Yo vivo aquí. ¿Quién diablos es usted?

—Santo cielo —exclama con un exagerado suspiro y la mano sobre el corazón.

—¿Qué está haciendo aquí? —pregunto, realmente enojado.

—Soy la esposa de Delbert.

—¿Quién diablos es Delbert? ¿Y cómo ha conseguido entrar?

—¿Quién es usted?

—Me llamo Rudy. Vivo aquí. Esto es una residencia privada.

Mira fugazmente a su alrededor y entorna los párpados, como para decir «menudo cuchitril».

—Birdie me ha dado la llave y me ha dicho que podía echar una ojeada.

—¡No es posible!

—¡Es verdad! —responde después de sacarse una llave del bolsillo de su ceñido pantalón corto y mostrármela, al tiempo que yo cierro los ojos y pienso en estrangular a la señorita Birdie—. Me llamo Vera y vivo en Florida. Sólo he venido a pasar unos días con Birdie.

Ahora lo recuerdo. Delbert es el hijo menor de la señorita Birdie, al que no ha visto desde hace tres años, y nunca llama ni escribe. No recuerdo si Vera, aquí presente, es la mujer a la que la señorita Birdie denomina una cualquiera, pero encajaría perfectamente. Tiene unos cincuenta años, y la piel cobriza y apergaminada propia de una devota del sol en Florida. Unos labios anaranjados brillan en el centro de su tostado rostro. Brazos marchitos. Pantalón corto ceñido sobre unas delgadas y arruga-

273

das piernas impecablemente morenas. Horribles sandalias amarillas.

—No tiene derecho a estar aquí —digo procurando sosegarme.

—Tranquilícese —dice cuando pasa frente a mí, con una oleada de perfume barato que huele a esencia de coco—. Birdie quiere verlo —agrega al salir de mi casa. Oigo el ruido de sus sandalias en los peldaños.

La señorita Birdie está sentada en el sofá, con los brazos cruzados, pendiente de otro estúpido culebrón y ajena al resto del mundo. Vera hurga en el frigorífico. Junto a la mesa de la cocina hay otro ente moreno, un corpulento individuo con el pelo artificialmente rizado, mal teñido, canoso y patillas al estilo Elvis. Gafas de montura dorada. Brazaletes de oro en ambas muñecas. Un típico chulo.

—Usted debe de ser el abogado —dice cuando cierro la puerta a mi espalda. Sobre la mesa hay unos papeles que ha estado examinando.

—Me llamo Rudy Baylor —respondo, de pie al otro extremo de la mesa.

—Yo soy Delbert Birdsong. El hijo menor de Birdie.

Está cerca de los sesenta y procura desesperadamente aparentar cuarenta.

—Encantado de conocerlo.

—Sí, mucho gusto —responde con un ademán—. Siéntese.

—¿Qué desea? —pregunto.

Es evidente que hace horas que están aquí. Sus conflictivas huellas están patentes en la cocina y sala de estar adjunta. Veo la nuca de la señorita Birdie, pero no sé si nos escucha o está pendiente del televisor. El volumen está bajo.

—Procuro ser amable —responde Delbert, como si fuera el propietario.

Vera no encuentra nada en el frigorífico y decide reunirse con nosotros.

—Me ha levantado la voz —solloza en dirección a Delbert—. Me ha ordenado salir de su casa con muy malos modales.

—¿Es cierto? —pregunta Delbert.

—Maldita sea, claro que es cierto. Yo vivo aquí y les advierto a ambos que no entren en mi casa. Es una residencia privada.

Echa los hombros atrás. Es evidente que ese individuo ha peleado muchas veces en los bares.

—Mi madre es la propietaria —responde.

—Y yo su inquilino. Pago el alquiler todos los meses.

—¿Cuánto?

—Eso, caballero, no es de su incumbencia. Su nombre no figura en la escritura.

—Yo diría que vale unos cuatrocientos, tal vez quinientos dólares mensuales.

—Estupendo. ¿Alguna otra opinión?

—Sí, es usted un listillo.

—De acuerdo. ¿Algo más? Su esposa me ha dicho que la señorita Birdie deseaba verme —digo con el volumen necesario para que la señorita Birdie me oiga, pero permanece impasible.

Vera coge una silla y se instala junto a Delbert. Intercambian significativas miradas. Él levanta el borde de una hoja de papel, se ajusta las gafas y me mira.

—¿Ha estado alterando el testamento de mamá? —pregunta.

—Eso es confidencial entre la señorita Birdie y yo.

Al mirar hacia la mesa, apenas logro ver la parte superior del documento y me parece que se trata de su testamento más reciente, redactado por su anterior abogado. Esto es muy desconcertante, porque la señorita Birdie siempre ha asegurado que ninguno de sus hijos, ni Delbert ni Randolph, conocían la existencia de su dinero. Pero en dicho testamento se habla claramente de la distribución de unos veinte millones de dólares. Delbert ahora lo sabe. Lo ha estado leyendo durante las últimas horas. En el párrafo tercero, si mal no recuerdo, se le otorgan dos millones.

Lo más preocupante es cómo se las ha arreglado Delbert para obtener dicho documento. La señorita Birdie nunca se lo habría entregado voluntariamente.

—Un auténtico listillo —afirma—. Y hay quien se pregunta por qué odia la gente a los abogados. Vengo a ver cómo está mamá y, maldita sea, tiene a un repugnante abogado viviendo con ella. ¿No es como para preocuparse?

Probablemente.

—Yo vivo en este piso —respondo—. Es un domicilio privado con una puerta cerrada con llave. Si vuelve a entrar en el mismo llamaré a la policía.

De pronto recuerdo que guardo una copia del testamento de la señorita Birdie, en una carpeta debajo de la cama. No la habrán encontrado allí. De repente siento náuseas ante la idea de que haya sido yo, y no la señorita Birdie, el responsable de que se divulgara un asunto tan confidencial.

No me asombra que me ignore.

Desconozco por completo el texto de sus anteriores testamentos, de modo que no sé si Delbert y Vera están encantados ante la perspectiva de convertirse en millonarios o enojados porque recibirán menos de lo que esperaban. Además, no puedo en modo alguno revelarles la verdad. Para ser sincero, realmente no quiero hacerlo.

Delbert se mofa de mi amenaza de llamar a la policía.

—Se lo preguntaré otra vez —dice, a guisa de mala imitación de Brando en *El padrino*—. ¿Ha redactado un nuevo testamento para mi madre?

—Es su madre. Pregúnteselo a ella.

—No dice palabra —interrumpe Vera.

—Estupendo. Tampoco lo haré yo. Es estrictamente confidencial.

Delbert no lo comprende plenamente, ni es lo suficientemente listo para atacar desde otro ángulo. A su entender puede que, en realidad, esté quebrantando la ley.

—Espero que no se esté entrometiendo, muchacho —dice, con la mayor agresividad posible.

—¡Señorita Birdie! —exclamo, dispuesto a retirarme.

Permanece unos segundos inmóvil, luego levanta el control remoto y sube el volumen del televisor.

Me parece bien, en lo que a mí concierne.

—Si vuelven a acercarse a mi piso llamaré a la policía. ¿Comprendido? —exclamo, mientras señalo con el dedo a Delbert y a Vera.

Delbert fuerza una carcajada y Vera aporta inmediatamente una risita. Doy un portazo.

No puedo determinar si alguien ha tocado los documentos de debajo de mi cama. El testamento de la señorita Birdie está en la carpeta, creo que tal como lo había dejado. Han transcurrido varias semanas desde que lo miré por última vez. Todo parece estar en orden.

Cierro la puerta con llave y la atranco con una silla.

Estoy acostumbrado a llegar temprano a la oficina, alrededor de las siete y media, no porque tenga mucho trabajo, citas con clientes, ni apariciones en el juzgado, sino porque me gusta tomar una taza de café tranquilamente a solas. Dedico por lo menos una hora diaria a preparar y organizar el caso Black. Deck y yo procuramos evitarnos por la oficina, pero a veces resulta difícil. Empezamos a recibir gradualmente llamadas telefónicas.

Me gusta el sosiego de este lugar antes de que empiece el día.

El domingo Deck llega tarde, casi a las diez. Charlamos unos minutos. Quiere almorzar temprano, dice que es importante.

Salimos a las once y caminamos un par de manzanas, hasta una cooperativa vegetariana con un pequeño restaurante en el fondo. Pedimos una pizza vegetariana y té de naranja. Deck está muy nervioso, su rostro se contorsiona más que de costumbre y vuelve la cabeza al mínimo ruido.

—Debo contarte algo —dice, apenas en un susurro.

Estamos solos, las otras seis mesas están vacías.

—Estamos a salvo, Deck —respondo, para procurar tranquilizarlo—. ¿De qué se trata?

—Salí de la ciudad el sábado, inmediatamente después de la declaración. Cogí un avión a Dallas y de allí a Las Vegas, donde me instalé en el hotel Pacific.

Lo que faltaba. Ha vuelto a salir de juerga, bebiendo y apostando. Se ha quedado sin blanca.

—Ayer por la mañana hablé con Bruiser por teléfono y me dijo que me marchara. Dijo que los federales me habían seguido desde Memphis y que debía marcharme. Dijo que alguien me había vigilado durante todo el camino y que había llegado el momento de regresar a Memphis. Me dijo que te advirtiera de que los federales vigilan todos tus pasos porque eres el único abogado que ha trabajado para Bruiser y para Prince.

Tomo un sorbo de té para refrescar mi paladar reseco.

—¿Sabes dónde... está Bruiser? —pregunto demasiado alto, aunque nadie nos escucha.

—No. No lo sé —responde sin dejar de mirar a su alrededor.

—Bueno, ¿está en Las Vegas?

—Lo dudo. Creo que me mandó allí porque eso pretende hacerles creer a los federales. Parece un lugar probable para Bruiser y, por consiguiente, no iría allí.

No logro enfocar la mirada ni reducir la velocidad de mi cerebro. Se me ocurren simultáneamente una docena de preguntas, pero no puedo formularlas todas. Hay infinidad de cosas que deseo saber, pero muchas no me convienen. Nos observamos momentáneamente.

Estaba francamente convencido de que Bruiser y Prince estaban en Singapur o en Australia, y de que nunca volveríamos a oír hablar de ellos.

—¿Por qué se puso en contacto contigo? —pregunto con suma cautela.

Se muerde el labio como si estuviera a punto de llorar y exhibe sus cuatro dientes de roedor. Se rasca la cabeza conforme transcurren los minutos. Pero el tiempo está paralizado.

—Parece ser que han dejado aquí algún dinero —responde, después de bajar aún más el tono de su voz—. Y ahora quieren recuperarlo.

—¿Quieren?

—Parece que siguen juntos, ¿no es cierto?

—Efectivamente. ¿Y quieren que tú se lo resuelvas?

—El caso es que no llegamos a hablar de los detalles. Pero parece que quieren que *nosotros* les ayudemos a *ellos* a recuperar el dinero.

—¿Nosotros?

—Sí.

—¿Tú y yo?

—Eso es.

—¿Cuánto dinero?

—Nunca se ha llegado a mencionar, pero puedes estar seguro de que si no se tratara de una fortuna no les preocuparía.

—¿Y dónde está?

—No me lo ha dicho con exactitud, sólo sé que es al contado y que está encerrado en algún lugar.

—¿Y quiere que nosotros lo saquemos?

—Exactamente. Supongo que el dinero está escondido en algún lugar de la ciudad, probablemente cerca de donde estamos ahora. De momento los federales no lo han encontrado y, por tanto, es probable que no lo hagan. Bruiser y Prince confían en ti y en mí. Además, ahora somos semirrespetables, con un auténtico bufete, y no un par de maleantes callejeros que robarían el dinero cuando le echaran la vista encima. Calculan que entre tú y yo podemos cargar el dinero en una furgoneta, llevárselo a algún lugar y todos felices.

Soy incapaz de decidir cuánto de lo que cuenta Deck es de su propia cosecha y cuánto lo que le ha propuesto Bruiser. No quiero saberlo. Pero me muerde la curiosidad.

—¿Y qué sacamos por nuestra colaboración?

—No llegamos a hablar de ello. Pero un montón. Podríamos cobrar por adelantado.

Deck ya lo ha calculado.

—De ningún modo, Deck. Olvídalo.

—Sí, lo sé —responde con tristeza, rendido al primer asalto.

—Es demasiado peligroso.

—Sí.

—Ahora todo parece maravilloso, pero podríamos acabar en la cárcel.

—Por supuesto, pero tenía que contártelo, compréndelo —responde, descartándolo con un ademán, como si no se atreviera siquiera a pensar en ello.

El camarero deja un plato de tiras de maíz fritas sobre la mesa, y se retira.

He pensado en el hecho de que, con toda seguridad, debo de ser la única persona que ha trabajado para ambos fugitivos, pero francamente nunca se me había ocurrido que los federales me vigilaran. Me quedo sin apetito. Mi garganta está seca. El más mínimo sonido me produce un sobresalto.

Adoptamos ambos una actitud meditabunda y nos dedicamos a observar los objetos de la mesa. No volvemos a hablar hasta que llega la pizza y comemos en silencio. Me gustaría conocer los detalles: ¿Cómo se ha puesto Bruiser en contacto con Deck? ¿Quién ha pagado el viaje a Las Vegas? ¿Ha sido ésta la primera vez que han hablado desde su desaparición? ¿Será la última? ¿Por qué se interesa Bruiser todavía por mí?

Dos ideas emergen de las tinieblas. En primer lugar, si Bruiser dispone de suficiente ayuda para vigilar a Deck hasta Las Vegas y saber que le han seguido todo el camino, sin duda puede contratar a alguien para que traslade el dinero desde Memphis. ¿Por qué preocuparse de nosotros? Porque no le importa que nos atrapen, he ahí el porqué. En segundo lugar, los federales no se han molestado en interrogarme porque no quieren ponerme sobre aviso. Les resulta mucho más fácil vigilarme, porque no me preocupo por ellos.

Y algo más. No cabe la menor duda de que mi compañero, al otro lado de la mesa, ha abierto la puerta a una discusión seria sobre dinero. Deck sabe más de lo que me ha contado y ha iniciado esta entrevista con un proyecto en mente.

No soy tan ingenuo como para suponer que se ha dado por vencido con tanta facilidad.

La correspondencia diaria es algo que he aprendido a temer. Deck la recoge después del almuerzo, como de costumbre, y la trae al despacho. Hay un grueso sobre tamaño folio de los buenazos de Tinley Britt y aguanto la respiración cuando lo abro. Es la instancia preliminar a las conclusiones de Drummond, en la que formula una serie de preguntas, solicita todos los documentos conocidos por el acusado o su abogado, y una serie de admisiones. Lo último es un ingenioso método para obligar a la parte contraria a admitir o negar ciertos hechos por escrito, en el plazo de treinta días. Todo lo que no se niega, se considera definitivamente admitido. Incluye también una solicitud para tomarles declaración a Dot y Buddy Black en mi despacho, dentro de dos semanas. Normalmente, según tengo entendido, los abogados charlan por teléfono y deciden conjuntamente la fecha, la hora y el lugar de la declaración. Se denomina cortesía profesional, tarda unos cinco minutos, y contribuye enormemente a la placidez del proceso. Evidentemente, Drummond ha olvidado sus buenos modales o ha decidido jugar duro. Sea como fuere, estoy decidido a cambiar de fecha y lugar. No porque me parezcan inoportunos, sino por principio.

Asombrosamente, en el sobre no hay ninguna petición. Veremos mañana.

La solicitud preliminar a las conclusiones debe responderse en un plazo de treinta días, y ambas partes pueden presentarla simultáneamente. La mía está casi lista y el recibo de la de Drummond me incita a actuar. Estoy decidido a mostrarle al «señor prócer» que también sé jugar a la guerra del papeleo. Le dejaré impresionado, o comprenderá una vez más que trata con un abogado que no tiene otra cosa que hacer.

Casi ha oscurecido cuando aparco silenciosamente frente a la casa. Junto al Cadillac de la señorita Birdie hay dos coches inusuales, dos relucientes Pontiac con el anagrama de Avis en el parachoques trasero. Oigo voces cuando rodeo sigilosamente la casa con la esperanza de llegar a mi piso sin ser visto.

Me he quedado hasta bastante tarde en el despacho, principalmente con el propósito de no encontrarme con Delbert y Vera. Pero no tendré tanta suerte. Están en el jardín con la señorita Birdie, tomando té. Y no están solos.

—Ahí está —exclama Delbert al verme, al tiempo que yo acelero el paso y miro hacia el jardín—. Acérquese, Rudy.

Es una orden, más que una invitación.

Se levanta lentamente cuando me acerco y otro individuo también se pone de pie.

—Rudy, le presento a mi hermano Randolph.

—Mi esposa June —dice Randolph después de estrecharnos la mano, mientras gesticula en dirección a otra apergaminada mujerzuela al estilo de Vera, con el cabello teñido.

La saludo con la cabeza y ella me lanza una mirada que fundiría el plomo.

—Señorita Birdie —digo educadamente para saludar a la propietaria de mi casa.

—Hola, Rudy —responde cariñosamente, sentada en un sofá de mimbre junto a Delbert.

—Siéntese —dice Randolph, al tiempo que me ofrece una silla.

—No, gracias —respondo—. Debo ir a mi casa para comprobar si la ha visitado algún intruso —agrego, mirando a Vera, que está sentada detrás del sofá, separada de los demás, probablemente lo más lejos posible de June.

June tiene entre cuarenta y cuarenta y cinco años. Su marido, si mal no recuerdo, cerca de los sesenta. Ahora me acuerdo de que es ella a quien la señorita Birdie denomina pécora. La tercera esposa de Randolph. Interesándose siempre por el dinero.

—No hemos estado en su piso —responde Delbert en tono quisquilloso.

Al contrario de su grotesco hermano, Randolph envejece con dignidad. No está gordo, no se tiñe ni riza el cabello, ni va cargado de oro. Lleva una camiseta de golf, unas bermudas, calcetines blancos y zapatillas del mismo color. Como todos los demás, está moreno. Podría pasar perfectamente por un ejecutivo jubilado, con su correspondiente mujercita de plástico.

—¿Cuánto tiempo piensa quedarse aquí, Rudy? —pregunta.

—No sabía que me marchara.

—No he dicho que lo hiciera. Es pura curiosidad. Mi madre me ha dicho que no han firmado ningún contrato y me interesa saberlo.

—¿Por qué le interesa?

Las cosas están cambiando con mucha rapidez. Hasta anoche, la señorita Birdie nunca había mencionado ningún contrato.

—Porque de ahora en adelante, voy a ayudar a mi madre con sus asuntos. El alquiler es muy bajo.

—Sin duda lo es —agrega June.

—¿Se ha quejado usted, señorita Birdie? —pregunto.

—Pues... no —responde vagamente, como si hubiera pensado en hacerlo, pero no hubiera encontrado todavía el momento oportuno.

Podría hablar del estiércol, la pintura y la jardinería, pero estoy decidido a no discutir con esos imbéciles.

—Ahí lo tienen. Si la propietaria está satisfecha, ¿de qué se preocupan?

—No queremos que nadie se aproveche de mamá —dice Delbert.

—Por Dios, Delbert —responde Randolph.

—¿Quién se aprovecha de ella? —pregunto.

—Bueno, nadie, pero...

—Lo que intenta decir —interrumpe Randolph—, es que a partir de ahora las cosas van a ser diferentes. Estamos aquí para ayudar a nuestra madre y nos interesamos simplemente por sus negocios. Eso es todo.

Observo a la señorita Birdie mientras habla Randolph y su rostro rebosa satisfacción. Sus hijos están aquí, preocupándose por ella, haciendo preguntas, exigiendo condiciones, protegiendo a su mamá. Aunque estoy seguro de que detesta a sus dos nueras, la señorita Birdie se siente ahora muy satisfecha.

—Me parece muy bien —respondo—. Pero no se metan conmigo y no se les ocurra entrar en mi piso.

Doy media vuelta y me alejo rápidamente, para dejarlos con muchos comentarios y preguntas que tenían previsto formular. Cierro la puerta de mi piso con llave, me como un bocadillo y, en la oscuridad, por la ventana, oigo que charlan a lo lejos.

Dedico unos minutos a intentar reconstruir la reunión. En algún momento de ayer, Delbert y Vera llegaron de Florida con algún propósito que probablemente nunca conoceré. De algún modo descubrieron el último testamento de la señorita Birdie, vieron que disponía de unos veinte millones para distribuir y se interesaron profundamente por su bienestar. Se enteraron de que vivía un abogado en la finca y eso también les preocupó. Delbert llamó a Randolph, que también vive en Florida, y éste corrió hacia la casa de su madre, acompañado de su mujercita de plástico. Hoy han pasado el día interrogando a su madre sobre todo lo imaginable y han llegado al punto de convertirse en sus protectores.

En el fondo no me importa. No puedo evitar reírme de la situación. Me pregunto cuánto tardarán en averiguar la verdad.

De momento la señorita Birdie es feliz. Y me alegro por ella.

TREINTA

Llego temprano a mi cita de las nueve con el doctor Walter Kord. No me sirve de nada. Espero una hora, leyendo los informes médicos de Donny Ray que me conozco ya de memoria. La sala de espera está llena de pacientes cancerosos. Procuro no fijarme en ellos.

Una enfermera viene a por mí a las diez. La sigo a un consultorio desprovisto de ventanas, al fondo de un laberinto. Entre todas las especialidades médicas, ¿cómo se le puede ocurrir a alguien elegir la oncología? Supongo que alguien debe hacerlo.

¿A quién se le ocurre ser abogado?

Me siento en una silla con mis documentos y espero otros quince minutos. Oigo voces en el pasillo, antes de que se abra la puerta. Un joven de unos treinta y cinco años entra en la sala.

—¿Señor Baylor? —pregunta al tiempo que me tiende una mano, me levanto y se la estrecho.

—Sí.

—Walter Kord. Tengo prisa. ¿Podemos resolver este asunto en cinco minutos?

—Supongo.

—Adelante, tengo muchos pacientes —dice, incluso con una sonrisa.

Soy perfectamente consciente de que los médicos odian a los abogados y, la verdad, no se lo reprocho.

—Gracias por su informe. Ha cumplido su cometido. Ya le hemos tomado declaración a Donny Ray.

—Estupendo.

Mide unos diez centímetros más que yo y me mira como si fuera imbécil.

—Necesitamos su testimonio —digo después de apretar los dientes.

Su reacción es la típica de los médicos. Detestan los juzgados y, para evitarlos, a veces acceden a que se les tome una declaración jurada en lugar de comparecer personalmente en la sala. No están obligados a hacerlo. Y, cuando no lo hacen, en algunas ocasiones a los abogados no les queda más alternativa que recurrir a su arma letal: la citación judicial. Los abogados tienen autoridad para citar judicialmente casi a cualquiera, incluidos los médicos. Así pues, en este limitado sentido, los abogados tienen poder sobre los médicos. Eso hace que los médicos odien aún más a los abogados.

—Estoy muy ocupado —responde.

—Lo sé. No es para mí, sino para Donny Ray.

Frunce el entrecejo y resopla, como si le resultara físicamente doloroso.

—Cobro quinientos dólares por hora para hacer declaraciones.

No me sorprende, porque me lo esperaba. En la facultad había oído hablar de médicos que cobraban incluso más. Pero ahora he venido a suplicar.

—No puedo permitírmelo, doctor Kord. Abrí el bufete hace seis semanas y estoy a punto de morirme de hambre. Éste es el único caso decente que tengo.

Es asombrosa la fuerza de la verdad. Ese individuo, que gana probablemente un millón de dólares anuales, sucumbe inmediatamente ante mi ingenuidad. Veo compasión en sus ojos. Titubea unos instantes, piensa tal vez en Donny Ray y en la frustración de no poder ayudarlo, o puede que se apiade de mí. ¿Quién sabe?

—Le mandaré la cuenta. Págueme cuando pueda.

—Gracias, doctor.

—Hable con mi secretaria para elegir la fecha. ¿Podemos hacerlo aquí?

—Desde luego.

—Bien. Debo marcharme.

Deck tiene un cliente en su despacho cuando regreso. Es una mujer madura, corpulenta y bien vestida. Me hace una seña cuando me ve aparecer y me presenta a la señora Madge Dresser, que quiere divorciarse. Ha estado llorando y cuando me apoyo en la mesa junto a Deck, éste me pasa una nota que dice: «Tiene dinero.»

Pasamos una hora con Madge y nos cuenta una lúgubre historia: alcohol, palizas, otras mujeres, apuestas, hijos malvados y ella no ha hecho nada de malo. Solicitó el divorcio hace un par de años y su marido rompió a balazos la ventana del bufete de su abogado. Juega con armas y es peligroso. Miro a Deck cuando nos lo cuenta. Él elude mi mirada.

Nos paga seiscientos dólares al contado y promete pagar más. Mañana presentaremos la petición de divorcio. Deck le asegura que en el bufete de Rudy Baylor está en buenas manos.

Cuando apenas acaba de retirarse, suena el teléfono. Un voz masculina pregunta por mí y me identifico.

—Hola, Rudy, me llamo Roger Rice y soy abogado. Creo que no nos conocemos.

Conocí a casi todos los abogados de Memphis cuando buscaba trabajo, pero no recuerdo a Roger Rice.

—No, creo que no. Soy nuevo.

—Sí, he tenido que llamar a información para conseguir su número. El caso es que tengo en mi despacho a dos hermanos, Randolph y Delbert Birdsong, acompañados de su madre, Birdie. Tengo entendido que los conoce.

Me la imagino sentada entre sus dos hijos, con una estúpida sonrisa en los labios, diciendo «estupendo».

—Por supuesto, conozco bien a la señorita Birdie —respondo, como si hubiera estado todo el día pendiente de aquella llamada.

—He salido a la sala de conferencias para poder hablar. Estoy redactando su testamento y la verdad es que hay un montón de dinero en juego. Según ellos, usted había intentado elaborarlo.

—Es cierto. Redacté un borrador hace varios meses, pero la verdad es que no ha mostrado mucho interés por firmarlo.

—¿Por qué no?

Es amable, se limita a hacer su trabajo y no es culpa suya que estén en su despacho. De modo que le resumo brevemente el proyecto de la señorita Birdie, de dejar su fortuna al reverendo Kenneth Chandler.

—¿Tiene realmente el dinero? —pregunta.

Simplemente no puedo revelarle la verdad. Quebrantaría todo código ético divulgar cualquier información sobre la señorita Birdie sin su previo consentimiento. Además, la información que Rice me solicita fue obtenida por medios, aunque no ilegales, sí cuestionables.

—¿Qué le ha contado? —pregunto.

—Poca cosa. Algo acerca de una fortuna en Atlanta, una herencia de su segundo marido, pero cuando intento concretar responde con vaguedades.

Resulta ciertamente familiar.

—¿Por qué quiere un nuevo testamento? —pregunto.

—Quiere dejarlo todo a su familia: hijos y nietos. Lo único que deseo saber es si tiene el dinero.

—No estoy seguro acerca del dinero. Hay un sumario de homologación testamentaria en Atlanta, declarado secreto por el tribunal, y eso es todo lo que sé.

Todavía no está satisfecho y no puedo decirle más. Prometo mandarle por fax el nombre y número de teléfono del abogado de Atlanta.

Hay todavía más coches alquilados frente a la casa cuando regreso después de las nueve. Me veo obligado a aparcar en la calle y eso realmente me molesta. Avanzo sigilosamente en la oscuridad y cruzo inadvertido el jardín.

Deben de ser los nietos. Junto a la ventana de mi pequeña sala de estar me como una tarta de pollo a oscuras y escucho las voces. Distingo las de Delbert y Randolph. Algún comentario aislado de la señorita Birdie se desplaza por el húmedo aire. Las otras voces son más jóvenes.

Todos parecen haber respondido como a una llamada de urgencia. ¡Daos prisa! ¡Está forrada! Sabíamos que la vieja tenía unos ahorrillos, pero no una fortuna. Una llamada condujo a otra. ¡Venid de prisa! Tu nombre figura en el testamento y junto al mismo está la cifra de un millón de dólares. Y está pensando en volver a redactarlo. Adelante, ha llegado el momento de amar a la abuelita.

TREINTA Y UNO

Siguiendo el consejo del juez Kipler y con su beneplácito, nos reunimos en su sala para tomarle declaración a Dot. Después de que Drummond la programara en mi despacho sin consultarme, me negué a aceptar la fecha y el lugar. Intervino Kipler, llamó a Drummond y el asunto se resolvió en pocos segundos.

Cuando le tomamos declaración a Donny Ray, todo el mundo vio a Buddy sentado en su Fairlane. Les he explicado tanto a Kipler como a Drummond que, en mi opinión, no debemos tomarle declaración a Buddy. No está bien de la cabeza, en palabras de Dot. El pobre hombre es inofensivo y no sabe nada del embrollo del seguro. En ninguno de los documentos aparece indicio alguno que vincule siquiera remotamente a Buddy. Nunca le he oído pronunciar una oración completa. No lo creo capaz de soportar la tensión de una prolongada declaración. Podría ponerse nervioso y apalear a unos cuantos abogados.

Dot lo deja en casa. Ayer pasé dos horas con ella, preparándola para las preguntas de Drummond. Dot declarará en el juicio, de modo que su testimonio actual no constituirá una prueba, sino parte del sumario. Drummond iniciará el interrogatorio, formulará prácticamente todas las preguntas y en general explorará a su antojo. Durará horas.

Kipler quiere estar también presente y nos reunimos alrededor de una de las mesas de los letrados, frente al estrado. El juez organiza a la operadora de vídeo y a la relatora. Éste es su territorio y quiere que las cosas se hagan a su manera.

Creo sinceramente que teme que Drummond me amilane si me abandona. La fricción entre ellos es tan intensa, que apenas son capaces de mirarse a la cara. Me parece maravilloso.

A la pobre Dot le tiemblan las manos, cuando se sienta sola al extremo de la mesa. Yo estoy bastante cerca y eso probablemente la pone todavía más nerviosa. Lleva su mejor blusa de algodón y sus mejores vaqueros. Le he explicado que no tenía por qué arreglarse particularmente, puesto que el vídeo no se muestra al jurado. Sin embargo, el día del juicio será importante que se ponga un vestido. Dios sabe qué haremos con Buddy.

Kipler está sentado a mi lado de la mesa, pero lo más lejos posible, cerca de la cámara de vídeo. Al otro lado está Drummond, con sólo tres acompañantes: B. Dewey Clay Hill III, M. Alec Plunk hijo y Brandon Fuller Grone.

Deck está en algún lugar del edificio, al acecho de insospechados clientes. Ha dicho que tal vez pasaría luego.

Cinco abogados y un juez observan a Dot Black cuando levanta la mano derecha para prestar juramento. A mí también me temblarían las manos. Drummond le brinda una radiante sonrisa a Dot, se presenta para que conste y dedica los primeros cinco minutos a explicar amablemente el propósito de la declaración. Buscamos la verdad. No intentará engañarla ni confundirla. Puede consultar en cualquier momento con su ilustre letrado, etcétera, etcétera. No tiene ninguna prisa. El tiempo corre.

Durante la primera hora explora la historia familiar. La preparación de Drummond, como de costumbre, es impecable. Pasa paulatinamente de un tema a otro: educación, trabajo, casa, aficiones... y formula preguntas que a mí nunca se me hubieran ocurrido. En su mayoría son puras divagaciones, pero es lo que hacen los abogados cuando toman declaración para el sumario. Hurgan, preguntan, vuelven a hurgar, y quién sabe lo que descubren. Pero aunque descubriera algo auténticamente sensacionalista, como por ejemplo un embarazo en la adolescencia, no le sería de utilidad alguna. No podría utilizarlo en el juicio. Sería completamente ajeno a la cuestión. Pero las normas lo permiten y su cliente le paga un montón de dinero para tentar en las tinieblas.

Kipler decreta un descanso y Dot sale corriendo al pasillo. Lleva un cigarrillo entre los labios antes de llegar a la puerta de la sala. Nos reunimos para charlar cerca de una fuente.

—Lo está haciendo muy bien —le digo, y no miento.

—¿Ese hijo de perra va a preguntarme por mi vida sexual? —refunfuña.

—Probablemente.

Casi tengo que pedirle disculpas para retirarme, sólo de imaginarla en cama con su marido, mientras ella chupa con avidez su cigarrillo, como si fuera el último de su vida.

—¿No puede impedírselo?

—Si se excede, lo haré. Pero tiene derecho a preguntar casi cualquier cosa.

—Maldito fisgón.

La segunda hora es tan lenta como la primera. Drummond investiga la economía de los Black y descubrimos cómo compraron la casa, sus coches, incluido el Fairlane, y sus principales pertenencias. Kipler empieza a hartarse y le ordena a Drummond que prosiga. Pregunta entonces por Buddy, sus heridas de guerra, sus trabajos y su pensión, así como sus aficiones y su forma de pasar el tiempo.

Kipler se enoja y le ordena a Drummond que procure encontrar algo significativo.

Dot dice que necesita ir al lavabo. Yo le he dicho que lo hiciera cuando estuviera cansada. Se fuma tres cigarrillos en el pasillo mientras charlamos, e intento eludir la humareda.

A mitad de la tercera hora, llegamos finalmente a la reclamación. He preparado una copia completa de todos los documentos, incluidos los informes médicos de Donny Ray, que guardo en un nítido montón sobre la mesa. Kipler los ha inspeccionado. Estamos en una situación inusual y envidiable, la de no poseer ningún documento irregular. No hay nada que deseemos ocultar. Drummond puede verlo todo.

Según Kipler, y también Deck, no es inusual que en estos casos las compañías de seguros les oculten algo a sus propios abogados. En realidad esto es bastante frecuente, especialmente cuando la compañía tiene trapos sucios que desea sepultar.

En una clase sobre procedimientos judiciales del año pasado, estudiamos con incredulidad caso tras caso en los que grandes empresas perdieron el juicio por intentar ocultarles documentos a sus propios abogados.

Al pasar a los documentos, estoy enormemente emocionado. También lo está Kipler. Drummond ha solicitado ya por escrito estos documentos para formular sus conclusiones, pero queda todavía una semana de plazo para su entrega. Quiero contemplar su rostro cuando vea la «estúpida carta». Kipler también.

Suponemos que ya ha visto la mayoría, si no todos, de los documentos que están sobre la mesa frente a Dot. Ha recibido los documentos de su cliente; a mí me los han entregado los Black. Pero suponemos que casi todos son iguales. En realidad, yo también he solicitado por escrito la presentación de documentos, al igual que él. Cuando responda a mi solicitud, me mandará documentos que están en mis manos desde hace tres meses. Las huellas del papeleo.

Más adelante, si todo funciona como está previsto, examinaré un nuevo conjunto de documentos de la oficina de Cleveland.

Empezamos con la solicitud y la póliza. Dot se las entrega a Drummond, que las examina rápidamente antes de pasárselas a Hill, quien a su vez las entrega a Plunk y éste finalmente a Grone. Pasa el tiempo, mientras esos payasos las examinan página por página. Hace meses que obran en su poder la póliza y la solicitud. Pero el tiempo es oro. Por fin la relatora cataloga los documentos como pruebas del testimonio de Dot.

El próximo documento es la primera carta de denegación, que circula por la mesa. El mismo procedimiento se sigue para las demás. Procuro desesperadamente no quedarme dormido.

La próxima es la «estúpida carta». Le he dicho a Dot que se limite a entregársela a Drummond, sin comentar nada acerca de su contenido. No quiero ponerlo sobre aviso, por si no la ha visto. Es difícil para ella, porque es tan ofensiva... Drummond la coge y la lee:

> Querida señora Black:
> En siete ocasiones anteriores, esta compañía ha denegado su petición por escrito. Ahora se la denegamos por octava y última vez. ¡Usted debe de ser sumamente estúpida!

Con treinta años de experiencia en los juzgados, Drummond es un actor excelente. No obstante, me percato inmediatamente de que nunca había visto esta carta. Su cliente no la había incluido en la ficha. Lo coge evidentemente por sorpresa, abre ligeramente la boca, se le forman tres profundos surcos en la frente y entorna los párpados para mirar con ira. La lee por segunda vez.

Entonces hace algo que más adelante tendría que lamentar. Levanta los ojos por encima de la carta y me mira. Yo, evidentemente, lo estoy observando con una expresión irónica como para decirle: «Te he sorprendido, muchacho.»

A continuación incrementa su agonía al mirar a Kipler. Su señoría está pendiente del más leve movimiento de sus facciones, sus tics y sus parpadeos, y descubre lo evidente. A Drummond le ha dejado estupefacto lo que tiene en las manos.

Recupera elegantemente su compostura, pero el mal ya está hecho. Le pasa la carta a Hill, que está medio dormido e inconsciente de la bomba que le entrega su jefe. Observamos a Hill unos segundos, hasta que reacciona.

—Hablemos extraoficialmente —dice Kipler, al tiempo que la relatora deja de taquigrafiar y la operadora para la cámara de vídeo—. Señor Drummond, me parece evidente que usted no había visto esta carta. Y tengo el presentimiento de que no será el primero ni el último documento que sus clientes intentan ocultarle. He acusado a suficientes compañías de seguros para saber que ciertos documentos suelen desaparecer —agrega el juez, inclinado sobre la mesa y señalando a Drummond—. Si les sorprendo a usted o a su cliente ocultando algún documento de la acusación, aplicaré sanciones contra ambos. Les impondré penas que incluirán costes y gastos jurídicos equivalentes a los honorarios que le pagan a usted sus clientes. ¿Me comprende usted, señor Drummond?

La vía de las sanciones es la única que me permitirá ganar doscientos cincuenta dólares por hora.

Drummond y su equipo están todavía desconcertados. Imagino el impacto que esa carta causará en el jurado y estoy seguro de que ellos piensan lo mismo.

—¿Me acusa usted de ocultar documentos, su señoría?

—Todavía no —responde Kipler, sin dejar de señalarle—. De momento es sólo una advertencia.

—Creo que debería usted inhibirse del caso, su señoría.

—¿Es una petición?

—Sí, señor.

—Denegada. ¿Algo más?

Drummond baraja papeles y pierde unos segundos. La tensión se aplaca. La pobre Dot está aterrada, convencida probablemente de que ha hecho algo para provocar el enfrentamiento. Yo también me siento ligeramente incómodo.

—Prosigamos oficialmente —dice Kipler, sin quitarle a Drummond los ojos de encima.

Se hacen varias preguntas y respuestas. Circulan otros documentos. A las doce y media se hace un receso para almorzar, y al cabo de una hora regresamos para iniciar la sesión de la tarde. Dot está agotada.

Kipler le ordena a Drummond, en un tono bastante severo, que se apresure. Lo intenta, pero no es fácil. Hace tanto tiempo que lo practica y ha ganado tanto dinero haciéndolo, que podría seguir formulando preguntas literalmente hasta el fin de los tiempos.

Mi cliente adopta una estrategia que me encanta. Les explica a todos, extraoficialmente, que tiene un problema de vejiga, nada grave, pero ya saben, tiene casi sesenta años. Y el caso es que conforme avanza el día, se ve obligada a acudir al retrete con mayor frecuencia. Drummond, como era de suponer, le formula un sinfín de preguntas sobre la vejiga, pero Kipler le interrumpe. De modo que cada quince minutos Dot se disculpa y abandona la sala. No se apresura en volver.

Estoy seguro de que no tiene ningún problema en la vejiga y lo que hace es fumar como una chimenea. Su estrategia le permite relajarse y acaba por agotar a Drummond.

A las tres treinta, seis horas y media después de haber empezado, Kipler decide que la declaración ha concluido.

Por primera vez desde hace más de dos semanas han desaparecido todos los coches de alquiler. El único coche frente a la casa es el Cadillac de la señorita Birdie. Aparco detrás del mismo, en mi lugar habitual, y rodeo la casa. No hay nadie.

Por fin se han marchado. No he hablado con la señorita Birdie desde el día en que llegó Delbert y tenemos cosas que aclarar. No es que esté enojado, pero debemos charlar.

Al llegar a la escalera de mi piso, oigo una voz. No es la de la señorita Birdie.

—Rudy, ¿dispone de un minuto? —pregunta Randolph, que acaba de levantarse de una mecedora en el jardín.

Dejo mi maletín y mi chaqueta sobre los peldaños y me acerco.

—Siéntese —dice—. Tenemos que hablar —agrega, aparentemente de muy buen humor.

—¿Dónde está la señorita Birdie? —pregunto, después de comprobar que la casa está a oscuras.

—Ha salido de viaje por algún tiempo. Quiere pasar una temporada con nosotros en Florida. Ha cogido un avión esta mañana.

—¿Cuándo regresa? —no puedo evitar preguntar, aunque no es de mi incumbencia.

—No lo sé. Puede que no lo haga. De ahora en adelante, Delbert y yo nos ocuparemos de sus negocios. Supongo que últimamente nos habíamos despreocupado bastante de ella, pero quiere que la cuidemos.

»Por otra parte, deseamos que se quede usted aquí. A decir verdad, queremos hacerle una propuesta. Se queda aquí, cuida de la casa y la propiedad, y no paga alquiler alguno.

—¿A qué se refiere cuando dice cuidar de la propiedad?

—Al mantenimiento general, nada extraordinario. Mamá nos ha contado que este verano se ha ocupado muy adecuadamente del jardín. Siga haciendo lo mismo. No deberá ocuparse del correo, porque se lo mandarán directamente a Florida. Si aparece algún problema de mayor importancia, llámeme. Es un buen trato, Rudy.

Sin duda lo es.

—Acepto.

—Bien. A mamá realmente le gusta usted, dice que es un joven excelente en quien se puede confiar. A pesar de ser abogado —dice y suelta una carcajada.

—¿Qué piensa hacer con el coche?

—Mañana me lo llevo a Florida —responde, al tiempo que

me entrega un grueso sobre—. Aquí tiene las llaves de la casa, los números de teléfono de la compañía aseguradora, del sistema de alarma y cosas por el estilo. También está mi dirección y número de teléfono.

—¿Dónde se hospeda?

—Con nosotros, cerca de Tampa. Tengo una bonita casa con una habitación para huéspedes. Cuidaremos de ella. Dos de mis hijos viven cerca, de modo que no le faltará compañía.

Ya los veo a todos ahora esforzándose para cuidar a la abuelita. Les encantará tratarla a cuerpo de rey durante algún tiempo, a condición de que no viva demasiado. No pueden esperar a que muera para ser ricos. Es difícil reprimir una sonrisa.

—Me alegro —respondo—. Se ha sentido muy sola.

—Usted realmente le gusta, Rudy. Ha sido muy bueno con ella —dice en un tono suave y sincero.

Me conmueve su tristeza.

Nos estrechamos la mano y nos despedimos.

Me mezo en la hamaca, ahuyento los mosquitos y contemplo la luna. Dudo seriamente de que vuelva a ver a la señorita Birdie y siento la extraña soledad que provoca la pérdida de una amiga. Esa gente la mantendrá vigilada hasta el día de su muerte para asegurarse de que no altere su testamento. Me siento ligeramente culpable por conocer la verdad respecto a su riqueza, pero es un secreto que no puedo compartir.

Por otra parte, me alegro de su destino. Ha abandonado esta vieja casa solitaria y ahora está rodeada de su familia. De pronto la señorita Birdie se ha convertido en el centro de atención, cosa que siempre ha anhelado. Pienso en ella en el Parque de los Cipreses, organizando a los demás, dirigiendo el coro, haciendo discursos, cuidando de Bosco y los demás ancianos. Tiene un corazón de oro, pero también aspira a que le presten atención.

Espero que le siente bien el sol. Deseo que sea feliz. Me pregunto quién la sustituirá en el Parque de los Cipreses.

TREINTA Y DOS

Sospecho que la razón por la que Booker ha elegido este restaurante tan elegante es porque tiene buenas noticias. Los cubiertos son de plata y las servilletas de lino. Debe de tener un cliente que paga la cuenta.

Llega con quince minutos de retraso, muy inusual en él, aunque ahora es un hombre muy ocupado. Sus primeras palabras son:

—He aprobado.

Tomamos un vaso de agua mientras me cuenta la animada historia de su apelación ante el tribunal examinador de la facultad. Han recalificado su examen, su puntuación global ha subido tres puntos y se ha convertido en un abogado colegiado de pleno derecho. Nunca le había visto tan sonriente. Sólo otros dos candidatos de nuestro grupo apelaron con éxito. Sara Plankmore no ha sido uno de ellos. Booker ha oído rumores de que su puntuación ha sido pésima y puede que peligre su empleo en la fiscalía federal.

Contra su voluntad, pido una botella de champán y le ordeno al camarero que me pase la cuenta. No puede ocultarse el dinero.

Llega la comida: unas admirables lonchas de salmón, cuya hermosura contemplamos antes de comérnoslas. Shankle manda a Booker en treinta direcciones distintas, quince horas al día, pero Charlene es una mujer muy paciente. Comprende que debe sacrificarse en los primeros años para cosechar el fruto más adelante. De momento, me siento afortunado de no tener esposa e hijos.

Hablamos de Kipler, que ha hablado un poco con Shankle y ha corrido la voz. A los abogados les resulta muy difícil guardar secretos. Shankle le ha mencionado a Booker, que Kipler le ha mencionado a él, que su amigo, es decir yo, tiene un caso que podría reportar varios millones. Evidentemente, Kipler está convencido de que tengo a la compañía Great Benefit completamente atrapada y la única incógnita consiste en la cantidad que otorgará el jurado. Kipler está decidido a llevarme sano y salvo ante el jurado.

Espléndidas habladurías.

Booker quiere saber qué más estoy haciendo. Da la impresión de que Kipler también ha mencionado que, al parecer, no tengo mucho que hacer.

Mientras degustamos un pastel de queso, Booker dice que tiene unos sumarios a los que tal vez yo estaría dispuesto a echar una ojeada. Se explica. La segunda cadena de muebles de Memphis es una empresa llamada Ruffin, de propiedad negra y con tiendas repartidas por toda la ciudad. Todo el mundo conoce las tiendas Ruffin, sobre todo debido a sus abundantes anuncios por televisión a altas horas de la noche, y a su gran variedad de ofertas sin depósito. Su facturación es de unos ocho millones anuales, según Booker, y Marvin Shankle es su abogado. Ofrecen su propia financiación y tienen muchos malos deudores. Es la naturaleza de su negocio. El bufete Shankle está saturado con centenares de deudas pendientes de clientes de Ruffin.

¿Me interesan algunos de dichos casos?

Cobrar deudas pendientes no es la razón por la que los jóvenes inteligentes acuden a la Facultad de Derecho. Los deudores son personas que empezaron por comprar muebles baratos. La empresa no quiere recuperar los muebles, sino el dinero. En la mayoría de los casos, el acusado no responde ni comparece, de modo que el abogado se ve obligado a embargar efectos personales o salarios. Eso puede ser peligroso. Hace tres años, un joven iracundo a quien habían embargado el sueldo disparó contra un abogado de Memphis, aunque no lo mató.

Para que sea rentable, el abogado necesita un montón de dichos casos, porque sólo reportan unos centenares de dólares cada uno. La ley permite la inclusión de costes y honorarios.

Es un trabajo desagradable, pero, y ésa es la razón por la que Booker me lo ofrece, a todos se les puede sacar algo. Los honorarios son humildes, pero sumados permiten pagar gastos y comprar comida.

—Puedo mandarte cincuenta —dice—, acompañados de los formularios correspondientes. Además, te ayudaré a presentar el primer lote. Hay un sistema.

—¿Cuáles son los honorarios medios?

—Es difícil de decir, porque en algunos casos no cobrarás un centavo. Han abandonado la ciudad o se declaran insolventes. Pero el promedio es de unos cien dólares por caso.

Cien veces cincuenta son quinientos dólares.

—La duración media de cada caso es de unos cuatro meses —aclara— y, si lo deseas, puedo mandarte aproximadamente veinte mensuales. Los presentas todos al mismo tiempo, en la misma sala, ante el mismo juez, con la misma fecha de vencimiento y compareces una sola vez en el juzgado. Cógelos y prueba. El noventa por ciento es papeleo.

—Lo haré —respondo—. ¿Algo más que os sobre?

—Tal vez. Mantengo siempre los ojos abiertos.

Llega el café y nos dedicamos a lo que mejor hacen los abogados: hablar de otros abogados. En nuestro caso, chismorreamos acerca de nuestros condiscípulos y de cómo se desenvuelven en el mundo real.

Booker ha resucitado.

Deck es capaz de escabullirse por la más mínima abertura de una puerta sin hacer el menor ruido. Me lo hace constantemente. A veces estoy en mi escritorio concentrado, inmerso en uno de mis sumarios, cuando de pronto ¡ahí está Deck! Preferiría que llamara a la puerta, pero tampoco quiero ofenderlo. Ahí está, inesperadamente, frente a mi escritorio, con un montón de cartas en las manos, cuando de pronto ve un montón de carpetas en un rincón.

—¿Qué es eso? —pregunta.

—Trabajo —respondo.

Levanta una carpeta y la mira.

—¿Ruffin?

—Sí, señor. Ahora somos los abogados de la segunda cadena de venta de muebles más importante de Memphis.

—Es el cobro de una deuda —exclama con asco, como si le hubiera manchado las manos.

Curiosa reacción para alguien que sueña en desastres como el del barco de ruedas.

—Es trabajo honrado, Deck.

—Eso es golpearse la cabeza contra las paredes.

—Vete a perseguir ambulancias.

Deja la correspondencia sobre la mesa y se retira tan sigilosamente como ha entrado. Respiro hondo y abro un grueso sobre de Trent & Brent. Contiene un montón de cuartillas por lo menos de cinco centímetros de grosor.

Drummond ha respondido a mis preguntas, denegado mis solicitudes de admisiones y aportado algunos de los documentos solicitados. Tardaré horas en examinarlo y otras muchas para deducir lo que no ha facilitado.

Son particularmente importantes sus respuestas a mis preguntas. Debo tomarle declaración a un ejecutivo de la compañía y ha nombrado a un caballero llamado Jack Underhall, de la oficina central en Cleveland. También le he preguntado por los cargos y direcciones de varios empleados de Great Benefit, cuyos nombres aparecen repetidamente en los documentos de Dot.

Mediante un formulario que me ha facilitado el juez Kipler, preparo una notificación para tomar declaración a seis personas. Elijo una fecha de la semana próxima, perfectamente consciente de que Drummond no estará de acuerdo. Eso fue lo que hizo con la declaración de Dot y es la forma habitual de proceder. Acudirá a Kipler, que no se mostrará muy compasivo.

Voy a pasar un par de días en Cleveland, en la oficina central de Great Benefit. No me apetece, pero no tengo otra alternativa. Será un desplazamiento caro: viajes, hospedaje, comida y relatores del juzgado. Deck y yo todavía no hemos hablado de ello. Francamente, prefiero esperar a que llegue con un siniestro automovilístico de solución rápida.

Los documentos del caso Black ocupan ya un tercer fichero, que guardo en una caja de cartón en el suelo, junto a mi escritorio. Lo miro muchas veces todos los días y me pregunto si sé lo que estoy haciendo. ¿Quién soy yo para soñar en una gran victoria ante los tribunales, para infligir una derrota al gran Leo F. Drummond?

Nunca he abierto la boca ante un jurado.

Donny Ray estaba demasiado débil para hablar por teléfono hace una hora y me dirijo en coche a su casa de Granger. Estamos a finales de setiembre y no recuerdo la fecha exacta, pero Donny Ray recibió su primer diagnóstico hace algo más de un año. Dot tiene los ojos irritados cuando acude a la puerta.

—Creo que casi le hemos perdido —dice entre sollozos.

No creí que pudiera tener peor aspecto, pero su cara está todavía más frágil y pálida. Está dormido con las luces apagadas. El sol se acerca al horizonte de poniente y las sombras forman rectángulos perfectos sobre las blancas sábanas de su estrecha cama. El televisor está apagado. La habitación silenciosa.

—Hoy no ha probado bocado —susurra Dot mientras ambos le observamos.

—¿Mucho dolor?

—No demasiado. Le he puesto dos inyecciones.

—Me quedaré un rato con él —susurro al tiempo que me instalo en una silla plegable.

Dot se retira y oigo sus sollozos por el pasillo.

Para mí podría estar muerto. Concentro la mirada en su pecho, a la espera de ver cómo sube y baja ligeramente, pero no detecto nada. Se oscurece la habitación. Enciendo una lamparilla de la mesa junto a la puerta y se mueve ligeramente. Abre y cierra los ojos.

De modo que así mueren quienes no tienen seguro. En una sociedad repleta de médicos ricos, hospitales impecables, los aparatos científicos más avanzados y casi todos los ganadores del premio Nobel del mundo, parece escandaloso que se le permita a Donny Ray deteriorarse y morir sin una atención médica adecuada.

Podían haberlo salvado. Legalmente estaba con toda claridad al amparo de la cobertura de Great Benefit, por dudosa que fuera, cuando contrajo esa terrible enfermedad. En el momento del diagnóstico, estaba cubierto por una póliza que a sus padres les había costado un buen dinero. Según la ley, Great Benefit tenía la obligación contractual de facilitarle tratamiento médico.

En un futuro muy próximo, espero conocer a la persona responsable de esta muerte. Puede que no sea más que un subordinado que obedece órdenes. O el vicepresidente que las pronuncia. Me gustaría tomar una fotografía de Donny Ray en este momento y mostrársela a esa patética persona cuando finalmente la conozca.

Tose, vuelve a moverse y creo que intenta decirme que sigue vivo. Apago la luz y nos quedamos a oscuras.

Estoy solo y desarmado, asustado y sin experiencia, pero me acompaña la razón. Si los Black no ganan este proceso, nuestro sistema judicial es injusto.

Se enciende una farola en la lejanía y un rayo de luz perdido que se filtra por la ventana ilumina el pecho de Donny Ray. Ahora se mueve, sube y baja lentamente. Creo que intenta despertarse.

Ya no viviré muchos más momentos sentado en esta habitación. Contemplo su esquelético cuerpo, apenas visible bajo las sábanas, y prometo vengarme.

TREINTA Y TRES

El juez está iracundo cuando sube al estrado, con la toga flameando a su alrededor. Hoy se celebra una vista destinada a resolver sin interrupción multitud de peticiones relacionadas con docenas de casos. La sala está llena de abogados.

Nosotros vamos en primer lugar, porque el juez Kipler está perturbado. Yo he presentado una notificación para tomar declaración a seis funcionarios de Great Benefit, a partir del próximo lunes en Cleveland. Drummond se ha opuesto alegando, naturalmente, que no está disponible debido a sus sagradas obligaciones en los juzgados. Pero no sólo él está ocupado, sino que también lo están los seis futuros testigos. ¡Todos y cada uno de ellos!

Kipler organizó una conferencia por teléfono con Drummond y conmigo, y las cosas se pusieron feas, por lo menos para la defensa. Drummond está realmente comprometido y ha mandado por fax la orden preliminar de otro juzgado para demostrarlo. Lo que ha enojado al juez ha sido la afirmación de Drummond, de que no podría trasladarse tres días a Cleveland hasta dentro de dos meses. Además, los funcionarios en cuestión eran personas muy ocupadas y podrían transcurrir varios meses antes de poderlos reunir a todos en un mismo lugar.

Kipler ha ordenado esta vista para poder ensañarse oficialmente con Drummond y dejar constancia de ello. Puesto que he hablado con su señoría a diario durante los últimos cuatro días, sé exactamente lo que está a punto de ocurrir. No será agradable, ni yo tendré mucho que decir.

—Se abre la sesión —dice Kipler en dirección a la relatora, y los clónicos de la otra mesa, que hoy son cuatro, se inclinan sobre sus cuadernos—. Con referencia al caso dos uno cuatro seis seis ocho, *Black contra Great Benefit*, el demandante ha presentado una notificación para tomar declaración al representante designado de la compañía y a otros cinco empleados del acusado el lunes día cinco de octubre, en sus oficinas centrales de Cleveland, Ohio. El abogado defensor previsiblemente ha protestado, alegando la existencia de previas obligaciones. ¿Es eso correcto, señor Drummond?

—Sí, señor —responde Drummond, después de levantarse lentamente—. He presentado ya a la sala la copia de una orden preliminar para comparecer ante un tribunal federal en un caso que se inicia el lunes, en el que actúo como abogado principal de la defensa.

Drummond y Kipler han discutido ya violentamente dos veces sobre el mismo tema, pero es importante hacerlo ahora para que quede constancia oficial de ello.

—¿Y cuándo podría usted incluir este asunto en su agenda? —pregunta Kipler, con mucho sarcasmo.

Yo estoy solo en mi mesa. Deck no me acompaña. Hay por lo menos cuarenta abogados a mi espalda, en los bancos de la sala, todos contemplando la paliza que está a punto de recibir el gran Leo F. Drummond. Deben preguntarse quién soy yo, ese desconocido novato, tan bueno como para que el juez luche por mí.

—Bueno, su señoría, tengo una agenda muy completa —responde Drummond, mientras se mueve con cierta incomodidad—. Tal vez podría...

—Tengo entendido que ha dicho dentro de dos meses. ¿Estoy en lo cierto? —pregunta Kipler con aparente estupor, como si le pareciera imposible que cualquier abogado pudiera estar tan ocupado.

—Sí, señor. Dos meses.

—¿Asistiendo a juicios?

—Juicios, declaraciones, peticiones y apelaciones. Tendré mucho gusto en mostrarle mi agenda.

—En este momento, señor Drummond, no se me ocurre nada peor —responde Kipler—. Le diré lo que vamos a hacer y le ruego que me escuche atentamente, porque lo voy a dictar por escrito en forma de orden. Le recuerdo, señor Drummond, que este caso procede por vía rápida y en mi sala eso significa sin demoras. Estas seis declaraciones se iniciarán a primera hora de la mañana del lunes en Cleveland —afirma el juez, al tiempo que Drummond se hunde en su silla y empieza a escribir afanosamente—. Si no puede asistir, lo siento por usted. Pero a juzgar por su última comparecencia, dispone de otros cuatro abogados que colaboran con usted en este caso: Morehouse, Plunk, Hill y Grone. Todos ellos, dicho sea de paso, tienen mucha más experiencia que el señor Baylor que, si mal no recuerdo, se colegió el verano pasado. Comprendo que no pueden mandar a un solo abogado a Cleveland, que deberán ser por lo menos dos, pero estoy seguro de que disponen de suficientes abogados para representar adecuadamente a su cliente.

Las palabras del juez retumban en el aire. Los abogados a mi espalda están increíblemente inmóviles y silenciosos. Intuyo que muchos de ellos esperaban esto desde hacía años.

—Además, los seis empleados citados en la notificación estarán disponibles el lunes por la mañana y lo seguirán estando hasta que el señor Baylor haya terminado con ellos. Esta empresa está registrada para ejercer sus actividades comerciales en Tennessee. Está bajo mi jurisdicción en este asunto y ordeno a las seis personas en cuestión que colaboren plenamente.

Drummond y sus compañeros se hunden aún más en sus asientos y escriben con mayor rapidez.

—Por otra parte, la acusación ha solicitado fichas y documentos —agrega Kipler antes de hacer una pausa para mirar fijamente a la mesa de la defensa—. Escúcheme, señor Drummond, no pretenda hacer juegos malabares con los documentos. Insisto en una plena cooperación, con todos los documentos sobre la mesa. El lunes y el martes estaré pendiente del teléfono, y si me llama el señor Baylor para comunicarme que no ha recibido los documentos a los que tiene derecho, lo llamaré a usted para asegurarme de que lo haga. ¿Me ha comprendido?

—Sí, señor —responde Drummond.

—¿Puede asegurarse de que su cliente también lo comprenda?

—Creo que sí.

Kipler se relaja un poco y respira hondo. La sala está sumida en el más absoluto silencio.

—Pensándolo mejor, señor Drummond, me gustaría ver su agenda. En el supuesto de que no le importe.

Drummond se la ha ofrecido hace unos minutos y claramente no puede negársela ahora. Es una gruesa libreta encuadernada en cuero negro, donde consta la vida y compromisos de un hombre muy ocupado. Es también algo muy personal y sospecho que Drummond no tenía realmente intención de mostrársela al juez.

Se acerca con orgullo al estrado, la entrega a su señoría y espera. Kipler la hojea rápidamente sin leerla. Sólo busca fechas libres.

—Veo que no tiene nada previsto para la semana del ocho de febrero.

Drummond se acerca y mira la agenda, que Kipler sostiene al borde de la mesa. Asiente sin decir palabra. El juez se la devuelve y el abogado regresa a su silla.

—El juicio se celebrará el lunes día ocho de febrero —declara su señoría.

Yo respiro hondo y procuro parecer seguro de mí mismo. Cuatro meses parecen mucho tiempo, un período bastante largo, pero para alguien que no ha participado siquiera en el juicio de un ratero de poca monta, es aterrador. He memorizado el sumario una docena de veces. He memorizado las normas del proceso y de las pruebas. He leído infinidad de libros sobre la presentación de conclusiones, la elección de jurados, el interrogatorio de los testigos y sobre cómo ganar el juicio, pero no tengo ni idea de lo que sucederá en esta sala el ocho de febrero.

Kipler nos da permiso para retirarnos, recojo rápidamente mis papeles y abandono la sala. Al salir, me percato de que varios de los abogados que esperan su turno me miran fijamente.

¿Quién es ese individuo?

Aunque nunca me lo ha confesado abiertamente, ahora sé que los contactos más íntimos de Deck son un par de fisgones privados, a los que conoció cuando trabajaba para Bruiser. Uno de ellos, Butch, es un ex policía que comparte su afición por los casinos y con quien se desplaza una o dos veces por semana a Tunica para jugar al póquer y al blackjack.

De algún modo, Butch se las ha arreglado para localizar a Bobby Ott, el agente que les vendió la póliza a los Black. Lo ha encontrado en la granja penitenciaria del condado de Shelby, donde cumple diez meses de condena por la entrega de cheques falsos. La investigación subsiguiente ha revelado que Ott se ha divorciado recientemente y ha sido declarado insolvente.

A Deck le disgustó no haberlo atrapado. Ott tiene un montón de problemas legales. ¡Cuántos honorarios perdidos!

Un joven funcionario de la institución penitenciaria me recibe, después de que un corpulento guardia con unas gruesas manos me registrara e inspeccionara mi maletín. Me acompaña a una sala, cerca de la entrada del edificio principal. Es un cuarto cuadrado, con cámaras en las cuatro esquinas. Una verja central separa a los reclusos de las visitas. No tengo ningún inconveniente en hablar a través de una verja y espero que mi visita sea lo más breve posible. A los cinco minutos aparece Ott al otro lado. Tiene unos cuarenta años, lleva gafas de montura metálica y un corte de pelo militar. Es poco corpulento y viste el mono azul marino de la cárcel. El guardia que le ha acompañado se retira y nos deja solos.

Le paso mi tarjeta por una abertura en la parte inferior de la verja.

—Me llamo Rudy Baylor. Soy abogado.

¿Por qué sonará a algo tan siniestro?

Se lo toma bien e intenta sonreír. En otra época este individuo se ganaba la vida llamando a las puertas de los pobres y vendiéndoles seguros baratos, de modo que a pesar de su evidente mala suerte, en el fondo debe ser una persona amable, capaz de convencer a la gente para que le permitan entrar en sus casas.

—Encantado de conocerlo —dice rutinariamente—. ¿Qué le trae por aquí?

—Esto —respondo, al tiempo que saco una copia del pleito de mi maletín y se la paso por debajo de la verja—. Es una demanda judicial que he presentado en representación de unos antiguos clientes suyos.

—¿Quiénes? —pregunta después de recoger la demanda y examinar la primera hoja, que es una citación.

—Dot y Buddy Black, y su hijo Donny Ray.

—Great Benefit, ¿no es cierto? ¿Le importa que lo lea?

Deck me ha explicado que con frecuencia los agentes representan a más de una compañía.

—En absoluto. Se le cita a usted como acusado. Adelante.

Su voz y sus movimientos son muy calculados. No desperdicia energía alguna. Lee con mucha lentitud y pasa las páginas con gran reticencia. Pobre hombre. Ha sufrido un divorcio, perdido todo lo demás al declararse insolvente, ahora cumple una condena en la cárcel y de pronto aparezco yo, con toda mi arrogancia, para demandarlo por diez millones.

Pero no parece afectarle. Acaba de leer y deja los papeles sobre el mostrador.

—Ya sabe que estoy al amparo del tribunal de insolvencia —dice.

—Sí, lo sé.

En realidad no es cierto. Según los datos que obran en el juzgado, presentó su solicitud de insolvencia en marzo, dos meses antes de que lo hiciera yo, y ya ha sido rehabilitado. Una antigua insolvencia no siempre evita demandas futuras, pero no se lo comento. Este individuo es más pobre que una rata. Goza de inmunidad.

—Nos hemos visto obligados a incluirlo como acusado porque fue usted quien vendió la póliza.

—Sí, lo comprendo. Usted se limita a cumplir con su obligación.

—Exactamente. ¿Cuándo sale?

—Dentro de dieciocho días. ¿Por qué?

—Es posible que queramos tomarle declaración.

—¿Aquí?

—Tal vez.

—¿Qué prisa tienen? Deje que salga y declararé.

—Me lo pensaré.

Mi visita es como unas pequeñas vacaciones para él y no tiene prisa para que me vaya. Hablamos unos minutos de la vida en la cárcel y empiezo a mirar hacia la puerta.

Nunca había estado en el primer piso de la casa de la señorita Birdie, y es tan húmedo y polvoriento como la planta baja. Abro las puertas de todas las habitaciones, enciendo las luces, miro rápidamente a mi alrededor, apago las luces y vuelvo a cerrar las puertas. El suelo del pasillo cruje al andar. Hay una escalerilla que sube a un segundo piso, pero me produce aprensión.

La casa es mucho mayor de lo que imaginaba. Y mucho más solitaria. Es difícil imaginarla aquí sola; me siento profundamente culpable de no haber pasado más tiempo con ella, de no haberla acompañado a ver sus culebrones y series repetidas por televisión, de no haber comido más bocadillos de pavo y tomado más tazas de café instantáneo con ella.

La planta baja parece tan tranquila como el primer piso y cierro la puerta del jardín a mi espalda. Es extraña su ausencia. No recuerdo que me reconfortara su presencia, pero siempre era agradable saber que había alguien ahí, en esa enorme casa, por si necesitaba algo. Ahora me siento aislado.

En la cocina contemplo el teléfono. Es uno de los antiguos modelos de disco giratorio y siento la tentación de llamar a Kelly. Si contesta, ya se me ocurrirá algo. Si oigo la voz de su marido, colgaré. La llamada puede ser localizada a esta casa, pero yo no vivo aquí.

Hoy he pensado en ella más que ayer. Esta semana más que la anterior.

Necesito verla.

TREINTA Y CUATRO

Me dirijo a la terminal de autobuses en la furgoneta de Deck. Es domingo, por la mañana temprano. Hace un tiempo claro y hermoso, con los primeros indicios de otoño en el aire. Memphis en octubre es un lugar encantador.

El viaje de ida y vuelta en avión a Cleveland cuesta casi setecientos dólares. Calculamos que una habitación en un motel barato, pero mínimamente seguro, costaría cuarenta dólares por noche y que el gasto de la comida iba a ser insignificante, porque con poco me basta. Somos nosotros quienes tomamos la declaración y, por consiguiente, su coste corre por cuenta nuestra. La relatora más barata con la que he hablado en Cleveland cobra cien dólares por comparecer, más dos dólares por página copiada y mecanografiada. No es inusual que dichas declaraciones consten de un mínimo de cien páginas. También me gustaría grabarlas en vídeo, pero eso es impensable.

También lo es, al parecer, la idea de viajar en avión. El bufete de Rudy Baylor no puede permitirse pagar el billete a Cleveland. No me atrevo en modo alguno a arriesgarme con mi Toyota por la autopista. Si se averiara me dejaría colgado y tendría que aplazar las declaraciones. Deck se ha ofrecido más o menos a prestarme su furgoneta, pero tampoco la considero fiable para un desplazamiento de mil seiscientos kilómetros.

Los autocares Greyhound son seguros, aunque terriblemente lentos. Siempre acaban por llegar. No es mi transporte predilecto, pero qué le vamos a hacer. Tampoco tengo mucha prisa. Así podré contemplar el paisaje y nos ahorraremos un valioso dinero. Hemos considerado muchos aspectos.

Deck conduce sin decir gran cosa. Creo que está un poco avergonzado porque no nos podemos permitir algo mejor. Además, sabe que él debería también viajar conmigo. Voy a enfrentarme a testigos hostiles y tendré que repasar montones de nue-

305

vos documentos con suma rapidez. Sería reconfortante tener otra mente cerca de mí.

Nos despedimos en el aparcamiento de la estación. Promete cuidar del despacho y procurar conseguir algún trabajo. Estoy seguro de que lo intentará. Se aleja en dirección a Saint Peter.

Nunca he viajado en un Greyhound. La terminal, pequeña pero limpia, está llena de viajeros de domingo por la mañana, la mayoría de los cuales son ancianos y negros. Me acerco a una ventanilla y compro mi billete. Le cuesta a mi bufete ciento treinta y nueve dólares.

El autocar sale a las ocho en punto en dirección a Arkansas, y luego hacia el norte, en dirección a San Luis. Afortunadamente, logro evitar la molestia de sentarme junto a alguien.

El autocar está casi lleno, con sólo tres o cuatro asientos libres. Según el horario, llegaremos a San Luis en seis horas, a Indianapolis a las siete de la tarde y a Cleveland a las once de la noche. Eso supone quince horas en este autocar. Las declaraciones comienzan a las nueve de la mañana.

Estoy seguro de que mis rivales de Trent & Brent duermen todavía, tomarán un buen desayuno cuando despierten, leerán el periódico del domingo en el jardín con sus respectivas esposas, tal vez alguno de ellos vaya a la iglesia, luego comerán un suculento almuerzo y jugarán un rato al golf. A eso de las cinco, sus esposas les llevarán al aeropuerto, donde les darán un beso de despedida como Dios manda y se embarcarán en primera clase. Al cabo de una hora aterrizarán en Cleveland, donde los recibirá indudablemente un lacayo de Great Benefit, que los trasladará en coche al mejor hotel de la ciudad. Después de una exquisita cena, con copas y vino, se reunirán en una lujosa sala de conferencias donde se confabularán contra mí hasta avanzada la noche. Cuando yo llegue a mi motel barato, ellos se acostarán tranquilos, relajados y listos para la batalla.

El edificio de Great Benefit está en un barrio lujoso de Cleveland, fundado por blancos adinerados. Le explico al taxista que busco un motel barato en las cercanías y sabe exactamente adónde llevarme. Para frente al Plaza Inn. Al lado está McDonald's y en frente Blockbuster Video. No es más que una calle con comercios a ambos lados: prostíbulos, comida rápida, anuncios luminosos que parpadean, centros comerciales y moteles baratos. Cerca de aquí debe de haber unas galerías comerciales. Parece un lugar seguro.

Hay muchas habitaciones libres y pago treinta y dos dólares

al contado por una noche. Pido el recibo, tal y como me ha dicho Deck que lo hiciera.

Dos minutos después de la medianoche me meto en la cama, me dedico a contemplar el techo y, entre otras cosas, me doy cuenta de que a excepción del recepcionista, nadie en el mundo sabe dónde estoy. No tengo a nadie a quien llamar.

Evidentemente, no logro conciliar el sueño.

Desde que empecé a odiar Great Benefit, he tenido una imagen mental de su oficina central. Imagino un edificio alto y moderno con mucho cristal reluciente, una fuente frente a la entrada principal, mástiles, y el nombre y logotipo de la empresa repujados en bronce. Un lugar rebosante de riqueza y prosperidad corporativa.

Pero no es exactamente así. El edificio es fácil de encontrar, porque la dirección está escrita en grandes letras negras junto a la entrada de hormigón: 5550 Baker Gap Road. Pero el nombre de Great Benefit no aparece por ninguna parte. En realidad, el edificio no es identificable desde la calle. No hay fuentes, ni mástiles, sólo una enorme plaza de bloques de cinco plantas, aparentemente adosados. Es todo muy moderno e increíblemente feo. Las fachadas son de cemento blanco con ventanas ahumadas.

Afortunadamente la entrada está señalizada y entro en un pequeño vestíbulo, con unas cuantas plantas en macetas de plástico junto a una pared y una atractiva recepcionista junto a otra. Lleva unos elegantes auriculares en la cabeza, con un fino cable junto a la mejilla que sostiene un pequeño micrófono cerca de sus labios. En la pared a su espalda figuran los nombres de indefinidas empresas: PinnConn Group, Green Lakes Marine y Great Benefit Life Insurance, cada una con su correspondiente logotipo repujado en bronce. ¿Cuál es propietaria de las demás?

—Me llamo Rudy Baylor y tengo una cita con el señor Paul Moyer —digo educadamente.

—Un momento, por favor —responde antes de pulsar un botón—. Señor Moyer, está aquí el señor Baylor —dice sin dejar de sonreír.

Su despacho debe de estar cerca, porque en menos de un minuto me recibe efusivamente, estrechándome la mano y colmándome de cumplidos. Le sigo por un pasillo hasta el ascensor. Es casi tan joven como yo y habla incesantemente sin decir nada. Nos apeamos en el cuarto piso y ya estoy completamente desorientado en esa horrenda monstruosidad arquitectónica. El suelo del cuarto piso está enmoquetado, las luces tenues y hay cuadros en las paredes. Moyer no deja de charlar mientras avanzamos por el pasillo, abre una gruesa puerta y me indica mi lugar.

Bienvenido a la casa de la fortuna. Me encuentro en una sala de reuniones, con una larga y ancha reluciente mesa elíptica en el centro de la misma, y por lo menos quince sillas tapizadas en cuero a su alrededor. Una brillante araña cuelga del centro del techo. A mi izquierda hay una barra. A mi derecha una bandeja con café, bollos y galletas. Alrededor de la comida hay un grupo de conspiradores, por lo menos ocho individuos, todos ellos con traje oscuro, camisa blanca, corbata a rayas y zapatos negros. Ocho contra uno. El temblor de mis entrañas se convierte en terremoto. ¿Dónde está Tyrone Kipler cuando lo necesito? En este momento, incluso la presencia de Deck sería reconfortante.

Cuatro de ellos son mis compinches de Trent & Brent. Otro me resulta familiar de la vista en Memphis y los otros tres me son desconocidos. Todos dejan inmediatamente de hablar cuando se percatan de mi llegada. Momentáneamente, dejan incluso de beber y masticar para mirarme fijamente. He interrumpido una conversación muy importante.

T. Pierce Morehouse es el primero en reaccionar.

—Adelante, Rudy —dice, pero sólo porque se siente obligado a ello.

Saludo con la cabeza a B. Dewey Clay Hill III, a Alec Plunk hijo y a Brandon Fuller Grone, y luego estrecho la mano de los otros cuatro conforme Morehouse recita sus nombres, que olvido inmediatamente. Jack Underhall es el rostro familiar de las escaramuzas en la sala de Kipler. Es uno de los abogados empleados por Great Benefit, a quien han nombrado como portavoz de la compañía.

Mis rivales parecen frescos y relajados después de un vuelo rápido, una tranquila cena y una descansada noche. Su ropa está planchada y almidonada, como si hubiera salido del armario esta mañana y no de una maleta. Mis ojos están cansados e irritados, mi camisa arrugada. Pero tengo cosas más importantes en que pensar.

Llega la taquígrafa y T. Pierce nos conduce a un extremo de la mesa. Señala aquí y allá, reservando la cabeza de la mesa para el testigo, y preguntándose momentáneamente dónde debería instalarse cada uno. Por fin lo decide. Me instalo en la silla indicada e intento acercarla a la mesa. No es fácil, pesa una tonelada. Al otro lado de la mesa, por lo menos a tres metros de distancia, los cuatro muchachos de Trent & Brent abren sus maletines con todo el ruido posible: cerrojos, cremalleras, carpetas, movimiento de papeles... En pocos segundos, la mesa está cubierta de hojas.

Los cuatro funcionarios de traje oscuro deambulan por detrás de la relatora, sin saber exactamente qué hacer, a la espera de las instrucciones de T. Pierce.

—Bien, Rudy —dice, después de organizar finalmente sus papeles—. Hemos considerado que podríamos empezar por tomarle declaración al portavoz de la compañía, Jack Underhall.

Lo suponía y ya he decidido no aceptarlo.

—No, creo que no —respondo, con cierto nerviosismo.

Procuro desesperadamente actuar con serenidad, a pesar de encontrarme en terreno ajeno y rodeado de enemigos. Hay varias razones por las que no deseo empezar por el portavoz de la compañía, primordialmente porque eso es lo que quieren ellos. Son mis declaraciones, no dejo de repetirme.

—¿Usted perdone? —exclama T. Pierce.

—Me ha oído perfectamente. Quiero empezar por Jackie Lemancyzk, la encargada de reclamaciones. Pero antes quiero la ficha.

El núcleo de cualquier caso de mala fe es la ficha de reclamaciones: conjunto de cartas y documentos que el encargado de reclamaciones guarda en la oficina central. En un buen caso de mala fe, la ficha de reclamaciones es una asombrosa relación cronológica de chapuza tras chapuza. Tengo acceso legal a la misma y debí haberla recibido hace diez días. Drummond se declaró inocente y acusó a su cliente de actuar con suma lentitud. Kipler ordenó categóricamente en una orden judicial que la ficha estuviera a mi disposición a primera hora de esta mañana.

—Consideramos que sería preferible empezar por el señor Underhall —repite sin autoridad T. Pierce.

—No me importa lo que ustedes consideren —respondo, sumamente perturbado e indignado, con la confianza de que el juez es mi amigo—. ¿Quiere que llamemos al juez? —pregunto en tono de desafío, como un auténtico chulo.

Aunque Kipler está ausente, su presencia domina el ambiente. Su orden especifica con toda claridad que los seis testigos que he solicitado deben estar a mi disposición a las nueve de esta mañana y que el orden de las declaraciones se hará sólo a mi discreción. Deben permanecer disponibles hasta que haya concluido con ellos. La orden también deja abierta la posibilidad de declaraciones adicionales, si la investigación y respuestas obtenidas así lo aconsejan. No he podido evitar amenazarlos con una llamada a su señoría.

—Bueno... el caso es que tenemos un problema con Jackie Lemancyzk —responde T. Pierce mientras mira con nerviosismo a los cuatro individuos de traje oscuro, que han retrocedido para acercarse a la puerta y tienen todos la mirada fija en sus zapatos.

T. Pierce está frente a mí, al otro lado de la mesa, y tiene dificultades.

—¿Qué clase de problema? —pregunto.

—Ya no trabaja en la empresa.

Se me abre inadvertidamente la boca. Estoy auténticamente estupefacto y durante unos momentos no se me ocurre nada. Lo miro e intento recapacitar.

—¿Cuándo se marchó? —pregunto.

—Al final de la semana pasada.

—¿Cuándo exactamente? Estuvimos en el juzgado el jueves. ¿Lo sabían entonces?

—No. Se marchó el sábado.

—¿Ha sido un despido?

—Ha dimitido.

—¿Dónde está ahora?

—Ya no trabaja para la compañía, ¿comprende? No podemos presentarla como testigo.

Examino momentáneamente mis notas, en busca de otros nombres.

—De acuerdo, ¿qué me dice de Tony Krick, segundo encargado de reclamaciones?

Más contorsiones, tics y nervios.

—También se ha marchado —responde T. Pierce—. Ha sido despedido.

Mi segundo bofetón. Pienso desesperadamente en cómo reaccionar.

En realidad, Great Benefit ha despedido a ciertas personas para evitar que hablaran conmigo.

—Vaya coincidencia —exclamo sin saber cómo proceder.

Plunk, Hill y Grone se niegan a levantar la mirada de sus cuadernos. Me pregunto qué escriben.

—En este momento nuestro cliente atraviesa un período de reducción de empleo —declara T. Pierce, con el rostro perfectamente impasible.

—¿Qué me dice de Richard Pellrod, el encargado decano de reclamaciones? Deje que lo adivine, también lo han despedido.

—No. Está aquí.

—¿Y Russell Krokit?

—El señor Krokit ha ido a trabajar en otra compañía.

—De modo que no lo han despedido.

—No.

—Ha dimitido, como Jackie Lemancyzk.

—Exactamente.

Russell Krokit era el encargado decano de reclamaciones cuando escribió la «estúpida carta». A pesar de los nervios y el miedo que me producía este viaje, esperaba con anhelo su declaración.

—¿Y Everett Lufkin, vicepresidente de reclamaciones? ¿Despedido?

—No. Está aquí.

Se hace un silencio increíblemente largo, durante el que todo el mundo finge hacer algo, hasta que las aguas vuelven a su cauce. Mi pleito ha causado víctimas. Escribo cuidadosamente en mi cuaderno una lista de lo que debo hacer a continuación.

—¿Dónde está la ficha? —pregunto.

T. Pierce levanta un montón de papeles que tiene a su espalda y me los acerca por encima de la mesa. Es un conjunto de pulcras copias, sujetas con gruesas gomas elásticas.

—¿Están por orden cronológico? —pregunto, puesto que así lo ha ordenado Kipler.

—Eso creo —responde T. Pierce, al tiempo que mira a los cuatro funcionarios de Great Benefit, como si estuviera dispuesto a estrangularlos.

La ficha mide casi once centímetros de grosor.

—Concédanme una hora —digo sin retirar las gomas elásticas—. Luego proseguiremos.

—Por supuesto —responde T. Pierce—. Ahí hay una pequeña sala de conferencias —agrega mientras señala la pared a mi espalda.

Junto con Jack, de traje oscuro, me acompaña a la sala adjunta, donde me dejan inmediatamente solo. Me instalo junto a la mesa y empiezo a examinar los documentos.

Al cabo de una hora entro de nuevo en la sala de juntas. Están tomando café y charlando angustiados.

—Es preciso llamar al juez —declaro, y T. Pierce presta inmediatamente atención—. Desde aquí —agrego señalando el cuarto donde he estado trabajando.

Con T. Pierce en un teléfono y yo en otro, marco el número del despacho del juez Kipler. Contesta a la segunda llamada. Nos identificamos y le damos los buenos días.

—Aquí han surgido ciertos problemas, su señoría —digo procurando iniciar la conversación en el tono adecuado.

—¿Qué clase de problemas? —pregunta.

T. Pierce escucha, con la mirada fija en el suelo.

—En primer lugar, de los seis testigos especificados en mi notificación, y su orden judicial, de repente tres han desapareci-

311

do. Han dimitido, han sido despedidos, o algo les ha sucedido, pero no están aquí. Sucedió al final de la semana pasada.

—¿Quiénes?

Estoy seguro de que tiene la ficha delante, con los nombres de los convocados.

—Jackie Lemancyzk, Tony Krick y Russell Krokit ya no trabajan en la compañía. Pellrod, Lufkin y Underhall, el portavoz, han sobrevivido milagrosamente a la abstersión.

—¿Y la ficha?

—Está en mi poder y la he hojeado.

—¿Y bien?

—Falta por lo menos un documento —respondo con la mirada fija en T. Pierce, que frunce con incredulidad el entrecejo.

—¿Cuál? —pregunta Kipler.

—La «estúpida carta». No está en la ficha. No he tenido tiempo de comprobar todo lo demás.

Los abogados de Great Benefit vieron la «estúpida carta» por primera vez la semana pasada. La copia que Dot le entregó a Drummond durante su declaración, tenía la palabra «copia» estampada tres veces sobre el encabezamiento. Lo hice deliberadamente para poder identificarla si aparecía de nuevo. La original está cuidadosamente guardada en mis ficheros. Habría sido demasiado arriesgado para Drummond y sus secuaces mandar dicha copia a Great Benefit, para incluirla en la ficha de reclamaciones.

—¿Es eso cierto, Pierce? —pregunta Kipler.

Pierce está sinceramente desconcertado.

—Lo siento, su señoría, no lo sé. He repasado la ficha pero, bueno, no lo sé, supongo que sí. No lo he comprobado todo.

—¿Están los dos en la misma sala? —pregunta Kipler.

—Sí, señor —respondemos simultáneamente.

—Bien. Pierce, abandone la sala. Rudy, quédese al teléfono.

T. Pierce empieza a decir algo, pero recapacita y cierra la boca. Confuso, cuelga el teléfono y abandona la sala.

—Bien, señor juez, ahora estoy solo —digo.

—¿Cuál es su actitud? —pregunta.

—Bastante tensa.

—No me sorprende. Eso es lo que vamos a hacer. El hecho de eliminar testigos y ocultar documentos me autoriza a ordenar que se tomen aquí las declaraciones. Es discrecional y se han merecido el castigo. Creo que debería tomarle declaración exclusivamente a Underhall. Pregúntele todo lo imaginable, pero procure obligarle a concretar respecto al cese de los tres testigos ausentes. Ensáñese con él. Cuando haya terminado, regrese a casa. Ordenaré una vista para más adelante esta semana y llegaremos al fondo de este asunto. Traiga también la ficha del cliente.

Tomo notas con la mayor rapidez posible.

—Ahora déjeme hablar con Pierce, y le pondré sobre aviso.

Jack Underhall es un pequeño personaje compacto, con un fino bigote y pronunciación entrecortada. Aclara aspectos de la compañía propiamente dicha. Great Benefit es propiedad de PinnConn, una corporación privada cuyos propietarios son de difícil identificación. Le formulo numerosas preguntas sobre las afiliaciones y vínculos de las tres empresas domiciliadas en este edificio, y el tema llega a ser terriblemente confuso. Hablamos durante una hora de la estructura corporativa, empezando por el director gerente del grupo. Hablamos de productos, ventas, mercados, divisiones y personal, todo ello hasta cierto punto interesante, pero en general inútil. Me muestra dos cartas de dimisión de los testigos ausentes y me asegura que su retirada no ha tenido nada que ver con el caso que nos ocupa.

Después de tres horas de interrogatorio, lo doy por concluido. Me había resignado a pasar por lo menos tres días en Cleveland, encerrado en una misma sala con los muchachos de Trent & Brent, luchando con un testigo hostil tras otro, y examinando montones de documentos por la noche.

Pero abandono el lugar poco antes de las dos, para no volver nunca más, cargado de nuevos documentos que Deck examinará meticulosamente, con la seguridad de que esos cretinos se verán ahora obligados a acudir a mi terreno y declarar en mi sala, en presencia de mi juez predilecto.

El regreso a Memphis en autocar parece mucho más rápido.

TREINTA Y CINCO

Deck tiene unas tarjetas de visita que lo describen como «seudo-abogado», una especie nueva para mí. Circula por los pasillos del juzgado y se acerca a los pequeños delincuentes, que esperan para comparecer por primera vez ante diversos jueces. Detecta a un individuo que parece asustado, con un papel en la mano, y se lanza al ataque. Deck lo denomina el doble paso del halcón, una oferta rápida de servicios jurídicos perfeccionada por numerosos abogados callejeros que deambulan por el juzgado. En una ocasión me invitó a que lo acompañara, para aprender los pasos básicos. Rechacé la oferta.

Derrick Dogan había sido elegido inicialmente como víctima potencial del doble paso de halcón, pero la operación fracasó cuando le preguntó a Deck:

—¿Qué diablos es un seudoabogado?

A pesar de que Deck siempre tiene una respuesta a mano, no logró satisfacer al cliente potencial y se retiró inmediatamente. Pero Dogan se guardó la tarjeta que Deck le había entregado. Aquel mismo día se precipitó contra él un adolescente que conducía con exceso de velocidad. Veinticuatro horas después de haber mandado a Deck a la porra en la puerta del juzgado, llamó al número de la tarjeta desde una habitación semiprivada de Saint Peter. Deck contestó el teléfono desde el despacho, donde yo intentaba descifrar una trama impenetrable de documentos del seguro. A los pocos minutos, nos desplazamos a toda prisa hacia el hospital. Dogan quería hablar con un verdadero abogado y no con un seudoabogado.

Ésta es una visita semilegítima al hospital, la primera en mi caso. Cuando encontramos a Dogan está solo, con una pierna rota, costillas y una muñeca fracturadas, y cortes y contusiones en la cara. Le hablo como un auténtico abogado y le suelto el habitual discurso bien ensayado, aconsejándole que no hable con ninguna compañía de seguros, ni le diga nada a nadie. Somos nosotros contra ellos y mi bufete resuelve más accidentes de tráfico que cualquier otro de la ciudad. Deck sonríe. Ha sido un buen profesor.

Dogan firma un contrato y un formulario que nos permitirá obtener su historial médico. Está bastante dolorido y nos quedamos poco rato. Su nombre está en el contrato. Nos despedimos y prometemos verlo mañana.

Al mediodía, Deck ha conseguido una copia del informe del accidente y ha hablado ya con el padre del adolescente. Están asegurados con State Farm. El padre, un tanto precipitadamente, le revela a Deck que, en su opinión, la póliza tiene un límite de veinticinco mil dólares. Tanto él como su hijo lamentan muchísimo lo sucedido. No se preocupe, responde Deck, agradecido de que el accidente haya tenido lugar.

Un tercio de veinticinco mil son algo más de ocho mil. Almorzamos en un maravilloso restaurante llamado Dux, en The Peabody. Yo tomo vino. Deck come postre. Es el momento más glorioso en la historia de nuestro bufete. Durante tres horas, contamos y gastamos el dinero.

El jueves de la semana de mi viaje a Cleveland nos encontramos en la sala de Kipler a las cinco y media de la tarde. Su señoría ha elegido la hora para que el gran Leo F. Drummond pueda estar presente, después de un largo día en el juzgado, y ensañarse una vez más con él. Con su presencia, el equipo de la defensa está completo y a pesar de la soberbia de sus cinco componentes, todo el mundo sabe que les tocan las de perder. Jack Underhall, uno de los abogados empleados de Great Benefit, está también en la sala, pero los demás funcionarios de traje oscuro han preferido permanecer en Cleveland. No se lo reprocho.

—Le advertí lo de los documentos, señor Drummond —dice su señoría desde el estrado. Todavía no han transcurrido cinco minutos desde que se abrió la sesión, y Drummond ya está recibiendo palos—. Creí haber sido suficientemente específico, incluso se lo entregué todo por escrito, como usted sabe, en forma de orden judicial. Dígame, ¿qué ha ocurrido?

Probablemente no es culpa de Drummond. Su cliente juega con él y tengo la firme sospecha de que ya se ha ensañado, a su vez, con los muchachos de Cleveland. Leo Drummond es un gran egocentrista y no asimila fácilmente la humillación. Casi me inspira compasión. Está plenamente inmerso en un pleito de muchísimos millones de dólares en el tribunal federal, probablemente duerme apenas tres horas diarias, tiene un montón de cosas en la cabeza y ahora le obligan a comparecer en esta sala para defender la sospechosa conducta de su avieso cliente.

Casi me inspira compasión.

—No hay excusa, su señoría —responde, con convincente sinceridad.

—¿Cuándo descubrió usted que esos tres testigos habían dejado de trabajar para su cliente?

—El domingo por la tarde.

—¿Intentó usted comunicárselo al abogado de la acusación?

—Sí, señor. No pude localizarlo. Llamamos incluso a las líneas aéreas. No hubo suerte.

Debieron llamar a Greyhound.

Kipler mueve exageradamente la cabeza para manifestar su desazón.

—Siéntese, señor Drummond —ordena el juez, cuando yo no he abierto todavía la boca—. Éste es mi plan, caballeros —prosigue su señoría—. Dentro de una semana, a partir del próximo lunes, nos reuniremos aquí para tomar declaraciones. Las siguientes personas comparecerán en representación del acusado: Richard Pellrod, encargado decano de reclamaciones, Everett Lufkin, vicepresidente de reclamaciones, Kermit Aldy, vicepresidente de contratación de pólizas, Bradford Barnes, vicepresidente administrativo, y M. Wilfred Keeley, director gerente.

Kipler me había ordenado elaborar una lista del personal requerido. Casi se oye cómo los muchachos al otro lado del pasillo succionan el aire de la sala.

—No habrá pretextos, retrasos, ni prórrogas. Se desplazarán evidentemente por cuenta propia. Se pondrán a disposición de la acusación para declarar y sólo podrán retirarse a discreción del señor Baylor. Todos los gastos de las declaraciones, incluidos los de taquigrafía y copias, correrán a cargo de Great Benefit. Anticipemos que dichas declaraciones durarán tres días.

»Además, el miércoles de la semana próxima a lo más tardar, cinco días antes de la fecha fijada para las declaraciones, le serán entregadas a la acusación copias de todos los documentos. Dichas copias deberán ser pulcras y estar en orden cronológico. En caso de incumplimiento, se impondrán severas sanciones.

»Y, a propósito de sanciones, por la presente condeno al acusado, Great Benefit, a pagarle al señor Baylor los gastos de su inútil desplazamiento a Cleveland. Señor Baylor, ¿cuánto cuesta el billete de ida y vuelta en avión a Cleveland?

—Setecientos dólares —respondo sin mentir.

—¿En primera clase o turista?

—Turista.

—Señor Drummond, ustedes mandaron a cuatro abogados a Cleveland. ¿Viajaron en primera clase o turista?

Drummond mira fugazmente a T. Pierce, que agacha la cabeza como un chiquillo sorprendido sisando.

—Primera clase —responde.

—Lo suponía. ¿Cuánto cuesta el billete de primera clase?

—Mil trescientos dólares.

—¿Cuánto gastó en comida y alojamiento, señor Baylor?

A decir verdad, menos de cuarenta dólares. Pero sería terriblemente embarazoso reconocerlo ante el público de la sala. Ojalá me hubiera hospedado en uno de los mejores hoteles.

—Unos sesenta dólares —respondo con cierta incomodidad, pero sin ser avaricioso.

Estoy seguro de que sus habitaciones costaron ciento cincuenta dólares por noche. Kipler lo anota todo con mucho melodrama, sin dejar de calcular mentalmente.

—¿Cuánto tiempo pasó viajando? ¿Un par de horas en cada desplazamiento?

—Aproximadamente —respondo.

—A doscientos dólares por hora, eso son ochocientos dólares. ¿Algún gasto adicional?

—Doscientos cincuenta para la taquígrafa.

Toma nota, suma y verifica sus cifras.

—Ordeno al acusado a pagarle al señor Baylor la suma de dos mil cuatrocientos diez dólares como sanción, en un plazo máximo de cinco días. En el caso de que transcurridos los cinco días el señor Baylor no lo haya recibido, dicha suma se duplicará automáticamente a diario hasta que el cheque obre en su poder. ¿Lo ha comprendido, señor Drummond?

No puedo reprimir una sonrisa.

Drummond se levanta despacio, ligeramente doblado por la cintura y las manos abiertas. Está furioso, pero se controla.

—Protesto —exclama.

—Se toma nota de su protesta. Su cliente dispone de cinco días.

—No hay ninguna prueba de que el señor Baylor viajara en primera clase.

Es propio del abogado defensor oponerse a todo, e instintivo buscarle cinco patas al gato. También es rentable. Pero la cantidad es insignificante para su cliente y Drummond debería comprender que está perdiendo el tiempo.

—Es evidente, señor Drummond, que el viaje de ida y vuelta

a Cleveland cuesta mil trescientos dólares. Y eso es lo que le ordeno pagar a su cliente.

—El señor Baylor no recibe una tarifa horaria —responde.

—¿Sugiere que su tiempo carece de valor?

—No.

Lo que pretende decir es que no soy más que un abogado novato de poca monta y que mi tiempo es mucho menos valioso que el suyo o el de sus colegas.

—En tal caso, le pagará doscientos dólares por hora. Y considérese afortunado, porque había pensado en obligarle a pagar todas las horas que pasó en Cleveland.

¡Por los pelos!

Drummond agita los brazos frustrado y vuelve a sentarse. Kipler lo mira fijamente. A los pocos meses de su nombramiento, es ya famosa su repulsión por las grandes empresas. Se ha mostrado pródigo con las sanciones en otros casos y no dejan de correr las voces por los círculos jurídicos. Con poco basta.

—¿Algo más? —exclama el juez en dirección a la defensa.

—No, señor —respondo en voz alta, sólo para que todos sepan que sigo ahí.

Se produce un movimiento colectivo de cabezas entre los conspiradores al otro lado del pasillo y Kipler golpea su martillo. Recojo rápidamente mis papeles y abandono la sala.

Para cenar me como un bocadillo de tocino con Dot. El sol se oculta lentamente tras los árboles del jardín, más allá del Fairlane donde Buddy está sentado y del que se niega a salir para comer. Dot me cuenta que cada día pasa más tiempo en el vehículo, a causa de Donny Ray. Le quedan pocos días de vida, y Buddy lo encaja ocultándose en el coche y emborrachándose. Se sienta con su hijo unos minutos todas las mañanas, suele salir de su habitación llorando y procura evitar a todo el mundo el resto del día.

Además, no acostumbra a salir cuando hay alguien de visita en la casa. No me importa. Ni tampoco a Dot. Hablamos del pleito, de la conducta de Great Benefit y de la increíble ecuanimidad del juez Tyrone Kipler, pero ha perdido interés. La enérgica mujer que conocí hace seis meses en el Parque de los Cipreses parece haberse dado por vencida. Entonces creía sinceramente que un abogado, cualquier abogado, incluso yo, podía asustar a Great Benefit para que actuara correctamente. Cabía todavía la posibilidad de un milagro. Ahora, ya no queda esperanza alguna.

Dot se culpará siempre a sí misma por la muerte de Donny

Ray. Me ha dicho en más de una ocasión que debió consultar inmediatamente a un abogado cuando Great Benefit denegó por primera vez la reclamación. Pero optó por escribirles ella misma. Ahora tengo la sensación de que Great Benefit habría reaccionado con rapidez si se les hubiera amenazado con un pleito, y facilitado el tratamiento necesario. Lo creo, en primer lugar, porque su actitud es completamente improcedente, y ellos lo saben. Y, en segundo lugar, porque ofrecieron setenta y cinco mil dólares cuando yo, un novato sin experiencia, acababa de iniciar los trámites del proceso. Están asustados. Sus abogados están asustados. Los muchachos de Cleveland están asustados.

Dot me sirve una taza de café instantáneo descafeinado y luego me deja para comprobar cómo sigue su marido. Me llevo el café a la casa, a la habitación de Donny Ray, que está dormido entre las sábanas, acurrucado sobre su lado derecho. La única luz es la de una pequeña lámpara en el rincón. Me siento cerca de la misma, de espaldas a la ventana abierta donde sopla una fresca brisa. El barrio está tranquilo y la habitación silenciosa.

Su testamento es un sencillo documento de dos párrafos, en el que se lo cede todo a su madre. Lo redacté hace una semana. No debe ni posee nada, y el testamento es innecesario. Pero hizo que se sintiera mejor. También ha planeado su funeral y Dot lo ha organizado. También quiere que yo sea uno de los dolientes.

Levanto el mismo libro que leo intermitentemente desde hace dos meses, un compendio de cuatro novelas. Tiene treinta años y es uno de los pocos libros en la casa. Lo dejo en el mismo lugar y leo unas cuantas páginas en cada visita.

Gime y se mueve ligeramente. Me pregunto cómo reaccionará Dot cuando entre una mañana y Donny Ray no despierte.

Nos deja solos cuando estoy con él. Oigo que lava los platos. Creo que Buddy está ahora en la casa. Paso una hora leyendo y miro de vez en cuando a Donny Ray. Si despierta charlaremos, o tal vez encenderé el televisor. Lo que le apetezca.

Oigo una voz extraña en la sala de estar, seguida de un golpe en la puerta. Se abre lentamente y tardo unos segundos en reconocer al joven que acaba de aparecer. Es el doctor Kord, que ha venido a visitar a su paciente. Nos estrechamos la mano, hablamos en voz baja al pie de la cama y luego nos acercamos a la ventana.

—Pasaba por aquí —dice todavía en un susurro, como si circulara todos los días por aquel barrio.

—Siéntese —digo ofreciéndole una silla.

Nos sentamos de espaldas a la ventana, con nuestras rodillas tocándose y la mirada fija en el joven moribundo a menos de dos metros.

—¿Cuánto hace que está aquí? —pregunta.

—Un par de horas. He cenado con Dot.

—¿Ha despertado?

—No.

Permanecemos sentados en la penumbra, con una fresca brisa en nuestros cogotes. El reloj marca el ritmo de nuestras vidas, pero en este momento ha desaparecido la sensación del tiempo.

—He estado pensando —dice Kord, casi para sus adentros—, sobre ese juicio. ¿Alguna idea de cuándo se celebrará?

—El ocho de febrero.

—¿Definitivamente?

—Eso parece.

—¿No sería preferible que declarara en persona, en lugar de dirigirme al jurado mediante un vídeo o una declaración jurada por escrito?

—De eso no cabe la menor duda.

Hace varios años que Kord ejerce como médico, y sabe lo que son los juicios y las declaraciones.

—Entonces olvidémonos de la declaración escrita —dice después de inclinarse hacia delante y apoyar los codos sobre las rodillas—. Lo haré personalmente y no cobraré un centavo.

—Eso es muy generoso.

—No tiene importancia. Es lo menos que puedo hacer.

Reflexionamos durante un buen rato. De vez en cuando se oye un pequeño ruido en la cocina, pero la casa está silenciosa. A Kord no le molestan los silencios prolongados.

—¿Sabes en qué consiste mi trabajo? —pregunta por fin.

—¿En qué?

—En hacer un diagnóstico y luego preparar a las personas para la muerte.

—¿Por qué elegiste la oncología?

—¿Quieres que te diga la verdad?

—Claro. ¿Por qué no?

—Hay demanda de oncólogos. Es fácil de comprender, ¿no es cierto? Es una de las especialidades menos solicitadas.

—Supongo que alguien tiene que hacerlo.

—En realidad no está tan mal. Me encanta mi trabajo —dice antes de hacer una pausa para mirar a su paciente—. Pero éste es un caso duro. Ver a un paciente que no recibe el tratamiento adecuado. Si los trasplantes de médula no fueran tan caros, tal vez habríamos podido hacer algo al respecto. Yo estaba dispuesto a donar mi tiempo y mi trabajo, pero sigue siendo una operación de doscientos mil dólares. Ningún hospital ni clínica del país puede permitirse un gasto semejante.

—Le despierta a uno el odio por la compañía de seguros, ¿no crees?

—Sí, qué duda cabe —responde—. Démosles su merecido —agrega después de una prolongada pausa.

—Estoy intentándolo.

—¿Estás casado? —pregunta, después de erguir la espalda y consultar su reloj.

—No. ¿Y tú?

—Tampoco. Divorciado. Vamos a tomar una cerveza.

—De acuerdo. ¿Dónde?

—¿Conoces la marisquería Murphy's?

—Por supuesto.

—Reunámonos allí.

Pasamos de puntillas junto a la cama de Donny Ray, nos despedimos de Dot, que se mece y fuma en el portal, y de momento nos retiramos.

Estoy profundamente dormido cuando suena el teléfono a las tres y veinte de la madrugada. O Donny Ray ha fallecido, o ha habido un desastre aéreo y Deck está al acecho. ¿Quién si no podría llamar a esas horas?

—¿Rudy? —pregunta por teléfono una voz familiar.

—¡Señorita Birdie! —exclamo al tiempo que me incorporo en la cama y enciendo la luz.

—Lamento llamarte a una hora tan intempestiva.

—No se preocupe. ¿Cómo está?

—Me tratan como a unos mezquinos.

Cierro los ojos, respiro hondo y me dejo caer de nuevo sobre la cama. ¿Por qué no me sorprende?

—¿Quién es mezquino con usted? —pregunto, pero sólo porque es lo que se supone que debo hacer.

En este momento es difícil compadecerse.

—La más ruin es June —responde, como si estuvieran catalogados—. No me quiere en la casa.

—¿Vive con Randolph y June?

—Sí y es horrible. Francamente horrible. Tengo miedo de comer lo que me ofrecen.

—¿Por qué?

—Porque temo que esté envenenado.

—No exagere, señorita Birdie.

—Hablo en serio. Todos esperan a que me muera, eso es todo. Hice un nuevo testamento cediéndoles lo que quieren, lo firmé en Memphis y cuando llegamos a Tampa, los primeros días, me trataron con mucho cariño. Mis nietos venían siempre a verme. Me traían flores y chocolates. Luego Delbert me llevó a un médico para que me hiciera un reconocimiento. El doctor me examinó de pies a cabeza y les dijo que mi salud era impecable. Creo que eso no era lo que esperaban. Parecían decepcionados con los resultados y cambiaron de actitud de la noche a la mañana. June volvió a comportarse como la mezquina pécora que es en realidad. Randolph volvió a dedicarse al golf y no está nunca en casa. Delbert no se mueve del canódromo. Vera odia a June y June detesta a Vera. Los nietos, la mayoría de los cuales no trabajan, se han limitado a desaparecer.

—¿Por qué me llama a estas horas, señorita Birdie?

—Porque sólo puedo utilizar el teléfono a escondidas. Ayer June me prohibió usarlo y cuando hablé con Randolph, me dijo que podía hacer dos llamadas diarias. Echo de menos mi casa, Rudy. ¿Cómo está?

—Muy bien, señorita Birdie.

—No puedo seguir mucho tiempo aquí. Vivo en una pequeña habitación, con un diminuto baño. Estoy acostumbrada a los grandes espacios, Rudy, tú lo sabes.

—Sí, señorita Birdie.

Espera que me ofrezca voluntario para traerla a casa, pero no es lo indicado en este momento. Hace menos de un mes que se ha marchado. Le sentará bien.

—Y Randolph quiere que le firme unos poderes notariales para actuar en mi nombre. ¿Qué opinas?

—Nunca le aconsejaría a un cliente que lo hiciera, señorita Birdie. No es una buena idea.

Nunca he tenido un cliente con dicho dilema, pero en su caso no es aconsejable.

Pobre Randolph. Se esfuerza como un condenado para hacerse con su fortuna de veinte millones de dólares. ¿Qué hará si descubre la verdad? La señorita Birdie cree que ahora están mal las cosas. Menuda sorpresa le espera.

—No sé qué hacer... —sus palabras se pierden en la lejanía.

—No lo firme, señorita Birdie.

—Otra cosa. Ayer, Delbert... Llega alguien. Debo cortar.

Se interrumpe la comunicación. Imagino a June dándole latigazos a la señorita Birdie por hacer una llamada telefónica no autorizada.

La llamada en sí no es un hecho significativo. Es casi cómico. Si la señorita Birdie desea regresar a su casa, me ocuparé de que lo haga.

Logro quedarme dormido.

TREINTA Y SEIS

Marco el número de la institución penitenciaria y pregunto por la misma señora con la que hablé la primera vez que visité a Ott. Las normas exigen que sea ella quien autorice todas las visitas. Quiero verlo de nuevo antes de tomarle declaración.

—Bobby Ott ya no está aquí —responde mientras la oigo teclear.

—¿Cómo?

—Salió en libertad hace tres días.

—Me dijo que le quedaban dieciocho días. Y de eso hace sólo una semana.

—Lo siento. Se ha marchado.

—¿Dónde está? —pregunto con incredulidad.

—¿Está bromeando? —exclama y me cuelga el teléfono.

Ott está libre. Me mintió. Tuvimos suerte de encontrarlo por primera vez y ahora se ha vuelto a esconder.

La llamada que temía llega por fin el domingo por la mañana. Estoy sentado en el jardín de la señorita Birdie como si fuera el dueño de la casa, leyendo el periódico dominical, tomando café y disfrutando del magnífico clima. Es Dot y me dice que lo ha encontrado hace aproximadamente una hora. Se durmió anoche y no ha vuelto a despertar.

Le tiembla un poco la voz, pero controla sus emociones. Hablamos unos momentos y me percato de que se me seca la garganta y humedecen mis ojos. Hay un vestigio de alivio en sus palabras. Por fin ha dejado de sufrir, repite en más de una ocasión.

Le digo que lo lamento y que iré a visitarla esta tarde.

Cruzo el jardín hasta acercarme a la hamaca, donde me apoyo contra un roble y seco las lágrimas de mis mejillas. Me siento al borde de la hamaca, con los pies en el suelo, la cabeza gacha y rezo la última de mis muchas oraciones por Donny Ray.

Llamo al juez Kipler a su casa para comunicarle la defunción. El funeral tendrá lugar mañana a las dos de la tarde, lo cual supone un problema. Las declaraciones del personal de la oficina central están programadas para las nueve de la mañana y durarán casi toda la semana. Estoy seguro de que los ejecutivos de Cleveland están ya en la ciudad, probablemente en el despacho de Drummond en estos momentos, ensayando frente a cámaras de vídeo. Es así de meticuloso.

Kipler me dice que acuda de todos modos a las nueve al juzgado, y él lo resolverá sobre la marcha. Le digo que estoy listo. Sin duda debería estarlo. He mecanografiado todas las preguntas posibles para cada uno de los testigos y su señoría en persona ha hecho ciertas sugerencias. Deck también las ha revisado.

Kipler insinúa que tal vez aplazará las declaraciones, porque mañana tiene dos vistas importantes.

Sea lo que Dios quiera. En este momento realmente no me importa.

Cuando llego a casa de los Black, el barrio entero ha acudido a dar el pésame. La calle está repleta de coches aparcados. Numerosos ancianos deambulan por el jardín y otros están sentados en el pórtico de la casa. Sonrío y saludo con la cabeza hasta que consigo entrar y llegar a la cocina, donde encuentro a Dot junto al frigorífico. La casa está llena de gente. La mesa y demás superficies de la cocina están cubiertas de tartas, cocidos y cazuelas con pollo frito.

Dot y yo nos damos un tierno abrazo. Expreso mi pésame diciéndole simplemente cuánto lo siento y ella me da las gracias por haber venido. Tiene los ojos irritados, pero intuyo que está harta de llorar. Me muestra la comida y me dice que me sirva yo mismo. La dejo con un grupo de mujeres del barrio.

De pronto tengo hambre. Lleno un gran plato de cartón con pollo, judías en salsa de tomate y col en escabeche, y me lo llevo al jardín trasero, donde como a solas. Buddy, bendito sea, no está en su coche. Probablemente, Dot lo ha encerrado en su habitación para que no la ponga en ridículo. Como despacio y escucho la charla que emana de las ventanas abiertas de la cocina y la sala de estar. Después de vaciar el plato, me sirvo una segunda ración y vuelvo a ocultarme en el jardín.

No tarda en acercarse a mí un joven con un aspecto curiosamente familiar.

—Soy Ron Black —dice, antes de sentarse junto a mí—. El hermano gemelo.

Es delgado, en buena forma y no muy alto.

—Encantado de conocerte —respondo.

—De modo que tú eres el abogado —dice, con una lata de refresco en la mano.

—Sí. Rudy Baylor. Siento lo de tu hermano.

—Gracias.

Soy muy consciente de lo poco que Dot y Donny Ray hablaban de Ron. Se marchó de casa poco después de terminar el bachillerato, se alejó de la familia y ha mantenido siempre las distancias. Hasta cierto punto lo comprendo.

No está de humor para charlar. Sus oraciones son cortas y forzadas, pero acabamos por hablar del trasplante de médula. Confirma lo que ya sabía, que estaba perfectamente dispuesto a donar su médula para salvar a su hermano y que el doctor Kord le había dicho que la compatibilidad era perfecta. Le explico que será necesario que se lo cuente a un jurado dentro de unos meses y me responde que le encantará hacerlo. Formula algunas preguntas sobre el pleito, pero no manifiesta curiosidad alguna respecto a lo que pueda reportarle.

Estoy seguro de que está afligido, pero domina muy bien su dolor. Abro la puerta de su infancia, con la esperanza de oír algunas cariñosas anécdotas propias de todos los gemelos, sobre bromas y travesuras compartidas. Nada. Se crió aquí, en esta casa y este barrio, y es evidente que el pasado no le interesa.

El funeral tendrá lugar mañana a las dos y apuesto cualquier cosa a que Ron Black estará en un avión de regreso a Houston a las cinco.

La muchedumbre decrece y aumenta de nuevo, pero la comida sigue ahí. Me como dos trozos de pastel de chocolate, mientras Ron se toma su refresco caliente. Después de dos horas sentado, estoy agotado. Me disculpo y me retiro.

El lunes hay una auténtica legión de individuos de rostro severo y traje oscuro sentados alrededor de Leo F. Drummond en un extremo de la sala.

Estoy preparado. Asustado, tembloroso e inseguro, pero con todas las preguntas escritas. Aunque se me trabe por completo la lengua, podré limitarme a leer las preguntas y obligarlos a contestarlas.

Es divertido ver a esos altos ejecutivos muertos de miedo. Sólo puedo imaginar las duras palabras que le dedicaron a Drummond, y a mí, y a Kipler, y a los abogados en general, y a este caso en particular, cuando se les comunicó que hoy debían presentarse aquí en masa, y no sólo presentarse y declarar, sino esperar horas y días hasta que termine con ellos.

Kipler sube al estrado y llama nuestro caso en primer lugar. Para las declaraciones se nos ha asignado una sala adjunta que está libre esta semana, de modo que su señoría pueda asomar la cabeza de vez en cuando y asegurarse de que Drummond no se extralimite. Nos llama al estrado porque tiene algo que decir.

—No es necesario que esto conste en acta —le comunica Kipler a la taquígrafa—. Señor Drummond, ¿sabía usted que Donny Ray falleció ayer por la mañana?

—No, señor —responde Drummond gravemente—. Lo siento mucho.

—El funeral tendrá lugar esta tarde y esto nos plantea un problema. El señor Baylor debe asistir al mismo en calidad de doliente. En realidad, debería estar ahora con la familia.

Drummond, de pie, nos mira alternativamente a mí y a Kipler.

—Vamos a aplazar estas declaraciones. Traiga a sus testigos el próximo lunes, a la misma hora y en el mismo lugar —dice Kipler con la mirada fija en Drummond, a la espera de la respuesta equivocada.

Los cinco importantes ejecutivos de Great Benefit se verán obligados a reorganizar y reajustar su atareada vida, para regresar a Memphis la próxima semana.

—¿Por qué no empezamos mañana? —pregunta Drummond estupefacto.

Su pregunta es perfectamente lógica.

—Soy yo quien preside esta sala, señor Drummond, quien dirige la instrucción del caso, y no le quepa le menor duda de que pienso dirigir también el proceso.

—Pero, con la venia de su señoría, y no pretendo ser contradictorio, su presencia no es necesaria para tomar las declaraciones. Esos cinco caballeros han tenido que hacer grandes esfuerzos para estar hoy aquí. Tal vez la semana próxima no les sea posible.

Eso es exactamente lo que Kipler esperaba oír.

—Estarán aquí, señor Drummond, no le quepa la menor duda. El próximo lunes a las nueve de la mañana.

—Con el debido respeto, su señoría, me parece injusto.

—¿Injusto? Estas declaraciones podían haberse tomado en Cleveland hace dos semanas, señor Drummond. Pero su cliente empezó a hacer jugarretas.

La autoridad del juez es ilimitada en asuntos como éste y no existe apelación alguna. Kipler está castigando a Drummond y a Great Benefit, y en mi modesta opinión, exagera un poco. Aquí se celebrará un juicio dentro de pocos meses y el juez establece su autoridad. Le está comunicando a ese importante abogado que él, su señoría, será quien dirija el proceso.

Me parece estupendo.

Tras una pequeña iglesia rural, a pocos kilómetros al norte de Memphis, depositan a Donny Ray para su eterno descanso. Puesto que yo soy uno de los ocho dolientes, se me indica que me ponga de pie tras las sillas donde está sentada la familia. Hace fresco y está nublado, un día propio de un entierro.

El último funeral al que había asistido era el de mi padre y procuro no pensar en ello.

La muchedumbre se apretuja bajo un palio color borgoña, mientras un joven sacerdote lee fragmentos de la Biblia. Contemplamos el ataúd gris rodeado de flores. Oigo los sollozos de Dot y veo a Buddy sentado junto a Ron. Alejo la mirada, procurando mentalmente ausentarme y pensar en algo agradable.

Deck está hecho un manojo de nervios cuando regreso al despacho. Su amigo Butch, el detective privado, está sentado sobre una mesa con sus protuberantes bíceps bajo un jersey de cuello rasgado. Es un individuo desaliñado de mejillas rojizas, con botas puntiagudas y aspecto de camorrista. Deck nos presenta, califica a Butch de cliente y me entrega un cuaderno con un mensaje escrito con un rotulador negro en la primera página: «Sigue hablando sin decir nada, ¿vale?»

—¿Cómo ha ido el funeral? —pregunta Deck, al tiempo que me coge del brazo y me conduce hacia la mesa donde Butch está esperando.

—Como todos los funerales —respondo, sin concentrar la mirada en esos dos individuos.

—¿Cómo está la familia? —pregunta Deck.

—Bien, supongo.

Butch destornilla la tapa del auricular del teléfono y señala a su interior.

—Por lo menos ahora ese chico ha dejado de sufrir, ¿no te parece? —dice Deck, mientras yo observo el auricular.

Butch me muestra un pequeño artefacto negro pegado al interior, que yo me limito a contemplar.

—¿No crees que es preferible que haya dejado de sufrir?

—insiste Deck levantando la voz, al tiempo que me hurga las costillas con el codo.

—Sí, por supuesto. Sin duda es preferible que haya dejado de sufrir. Pero no deja de ser muy triste.

Vemos cómo Butch vuelve a colocar el teléfono hábilmente en su lugar y se encoge de hombros, como si yo supiera exactamente qué hay que hacer a continuación.

—Vamos a tomar un café —dice Deck.

—Buena idea —respondo, con un enorme nudo en el estómago.

Al llegar a la acera, me paro y los miro.

—¿Qué diablos sucede? —pregunto.

—Vamos por ahí —responde Deck.

Hay un café de ambiente artístico a una manzana y media a lo largo de la calle, y nos acercamos al mismo sin decir palabra. Nos ocultamos en un rincón, como si nos acecharan unos pistoleros.

No tarda en revelarse la historia. Deck y yo hemos estado preocupados por los federales, desde la desaparición de Bruiser y Prince. Esperábamos que como mínimo nos visitaran e hicieran algunas preguntas. Hemos hablado muchas veces de ello pero, sin que yo lo supiera, Deck también se lo ha consultado a su amigo Butch. Personalmente, no confiaría tanto en él.

Butch ha llegado hace una hora a nuestras oficinas y Deck le ha pedido que echara una ojeada a los teléfonos. Reconoce que no es un experto en electrónica, pero es un gato viejo. Los artilugios de escucha son fáciles de detectar. Un aparato idéntico en cada uno de los tres teléfonos. Se disponían a buscar más micrófonos, pero han decidido esperarme.

—¿Más micrófonos? —pregunto.

—Sí, pequeños artilugios escondidos por la oficina, para captar lo que no reciban los teléfonos —responde Butch—. Es bastante sencillo. No tenemos más que examinarlo todo con una lupa.

A Deck le tiemblan literalmente las manos. Me pregunto si habrá hablado con Bruiser por el teléfono del despacho.

—¿Y si los encontramos? —pregunto, antes de probar el café.

—Legalmente puedes retirarlos —responde Butch—. O limitarte a prestar atención a lo que dices. Fingir que no conoces su existencia.

—¿Y si los retiramos?

—Los federales sabrán que los has encontrado. Crecerán sus sospechas y probablemente incrementarán otras formas de vigilancia. Lo mejor, en mi opinión, es seguir como si nada.

—Para ti es fácil decirlo.

Deck se seca la frente y se niega a mirarme. Me pone muy nervioso.

—¿Conoces a Bruiser Stone? —le pregunto a Butch.

—Por supuesto. He trabajado para él.

—Bien —respondo sin asombrarme, antes de dirigirme a Deck—. ¿Has hablado con Bruiser por nuestros teléfonos?

—No —responde—. No he hablado con Bruiser desde su desaparición.

Con esa mentira me comunica que no hable en presencia de Butch.

—Me gustaría saber si hay otros micrófonos —digo dirigiéndome a Butch—. Sería interesante saber cuánto oyen en nuestro despacho.

—Será preciso escudriñar toda la oficina.

—Adelante.

—No tengo ningún inconveniente. Empezaremos por las mesas, las sillas y los escritorios. Examinaremos las papeleras, los libros, los relojes, las grapadoras... todo. Esos artefactos pueden ser más diminutos que una pasa.

—¿Pueden detectar que estamos buscándolos? —pregunta Deck, muerto de miedo.

—No. Vosotros seguid hablando como de costumbre. Yo no diré palabra y no sabrán que estoy ahí. Si encontráis algo, haced señales con la mano.

Nos llevamos el café al bufete, que de pronto se ha convertido en un lugar aborrecible y aterrador. Deck y yo iniciamos una conversación superficial sobre el caso de Derrick Dogan, mientras damos cuidadosamente la vuelta a mesas y sillas. Cualquier persona medianamente inteligente detectaría que nuestra conducta es inusual y que intentamos ocultar algo.

Nos desplazamos a gatas. Examinamos las papeleras y los ficheros. Inspeccionamos las bocas de ventilación y las tablas del suelo. Por primera vez, me alegra disponer de tan pocos muebles.

Buscamos durante cuatro horas y no encontramos nada. Sólo nuestros teléfonos han sido violados. Deck y yo invitamos a Butch a comer un plato de espagueti con nosotros en la taberna de la esquina.

A medianoche estoy tumbado en la cama, sin pensar siquiera en la posibilidad de dormir. Leo el periódico de la mañana y echo de vez en cuando una ojeada al teléfono. No es posible, me repito constantemente, no es posible que se hayan tomado la molestia de intervenirlo. Durante toda la tarde y noche no he dejado de ver sombras y oír ruidos. Me han sobresaltado sonidos inexistentes. Se me han puesto todos los pelos de punta. He perdido el apetito. Me siguen, lo sé, ¿pero están muy cerca de mí?

¿Y cuánto piensan acercarse?

A excepción de los anuncios, leo de cabo a rabo el periódico. Ayer Sara Plankmore Wilcox dio a luz una niña de tres kilos. Enhorabuena. Ya no la detesto. Desde la muerte de Donny Ray, me siento más amable con todo el mundo. A excepción, claro está, de Drummond y su repugnante cliente.

PFX Freight no ha perdido ningún partido de liga.

Me pregunto si la llevará consigo a todos los partidos.

Leo el informe de estadísticas vitales todos los días. Presto particular atención a las peticiones de divorcio, pero no me siento muy optimista. También leo la lista de detenidos, para comprobar si Cliff Riker ha vuelto a apalear a su esposa.

TREINTA Y SIETE

Los documentos cubren cuatro mesas plegables alquiladas, colocadas en fila en el vestíbulo de nuestro bufete. Están en nítidos montones, por orden cronológico, todos identificados, numerados, clasificados, e incluso informatizados.

Y memorizados. He estudiado tantas veces estos documentos que conozco el contenido de cada página. Los documentos que me ha entregado Dot constan de un total de doscientas veintiuna páginas. La póliza, por ejemplo, que será considerada como un solo documento en el juicio, tiene treinta páginas. Los documentos facilitados hasta el momento por Great Benefit, algunos de ellos duplicados de los de los Black, constan de un total de setecientas cuarenta y ocho páginas.

Deck ha dedicado también innumerables horas al papeleo. Ha redactado un análisis detallado de la ficha de reclamación. Se ha ocupado asimismo de la mayor parte del trabajo informático y me ayudará durante las declaraciones. Su trabajo consiste en mantener los documentos ordenados y encontrar rápidamente los que necesitemos.

No está exactamente entusiasmado con este tipo de trabajo, pero quiere a toda costa que yo esté satisfecho. Está convencido de que hemos sorprendido a Great Benefit con las manos en la masa, pero también considera que este caso no se merece tanto esfuerzo como yo le dedico. Me temo que Deck tiene graves dudas respecto a mi habilidad en la sala. Sabe que independientemente de las doce personas que elijamos, los componentes del jurado considerarán que cincuenta mil dólares es una fortuna.

Tomo una cerveza en el despacho el domingo por la noche y repaso una vez más una mesa tras otra. Falta algo. Deck está seguro de que Jackie Lemancyzk, la encargada de reclamaciones, no habría tenido suficiente autoridad para denegar por cuenta propia la reclamación. Cumplió con su obligación y transfirió la ficha al departamento de contratación. Hay cierta interrelación entre los departamentos de reclamaciones y contratación, intercambio de circulares, y ahí es donde se pierde la pista del papeleo.

Se elaboró un programa para denegar la reclamación de Donny Ray y probablemente muchas otras. Debemos dilucidarlo.

Después de mucha deliberación y estudio con los miembros de mi bufete, he decidido tomarle declaración en primer lugar a M. Wilfred Keeley, director gerente de la compañía. Me ha parecido que sería una buena idea empezar con el más importante, e ir bajando. Es un individuo de cincuenta y seis años, robusto, con una cálida sonrisa incluso para mí. Me da las gracias por permitirle ser el primero. Necesita desesperadamente regresar cuanto antes a la oficina central.

Hurgo por la periferia durante la primera hora. Estoy sentado junto a mi mesa con unos vaqueros, camisa de franela, mocasines y calcetines blancos. Me ha parecido que contrastaría agradablemente con los diversos tonos de negro que predominan en el otro bando. A Deck le parece irrespetuoso.

Después de dos horas de declaración, Keeley me entrega un informe financiero y hablamos un rato de dinero. Deck estudia las cifras y me pasa una retahíla de preguntas. Drummond y tres de los muchachos intercambian algunas notas, pero parecen sumamente aburridos. Kipler preside una vista en la sala adjunta.

Keeley conoce otros varios pleitos contra Great Benefit pendientes actualmente en diferentes lugares del país. Hablamos un rato de los mismos: nombres, juzgados, otros abogados, hechos parecidos. No se le ha obligado a declarar en ninguno de ellos. Me muero de impaciencia por hablar con los demás abogados que han demandado a Great Benefit. Compararemos documentos y estrategias jurídicas.

Lo emocionante de dirigir una compañía de seguros no es definitivamente el negocio mundano de venta de pólizas y satisfacción de reclamaciones. Consiste en invertir el dinero de las primas. Keeley está mucho más versado sobre inversiones, dice que por ahí empezó y siguió progresando. No sabe mucho acerca de las reclamaciones.

Puesto que no soy responsable de los gastos de las declaraciones, no tengo prisa. Formulo un sinfín de preguntas innecesarias, sólo para indagar y dar palos en la oscuridad. Drummond parece aburrido y a veces frustrado, pero él ha marcado la pauta en cuanto a cómo prolongar un día entero una declaración y su contador también corre. De vez en cuando le gustaría protestar, pero sabe que acudiré inmediatamente a la sala adjunta para hablar con el juez Kipler, que me dará la razón y le hará una advertencia.

Por la tarde aparece otro millar de preguntas y cuando concluimos la sesión a las cinco y media, estoy físicamente agotado. La sonrisa de Keeley se esfuma después del mediodía, pero sigue dispuesto a contestar mientras yo sea capaz de preguntar. Me da de nuevo las gracias por haberle permitido acabar primero y por dejar que se retire sin formularle más preguntas. Regresa inmediatamente a Cleveland.

El martes se animan un poco las cosas, en parte porque me he cansado de perder el tiempo y en parte porque los testigos saben poco o no recuerdan. Empiezo por Everett Lufkin, vicepresidente de reclamaciones, un individuo que no pronuncia una sola sílaba, a no ser en respuesta a una pregunta directa. Lo obligo a examinar algunos documentos y a media mañana por fin reconoce que la política de su compañía es hacer algo denominado «indagación posreclamación», que es algo odioso aunque no ilegal. Cuando un asegurado presenta una reclamación, el funcionario que la recibe inicialmente solicita todos los informes médicos del asegurado durante los cinco años precedentes. En nuestro caso, Great Benefit consiguió los informes del médico de cabecera de la familia Black, que cinco años antes había tratado a Donny Ray cuando padeció una virulenta gripe. Dot no la había mencionado en la solicitud. Aunque la gripe no tiene nada que ver con la leucemia, Great Benefit basó una de sus primeras denegaciones en el hecho de que la gripe era una condición preexistente.

En este momento siento la tentación de clavarle una estaca en el corazón, y no sería difícil hacerlo. Pero tampoco inteligente. Lufkin declarará en el juicio y es preferible guardar la munición para entonces. Algunos abogados son partidarios de demostrar el caso durante las declaraciones, pero mi vasta experiencia me aconseja conservar lo bueno para el jurado. En realidad, lo he leído en algún libro. Además, es la estrategia que utiliza Jonathan Lake.

Kermit Aldy, vicepresidente de contratación, es tan lúgubre e impreciso como Lufkin. El proceso de contratación consiste en recibir y analizar la propuesta del agente, y finalmente decidir si extender o no una póliza. Es mucho papeleo con pocas recompensas y Aldy parece la persona perfecta para dicha misión. Termino con él en menos de dos horas y sin causarle ningún daño.

Bradford Barnes es el vicepresidente administrativo y tardamos casi una hora en averiguar exactamente lo que hace. Estamos a miércoles por la mañana. Estoy harto de esa gente. Los muchachos de Trent & Brent, a menos de dos metros, con los mismos trajes oscuros y ceño de autosuficiencia que exhiben desde hace varios meses, me producen náuseas. Incluso la taquígrafa me da asco. Barnes no sabe nada de nada. Lo ataco y se agacha, sin recibir un solo golpe. No declarará en el juicio porque no tiene ni idea.

El miércoles por la tarde llamo al último testigo, Richard Pellrod, encargado decano de reclamaciones que escribió por lo menos dos cartas de denegación a los Black. Ha esperado sentado en el vestíbulo desde el lunes por la mañana y odia mis entrañas. Me levanta varias veces la voz durante las primeras preguntas y eso refuerza mi ánimo. Le muestro sus cartas de denegación y se pone quisquilloso. Según su criterio, que es todavía el de Great Benefit, los trasplantes de médula son sencillamente demasiado experimentales para aceptarlos como método de tratamiento. Pero una de sus denegaciones se basaba en el hecho de que Donny Ray no había declarado una condición preexistente. Se lo atribuye a otro, un simple lapso. Es un cabrón mentiroso y decido hacerle sufrir. Cojo un montón de documentos y los repasamos uno por uno. Lo obligo a explicármelos y a responsabilizarse de cada uno de ellos. Él era, después de todo, el supervisor de Jackie Lemancyzk que, evidentemente, ya no está con nosotros. Según él, puede que haya regresado a su ciudad natal, en algún lugar del sur de Indiana. Periódicamente le formulo alguna pregunta puntual relacionada con su dimisión, y eso realmente le molesta. Más documentos. Más culpabilidad transferida a otros. Persisto. Puedo preguntar lo que quiera y cuando se me antoje, y nunca sabe lo que viene. Después de cuatro horas de bombardeo constante, solicita un descanso.

Concluimos con Pellrod a las siete y media del miércoles por la tarde, y las declaraciones de los ejecutivos han terminado. Tres días, diecisiete horas, probablemente mil páginas de testimonio. Las declaraciones, al igual que los documentos, habrá que leerlas docenas de veces.

Mientras sus muchachos guardan los documentos en sus maletines, Leo F. Drummond me llama a un lado.

—Buen trabajo, Rudy —dice sin levantar la voz, como si realmente le hubiera impresionado pero prefiriera mantener discreta su evaluación.

—Gracias.

Respira hondo. Estamos los dos agotados y hartos de vernos las caras.

—¿Quién nos falta? —pregunta.

—Yo he terminado —respondo, sin que se me ocurra nadie a quien quiera tomarle declaración.

—¿Y el doctor Kord?

—Declarará en el juicio.

Eso le sorprende. Me mira atentamente, al tiempo que sin duda se pregunta cómo puedo permitirme pagar a un médico para que declare ante el jurado.

—¿Qué dirá?

—Ron Black era perfectamente compatible para efectuarle un trasplante a su hermano gemelo. El trasplante de médula es un tratamiento rutinario. Se le podía haber salvado la vida al muchacho. Su cliente lo mató.

Se lo toma bien y es evidente que no le sorprende.

—Probablemente nosotros le tomaremos declaración —dice.

—Quinientos por hora.

—Sí, lo sé. Escúcheme, Rudy, ¿quiere tomar una copa conmigo? Hay algo de lo que me gustaría hablar con usted.

—¿Qué?

No se me ocurre nada peor en este momento que tomar una copa con Drummond.

—Negocios. La posibilidad de llegar a un acuerdo. ¿Podría pasarse por mi despacho, tal vez dentro de unos quince minutos? Estamos a la vuelta de la esquina.

Es tentadora la perspectiva de «llegar a un acuerdo». Además, siempre he querido ver su bufete.

—Tendré que darme prisa —respondo, como si me esperara un harén de hermosas e importantes mujeres.

—De acuerdo. Vamos ahora mismo.

Le digo a Deck que me espere en la esquina y camino con Drummond tres manzanas, hasta el edificio más alto de Memphis. Charlamos del tiempo mientras subimos al cuadragésimo piso. Las salas son todas de mármol y bronce, y están llenas de gente como en pleno día. Es una fábrica en cuya decoración predomina el buen gusto. Intento ver a mi viejo amigo Loyd Beck, el mequetrefe de Broadnax & Speer, con la esperanza de no encontrarme con él.

El despacho de Drummond está elegantemente decorado, pero no es excesivamente grande. En este edificio se pagan los alquileres más altos de la ciudad y aprovechan el espacio.

—¿Qué le apetece? —pregunta después de arrojar su maletín y la chaqueta sobre la mesa.

No quiero tomar alcohol. Además, estoy tan cansado que bastaría una copa para derribarme.

—Una Coca-cola —respondo.

Le decepciona momentáneamente mi elección. Él se prepara un whisky con agua en la barra de un rincón de su despacho.

Alguien llama a la puerta y me sorprende enormemente ver que aparece el señor M. Wilfred Keeley. No nos hemos visto desde que le interrogué durante ocho horas el lunes. Se comporta como si estuviera encantado de verme. Nos saludamos y estrechamos la mano como viejos amigos. Se acerca a la barra y se prepara una copa.

Saborean sus whiskies, mientras nos sentamos alrededor de una mesilla redonda en un rincón. El hecho de que Keeley haya regresado tan pronto sólo puede significar una cosa: quieren llegar a un acuerdo. Los escucho atentamente.

El mes pasado ingresé seiscientos dólares en mi precario bufete. Drummond gana por lo menos un millón anual. Keeley dirige una compañía con un volumen de ventas de por lo menos mil millones anuales y gana probablemente más que su abogado. Y quieren hablar de negocios conmigo.

—El juez Kipler me preocupa enormemente —declara de pronto Drummond.

—Nunca he visto nada parecido —agrega inmediatamente Keeley.

Drummond es célebre por su preparación impecable y estoy seguro de que este diálogo ha sido cuidadosamente ensayado.

—Con franqueza, Rudy, me da miedo lo que pueda hacer en el juicio —dice Drummond.

—Está canalizándonos —agrega Keeley mientras mueve con incredulidad la cabeza.

Es comprensible que Kipler les preocupe, pero sudan sangre porque han sido sorprendidos con las manos en la masa. Han matado a un joven y su conducta asesina está a punto de ser divulgada. Decido ser amable y escuchar lo que tengan que decir.

—Nos gustaría llegar a un acuerdo, Rudy —dice Drummond, después de sorber simultáneamente sus respectivas copas—. Tenemos confianza en nuestra defensa y se lo digo sinceramente. En condiciones igualitarias, estamos listos para enfrentarnos mañana mismo. No he perdido un solo caso en once años. Me encantan las buenas disputas en la sala. Pero ese juez es tan parcial, que da miedo.

—¿Cuánto? —pregunto, para ahorrarme las divagaciones.

Se retuercen en perfecta armonía hemorroidal.

—Doblaremos la oferta inicial —responde Drummond después de unos momentos de dolor—. Ciento cincuenta mil. Usted cobrará unos cincuenta y sus clientes...

—Sé contar —interrumpo.

Mis honorarios no son de su incumbencia. Estoy sin blanca y con cincuenta mil sería rico.

¡Cincuenta mil dólares!

—¿Qué se supone que debo hacer con esta oferta? —pregunto.

Se miran confundidos.

—Mi cliente ha fallecido. Su madre lo enterró la semana pasada y ahora esperan que le diga que hay más dinero sobre la mesa.

—La ética le obliga a decirle...

—No me dé lecciones de ética, Leo. Se lo diré. Le comunicaré su oferta y apuesto a que responderá que no le interesa.

—Lamentamos mucho su muerte —dice Keeley con tristeza.

—Me doy cuenta de que está usted sumamente afligido, señor Keeley. Transmitiré su pésame a la familia.

—Escúcheme, Rudy, estamos haciendo un esfuerzo de buena fe para llegar a un acuerdo —dice Drummond.

—Ha elegido un pésimo momento.

Se hace una pausa mientras todos bebemos. Drummond es el primero en empezar a sonreír.

—¿Qué desea esa dama? Díganoslo, Rudy, ¿qué necesita para sentirse satisfecha?

—Nada.

—¿Nada?

—Nada que usted pueda hacer. Su hijo ha muerto y usted no puede hacer nada para remediarlo.

—¿Entonces a qué viene el juicio?

—Para dar a conocer lo que han hecho.

Más contorsiones. Más expresiones de dolor. Más whisky al gaznate.

—Quiere dar a conocer lo que han hecho y destruirlos.

—Somos demasiado grandes —dice afectadamente Keeley.

—Ya lo veremos —respondo después de ponerme de pie y recoger mi maletín—. No se molesten en acompañarme.

Salgo del despacho y los dejo sentados.

TREINTA Y OCHO

Nuestro bufete adquiere lentamente el aspecto de actividad comercial, por modesta y poco lucrativa que sea. Hay montoncitos de pequeñas fichas aquí y allá, siempre a la vista de los clientes que nos visiten. Tengo casi una docena de casos penales de oficio, todos ellos de faltas graves o delitos de poca monta. Deck asegura tener treinta fichas abiertas, pero creo que exagera.

Ahora el teléfono suena con mayor frecuencia. Hay que ser muy disciplinado para hablar por un teléfono intervenido y eso es algo con lo que lucho todos los días. Me repito a mí mismo que antes de intervenir los teléfonos, alguien firmó una orden judicial autorizando dicha invasión de la intimidad. Un juez debe haberlo autorizado y por consiguiente hay cierto elemento de legitimidad en ello.

El vestíbulo está todavía lleno de mesas alquiladas, cubiertas con los documentos del caso Black, y su presencia da la impresión de un trabajo monumental en progreso.

Por lo menos el despacho parece más ocupado. Después de varios meses, el mísero promedio de nuestros gastos es de mil setecientos dólares mensuales. Nuestros ingresos brutos medios son de tres mil doscientos, de modo que teóricamente Deck y yo nos repartimos mil quinientos, sin deducir retenciones ni impuestos.

Sobrevivimos. Nuestro mejor cliente es Derrick Dogan y si logramos saldar su caso por veinticinco mil, el límite de la póliza, respiraremos con más tranquilidad. Esperamos que se resuelva antes de Navidad, aunque no sé exactamente por qué. Ni Deck ni yo tenemos a nadie a quien queramos obsequiar.

Pasaré las vacaciones trabajando en el caso de los Black. Febrero no está lejos.

El correo de hoy es rutinario, con dos excepciones. No hay una sola comunicación de Trent & Brent. Es tan inusual que resulta emocionante. La segunda sorpresa me trastorna de tal modo, que me veo obligado a caminar por la oficina para serenarme.

El sobre es grande y cuadrado, con mi nombre y dirección escritos a mano. En su interior hay una invitación impresa para asistir a una promoción prenavideña de cadenas, brazaletes y collares de oro, en una joyería de unas galerías del barrio. Es pura propaganda, que habitualmente arrojaría de inmediato a la papelera, si el nombre y la dirección estuvieran impresos.

En el margen inferior, debajo de las horas de apertura de la joyería, con una letra bastante hermosa está escrito el nombre de Kelly Riker. Ningún mensaje. Nada. Sólo el nombre.

Paseo una hora por las galerías. Contemplo a unos chiquillos que patinan sobre hielo en una pista cubierta. Veo grandes grupos de adolescentes que circulan de un lado para otro. Compro un paquete de comida china recalentada y me la como en el paseo sobre la pista de patinaje.

La joyería es una de las más de cien tiendas bajo el mismo techo. La he visto cómo manipulaba una caja al mirar por primera vez.

Entro detrás de una pareja y me dirijo lentamente al mostrador, donde Kelly Riker está atendiendo a un cliente. Levanta la cabeza, me ve y sonríe. Retrocedo unos pasos, apoyo los codos en una estantería y contemplo el deslumbrante surtido de cadenas de oro, gruesas como sogas. La tienda está llena de gente. Media docena de dependientes charlan con clientes y les muestran diversos artículos.

—¿En qué puedo servirle, caballero? —pregunta, a medio metro de distancia.

La miro y me derrito.

Nos miramos sonrientes hasta el límite de nuestra audacia.

—Sólo miraba —respondo, con la esperanza de que nadie esté observándonos—. ¿Cómo estás?

—Bien, ¿y tú?

—Estupendo.

—¿Puedo mostrarte algo? Esto está de rebaja —dice, al tiempo que señala unas cadenas dignas de un chulo.

—Muy bonitas. ¿Podemos hablar? —pregunto de manera que sólo ella lo oiga.

—Aquí no —responde después de acercarse todavía más, y yo huelo su perfume, abre el cerrojo de una caja, desliza la tapa, saca una cadena de veinticinco centímetros para mostrármela y prosigue—: Hay un cine a lo largo de las galerías. Compra una entrada para la película de Eddie Murphy. Sección central, última fila. Estaré allí dentro de treinta minutos.

—¿Eddie Murphy? —repito mientras admiro la cadena.

—Bonita, ¿no le parece?

—Lo que andaba buscando. Realmente hermosa. Pero déjeme mirar un poco más.

—Vuelva pronto —dice como una perfecta dependienta, después de quitármela de las manos.

Se me derriten las rodillas cuando floto por las galerías. Sabía que vendría y lo había planeado todo: el cine, la película, la butaca y el lugar. Tomo un café junto a un ajetreado Papá Noël, e intento imaginar lo que me contará, lo que barrunta por su mente. Para evitar un tostón de película, compro la entrada en el último momento.

Hay menos de cincuenta espectadores en la sala. Un grupo de chiquillos, demasiado jóvenes para una película clasificada «X», en una de las primeras filas, se ríen de las obscenidades. Hay otras tristes almas repartidas por la oscuridad. La última fila está vacía.

Llega con unos minutos de retraso y se sienta junto a mí. Cruza las piernas y no puedo evitar percatarme de que la falda se le levanta por encima de las rodillas.

—¿Vienes aquí a menudo? —pregunta.

Suelto una carcajada. No parece nerviosa, pero yo ciertamente lo estoy.

—¿Estamos a salvo? —pregunto.

—¿A salvo de quién?

—De tu marido.

—Sí, ha salido con los muchachos esta noche.

—¿Vuelve a beber?

—Sí.

Ésa es una afirmación de gran alcance.

—Pero no mucho —agrega, a guisa de coletilla.

—Entonces no te ha...

—No. Hablemos de otro tema.

—Lo siento. Me preocupo por ti, eso es todo.

—¿Por qué te preocupas por mí?

—Porque no logro alejarte nunca de mi mente. ¿Piensas tú alguna vez en mí?

Miramos la pantalla, pero sin ver nada.

—Constantemente —responde, y se me para el corazón.

De pronto en la pantalla, un individuo y una muchacha están arrancándose mutuamente la ropa del cuerpo. Se desploman sobre la cama, almohadas y paños menores vuelan por los aires, se dan un apasionado beso y empieza a temblar la cama. Conforme los amantes se revuelcan, Kelly coloca su brazo debajo del mío y se me acerca. No hablamos hasta que termina la escena. Entonces empiezo a respirar de nuevo.

—¿Cuándo empezaste a trabajar? —pregunto.

—Hace dos semanas. Necesitamos un poco más de dinero para Navidad.

Probablemente ganará más que yo entre ahora y la Navidad.

—¿Te permite que trabajes?

—Prefiero no hablar de él.

—¿De qué quieres hablar?

—¿Cómo va la abogacía?

—Ajetreada. Tengo un juicio muy importante en febrero.

—¿De modo que estás satisfecho?

—Es una lucha, pero el bufete prospera. Los abogados pasamos hambre y luego, si hay suerte, nos hacemos ricos.

—¿Y si no hay suerte?

—Seguimos pasando hambre. Prefiero no hablar de abogados.

—De acuerdo. Cliff quiere tener un hijo.

—¿De qué servirá eso?

—No lo sé.

—No lo hagas, Kelly —digo con una pasión que me deja asombrado.

Nos miramos y estrechamos la mano.

¿Por qué estoy sentado en un cine a oscuras y cogido de la mano con una mujer casada? He ahí la pregunta del siglo. ¿Qué sucedería si de pronto apareciera Cliff y me sorprendiera abrazado a su esposa? ¿Quién mataría a quién?

—Me ha dicho que deje de tomar la píldora.

—¿Lo has hecho?

—No. Pero me preocupa lo que pueda suceder cuando no quede embarazada. Como recordarás, hasta ahora ha sido relativamente fácil.

—Es tu cuerpo.

—Sí, y lo quiere constantemente. Está obsesionado con el sexo.

—Preferiría hablar de otro tema, si no te importa.

—De acuerdo. Ya casi no nos queda nada de qué hablar.

—Tienes razón.

Nos soltamos la mano y dedicamos unos momentos a mirar

la película. Kelly se gira lentamente y se apoya sobre el codo. Nuestras caras están a escasos centímetros.

—Sólo deseaba verte, Rudy —dice, casi en un susurro.

—¿Eres feliz? —pregunto, al tiempo que le acaricio la mejilla con el reverso de la mano.

¿Cómo puede ser feliz?

—No, realmente no.

—¿Qué puedo hacer?

—Nada —responde después de morderse el labio y me parece detectar lágrimas en sus ojos.

—Debes tomar una decisión.

—¿Tú crees?

—Olvídate de mí, o solicita el divorcio.

—Creí que eras mi amigo.

—Eso creía yo también. Pero no es cierto. Es más que amistad y ambos lo sabemos.

Miramos unos momentos la película.

—Debo marcharme —dice—. Mi descanso ya casi ha terminado. Lamento haberte molestado.

—No me has molestado, Kelly. Estoy encantado de verte. Pero no pienso ocultarme de este modo. Solicita el divorcio, u olvídate de mí.

—No puedo olvidarte.

—Entonces solicitemos el divorcio. Podemos hacerlo mañana mismo. Te ayudaré a deshacerte de ese patán y luego podremos divertirnos.

Se me acerca, me da un fugaz beso en la mejilla y desaparece.

Sin consultármelo previamente, Deck saca a escondidas el teléfono de su despacho y se lo lleva a Butch para mostrárselo a un conocido que ha trabajado supuestamente en algún servicio secreto del ejército. Según dicho conocido, los artefactos todavía ocultos en nuestros teléfonos son bastante diferentes de los habitualmente utilizados por el FBI y otros servicios gubernamentales. Están fabricados en Checoslovaquia, son de una calidad media, y el receptor debe estar situado en las cercanías. Está casi seguro de que no han sido instalados por la policía ni los federales.

Recibo dicha información mientras tomamos un café, una semana antes del día de Acción de Gracias.

—Son otros los que nos escuchan —dice Deck muy nervioso.

Estoy demasiado aturdido para reaccionar.

—¿De quién puede tratarse? —pregunta Butch.

—¿Cómo diablos puedo saberlo? —exclamo enojado.

Ese individuo no tiene derecho a formularnos esta clase de preguntas. Cuando se haya marchado hablaré severamente con Deck por haberlo involucrado hasta tal punto. Le echo una mala mirada a mi socio, que no deja de moverse y observar a su alrededor, a la espera de que algún desconocido le ataque.

—El caso es que no son los federales —afirma categóricamente Butch.

—Gracias.

Pagamos el café y regresamos al despacho. Butch verifica una vez más los teléfonos, innecesariamente. Ahí siguen los diminutos botones.

La cuestión ahora es: ¿quién nos escucha?

Me encierro en mi despacho a la espera de que Butch nos abandone y empiezo a concebir un plan magistral. Al cabo de un rato Deck llama a mi puerta, sólo con la fuerza suficiente para que lo oiga.

Hablamos unos minutos de mi proyecto. Deck abandona el bufete y se dirige al juzgado, en el centro de la ciudad. Al cabo de media hora, me llama para ponerme al corriente de los casos de varios clientes ficticios. También me pregunta si necesito algo del centro de la ciudad.

—¿A que no adivinas quién quiere llegar ahora a un acuerdo? —pregunto después de unos minutos de charla.

—¿Quién?

—Dot Black.

—¿Dot Black? —pregunta con fingida incredulidad.

Deck no es el mejor actor del mundo.

—Sí, he pasado esta mañana por su casa y le he llevado un pastel de fruta. Dice que no tiene fuerzas para soportar el juicio y quiere llegar a un acuerdo cuanto antes.

—¿Cuánto?

—Ha dicho que aceptaría ciento sesenta. Ha estado pensando en ellos y puesto que su máxima oferta son ciento cincuenta, considera que los habrá vencido si pagan más de lo que se proponen. Cree que es una astuta negociadora. He intentado explicárselo, pero ya sabes lo testaruda que es.

—No lo hagas, Rudy. Este caso vale una fortuna.

—Lo sé. Kipler cree que obtendremos una recompensa punitiva gigantesca, pero ya sabes que éticamente estoy obligado a hablar con Drummond e intentar llegar a un acuerdo. Es la voluntad del cliente.

—No lo hagas. Ciento sesenta es una limosna —dice Deck, ahora con razonable convicción, y no puedo evitar una sonrisa, consciente de que calcula mentalmente su parte de los honorarios—. ¿Crees que subirán a ciento sesenta? —pregunta.

—No lo sé. Me dio la impresión de que ciento cincuenta era el máximo. Pero tampoco se lo discutí.

Si Great Benefit está dispuesta a pagar ciento cincuenta, no cabe la menor duda de que subirá a ciento sesenta.

—Lo hablaremos cuando regrese —dice.

—De acuerdo.

Colgamos y al cabo de media hora, Deck está sentado en mi despacho.

A las nueve menos cinco de la mañana siguiente suena el teléfono. Deck lo contesta en su despacho y luego viene corriendo hasta el mío.

—Es Drummond —dice.

Nuestro pequeño bufete, en un alarde de magnanimidad, ha adquirido un magnetófono de cuarenta dólares, que está conectado a mi teléfono, y confiamos en que no afecte al aparato de escucha. Butch dijo que no lo creía.

—Hola —respondo, procurando ocultar mis nervios y mi angustia.

—Hola Rudy, soy Leo Drummond —dice amablemente—. ¿Cómo está?

Éticamente, en este momento debería comunicarle que está grabándose la conversación y brindarle la oportunidad de reaccionar. Pero por razones evidentes, Deck y yo hemos decidido no hacerlo. Nuestro plan sería inútil. ¿Qué es la ética entre compañeros?

—Muy bien, señor Drummond, ¿y usted?

—No puedo quejarme. Escúcheme, debemos ponernos de acuerdo para tomarle declaración al doctor Kord. He hablado con su secretaria. ¿Qué le parece el doce de febrero? A las diez de la mañana, por supuesto en su despacho.

La declaración de Kord será la última, creo, a no ser que a Drummond se le ocurra alguien más remotamente interesado en el caso. Sin embargo, no deja de ser curioso que se le haya ocurrido llamarme con antelación, para interesarse por lo que pudiera ser conveniente.

—Me parece bien —respondo, mientras Deck circula hecho un manojo de nervios por mi despacho.

—Estupendo. No creo que dure mucho. O por lo menos eso espero a quinientos dólares por hora. Es obsceno, ¿no le parece?

¿No es asombroso lo amiguetes que somos ahora? Nosotros, los abogados, contra los médicos.

—Realmente obsceno.

—Bueno, qué le vamos a hacer. Por cierto, Rudy, ¿sabe lo que mi cliente realmente desea?

—¿Qué?

—Bueno, no les apetece la perspectiva de pasar una semana en Memphis soportando ese juicio. Son altos ejecutivos, ya sabe, personas de mucho dinero que deben proteger su reputación y su carrera. Quieren llegar a un acuerdo, Rudy, y me han encargado que se lo diga. Hablamos sólo de llegar a un acuerdo, no de admisión de responsabilidades, compréndalo.

—Por supuesto —respondo, al tiempo que le guiño un ojo a Deck.

—Su perito afirma que el coste del trasplante de médula habría costado entre ciento cincuenta y doscientos mil dólares, y no discutimos sus cifras. En el supuesto, y no es más que un supuesto, que mi cliente fuera realmente responsable del trasplante. Supongamos, limitémonos a suponer, que estuviera cubierto. En tal caso, mi cliente habría tenido que pagar alrededor de ciento setenta y cinco mil.

—Si usted lo dice.

—Ésa es la cantidad que le ofrecemos para saldar el asunto inmediatamente. ¡Ciento setenta y cinco mil! Y dejamos de tomar declaraciones. Puedo hacerle llegar un cheque en menos de siete días.

—No lo creo.

—Por Dios, Rudy. Ni todo el dinero del mundo podría resucitar al muchacho. Debe procurar que su cliente sea razonable. Creo que ella desea llegar a un acuerdo. Llega un momento en el que el abogado debe actuar como tal y responsabilizarse de la situación. Esa pobre mujer no tiene ni idea de lo que sucederá en el juicio.

—Hablaré con ella.

—Llámela ahora mismo. Lo esperaré una hora antes de salir. Llámela.

Probablemente ese taimado cabrón tiene nuestros micrófonos conectados a su despacho. Le encantaría que la llamara para escuchar nuestra conversación.

—Le llamaré, señor Drummond. Buenos días.

Cuelgo el teléfono, rebobino la cinta y escuchamos la grabación.

Deck se acomoda en una silla, con la boca completamente abierta y exhibiendo sus cuatro dientes relucientes.

—Han intervenido nuestros teléfonos —dice estupefacto, cuando acabamos de escuchar la grabación.

Contemplamos el magnetófono, como si por sí mismo lo explicara todo. Durante varios minutos permanezco literalmente aturdido y paralizado de estupor. Nada se mueve. Nada funciona. De pronto suena el teléfono, pero ninguno de nosotros lo levanta. En este momento nos tiene a ambos aterrados.

—Supongo que debemos comunicárselo a Kipler —digo por fin, con lentitud y parsimonia.

—No lo creo —responde Deck después de quitarse sus gruesas gafas y frotarse los ojos.

—¿Por qué no?

—Reflexionemos. Sabemos, o por lo menos creemos saber, que Drummond, o tal vez su cliente, ha pinchado nuestros teléfonos. Es evidente que Drummond está al corriente, porque acabamos de sorprenderlo. Pero no hay forma de demostrarlo irrefutablemente, de sorprenderlo con las manos en la masa.

—Lo negará hasta el día de su muerte.

—Exactamente. En cuyo caso, ¿qué puede hacer Kipler? ¿Acusarlo sin pruebas contundentes? ¿Ensañarse un poco más con él?

—A estas alturas ya está acostumbrado.

—Y no surtirá efecto alguno en el juicio. No se le puede comunicar al jurado que el señor Drummond y su cliente han jugado sucio durante la instrucción del caso.

Seguimos contemplando un rato el magnetófono mientras digerimos la noticia e intentamos abrirnos paso entre las tinieblas. El año pasado, en una clase de ética, leímos el caso de un abogado que fue severamente sancionado por grabar en secreto una conversación telefónica con otro abogado. Soy culpable, pero mi delito es insignificante comparado con la repugnante actitud de Drummond. Sin embargo, el problema estriba en que si muestro la grabación me inculpo automáticamente, mientras que Drummond nunca será condenado, porque no habrá forma de demostrar su responsabilidad. ¿A qué nivel está involucrado? ¿Ha sido idea suya la de intervenir nuestros teléfonos? ¿O se limita a utilizar información robada que le facilita su cliente?

Una vez más, nunca lo sabremos. Además, curiosamente, no importa. Y él lo sabe.

—Podemos utilizarlo en beneficio propio —digo.

—Eso era exactamente lo que yo estaba pensando.

—Pero debemos ser cautelosos, para no despertar sus sospechas.

—Sí, reservémoslo para el juicio. Esperemos el momento perfecto, cuando nos convenga mandar a esos payasos a la caza de fantasmas.

Empezamos ambos a sonreír.

Espero dos días y llamo a Drummond para comunicarle la triste noticia de que mi cliente no quiere su asqueroso dinero. Actúa de un modo un poco extraño, le confieso. Un día tiene miedo de asistir al juicio y al día siguiente quiere pelear en la sala. En este momento, quiere pelea.

No sospecha en absoluto. Adopta su acostumbrada actitud de hombre duro, con la amenaza de que se retirará permanentemente la oferta y de que será un juicio desagradable hasta las últimas consecuencias. Estoy seguro de que eso debe gustarles a los que escuchan desde Cleveland. Me pregunto cuánto deben tardar en escuchar estas conversaciones.

Deberíamos aceptar el dinero. Dot y Buddy cobrarían más de cien mil, una cantidad superior a la que podrían gastar en el resto de su vida. Su abogado recibirá casi sesenta mil, una auténtica fortuna. Pero el dinero no significa nada para los Black. Nunca lo han tenido y no sueñan con hacerse ricos. Dot sólo pretende que quede constancia oficial de lo que Great Benefit le ha hecho a su hijo. Quiere un juicio definitivo que le otorgue la razón y afirme que Donny Ray ha muerto porque Great Benefit lo ha asesinado.

En lo que a mí concierne, me asombra mi propia habilidad para despreocuparme del dinero. Es tentador, qué duda cabe, pero no me obsesiona. No me muero de hambre. Soy joven y habrá otros casos.

Además, estoy convencido de que si Great Benefit está lo suficientemente asustada para intervenir nuestros teléfonos, ocultan indudablemente secretos muy nefastos. A pesar de lo preocupado que estoy, me sorprendo a mí mismo soñando con el juicio.

Booker y Charlene me invitan a comer con la familia Kane el día de Acción de Gracias. Su abuela vive en una pequeña casa al sur de Memphis y evidentemente ha estado cocinando toda la semana. Llueve, hace frío, y nos vemos obligados a pasar la tarde dentro de la casa. Somos por lo menos cincuenta, de edades que oscilan entre los seis meses y los ochenta años, y el único rostro blanco es el mío. Pasamos varias horas comiendo, los hombres apretujados en la sala de estar viendo un partido tras otro por televisión. Booker y yo nos comemos nuestra tarta y tomamos café en el garaje, sobre el capó del coche, temblando mientras charlamos. Siente curiosidad por mi vida sexual y le aseguro que actualmente es inexistente. Le comunico que el negocio prospera. Él trabaja día y noche. Charlene quiere tener otro hijo, pero puede que no sea fácil dejarla embarazada. No está nunca en casa.

La vida de un abogado ajetreado.

TREINTA Y NUEVE

Sabíamos que estaba en el correo, pero la decisión con que pisa al andar me indica que ha llegado. Deck entra alegremente en mi despacho, agitando el sobre en la mano.

—¡Ha llegado! ¡Ha llegado! ¡Somos ricos!

Abre el sobre, extrae delicadamente el cheque y lo deposita con suavidad sobre mi escritorio. Lo admiramos. ¡Veinticinco mil dólares de State Farm! Es Navidad.

Puesto que Derrick Dogan utiliza todavía muletas para andar, acudimos inmediatamente a su casa con los documentos necesarios. Firma donde le indicamos y le entregamos el dinero. Él recibe exactamente dieciséis mil seiscientos sesenta y siete dólares, y nosotros ocho mil trescientos treinta. Deck quería cobrarle los gastos de copias, correo, llamadas telefónicas y otros varios, que la mayoría de los abogados acostumbra a cobrar a sus clientes en el momento de la liquidación, pero yo me he negado.

Nos despedimos de él, le deseamos buena suerte y procuramos manifestar cierta tristeza respecto a lo sucedido. No es fácil.

Hemos decidido quedarnos con tres mil cada uno y dejar el resto en el fondo del bufete, para los inevitables meses de penuria en el futuro. Vamos a almorzar en un elegante restaurante del este de Memphis, por cuenta del bufete. El bufete tiene ahora una tarjeta de crédito oro, expedida por una sucursal bancaria desesperada, cuyo director está impresionado por mi rango social como abogado. Contesté con evasivas las preguntas referentes a insolvencias previas. Deck y yo nos hemos comprometido con un apretón de manos a no utilizar dicha tarjeta sin el consentimiento de ambos.

Cojo mis tres mil y me compro un coche. Evidentemente no es nuevo, pero no he dejado de soñar con él desde que supimos con certeza que el caso Dogan estaba resuelto. Es un Volvo DL de mil novecientos ochenta y cuatro, azul, con cuatro velocidades y *overdrive*, en muy buen estado y con sólo doscientos mil kilómetros. Es poco para un Volvo. Su primer y único propietario era un banquero, a quien le gustaba revisarlo personalmente.

He considerado la posibilidad de comprarme un coche nuevo, pero no puedo soportar la idea de endeudarme.

Es mi primer coche de abogado. Me dan trescientos dólares por mi Toyota y los invierto en comprar un teléfono para mi nuevo vehículo. Rudy Baylor va llegando lentamente.

Hace varias semanas decidí que no pasaría la Navidad en esta ciudad. Los recuerdos del año pasado son todavía demasiado dolorosos. Estaré solo y será más fácil si me ausento. Deck ha mencionado la posibilidad de que pasáramos juntos las fiestas, pero no ha sido más que una sugerencia vaga desprovista de detalles. Le he dicho que probablemente me reuniría con mi madre.

Cuando mi madre y Hank no están de viaje en su furgoneta aparcan el vehículo tras una pequeña casa que él tiene en Toledo. Nunca he visto la casa, ni la furgoneta, ni estoy dispuesto a pasar la Navidad con Hank. Mi madre me llamó poco después del día de Acción de Gracias, con una vaga invitación para pasar las fiestas con ellos. Le respondí que no podría porque estaba muy ocupado. Le mandaré una felicitación.

No me desagrada mi madre, simplemente hemos dejado de hablarnos. El distanciamiento ha sido gradual, sin ningún incidente desagradable con austeras palabras que uno tarda años en olvidar.

Según Deck, el sistema jurídico se paraliza desde el quince de diciembre hasta después de Año Nuevo. No se celebran juicios ni vistas. Los abogados se dedican a celebrar fiestas en sus bufetes y almuerzos para el personal. Es un momento ideal para abandonar la ciudad.

Guardo los documentos del caso Black en el maletero de mi reluciente Volvo, junto con unas mudas, y me lanzo a la carretera. Circulo sin rumbo fijo por pequeñas carreteras de dos carriles, en dirección noroeste, hasta encontrarme con nieve en Kansas y Nebraska. Duermo en moteles baratos, me alimento de comida rápida y contemplo el paisaje. Una tormenta invernal ha asolado las praderas del norte. Hay montañas de nieve junto a las carreteras. Las llanuras están tan blancas e inmóviles como cúmulos caídos del cielo.

Me siento estimulado por la soledad de la carretera.

Es el veintitrés de diciembre cuando llego finalmente a Madison, Wisconsin. Encuentro un pequeño hotel, con comida caliente en su acogedor restaurante, y recorro las calles del centro de la ciudad, de tienda en tienda como cualquiera. Hay ciertos aspectos de la Navidad que no echo de menos.

Me siento en un banco helado del parque, con los pies sobre la nieve, y escucho un apasionado concierto de villancicos. Nadie en el mundo sabe dónde estoy, en qué ciudad ni en qué estado. Adoro esa libertad.

Después de cenar y tomar unas copas en el bar del hotel llamo a Max Leuberg, que ha recuperado su cátedra de Derecho en esta facultad. He hablado con él aproximadamente una vez al mes para pedirle consejos, y me ha invitado a que lo visitara. Le he mandado copias de los documentos más importantes, junto a copias de las alegaciones, la instrucción escrita y la mayoría de las declaraciones. La caja pesaba seis kilos y me costó casi treinta dólares el envío. Deck estuvo de acuerdo.

Max parece sinceramente feliz de que esté en Madison. Puesto que es judío, participa muy poco en los festejos navideños y el otro día me dijo por teléfono que era un período maravilloso para trabajar. Me da las direcciones oportunas.

A las nueve de la mañana del día siguiente, la temperatura es de once grados bajo cero cuando entro en la facultad. Está abierta, pero desierta. Leuberg me espera en su despacho con café caliente. Charlamos durante una hora sobre cosas que echa de menos en Memphis, entre las que no se incluye la Facultad de Derecho. Su estudio aquí es muy parecido al que tenía en Memphis: abarrotado, desordenado, y con las paredes cubiertas de provocativos carteles y pegatinas. Su aspecto es también el mismo: una frondosa cabellera despeinada, vaqueros y zapatillas blancas. Lleva calcetines, pero sólo porque en la calle hay dos palmos de nieve. Rebosa energía y actividad.

Le sigo por el pasillo hasta una pequeña aula, con una larga mesa en el centro de la misma. Abre la puerta con una llave. Los documentos que le mandé están ordenados sobre la mesa. Nos sentamos uno frente a otro y sirve más café de un termo. Sabe que faltan seis semanas para el juicio.

—¿Alguna oferta? —pregunta.

—Sí, varias. Han llegado a ciento setenta y cinco mil, pero mi cliente los ha rechazado.

—Es inusual, pero no me sorprende.

—¿Por qué no le sorprende?

—Porque los tiene atrapados. Aquí hay muchos trapos sucios, Rudy. Es uno de los mejores casos de mala fe que he visto, y he examinado millares.

—Hay algo más —digo, antes de contarle que nuestros teléfonos están pinchados y que tenemos pruebas contundentes de que Drummond escucha nuestras conversaciones.

—No es la primera vez que lo oigo —responde—. Sucedió en un caso de Florida, pero el abogado de la acusación no descubrió que sus teléfonos estaban intervenidos hasta después del juicio. Empezó a sospechar porque la defensa parecía saber lo que se proponía. Pero, caramba, esto es harina de otro costal.

—Deben estar asustados.

—Están muertos de miedo, pero no nos confiemos. Juegan en un terreno que les es favorable. En su condado no son partidarios de otorgar daños y perjuicios.

—¿Qué está diciéndome?

—Que acepte el dinero y cierre el caso.

—No puedo hacerlo. No quiero hacerlo. Mi cliente no desea hacerlo.

—Estupendo. Ha llegado el momento de trasladar a esa gente al siglo veinte. ¿Dónde está su magnetófono?

Se incorpora de un brinco y da saltos por la sala. En la pared hay una pizarra y el profesor se dispone a dar una conferencia. Saco el magnetófono del maletín y lo coloco sobre la mesa. Mi pluma y mi cuaderno están listos para entrar en acción.

Max despega y durante una hora tomo apuntes sin parar y le formulo innumerables preguntas. Habla de mis testigos, sus testigos, los documentos y diversas estrategias. Max se ha estudiado el material que le he mandado. Le encanta la idea de atrapar a esa gente.

—Guárdese lo mejor para el final —dice el profesor—. Muéstreles la grabación de la declaración de ese pobre chico antes de morir. Supongo que su aspecto es lamentable.

—Peor.

—Estupendo. Es una imagen maravillosa para dejar en la mente del jurado. Si todo funciona a pedir de boca, podrá concluir su exposición en tres días.

—¿Y luego?

—Siéntese tranquilo y vea cómo intentan justificarse.

De pronto deja de hablar, coge algo de la mesa y me lo entrega.

—¿De qué se trata?

—Es la nueva póliza de Great Benefit, expedida el mes pasado a uno de mis alumnos. Yo la pagué y la anularemos el mes próximo. Sólo pretendía ver la redacción del texto. Adivine lo que han excluido, en mayúsculas.

352

—Los trasplantes de médula ósea.

—Todos los trasplantes, incluidos los de médula. Guárdesela y utilícela en el juicio. Creo que debería preguntarle al director gerente por qué modificaron la póliza cuando los Black presentaron su demanda judicial. ¿Por qué excluyen ahora específicamente el trasplante de médula? Y si no estaba excluido en la póliza de los Black, ¿por qué no pagaron la reclamación? Un buen caso, Rudy. Maldita sea, tal vez vaya a ver el juicio.

—Por favor, hágalo.

Sería muy reconfortante disponer de otro amigo, además de Deck, a quien poder consultar.

A Max le parece problemático nuestro análisis de la ficha de reclamación y no tardamos en perdernos entre el papeleo. Traslado las cuatro cajas de cartón de mi maletero al aula y a mediodía el lugar parece un campo de batalla.

Su energía es contagiosa. Durante el almuerzo recibo la primera de varias clases sobre la contabilidad de las compañías de seguros. Puesto que el sector está exento de la legislación federal antimonopolios, ha elaborado sus propios métodos de contabilidad. Ningún inspector contable competente es capaz de entender las cifras de una compañía de seguros. Son deliberadamente arcanas, porque ninguna compañía de seguros desea que el mundo exterior sepa lo que está haciendo. Pero Max me ofrece algunas directrices.

Great Benefit dispone de un capital social de cuatrocientos a quinientos millones de dólares, aproximadamente la mitad del cual está oculto en reservas y excedentes. Eso es lo que hay que explicarle al jurado.

No me atrevo a sugerir lo inimaginable, trabajar el día de Navidad, pero Max está dispuesto a todo. Su esposa está en Nueva York, visitando a su familia. No tiene otra cosa que hacer y quiere realmente examinar los documentos de las dos cajas restantes. Estoy agotado, y por fin declara que hemos terminado, cuando ya ha oscurecido el veinticinco de diciembre. Me ayuda a guardar de nuevo los documentos en las cajas y a trasladarlas a mi coche. Está nevando de nuevo intensamente.

Max y yo nos despedimos en la puerta de la facultad. No tengo palabras para darle las gracias. Me desea buena suerte y me obliga a prometerle que lo llamaré una vez por semana antes del juicio, y a diario durante el mismo. Repite que tal vez haga un viaje relámpago.

Me despido con la mano desde la nieve.

Tardo tres días dando vueltas hasta llegar a Spartanburg, en Carolina del Sur. El Volvo se porta de maravilla por carretera, especialmente en la nieve y el hielo del medio oeste septentrional. Llamo a Deck en una ocasión desde el teléfono de mi coche. Dice que el bufete está tranquilo y que nadie ha preguntado por mí.

He pasado los últimos tres años y medio estudiando intensamente para obtener mi título de abogado, además de trabajar en Yogi's siempre que podía. No he disfrutado de mucho tiempo libre. Este viaje barato por diferentes lugares del país puede parecerle aburrido a la mayoría de la gente, pero para mí son unas vacaciones de lujo. Me aclara la mente y el alma, me permite pensar en otras cosas aparte de las leyes. Me libero de ciertos fantasmas, Sara Plankmore entre otros. Desaparecen viejos rencores. La vida es demasiado corta para odiar a personas que sencillamente no pueden evitar comportarse como lo hacen. Los graves pecados de Loyd Beck y Barry X. Lancaster son redimidos en algún lugar del oeste de Virginia. Prometo dejar de preocuparme por la señorita Birdie y su detestable familia. Pueden resolver sus propios problemas sin mi ayuda.

A lo largo de los kilómetros no dejo de soñar en Kelly Riker, su perfecta dentadura, sus morenas piernas y su dulce voz.

Cuando pienso en asuntos jurídicos, me concentro en el juicio que se avecina. Hay sólo un sumario en el bufete que podría acabar ante el juez, de modo que tengo únicamente un juicio en que pensar. Ensayo mi introducción ante el jurado. Interrogo a los maleantes de Great Benefit. Casi echo a llorar durante las conclusiones.

Me miran algunos de los motoristas con los que me cruzo, pero qué diablos, nadie me conoce.

He hablado con cuatro abogados que han demandado, o están demandando actualmente, a Great Benefit. Los tres primeros no me han sido de ninguna ayuda. El cuarto está en Spartanburg. Su nombre es Cooper Jackson y su caso tiene algo de extraño. No pudo contármelo por teléfono, el de mi casa, pero dijo que le encantaría recibirme en su despacho y mostrarme su ficha.

Su bufete, situado en un moderno edificio de un banco en el centro de la ciudad, tiene seis abogados. Lo llamé ayer por el teléfono de mi coche desde algún lugar de Carolina del Norte y hoy está disponible. Dice que hay poca actividad durante las vacaciones de Navidad.

Es un individuo corpulento, de pecho ancho y gruesas extre-

midades, con una barba oscura y ojos negros que brillan y dan-
zan animadamente con cada expresión. Tiene cuarenta y seis
años, y dice que se ha enriquecido trabajando a comisión. Se
asegura de que la puerta de su despacho esté cerrada antes de
proseguir.

Se supone que no debería revelarme la mayor parte de lo que
está a punto de contarme. Ha llegado a un acuerdo con Great
Benefit, y él y sus clientes han firmado un pacto estrictamente
confidencial, con severas sanciones en caso de que una u otra
parte revelen las condiciones del acuerdo. No le gustan esos pac-
tos, pero no son inusuales. Presentó la demanda hace un año, en
representación de una señora con problemas sinusoidales que
precisaba una intervención quirúrgica. Great Benefit denegó la
reclamación, basándose en que dicha señora no había declarado
en la solicitud que, cinco años antes de contratar la póliza, le
habían extirpado un quiste de los ovarios. El quiste suponía una
condición preexistente, según la carta de denegación. La reclamación ascendía a once mil dólares. Se intercambiaron otras
cartas, seguidas de denegaciones adicionales, hasta que contrató a Cooper Jackson, que se desplazó cuatro veces a Cleveland,
en su propio avión, para tomar ocho declaraciones.

—El mayor puñado de cretinos y taimados cabrones con que
me he encontrado en mi vida —dice refiriéndose al personal de
Cleveland.

A Jackson le encantan los juicios difíciles y va a por todas. Se
preparó concienzudamente para el juicio y de pronto Great Benefit propuso con suma discreción un acuerdo.

—Y ahora viene la parte confidencial —dice, evidentemente
encantado de violar el acuerdo y contármelo todo, como seguramente lo ha hecho con un centenar de personas—. Nos pagaron
los once mil y luego nos dieron otros doscientos mil, para que
no volviéramos a importunarlos.

Le brillan los ojos como si esperara mi respuesta. Es un
acuerdo extraordinario, porque en realidad Great Benefit pagó
un montón de dinero en daños y perjuicios. No me sorprende
que quisieran ocultarlo.

—Asombroso —exclamo.

—Sí, lo es. Yo no quería aceptar el acuerdo, pero mi pobre
cliente necesitaba el dinero. Estoy seguro de que podíamos haber obtenido un buen veredicto contra ellos.

Me cuenta unas cuantas batallitas para convencerme de que
ha ganado un montón de dinero y luego le sigo a una pequeña
sala desprovista de ventanas, con estantes repletos de cajas idén-
ticas de cartón. Señala tres de ellas y apoya su voluminoso cuerpo en la estantería.

—Aquí está su estrategia —dice al tiempo que toca una de las cajas, como si contuviera grandes misterios—. Llega la reclamación y se asigna a un administrativo, un simple oficinista mal pagado. El personal de reclamaciones es el peor formado y menos remunerado. Ocurre en todas las compañías de seguros. El sector fascinante es el de inversiones, no los de reclamaciones ni contratación. El administrativo en cuestión manda una carta de denegación al asegurado. Estoy convencido de que usted debe tener una. A continuación, el encargado de la reclamación solicita los informes médicos de los últimos cinco años. Se estudian dichos informes. El asegurado recibe otra carta del departamento de reclamaciones, en la que se le informa de que su reclamación ha sido denegada, a la espera de otras investigaciones. Ahí es donde se pone interesante. El encargado de reclamaciones manda la ficha al departamento de contratación, y el departamento de contratación manda una circular al departamento de reclamaciones, donde se dice algo así como: «No paguen esta reclamación hasta que tengan noticias nuestras.» Se intercambian numerosas cartas y circulares entre contratación y reclamaciones, aumenta el papeleo, aparecen discrepancias, se discuten cláusulas y subcláusulas de la póliza, y se entabla una guerra entre ambos departamentos. No olvide que todas esas personas trabajan en la misma compañía y en el mismo edificio, pero raramente se conocen. Tampoco tienen conocimiento alguno de lo que el otro departamento hace. Eso es perfectamente deliberado. Entretanto, su cliente va recibiendo cartas en su casa, algunas del departamento de reclamaciones y otras de contratación. La mayoría de la gente se da por vencida y eso, evidentemente, es lo que se proponen. Aproximadamente uno de cada veinticinco consulta a un abogado.

Recuerdo documentos y fragmentos de declaraciones mientras Jackson habla y, de pronto, las cosas empiezan a caer en su lugar.

—¿Cómo puede demostrarlo? —pregunto.

—Está todo aquí —responde, al tiempo que golpea las cajas—. La mayoría de estos documentos no le servirían para nada, pero tengo los manuales.

—Yo también.

—No tengo ningún inconveniente en que lo examine todo. Está perfectamente organizado. Tengo un excelente pasante, a decir verdad, dos.

Sí, pero yo, Rudy Baylor, tengo un ¡seudoabogado!

Me deja con las cajas y busco inmediatamente los manuales de color verde oscuro. Uno es para contratación y el otro para reclamaciones. Al principio parecen casi idénticos a los que he obtenido durante la instrucción. Los procedimientos están clasificados por secciones. Hay un sumario al principio, un glosario al final y no son más que manuales para oficinistas.

Luego veo algo diferente. Al final del manual de reclamaciones descubro la sección «u». En mi manual no aparece dicha sección. La leo lentamente y se desvela la conspiración. El manual de contratación también tiene una sección «u». Es la otra mitad de la estrategia, exactamente como Cooper Jackson la ha descrito. Los manuales, al leerlos conjuntamente, ordenan a cada departamento denegar la reclamación a la espera de otras investigaciones y luego, evidentemente, mandar la ficha al otro departamento con instrucciones de no pagar la reclamación a la espera de noticias.

Las noticias nunca llegan. Ningún departamento puede pagar hasta que el otro lo autorice.

Ambas secciones «u» facilitan abundantes directrices en cuanto a la forma de documentar cada paso, construir en realidad una autopista de papeleo, para demostrar algún día, si fuera necesario, el muchísimo trabajo que se invirtió en la evaluación de la reclamación antes de denegarla.

En ninguno de mis manuales aparece la sección «u». La retiraron convenientemente antes de entregármelos. Esos estafadores de Cleveland, y tal vez sus abogados de Memphis, me han ocultado deliberadamente la sección «u». Eso es, sin exageración alguna, un descubrimiento asombroso.

No tardo en recuperarme de la sorpresa y echo a reír ante la idea de presentar dichas secciones en el juicio y mostrárselas al jurado.

Paso horas examinando el resto de los documentos, pero no puedo alejar la mirada de los manuales.

A Cooper le gusta tomar vodka en su despacho, pero sólo después de las seis de la tarde. Me invita a tomar una copa. Guarda la botella en un pequeño frigorífico de un armario que utiliza como mueble bar. Yo saboreo también el mío. Bastan un par de gotitas para que me ardan hasta las entrañas.

—Estoy seguro de que tiene copias de las diversas investigaciones gubernamentales de Great Benefit —dice, después de vaciar la primera copa.

No sé de qué está hablándome y sería absurdo mentir.

—Pues, a decir verdad, no.

—Le conviene repasarlas. Yo denuncié a la compañía al fiscal general de Carolina del Sur, un antiguo compañero de facultad, y actualmente están investigándola. Otro tanto ocurre en

Georgia. El comisario de seguros de Florida ha iniciado una investigación oficial. Parece que se ha denegado un número excesivo de reclamaciones en poco tiempo.

Hace unos meses, cuando estudiaba todavía en la facultad, Max Leuberg mencionó haber denunciado una compañía al Departamento de Seguros del estado. También mencionó que probablemente no serviría de nada, porque el sector de los seguros estaba en muy buenas relaciones con quienes pretendían regularlo.

No puedo evitar la sensación de que me ha pasado algo por alto. Bueno, después de todo, éste es mi primer caso de mala fe.

—¿Sabía que se habla de la posibilidad de un pleito colectivo? —pregunta, mientras sus brillantes ojos parpadean con suspicacia, consciente de que no sé nada del tema.

—¿Dónde?

—Unos abogados de Raleigh. Tienen un puñado de pequeñas demandas de mala fe contra Great Benefit, pero esperan pacientemente. La compañía todavía no ha recibido un buen golpe. Sospecho que llegan a acuerdos discretos con los que les preocupan.

—¿Cuántas pólizas hay en el mercado?

En realidad he formulado esta pregunta durante la instrucción, pero todavía espero una respuesta.

—Casi cien mil. Si calcula una media de reclamaciones del diez por ciento, eso supone diez mil reclamaciones anuales, aproximadamente lo normal en dicho sector. Digamos, por ejemplo, que denieguen la mitad de las reclamaciones. Quedan reducidas a cinco mil. La cantidad media por reclamación es de diez mil dólares. Cinco mil por diez mil son cincuenta millones de dólares. Y supongamos que se gasten diez millones, por decir algo, para saldar los pleitos que aparezcan. Se habrán ahorrado cuarenta millones con sus pequeñas estratagemas y puede que al año siguiente vuelvan a pagar las reclamaciones legítimas. Al cabo de otro año, aplican de nuevo la política de las denegaciones. Elaboran otra estrategia. Ganan tanto dinero que pueden permitirse el lujo de estafar a cualquiera.

—¿Puede demostrarlo? —pregunto después de mirarle fijamente un buen rato.

—No. Es sólo un presentimiento. Probablemente es imposible demostrarlo, porque es tan incriminador. Esta compañía comete verdaderas estupideces, pero dudo que sean tan idiotas como para poner algo como esto por escrito.

Empiezo a mencionarle lo de la «estúpida carta», pero opto por no hacerlo. Lleva las de ganar. Saldrá victorioso de cualquier contienda.

—¿Forma parte de alguna asociación de abogados? —pregunta.

—No. Ejerzo desde hace sólo unos meses.

—Yo estoy bastante involucrado. Hay una red relativamente indefinida de abogados, a los que nos gusta demandar a las compañías de seguros por casos de mala fe. Nos mantenemos en contacto. Intercambiamos rumores. Oigo muchas cosas acerca de Great Benefit. Creo que han denegado demasiadas reclamaciones. Todo el mundo está a la espera del primer gran juicio que les ponga de manifiesto. Un buen veredicto iniciará la estampida.

—No estoy seguro en cuanto al veredicto, pero puedo garantizarle que se celebrará el juicio.

Me dice que hablará probablemente con sus compañeros, activará la red y sus contactos, recogerá los rumores y averiguará lo que sucede en otras partes del país. Y puede que acuda a Memphis en febrero para presenciar el juicio. Un buen veredicto, repite, romperá el dique.

Paso la mitad del día siguiente repasando la ficha de Jackson, le doy las gracias y me marcho. Insiste en que me mantenga en contacto. Tiene el presentimiento de que muchos abogados estarán pendientes del juicio.

¿Por qué me da miedo?

Tardo doce horas en regresar a Memphis. Cuando descargo el Volvo tras la oscura casa de la señorita Birdie, empieza a caer una suave nevada. Mañana es Año Nuevo.

CUARENTA

La entrevista preliminar al juicio se celebra a mitad de enero, en la sala del juez Kipler. Su señoría nos organiza alrededor de la mesa de la defensa y ordena a un alguacil que vigile la puerta para impedir la entrada de cualquier abogado en el juzgado. Él se sienta en un extremo, sin toga, con su secretaria a un lado y la relatora al otro. Yo estoy a su derecha, de espaldas a la sala, y frente a mí está todo el equipo de la defensa. Es la primera vez que veo a Drummond desde la declaración de Kord, el doce de diciembre, y tengo que hacer un esfuerzo para no perder los buenos modales. Cada vez que descuelgo el teléfono de mi despacho veo a ese maleante de impecable compostura, elegantemente vestido y sumamente respetado, que escucha mi conversación.

Ambas partes hemos solicitado órdenes preliminares y hoy se resolverán las discrepancias. La orden definitiva servirá de programa para el juicio.

Kipler no se sorprendió excesivamente cuando le mostré los manuales que me ha prestado Cooper Jackson. Los ha comparado cuidadosamente con los que me ha entregado Drummond. Según su señoría, no estoy obligado a comunicarle a Drummond que sé que me han ocultado documentos. Las normas me autorizan a esperar al juicio y poner a Great Benefit en evidencia ante el jurado.

El efecto será devastador. Les bajaré los pantalones ante el jurado y veré cómo echan a correr.

Llegamos a la cuestión de los testigos. He confeccionado una lista de casi todos los nombres relacionados con el caso.

—Jackie Lemancyzk ya no trabaja para mi cliente —dice Drummond.

—¿Sabe dónde está? —me pregunta Kipler.

—No —respondo sinceramente.

He hecho un centenar de llamadas a la región de Cleveland y

no he encontrado ni rastro de Jackie Lemancyzk. También he convencido a Butch para que procurara localizarla por teléfono, pero ha corrido la misma suerte.

—¿Lo sabe usted? —le pregunta a Drummond.

—No.

—En tal caso, la consideraremos como posible testigo.

—Exactamente.

A Drummond y T. Pierce Morehouse les parece gracioso, e intercambian sonrisas de frustración. No lo hallarán tan divertido si logramos localizarla y acude a declarar. Aunque parece bastante improbable.

—¿Qué me dicen de Bobby Ott? —pregunta Kipler.

—Otro testigo posible —respondo.

Ambas partes podemos nombrar a las personas que esperamos que se presenten al juicio. Ott parece dudoso, pero si lo encontramos, quiero poder llamarlo como testigo. Una vez más le he pedido a Butch que lo buscara.

Hablamos de los peritos. Sólo tengo dos, el doctor Walter Kord y Randall Gaskin, administrador de la clínica oncológica. Drummond ha incluido a uno en su lista, el doctor Milton Juffy, de Syracuse. He decidido no tomarle declaración por dos razones. En primer lugar, sería demasiado caro viajar hasta allí para hacerlo y, lo que es más importante, sé lo que va a decir. Declarará que los trasplantes de médula son demasiado experimentales para ser considerados como un tratamiento médico adecuado y razonable. Walter Kord está furioso y me ayudará a preparar el interrogatorio.

Kipler duda que llegue a declarar.

Discutimos sobre documentos durante una hora. Drummond le asegura al juez que han actuado con toda honradez y entregado todos los documentos. A cualquiera le parecería convincente, pero yo sospecho que miente. También lo sospecha Kipler.

—¿Qué me dice de la información solicitada por la acusación sobre el total de pólizas en existencia durante los dos últimos años, el total de reclamaciones durante el mismo período y el total de reclamaciones denegadas?

Drummond respira hondo y parece sumamente perplejo.

—Estamos en ello, su señoría, se lo juro. La información está dispersa por distintas agencias regionales a lo largo y ancho del país. Mi cliente tiene treinta y una agencias estatales, diecisiete agencias provinciales, cinco regionales, es difícil...

—¿Tiene su cliente ordenadores?

—Por supuesto —responde frustrado—. Pero no se trata simplemente de pulsar unas teclas y ¡ahí está la información!

—El juicio empieza dentro de tres semanas, señor Drummond. Quiero esa información.

—Estamos intentándolo, su señoría. Se lo recuerdo a mi cliente todos los días.

—¡Obténgala! —exclama Kipler, señalando incluso al gran Leo F. Drummond.

Morehouse, Hill, Plunk y Grone se hunden simultáneamente unos centímetros en sus asientos, pero sin dejar de tomar notas.

Pasamos a asuntos menos delicados. Estamos todos de acuerdo en que debemos reservar dos semanas para el juicio, aunque Kipler me ha confiado que se propone presionar todo lo posible para resolverlo en cinco días. Concluimos la vista en dos horas.

—Bien, caballeros, ¿alguna negociación para llegar a un acuerdo? —pregunta el juez.

Evidentemente, ya le he hablado de la última oferta de ciento setenta y cinco mil. También sabe que Dot Black no tiene ningún interés en llegar a un acuerdo. No quiere el dinero. Quiere sangre.

—¿Cuál es su mejor oferta, señor Drummond?

Hay expresiones de satisfacción entre los cinco componentes de la defensa, como si algo dramático estuviera a punto de ocurrir.

—Bien, su señoría, desde esta mañana mi cliente me ha autorizado a ofrecer doscientos mil dólares para saldar el caso —responde Drummond, con un pequeño esfuerzo melodramático.

—Señor Baylor.

—Lo siento. Mi cliente me ha ordenado no aceptar su oferta.

—¿Por cualquier cantidad?

—Exactamente. Quiere un jurado en ese palco y que el mundo sepa lo que le ha ocurrido a su hijo.

Estupefacción y desconcierto al otro lado de la mesa. Nunca había visto tanto movimiento de cabezas. Incluso el juez parece perplejo.

Apenas he hablado con Dot desde el funeral. Nuestras escasas conversaciones han sido satisfactorias. Está afligida y enojada, y es perfectamente comprensible. Responsabiliza a Great Benefit, a la administración, a los médicos, a los abogados, e incluso a veces a mí de la muerte de Donny Ray. Y también lo comprendo. No necesita ni quiere el dinero. Lo que quiere es justicia. Como dijo en la puerta de su casa la última vez que nos vimos: Quiero arruinar a esos hijos de puta.

—Esto es espantoso —dice con dramatismo Drummond.

—Habrá juicio, Leo —respondo—. Prepárese.

Kipler señala una carpeta y su secretaria se la acerca. Entonces le entrega a Drummond algún tipo de lista y otra a mí.

—Aquí están los nombres y direcciones de los componentes potenciales del jurado. Creo que hay noventa y dos, aunque puede que algunos hayan cambiado de domicilio o se hayan trasladado.

Cojo la lista y empiezo a leer inmediatamente los nombres. Hay un millón de habitantes en este condado. ¿Espero realmente conocer a alguien de la lista? Todos desconocidos.

—Elegiremos el jurado una semana antes del juicio, estén preparados para el primero de febrero. Pueden investigar a los candidatos pero, evidentemente, cualquier contacto directo constituiría una falta grave.

—¿Dónde están las fichas? —pregunta Drummond.

Cada miembro potencial del jurado rellena una ficha con ciertos datos básicos como su edad, raza, sexo, lugar de trabajo, tipo de trabajo y nivel de educación. A menudo ésa es toda la información que el abogado posee cuando se inicia el proceso de selección.

—Estamos elaborándolas. Saldrán por correo mañana. ¿Algo más?

—No, señor —respondo.

Drummond mueve la cabeza.

—Quiero esa información sobre pólizas y reclamaciones cuanto antes, señor Drummond.

—Estamos intentándolo, su señoría.

Almuerzo solo en la cooperativa vegetariana cerca de nuestro despacho. Habichuelas negras, arroz con salsa de tomate, y una infusión de hierbas. Siempre que vengo aquí me siento más sano. Como lentamente, revolviendo las alubias y con la mirada fija en los noventa y dos nombres de la lista. Drummond, con sus ilimitados recursos, utilizará un equipo de investigadores para localizar a esas personas y explorar sus vidas. Harán cosas como fotografiar en secreto sus casas y sus coches, averiguar si han estado involucrados en algún proceso judicial, obtener sus referencias financieras e historial laboral, e investigar los trapos sucios, como posibles divorcios, insolvencias, o cargos penales. Consultarán los archivos públicos para averiguar cuánto han pagado por sus casas. Lo único prohibido es el contacto personal, ya sea directamente o a través de un intermediario.

Cuando nos reunamos en la sala para elegir a los doce componentes del jurado, Drummond y compañía dispondrán de una amplia ficha para cada una de esas personas. Dichas fichas serán evaluadas no sólo por él y sus compañeros, sino que también serán meticulosamente analizadas por un equipo de asesores profesionales para la elección del jurado. En la historia de la jurisprudencia norteamericana, los asesores para la elección del jurado son una especie relativamente nueva. Suelen ser abogados con cierto grado de pericia y experiencia en el estudio de la naturaleza humana. Muchos de ellos son también siquiatras o sicólogos. Circulan por el país y venden sus conocimientos a precios exorbitantes a abogados que puedan permitírselos.

En la facultad oí la anécdota de un asesor contratado por Jonathan Lake por ochenta mil dólares. El jurado dictó un veredicto de varios millones y, por consiguiente, los honorarios del asesor eran una menudencia.

Los asesores de Drummond estarán en la sala cuando seleccionemos a los miembros del jurado. Observarán discretamente sus rostros, el lenguaje corporal, sus atuendos, sus modales...

Yo, por otra parte, tengo a Deck, que es un ejemplar inusual del género humano por derecho propio. Les entregaremos una copia de la lista a Butch, Booker y cualquier otra persona que pueda reconocer uno o dos nombres. Haremos llamadas telefónicas, tal vez comprobaremos un par de direcciones, pero nuestro trabajo es mucho más difícil. En general, nos veremos obligados a elegir a las personas por su aspecto en la sala.

CUARENTA Y UNO

Ahora voy a las galerías por lo menos tres veces por semana, normalmente a la hora de cenar. En realidad, tengo mi propia mesa en el paseo, junto a la verja del mirador de la pista de patinaje sobre hielo, donde como pollo *chow mein* y contemplo cómo patinan los chiquillos. Desde mi mesa tengo también una buena vista de los transeúntes, para que nadie pueda cogerme por sorpresa. Ha pasado una única vez, sola y, aparentemente, sin dirigirse a ningún lugar en particular. Sentí un poderoso deseo de unirme a ella, cogerla de la mano y llevarla a alguna tienda elegante donde pudiéramos ocultarnos entre los estantes y charlar.

Éste es el mayor centro comercial en muchos kilómetros a la redonda y a veces está bastante abarrotado de gente. Observo a las personas que deambulan y me pregunto si alguna de ellas formará parte de mi jurado. ¿Cómo encuentro noventa y dos personas entre un millón?

Imposible. Hago lo que puedo con mis recursos. Deck y yo copiamos inmediatamente en cartulinas las fichas de los candidatos, y llevo permanentemente un juego conmigo.

Estoy sentado aquí esta noche, en el paseo del centro comercial, observando a las personas que circulan, y me saco otra cartulina del bolsillo: R. C. Badley, dice en mayúsculas. Cuarenta y siete años de edad, blanco, fontanero, acabado el bachillerato, vive en un suburbio del sudeste de Memphis. Tapo la cartulina para asegurarme de que mi memoria es correcta. Lo es. He practicado tanto que ya estoy harto de esa gente. Sus nombres están pegados a la pared de mi despacho y paso por lo menos una hora diaria estudiando lo que ya he memorizado. Próxima ficha: Lionel Barton, veinticuatro años de edad, varón negro, estudiante universitario a tiempo partido y dependiente en un almacén de repuestos de automóvil, vive en un piso del sur de Memphis.

Mi modelo ideal como miembro del jurado es un joven negro, que haya terminado por lo menos el bachillerato. La sabiduría popular confirma que el mejor jurado para la acusación lo constituyen los negros. Sienten afinidad con la víctima y desconfían de la Norteamérica blanca corporativa. ¿Quién puede reprochárselo?

Mis sentimientos son ambiguos respecto a hombres y mujeres. Según la sabiduría tradicional, las mujeres son más tacañas con el dinero porque sufren las adversidades de la economía familiar. Son menos propensas a otorgar generosas recompensas, porque el dinero no acabará nunca en su bolso. Sin embargo, en este caso particular, Max Leuberg es partidario de las mujeres porque son madres. Ellas sienten el dolor de perder un hijo. Se identificarán con Dot, y si hago bien mi trabajo y logro enfurecerlas debidamente, procurarán arruinar a Great Benefit. Creo que tiene razón.

Por consiguiente, si pudiera hacerlo a mi manera, el jurado lo formarían doce mujeres negras, preferiblemente con hijos.

Deck, evidentemente, tiene otra teoría. Teme a los negros, porque Memphis está tan racialmente polarizado. Acusador blanco, acusado blanco, todo el mundo blanco a excepción del juez. ¿Qué puede importarles a los negros?

Éste es un ejemplo perfecto de la falacia que supone estereotipar al jurado según la raza, clase social, edad y educación de sus componentes. En realidad, nadie puede prever lo que hará cualquiera a la hora de deliberar. He leído todos los libros de la biblioteca sobre la selección de jurados y tengo tantas dudas ahora como antes de leerlos.

Sólo hay un tipo de persona al que es preciso evitar en este caso: los ejecutivos blancos. Son atroces en casos de daños y perjuicios. Suelen dirigir las deliberaciones. Son educados, autoritarios, organizados y desprecian a los abogados. Afortunadamente, suelen estar demasiado ocupados para formar parte de un jurado. He detectado sólo cinco en mi lista y estoy seguro de que cada uno de ellos tendrá una docena de razones para ser eximido. Kipler, en otras circunstancias, se lo pondría difícil. Pero en este caso, estoy prácticamente convencido de que tampoco desea que formen parte del jurado. Apostaría cualquier cosa a que su señoría quiere rostros negros en el palco.

Estoy seguro de que si sigo en este oficio, algún día se me ocurrirá otra jugada más sucia, pero actualmente parece inimaginable. Pienso en ello desde hace varias semanas y por fin se lo he mencionado a Deck. Casi le da un ataque.

Si a Drummond y su pandilla les gusta escuchar lo que hablamos por teléfono, vamos a ofrecerles algo sabroso. Esperamos a última hora de la tarde. Yo estoy en mi despacho. Deck en una cabina a la vuelta de la esquina. Me llama. Lo hemos ensayado varias veces, tenemos incluso un guión.

—Rudy, soy Deck. Por fin he encontrado a Dean Goodlow.

Goodlow es un varón blanco, treinta y nueve años de edad, educación universitaria, propietario de una franquicia de limpieza de alfombras. Le hemos otorgado un cero en nuestra calificación, es definitivamente el tipo de persona que no queremos en el jurado. A Drummond le encantaría.

—¿Dónde? —pregunto.

—Le he sorprendido en su despacho. Había pasado una semana fuera de la ciudad. Estábamos completamente equivocados, es un personaje encantador. No le gustan en absoluto las compañías de seguros, dice que discute permanentemente con la suya y considera que deberían ser sometidas a una estricta regulación. Le he contado los detalles de nuestro caso y no puedes imaginarte lo furioso que se ha puesto. Será un excelente miembro del jurado.

A las palabras de Deck les falta un poco de naturalidad, probablemente está leyéndolas, pero para un oído incauto parece creíble.

—¡Vaya sorpresa! —exclamo claramente junto al teléfono, para que Drummond no se pierda una sola sílaba.

La idea de que los abogados hablen con miembros potenciales del jurado, durante el proceso de selección, es increíble, casi inverosímil. A Deck y a mí nos preocupa que nuestra estratagema parezca tan absurda que Drummond comprenda que estamos fingiendo. ¿Pero quién creería que un abogado, para espiar a su rival, le pincha ilegalmente el teléfono? También hemos decidido que Drummond se tragaría el anzuelo, porque yo no soy más que un ignorante novato y Deck, después de todo, un simple seudoabogado. Hacemos lo que podemos.

—¿Se sentía incómodo hablando contigo? —pregunto.

—Un poco. Le he contado lo mismo que a los demás, que no soy más que un investigador, no un abogado. Y que si no mencionan a nadie nuestra conversación, no habrá ningún problema.

—Bien. ¿Y crees que Goodlow está con nosotros?

—Sin lugar a dudas. Debemos elegirlo.

Muevo papeles cerca del teléfono.

—¿Quién queda en la lista? —pregunto.

—Déjame ver —responde Deck, e inmediatamente oigo el ruido de papeles por la línea—. Hemos hablado con Dermont

King, Jan DeCell, Lawrence Perotti, Hilda Hinds y RaTilda Browning.

A excepción de RaTilda Browning, son todos blancos que no queremos en el jurado. Si logramos contaminar suficientemente sus nombres, Drummond hará todo lo posible para excluirlos.

—¿Qué me dices de Dermont King? —pregunto.

—Perfecto. En una ocasión tuvo que echar a un inspector de seguros de su casa. Se merece un nueve.

—¿Y Perotti?

—Un tipo estupendo. No podía creer que una compañía de seguros fuera capaz de matar a alguien. Está con nosotros.

—¿Jan DeCell?

Más movimiento de papeles.

—Déjame ver. Es una señora muy agradable, de pocas palabras. Parecía tener la sensación de que no era correcto que habláramos. Hemos charlado sobre las compañías de seguros y le he contado que Great Benefit tiene un capital de cuatrocientos millones. Creo que estará con nosotros. Pongámosle un cinco.

Es difícil no echar a reír. Presiono el auricular contra mi oreja.

—¿RaTilda Browning?

—Una negra radical, no le interesan los blancos. Me ha echado de su despacho, trabaja en un banco negro. No nos dará ni los buenos días —responde Deck, antes de hacer una prolongada pausa y mover papeles cerca del auricular—. Y a ti, ¿cómo te ha ido?

—He localizado a Esther Samuelson en su casa, hace aproximadamente una hora. Una señora muy agradable, con cerca de sesenta años. Hemos hablado mucho de Dot y de lo terrible que sería perder un hijo. Está con nosotros.

El difunto marido de Esther Samuelson fue, durante muchos años, funcionario de la Cámara de Comercio. Marvin Shankle me lo ha contado. No puedo imaginarla en el jurado para un caso como el nuestro. Hará lo que a Drummond se le antoje.

—Luego he encontrado a Nathan Butts en su despacho. Le ha sorprendido un poco saber que yo era uno de los abogados involucrados en el caso, pero se ha relajado. Odia las compañías de seguros.

Si a estas alturas a Drummond todavía le late el corazón, su pulso debe ser inapreciable. La idea de que precisamente yo, el abogado, y no mi investigador, circule por las calles hablando de los detalles del caso con miembros potenciales del jurado, basta para provocar un infarto. Sin embargo, también habrá comprendido que no puede hacer absolutamente nada al respecto. Cualquier reacción por su parte delataría que escucha mis llamadas telefónicas. Eso bastaría para que lo expulsaran inmediatamente del Colegio de Abogados y, probablemente, para que se presentaran cargos contra él.

Su única reacción posible consiste en mantener la boca cerrada y procurar evitar a las personas cuyos nombres mencionamos.

—Tengo unos cuantos más —digo—. Sigamos hasta eso de las diez y luego reunámonos aquí, en mi despacho.

—De acuerdo —responde Deck cansado, en un tono ahora mucho más verosímil.

Colgamos y, al cabo de quince minutos, suena el teléfono.

—¿Puedo hablar con Rudy Baylor? —pregunta una voz vagamente familiar.

—Rudy Baylor al habla.

—Soy Billy Porter. Usted ha pasado hoy por nuestro almacén.

Billy Porter es un varón blanco, lleva corbata para acudir al trabajo y dirige un almacén de Western Auto. En nuestra escala del cero al diez ha merecido un simple uno. No lo queremos en el jurado.

—Sí, señor Porter, gracias por llamarme.

En realidad es Butch, a quien hemos decidido conceder un pequeño papel en nuestra farsa. Está con Deck, probablemente ambos acurrucados en una cabina para protegerse del frío. Butch, como buen profesional, ha pasado por Western Auto y ha hablado con Porter de un juego de neumáticos. Intenta imitar su voz. Nunca volverán a verse.

—¿Qué desea? —pregunta Billy/Butch.

Le hemos dicho que pareciera agresivo al principio y que rápidamente cambiara de actitud.

—Pues usted verá, es acerca del juicio, ya sabe, relacionado con la citación que habrá recibido. Yo soy uno de los abogados del caso.

—¿Es esto legal?

—Claro que es legal, pero no se lo comente a nadie. Escúcheme, yo represento a esa anciana cuyo hijo fue asesinado por una compañía llamada Great Benefit Life Insurance.

—¿Asesinado?

—Efectivamente. El muchacho necesitaba una operación, pero la compañía le negó indebidamente el tratamiento. Murió hace unos tres meses de leucemia. Ésa es la razón por la que los hemos demandado. Necesitamos realmente su ayuda, señor Porter.

—Esto es terrible.

—El peor caso que he visto, y eso que he participado en muchísimos. Le aseguro, señor Porter, con perdón por el lenguaje, que son más culpables que la madre que los parió. Nos han ofrecido ya doscientos mil dólares para cerrarnos la boca, pero queremos mucho más. Pedimos daños y perjuicios, y necesitamos su ayuda.

—¿Me elegirán? En realidad no puedo faltar al trabajo.

—Elegiremos doce entre unos setenta, es todo lo que le puedo decir. Pero se lo ruego, procure ayudarnos.

—De acuerdo. Haré lo que pueda. Pero prefiero no estar en el jurado, ¿comprende?

—Sí, señor. Gracias.

Deck llega al despacho, donde nos comemos un bocadillo. Sale otras dos veces y me llama. Mencionamos unos cuantos nombres de personas con las que presuntamente hemos hablado, y todas ellas están más que dispuestas a castigar a Great Benefit por su perversidad. Damos la impresión de que ambos circulamos por las calles, llamando a las puertas, suplicando su apoyo y quebrantando suficientes normas éticas para que me expulsen eternamente del Colegio. ¡Y esto ocurre la noche anterior al día previsto para la elección del jurado!

De las sesenta y tantas personas que se presentarán para ser interrogadas, hemos logrado proyectar graves dudas sobre un tercio de ellas, después de seleccionar cuidadosamente las que más nos preocupan.

Apuesto a que Leo Drummond no pegará ojo esta noche.

CUARENTA Y DOS

La primera impresión es decisiva. Los componentes potenciales del jurado llegan entre las ocho y media y las nueve. Cruzan nerviosos la doble puerta de madera de la sala y avanzan por el pasillo, contemplando casi boquiabiertos el entorno. Dot y yo estamos solos a un extremo de nuestra mesa, mirando hacia los bancos acolchados donde se instalan los recién llegados. Estamos de espaldas al estrado. Lo único que hay sobre nuestra mesa es un cuaderno. Deck está en una silla cerca del palco del jurado, lejos de nosotros. Dot y yo susurramos y procuramos sonreír. Siento un hormigueo en el estómago.

Alrededor de la mesa de la defensa, situada al otro lado del pasillo, contrastando enormemente con la nuestra, hay cinco individuos de traje negro y rostro severo, todos ellos con montones de papeles que cubren la superficie.

Mi emulación de David contra Goliat es decisiva y empieza ahora. Lo primero de lo que se percatan los miembros del jurado es de mi carencia de personal, munición y, evidentemente, recursos. Mi pobre cliente es frágil y débil. No podemos competir con esos ricos de la otra mesa.

Ahora que ha concluido la instrucción del caso me he percatado de lo innecesario que es disponer de cinco abogados para la defensa. Cinco excelentes abogados. También me asombra que Drummond no sea consciente de la amenaza que eso supone a los ojos del jurado. Su cliente debe ser culpable de algo. De lo contrario, ¿por qué emplearía cinco abogados contra uno solo, que soy yo?

Esta mañana se han negado a hablar conmigo. Hemos mantenido las distancias, pero sus muecas y ceño de desdén delatan su repugnancia por mi contacto directo con miembros potenciales del jurado. Les produce asco y repulsión, pero no saben qué hacer al respecto. A excepción de robarle dinero a un cliente, ponerse en contacto con miembros potenciales del jurado es

371

probablemente el pecado más grave que un abogado puede cometer. Está en la misma categoría que pinchar los teléfonos de su rival. Su aspecto es estúpido aparentando indignación.

El secretario del juzgado reúne a los candidatos a un lado del pasillo y luego les indica que se sienten sin ningún orden específico al otro lado, frente a nosotros. De los noventa y dos de la lista, sesenta y uno están presentes. Algunos no pudieron ser localizados. Dos habían fallecido. Unos cuantos alegaron estar enfermos. Tres se ampararon en su avanzada edad para eximirse. Kipler disculpó a otros varios por razones personales diversas. Conforme el secretario pasa lista, yo tomo notas. Tengo la misma sensación que si los conociera desde hace meses. El número seis es Billy Porter, el director de Western Auto que presuntamente me llamó anoche. Será interesante ver cómo le trata Drummond.

Jack Underhall y Kermit Aldy están presentes en representación de Great Benefit, sentados detrás de Drummond y su equipo. Eso significa siete trajes oscuros, siete rostros graves e implacables con la mirada fija en los miembros potenciales del jurado. ¡Alegrad esas caras, muchachos! Yo mantengo una expresión agradable en la mía.

Kipler entra en la sala y todo el mundo se levanta. Se abre la sesión. Da la bienvenida a los jurados potenciales y pronuncia un breve y claro discurso sobre las obligaciones del jurado y la responsabilidad de un buen ciudadano. Se levantan varias manos cuando pregunta si alguien tiene una buena razón para ser eximido. Les ordena que se acerquen al estrado uno por uno, donde cuentan su caso en voz baja. Cuatro de los cinco ejecutivos de mi lista negra susurran con el juez. Comprensiblemente, los exime.

Esto dura cierto tiempo, pero nos permite observar a los presentes. Tal como están sentados, probablemente no pasaremos de las tres primeras filas. Es decir, treinta y seis. Necesitamos sólo doce, más dos de reserva.

Tras la mesa de la defensa veo a dos desconocidos elegantemente vestidos. Asesores para la elección del jurado, supongo. Están pendientes de todos sus movimientos. Me pregunto cómo habrá afectado nuestra estratagema sus profundos perfiles sicológicos. Me río para mis adentros. Apuesto a que hasta ahora nunca habían intervenido en sus evaluaciones un par de chiflados que la noche anterior se dedican a charlar con los miembros potenciales del jurado.

Su señoría exime a otros siete y quedan reducidos a cincuenta. A continuación hace un breve resumen del caso y presenta a ambas partes y a los abogados. Buddy no está en la sala, está en su Fairlane.

Luego Kipler empieza a formular preguntas serias y les ordena a los presentes que levanten la mano si necesitan responder a alguna de ellas. ¿Alguno de ustedes conoce a alguna de las partes, alguno de los abogados o alguno de los testigos? ¿Alguno de ustedes tiene una póliza extendida por Great Benefit? ¿Alguno de ustedes está involucrado en algún pleito? ¿Alguno de ustedes ha demandado a una compañía de seguros?

Hay varias respuestas. Levantan la mano, se levantan y se acercan a su señoría. Los primeros están nerviosos, pero después de un comentario humorístico se rompe el hielo y todo el mundo parece un poco más tranquilo. En algunos momentos, fugazmente, me digo a mí mismo que éste es mi lugar. Puedo hacerlo. Soy abogado. Evidentemente, todavía no he abierto la boca.

Kipler me ha entregado la lista de preguntas que él formulará, e incluyen todo lo que yo deseo saber. No tiene nada de malo. Le ha entregado a Drummond la misma lista.

Tomo notas, observo a la gente y escucho atentamente lo que dicen. Deck hace lo mismo. Es una crueldad, pero casi prefiero que los miembros del jurado no sepan que está conmigo.

Se prolonga la sesión mientras Kipler hace sus preguntas. Después de casi dos horas, ha terminado. Se me forma de nuevo un terrible nudo en el estómago. Ha llegado el momento de que Rudy Baylor diga sus primeras palabras en un juicio real. Será una comparecencia muy breve.

Me levanto, me acerco a la barra, les brindo una cálida sonrisa y pronuncio las palabras que he ensayado un millar de veces:

—Buenos días. Me llamo Rudy Baylor y represento a la familia Black.

Hasta aquí todo bien. Después de dos horas de bombardeo desde el estrado están listos para algo diferente. Los miro con simpatía y sinceridad.

—El juez Kipler les ha formulado muchas preguntas —prosigo—, que son muy importantes. Les ha preguntado todo lo que yo deseaba saber y, por consiguiente, no les haré perder el tiempo. En realidad, sólo deseo saber una cosa. ¿Puede alguien de ustedes pensar en cualquier razón por la que no deberían formar parte del jurado en este caso?

Previsiblemente, nadie responde. Han estado observándome durante más de dos horas, sólo quiero saludarlos, brindarles otra sonrisa y ser muy breve. Hay pocas cosas en la vida peores que un abogado que se extiende demasiado. Además, tengo la sensación que Drummond los golpeará con bastante dureza.

—Gracias. —Sonrío y vuelvo la cabeza hacia el estrado—. No

veo ningún problema con estos candidatos, su señoría —agrego en voz alta, después regreso a mi asiento y le doy a Dot unos golpecitos en el hombro.

Drummond se ha puesto de pie. Procura parecer tranquilo y amable, pero está furioso. Se presenta y empieza a hablar de su cliente y del hecho que Great Benefit es una gran compañía con un balance muy positivo. Deben comprender que ésa no es razón para castigarla. ¿Influirá eso en alguno de ustedes? En realidad está argumentando el caso, lo cual es improcedente, pero permanece lo suficientemente cerca de la frontera para que no le llamen la atención. No estoy seguro de si debería protestar. He decidido que sólo lo haré cuando esté seguro de tener razón. Esta forma de interrogar es muy eficaz. El suave tono de su voz empieza a inspirar confianza. Sus canas sugieren sabiduría y experiencia.

Cubre otras cuantas áreas sin una sola respuesta. Está sembrando. De pronto se lanza al ataque.

—La pregunta que voy a formularles es la más importante del día —dice con gravedad—. Les ruego que me escuchen con atención. Esto es esencial —agrega antes de hacer una dramática y prolongada pausa, acompañada de un profundo suspiro—. ¿Se ha puesto alguien en contacto con alguno de ustedes, con relación a este caso?

En la sala reina un silencio sepulcral y sus palabras se posan lentamente después de retumbar en el aire. Era más una acusación que una pregunta. Echo una ojeada a su mesa. Hill y Plunk me miran fijamente. Morehouse y Grone están pendientes del jurado.

Drummond permanece unos segundos inmóvil, dispuesto a lanzarse contra el primero que tenga el valor de levantar la mano y decir: ¡Sí! ¡El abogado de la acusación pasó por mi casa anoche!

Drummond sabe que está a punto de suceder. Está convencido de ello. Extraerá la verdad, nos desenmascarará a mí y a mi corrupto seudoabogado, solicitará que se me abra un expediente, que se me sancione y finalmente se me expulse del Colegio de Abogados. El caso se aplazará varios años. ¡Está a punto de suceder!

Pero se le hunden lentamente los hombros. El aire sale lentamente de sus pulmones. ¡Maldita pandilla de embusteros!

—Es muy importante —insiste—. Debemos saberlo —agrega en un tono de desconfianza.

Nada. Ni el más mínimo movimiento. Pero lo miran fijamente y logra que se sientan muy incómodos. Sigue, muchacho, sigue.

—Permítanme que se lo pregunte de otro modo —dice con mucho aplomo—. ¿Alguno de ustedes mantuvo ayer una conversación con el señor Baylor, aquí presente, o con el señor Deck Shifflet, en esa esquina?

—¡Protesto, su señoría! —exclamo después de levantarme—. ¡Esto es absurdo!

Kipler está a punto de saltar del estrado.

—¡Se admite la protesta! ¿Qué se propone, señor Drummond? —exclama frente al micrófono de tal modo que retumban las paredes de la sala.

—Con la venia de su señoría, tenemos razones para suponer que ha habido intento de manipulación del jurado.

—Claro y me acusa a mí —respondo enojado.

—No comprendo qué está usted haciendo, señor Drummond —dice Kipler.

—Tal vez deberíamos hablarlo en su despacho —responde Drummond sin dejar de mirarme fijamente.

—Adelante —exclamo, como si estuviera ansioso por pelear.

—Un breve recésit —dice Kipler en dirección al alguacil.

Drummond y yo estamos sentados frente a la mesa de su señoría. Los otros cuatro de Trent & Brent están de pie a nuestra espalda. Kipler está sumamente perturbado.

—Espero que tenga buenas razones —dice el juez dirigiéndose a Drummond.

—Se ha intentado manipular a estas personas —afirma Drummond.

—¿Cómo lo sabe?

—No puedo responderle, pero lo sé con toda certeza.

—No juegue conmigo, Leo. Quiero pruebas.

—No puedo dárselas, su señoría, sin divulgar información confidencial.

—¡Bobadas! Cuéntemelo.

—Es cierto, su señoría.

—¿Está acusándome a mí? —pregunto.

—Sí.

—Se ha vuelto loco.

—Su conducta es un poco extraña, Leo —dice su señoría.

—Creo poder demostrarlo —responde afectadamente.

—¿Cómo?

—Permítame que acabe de interrogar a los candidatos. La verdad saldrá a relucir.

—Nadie ha reaccionado todavía.

—Apenas he empezado.

Kipler reflexiona unos instantes. Cuando este juicio haya concluido le contaré la verdad.

—Me gustaría hablar individualmente con ciertos candidatos —dice Drummond.

Eso no es habitual, pero puede hacerse a discreción del juez.

—¿Qué opina, Rudy?

—Nada que objetar —respondo, con el deseo de que Drummond empiece a interrogar cuanto antes a las personas con las que supuestamente hemos hablado—. No tengo nada que ocultar —agrego al tiempo que un par de cretinos tosen a mi espalda.

—Muy bien. Está cavando su propia fosa, Leo. Pero no se extralimite.

—¿Qué han estado haciendo ahí? —pregunta Dot cuando regreso a la mesa.

—Cosas de abogados —susurro.

Drummond ha regresado ya junto a la barra y los jurados potenciales le observan con suma suspicacia.

—Como iba diciéndoles, es muy importante que nos digan si alguien se puso en contacto con ustedes y les habló de este caso. Les ruego que levanten la mano si eso ha sucedido —dice, como un maestro de escuela.

Ninguna mano se levanta. Ningún movimiento. Sólo un montón de personas progresivamente enojadas.

Mueve los pies, se frota la barbilla y mira directamente a Billy Porter.

—Señor Porter —dice en un tono grave.

Billy se incorpora de un brinco y asiente. Se ha ruborizado.

—Señor Porter, voy a hacerle una pregunta directa y le agradeceré que me responda sinceramente.

—Hágame una pregunta sincera y recibirá una respuesta sincera —responde Porter enojado.

A ese individuo le cuesta poco enfurecerse. Francamente, yo no me metería con él.

Drummond titubea unos instantes, pero sigue adelante.

—Muy bien, señor Porter, dígame, ¿mantuvo usted o no una conversación telefónica anoche con el señor Rudy Baylor?

Me pongo de pie y miro a Drummond con los brazos abiertos, como si yo fuera completamente inocente y él se hubiera vuelto loco, pero no digo nada.

—Claro que no —responde Porter con las mejillas todavía más rojas.

Drummond se apoya con ambas manos a la baranda de caoba y mira fijamente a Billy Porter, en primera fila, a poco más de un metro de distancia.

—¿Está usted seguro, señor Porter? —exclama.

—¡Claro que lo estoy!

—Creo que lo hizo —dice Drummond, que ha perdido ahora los estribos.

Antes de darme tiempo a protestar o de que Kipler tenga oportunidad de llamarle la atención, el señor Billy Porter se separa de su asiento y se lanza contra el gran Leo F. Drummond.

—¡No me llames embustero, hijo de puta! —exclama Porter, al tiempo que agarra a Drummond por el cuello.

Drummond vuela por encima de la barra y sus mocasines salen despedidos por el aire. Las mujeres chillan. Los miembros del jurado saltan de sus asientos. Porter está sobre Drummond, que intenta luchar, patalear y dar algún puñetazo.

T. Pierce Morehouse y M. Alec Plunk hijo abandonan sus asientos y se acercan a la pelea. Otros los siguen. No tarda en aparecer el alguacil. Dos hombres intentan separarlos.

Yo permanezco en mi asiento disfrutando del espectáculo. Kipler llega junto a la barra en el momento en que sujetan a Porter, Drummond se levanta y logran separar a los contendientes. Uno de los mocasines de Leo aparece bajo la segunda fila y alguien va a devolvérselo mientras él se quita el polvo, sin dejar de mirar a Porter con recelo. Porter recupera inmediatamente la compostura.

Los asesores para la elección del jurado están aturdidos. Sus modelos informáticos han sido un fracaso. Sus sofisticadas teorías desvanecidas. A estas alturas son perfectamente inútiles.

Después de un breve recésit, Drummond solicita que se exima a todos los miembros potenciales del jurado. Kipler se lo deniega.

Se exime al señor Billy Porter, que se retira ofendido de la sala. Me parece que quería ensañarse un poco más con Drummond. Ojalá le espere a la salida para acabar con él.

Pasamos las primeras horas de la tarde en el despacho del juez, con el tedioso proceso de elegir a los miembros del jurado. Drummond y sus secuaces excluyen a todas las personas cuyos nombres Deck y yo mencionamos anoche por teléfono. Están convencidos de que hemos influido en ellas y de algún modo las hemos persuadido para que no hablen. Tanto es su rencor que ni siquiera me miran.

El resultado es el jurado de mis sueños. Seis mujeres negras, todas madres. Dos hombres negros, uno de ellos licenciado universitario y el otro ex conductor de camión lesionado. Tres hombres blancos, dos de los cuales son sindicalistas. El tercero vive a cuatro manzanas de los Black. Una mujer blanca, casada con un conocido agente inmobiliario. No he podido evitarla, pero no me preocupa. Sólo se necesitan nueve de los doce para promulgar un veredicto.

Kipler los reúne a las cuatro de la tarde y se les toma juramento. Les explica que el juicio empezará dentro de una semana. No deben hablar del caso con nadie. A continuación hace algo que al principio me aterroriza, pero luego me parece una excelente idea. Nos pregunta a mí y a Drummond si queremos dirigirnos extraoficialmente al jurado. Limítense a esbozarles un poco el caso. Nada extraordinario.

Yo, evidentemente, no me lo esperaba, primordialmente porque nunca había oído hablar de ello. No obstante, sacudo mis temores y me sitúo ante el palco del jurado. Les hablo un poco de Donny Ray, de la póliza y de las razones que nos inducen a creer que Great Benefit es culpable. En cinco minutos he terminado.

Drummond se acerca al jurado y hasta un ciego se percataría de la desconfianza que ha provocado. Se disculpa por el incidente, pero se lo atribuye estúpidamente a Porter. Menudo egocentrista. Habla de su versión de los hechos, dice que lamenta la muerte de Donny Ray, pero sugerir que su cliente es responsable de la misma es absurdo.

Observo a su equipo y a los muchachos de Great Benefit, que están indudablemente asustados. Las circunstancias que los rodean son sumamente desfavorables. El jurado es partidario de la acusación. El juez es su enemigo. Y su estrella no sólo ha perdido toda credibilidad ante el jurado, sino que además ha recibido una paliza.

Kipler levanta la sesión y el jurado se retira.

CUARENTA Y TRES

Seis días después de elegir el jurado y cuatro días antes del juicio, llama un abogado de Cleveland al bufete preguntando por mí y Deck contesta el teléfono. Siento un recelo inmediato porque no conozco a ningún abogado en Cleveland y hablo con él sólo el tiempo suficiente para averiguar su nombre. Lo consigo en unos diez segundos y luego corto la llamada y le dejo con la palabra en la boca, como si hubiera un fallo técnico en la línea. Últimamente esto ocurre con mucha frecuencia, digo en voz alta dirigiéndome a Deck antes de colgar para que quede grabado. Descolgamos los tres teléfonos del bufete y salgo corriendo a la calle, donde está aparcado mi Volvo. Butch lo ha inspeccionado y parece estar libre de micrófonos. Con la ayuda del servicio de información llamo al abogado de Cleveland.

Resulta ser una importantísima llamada.

Su nombre es Peter Corsa. Está especializado en Derecho laboral y en toda clase de discriminación en el trabajo, y representa a una joven llamada Jackie Lemancyzk. Acudió a su despacho cuando la despidieron inesperadamente de Great Benefit sin ninguna razón aparente, y juntos esperan obtener satisfacción por una multitud de agravios. Al contrario de lo que me habían dicho, la señorita Lemancyzk no ha abandonado Cleveland. Ha cambiado de piso y su número de teléfono no figura en la guía.

Le cuento a Corsa que hemos hecho innumerables llamadas a Cleveland, sin hallar rastro de Jackie Lemancyzk. Uno de los ejecutivos de la compañía, Richard Pellrod, me había dicho que se había trasladado a algún lugar del sur de Indiana.

Corsa me confirma que no es cierto. No ha abandonado Cleveland en ningún momento, pero se ha ocultado.

Es una historia extraordinariamente sensacional y Corsa no ahorra detalles.

Su cliente ha mantenido relaciones sexuales con varios de

sus jefes en Great Benefit. Me asegura que es muy atractiva. Sus promociones y salario dependían directamente de su disposición a acostarse con uno y otro. En un momento dado había sido la única mujer en llegar a ocupar el cargo de encargado decano de reclamaciones, pero fue degradada cuando rompió sus relaciones con el vicepresidente de reclamaciones, Everett Lufkin, que parece una comadreja, pero le gusta el sexo retorcido.

Estoy de acuerdo en que parece una comadreja. Le tomé declaración durante cuatro horas y me ensañaré con él la semana próxima, cuando comparezca como testigo.

Su pleito se basará en acoso sexual y otras infracciones laborales, pero también sabe mucho acerca de los trapos sucios en el departamento de reclamaciones de Great Benefit. ¡Se acostaba con el vicepresidente de reclamaciones! Pronostica que hay muchos pleitos en camino.

Por fin le formulo la pregunta esencial:

—¿Vendrá a declarar?

No lo sabe. Tal vez. Pero tiene miedo. Son gente nefasta con mucho dinero. Actualmente se siente muy débil y está bajo tratamiento.

Accede a que hable con ella por teléfono y organizamos una conferencia nocturna desde mi piso. Le explico que no es buena idea llamarme al despacho.

Lo único en lo que logro pensar es en el juicio. Cuando Deck no está en el despacho, camino de un lado para otro hablando solo y le cuento al jurado lo nefasta que es la compañía Great Benefit, interrogo testigos, hablo delicadamente con Dot y el doctor Kord, y dejo al jurado embelesado con mis conclusiones. No obstante, sigue siendo difícil pedirle al jurado diez millones en daños y perjuicios, y mantengo seria la cara. Tal vez si tuviera cincuenta años, hubiera intervenido en centenares de casos y me sintiera seguro de lo que estoy haciendo, osaría pedirle diez millones al jurado. Pero para un novato que ha terminado la carrera hace nueve meses, parece absurdo.

Pero los pido de todos modos. Los pido en mi despacho, en el coche y especialmente en mi casa, a menudo a las dos de la madrugada, cuando no logro conciliar el sueño. Hablo con esas doce personas, esos doce rostros que ahora tienen nombres, esos seres humanos maravillosamente justos que me escuchan, asienten y están impacientes por hacer justicia.

Estoy a punto de ganar la batalla, de destruir públicamente a Great Benefit en la sala y lucho constantemente para controlar dichos pensamientos. Maldita sea, no es fácil. Los hechos, el jurado, el juez, los abogados asustados de la otra parte. Todo suma mucho dinero.

Algo tiene que fallar.

Hablo una hora con Jackie Lemancyzk. En algunos momentos parece fuerte y decidida, en otros está a punto de desmoronarse. No quería acostarse con esos individuos, repite una y otra vez, pero era la única forma de progresar. Está divorciada y tiene un par de hijos.

Accede a venir a Memphis. Ofrezco pagarle el billete de avión y los gastos de su estancia, con la tranquilidad y seguridad de que mi bufete dispone de los medios necesarios. Me obliga a prometerle que si declara lo hará por sorpresa y sin previo aviso a Great Benefit.

La tienen aterrorizada. Creo que la sorpresa será maravillosa.

Pasamos el fin de semana en el bufete, durmiendo sólo unas horas en nuestros pisos respectivos, y luego regresando como almas en pena al despacho para seguir preparándonos.

Mis escasos momentos de relajación los debo a Tyrone Kipler. Le he agradecido en silencio un millar de veces que seleccionara el jurado con una semana de antelación al juicio y que me permitiera dirigirles extraoficialmente unos comentarios. Antes, el jurado constituía una gran parte de lo desconocido, un elemento inmensamente temible. Ahora conozco sus nombres y sus rostros, y he charlado con ellos sin la ayuda de notas escritas. Les gusto, y desconfían de mi rival.

A pesar de mi descomunal inexperiencia, estoy plenamente convencido de que el juez Kipler me salvará de mí mismo.

Deck y yo nos despedimos alrededor de la medianoche del domingo. Cae una ligera nevada cuando salgo del bufete. Una ligera nevada en Memphis suele suponer una semana de vacaciones en las escuelas y el cierre de todas las dependencias gubernamentales. La ciudad nunca ha adquirido una pala mecánica para limpiar las calles. Parte de mí anhela una tormenta para que mañana se postergue. Parte de mí desea resolverlo todo cuanto antes.

Cuando llego a mi casa ha dejado de nevar. Me tomo dos cervezas calientes con el ferviente deseo de quedarme dormido.

—¿Algún asunto preliminar? —pregunta Kipler a un tenso grupo en su despacho.

Estoy sentado junto a Drummond y ambos miramos a su señoría. Tengo los ojos irritados de una noche de insomnio, me duele la cabeza y en mi cerebro se acumula un tropel de pensamientos simultáneos.

Me sorprende el aspecto cansado de Drummond. Para alguien que pasa la vida en los juzgados, parece excepcionalmente agotado. Me alegro. Espero que haya trabajado también todo el fin de semana.

—No se me ocurre nada —respondo previsiblemente.

Mis contribuciones son escasas en esas pequeñas reuniones. Drummond mueve la cabeza.

—¿Es posible estipular el coste de un trasplante de médula? —pregunta Kipler—. De ser así, podemos prescindir del testimonio de Gaskin. Parece que asciende a unos ciento setenta y cinco mil dólares.

—Me parece correcto —respondo.

Los abogados de la defensa incrementan sus ingresos si se estipula un coste inferior, pero no supone ninguna ventaja para Drummond.

—Parece razonable —responde con indiferencia.

—¿Significa esto que está de acuerdo? —insiste acerbadamente Kipler.

—Sí.

—Gracias. Respecto a los demás costes, parecen ascender a unos veinticinco mil. ¿Podemos aceptar que la petición de costes por parte de la acusación es de doscientos mil? ¿Les parece aceptable? —pregunta el juez, con la mirada fija en Drummond.

—Me parece correcto —respondo, con la seguridad de que Drummond se siente realmente molesto.

—Sí —dice Drummond.

Kipler toma nota.

—Gracias. ¿Algo más antes de empezar? ¿Alguna posibilidad de llegar a un acuerdo?

—Con la venia de su señoría —respondo firmemente, como lo hemos proyectado con todo esmero—. En nombre de mi cliente, propongo saldar este asunto por un millón doscientos mil.

Previsiblemente los abogados de la defensa fingen escandalizarse y expresar incredulidad ante cualquier propuesta de la acusación, y mi oferta es recibida con movimiento de cabezas, toses, e incluso una pequeña carcajada entre los esbirros agrupados a mi espalda.

—Qué más quisiera usted —responde acerbadamente Drummond.

Creo sinceramente que Leo está a punto de perder los cabales. Cuando se inició el proceso era un auténtico caballero, con una conducta siempre impecable tanto en la sala como fuera de ella, propia de un verdadero profesional. Ahora se comporta como un novato enfurruñado.

—¿Alguna propuesta por su parte, señor Drummond? —pregunta Kipler.

—Nuestra oferta sigue siendo de doscientos mil dólares.

—Muy bien. Empecemos. Cada parte dispondrá de quince minutos para comentarios iniciales, pero evidentemente pueden ser más breves.

He cronometrado una docena de veces mi comentario introductorio, y dura seis minutos y medio. Entra el jurado, su señoría le saluda, le da ciertas instrucciones y me cede la palabra.

Si lo repito con suficiente frecuencia, puede que algún día llegue a tener talento dramático. Pero eso tendrá que esperar. De momento me contento con poder hacerlo. Consulto un par de veces el cuaderno que tengo en la mano y ofrezco al jurado mi versión del caso. Me sitúo detrás del atril con la esperanza de tener aspecto de abogado con mi nuevo traje gris. Los hechos a mi favor son tan abrumadores que no siento la necesidad de insistir. Había una póliza, las cuotas se habían pagado regularmente todas las semanas, cubría a Donny Ray, enfermó y se le negó la atención necesaria. Murió por razones evidentes. Ustedes, miembros del jurado, conocerán a Donny Ray, pero sólo mediante una grabación en vídeo. Está muerto. El propósito de este juicio no es sólo el de cobrar de Great Benefit lo que debió haber pagado en primer lugar, sino el de castigar su pecado. Es una compañía inmensamente rica, que ha ganado su dinero cobrando primas y no pagando las reclamaciones. Cuando hayan escuchado a todos los testigos volveré con el propósito de pedirles a ustedes, miembros del jurado, una gran cantidad de dinero para castigar a Great Benefit.

Es esencial plantar cuanto antes esa semilla. Quiero que sepan que aspiramos a una fortuna y que Great Benefit merece un castigo.

Mi introducción transcurre sin contratiempos. No tartamudeo, ni tiemblo, ni provoco ninguna objeción por parte de Drummond. Preveo que Drummond permanecerá sentado durante la mayor parte del juicio. No desea que Kipler le ponga en ridículo, especialmente ante el jurado.

Me siento junto a Dot. Estamos solos en nuestra larga mesa.

Drummond se acerca muy seguro de sí mismo al palco del jurado con una copia de la póliza en la mano.

—Esta póliza fue adquirida por el señor y la señora Black —declara en un tono melodramático, después de levantar el documento para que todo el mundo lo vea—. Y en ningún lugar de la misma se dice que Great Benefit deba pagar los trasplantes —agrega, e inmediatamente hace una prolongada pausa para que digieran sus palabras, que son escuchadas por los miembros del jurado con suma atención—. Esta póliza cuesta dieciocho dólares semanales y no cubre los trasplantes de médula, pero la acusación esperaba que mis clientes pagaran doscientos mil dólares para, a que lo han adivinado, un trasplante de médula. Mi cliente se negó a hacerlo y no por malicia hacia Donny Ray Black. Para mi cliente no era una cuestión de vida o muerte, sino de lo que está incluido en la póliza —dice mientras agita con dramatismo el documento y crea bastante impacto—. No sólo pretenden obtener doscientos mil dólares a los que no tienen derecho, sino que le reclaman a mi cliente *diez millones de dólares* en daños adicionales. Lo llaman daños y perjuicios. Yo lo llamo absurdo. Yo lo llamo avaricia.

Está alcanzando su objetivo, pero es arriesgado. La póliza excluye explícitamente los trasplantes de todos los órganos trasplantables, pero no menciona el de médula ósea. Sus redactores metieron la pata y no lo incluyeron en la póliza. La nueva póliza que me ha entregado Max Leuberg excluye explícitamente los trasplantes de médula.

La estrategia de la defensa está clara. En lugar de reconocer un error cometido por incompetentes desconocidos en el seno de una compañía gigantesca, Drummond no admite nada. Alegará que los trasplantes de médula son poco fiables, impropios de una buena medicina, y claramente inaceptables como método de tratamiento rutinario de una leucemia aguda.

Parece un médico cuando habla de las escasas posibilidades de encontrar a un donante adecuado, una entre varios millones en algunos casos, y de las escasas probabilidades de éxito en los trasplantes.

—Simplemente no está incluido en la póliza —repite una y otra vez.

Decide meterse conmigo. La segunda vez que menciona la palabra «avaricia» me levanto y protesto. El discurso introductorio no es para discutir. Eso se reserva para el final. Sólo está autorizado a expresar lo que, a su entender, demostrarán las pruebas.

—Se admite la protesta —responde inmediatamente Kipler, mi buen amigo.

He ganado el primer punto.

—Lo siento, su señoría —dice sinceramente Drummond.

Habla de sus testigos, quiénes son y qué dirán. A los diez minutos pierde empuje y debería terminar. Kipler le llama la atención a los quince minutos y Drummond da las gracias al jurado.

—Llame a su primer testigo, señor Baylor —dice Kipler.

No tengo tiempo de asustarme.

Dot Black se acerca nerviosa al estrado, presta juramento, se sienta y mira al jurado. Lleva un sencillo vestido de algodón, muy viejo, pero su aspecto es pulcro.

Dot y yo hemos elaborado un guión. Se lo entregué hace una semana y lo hemos ensayado diez veces. Yo hago las preguntas y ella las contesta. Comprensiblemente, está muerta de miedo y sus respuestas parecen artificiales y fingidas. Le he dicho que no se preocupe por los nervios. Los miembros del jurado son simples seres humanos. Nombres, marido, familia, empleo, póliza, la vida con Donny Ray antes de la enfermedad, durante la misma y después de su muerte. Se seca los ojos varias veces, pero no pierde la compostura. Le he dicho a Dot que procure evitar las lágrimas. Todo el mundo puede imaginar su aflicción.

Describe la frustración de ser madre y no poder ofrecerle atención médica a su hijo moribundo. Escribió y llamó muchas veces a Great Benefit. Escribió y llamó a congresistas, senadores y alcaldes en un esfuerzo vano por obtener ayuda. Suplicó a los hospitales locales que le ofrecieran tratamiento gratuito. Organizó a amigos y vecinos para intentar recaudar fondos, pero fracasó rotundamente. Identifica la póliza y la solicitud. Responde a mis preguntas sobre su adquisición y explica las visitas semanales de Bobby Ott para cobrar las cuotas.

Luego llegamos a lo bueno. Le entrego las primeras siete cartas de denegación y Dot se las lee al jurado. Suenan peor de lo que suponía. Denegación absoluta sin razón alguna. Denegación de reclamaciones a la espera de revisión por parte de contratación. Denegación de contratación a la espera de revisión por parte de reclamaciones. Denegación de reclamaciones basada en condición preexistente. Denegación de contratación basada en el hecho de que Donny Ray, como persona adulta, estaba excluido de la póliza familiar. Denegación de reclamaciones basaba en la alegación de que los trasplantes de médula ósea están excluidos de la póliza. Denegación de reclamaciones basada en la alegación de que los trasplantes de médula son excesivamente experimentales y, por consiguiente, inaceptables como método de tratamiento médico.

Los miembros del jurado están pendientes de todas y cada una de las palabras. Les va llegando la putrefacción.

Y entonces, la «estúpida carta». Cuando Dot se la lee al jurado observo atentamente sus rostros. Algunos quedan visible-

...nte aturdidos. Otros parpadean con incredulidad. Varios mi-
...an a la mesa de la defensa, donde, curiosamente, todos tienen
la cabeza gacha en actitud meditabunda.

Cuando termina hay un silencio sepulcral en la sala.

—Por favor, vuelva a leerla —digo.

—Protesto —exclama inmediatamente Drummond, después
de ponerse de pie.

—No se admite la protesta —responde Kipler.

Dot vuelve a leerla, en esta ocasión con más sentido y emoción. Ahí es exactamente donde quiero dejar a Dot y cedo la testigo a la defensa. Drummond sube al estrado. Sería un error ponerse duro con ella y me sorprendería que lo hiciera.

Empieza con vagas preguntas sobre pólizas anteriores y las
razones por las que compró esta póliza en particular. ¿Qué se
proponía cuando lo hizo? Dot sólo pretendía asegurar a la familia, eso es todo. Y eso fue lo que le prometió el agente. ¿Le prometió el agente que cubriría los trasplantes?

—Yo no pensaba en trasplantes —responde—. Nunca había
necesitado ninguno.

Eso provoca algunas sonrisas entre los componentes del jurado, pero nadie se ríe.

Drummond insiste en que si al adquirir la póliza pretendía
que cubriera los trasplantes de médula. Nunca los había oído siquiera mencionar, repite Dot una y otra vez.

—¿De modo que no solicitó una póliza que los cubriera?
—pregunta Drummond.

—No pensaba en eso cuando adquirí la póliza. Sólo quería
un seguro completo.

Drummond anota un pequeño punto a su favor, pero espero
y confío que el jurado pronto lo olvidará.

—¿Por qué ha demandado a Great Benefit por diez millones?
—pregunta.

Esta pregunta puede producir unos resultados catastróficos
al principio del juicio, porque puede dar la impresión de que el
demandante es avaricioso. Las cantidades que se solicitan en los
pleitos por daños y perjuicios las deciden frecuentemente
los abogados sin consultar siquiera a sus clientes. Ciertamente
no le pregunté a Dot por cuánto quería demandarlos.

Pero sabía que esta pregunta aparecería, porque he estudiado las transcripciones de antiguos juicios de Drummond. Dot
está preparada.

—¿Diez millones? —pregunta.

—Eso es, señora Black. Usted ha demandado a mis clientes
por diez millones de dólares.

—¿Solamente?

—Usted perdone.

—Creí que les pedíamos mucho más.

—¿Habla usted en serio?

—Desde luego. Su cliente tiene mil millones de dólares y ha matado a mi hijo. Maldita sea, quería demandarles por mucho más.

A Drummond le flaquean ligeramente las rodillas y mueve los pies. Pero tiene un talento extraordinario y no deja de sonreír. En lugar de refugiarse en una pregunta inofensiva o regresar a su asiento, comete un último error con Dot Black. Es otra de sus preguntas habituales.

—¿Qué piensa hacer con el dinero si el jurado le otorga los diez millones de dólares?

Imagínense responder de sopetón a esta pregunta ante el público de la sala. Pero Dot está perfectamente preparada.

—Entregárselo a la Sociedad Norteamericana de la Leucemia. Hasta el último centavo. No quiero ni un penique de su asqueroso dinero.

—Gracias —dice Drummond antes de retirarse inmediatamente a su mesa.

Dos miembros del jurado se ríen cuando Dot abandona el estrado para sentarse junto a mí. Drummond está pálido.

—¿Cómo lo he hecho? —me pregunta en un susurro.

—De maravilla, Dot —respondo.

—Necesito fumarme un cigarrillo.

—Haremos un descanso dentro de un momento.

Llamo a Ron Black al estrado. Él también tiene un guión y su testimonio dura menos de treinta minutos. Lo único que quiero de Ron es que confirme que se le hicieron unos análisis, que su médula era perfectamente compatible con la de su hermano gemelo y que en todo momento estuvo dispuesto a actuar como donante. Drummond no le formula ninguna pregunta. Son casi las diez y Kipler ordena un recésit de diez minutos.

Dot corre a los servicios para encerrarse a fumar en un retrete. Le he advertido que no fume delante de los miembros del jurado. Deck y yo nos sentamos a nuestra mesa y comparamos notas. Durante el juicio está a mi espalda y observa a los miembros del jurado. Las cartas de denegación despertaron su interés. La «estúpida carta» los puso furiosos.

Manténlos enojados, dice. Procura que sigan furiosos. Sólo los jurados iracundos conceden daños y perjuicios.

El doctor Walter Kord tiene un aspecto muy elegante cuando sube al estrado. Lleva una chaqueta deportiva de mezclilla, pantalón oscuro y corbata roja, como un joven médico a quien sonríe la prosperidad. Es oriundo de Memphis, donde estudió el

rato, para seguir luego sus estudios en Vanderbilt y fi-
nte en la Facultad de Medicina de Duke. Impecables refe-
as. Después de haber repasado su currículum no me cabe
ninguna duda de que se trata de un experto en oncología. Le
entrego el historial médico de Donny Ray y le hace al jurado
un claro resumen de su tratamiento. Kord utiliza lenguaje común a ser posible y aclara inmediatamente los términos técnicos.
Como médico, está acostumbrado a odiar los juzgados, pero se
siente muy a gusto consigo mismo y con el jurado.

—¿Puede explicarle la enfermedad al jurado, doctor Kord?
—pregunto.

—Por supuesto. La leucemia mielocítica aguda, o LMA, es
una enfermedad que afecta a dos grupos generacionales, el primero de los cuales son adultos de edades comprendidas entre
los veinte y los treinta años, y el segundo ancianos, generalmente de más de setenta años. Los blancos son más propensos a la
LMA que los de otros grupos raciales y, por alguna razón desconocida, la enfermedad es más común entre personas de ascen-
dencia judía. Los hombres son más propensos que las mujeres.
En general, la causa de la enfermedad es desconocida.

»El cuerpo elabora la sangre en la médula ósea y ahí es donde ataca la LMA. Los glóbulos blancos, encargados de luchar
contra las infecciones, se convierten en malignos en la leucemia
aguda y su número suele aumentar cien veces más de lo normal.
Cuando eso sucede, se reprimen los glóbulos rojos y el paciente
está pálido, débil y anémico. Con el crecimiento incontrolado de
los glóbulos blancos disminuye también la producción normal
de plaquetas, tercer tipo de células de la médula ósea. Eso produce moratones, hemorragias y jaquecas. Cuando Donny Ray
acudió por primera vez a mi consultorio se quejaba de mareos,
asfixia, fatiga, fiebre y síntomas parecidos a los de la gripe.

Cuando Kord y yo ensayábamos la semana pasada, le pedí
que no le llamara señor Black, ni paciente fulano o mengano,
sino Donny Ray.

—¿Y qué hizo usted? —pregunto, convencido de que todo va
sobre ruedas.

—Le practiqué un procedimiento diagnóstico conocido
como aspiración de médula ósea.

—¿Puede explicárselo al jurado?

—Por supuesto. En el caso de Donny Ray, efectué la extrac-
ción del hueso ilíaco. Lo coloqué boca abajo, anestesié una pequeña zona cutánea, practiqué una diminuta incisión e introdu-
je una gran aguja. Dicha aguja consta de dos partes, la exterior
es un tubo flexible y la interior un tubo sólido. Después de introducir la aguja hasta la médula ósea, se retira el tubo sólido y

se une un tubo de succión a la aguja. Esto actúa como jeringa y se extrae una pequeña cantidad de médula ósea líquida. A continuación llevamos a cabo los análisis de medición de glóbulos blancos y glóbulos rojos. No cabía la menor duda de que padecía leucemia aguda.

—¿Cuánto cuesta esa prueba? —pregunto.

—Unos mil dólares.

—¿Y cómo los pagó Donny Ray?

—Cuando acudió por primera vez al consultorio rellenó los formularios habituales y dijo que estaba cubierto por una póliza médica expedida por Great Benefit Life Insurance Company. Mi personal administrativo se puso en contacto con la compañía y comprobó que dicha póliza efectivamente existía. Proseguí con el tratamiento.

Le muestro copias de los documentos pertinentes y los identifica.

—¿Cobró de Great Benefit?

—No. La compañía nos comunicó que denegaban la reclamación por varias razones. Al cabo de seis meses anulamos la factura y la señora Black nos ha estado pagando cincuenta dólares mensuales.

—¿En qué consistió el tratamiento de Donny Ray?

—Lo denominamos terapia de inducción. Ingresó en el hospital y le inserté una sonda en una vena del cuello. La primera inducción de quimioterapia consistió en la administración de un medicamento llamado ara-C, que se introduce en el cuerpo veinticuatro horas al día, durante siete días consecutivos. Durante los tres primeros se le administró también un medicamento llamado idarubicín, conocido con el nombre de «muerte roja» por su color encarnado y su extraordinaria capacidad para destruir células en la médula ósea. Se le administró también allopurinol, un medicamento contra la gota, porque existe gran propensión a dicha enfermedad cuando se destruyen enormes cantidades de glóbulos sanguíneos. Se le administró abundante líquido por vía endovenosa, para limpiarle los riñones. Recibió también antibióticos y fungicidas, para evitar infecciones. Y por último un medicamento llamado amphotericín B, para el tratamiento de hongos. Es sumamente tóxico y le subió la temperatura a cuarenta grados. También le provocó temblores incontrolados, de ahí que dicho medicamento se conozca popularmente como «temblar y cocerse». No obstante, soportó bien el tratamiento, con una actitud muy positiva para un joven tan gravemente enfermo.

»La teoría de la terapia de inducción intensiva supone la eliminación de todas las células de la médula ósea y la creación de un ambiente en el que las células normales se reproduzcan con mayor rapidez que las leucémicas.

—¿Y eso sucede?

—Durante un breve período. Pero tratamos a todos los pacientes con la convicción de que la leucemia reaparecerá, a no ser, evidentemente, que se someta al paciente a un trasplante de médula.

—Doctor Kord, ¿puede explicarle al jurado cómo efectúa usted un trasplante de médula?

—Por supuesto. No es un procedimiento complicado. Después de someter al paciente a la quimioterapia que acabo de describir, y si halla a un donante que sea compatible genéticamente con él, extraemos la médula del donante y se la insertamos al paciente por vía endovenosa. La idea consiste en trasladar de un paciente a otro la población entera de células de la médula ósea.

—¿Era Ron Black un donante adecuado para Donny Ray?

—Sin la menor duda. Es un gemelo idéntico y ésos son los casos más fáciles. Les hicimos análisis a ambos y le aseguro que el trasplante habría sido un éxito.

—Protesto —exclama Drummond poniéndose de pie—. Especulación. El doctor no puede afirmar que el trasplante hubiera sido un éxito.

—No se admite la protesta. Guárdesela para su turno de preguntas.

Hago otras cuantas preguntas sobre el procedimiento y mientras Kord responde presto atención al jurado. Escuchan y lo siguen atentamente, pero ha llegado el momento de terminar.

—¿Recuerda cuándo estaba usted listo para efectuar el trasplante?

Consulta sus notas, aunque conoce la respuesta.

—En agosto del noventa y uno. Hace aproximadamente dieciocho meses.

—¿Habría incrementado dicho trasplante la probabilidad de superar la leucemia aguda?

—Indudablemente.

—¿En qué proporción?

—Ochenta o noventa por ciento.

—¿Y cuáles eran las probabilidades de supervivencia sin el trasplante?

—Nulas.

—He terminado con este testigo.

Son más de las doce, hora de almorzar. Kipler levanta la sesión hasta la una y media. Deck se ofrece para ir en busca de bocadillos, y Kord y yo nos preparamos para el próximo asalto. Le encanta la idea de discutir con Drummond.

Nunca sabré a cuántos asesores médicos consultó Drummond para el juicio. No tiene ninguna obligación de revelarlo. Sólo ha mencionado a un especialista, como testigo pericial en potencia. El doctor Kord me ha asegurado en más de una ocasión que los trasplantes de médula ósea están tan aceptados en la actualidad que sólo un curandero alegaría lo contrario. Me ha mostrado una docena de artículos y ponencias, incluso libros, que apoyan su convicción de que el trasplante es el mejor tratamiento para la leucemia aguda.

Evidentemente, Drummond también lo ha descubierto. Además de que no es médico, defiende un punto de vista muy precario, de modo que no discute demasiado con Kord. La escaramuza es breve. Su argumento principal se basa en que muy pocos enfermos de leucemia aguda reciben trasplantes, comparados con los que no los reciben. Menos del cinco por ciento, afirma Kord, pero sólo debido a la dificultad para encontrar donantes. En todo el país se efectúan unos siete mil trasplantes anuales.

Los pacientes que tienen la suerte de encontrar un donante tienen muchas más probabilidades de sobrevivir. Donny Ray era uno de los afortunados. Tenía un donante.

Kord parece casi decepcionado al ver que Drummond se da por vencido después de pocas preguntas. Yo no deseo preguntarle nada más, así que se le concede permiso para retirarse.

El próximo es un momento de gran tensión, porque estoy a punto de anunciar a qué ejecutivo de la compañía deseo interrogar. Drummond me lo ha preguntado esta mañana y le he respondido que todavía no lo había decidido. Se ha quejado a Kipler, pero el juez le ha respondido que no estoy obligado a comunicárselo hasta que esté listo para hacerlo. Están retenidos en la sala de los testigos, a lo largo del pasillo, esperando furiosos.

—El señor Everett Lufkin —anuncio.

Mientras el alguacil va en su busca, se desata un torbellino de actividad en la mesa de la defensa, que yo sepa para nada, ya que se limitan a trasladar papeles de un lado a otro, intercambiarse notas y buscar fichas.

Lufkin entra en la sala, mira anhelante a su alrededor, como si acabara de despertar de un letargo, se ajusta la corbata y sigue al alguacil por el pasillo. Mira nervioso a su grupo de apoyo, situado a su izquierda, y sube al estrado.

Drummond es famoso por la preparación a la que somete a sus testigos, con brutales interrogatorios que llevan a cabo cuatro o cinco abogados. Lo graban todo en vídeo y luego pasan horas juntos viendo la grabación y perfeccionando la técnica para este momento.

Sé que estos ejecutivos habrán recibido una preparación impecable.

Lufkin me mira, después se dirige al jurado, procurando en todo momento parecer tranquilo, pero sabe que no podrá responder todas las preguntas que se avecinan. Tiene unos cincuenta y cinco años, pelo canoso, facciones armoniosas y voz agradable. Jackie Lemancyzk me contó que quería atarla.

Evidentemente, no tienen ni idea de que ella declarará mañana.

Hablamos del departamento de reclamaciones y de su función en el esquema general de Great Benefit. Lleva ocho años trabajando en la compañía y desde hace seis ocupa el cargo de vicepresidente de reclamaciones y controla perfectamente su departamento. Quiere parecer importante ante el jurado y en pocos minutos establecemos que su trabajo consiste en supervisar todos los aspectos de las reclamaciones. No se ocupa personalmente de todas las reclamaciones, pero es responsable del departamento. Logro conducirle a una discusión aburrida sobre la burocracia corporativa, y de pronto le pregunto:

—¿Quién es Jackie Lemancyzk?

Se le sacuden ligeramente los hombros.

—Una ex encargada de reclamaciones.

—¿Trabajaba en su departamento?

—Sí.

—¿Cuándo dejó de trabajar para Great Benefit?

Se encoge de hombros, no recuerda la fecha.

—¿Pudo ser el tres de octubre del año pasado?

—Puede ser.

—Es decir, dos días antes de la fecha prevista para declarar para este caso.

—Sinceramente no lo recuerdo.

Le muestro dos documentos para refrescarle la memoria. El primero es su carta de dimisión del tres de octubre, y el segundo mi notificación para tomarle declaración el día cinco. Ahora lo recuerda. Admite con reticencia que abandonó Great Benefit cuando faltaban dos días para declarar para este juicio.

—¿Y ella era la persona responsable de esta reclamación en su compañía?

—Exactamente.

—¿Y usted la despidió?

—Claro que no.

—¿Cómo se libró de ella?

—Presentó su dimisión. Puede leerla, la tengo por escrito.

—¿Por qué dimitió?

Se acerca la carta como un verdadero listillo y lee, mirando al jurado:

—Por la presente dimito por razones personales.

—¿De modo que fue idea suya dejar el trabajo?

—Eso dice la carta.

—¿Cuánto tiempo trabajó para usted?

—Mucha gente trabaja para mí. No recuerdo esos detalles.

—¿Entonces no lo sabe?

—No estoy seguro. Varios años.

—¿La conocía bien?

—No demasiado. Era uno de los muchos encargados de reclamaciones.

Mañana, ella declarará que su idilio duró tres años.

—¿Está usted casado, señor Lufkin?

—Sí, y soy muy feliz.

—¿Tiene hijos?

—Sí. Dos hijos mayores.

Lo abandono unos momentos para dirigirme a mi mesa en busca de unos documentos. Es la ficha de reclamación de los Black y se la entrego a Lufkin. La examina lentamente, repasa su contenido y luego afirma que parece completa. Me aseguro de que prometa que está completa y no falta nada.

Para satisfacer al jurado le formulo una serie de preguntas rutinarias, con repuestas igualmente rutinarias, destinadas a facilitar una explicación básica sobre cómo se supone que debe tratarse una reclamación. Evidentemente, en nuestra hipótesis, Great Benefit actúa con absoluta corrección.

Luego llegamos a la parte escabrosa. Le hago leer ante el micrófono y para que quede constancia de ello cada una de las siete cartas de denegación. ¿Quién las escribió? ¿Por qué? ¿Se siguieron las directrices del manual de reclamaciones? ¿Qué sección del manual? ¿Vio él personalmente la carta?

Le hago leer también todas las cartas de Dot. Suplican ayuda. Su hijo está muriéndose. ¿Hay alguien que la escuche? Le interrogo sobre cada una de ellas. ¿Quién la recibió? ¿Qué se hizo con ella? ¿Qué indica el manual? ¿La vio él personalmente?

El jurado parece ansioso por llegar a la «estúpida carta» pero, evidentemente, Lufkin está preparado. La lee al jurado y luego explica en un tono seco y completamente desprovisto de compasión que la escribió un individuo que luego abandonó la compañía. Fue un error por parte de quien la escribió, por parte de la compañía, y ahora, en este momento, ante el público de la sala, la compañía se disculpa por dicha carta.

Dejo que se explaye. Si le doy bastante cuerda acabará por ahorcarse a sí mismo.

—¿No le parece un poco tarde para disculparse? —pregunto por fin.

—Tal vez.

—El muchacho está muerto, ¿no es cierto?

—Sí.

—Y para que conste en acta, señor Lufkin, ¿es cierto que no se han disculpado ustedes por escrito?

—Así es, que yo sepa.

—Ninguna disculpa hasta este momento, ¿no es cierto?

—Es cierto.

—Que usted sepa, señor Lufkin, ¿se ha disculpado Great Benefit alguna vez por algo?

—Protesto —exclama Drummond.

—Se acepta la protesta. Prosiga, señor Baylor.

Hace casi dos horas que Lufkin está en el estrado. Puede que el jurado esté harto de él. Yo ciertamente lo estoy. Ha llegado el momento de ser cruel.

He dado deliberadamente mucha importancia al manual de reclamaciones, como pronunciamiento inviolable de la política de la empresa. Le entrego a Lufkin el ejemplar del manual, que recibí durante la instrucción del caso. Le formulo una serie de preguntas que contesta a la perfección y establece que sí, efectivamente, éste es el libro que contiene la palabra sagrada sobre los procedimientos de reclamación. Ha sido probado, experimentado y verificado. Se revisa periódicamente, se modifica, actualiza y corrige con el paso del tiempo, con el propósito de facilitar el mejor servicio posible a sus clientes.

Cuando llegamos a un punto casi de hastío sobre el maldito manual le pregunto:

—Dígame, señor Lufkin, el ejemplar que tiene en las manos, ¿es una copia completa del manual de reclamaciones?

Lo hojea con rapidez, como si lo conociera al dedillo, sección por sección y palabra por palabra.

—Sí —responde.

—¿Está usted seguro?

—Sí.

—¿Y es éste el ejemplar que se le pidió que me entregaran durante la instrucción del caso?

—Efectivamente.

—Solicité un ejemplar a sus abogados y éste fue el que me entregaron, ¿no es cierto?

—Sí.

—¿Seleccionó usted este ejemplar para que me lo entregaran?

—Sí.

Respiro hondo y me acerco a mi mesa. Debajo de la misma hay una pequeña caja de cartón, llena de fichas y papeles. Después de hurgar unos momentos en la misma me incorporo con las manos vacías y me dirijo al testigo.

—¿Le importaría abrir el manual y dirigirse a la sección «u», por favor?

Al pronunciar la última palabra miro directamente a Jack Underhall, el abogado de la compañía que está sentado detrás de Drummond. Tiene los ojos cerrados. Deja caer la cabeza y se apoya sobre los codos, con la mirada fija en el suelo. Junto a él, Kermit Aldy parece que se asfixia.

Drummond no sabe qué sucede.

—¿Cómo dice? —pregunta Lufkin, en un tono por encima de lo normal.

A la vista de todo el mundo, saco la copia del manual que me entregó Cooper Jackson y la coloco sobre mi mesa. Todo el mundo en la sala la mira fijamente. Miro fugazmente a Kipler, que está divirtiéndose de lo lindo.

—La sección «u», señor Lufkin. Abra el manual y encuéntrela. Quiero hablar de ella.

Abre el manual y vuelve a hojearlo. En este preciso momento estoy seguro de que vendería a sus hijos para que de algún modo se produjera un milagro y se materializara la sección «u».

Pero no ocurre.

—No hay ninguna sección «u» —responde con tristeza, casi incoherentemente.

—Le importaría repetirlo —digo levantando la voz—. No lo he oído.

—Pues... el caso es que en este ejemplar no está la sección «u» —dice aturdido, no por la ausencia de dicha sección, sino por haber sido descubierto.

Mira desesperadamente a Drummond y a Underhall, como si esperara que pidieran tiempo muerto, o algo por el estilo.

Leo F. Drummond no tiene ni idea de lo que le ha hecho su cliente. Han manipulado el manual sin comunicárselo a su abogado. Habla en un susurro con Morehouse. ¿Qué diablos ocurre?

Me acerco ostentosamente al estrado, con el otro manual en la mano. Tiene el mismo aspecto que el del testigo. En la primera página aparece a misma fecha de edición, revisada el uno de enero de 1991. Son dos ejemplares idénticos, a excepción de que en uno de ellos hay una última sección denominada «u», pero no en el otro.

—¿Lo reconoce, señor Lufkin? —pregunto, al tiempo que le entrego el ejemplar de Jackson y retiro el mío.

—Sí.

—Dígame, ¿qué es?

—Un ejemplar del manual de reclamaciones.

—¿Y hay en este ejemplar una sección llamada «u»?

Lo hojea y asiente.

—¿Cuál es su respuesta, señor Lufkin? La relatora del juzgado no registra los movimientos de cabeza.

—Contiene una sección titulada «u».

—Gracias. Dígame, ¿retiró usted personalmente la sección «u» de mi ejemplar, o le ordenó a alguien que lo hiciera?

Deposita con suavidad el ejemplar sobre la barandilla y se cruza decididamente de brazos. Baja la mirada al suelo y espera. Creo que está quedándose dormido. Pasan los segundos y estamos todos a la espera de su respuesta.

—Conteste a la pregunta —exclama Kipler desde el estrado.

—No sé quién lo hizo.

—Pero alguien lo ha hecho, ¿no es cierto?

—Evidentemente.

—De modo que admite que Great Benefit ha ocultado documentos.

—No admito nada. Estoy seguro de que ha sido un descuido.

—¿Un descuido? Por favor, señor Lufkin, no bromee. ¿No es cierto que alguien en Great Benefit retiró deliberadamente la sección «u» de mi ejemplar del manual?

—No lo sé. Sencillamente ha ocurrido, supongo.

Regreso a mi mesa, sin buscar nada en particular. Sólo pretendo dejarlo ahí unos segundos, para que el jurado llegue a odiarlo lo suficiente. Mira vagamente al suelo, hundido, derrotado, con el deseo de estar en cualquier otro lugar.

Me acerco a la mesa de la defensa y le entrego a Drummond una copia de la sección «u» con una radiante y perversa sonrisa dedicada a él y a Morehouse. Luego le entrego otra copia a Kipler. No me apresuro, a fin de que el jurado observe y espere con gran anticipación.

—Bien, señor Lufkin, hablemos de la misteriosa sección «u». Deberíamos explicársela al jurado. ¿Le importaría mirársela?

Abre el manual y pasa las páginas.

—Entró en vigor el uno de enero de mil novecientos noventa y uno, ¿no es cierto?

—Sí.

—¿La redactó usted?

—No.

Por supuesto.

—Bien, ¿quién lo hizo?

Otra sospechosa pausa mientras procura elaborar una mentira apropiada.

—No estoy seguro —responde.

—¿No está usted seguro? ¿Pero no acaba de declarar que esto era plenamente de su responsabilidad en Great Benefit?

Vuelve a mirar al suelo, con la esperanza de que yo desaparezca.

—Dejemos el primero y segundo párrafos —digo— y leamos el tercero.

El párrafo tercero ordena al encargado de reclamaciones que deniegue inmediatamente toda reclamación en el plazo máximo de tres días a partir de su recibo. Sin excepción alguna. Toda reclamación. El párrafo cuarto autoriza la revisión subsiguiente de algunas reclamaciones y especifica la documentación necesaria que indique que la reclamación no será cara, pero sí muy válida y, por tanto, pagadera. El párrafo quinto le ordena al encargado que mande todas las reclamaciones, con un valor potencial superior a los cinco mil dólares, a contratación, con una carta de denegación al asegurado, evidentemente pendiente de revisión por parte de contratación.

Y así sucesivamente. Obligo a Lufkin a leer fragmentos del manual y luego le formulo preguntas que no puede responder. Uso repetidamente la palabra «estratagema», sobre todo cuando Drummond ha protestado y Kipler no ha admitido la protesta. En el párrafo undécimo aparece un verdadero glosario de códigos secretos, que se supone que los encargados de reclamaciones deben utilizar en la ficha, para indicar las reacciones importantes de los asegurados. Es evidente que el sistema está diseñado para jugar a suertes. Si el asegurado amenaza con abogados y pleitos, un supervisor inspecciona inmediatamente la ficha. Si el asegurado no presiona, la denegación persiste.

El párrafo decimoctavo «b» le ordena al encargado que extienda un cheque por el valor de la reclamación y que lo mande junto con la ficha a contratación, acompañado de instrucciones de no mandar el cheque hasta nueva orden de reclamaciones. La nueva orden, evidentemente, no llega jamás.

—¿Qué ocurre con el cheque? —le pregunto a Lufkin.

No lo sabe.

La otra mitad de la estratagema está en la sección «u» del manual de contratación, de modo que mañana repetiré esta misma operación con otro vicepresidente.

En realidad, es innecesario. Si pudiéramos parar ahora, el jurado me concedería lo que le pidiera, y todavía no han visto a Donny Ray.

A las cuatro y media se hace un breve recésit. Hace dos horas y media que Lufkin declara y ha llegado el momento de despedirle. Cuando salgo al pasillo de camino a los servicios, veo a Drummond que señala una puerta por donde quiere que pasen Lufkin y Underhall. Me encantaría oírle.

Al cabo de veinte minutos, Lufkin está de nuevo en el estrado. He terminado con los manuales por ahora. Los miembros del jurado podrán leerlos detalladamente cuando deliberen.

—Sólo unas cuantas preguntas breves —sonrío reanimado—. ¿Cuántas pólizas de seguro médico expidió Great Benefit y estaban en vigor en mil novecientos noventa y uno?

Una vez más, la comadreja mira con desesperación a su abogado. Debían haberme facilitado esa información hace tres semanas.

—No estoy seguro —responde.

—¿Cuántas reclamaciones se recibieron en mil novecientos noventa y uno?

—No estoy seguro.

—Usted es el vicepresidente de reclamaciones, ¿no es cierto?

—Es una gran compañía.

—¿Cuántas reclamaciones se denegaron?

—No lo sé.

—Por ahora, el testigo puede retirarse —dice en aquel preciso momento el juez Kipler—. Vamos a hacer un breve recésit para que los miembros del jurado puedan irse a sus casas.

Se despide del jurado, les da de nuevo las gracias y les recuerda sus obligaciones. Recibo unas cuantas sonrisas cuando desfilan junto a nuestra mesa. Esperamos a que se hayan retirado todos.

—Tome nota —le dice el juez Kipler a la taquígrafa cuando el último miembro del jurado ha abandonado la sala—. Señor Drummond, los condeno a usted y a su cliente por desacato. Insistí en que facilitaran esa información a la acusación hace varias semanas. No lo han hecho. Es muy importante y pertinente, y ustedes se han negado a facilitarla. ¿Están usted y su cliente dispuestos a ser encarcelados hasta que dicha información se reciba?

Leo se levanta, cansado y precozmente envejecido.

—Con la venia de su señoría, he intentado obtener dicha información. He hecho todo lo que he podido.

Pobre Leo. Todavía está intentando comprender la sección «u». En este momento es perfectamente creíble. Su cliente ha demostrado públicamente que le oculta documentos a su propio abogado.

—¿Está aquí el señor Keeley? —pregunta su señoría.

—Sí, en la sala de los testigos —responde Drummond.

—Tráiganlo.

A los pocos segundos llega el alguacil a la sala acompañado del director gerente.

Dot está harta. Necesita ir al retrete y fumarse un cigarrillo.

Kipler ordena a Keeley subir al estrado, le toma él mismo juramento y le pregunta si existe alguna razón que justifique el hecho de que la compañía se haya negado a facilitar la información solicitada.

Tose, tartamudea e intenta culpar a las agencias provinciales y regionales.

—¿Comprende usted el concepto de desacato? —pregunta Kipler.

—Tal vez, bueno, en realidad no.

—Es muy simple. Su compañía ha sido condenada por desacato, señor Keeley. Puedo imponerle una multa a su compañía, o mandarle a usted, como director gerente, a la cárcel. ¿Qué prefiere?

Estoy seguro de que algunos de sus amigos han pasado temporadas en los clubes de campo federales, pero Keeley sabe que aquí la cárcel significa los calabozos del centro de la ciudad, llenos de maleantes callejeros.

—No quiero ir a la cárcel, su señoría.

—Lo suponía. Por la presente condeno a Great Benefit a pagar la suma de diez mil dólares, pagaderos a la acusación antes de las cinco de la tarde de mañana. Llame a su oficina y ordene que le manden el cheque urgentemente.

Keeley sólo puede asentir.

—Además, si la información solicitada no ha llegado aquí por fax a las nueve de la mañana, ingresará usted en la cárcel de la ciudad de Memphis, donde permanecerá hasta que obedezca la orden. Asimismo, mientras usted permanece en la cárcel, su compañía pagará una multa de cinco mil dólares diarios.

Entonces Kipler vuelve la cabeza y señala a Drummond.

—Le he advertido repetidamente lo de estos documentos, señor Drummond. Esta conducta es completamente inaceptable.

Golpea enojado su martillo y abandona el estrado.

CUARENTA Y CUATRO

En otras circunstancias podría sentirme ridículo con una gorra azul y gris con un tigre, junto con mi traje, apoyado contra la pared de la terminal A del aeropuerto de Memphis. Pero hoy es un día que no ha tenido nada de normal. Es tarde y estoy cansado, aunque la adrenalina circula en abundancia por mi organismo. Un mejor inicio del juicio sería inimaginable.

El vuelo de Chicago llega a su debido tiempo y pronto se me reconoce por mi gorra. Una mujer tras unas enormes gafas de sol se me acerca, me mira de pies a cabeza y por fin dice:

—¿Señor Baylor?

—Soy yo.

Estrecho la mano de Jackie Lemancyzk y la de su acompañante, un individuo que sólo se identifica como Carl. Lleva una bolsa en la mano y, aunque ambos parecen nerviosos, están listos para seguir adelante.

Hablamos de camino al hotel Holiday Inn, en el centro de la ciudad, a seis manzanas del juzgado. Ella está sentada delante conmigo. Carl, en el asiento trasero, no dice palabra, pero la protege como un sabueso. Le relato los hechos más emocionantes del primer día. No, no saben que va a comparecer. Le tiemblan las manos. Es frágil y delicada, asustada de su propia sombra. A excepción de la venganza, no se me ocurre otra razón para explicar su presencia.

La reserva del hotel está a mi nombre, tal como ella me lo ha pedido. Nos sentamos los tres alrededor de una mesilla de su habitación, en el decimoquinto piso, y examinamos mi interrogatorio directo. Las preguntas están ordenadas y mecanografiadas.

Si ahí hay belleza, está bien escondida. Lleva el cabello cortado y precariamente teñido de un rojo oscuro. Su abogado me dijo que estaba bajo tratamiento y no pienso preguntarle nada al respecto. Sus ojos, desprovistos de maquillaje, están tristes e irritados. Tiene treinta y un años, dos hijos menores, un divorcio, y a juzgar por su aspecto y modales, es difícil imaginar que a lo largo de su carrera en Great Benefit ha ido saltando de cama en cama.

La actitud de Carl es sumamente protectora. Le acaricia el brazo y de vez en cuando expresa su opinión, en respuesta a preguntas concretas. Ella quiere declarar cuanto antes por la mañana, regresar al aeropuerto y abandonar la ciudad.

Los dejo a medianoche.

A las nueve de la mañana del martes, el juez Kipler abre la sesión, pero ordena que el jurado permanezca unos momentos en su sala. Le pregunta a Drummond si se ha recibido la información sobre reclamaciones. Por cinco mil dólares diarios, casi preferiría que no hubiera llegado.

—Se ha recibido hace aproximadamente una hora, su señoría —responde, evidentemente aliviado.

Me entrega un nítido fajo de documentos de cinco centímetros de grosor, e incluso sonríe ligeramente cuando le entrega a Kipler el suyo.

—Señor Baylor, necesitará un poco de tiempo —dice su señoría.

—Concédame treinta minutos —respondo.

—De acuerdo. Llamaremos al jurado a las nueve y media.

Deck y yo nos refugiamos inmediatamente en un cuarto a lo largo del pasillo, destinado a abogados, y examinamos la información. A primera vista parece griego y casi imposible de descifrar. Lo lamentarán.

A las nueve y media entra el jurado en la sala y el juez Kipler los recibe amablemente. Declaran que no ha habido ninguna novedad, enfermedad, ni contacto con nadie relacionado con el caso.

El segundo día está a punto de comenzar:

—Su testigo, señor Baylor —dice Kipler.

—Desearíamos continuar con Everett Lufkin —respondo.

Traen a Lufkin de la sala de los testigos y sube al estrado. Después de la farsa de la sección «u» del día anterior, nadie creerá una palabra de lo que declare. Estoy seguro de que Drummond se ha ensañado con él hasta medianoche. Tiene aspecto macilento. Le entrego la copia oficial de la información sobre reclamaciones y le pregunto si puede identificarla.

—Es la copia informatizada de un resumen de varias reclamaciones.

—¿Preparada por los ordenadores de Great Benefit?

—Efectivamente.

—¿Cuándo?

—Ayer, tarde y noche.

—¿Bajo su supervisión, como vicepresidente de reclamaciones?

—Sí, en cierto modo.

—Estupendo. Ahora, señor Lufkin, puede decirle por favor al jurado cuántas pólizas médicas existían en mil novecientos noventa y uno.

Titubea y empieza a manosear los papeles. Esperamos mientras busca entre las páginas. El único ruido, durante la prolongada y angustiosa espera, es el de los papeles sobre las rodillas de Lufkin.

La «saturación» de documentos es una táctica predilecta de las compañías de seguros y sus abogados. Les encanta esperar al último momento, preferiblemente el día anterior al juicio, y entregarle al abogado de la acusación cuatro cajas llenas de papeles. En mi caso se ha evitado gracias a Tyrone Kipler.

Esto no es más que una pequeña muestra. Al parecer creían que podían llegar aquí esta mañana, entregarme setenta páginas de copias informatizadas, aparentemente carentes de significado, y quedarse tan tranquilos.

—No es fácil saberlo —responde en un tono apenas audible—. Si tuviera un poco de tiempo.

—Ha tenido usted dos meses —declara Kipler cerca del micrófono, que funciona a la perfección, en un tono y volumen sorprendentes—. Y ahora conteste a la pregunta.

Ya han empezado a moverse en la mesa de la defensa.

—Quiero saber tres cosas, señor Lufkin —digo—. El número de pólizas en existencia, el número de reclamaciones basadas en dichas pólizas y el número de reclamaciones denegadas. Todo ello durante el año mil novecientos noventa y uno.

—Si no me falla la memoria —responde después de seguir mirando páginas—, teníamos unas noventa y siete mil pólizas.

—¿No puede usted consultar sus propias cifras y responder con exactitud?

Es evidente que no puede. Finge estar tan inmerso en los datos que no puede responder a mi pregunta.

—¿Y usted es el vicepresidente de reclamaciones? —pregunto con sarcasmo.

—¡Efectivamente! —responde.

—Permítame que le haga otra pregunta, señor Lufkin. ¿Usted cree que estos documentos contienen la información que le he pedido?

—Sí.

—Por consiguiente, es sólo cuestión de encontrarla.

—Si se calla un momento, la encontraré —exclama como un animal malherido. Acaba de ponerse en evidencia.

—No estoy obligado a callarme, señor Lufkin.

Drummond se levanta con los brazos abiertos.

—Con la venia de su señoría, el testigo intenta encontrar la información.

—Señor Drummond, el testigo ha tenido dos meses para obtener dicha información. Como vicepresidente de reclamaciones, es de esperar que sea capaz de leer las cifras. No se admite la protesta.

—Olvídese momentáneamente de esas copias, señor Lufkin —digo—. ¿Cuál suele ser la proporción anual entre pólizas y reclamaciones? Limítese a darnos el porcentaje.

—Habitualmente recibimos del ocho al diez por ciento de reclamaciones respecto al número de pólizas vigentes.

—¿Y qué porcentaje de las reclamaciones acaba por ser denegado?

—Se deniega aproximadamente un diez por ciento del total de reclamaciones —responde.

Aunque de pronto conoce las respuestas, no siente el más mínimo deseo de compartirlas.

—¿Cuál es el valor medio en dólares de las reclamaciones, aprobadas o denegadas?

Se hace una larga pausa mientras reflexiona. Creo que se ha dado por vencido. Lo único que pretende ahora es acabar con el interrogatorio, abandonar el estrado y salir de Memphis.

—Una media aproximada de cinco mil dólares por reclamación.

—¿Es cierto que algunas de las reclamaciones son solamente por unos centenares de dólares?

—Sí.

—¿Y otras por decenas de millares?

—Sí.

—Por consiguiente, es difícil calcular la media, ¿no es cierto?

—Sí.

—Dígame, estas medias y porcentajes que usted ha citado, ¿son normales en el sector de los seguros, o únicamente característicos de Great Benefit?

—No puedo hablar por el sector en general.

—¿Quiere decir que no lo sabe?

—No he dicho eso.

—¿De modo que lo sabe? Entonces responda a mi pregunta.

Se le hunden ligeramente los hombros. Lo único que desea es abandonar la sala.

—Diría que son bastante normales.

—Gracias —digo antes de hacer una dramática pausa, consultar momentáneamente mis notas y guiñarle el ojo a Deck, que en este momento abandona la sala—. Sólo un par de preguntas, señor Lufkin. ¿Le sugirió usted a Jackie Lemancyzk que abandonara la compañía?

—No.

—¿Cómo calificaría usted su conducta laboral?

—Media.

—¿Sabe usted por qué fue degradada de su cargo de encargada decana de reclamaciones?

—Si mal no recuerdo, estaba relacionado con su poco tacto para tratar con los clientes.

—¿Recibió algún tipo de bonificación cuando dimitió?

—No. Simplemente dimitió.

—¿No fue compensada de ningún modo?

—No.

—Gracias. Su señoría, he terminado con este testigo.

Drummond tiene dos alternativas. Puede interrogar ahora a Lufkin sin preguntas preparadas, o reservárselo para más adelante. En este momento sería imposible levantar los ánimos de ese individuo y no me cabe la menor duda de que Drummond querrá retirarlo cuanto antes de la sala.

—Con la venia de su señoría, interrogaremos a este testigo más adelante —declara previsiblemente Drummond.

El jurado no volverá a verlo jamás.

—Muy bien. Señor Baylor, llame a su próximo testigo.

—La acusación llama a Jackie Lemancyzk —exclamo a pleno pulmón, y vuelvo inmediatamente la cabeza para observar la reacción de Underhall y Aldy.

Estaban hablándose en voz baja y quedan paralizados al oír el nombre. Se les abren enormemente los ojos y la boca de asombro.

El pobre Lufkin está a medio camino de la puerta cuando oye la noticia. Se detiene, mira aterrado a la mesa de la defensa y abandona apresuradamente la sala.

Rodeado de sus secuaces, Drummond se pone de pie.

—Con la venia de su señoría, ¿permite que nos acerquemos al estrado?

Kipler nos hace una seña para que nos acerquemos y separa el micrófono. Mi rival finge estar furioso. No me cabe la menor duda de que está sorprendido, pero no tiene ningún derecho a quejarse. Casi jadea.

—Su señoría, nos ha cogido completamente por sorpresa —dice sin levantar la voz, para que el jurado no lo oiga ni se percate de su espanto.

—¿Por qué? —pregunto afectadamente—. Figura en la orden preliminar como testigo potencial.

—Tenemos derecho a que se nos notifique con antelación. ¿Cuándo la ha encontrado?

—No sabía que estuviera perdida.

—Es una pregunta razonable, señor Baylor —dice su señoría, mirándome con ceño por primera vez en la vida.

Los miro con ingenuidad a ambos, como para decirles «oigan, no soy más que un novato, no se metan conmigo».

—Está en la orden preliminar —insisto.

Además, los tres sabemos que va a declarar. Tal vez debí haber informado ayer a la sala de que estaba en la ciudad pero, después de todo, éste es mi primer juicio.

Entra detrás de Deck en la sala. Underhall y Aldy se niegan a mirarla. Los cinco monigotes de Trent & Brent la observan atentamente. Tiene muy buen aspecto. Un holgado vestido azul cubre su delgado cuerpo hasta la parte superior de las rodillas. Su cara ha cambiado enormemente desde anoche, ahora es mucho más atractiva. Presta juramento, se sienta en la silla de los testigos, lanza una mirada de odio a los muchachos de Great Benefit y está lista para declarar.

Me pregunto si se habrá acostado con Underhall o Aldy. Anoche mencionó a Lufkin y a otro, pero sé que no me lo contó todo.

Cubrimos rápidamente los puntos básicos y entramos a matar.

—¿Cuánto tiempo trabajó en Great Benefit?

—Seis años.

—¿Y cuándo concluyó su empleo?

—El tres de octubre.

—¿Qué ocurrió?

—Me expulsaron.

—¿No dimitió usted?

—No. Me despidieron.

—¿Quién la despidió?

—Fue una conspiración. Everett Lufkin, Kermit Aldy, Jack Underhall y otros —dice al tiempo que mueve la cabeza hacia los culpables, y todo el mundo mira a los muchachos de Great Benefit.

Me acerco a la testigo y le entrego una copia de su carta de dimisión.

—¿Reconoce esto? —pregunto.

—Es una carta que yo mecanografié y firmé —responde.

—La carta dice que usted dimite por razones personales.

—Esta carta es una mentira. Me despidieron por el hecho de

estar involucrada en la reclamación de Donny Ray Black y para evitar que declarara el día cinco de octubre, como estaba previsto. Me despidieron para poder alegar que ya no trabajaba en la compañía.

—¿Quién le obligó a escribir esta carta?

—Los mismos. Fue una conspiración.

—¿Puede explicarse?

Mira por primera vez al jurado y están todos pendientes de ella.

—El sábado anterior a la fecha prevista para mi declaración, me llamaron para que acudiera a la oficina —empieza a decir, después de respirar hondo—. Allí me encontré con Jack Underhall, el hombre que está sentado ahí de traje gris. Es uno de los abogados de la compañía. Me dijo que me marchara inmediatamente y que tenía dos opciones. Podía considerarme despedida y marcharme sin nada. O podía escribir una carta y llamarlo dimisión, en cuyo caso la compañía me entregaría diez mil dólares al contado para que no hablara. Y tuve que tomar la decisión en aquel mismo momento, en su presencia.

Anoche logró contármelo sin emocionarse, pero es diferente en la sala. Se muerde el labio y titubea unos instantes antes de proseguir.

—Soy una madre divorciada con dos hijos menores y muchas facturas. No tenía otra alternativa. De pronto me había quedado sin trabajo. Escribí la carta, cogí el dinero y firmé un compromiso de no hablar jamás con nadie de ninguna de las reclamaciones.

—¿Incluida la de los Black?

—Especialmente la de los Black.

—Entonces cogió el dinero y firmó el acuerdo. ¿Por qué está ahora aquí?

—Cuando me recuperé del susto, hablé con un abogado. Muy buen abogado. Y me aseguró que el acuerdo que había firmado era ilegal.

—¿Tiene una copia de dicho acuerdo?

—No. El señor Underhall no quiso entregarme ninguna. Pero puede preguntárselo a él. Estoy segura de que tiene el original.

Vuelvo lentamente la cabeza para mirar a Jack Underhall, al igual que el resto de los presentes en la sala. Los cordones de sus zapatos se han convertido de pronto en el centro de su vida y se los toca con los dedos, aparentemente ajeno a la declaración de Jackie.

Miro a Leo Drummond y, por primera vez, le veo completamente derrotado. Su cliente, evidentemente, no le había hablado del soborno ni del acuerdo firmado bajo presión.

—¿Por qué acudió a un abogado?

—Porque necesitaba asesoramiento. Me habían despedido injustamente. Pero antes de que me despidieran, era objeto de discriminación por ser mujer y varios ejecutivos de Great Benefit me atosigaron sexualmente.

—¿Alguien en particular?

—Protesto, su señoría —dice Drummond—. Puede que esto sea muy interesante, pero no guarda relación con el caso que nos ocupa.

—Veamos adónde nos conduce. De momento no se admite la protesta. Responda, señora Lemancyzk.

—Mantuve relaciones sexuales con Everett Lufkin durante tres años —responde, después de respirar hondo—. Incrementó mi paga y subí de categoría, siempre a condición de que hiciera todo lo que él deseaba. Un buen día me harté y me degradaron de encargada decana de reclamaciones a simple administrativa. Redujeron mi salario en un veinte por ciento. Entonces Russell Krokit, a quien habían nombrado encargado decano de reclamaciones, después de haberle despedido cuando yo ocupaba el cargo, decidió que quería tener relaciones conmigo. Me obligó, bajo amenaza de despedirme si no accedía a sus deseos. Por otra parte, si me convertía durante algún tiempo en su amante, se aseguraría de que me ascendieran. Las alternativas eran complacerle o largarme.

—¿Estaban ambos casados?

—Sí, y con hijos. Era conocido su afán por las jovencitas en el departamento de reclamaciones. Podría facilitarle muchos nombres. Y ésos no son los dos únicos ejecutivos que cambian promoción por sexo.

Una vez más, todas las miradas se dirigen a Underhall y Aldy.

Hago una pausa para comprobar algo en mi mesa. No es más que un pequeño truco, que de algún modo he aprendido, para permitir que se asimile debidamente algo interesante antes de proseguir.

Miro a Jackie y se seca los ojos con un pañuelo. Ahora están ambos irritados. El jurado está con ella, dispuesto a matar para defenderla.

—Hablemos de la ficha de los Black —digo—. Le fue asignada a usted.

—Exactamente. Se me asignó la reclamación inicial de la señora Black. De acuerdo con la política vigente de la compañía, le mandé una carta de denegación.

—¿Por qué?

—¿Por qué? Porque todas las reclamaciones se denegaban inicialmente, por lo menos en mil novecientos noventa y uno.

—¿Todas las reclamaciones?

—Sí. Nuestra política consistía en denegar inicialmente todas las reclamaciones y luego revisar las de menor cuantía que parecían legítimas. Acabábamos por pagar algunas de ellas, pero ninguna de las cuantiosas a no ser que interviniera algún abogado.

—¿Cuándo entró en vigor dicha política?

—El uno de enero de mil novecientos noventa y uno. Era un experimento, una especie de estratagema —dice al tiempo que yo asiento, para que prosiga—. La compañía decidió denegar todas las reclamaciones superiores a los mil dólares, durante un período de doce meses. No importaba lo legítima que fuera la reclamación, simplemente se denegaba. Muchas de las reclamaciones de menor cuantía también se denegaban, si encontrábamos alguna razón para hacerlo. Se pagaron muy pocas reclamaciones de mayor cuantía, y sólo cuando el asegurado había contratado a un abogado y empezado a amenazarnos.

—¿Durante cuánto tiempo estuvo vigente dicha política?

—Doce meses. Fue un experimento de un año. Nunca se había hecho en el sector de los seguros y la dirección en general lo consideró una idea maravillosa. Denegar durante un año, sumar el dinero ahorrado, deducir lo gastado en acuerdos en los juzgados, y lo que queda es un buen saco de oro.

—¿Cuánto oro?

—Esa estratagema les permitió ganar unos cuarenta millones adicionales.

—¿Cómo lo sabe?

—Cualquiera que pase el tiempo suficiente con esos cretinos en la cama oye toda clase de basura. Te lo cuentan todo. Hablan de sus esposas y del trabajo. No me siento orgullosa de ello. No me proporcionó un solo momento de placer. Era una víctima.

Vuelve a tener los ojos irritados y le tiembla ligeramente la voz.

Hago otra pausa mientras repaso mis notas.

—¿Qué tratamiento se otorgó a la reclamación de los Black?

—Inicialmente se denegó, como todas las demás. Pero era una reclamación cuantiosa y se codificó de otro modo. Cuando detectaron las palabras «leucemia aguda», Russell Krokit pasó a supervisar todo lo que hacía. Se percataron casi desde el primer momento de que la póliza no excluía los trasplantes de médula. Se convirtió en una ficha muy importante por dos razones. En primer lugar, suponía un montón de dinero, que la compañía evidentemente no quería pagar. Y en segundo lugar, el asegurado padecía una enfermedad terminal.

—¿De modo que el departamento de reclamaciones sabía que Donny Ray Black moriría?

—Por supuesto. Sus informes médicos eran perfectamente claros. Recuerdo un informe de su médico en el que declaraba que la quimioterapia había sido satisfactoria, pero que la leucemia reaparecería, probablemente en menos de un año, y que por fin acabaría con la vida del paciente si no recibía un trasplante de médula.

—¿Se lo mostró usted a alguien?

—Se lo mostré a Russell Krokit, quien a su vez lo entregó a su jefe, Everett Lufkin. En algún lugar de la cúpula se decidió proseguir con la denegación.

—¿Pero usted sabía que debían pagar la reclamación?

—Todo el mundo lo sabía, pero la compañía jugaba a apuestas.

—¿Puede explicarse?

—Apostaba a que el asegurado no consultaría a ningún abogado.

—¿Sabe usted cuál era entonces el margen de posibilidades?

—Por lo general se consideraba que, a lo sumo, uno de cada veinticinco consultaba a un abogado. Ésa fue la única razón por la que iniciaron dicho experimento. Sabían que no podían fracasar. Venden esas pólizas a personas de escasa formación y confían en que acepten las denegaciones por ignorancia.

—¿Qué ocurría cuando recibían una carta de algún abogado?

—La situación cambiaba radicalmente. Si la reclamación era legítima e inferior a los cinco mil dólares, la pagábamos inmediatamente y enviábamos una carta pidiendo disculpas. Se alegaba un error administrativo, ya sabe a qué clase de carta me refiero. O a veces lo atribuían a un error informático. He mandado montones de cartas parecidas. Si la reclamación superaba los cinco mil dólares, la ficha abandonaba mis manos y pasaba a las del supervisor. Creo que casi siempre las pagaban. Si el abogado había presentado ya una demanda o estaba a punto de hacerlo, la compañía negociaba un acuerdo confidencial.

—¿Con qué frecuencia sucedía?

—Realmente no lo sé.

—Gracias —digo, al tiempo que me retiro del estrado y vuelvo la cabeza para mirar a Drummond con una agradable sonrisa—. Su testigo.

Me siento junto a Dot, que solloza discretamente. Siempre se ha culpado a sí misma por no acudir antes a un abogado, y esta declaración ha sido particularmente dolorosa para ella. Independientemente de lo que ocurra, nunca se perdonará a sí misma.

Afortunadamente, varios miembros del jurado se percatan de que está llorando.

El pobre Leo se sitúa lentamente lo más lejos posible del jurado, desde donde se le permita formular sus preguntas. No tengo la más remota idea de lo que piensa preguntar, pero estoy seguro de que ya le han tendido otras emboscadas.

Se presenta con suma cordialidad y le dice a Jackie que, evidentemente, no se conocen. Ésta es una forma de comunicarle al jurado que no sabe en modo alguno lo que le responderá. Ella le pone mala cara. No sólo odia Great Benefit, sino a cualquier abogado dispuesto a representar a la compañía.

—¿Es cierto, señora Lemancyzk, que recientemente tuvieron que ingresarla en cierta institución porque tenía varios problemas? —pregunta delicadamente Drummond.

En un juicio no deben formularse preguntas cuya respuesta se desconozca, pero en este caso tengo la impresión de que Leo avanza casi a ciegas. Su fuente de información han sido unos susurros desesperados durante los últimos quince minutos.

—¡No! No es cierto —exclama Jackie.

—Usted perdone. ¿Pero no ha estado recibiendo tratamiento?

—Nadie me ha obligado a ingresar en ningún lugar. Acudí voluntariamente a cierta clínica, donde permanecí dos semanas. Podía marcharme cuando se me antojara. El tratamiento debía estar cubierto por una póliza de Great Benefit, que se supone vigente durante doce meses a partir de la fecha en que abandoné la compañía. Como era de suponer, han denegado la reclamación.

Drummond se lo traga y consulta su cuaderno, como si no hubiera oído la respuesta.

—¿Es ésa la razón por la que está aquí? ¿Porque está enojada con Great Benefit?

—Detesto Great Benefit y a la mayoría de los gusanos que trabajan en la compañía. ¿Responde eso a su pregunta?

—¿Está inspirada su declaración por el odio?

—No. Estoy aquí porque conozco la verdad en cuanto a la forma sistemática en que han estafado a millares de personas. Es preciso que se sepa.

Más te valdría abandonarlo, Leo.

—¿Por qué acudió a una clínica en busca de tratamiento?

—Tengo problemas de alcoholismo y depresión. Ahora estoy bien. La semana próxima, ¿quién sabe? Durante seis años, sus clientes me han tratado como un trozo de carne. Circulé por la oficina como una caja de bombones y cada uno tomó lo que le apeteció. Se aprovecharon de mí porque no tenía dinero, estaba sola con dos hijos menores y tenía un bonito culo. Me han desposeído de mi dignidad. Lucho para recuperarme, señor Drummond. Intento salvarme a mí misma y si creo que algún tratamiento puede ayudarme, no vacilaré en solicitarlo. Si por lo menos su cliente pagara las malditas cuentas.

—He terminado, su señoría —dice Drummond antes de retirarse rápidamente a su mesa.

Acompaño a Jackie casi hasta la puerta. Le doy varias veces las gracias y prometo llamar a su abogado. Deck sale con ella para llevarla al aeropuerto.

Son casi las once y media. Quiero que el jurado reflexione sobre su declaración durante el almuerzo y le solicito al juez Kipler un temprano recésit. Alego oficialmente que necesito analizar unas copias informáticas, antes de llamar al próximo testigo.

Los diez mil dólares de multa han llegado mientras estábamos en la sala y Drummond los ha depositado en plica, junto a un recurso de apelación y un informe de veinte páginas. Se propone apelar contra dicha sanción y el dinero quedará depositado en una cuenta del juzgado, a la espera de la decisión definitiva. Tengo otras cosas en que pensar.

CUARENTA Y CINCO

Recibo algunas sonrisas de los miembros del jurado cuando regresan a sus asientos después del almuerzo. Se supone que no deben hablar del caso hasta que se les haga entrega oficial del mismo, pero todo el mundo sabe que lo comentan cada vez que abandonan la sala. Hace unos años, dos miembros del jurado se liaron a puñetazos al discutir la veracidad de cierto testigo. El problema fue que se trataba del segundo testigo, en un juicio cuya duración prevista era de dos semanas. El juez decretó el juicio nulo y empezaron de nuevo.

Han tenido dos horas para digerir y asimilar el testimonio de Jackie. Ha llegado el momento de que les muestre la forma de corregir algunas de dichas maldades. Es hora de hablar de dinero.

—Con la venia de su señoría, la acusación llama al señor Wilfred Keeley al estrado.

Encuentran a Keeley cerca de la sala, y entra cargado de energía y con anhelo por declarar. Parece vigoroso y amable, al contrario de Lufkin, y a pesar de las mentiras irrefutables de su compañía. Evidentemente quiere asegurarle al jurado que está al mando y que se puede confiar en él.

Le formulo algunas preguntas generales para establecer que es en efecto el director gerente, el jefe supremo de Great Benefit. Lo admite con toda franqueza. A continuación le entrego una copia del último informe financiero de la compañía y lo examina como si lo leyera todas las mañanas.

—Dígame, señor Keeley, ¿puede decirle al jurado cuál es el valor activo de su compañía?

—¿A qué se refiere por valor activo? —replica.

—Me refiero al valor neto.

—Éste no es un concepto claro.

—Claro que lo es. Observe el informe financiero que tiene delante, tome por una parte los haberes, reste los débitos, y dígale al jurado cuál es el saldo. Ése es el valor neto.

412

—No es tan simple.

Muevo con incredulidad la cabeza.

—¿Admite usted que el valor neto de su compañía es de aproximadamente cuatrocientos cincuenta millones de dólares?

Además de la utilidad evidente de sorprender a un ejecutivo mintiendo, otra ventaja es que los demás testigos tienen que decir la verdad. Keeley debe ser completamente honrado y estoy seguro de que Drummond ha insistido mucho en ello. No habrá sido fácil.

—Es una estimación razonable. Estoy de acuerdo.

—Gracias. Ahora, dígame, ¿de cuánto dinero líquido dispone su compañía?

La pregunta era inesperada. Drummond se levanta y protesta. Kipler no admite la protesta.

—Bueno, es difícil saberlo —responde antes de sumirse en el estado de angustia que al parecer cabe esperar de Great Benefit.

—Vamos, señor Keeley, usted es el director gerente. Hace dieciocho años que está en la compañía. Procede del mundo de las finanzas. ¿De cuánto dinero líquido disponen?

Espero pacientemente mientras examina las páginas como un endemoniado. Por fin me da una cifra y ahí es donde le doy las gracias a Max Leuberg. Levanto mi copia y le pido que me aclare cierta cuenta de reserva en particular. Cuando les demandé por diez millones de dólares, depositaron el dinero en una cuenta de reserva para pagar la demanda. Lo mismo hacen con todos los pleitos. Sigue siendo su dinero, que se invierte y gana dividendos, pero ahora está calificado de *obligación*. A las compañías de seguros les encanta que las demanden por muchos millones de dólares, porque pueden reservar el dinero y alegar que son casi insolventes.

Y todo es perfectamente legal. Es un sector no regulado, con su propio conjunto de tenebrosos métodos de contabilidad.

Keeley empieza a utilizar complicados términos financieros, que nadie alcanza a comprender. Prefiere confundir al jurado, a admitir la verdad.

Le pregunto por otra cuenta de reserva, antes de pasar a una de excedentes. Excedentes limitados. Excedentes ilimitados. Le formulo un sinfín de preguntas y parezco bastante inteligente. Con la ayuda de las notas de Leuberg, compagino las cifras y le pregunto a Keeley si la compañía dispone de unos cuatrocientos ochenta y cinco millones en dinero líquido.

—Ojalá —responde con un carcajada, sin provocar siquiera una sonrisa.

—¿Entonces de cuanto dinero líquido dispone, señor Keeley?

—Pues no lo sé. Supongo que alrededor de cien millones.

Eso basta por ahora. Al llegar a las conclusiones, puedo escribir las cifras en una pizarra y explicar dónde está el dinero.

Le entrego una copia informática de los datos de reclamaciones y la mira sorprendido. Durante el almuerzo he tomado la decisión de tenderle una emboscada cuando estuviera en el estrado, en lugar de llamar a Lufkin para una segunda comparecencia. Mira a Drummond en busca de ayuda, pero el abogado no puede hacer nada por él. El señor Keeley es el director gerente, e indudablemente tendría que poder ayudarnos a descubrir la verdad. Parto de la suposición de que esperan que llame de nuevo a Lufkin para que aclare dichos datos. Pero por mucho que me gustaría hacerlo, he terminado con él. No pienso brindarle la oportunidad de refutar la declaración de Jackie Lemancyzk.

—¿Reconoce esa copia, señor Keeley? Es la que su compañía me ha entregado esta mañana.

—Por supuesto.

—Estupendo. ¿Puede decirle al jurado cuántas pólizas médicas tenía en vigencia su compañía en mil novecientos noventa y uno?

—Pues no lo sé. Déjeme ver —responde mientras examina una página tras otra.

—¿Le parece correcta la cifra de noventa y ocho mil, aproximadamente?

—Tal vez. Sí, creo que debe de ser eso.

—¿Y cuántas reclamaciones se recibieron basadas en dichas pólizas durante el mismo año?

Vuelve a mirar páginas. Examina el documento farfullando cifras para sí. Da casi vergüenza ajena.

—¿Le parece correcta la cifra de once mil cuatrocientas, más o menos? —pregunto al cabo de unos minutos.

—Podría ser, pero tendría que comprobarlo, ¿comprende?

—¿Cómo lo comprobaría?

—Tendría que estudiar un poco más estos documentos.

—¿Entonces está aquí la información?

—Eso creo.

—¿Puede decirle al jurado cuántas de dichas reclamaciones fueron denegadas por su compañía?

—Una vez más tendría que analizar estas cifras —responde levantando los papeles con ambas manos.

—¿De modo que esta información también está contenida en esos papeles?

—Tal vez. Sí, eso creo.

—Estupendo. Fíjese en las páginas once, dieciocho, treinta y tres y cuarenta y uno.

Obedece inmediatamente. Cualquier cosa a cambio de no hablar. Se oye el ruido de los papeles.

—¿Le parece la cifra de nueve mil cien correcta, aproximadamente?

La atroz sugerencia le produce estupor.

—Claro que no. Eso es absurdo.

—¿Pero usted no lo sabe?

—Sé que no es tan elevada.

—Gracias —digo antes de acercarme al testigo, recoger los documentos que tiene en la mano y entregarle la póliza de Great Benefit que me dio Max Leuberg—. ¿Reconoce esto?

—Por supuesto —responde aliviado.

—¿Qué es?

—Una póliza de seguro médico expedida por mi compañía.

—¿Cuándo fue expedida?

La examina momentáneamente.

—En setiembre de mil novecientos noventa y dos. Hace cinco meses.

—Mire por favor la página once, sección F, párrafo cuarto, subpárrafo «c», cláusula trece. ¿La ha encontrado?

La letra es tan menuda que casi tiene que acercarse la póliza a la nariz. Me río y miro al jurado. El humor no pasa inadvertido.

—Ya lo tengo —dice por fin.

—Estupendo. Léalo, por favor.

Lo lee forzando la vista y frunciendo el entrecejo, como si fuera una gran molestia. Cuando ha terminado sonríe.

—Ya está.

—¿Cuál es el propósito de dicha cláusula?

—Excluye ciertos tratamientos médicos de la cobertura.

—¿Concretamente?

—Concretamente todos los trasplantes.

—¿Figura el trasplante de médula ósea como una de las exclusiones?

—Sí. El trasplante de médula figura en la lista.

Me acerco al testigo y le entrego una copia de la póliza de los Black. Le pido que lea una sección concreta. La diminuta letra le obliga a forzar la vista, pero se esfuerza y la lee.

—¿Qué excluye esta póliza en cuanto a trasplantes?

—Todos los órganos principales: riñones, hígado, corazón, pulmones, ojos. Aquí está la lista completa.

—¿Se menciona la médula ósea?

—No figura en la lista.

—¿De modo que no está específicamente excluida?

—Exactamente.

—¿Cuándo se presentó esta demanda, señor Keeley? ¿Lo recuerda?

Mira fugazmente a Drummond, que evidentemente en este momento no puede ayudarle.

—A mediados del verano pasado, si mal no recuerdo. ¿Tal vez en junio?

—Sí, señor —respondo—. Fue en junio. ¿Sabe cuándo se cambió el texto de la póliza para excluir específicamente los trasplantes de médula ósea?

—No. No lo sé. No me ocupo de redactar las pólizas.

—¿Quién las redacta? ¿Quién escribe estas cláusulas?

—Lo hacen en el departamento jurídico.

—Comprendo. ¿Cabe suponer que se modificó el texto de la póliza después de presentar esta demanda?

Me observa momentáneamente antes de responder.

—No. Me parece que se modificó antes de la demanda.

—¿Se modificó después de presentar la reclamación, en agosto de mil novecientos noventa y uno?

—No lo sé.

Su respuesta parece sospechosa. O no presta demasiada atención a su compañía, o está mintiendo. En realidad, no me importa. He conseguido lo que me proponía. Puedo explicarle al jurado que la nueva póliza demuestra claramente que en la de los Black no había intención alguna de excluir los trasplantes de médula. En ambas se especifica claramente todo lo que se excluye, de modo que su propia redacción los ha comprometido.

Sólo me queda un pequeño asunto para Keeley.

—¿Tiene usted una copia del acuerdo que Jackie Lemancyzk firmó el día en que la despidieron?

—No.

—¿Ha visto usted alguna vez dicho acuerdo?

—No.

—¿Autorizó usted el pago de diez mil dólares al contado a Jackie Lemancyzk?

—No. Eso es mentira.

—¿Mentira?

—Eso he dicho.

—¿Qué me dice de Everett Lufkin? ¿No mintió ante el jurado respecto al manual de reclamaciones?

Keeley está a punto de responder, pero recapacita. Ninguna respuesta puede ayudarle ahora. Los miembros del jurado saben perfectamente que Lufkin les ha mentido y no puede convencerlos de lo contrario. Tampoco puede admitir que uno de sus vicepresidentes ha mentido en la sala.

No había previsto esa pregunta, simplemente ha surgido.

—Le he hecho una pregunta, señor Keeley. ¿Mintió el señor Everett ante este jurado respecto al manual de reclamaciones?

—No creo tener obligación de responder a esta pregunta.

—Conteste la pregunta —exclama severamente Kipler.

Se hace una dolorosa pausa, mientras Keeley me mira fijamente. La sala está silenciosa. Todos y cada uno de los miembros del jurado le observan, a la espera de su respuesta. La verdad es evidente para todos y decido ser amable.

—No puede responder, ¿no es cierto? Porque tendría que admitir que un vicepresidente de su compañía ha mentido en esta sala.

—Protesto.

—Se admite la protesta.

—No hay más preguntas.

—Por ahora me abstengo, su señoría —dice Drummond.

Evidentemente quiere que se tranquilicen los ánimos antes de interrogar a esos individuos. De momento, lo que Drummond pretende es distanciar al jurado de Jackie Lemancyzk.

Kermit Aldy, vicepresidente de contratación, es mi próximo y último testigo. A decir verdad, en este momento no necesito su testimonio, pero debo rellenar el tiempo. Son las dos y media del segundo día del juicio, y seguramente terminaré esta tarde. Quiero que los miembros del jurado regresen a sus casas pensando en dos personas: Jackie Lemancyzk y Donny Ray Black.

Aldy está asustado y habla poco, teme decir más de lo indispensable. No sé si se ha acostado con Jackie, pero en estos momentos todos los miembros de Great Benefit son sospechosos. Intuyo que el jurado también lo cree.

Cubrimos con rapidez la suficiente información de fondo. La contratación es tan terriblemente aburrida que sólo quiero facilitarle al jurado un mínimo de detalles. Aldy también es aburrido y, por consiguiente, apto para su labor. Para no aburrir al jurado, me apresuro.

Llega el momento de la diversión. Le entrego el manual de contratación, que recibí durante la instrucción del caso. Las cubiertas son verdes y es muy parecido al manual de reclamaciones. Ni Aldy, ni Drummond, ni ninguna otra persona, sabe si tengo en mi posesión otra copia del manual de contratación que incluya la sección «u».

Lo mira como si nunca lo hubiera visto, pero lo identifica cuando se lo pido. Todo el mundo conoce la próxima pregunta.

—¿Está completo este manual?

Lo hojea lentamente, sin apresurarse. Evidentemente cuenta con la experiencia de Lufkin del día anterior. Si dice que está completo y saco el ejemplar que me ha prestado Cooper Jackson, está acabado. Si admite que falta algo, pagará por ello. Apuesto a que Drummond le ha aconsejado lo segundo.

—Déjeme ver, parece completo, pero no, espere un momento. Falta una sección al final.

—¿Podría tratarse de la sección «u»? —pregunto con incredulidad.

—Sí, creo que sí.

Finjo asombrarme.

—¿Qué razón podría tener alguien para eliminar la sección «u» de este manual?

—No lo sé.

—¿Sabe usted quién la retiró?

—No.

—Claro que no. ¿Quién seleccionó este ejemplar para entregármelo?

—A decir verdad, no lo recuerdo.

—¿Pero es evidente que la sección «u» fue retirada antes de entregármelo?

—No está aquí, si es eso lo que pretende saber.

—Lo que pretendo es averiguar la verdad, señor Aldy. Le ruego que me ayude. ¿Se retiró la sección «u» de este manual antes de entregármelo?

—Eso parece.

—¿Es eso una respuesta afirmativa?

—Sí. La sección en cuestión fue retirada.

—¿Está usted de acuerdo en que el manual de contratación es muy importante para las operaciones de su departamento?

—Por supuesto.

—¿De modo que está usted muy familiarizado con el mismo?

—Sí.

—En tal caso, podría resumir fácilmente lo esencial de la sección «u» para el jurado, ¿no es cierto?

—No estoy seguro. Hace algún tiempo que no lo consulto.

Todavía no sabe si tengo una copia de la sección «u» del manual de contratación.

—¿Por qué no lo intenta? Haga un breve resumen de la sección «u» para el jurado.

Reflexiona unos instantes y luego explica que dicha sección contiene un sistema de comprobaciones y balances entre reclamaciones y contratación. Ambos departamentos deben supervisar ciertas reclamaciones. Se necesita una cantidad abundante de papeleo para asegurarse de que la reclamación se tramita debidamente. Divaga, adquiere más confianza en sí mismo y puesto que todavía no he mostrado ninguna copia de la sección «u», me parece que empieza a creer que no la tengo.

—De modo que el propósito de la sección «u» es el de garantizar que cada reclamación se tramite debidamente.

—Sí.

Saco un manual de debajo de mi mesa y me acerco al testigo.

—En tal caso, explíqueselo al jurado —digo al tiempo que le entrego un ejemplar completo del manual.

Se desanima ligeramente. Drummond procura dar la impresión de que está tranquilo, pero le resulta imposible.

La sección «u» en contratación es tan escabrosa como la sección «u» en reclamaciones, y después de una hora de poner a Aldy en aprieto, llega el momento de parar. La estratagema ha sido expuesta abiertamente, a la vista del jurado.

Drummond se abstiene de formular preguntas. Kipler ordena un recésit de quince minutos para que Deck y yo podamos instalar los monitores.

Nuestro último testigo es Donny Ray Black. El alguacil baja las luces de la sala y los miembros del jurado se inclinan hacia delante, ansiosos por ver su cara en la pantalla de veinte pulgadas. Hemos editado la declaración, que ahora dura sólo treinta y un minutos, y los miembros del jurado absorben cada una de sus roncas y débiles palabras.

En lugar de mirarlo por enésima vez, me siento junto a Dot y observo los rostros del jurado. Detecto mucha compasión. Dot se seca las mejillas con el reverso de la mano. Hacia el final, tengo un nudo en la garganta.

Cuando se apagan las pantallas y el alguacil se dispone a encender las luces, la sala está muy silenciosa durante un largo minuto. En la penumbra se oye el suave sollozo inconfundible de una madre que procede de nuestra mesa.

Hemos infligido todo el mal del que he sido capaz. He ganado el caso. Ahora, el reto es no perderlo.

—Con la venia de su señoría, la acusación ha concluido —anuncio solemnemente cuando se encienden las luces.

A pesar de que ya hace bastante rato que los miembros del jurado se han marchado, Dot y yo permanecemos sentados en una sala vacía, y hablamos de las extraordinarias declaraciones que hemos oído en los dos últimos días. Desde los primeros momentos se demostró que ella tenía razón y ellos no la tenían, pero la gratificación es mínima. Seguirá atormentándose hasta el día de su muerte por no haber luchado con más ahínco cuando era necesario.

Me dice que no le importa lo que ocurra de ahora en adelante. Ha gozado de su oportunidad en la sala. Quiere regresar a su casa y no volver jamás. Le explico que eso es imposible. Estamos sólo a medio camino. Faltan sólo unos días.

CUARENTA Y SEIS

Estoy fascinado por lo que Drummond intentará en su defensa. Se expone a empeorar la situación si presenta más testigos de la oficina central e intenta justificar sus estratagemas para denegar las reclamaciones. Sabe que me limitaré a exhibir las secciones «u» y formular toda clase de preguntas maliciosas. Que yo sepa, puede que haya más mentiras y tapaderas. Y la única forma de averiguarlo será en los interrogatorios.

Ha presentado una lista de dieciocho personas como testigos potenciales. No puedo imaginarme a quién llamará primero. En mi presentación del caso he gozado de la ventaja de saber lo que ocurriría a continuación, quién sería el próximo testigo, el próximo documento. Ahora es muy diferente. Tendré que reaccionar con rapidez.

Ya avanzada la noche llamo a Max Leuberg a Wisconsin y le cuento encantado los sucesos de los dos primeros días. Me ofrece algunos consejos y opiniones respecto a lo que sucederá a partir de ahora. Se emociona muchísimo y dice que tal vez cogerá un avión.

Paseo de un lado para otro hasta las tres de la madrugada, hablando a solas e intentando imaginar lo que Drummond se propone.

Me alegra ver a Cooper Jackson sentado en la sala cuando llego a las ocho y media. Me presenta a otros dos abogados, ambos de Raleigh, Carolina del Norte. Han venido en avión para presenciar mi juicio. ¿Cómo va?, me preguntan. Les ofrezco un resumen cauteloso de lo sucedido. Uno de los abogados estaba en la sala el lunes y vio el melodrama de la sección «u». Entre los tres tienen ahora unos veinte casos, han puesto anuncios en los periódicos y cosas por el estilo, y aparecen más casos por todas partes. Se proponen presentar pronto las demandas.

Cooper me entrega un periódico y me pregunta si lo he visto. Es el *The Wall Street Journal*, con fecha de ayer, y hay un artículo en primera plana sobre Great Benefit. Les digo que no he leído un periódico desde hace una semana, incluso he olvidado la fecha. Me comprenden perfectamente.

Leo rápidamente el artículo. Trata del creciente número de quejas sobre Great Benefit y su tendencia a denegar reclamaciones. Muchos estados investigan. Se presentan copiosas demandas. En el último párrafo se menciona cierto pequeño juicio en Memphis, que conviene observar porque podría producir el primer veredicto sustancial contra la compañía.

Le muestro el artículo a Kipler en su despacho y no le preocupa. Se limitará a preguntarles a los miembros del jurado si lo han visto. Se les ha advertido que no lean los periódicos. Ambos dudamos de que el *Journal* sea un periódico popular entre los miembros de nuestro jurado.

La defensa llama a André Weeks, vicecomisario de seguros del estado de Tennessee. Es un funcionario de alto rango en el departamento de seguros, un testigo que Drummond ya ha utilizado en otras ocasiones. Su misión consiste en colocar incuestionablemente al gobierno en el bando de la defensa.

Es un individuo muy apuesto, de unos cuarenta años, viste un bonito traje, y tiene una agradable sonrisa y cara de honradez. Además, en estos momentos cuenta con algo muy importante a su favor, no trabaja para Great Benefit. Drummond le formula un montón de preguntas mundanas sobre las obligaciones reguladoras de su departamento, intenta dar la impresión de que son muy rigurosos con el sector de los seguros y realmente lo controlan. Por consiguiente, puesto que Great Benefit goza todavía de buena reputación en este estado, eso significa que su conducta es correcta. De no ser así, André y sus sabuesos estarían acosando la compañía.

Drummond necesita tiempo. Necesita ofrecer al jurado cierta cantidad de testimonios, con la esperanza de que olviden algunas de las cosas horribles que ya han escuchado. Se lo toma con calma. Avanza lentamente, habla despacio, como un viejo catedrático. Y lo hace muy bien. En otras circunstancias sería temible.

Le entrega a Weeks la póliza de los Black y pasan media hora para explicarles al jurado que *todas y cada una de las pólizas* deben ser aprobadas por el departamento de seguros. Se hace gran hincapié en el término «aprobadas».

Puesto que no estoy de pie, puedo dedicarme a mirar a mi

alrededor. Examino los rostros de los miembros del jurado, algunos de los cuales me miran a los ojos. Están conmigo. Me percato de la presencia de desconocidos en la sala, jóvenes trajeados que antes no había visto. Cooper Jackson y sus compañeros están en la última fila, cerca de la puerta. Hay menos de quince espectadores. ¿Por qué querría presenciar alguien un juicio civil?

Después de una hora y media de aburridísimo testimonio sobre las complejidades de las normas de los seguros en todo el estado, los miembros del jurado empiezan a desinteresarse. A Drummond no le importa. Quiere prolongar el juicio hasta la semana próxima sea como sea. Finalmente me cede el testigo poco antes de las once, habiendo consumido efectivamente toda la mañana. Hacemos un descanso de quince minutos y ahora me toca a mí disparar a ciegas.

Weeks asegura que ahora hay más de seiscientas compañías de seguros en el estado, que en su departamento trabajan cuarenta y una personas, y que de ellos sólo dieciocho revisan pólizas. Reconoce con reticencia que cada una de las seiscientas compañías tiene por lo menos diez tipos diferentes de pólizas en el mercado y, por consiguiente, hay un mínimo de seis mil pólizas en los ficheros de su departamento. También admite que las pólizas se modifican y corrigen constantemente.

Calculamos un poco más y logro transmitir el mensaje de que es imposible que cualquier organismo burocrático controle el océano de letra menuda generada por el sector de los seguros. Le entrego la póliza de los Black. Alega haberla leído, pero admite haberlo hecho sólo en preparación para este juicio. Le formulo una pregunta sobre la remuneración semanal de invalidez temporal, sin estar hospitalizado. De pronto, la póliza parece haber aumentado de peso en sus manos y pasa rápidamente las páginas, con la esperanza de encontrar la sección apropiada y darme una respuesta. No sucede. Dobla y traspone papeles, entorna los párpados y frunce el entrecejo, hasta que por fin lo encuentra. Su respuesta es más o menos correcta y la acepto. Luego le pregunto sobre el método apropiado para cambiar de beneficiario en la póliza y casi me da pena. Examina la póliza durante mucho tiempo, mientras todos esperamos. El jurado se divierte. Kipler sonríe maliciosamente. Drummond está furioso, pero no puede hacer nada.

Nos da una respuesta, cuya corrección no importa. He demostrado lo que quería. Coloco los dos manuales verdes sobre mi mesa, como si Weeks y yo estuviéramos a punto de repasarlos de nuevo. Todo el mundo nos observa. Con el manual de reclamaciones en la mano, le pregunto si revisa periódicamente los procesos internos de tramitación de reclamaciones en alguna de las compañías que tan celosamente controla. Quiere responder que sí, pero evidentemente ha oído hablar de la sección «u». De modo que dice no y yo, naturalmente, quedo atónito. Le formulo algunas preguntas sarcásticas y le suelto del anzuelo. El daño está hecho y registrado.

Le pregunto si es consciente de que el comisario de seguros de Florida está investigando Great Benefit. No lo sabía. ¿Y en Carolina del Sur? Tampoco. ¿Qué me dice de Carolina del Norte? Cree haber oído algo al respecto, pero no ha visto nada. ¿Kentucky? ¿Georgia? Nada. Además, y para que conste, realmente no le preocupa lo que suceda en otros estados. Le doy las gracias.

El próximo testigo de Drummond tampoco trabaja para Great Benefit, pero casi. Su nombre es Payton Reisky y ostenta el rimbombante título de director ejecutivo y presidente de la National Insurance Alliance. Tiene el aspecto y los modales de una persona muy importante. No tardamos en descubrir que su institución es un organismo político con base en Washington, fundado por las compañías de seguros para actuar de portavoz en el Capitolio. Son un simple grupo de activistas, indudablemente con un presupuesto de oro. Hacen muchas cosas maravillosas, se nos dice, para promulgar una conducta justa en el sector de los seguros.

Esta pequeña introducción se prolonga durante mucho rato. Empieza a la una y media de la tarde, y a las dos estamos convencidos de que la NIA va por camino de salvar a la humanidad. ¡Qué gente tan maravillosa!

Reisky se ha dedicado treinta años a los negocios, y pronto se nos informa de su historial y su currículum. Drummond quiere que se le admita como perito en el trámite y procedimiento de reclamaciones. No tengo nada que objetar. He estudiado su declaración en otro juicio y creo que puedo con él. Tendría que ser un perito excepcionalmente diestro para que la sección «u» pareciera correcta.

Prácticamente sin que se lo pregunten detalla el proceso completo de la tramitación de una reclamación. Drummond asiente gravemente, como si estuvieran ganando terreno. ¡Menuda sorpresa! Great Benefit se ajustó a las normas en este caso. Tal vez cometió un par de errores insignificantes, pero es una gran compañía con muchísimas reclamaciones. Ningún alejamiento importante de lo razonable.

En términos generales, Reisky opina que Great Benefit estaba en su derecho a denegar esta reclamación, debido a su magnitud. Le explica con mucha seriedad al jurado que no se puede esperar que una póliza que cuesta dieciocho dólares semanales cubra unos trasplantes que cuestan doscientos mil dólares. El propósito de dicho género de pólizas es facilitar sólo una cobertura básica, no el oro y el moro.

Drummond saca a relucir el tema de los manuales y de las secciones ausentes. Lamentablemente, Reisky no lo considera importante. Los manuales cambian constantemente en un sector en modificación permanente, y los encargados de reclamaciones expertos no les prestan demasiada atención, porque saben lo que se hacen. Pero puesto que se le ha dado tanta importancia, hablemos de ello. Levanta con sumo gusto el manual de reclamaciones y explica varias secciones del mismo al jurado. Está todo aquí, en blanco y negro. ¡Funciona todo de maravilla!

Pasan de los manuales a las cifras. Drummond le pregunta si ha tenido oportunidad de revisar la información relativa a pólizas, reclamaciones y denegaciones. Reisky asiente gravemente y coge la copia informatizada que Drummond le entrega.

No cabe duda de que la media de denegaciones de Great Benefit fue muy elevada en 1991, pero puede que hubiera razones para ello. No es inaudito en el sector de los seguros. Además, no se puede confiar siempre en las cifras. En realidad, si se examinan los diez últimos años, la media de denegaciones de Great Benefit es ligeramente inferior al doce por ciento, que es un porcentaje perfectamente habitual en el sector de los seguros. A unas cifras siguen otras y pronto estamos completamente confusos, que es precisamente lo que Drummond se propone.

Reisky desciende del estrado y empieza a señalar sobre un cuadro multicolor. Habla con el jurado como un experto conferenciante y me pregunto con qué frecuencia actúa. Las cifras se ajustan perfectamente a la media.

Afortunadamente, Kipler nos concede un descanso a las tres y media. Me reúno en el pasillo con Cooper Jackson y sus amigos. Son todos veteranos y dispuestos a aconsejarme. Coincidimos en que Drummond prolonga deliberadamente la sesión, con la esperanza de llegar al fin de semana.

No digo una sola palabra en toda la tarde. Reisky declara hasta muy tarde y finaliza con una retahíla de opiniones sobre la corrección con que todo se ha tramitado. A juzgar por los rostros del jurado, se alegran de que haya terminado. Agradezco las horas adicionales para preparar su interrogatorio.

Deck y yo disfrutamos de una prolongada cena con Cooper Jackson y los otros tres abogados en un restaurante italiano llamado Grisanti's. El enorme John Grisanti, pintoresco propietario del restaurante, nos instala en un comedor privado llamado «sala de prensa». Nos trae un exquisito vino que no hemos pedido y nos dice exactamente lo que debemos comer.

El vino es muy agradable y, por primera vez en muchos días, casi me relajo. Puede que esta noche duerma debidamente.

La cuenta asciende a más de cuatrocientos dólares y Cooper Jackson la coge inmediatamente. Menos mal. Puede que el bufete de Rudy Baylor esté al borde de la prosperidad, pero de momento todavía es menesteroso.

CUARENTA Y SIETE

Poco después de que Payton Reisky suba al estrado a primera hora del jueves por la mañana le entrego una copia de la «estúpida carta» y le pido que la lea.

—Dígame, señor Reisky —pregunto cuando la ha leído—, en su experta opinión, ¿es ésta una respuesta justa y razonable por parte de Great Benefit?

Está sobre aviso.

—Claro que no —responde—. Es horrible.

—Espantoso, ¿no le parece?

—Efectivamente. Pero tengo entendido que el autor de esta carta ya no trabaja en la compañía.

—¿Quién se lo ha contado? —pregunto con sumo recelo.

—Bueno, no estoy seguro. Alguien de la compañía.

—¿Le ha contado también ese desconocido por qué el señor Krokit ha abandonado la compañía?

—No lo sé. Tal vez tuviera algo que ver con la carta.

—¿Tal vez? ¿Está usted seguro, o simplemente especula?

—No estoy seguro.

—Gracias. ¿Le ha contado ese desconocido que el señor Krokit abandonó la compañía dos días antes de la fecha prevista para declarar en este caso?

—Me parece que no.

—Usted no sabe por qué se marchó, ¿no es cierto?

—No.

—Estupendo. Me había dado la impresión de que intentaba comunicarle al jurado que había abandonado la compañía a causa de esta carta. No era eso lo que pretendía, ¿verdad?

—No.

—Gracias.

Anoche, mientras degustábamos el vino, decidimos que sería un error atacar a Reisky con los manuales. Lo hicimos por varias razones. En primer lugar, las pruebas ya han sido presentadas al jurado. En segundo lugar, la presentación inicial fue muy dramática y eficaz, al sorprender a Lufkin mintiendo. En tercer lugar, Reisky es ágil con el lenguaje y sería difícil acorralarlo. En cuarto lugar, ha tenido tiempo para prepararse para el ataque y sabrá defenderse. En quinto lugar, aprovechará la oportunidad para confundir aún más al jurado. Y, lo más importante, ocuparía demasiado tiempo. Se podría perder todo el día discutiendo con Reisky sobre manuales y estadísticas. Sería un día perdido que no conduciría a nada.

—¿Quién paga su salario, señor Reisky?

—Mi empresa. La National Insurance Alliance.

—¿Quién financia la NIA?

—El sector de los seguros.

—¿Contribuye Great Benefit a la NIA?

—Sí.

—¿Con cuánto capital contribuye?

Mira a Drummond, que ya se ha puesto de pie.

—Protesto, su señoría, no guarda relación con el caso.

—No se admite la protesta. Me parece bastante pertinente.

—¿Cuánto, señor Reisky? —repito amablemente.

Evidentemente no le apetece contestar y se finge escrupuloso.

—Diez mil dólares anuales —responde.

—¿De modo que le pagan más a usted que a Donny Ray Black?

—Protesto.

—Se admite la protesta.

—Lo siento, su señoría. Retiro el comentario.

—Con la venia de su señoría, ordene que lo borren del acta —exclama Drummond enojado.

—Así se ordena.

—Lo siento, señor Reisky —digo con toda mi modestia y aspecto arrepentido después de una pausa para que se tranquilizaran los ánimos—. ¿Proceden todos sus ingresos de las compañías de seguros?

—No tenemos otra fuente de ingresos.

—¿Cuántas compañías contribuyen a la NIA?

—Doscientas veinte.

—¿Y cuál fue la suma total aportada el año pasado?

—Seis millones de dólares.

—¿Y utilizan ese dinero para ganar influencias?

—Sí, en parte.

—¿Cobra algo más por declarar en este juicio?

—No.

—¿Por qué ha venido?

—Porque Great Benefit se ha puesto en contacto conmigo. Me han pedido que declarara.

Vuelvo la cabeza muy lentamente y señalo a Dot Black.

—Señor Reisky, ¿es usted capaz de mirar fijamente a los ojos de la señora Black y decirle que la reclamación de su hijo fue tramitada justa y debidamente por Great Benefit?

Tarda un par de segundos en enfocar la cara de Dot, pero no tiene alternativa.

—Sí —asiente por fin—. Sin duda lo fue.

Evidentemente lo había planeado. Quería dar por terminado el testimonio de Reisky con un toque dramático, pero no espera el giro humorístico. La señora Beverdee Hardaway, una robusta negra de cincuenta y un años, que es el miembro número tres del jurado y está sentada en medio de la primera fila, no puede evitar reírse ante la absurda respuesta de Reisky. Es un estallido inesperado de risa, evidentemente espontáneo, que intenta sofocar inmediatamente. Se lleva ambas manos a la boca. Aprieta los dientes y las mandíbulas, y mira desconcertada a su alrededor, pero todavía se le convulsiona ligeramente el cuerpo.

Lamentablemente para la señora Hardaway y por suerte para nosotros, la risa es contagiosa. Al señor Ranson Pelk, sentado a su espalda, algo le hace gracia. Otro tanto le ocurre a la señora Ella Faye Salter, sentada junto a la señora Hardaway. A los pocos segundos, la risa se generaliza en el palco del jurado. Algunos miran a la señora Hardaway como si fuera la causante de la travesura. Otros miran directamente a Reisky y mueven la cabeza con asombro.

Reisky supone lo peor, que él es la causa de la risa. Agacha la cabeza y mira fijamente al suelo. Drummond opta por no darse por enterado, aunque debe ser doloroso para él. No se ve un solo rostro entre sus brillantes halcones. Todos consultan papeles y libros. Aldy y Underhall se examinan los calcetines.

Kipler también tiene ganas de reírse. Tolera unos instantes el humor y luego da unos golpes con su martillo, como para dejar constancia de que el jurado se ha reído del testimonio de Payton Reisky.

Ocurre con suma rapidez. La absurda respuesta, la carcajada, la vergüenza, la risa, los movimientos de cabeza con escepticismo, todo en pocos segundos. Pero detecto cierto alivio por parte de algunos miembros del jurado. Quieren reírse, expresar su incredulidad y, al hacerlo, aunque sólo sea momentáneamente, le comunican a Reisky y a Great Benefit lo que opinan sobre lo que cuentan.

Aunque breve, el momento ha sido absolutamente glorioso.

Les sonrío. Me devuelven la sonrisa. Creen plenamente a mis testigos, pero nada de lo que declaran los de Drummond.

—He terminado, su señoría —digo con desdén, como si estuviera harto de ese mequetrefe embustero.

Drummond está evidentemente sorprendido. Creía que pasaría el resto del día interrogándole sobre los manuales y las estadísticas. Mueve papeles, le susurra algo a T. Price y luego dice:

—Nuestro próximo testigo es Richard Pellrod.

Pellrod era el encargado decano de reclamaciones, para el que trabajaba Jackie Lemancyzk. Fue un terrible testigo cuando le tomé declaración con anterioridad al juicio, cargado de complejos, pero no es sorprendente su presencia. Tienen que hacer algo para mancillar la reputación de Jackie. Pellrod era su inmediato superior.

Tiene cuarenta y seis años, de estatura media y barrigudo, poco cabello, facciones desproporcionadas, granos en la cara y unas insípidas gafas. Ese pobre hombre no tiene ningún atractivo físico, ni evidentemente le importa. Si declara que Jackie Lemancyzk no era más que una cualquiera, que deseaba acostarse incluso con él, apuesto a que el jurado volverá a reírse.

Pellrod tiene la personalidad irascible propia de alguien que ha trabajado veinte años tramitando reclamaciones. Apenas más amable que un cobrador, e incapaz de transmitir calor o confianza al jurado. Es un mero funcionario de bajo rango, que ha trabajado probablemente toda su vida en el mismo escritorio.

¡Y es lo mejor que tienen! No pueden traer a Lufkin, ni a Aldy, ni a Keeley, porque han perdido toda credibilidad con el jurado. Drummond tiene una lista con media docena de nombres de la oficina central, pero dudo que los llame a todos. ¿Qué pueden decir? ¿Que los manuales no existen? ¿Que su compañía no miente ni oculta documentos?

Drummond y Pellrod reproducen durante media hora un diálogo perfectamente ensayado sobre el funcionamiento interno del departamento de reclamaciones, los heroicos esfuerzos de Great Benefit para tratar justamente a los asegurados, y provocan los bostezos del jurado.

El juez Kipler decide poner fin al aburrimiento, e interrumpe el diálogo.

—Abogado, ¿le importaría darse prisa?

Drummond aparenta estupor.

—Con la venia de su señoría, creo que tengo derecho a examinar detenidamente al testigo —responde ofendido.

—Por supuesto. Pero la mayor parte de lo que ha dicho hasta ahora es ya del conocimiento del jurado. Es repetitivo.

A Drummond le parece increíble que le llamen la atención. Finge, en vano, que el juez le tiene ojeriza.

—No recuerdo que le haya llamado la atención al abogado de la acusación.

Acaba de cometer un error. Intenta prolongar la discusión y se ha equivocado de juez.

—El señor Baylor ha mantenido despierto al jurado, señor Drummond. Prosiga.

La carcajada de la señora Hardaway y la subsiguiente risa han relajado al jurado. Ahora están más animados y dispuestos a reírse de nuevo a costa de la defensa.

Drummond mira fijamente a Kipler, como para indicarle que hablarán de ello más tarde. Vuelve a concentrarse en Pellrod, que está sentado ahí como un sapo, con los ojos medio abiertos y la cabeza ladeada. Admite, con un mínimo vestigio de remordimiento, pero no mucho, que se cometen errores. Y, asombrosamente, atribuye la mayoría de ellos a Jackie Lemancyzk, una joven perturbada.

Habla de nuevo de la ficha Black y comenta algunos de los documentos más inofensivos. No llega a hablar de las cartas de denegación, pero dedica mucho tiempo a documentos insignificantes que carecen de interés.

—Señor Drummond —interrumpe gravemente Kipler—. Le he pedido que prosiguiera. Esos documentos están a disposición del jurado. Y este testimonio ya ha sido cubierto por otros testigos. Prosiga.

Drummond está realmente ofendido. Está siendo atosigado por un injusto juez. Tarda un poco en recuperar su compostura. Sus dotes de actor no son las habituales.

Optan por otra estrategia respecto al manual de reclamaciones. Pellrod afirma que no es más que un libro, ni más ni menos. Personalmente, no lo ha consultado desde hace años. Lo modifican con tanta frecuencia que la mayoría de los encargados de reclamaciones veteranos lo ignoran por completo. No significa nada para él. No significa nada para la mayoría de los encargados de reclamaciones que trabajan a sus órdenes. Drummond le muestra la sección «u» y ese hijo de perra afirma que nunca la había visto. Asegura que no conoce a ningún encargado de reclamaciones que se moleste en consultar el manual.

¿Cómo se tramitan entonces las reclamaciones? Pellrod nos lo cuenta. Con la ayuda de Drummond, habla de una reclamación hipotética y describe los canales normales. Paso a paso, formulario por formulario, circular por circular. La voz de Pellrod es sumamente monótona y aburre soberanamente al jurado. Lester Days, miembro número ocho del jurado, sentado en la última fila, se queda dormido. Hay bostezos y ojos que se mantienen difícilmente abiertos, en un esfuerzo por no dormirse.

No pasa inadvertido.

Si a Pellrod le importa no haber estimulado al jurado, no lo manifiesta. No cambia su voz ni su actitud. Concluye su testimonio con unas revelaciones alarmantes sobre Jackie Lemancyzk. Su problema con el alcohol era sobradamente conocido y a menudo apestaba a licor cuando llegaba al trabajo. Se ausentaba con mucha mayor frecuencia que los demás encargados de reclamaciones. Pasó a ser crecientemente irresponsable y su despido era inevitable. ¿Y sus abusos sexuales?

Pellrod y Great Benefit tienen que ser cautelosos en ese aspecto, porque dicho tema se discutirá en otro momento ante otro tribunal. Lo que se diga aquí queda registrado y puede utilizarse en el futuro. Por consiguiente, en lugar de presentarla como a una cualquiera que se acostaba con todo el mundo, Drummond opta acertadamente por no insistir en el tema.

—Realmente no sé nada al respecto —responde Pellrod, y se anota un pequeño punto con el jurado.

Pierden un poco más de tiempo y llegan casi a las doce, antes de que Drummond me ceda el testigo. Kipler quiere levantar la sesión para almorzar, pero lo convenzo de que seré muy rápido. Accede con reticencia.

Empiezo por entregarle a Pellrod una copia de la carta que firmó y le mandó a Dot Black. Fue la cuarta carta de denegación y se basaba en que la leucemia de Donny Ray era una condición preexistente. Le ordeno que la lea al jurado y admita que es suya. Le permito que intente explicar por qué la mandó, pero evidentemente no tiene explicación. La carta era un asunto privado entre Pellrod y Dot Black, sin ninguna intención de que la vieran otras personas, ni mucho menos leerla en la sala.

Habla de un formulario rellenado erróneamente por Jackie y de una confusión con el señor Krokit. En fin, que todo fue un error. Y lo lamenta muchísimo.

—Es un poco tarde para lamentarlo, ¿no le parece? —pregunto.

—Supongo.

—Cuando mandó su carta, ¿sabía que habría otras cuatro cartas de denegación?

—No.

—De modo que la suya pretendía ser la última carta de denegación a la señora Black, ¿no es cierto?

La carta en cuestión contiene las palabras «denegación definitiva».

—Supongo que sí.

432

—¿Cuál fue la causa de la muerte de Donny Ray Black?

—Leucemia —responde encogiéndose de hombros.

—¿Y qué condición médica provocó la presentación de esta demanda?

—Leucemia.

—En su carta, ¿a qué condición preexistente hace referencia?

—La gripe.

—¿Y cuándo tuvo la gripe?

—No estoy seguro.

—Puedo traer la ficha, si desea repasarla conmigo.

—No es necesario. Creo que tenía quince o dieciséis años —responde.

—De modo que tuvo la gripe a los quince o dieciséis años, antes de extender la póliza, y no lo mencionó en la solicitud.

—Exactamente.

—Dígame, señor Pellrod, con su vasta experiencia en reclamaciones, ¿ha conocido usted algún caso en el que una gripe estuviera de algún modo relacionada con la aparición de leucemia aguda al cabo de cinco años?

Hay sólo una respuesta, pero no puede dármela.

—Creo que no.

—¿Significa eso que no?

—Eso es, no.

—¿De modo que la gripe no tuvo nada que ver con la leucemia?

—No.

—Entonces usted mintió en su carta, ¿no es cierto?

Claro que mintió en su carta, y mentirá ahora si afirma que no mintió entonces. El jurado lo comprenderá. Está atrapado, pero Drummond ha tenido tiempo de prepararlo.

—La carta fue un error —responde Pellrod.

—¿Un error o una mentira?

—Un error.

—¿Un error que contribuyó a la muerte de Donny Ray Black?

—¡Protesto! —exclama Drummond desde su asiento.

Kipler reflexiona unos instantes. Esperaba la protesta y creo que será admitida. Pero el parecer de su señoría es otro.

—No se admite la protesta. Conteste la pregunta.

—Deseo agregar otra protesta en cuanto a esta forma de interrogar —exclama Drummond furioso.

—Me doy por enterado. Le ruego que responda, señor Pellrod.

—Fue un error, es todo lo que puedo decir.

—¿No una mentira?

—No.

—¿Qué me dice de su testimonio ante este jurado? ¿Está lleno de mentiras o de errores?

—Ni lo uno ni lo otro.

Vuelvo la cabeza y señalo a Dot Black antes de dirigirme de nuevo al testigo.

—Señor Pellrod, como encargado decano de reclamaciones, ¿puede usted mirar directamente a los ojos de la señora Black y decirle que la reclamación de su hijo fue tramitada correctamente por su departamento? ¿Es usted capaz de hacerlo?

Entorna los párpados, mueve la cara, frunce el entrecejo y mira a Drummond en busca de apoyo.

—Creo que no puede obligarme a hacerlo —responde después de aclararse la garganta, fingiéndose ofendido.

—Gracias. Eso es todo.

Termino en menos de cinco minutos y la defensa está desconcertada. Calculaban que pasaría el resto del día con Reisky, y mañana con Pellrod. Pero no quiero perder el tiempo con esos mequetrefes. Quiero dirigirme al jurado.

Kipler decreta un descanso de dos horas para comer. Llamo a Leo a un lado y le entrego una lista de seis testigos adicionales.

—¿Qué diablos es eso? —pregunta.

—Seis médicos, todos de aquí, todos oncólogos, todos dispuestos a declarar en la sala si su curandero sube al estrado.

Walter Kord está furioso con la estrategia de Drummond, de presentar los trasplantes de médula como algo experimental. Ha presionado a sus socios y amigos, y están todos dispuestos a declarar.

—No es un curandero.

—Usted sabe perfectamente que no es más que un curandero. Un chiflado de Nueva York o algún país extranjero. Aquí tengo a seis muchachos de la región. Llámelo al estrado. Será divertido.

—Estos testigos no están en la orden preliminar. Es una sorpresa injusta.

—Son testigos de refutación. Vaya a protestar al juez.

Lo dejo junto al estrado, con mi lista en la mano.

Después del almuerzo, pero antes de que Kipler ordene que se haga silencio en la sala, charlo cerca de mi mesa con el doctor Walter Kord y dos de sus socios. Sentado solo en primera fila, tras la mesa de la defensa, está el doctor Milton Jiffy, el curandero de Drummond. Cuando los abogados se preparan para la sesión de la tarde, llamo a Drummond y le presento a los socios de Kord. Es un momento difícil. Drummond está enojado por su presencia en la sala. Se sientan los tres en primera fila, detrás de mi mesa. Los cinco muchachos de Trent & Brent no pueden evitar mirarlos fijamente.

Entra el jurado y Drummond llama a Jack Underhall al estrado. Se le toma juramento, ocupa su asiento y sonríe como un idiota al jurado. Han estado observándolo durante tres días y no comprendo cómo Drummond puede esperar que alguien le crea.

El propósito de su testimonio pasa a ser perfectamente evidente. Todo está relacionado con Jackie Lemancyzk. Mintió en lo referente a los diez mil dólares al contado, en cuanto a la firma de un acuerdo, porque no existe dicho acuerdo, en cuanto a la estratagema para denegar reclamaciones, en lo referente al sexo con sus superiores, e incluso en cuanto a la denegación de la compañía de pagar sus gastos médicos. Underhall empieza en un tono ligeramente compasivo, pero no tarda en ponerse duro y vengativo. Es imposible decir cosas tan horribles con una sonrisa en los labios, pero está particularmente ansioso por denigrarla.

Es una maniobra audaz y arriesgada. El hecho de que ese maleante acuse a alguien de mentir no deja de ser paradójico. Han decidido que este juicio es mucho más importante que cualquier acción jurídica subsecuente por parte de Jackie. Aparentemente, Drummond está dispuesto a arriesgar su enajenación completa del jurado, con la esperanza de generar suficientes dudas como para enturbiar las aguas. Probablemente considera que no tiene mucho que perder, con un malicioso ataque contra una joven que no está presente y no puede defenderse.

Underhall nos comunica que la conducta laboral de Jackie era atroz. Se emborrachaba y se llevaba muy mal con sus compañeros de trabajo. Algo había que hacer. Le ofrecieron la oportunidad de dimitir, para no estropear sus perspectivas laborales. No tuvo nada que ver con el hecho de que estuviera a punto de declarar, ni nada en absoluto con la reclamación de los Black.

Su testimonio es extraordinariamente breve. Confían en que suba y baje del estrado sin causar demasiado daño. No es mucho lo que puedo hacer, a excepción de esperar que al jurado le repugne tanto como a mí. Es abogado y no quiero discutir con él.

—Señor Underhall, ¿tiene su compañía fichas del personal empleado en la misma? —pregunto amablemente.

—Sí.

—¿Tienen una ficha de Jackie Lemancyzk?

—Sí.

—¿La tiene aquí?

—No, señor.

—¿Dónde está?

—En nuestras oficinas, supongo.

—¿En Cleveland?

—Sí. En nuestras oficinas.

—¿De modo que no podemos verla?

—No la tengo, ¿comprende? Nadie me ha pedido que la trajera.

—¿Incluye evaluación laboral y cosas por el estilo?

—Sí.

—Si un empleado recibe una amonestación, degradación o traslado, ¿figura en su ficha personal?

—Sí.

—¿Aparece alguna de dichas anotaciones en la ficha de Jackie?

—Eso creo.

—¿Contiene su ficha una copia de su carta de dimisión?

—Sí.

—Pero tendremos que confiar en su palabra en cuanto al contenido de dicha ficha, ¿no es cierto?

—Nadie me ha pedido que la trajera, señor Baylor.

Consulto mis notas y me aclaro la garganta.

—Señor Underhall, ¿tiene usted una copia del acuerdo que Jackie firmó cuando usted le dio el dinero y ella prometió no hablar?

—Parece que usted no oye muy bien.

—¿Cómo dice?

—Acabo de declarar que no hay tal acuerdo.

—¿Quiere decir que no existe?

—Nunca ha existido. Jackie Lemancyzk miente —afirma categóricamente.

Finjo sorprenderme, me dirijo lentamente a mi mesa, que está cubierta de papeles. Encuentro el que busco, lo examino atentamente ante la mirada de todo el mundo y me acerco de nuevo al testigo. Underhall yergue la espalda y mira desesperadamente a Drummond, que en este momento mira fijamente el papel que yo tengo en la mano. ¡Están pensando en las secciones «u»! ¡Baylor nos la ha vuelto a jugar! Ha encontrado los documentos escondidos y nos ha sorprendido mintiendo.

—Pero Jackie Lemancyzk fue muy específica cuando le contó al jurado lo que le habían obligado a firmar. ¿Recuerda usted su declaración? —pregunto mientras agito ligeramente el papel que llevo en la mano.

—Sí, oí su testimonio —responde en un tono ligeramente más agudo y la voz un poco forzada.

—Dijo que usted le había entregado diez mil dólares al contado y obligado a firmar un acuerdo. ¿Lo recuerda? —pregunto sin dejar de mirar mi papel, como si estuviera leyendo.

Jackie me comentó que la cantidad se mencionaba en el primer párrafo del documento.

—Lo oí —responde mirando a Drummond.

Underhall sabe que no tengo una copia del acuerdo, porque ha ocultado el original en algún lugar. Pero no puede estar seguro. A veces ocurren cosas inusuales. ¿Cómo diablos encontré las secciones «u»?

No puede admitir que existe el acuerdo. Pero tampoco puede negarlo. Si lo niega y de pronto le muestro una copia, el daño causado será incalculable hasta que el jurado pronuncie su veredicto. Se mueve, se contorsiona y se seca el sudor de la frente.

—¿Y usted no tiene una copia del acuerdo para mostrársela al jurado? —pregunto, sin dejar de agitar el papel que llevo en la mano.

—No. No existe tal acuerdo.

—¿Está usted seguro? —pregunto mientras acaricio el borde del documento.

—Completamente seguro.

Le miro fijamente unos segundos, encantado de verlo sufrir. A ningún miembro del jurado se le ha ocurrido dormirse. Están a la espera del hachazo, de que muestre el acuerdo y verle empequeñecerse.

Pero no puedo. Arrugo el inútil papel que tengo en la mano y lo arrojo sobre mi mesa.

—He terminado —declaro.

Underhall respira hondo. Acaba de evitarse un infarto. Baja del estrado y abandona la sala.

Drummond solicita un recésit de cinco minutos. Kipler decide que el jurado merece un descanso más prolongado y nos concede un cuarto de hora.

La estrategia de la defensa de prolongar las declaraciones, con la esperanza de confundir al jurado, claramente no funciona. Los miembros del jurado se han reído de Reisky y se han dormido con Pellrod. Underhall ha sido un desastre casi fatal, por el terrible miedo de Drummond a que yo tuviera la copia de un documento, que su cliente le había asegurado que no existía.

Drummond está harto. Se arriesgará con una buena argumentación en las conclusiones finales, que es algo que puede controlar. Declara después del recésit que la defensa ha terminado.

El juicio ya casi ha acabado. Kipler programa los discursos de clausura para el viernes a las nueve de la mañana. Les promete a los miembros del jurado que el caso estará en sus manos a las once.

CUARENTA Y OCHO

El jurado ha abandonado la sala hace bastante rato, Drummond y su equipo han regresado apresuradamente a su bufete, para analizar una vez más lo que ha fallado, pero nosotros permanecemos sentados alrededor de la mesa de la acusación y hablamos de mañana. Cooper Jackson y los dos abogados de Raleigh, Hurley y Grunfeld, procuran no excederse con consejos no solicitados, pero me gusta oír sus opiniones. Todos saben que es mi primer juicio y les parece asombroso lo que he logrado. Estoy cansado, todavía bastante nervioso y muy realista en cuanto a lo sucedido. He dispuesto de un conjunto de hechos maravillosos, un acusado corrupto pero rico, un juez increíblemente comprensivo y una situación afortunada tras otra durante el juicio. Sin olvidar al estupendo jurado, aunque todavía no se ha pronunciado.

De ahora en adelante, según ellos, mis casos sólo pueden ser peores. Están convencidos de que el veredicto será de siete cifras. Hacía doce años que Jackson ejercía cuando consiguió su primer veredicto de un millón de dólares.

Me cuentan batallitas con el propósito de levantarme los ánimos. Es una forma agradable de pasar la tarde. Deck y yo trabajaremos toda la noche, pero de momento disfruto de la compañía de espíritus gemelos, cuyo ferviente deseo es el de que crucifique a Great Benefit.

Jackson está ligeramente decepcionado por las noticias que ha recibido de Florida. Un abogado de aquel estado se ha precipitado y esta mañana ha presentado cuatro demandas contra Great Benefit. Contaban con que se uniera a su juicio colectivo, pero evidentemente se ha dejado dominar por la codicia. Hasta el momento, disponen entre los tres de diecinueve demandas contra Great Benefit y se proponen presentarlas a principios de la semana próxima.

Procuran alentarme. Quieren invitarnos a una suculenta

cena, pero tenemos que trabajar. Lo último que necesito esta noche es una copiosa cena, con vino y copas.

Cenamos por fin en el despacho, con bocadillos y refrescos. Obligo a Deck a sentarse en una silla de mi despacho y ensayo mis conclusiones ante el jurado. He memorizado tantas versiones que emergen mezcladas. Utilizo una pequeña pizarra y escribo nítidamente las cifras esenciales. Suplico ecuanimidad y, al mismo tiempo, pido una cantidad descabellada de dinero. Deck me interrumpe con frecuencia y discutimos como colegiales.

Ninguno de nosotros ha pronunciado un discurso ante un jurado, pero él ha escuchado más que yo y eso le convierte en el experto. Hay momentos en los que me siento invencible, verdaderamente arrogante de haber llegado hasta aquí en tan buena forma. Deck lo detecta y me corta inmediatamente la cresta. Me recuerda repetidamente que todavía podemos perder o ganar el caso mañana por la mañana.

Sin embargo, la mayor parte del tiempo estoy simplemente asustado. El miedo es controlable, pero nunca me abandona. Me motiva y me incita a seguir adelante, pero me alegraré cuando desaparezca.

Apagamos las luces a eso de las diez y nos vamos a casa. Me tomo una cerveza como somnífero y surte efecto. Poco después de las once me quedo dormido, con visiones de triunfo en la mente.

Al cabo de menos de una hora suena el teléfono. Es una voz femenina desconocida, joven y muy angustiada.

—Usted no me conoce, pero soy amiga de Kelly —dice casi en un susurro.

—¿Qué ocurre? —pregunto, inmediatamente despierto.

—Kelly tiene problemas. Necesita su ayuda.

—¿Qué ha sucedido?

—Le ha dado otra paliza. Regresó borracho, como de costumbre.

—¿Cuándo? —pregunto de pie junto a mi cama, intentando encontrar el interruptor.

—Anoche. Necesita ayuda, señor Baylor.

—¿Dónde está?

—Aquí conmigo. Cuando la policía se llevó a Cliff, acudió a urgencias para que la viera un médico. Afortunadamente, no tiene nada roto. Yo fui a recogerla y está escondida aquí, en mi casa.

—¿Está muy malherida?

—Es bastante aparatoso, pero no tiene ningún hueso fracturado. Cortes y contusiones.

Me da su nombre y dirección, cuelgo y me visto apresuradamente. Es un gran complejo de pisos en los suburbios, no muy lejos del de Kelly, y entro en varias calles sin salida antes de encontrar el edificio indicado.

Robin, la amiga, entreabre la puerta sin quitar la cadena, y me obliga a identificarme claramente antes de permitir que entre en su casa. Me da las gracias por haber venido. Robin, a su vez, no es más que una niña, probablemente divorciada y trabajando por poco más del sueldo mínimo. Entro en la sala de estar, un pequeño cuarto con muebles de alquiler. Kelly está en el sofá, con una bolsa de hielo en la cabeza.

Su ojo izquierdo está completamente hinchado y su abultada piel está adquiriendo ya unos tonos azulados. Lleva un vendaje sobre la ceja, ligeramente manchado de sangre. Tiene las dos mejillas abultadas. Su labio inferior, cortado, sobresale de un modo grotesco. Lleva sólo una holgada camiseta y tiene morados en los muslos y alrededor de las rodillas.

Me agacho, le doy un beso en la frente y me siento en un taburete frente a ella. Veo una lágrima en su ojo derecho.

—Gracias por haber venido —musita, con una voz entorpecida por sus mejillas y labios lastimados.

Le doy unos suaves golpecitos en la rodilla y me acaricia el reverso de la mano.

Podría matarlo.

—Es preferible que no hable —dice Robin, después de sentarse junto a ella—. El médico dice que debe moverse lo menos posible. En esta ocasión la ha golpeado con los puños, no encontró el bate de béisbol.

—¿Qué ha ocurrido? —le pregunto a Robin, pero sin dejar de mirar a Kelly.

—Se han peleado por una tarjeta de crédito. Había que saldar las cuentas de Navidad. Ha estado bebiendo mucho. El resto ya lo conoce —cuenta someramente Robin, que parece haber vivido lo suyo y me percato de que no lleva ninguna alianza—. Se pelean, como de costumbre él gana y los vecinos llaman a la policía. Él va a la cárcel y ella al hospital. ¿Quiere una Coca-cola o algo por el estilo?

—No, gracias.

—La traje aquí anoche y esta mañana la he acompañado a un centro para mujeres maltratadas. Ha hablado con una asesora que le ha dicho lo que debía hacer y le ha dado un montón de folletos. Están ahí si quiere verlos. En resumen, debe solicitar el divorcio y salir corriendo.

—¿Te han fotografiado? —pregunto al tiempo que le acaricio la rodilla.

Kelly asiente. Las lágrimas han emergido del ojo abultado y le ruedan por ambas mejillas.

—Sí, le han tomado un montón de fotografías. Hay mucho más de lo que ve. Muéstraselo, Kelly. Es tu abogado. Debe verlo.

Con la ayuda de Robin, se levanta cuidadosamente, se vuelve de espaldas y se levanta la camiseta por encima de la cintura. No lleva nada debajo, a excepción de cardenales en sus piernas y trasero. Asciende la camiseta y veo más morados en la espalda. Desciende la camiseta y vuelve a sentarse con todo cuidado en el sofá.

—La ha azotado con un cinturón —aclara Robin—. La ha colocado sobre sus rodillas y le ha dado una soberana paliza.

—¿Tienes un pañuelo? —le pregunto a Robin mientras seco cuidadosamente las lágrimas de las mejillas de Kelly.

—Por supuesto —responde, y me entrega una caja de pañuelos de papel.

—¿Qué quieres hacer, Kelly? —pregunto.

—¿Bromea? —pregunta Robin—. Debe solicitar el divorcio, de lo contrario la matará.

—¿Es cierto? ¿Quieres solicitar el divorcio?

—Sí. Cuanto antes —asiente Kelly.

—Lo haré mañana.

Me aprieta la mano y cierra el ojo derecho.

—Lo cual nos lleva al segundo problema —dice Robin—. No puede quedarse aquí. Cliff ha salido esta mañana de la cárcel y ha empezado a llamar a las amigas de Kelly. Hoy no he acudido al trabajo, que es algo que no puedo repetir, y Cliff me ha llamado alrededor del mediodía. Le he dicho que no sabía nada. Me ha vuelto a llamar al cabo de una hora y me ha amenazado. Kelly tiene muy pocos amigos y no tardará en encontrarla. Además, comparto el piso con otra persona y no funcionaría.

—No puedo quedarme aquí —dice torpemente Kelly en voz baja.

—¿Adónde quieres ir entonces? —pregunto.

Robin ha estado pensándoselo.

—La asesora con la que hemos hablado esta mañana nos ha explicado que hay un hogar para mujeres maltratadas en la ciudad, una especie de lugar secreto, que no está oficialmente registrado en el condado ni el estado. Es como una residencia que conoce muy poca gente. Allí las mujeres están a salvo, porque sus queridos compañeros no pueden encontrarlas. El problema es que cuesta cien dólares diarios y sólo le permiten quedarse una semana. Desde luego, yo no gano esa cantidad de dinero.

—¿Es ahí donde quieres ir, Kelly? —pregunto.

Asiente dolorosamente.

—De acuerdo. Te llevaré mañana.

Robin suspira de alivio y entra en la cocina, de donde regresa con la dirección de la residencia.

—Déjame ver tus dientes —le digo a Kelly.

Abre todo lo que puede la boca, sólo lo suficiente para permitirme ver sus dientes delanteros.

—¿Nada roto? —pregunto.

Mueve la cabeza y toco el vendaje de su frente.

—¿Cuántos puntos?

—Seis.

—Esto no volverá a ocurrirte jamás, ¿comprendes? —digo después de acercarme un poco más y apretarle las manos.

—¿Me lo prometes? —susurra.

—Te lo prometo.

Robin se sienta de nuevo junto a Kelly y me entrega la tarjeta con la dirección.

—Escúcheme, señor Baylor, usted no conoce a Cliff, pero yo sí. Está loco, y es cruel y violento cuando está borracho. Le aconsejo que tenga cuidado.

—No te preocupes.

—Ahora mismo podría estar en la calle vigilando esta casa.

—No me preocupa —respondo después de ponerme de pie y darle a Kelly un beso en la frente—. Presentaré la solicitud de divorcio por la mañana y luego vendré a recogerte. En este momento tengo un juicio muy importante, pero me ocuparé de ello.

Robin me acompaña a la puerta y nos damos mutuamente las gracias. Se cierra a mi espalda y oigo el ruido de pestillos, cadenas y cerrojos.

Es casi la una de la madrugada. Hace una noche clara y muy fría. Nadie acecha en las tinieblas.

Dormir sería una broma a estas alturas, de modo que me dirijo al despacho, aparco junto a la acera, exactamente debajo de mi ventana, y entro corriendo en el edificio. No es un barrio seguro en cuanto cae la noche.

Cierro las puertas con llave a mi espalda y me instalo en mi despacho. Por muy terrible que pueda ser en otros sentidos, el divorcio es un trámite relativamente fácil de iniciar, por lo menos jurídicamente. Empiezo a mecanografiar, labor dura para mí, pero cuyo fin en este caso mitiga el esfuerzo. Estoy realmente convencido de que ayudo a salvar una vida.

Deck llega a las siete y me despierta. Poco después de las cuatro me he quedado dormido en mi silla. Me dice que parezco

cansado y macilento, y me pregunta qué ha sucedido con mi noche de reposo.

Se lo cuento y reacciona mal.

—¿Has pasado la noche preparando un maldito divorcio?
¡Debes presentar tus conclusiones en menos de dos horas!

—Tranquilízate, Deck, todo saldrá bien.

—¿A qué viene esa risita?

—Vamos a vencer, Deck. Great Benefit sufrirá una derrota.

—No, no se trata de eso. Por fin vas a conseguir la chica, de
ahí la sonrisa.

—Pamplinas. ¿Dónde está mi café?

Deck se estremece y se contorsiona. Está hecho un manojo
de nervios.

—Voy a por él —responde antes de salir de mi despacho.

La solicitud de divorcio está sobre mi mesa, lista para su presentación. Me ocuparé de que le entreguen a mi amigo Cliff la
citación en el trabajo, ya que de lo contrario puede que no sea
fácil encontrarlo. Junto al divorcio solicito también una orden
judicial que le prohíba acercarse a ella.

CUARENTA Y NUEVE

Una gran ventaja de ser novato es que se espera que esté nervioso y asustado. El jurado sabe que no soy más que un chiquillo sin experiencia. Por consiguiente, las expectativas son mínimas. No he desarrollado la pericia ni el talento necesarios para pronunciar grandes discursos.

Sería un error fingir ser algo que no soy. Tal vez cuando tenga una edad avanzada, cabello canoso y voz aterciopelada, y montones de casos a mis espaldas, tal vez entonces podré situarme ante un jurado y ofrecerles una actuación espléndida. Pero no hoy. Hoy soy sólo Rudy Baylor, un chiquillo nervioso que les pide a sus amigos del jurado que lo ayuden.

Me sitúo ante ellos, bastante tenso y nervioso, y procuro relajarme. Sé lo que diré, porque lo he dicho un centenar de veces. Pero es importante que no parezca ensayado. Empiezo por decirles que éste es un día muy importante para mis clientes, porque es su única oportunidad de obtener un compensación justa por parte de Great Benefit. No hay un mañana, una segunda oportunidad en la sala, ningún otro jurado a la espera para ayudarles. Les hablo de Dot y de todo lo que ha sufrido, y también de Donny Ray, pero sin ponerme excesivamente melodramático. Les pido a los miembros del jurado que imaginen cómo se sentirían si se estuvieran muriendo lenta y dolorosamente, sabiendo que deberían recibir un tratamiento al que tienen derecho. Mis palabras son lentas y comedidas, muy sinceras, y llegan a su destino. Hablo en un tono relajado y mirando directamente a la cara de las doce personas que están listas para cumplir su cometido.

Comento las características básicas de la póliza, sin entrar en detalles, y hablo someramente de los trasplantes de médula ósea. Señalo que la defensa no ha ofrecido ninguna prueba contraria al testimonio del doctor Kord. Este procedimiento médico está lejos de ser experimental y, con toda probabilidad, le habría salvado la vida a Donny Ray.

Mi voz se anima ligeramente al llegar a la parte entretenida. Hablo de los documentos que Great Benefit nos ha ocultado y de las mentiras que nos ha contado. Esto ha sido tan espectacular durante el juicio que sería un error insistir en ello. Lo maravilloso de un juicio de cuatro días es que las declaraciones importantes están todavía frescas en la mente del jurado. Utilizo el testimonio de Jackie Lemancyzk y los datos estadísticos de Great Benefit para escribir unas cifras en el encerado: el número de pólizas en 1991, el número de reclamaciones y, lo más importante, el número de denegaciones. Lo presento con rapidez y claridad, para que pueda entenderlo y no olvidarlo incluso un niño de diez años. El mensaje es claro e irrefutable. Los poderes anónimos que controlan Great Benefit decidieron implantar una estrategia de denegación de reclamaciones durante un período de doce meses. En palabras de Jackie, fue un experimento para comprobar cuánto dinero adicional podían ganar en un año. Fue una decisión tomada a sangre fría e inspirada exclusivamente en la avaricia, sin consideración alguna por personas como Donny Ray Black.

Al hablar de dinero muestro los informes financieros al jurado y explico que, después de estudiarlos durante cuatro meses, sigo sin comprenderlos. El sector de los seguros tiene su propio sistema de contabilidad. Pero a juzgar por las cifras de la propia compañía, disponen de un montón de dinero. Sumo en la pizarra el líquido disponible a los fondos de reserva y al superávit no distribuido, y leo la cifra de cuatrocientos setenta y cinco millones.

¿Cómo se castiga a una compañía tan adinerada? Cuando formulo esta pregunta, veo el brillo de los ojos que me observan. ¡Están impacientes!

Utilizo un ejemplo clásico, favorito de los abogados, y del que he oído una docena de versiones. Funciona porque es simple. Les cuento al jurado que no soy más que un joven abogado que lucha por sobrevivir, con dificultades para pagar sus cuentas, salido hace poco de la facultad. Supongamos que trabajo mucho, vivo austeramente, ahorro dinero y dentro de dos años tengo diez mil dólares en el banco. He hecho muchos esfuerzos para ganar ese dinero y quiero protegerlo. ¿Qué ocurre entonces si cometo alguna barbaridad, como perder por ejemplo la paciencia con alguien, darle un puñetazo en la nariz y fracturársela? Evidentemente, se me exigirá que pague los gastos sufridos por la víctima, pero también mereceré un castigo para que no se repita. Dispongo sólo de diez mil dólares. ¿Qué penalización habrá que imponerme para que me afecte? El uno por ciento serían cien dólares, puede que eso me importe o deje de importarme. No me gustaría desembolsar más de cien dólares, pero tampoco me trastornaría demasiado hacerlo. ¿Y el cinco por ciento? ¿Sería una penalización de quinientos dólares suficiente para castigarme por haberle fracturado la nariz a alguien? ¿Sufriría lo suficiente cuando extendiera el cheque? Puede que sí y puede que no. ¿Y el diez por ciento? Apuesto a que si me viera obligado a pagar mil dólares ocurrirían dos cosas. En primer lugar, estaría profundamente arrepentido. Y en segundo lugar, modificaría mi conducta.

¿Cómo se castiga a Great Benefit? Del mismo modo en que se me castigaría a mí, o al vecino de enfrente. Se consulta la cuenta bancaria, se decide de cuánto dinero dispones y se impone una penalización que duela, pero no que destruya. La lógica es la misma para una próspera corporación. No son mejores que cualquiera de nosotros.

Les digo a los miembros del jurado que son ellos quienes deben tomar una decisión. Nuestra demanda es por diez millones, pero no están en modo alguno sujetos a dicha cifra. Pueden decidir lo que les parezca justo y no soy yo quien deba sugerirles la cantidad.

Para concluir, después de darles las gracias con una sonrisa, les recuerdo que si no le paran los pies a Great Benefit, cualquiera de ellos podría ser la próxima víctima. Varios asienten y otros sonríen. Otros observan las cifras de la pizarra.

Regreso a mi mesa. Deck está en un rincón, con una sonrisa de oreja a oreja. Desde la última fila, Cooper Jackson expresa su aprobación levantando el pulgar. Me siento junto a Dot y espero ansioso a comprobar si el gran Leo F. Drummond es capaz de convertir en victoria una derrota.

Empieza con una empalagosa disculpa por su comportamiento durante el proceso de selección del jurado, teme haber empezado con el pie equivocado y suplica que confíen ahora en él. Prosiguen las disculpas cuando habla de su cliente, una de las compañías de seguros más antiguas y respetadas de Norteamérica. Pero ha cometido errores con esta reclamación. Errores graves. Aquellas horribles cartas de denegación eran terriblemente insensibles y ofensivas. Su cliente no había actuado como era debido. Pero su cliente tiene más de seis mil empleados y es difícil controlar la conducta de todos ellos, difícil revisar toda la correspondencia. No hay excusa, ni se niega la culpa. Se cometieron errores.

Desarrolla este tema unos minutos y expone con mucha destreza que la conducta de su cliente fue puramente fortuita, y ciertamente no deliberada. Elude la ficha de reclamaciones, los manuales, los documentos ocultos y las mentiras descubiertas.

Los hechos son como un campo minado para Drummond y quiere ir en otras direcciones.

Admite con toda franqueza que su cliente debió haber pagado la reclamación, el total de doscientos mil dólares que suponía. Es una admisión grave y los miembros del jurado la asimilan. Intenta suavizarlos y lo logra. Ahora llega a los daños y perjuicios. No puede por menos que estar atónito ante mi sugerencia de que el jurado considere otorgarle a Dot Black un porcentaje del capital de Great Benefit. ¡Es espantoso! ¿De qué serviría? Ha admitido que su cliente no había actuado debidamente. Los responsables de aquella injusticia habían sido expulsados. Great Benefit se había reformado.

¿Qué objetivo alcanzaría un cuantioso veredicto? Ninguno, absolutamente ninguno.

Drummond introduce con sumo tacto un argumento contra el enriquecimiento injusto. Debe ser cauteloso para no ofender a Dot, porque si lo hace ofende a los miembros del jurado. Menciona algunos detalles sobre los Black: dónde viven, desde cuándo, la casa, el barrio, etcétera. Los describe como personas corrientes, una familia de clase media con una vida sencilla pero feliz. Se muestra bastante generoso. Norman Rockwell no haría un mejor retrato. Casi veo los grandes árboles y al amable repartidor de periódicos. Su puesta en escena es magnífica y el jurado está atento. Describe cómo viven, o cómo les gustaría hacerlo.

¿Qué resolvería el jurado quitándole el dinero a Great Benefit y entregándoselo a los Black? Trastornaría su agradable equilibrio. Aportaría el caos a sus vidas. Les diferenciaría enormemente de sus vecinos y amigos. En resumen, les destrozaría la vida. Además, ¿tiene alguien derecho a la cantidad de dinero que yo, Rudy Baylor, he sugerido? Claro que no. No es justo ni permisible arrebatarle dinero a una corporación simplemente porque dispone del mismo.

Se acerca al encerado, escribe la cifra de setecientos cuarenta y seis dólares y le comunica al jurado que ésos son los ingresos mensuales de los Black. Junto a la misma escribe la cifra de doscientos mil dólares y la multiplica por el seis por ciento, para obtener la cifra de doce mil dólares. Le dice al jurado que lo que realmente se propone es doblar los ingresos mensuales de los Black. ¿No lo desearíamos todos? Es fácil. Entreguémosles a los Black la cantidad de doscientos mil dólares, que es lo que habría costado el trasplante, y si los invierten en bonos libres de impuestos al seis por ciento, obtendrán unos intereses netos de mil dólares mensuales. Great Benefit se ocupará incluso de la inversión en nombre de Dot y Buddy.

¡Menudo trato!

Tiene tanta experiencia como para lograr que funcione. El argumento es convincente y cuando observo los rostros de los miembros del jurado, me percato de que lo consideran. Estudian la pizarra. Parece un compromiso perfectamente equitativo.

Es en ese momento cuando espero que recuerden que Dot ha prometido entregar el dinero a la Sociedad Norteamericana de la Leucemia.

Drummond concluye con una apelación al sentido común y la ecuanimidad. Su voz adquiere un tono más grave y habla con mayor lentitud. Es la sinceridad personificada. Por favor, hagan lo que es justo, dice antes de sentarse.

Puesto que yo soy el acusador, tengo la última palabra. Me he reservado diez minutos de la media hora asignada para refutar sus argumentos, y me acerco al jurado con una sonrisa. Les digo que espero ser capaz de hablar algún día como el señor Drummond acaba de hacerlo. Le felicito por su pericia en la sala, es uno de los abogados más expertos del país. La amabilidad de ese joven que soy yo no tiene límites.

Sólo un par de comentarios. En primer lugar, Great Benefit reconoce ahora ser culpable y ofrece doscientos mil dólares como donativo pacificador. ¿Por qué? Porque ahora están mordiéndose las uñas y rogándole a Dios que no les impongan una sanción superior a los doscientos mil dólares. En segundo lugar, ¿reconoció el señor Drummond esos errores y ofreció ese dinero cuando se dirigió al jurado el lunes por la mañana? No, no lo hizo. Puesto que sabía entonces todo lo que sabe ahora, ¿por qué no reconoció desde el primer momento que su cliente era culpable? ¿Por qué? Porque tenían la esperanza de que ustedes no descubrieran la verdad. Y ahora que la han descubierto, ellos adoptan una actitud de humildad.

Concluyo provocando realmente al jurado.

—Si lo mejor que pueden hacer es otorgar doscientos mil dólares, no se molesten. No los queremos. Eran para una operación que nunca tendrá lugar. Si no consideran que los actos de Great Benefit merecen un castigo, quédense los doscientos mil dólares y regresemos todos a nuestras casas —digo mirando lentamente a cada uno de ellos a los ojos mientras camino frente al palco del jurado, convencido de que no me defraudarán—. Gracias —agrego, antes de regresar a mi mesa, para sentarme junto a mi cliente.

Mientras el juez Kipler les da las últimas instrucciones, me invade una intoxicante sensación de alivio. Me relajo como no lo había hecho hasta ahora. Ya no hay más testigos, documentos, peticiones ni informes, han concluido las vistas y las fechas límite, y han acabado las preocupaciones por uno u otro miembro del jurado. Respiro hondo y me hundo en mi butaca. Podría pasarme varios días durmiendo.

Esa tranquilidad dura unos cinco minutos, hasta que se retira el jurado para deliberar. Son casi las diez y media.

Empieza la espera.

Deck y yo subimos al segundo piso del juzgado y presentamos la petición de divorcio de los Riker antes de dirigirnos al despacho de Kipler. El juez me felicita por mi buena actuación y yo le doy las gracias por enésima vez. Pero hay algo más que me preocupa y le muestro la petición de divorcio. Le hablo someramente de Kelly Riker, de las palizas de su marido demente, y le solicito una orden judicial urgente que le prohíba al señor Riker acercarse a la señora Riker. Kipler detesta los divorcios, pero he logrado despertar su interés. Lo que le pido es bastante común en casos de disputas domésticas. Confía en mí y firma la orden. No se sabe nada del jurado. Hace quince minutos que se han retirado.

Butch se reúne con nosotros en el vestíbulo para recoger una copia de la petición de divorcio, la orden que acaba de firmar Kipler y la citación. Está de acuerdo en entregárselos a Cliff Riker en su lugar de trabajo. Le pido una vez más que procure hacerlo sin ponerlo en ridículo.

Esperamos una hora en la sala, Drummond y su equipo agrupados en una esquina. Deck, Cooper Jackson, Hurley, Grunfeld y yo en otra. Me divierte comprobar que los ejecutivos de Great Benefit se mantienen alejados de sus abogados, o puede que sea a la inversa. Underhall, Aldy y Lufkin están sentados en la última fila, con aspecto lúgubre. Esperan al pelotón de ejecución.

A las doce se manda el almuerzo a la sala del jurado y Kipler nos ordena regresar a la una y media. Con los vuelcos que me da el estómago, sería incapaz de asimilar la comida. Llamo a Kelly por el teléfono de mi coche mientras cruzo velozmente la ciudad en dirección a la casa de Robin. Kelly está sola. Lleva un holgado pantalón prestado y zapatillas. No tiene ropa consigo, ni artículos de baño. Camina con dificultad y le duele todo el cuerpo. La ayudo a llegar a mi coche, abro la puerta y la instalo en el asiento. Aprieta los dientes, pero no se queja. Los cardenales de su cara y cuello son mucho más oscuros a la luz del sol.

Cuando nos alejamos del bloque de pisos, me percato de que mira a su alrededor, como si temiera que Cliff apareciera entre los matorrales.

—Acabamos de presentar esto —digo al tiempo que le entrego una copia de la petición de divorcio.

Levanta el documento y lo lee mientras sorteamos el tráfico.

—¿Cuándo se lo entregaréis a él? —pregunta.

—Estará a punto de recibirlo.

—Se pondrá como un loco.

—Está loco.

—Irá a por ti.

—Eso espero. Pero no lo hará. Los hombres que maltratan a sus esposas no son más que unos cobardes. No te preocupes. Tengo una pistola.

La casa es vieja, sin ningún distintivo y no se diferencia de las demás. El jardín frontal es largo, ancho y está lleno de árboles. Los vecinos tendrían que esforzarse para llegar a ver algún movimiento. Paro al final del camino de la casa y aparco. Dejo a Kelly en el coche y llamo a una puerta lateral. Una voz por un intercomunicador me pide que me identifique. La seguridad aquí es primordial. Todas las ventanas tienen los cristales ahumados. El jardín trasero está rodeado de una valla de madera de por lo menos dos metros y medio de altura.

Se entreabre la puerta y una robusta joven me observa. No pretendo discutir. Después de cinco días en la sala no estoy de ánimo para el diálogo.

—Busco a Betty Norvelle —digo.

—Soy yo. ¿Dónde está Kelly?

Muevo la cabeza en dirección al coche.

—Tráigala.

Podría llevarla fácilmente en brazos, pero le duele tanto el reverso de sus piernas que le resulta más fácil andar. Avanzamos lentamente por la acera y entramos en la casa. Parece que acompañe a una anciana de noventa años. Betty le sonríe y nos acompaña a una pequeña sala, una especie de despacho, donde nos sentamos frente a una mesa. He hablado con ella esta mañana y quiere los papeles del divorcio. Los repasa rápidamente. Kelly y yo nos cogemos de la mano.

—¿De modo que usted es su abogado? —pregunta Betty después de percatarse de nuestra intimidad.

—Sí. Y amigo.

—¿Cuándo tienes que ver de nuevo al médico?

—Dentro de una semana —responde Kelly.

—¿De modo que de momento no necesitas atención médica?

—No.

—¿Tomas algún medicamento?

—Sólo analgésicos.

Los documentos parecen en orden. Extiendo un cheque por doscientos dólares: cien de depósito más la tarifa del primer día.

—No somos un organismo registrado —aclara Betty—. Esto es un hogar para mujeres maltratadas, cuyas vidas corren peligro. Es propiedad de una persona privada, una mujer maltratada, y hay varias como ésta en la zona. Nadie sabe que estamos aquí. Nadie sabe lo que hacemos. Y queremos que siga así. ¿Están ambos dispuestos a guardar el secreto?

—Por supuesto —asentimos simultáneamente y Betty nos ofrece un formulario para que lo firmemos.

—¿No será ilegal? —pregunta Kelly.

La pregunta es comprensible, dado lo siniestro del entorno.

—No exactamente. Lo peor que puede ocurrir es que nos clausuren el centro. Entonces nos trasladaríamos simplemente a otro lugar. Hace cuatro años que estamos aquí y nadie ha protestado. ¿Son conscientes de que siete días es el período máximo de estancia?

Lo sabíamos.

—Deben empezar a organizar su próximo paso.

Me encantaría que fuera mi casa, pero todavía no hemos hablado de ello.

—¿Cuántas mujeres hay aquí? —pregunto.

—Hoy cinco. Kelly, tú tendrás una habitación privada con baño. La comida no está mal. Puedes comer en tu habitación o con las demás. No disponemos de servicios médicos ni jurídicos. No ofrecemos terapia ni asesoramiento. Lo único que ofrecemos es amor y protección. Aquí estás a salvo. Nadie te encontrará. Y tenemos un guardia armado que circula por aquí.

—¿Puede venir a verme? —pregunta Kelly al tiempo que mueve la cabeza en dirección a mí.

—Sólo permitimos una visita, que debe ser autorizada previamente. Llame cuando quiera venir y asegúrese de que no le siguen. Lamento no poder permitir que pase la noche aquí.

—No tiene importancia —respondo.

—¿Desea saber algo más? De lo contrario, debo mostrarle a Kelly la casa. Puede venir a verla esta noche si lo desea.

Sé captar una indirecta. Me despido de Kelly y prometo visitarla esta noche. Me pide que le traiga una pizza. Después de todo, es viernes por la noche.

Cuando me alejo tengo la impresión de haberla introducido en los bajos fondos.

Un periodista de la prensa de Cleveland se me acerca en el vestíbulo del juzgado con la intención de hablar de Great Benefit. ¿Sabía que el fiscal general de Ohio, según los rumores, está investigando la compañía? No respondo. Me sigue hasta la sala. Deck está solo en la mesa de la acusación. Kipler brilla por su ausencia. Todo el mundo espera.

Butch le ha entregado los documentos a Cliff Riker cuando salía a almorzar. Riker ha intentado discutir con él, pero Butch no se ha dejado amilanar, le ha respondido que no le importaba resolverlo con los puños y Riker se ha retirado inmediatamente. Mi nombre figura en la citación, por tanto, de ahora en adelante, tendré que ser precavido.

Llega más gente a la sala, cuando son casi las dos. Aparece Booker y se sienta con nosotros. Cooper Jackson, Hurley y Grunfeld regresan de su almuerzo. Han tomado varias copas. El periodista se sienta en la última fila. Nadie quiere hablar con él.

Hay muchas teorías sobre las deliberaciones del jurado. Se supone que un veredicto rápido es favorable a la acusación en un caso como éste. El hecho de que la deliberación se prolongue significa que no hay acuerdo entre los miembros del jurado. Escucho esas especulaciones infundadas y no puedo estarme quieto. Salgo a tomar un vaso de agua, a continuación voy al retrete y luego al bar. Prefiero caminar a estar sentado en la sala. Tengo un nudo terrible en el estómago y me late violentamente el corazón.

Booker me conoce mejor que nadie y me acompaña. También está nervioso. Deambulamos sin rumbo fijo por los pasillos de mármol, sólo para matar el tiempo. Y esperar. En tiempos difíciles es importante estar con amigos. Le doy las gracias por haber venido. Responde que no se lo habría perdido por nada en el mundo.

A las tres y media estoy convencido de que he perdido. Tenía que haber sido una decisión sumamente fácil, una simple cuestión de elegir un porcentaje y calcular el resultado. Puede que haya confiado excesivamente en mí mismo. Recuerdo un caso tras otro de veredictos miserables en este condado. Estoy a punto de convertirme en una estadística, un ejemplo más de por qué a un abogado de Memphis le conviene aceptar una oferta razonable. El tiempo transcurre con una lentitud pasmosa.

Alguien me llama desde algún lugar lejano. Es Deck, está en la puerta de la sala y agita los brazos desesperadamente.

—Dios mío —exclamo.

—Tranquilízate —dice Booker, y al instante echamos a correr hacia la sala.

Respiro hondo, rezo una rápida oración y entro en la sala. Drummond y sus cuatro secuaces están sentados a su mesa. Dot está sola en la nuestra. Todo el mundo ocupa sus lugares. El jurado entra en la sala cuando me acerco para sentarme junto a mi cliente. Sus rostros no revelan nada. Cuando están todos sentados, su señoría les pregunta:

—¿Ha alcanzado el jurado un veredicto?

—Sí, su señoría —responde Ben Charnes, el joven negro licenciado encargado del jurado.

—¿Está escrito en un papel de acuerdo con mis instrucciones?

—Sí, señor.

—Le ruego que se levante y lo lea.

Charnes se pone de pie lentamente. Tiene un papel en las manos que tiembla visiblemente. No tanto como mis manos. Respiro con cierta dificultad. Me siento tan mareado que tengo la sensación de que voy a desmayarme. Dot, sin embargo, está muy serena. Ya ha ganado la batalla contra Great Benefit. Han reconocido en la sala que eran culpables. Ya no le importa nada de lo que pueda suceder.

Estoy decidido a permanecer impasible, sin manifestar mis emociones, sea cual fuere el veredicto. Lo hago tal como me han enseñado. Hago garabatos en un cuaderno. Una fugaz ojeada a mi izquierda confirma que los cinco abogados de la defensa emplean la misma táctica.

—Nosotros, los miembros del jurado —lee Charnes después de aclararse la garganta—, fallamos a favor del demandante y concedemos los doscientos mil dólares de gastos. —Hace una pausa, con todas las miradas fijas en el papel—. Además, nosotros, los miembros del jurado —agrega después de aclararse de nuevo la garganta—, fallamos a favor del demandante en lo referente a daños y perjuicios y otorgamos la cantidad de cincuenta millones de dólares.

Se oye un suspiro a mi espalda y una tensión inmediata en la mesa de la defensa. Por lo demás, todo permanece tranquilo durante unos segundos. Cae la bomba, estalla y después de un breve compás de espera, cuando todo el mundo ha comprobado que está sano y salvo, se respira de nuevo.

Escribo la cifra en mi cuaderno, aunque mis garabatos son ilegibles. Me niego a sonreír, aunque para ello debo morderme fuertemente el labio inferior. Son muchas las cosas que deseo hacer. Me gustaría subirme a la mesa y dar volteretas, me acercaría al palco del jurado y les besaría los pies, iría hasta la mesa de la defensa y les restregaría el éxito por las narices, y saltaría al estrado y le daría un abrazo a Tyrone Kipler.

Pero conservo la compostura y me limito a susurrarle a mi cliente:

—Enhorabuena.

Dot no responde.

Miro al estrado y veo a su señoría inspeccionando el veredicto escrito que el secretario le acaba de entregar. La mayoría de los miembros del jurado están mirándome. En ese momento es imposible no sonreír. Asiento para darles silenciosamente las gracias.

Dibujo una cruz en mi cuaderno y bajo la misma escribo el nombre de Donny Ray Black. Cierro los ojos y evoco mi imagen predilecta de él, lo veo en la silla plegable junto al campo de béisbol, comiendo palomitas de maíz y sonriendo simplemente por estar ahí. Se me forma un nudo en la garganta y se me humedecen los ojos. No tenía por qué haber muerto.

—El veredicto parece correcto —anuncia su señoría.

Yo diría que sumamente correcto. Se dirige al jurado para agradecerles el servicio prestado, les dice que la semana próxima recibirán sus míseros cheques, les pide que no hablen del caso con nadie y les concede permiso para retirarse. Bajo las direcciones del alguacil, abandonan por última vez la sala. Nunca volveremos a vernos. En estos momentos me gustaría poder regalarles un millón a cada uno.

Kipler también se esfuerza para mantener el rostro impasible.

—Hablaremos de peticiones posteriores al juicio dentro de una semana aproximadamente. Mi secretaria se pondrá en contacto con ustedes. ¿Algo más?

Me limito a mover la cabeza. ¿Qué más podría pedir?

—Nada, su señoría —responde Leo sin levantarse de su silla.

Su equipo está de pronto atareado guardando documentos en maletines y llenando cajas con informes. Están impacientes por retirarse. Es sobradamente el mayor veredicto de la historia de Tennessee y quedarán para siempre marcados como los muchachos que lo encajaron. Si no estuviera tan cansado y aturdido, tal vez me acercaría a ellos para tenderles la mano. Sería lo elegante, pero simplemente no me apetece. Es mucho más fácil seguir aquí, sentado junto a Dot y contemplar el nombre de Donny Ray en mi cuaderno.

No soy exactamente rico. La apelación tardará un año, tal vez dos, y el veredicto es tan importante que provocará un virulento ataque. De modo que tengo mucho trabajo en perspectiva.

Pero ahora estoy harto de trabajar. Quiero subirme a un avión y encontrar una playa.

Kipler da unos golpes con su martillo y este juicio ha concluido oficialmente. Miro a Dot y veo lágrimas. Le pregunto cómo se siente. Deck se nos acerca inmediatamente para felicitarnos. Está pálido, pero sonriente, con sus cuatro impecables dientes relucientes. Estoy pendiente de Dot. Es una mujer fuerte que se resiste a llorar, pero está perdiendo lentamente el control. Le acaricio el brazo y le entrego un pañuelo.

Booker me da un apretón en la nuca y dice que me llamará la semana próxima. Cooper Jackson, Hurley y Grunfeld se acercan a nuestra mesa, con grandes sonrisas y rebosantes de cumplidos. Tienen que coger un avión. Hablaremos el lunes. El periodista se me acerca, pero le indico con la mano que me deje tranquilo. Les presto escasa atención, porque me preocupa mi cliente, que está deshaciéndose en llanto, cada vez más desconsolada.

Tampoco presto atención a Drummond y sus muchachos, que se dirigen a la puerta cargados como mulas. No intercambiamos una sola palabra. Ahora me gustaría ser una mosca en la pared de Trent & Brent.

La relatora, el alguacil y la secretaria recogen sus bártulos y se retiran. Sólo quedamos Dot, Deck y yo en la sala. Tengo que hablar con Kipler y darle las gracias por llevarme de la mano y lograr que eso fuera posible. Lo haré luego. Ahora sostengo la mano de Dot mientras descarga un torrente de lágrimas. Deck está junto a nosotros sin decir nada. Yo tampoco hablo. Mis ojos están húmedos y me duele el corazón. A ella no le importa en absoluto el dinero. Sólo quiere que le devuelvan a su hijo.

Alguien, probablemente el alguacil, pulsa un interruptor en el pequeño pasillo, cerca de la sala del jurado, y se apagan las luces. La sala está semioscura. Ninguno de nosotros se mueve. Cede el llanto. Se seca las mejillas con un pañuelo y a veces con los dedos.

—Lo siento —digo con la voz ronca.

Ahora quiere marcharse, de modo que decidimos retirarnos. Le acaricio el brazo, y Deck se encarga de guardar nuestros papeles en tres maletines.

Salimos de la oscura sala al vestíbulo de mármol. Son casi las cinco del viernes por la tarde y hay poca actividad. No hay cámaras, periodistas ni muchedumbre alguna para captar unas palabras y unas imágenes del abogado del momento.

A decir verdad, pasamos completamente desapercibidos.

CINCUENTA

El último lugar al que me apetece ir es el despacho. Estoy demasiado cansado y aturdido para celebrarlo en un bar y, además, mi único compañero en este momento es Deck, que es abstemio. Por otra parte, con un par de copas entraría en coma, de modo que no me tientan. Deberíamos haber organizado una gran fiesta en algún lugar, pero esas cosas son difíciles de preparar con antelación cuando dependen de la decisión de un jurado.

Tal vez mañana. Estoy seguro de que habré superado el trauma y tendré una reacción tardía al veredicto. Para entonces se habrá impuesto la realidad. Mañana lo celebraré.

Me despido de Deck en la puerta del juzgado, le digo que estoy agotado y le prometo que nos veremos más tarde. Todavía estamos los dos aturdidos y necesitamos tiempo a solas para reflexionar. Me dirijo a casa de la señorita Birdie y llevo a cabo mi inspección cotidiana de todas las habitaciones de la casa. Es un día como otro cualquiera, no tiene nada de especial. Me siento en el jardín, contemplo mi pequeño piso y, por primera vez, empiezo a gastar dinero. ¿Cuánto tiempo transcurrirá, antes de que adquiera o construya mi propia casa? ¿Qué coche nuevo me compraré? Procuro alejar estos pensamientos de mi cabeza, pero no lo logro. ¿Qué hace alguien con dieciséis millones y medio de dólares? Ni siquiera soy capaz de comprenderlo. Sé que puede haber todavía un sinfín de problemas: puede anularse el veredicto y ordenar un nuevo juicio, podría invertirse el veredicto y dejarme sin blanca, la cantidad por daños y perjuicios podría reducirse enormemente en el tribunal de apelación, o ser anulada por completo. Sé que esas terribles cosas pueden suceder, pero de momento el dinero es mío.

Sueño mientras se pone el sol. La atmósfera está clara, pero muy fría. Tal vez mañana empiece a asimilar la magnitud de lo que he hecho. De momento me reconforta la idea de haber liberado de mi alma una enorme cantidad de veneno. Durante casi un año me ha atormentado el odio por esa entidad mística que es Great Benefit Life. He detestado a los que trabajan en la misma, a las personas que provocaron una secuencia de sucesos que acabaron con la vida de una víctima inocente. Espero que Donny Ray descanse en paz. Sin duda, algún ángel le comunicará lo sucedido hoy.

Se les ha puesto en evidencia y se ha demostrado que eran culpables. He dejado de odiarles.

Kelly corta pequeños trozos de pizza con el tenedor y da minúsculos mordiscos. Todavía tiene los labios hinchados y le duelen las mejillas y la mandíbula. Estamos sentados en su cama individual, de espaldas a la pared, con las piernas estiradas y la caja de la pizza entre los dos. Miramos una película de John Wayne en la pantalla de dieciocho pulgadas de un Sony colocado sobre la cómoda, a poca distancia al otro lado de la pequeña habitación.

Lleva el mismo pantalón gris, sin calcetines ni zapatos, y veo una pequeña cicatriz en su tobillo derecho, el que le fracturó el verano pasado. Se ha lavado el cabello y recogido en una cola de caballo. Se ha pintado las uñas rojo claro. Intenta estar alegre y charlar, pero le duele todo el cuerpo y es difícil pasárselo bien. Hablamos poco. Nunca he recibido una fuerte paliza y es difícil imaginar sus efectos secundarios. Los dolores físicos son bastante fáciles de comprender. El horror mental no lo es. Me pregunto en qué momento decidió parar, detenerse y admirar su obra.

Procuro no pensar en ello. No hemos hablado de ello, ni tengo intención alguna de sacarlo a relucir. Cliff no ha dado señales de vida desde que recibió los papeles.

Ha conocido a otra mujer aquí en el hogar, como prefieren llamarlo, una madre madura de tres adolescentes, tan asustada y traumatizada que tiene dificultad en pronunciar una oración completa. Está en la habitación contigua. El lugar es sumamente silencioso. Kelly ha salido sólo una vez de su habitación, para sentarse en el jardín trasero a tomar el fresco. Ha intentado leer, pero es difícil. Su ojo izquierdo sigue casi completamente cerrado y el derecho a veces empañado. El médico dijo que el daño no era permanente.

Ha llorado varias veces y le he prometido repetidamente que ésta ha sido su última paliza. Nunca volverá a ocurrir, aunque tenga que matar a ese cabrón con mis propias manos. Y lo digo en serio. Si se acercara a ella, estoy convencido de que sería capaz de volarle la tapa de los sesos.

Me da lo mismo que me detengan, me acusen y me juzguen. Dejen mi suerte en manos de doce componentes de un jurado. Nada puede impedir mi ímpetu.

No le menciono el veredicto. Sentado aquí con ella en esta pequeña habitación semioscura, viendo cómo cabalga John Wayne, parece que la sala de Kipler esté a días y kilómetros de distancia.

Y ahí es exactamente donde quiero estar.

Terminamos la pizza y nos acercamos. Nos cogemos de la mano como unos chiquillos. Pero debo ser cauteloso, porque está literalmente magullada de pies a cabeza.

Acaba la película y comienzan las noticias de las diez. De pronto tengo curiosidad por ver si mencionan el caso Black. Después de las violaciones y asesinatos obligatorios, y del primer interludio publicitario, el presentador anuncia en un tono bastante grandilocuente:

—Hoy ha sucedido algo insólito en un juzgado de Memphis. Un jurado civil ha otorgado la inusitada cantidad de cincuenta millones de dólares en daños y perjuicios contra Great Benefit Life Insurance Company de Cleveland, Ohio. Rodney Frate nos cuenta lo sucedido.

No puedo evitar sonreírme. Vemos a continuación a Rodney Frate en directo, temblando de frío frente al juzgado del condado de Shelby, que evidentemente está desierto desde hace horas.

—Hola Arnie, hace aproximadamente una hora he hablado con Pauline MacGregor, secretaria del tribunal del circuito, y me ha confirmado que alrededor de las cuatro de esta tarde, un jurado en la división octava, que es la sala del juez Kipler, ha dictado un veredicto de doscientos mil dólares por daños sufridos y cincuenta millones en concepto punitivo. He hablado también con el juez Kipler, que no ha querido posar para la cámara, y me ha dicho que se trataba de un caso de mala fe contra Great Benefit. No ha hecho otra declaración, a excepción de que cree que la cantidad otorgada excede en mucho a cualquier otra concedida en Tennessee. He hablado con varios abogados de la ciudad y ninguno de ellos había oído hablar de un veredicto tan cuantioso. Leo F. Drummond, abogado de la defensa, se ha negado a comentar. Rudy Baylor, abogado de la acusación, era inaccesible. Te devuelvo la conexión, Arnie.

Pasan inmediatamente a hablar de un siniestro automovilístico en la interestatal cincuenta y cinco.

—¿Has ganado? —pregunta Kelly, no asombrada sino insegura.

—He ganado.

—¿Cincuenta millones de dólares?

—Sí. Pero el dinero no está todavía en el banco.

—¡Rudy!

—He tenido suerte —respondo encogiéndome de hombros, como si se tratara de un día más en la oficina.

—Pero si acabas de salir de la facultad.

¿Qué puedo decirle?

—No es tan difícil. Teníamos un buen jurado y las cosas se pusieron automáticamente en su lugar.

—Sí, claro, como si ocurriera todos los días.

—Ojalá.

Coge el control remoto y apaga el volumen del televisor.

—Tu modestia no es sincera —insiste—. Finges.

—Tienes razón. En este momento, soy el mejor abogado del mundo.

—Eso está mejor —responde con una sonrisa.

Ya estoy casi acostumbrado a su cara morada y apaleada. No presto atención a las heridas, como lo hacía en el coche esta tarde. Estoy impaciente para que transcurra una semana y recupere su hermosura.

Juro que podría matarlo.

—¿Cuánto te corresponde? —pregunta.

—Veo que vas directamente al grano.

—Siento curiosidad —responde en un tono casi infantil.

Espiritualmente ya somos amantes y es divertido coquetear y reírse.

—La tercera parte, pero tardaré mucho en recibirla.

Se inclina hacia mí y de pronto le duele hasta el punto de gemir. La ayudo a acostarse boca abajo. Hace un esfuerzo para no llorar y su cuerpo está tenso. No puede dormir de espaldas, debido a las heridas.

Le acaricio el cabello y le susurro al oído, hasta que nos interrumpe el intercomunicador desde la planta baja. Es Betty Norvelle. Ha acabado la hora de visita.

Kelly me aprieta fuertemente la mano mientras beso su morada mejilla y le prometo regresar mañana. Me suplica que no me vaya.

Las ventajas de obtener un veredicto semejante en mi primer juicio son evidentes. La única desventaja, por lo que he podido percibir en las últimas horas, es que el rumbo en adelante sólo puede ser descendente. Todos los clientes esperarán ahora la misma magia. Me preocuparé de ello más adelante.

Estoy solo en mi despacho el sábado por la mañana, a la espera de un periodista y su fotógrafo, cuando suena el teléfono.

—Soy Cliff Riker —dice una voz ronca, y pulso inmediatamente el botón de grabación del magnetófono.

—¿Qué desea?

—¿Dónde está mi mujer?

—Tiene suerte de que no esté en el depósito de cadáveres.

—Voy a ajustarle las cuentas, matón.

—Siga hablando, muchacho. Estoy grabando la conversación.

Cuelga inmediatamente y me quedo mirando el teléfono. Es un modelo barato que el bufete ha adquirido en unos grandes almacenes. Durante el juicio lo sustituíamos alguna que otra vez, cuando no queríamos que Drummond escuchara.

Llamo a Butch a su casa y le cuento mi breve charla con el señor Riker. Butch quiere ajustarle las cuentas, por la confrontación de ayer cuando le entregó los documentos. Cliff le obsequió con abundantes improperios, dirigidos incluso contra su madre. La presencia de dos de sus compañeros de trabajo en las cercanías le impidieron a Butch reaccionar inmediatamente. Anoche me dijo que si había alguna amenaza debía comunicárselo. Tiene un compañero llamado Rocky, que a veces trabaja de portero en una discoteca, y entre los dos forman una pareja aterradora. Le hago prometer que sólo asustarán al muchacho, sin maltratarlo. Butch me asegura que se acercarán a él cuando esté a solas, le dirán que son mis guardaespaldas, le hablarán de la llamada telefónica y le advertirán que si se repite lo pagará caro. Me gustaría verlo. Estoy decidido a no vivir asustado.

Ésta es la idea de Butch de pasárselo bien.

El periodista del *Memphis Press* llega a las once. Hablamos mientras un fotógrafo toma una sinfín de fotografías. Quiere saberlo todo respecto al caso y al juicio, y le lleno los oídos. Ahora es información pública. Hablo bien de Drummond, maravillosamente de Kipler y divinamente del jurado.

Me promete que será un gran artículo en el dominical.

Circulo por el despacho leyendo la correspondencia y examinando algunos mensajes telefónicos, recibidos la semana pasada. Es imposible trabajar y me percato de los pocos casos y clientes que tengo. Paso la mitad del tiempo reviviendo el juicio, y la otra mitad soñando en mi futuro con Kelly. ¿Cómo podría ser más afortunado?

Llamo a Max Leuberg y le cuento los detalles. Una tormenta de nieve azota O'Hare, y le ha impedido venir a Memphis para presenciar el juicio. Charlamos durante una hora.

Nuestra cita del sábado por la noche es muy parecida a la del viernes, a excepción de que la comida y la película son diferentes. Le encanta la comida china y he traído un montón. Vemos una comedia sentados en la misma posición de la noche anterior.

Pero es cualquier cosa menos aburrido. Empieza a alejarse de su pesadilla personal. Las heridas físicas empiezan a curarse. Su risa fluye con mayor facilidad y sus movimientos se agilizan ligeramente. Hay un poco más de toqueteo, pero no excesivo. No el suficiente.

Anhela quitarse el jersey. Se lo lavan una vez al día, pero la tiene harta. Quiere volver a ser atractiva y quiere su ropa. Hablamos de entrar a escondidas en su piso y recuperar sus pertenencias.

Todavía no mencionamos el futuro.

CINCUENTA Y UNO

Lunes por la mañana. Ahora que soy un hombre rico y de holganza, me levanto a las nueve, me pongo un pantalón deportivo y unas zapatillas, y llego a mi despacho a las diez sin corbata. Mi socio está atareado guardando los documentos del caso Black y retirando las mesas plegables que han abarrotado nuestro vestíbulo desde hace meses. Todo nos parece gracioso. Ha desaparecido la presión, hemos descansado y ha llegado el momento de saborear el triunfo. Deck va en busca de café, nos sentamos junto a mi escritorio y recordamos los momentos más emocionantes.

Deck ha recortado el artículo del *Memphis Press* de ayer, por si necesitaba otra copia. Le doy las gracias, nunca se sabe, aunque tengo una docena de ejemplares en mi piso. Estoy en primera plana de la sección metropolitana, con un largo artículo muy bien redactado sobre mi victoria, acompañado de una fotografía mía bastante grande, sentado a mi escritorio. Ayer no pude dejar de admirar la fotografía en todo el día. El periódico entra en trescientos mil hogares. Ninguna suma de dinero podría conseguirme tanta publicidad.

Recibo algunos faxes. Un par de condiscípulos me felicitan y para bromear me piden un préstamo. Una encantadora comunicación de Madeline Skinner, de la facultad. Y dos de Max Leuberg. El primero es una copia de un breve artículo en un periódico de Chicago sobre el veredicto. El segundo el de otro artículo con fecha de ayer, en un periódico de Cleveland. Describe detalladamente el juicio y luego habla de los crecientes problemas de Great Benefit. Por lo menos siete estados investigan ahora la compañía, incluido el de Ohio. Multitud de asegurados presentan demandas a lo largo y ancho del país, y se espera que muchos más lo hagan. Se cree que el veredicto de Memphis iniciará una marea de acciones judiciales.

Estupendo. Nos deleitamos en el infortunio que hemos generado. Nos reímos al recordar a M. Wilfred Keeley consultando de nuevo los informes financieros y procurando encontrar más dinero. ¡Aquí está, en algún lugar!

Llega el repartidor de la floristería con un hermoso ramo de flores, que nos mandan para felicitarnos Booker Kane y sus compañeros del bufete de Marvin Shankle.

Esperaba que los teléfonos no dejaran de sonar, con nuevos clientes en busca de una sólida representación jurídica. Todavía no ha ocurrido. Deck dice que se han recibido un par de llamadas antes de las diez, una de las cuales se había equivocado de número. No estoy preocupado.

Kipler llama a las once y utilizo el nuevo teléfono, por si Drummond está escuchando. Me cuenta una interesante historia, en la que puede que yo esté involucrado. Antes de que se iniciara el juicio, el lunes pasado, le dije a Drummond en el despacho del juez que aceptaría un millón doscientos mil para saldar el caso. Drummond lo rechazó y se celebró el juicio. Evidentemente, no se lo comunicó a su cliente, que ahora asegura que habría pensado seriamente en pagar lo que yo pedía. Si la compañía lo hubiese aceptado o no en aquel momento no se sabe, pero retrospectivamente, un millón doscientos mil es mucho más fácil de digerir que cincuenta millones doscientos mil. En todo caso, la compañía ahora alega que habría pagado dicha suma y que su abogado, el gran Leo F. Drummond, cometió un lastimoso error cuando olvidó o se negó a comunicarles mi oferta.

Underhall, el abogado de la compañía, se ha pasado la mañana hablando por teléfono con Drummond y con Kipler. La compañía, furiosa, humillada y dolorida, busca evidentemente a alguien que pague el pato. Al principio, Drummond negó que hubiera sucedido, pero Kipler le delató. Y ahí es donde yo intervengo. Puede que necesiten de mí una declaración jurada de los hechos como yo los recuerdo. Con mucho gusto, he respondido. La prepararé inmediatamente.

Great Benefit ha despedido ya a Drummond y Trent & Brent, y la situación podría empeorar muchísimo. Underhall ha mencionado la presentación de una demanda por representación inadecuada contra el bufete. Las consecuencias serían devastadoras. Como todos los bufetes, Trent & Brent tiene un seguro que cubre la representación inadecuada, pero de responsabilidad limitada. Una póliza de cincuenta millones de dólares es inaudita. Un error de cincuenta millones de dólares por parte de Leo Drummond dejaría al bufete en una situación financiera sumamente precaria.

No puedo evitar reírme. Después de colgar le cuento la conversación a Deck. La idea de un pleito contra Trent & Brent por parte de una compañía de seguros es para troncharse de risa.

La próxima llamada es de Cooper Jackson. Él y sus amigos han presentado la demanda esta mañana, en el tribunal federal de Charlotte. Representan a más de veinte asegurados que fueron víctimas de alguna estafa por parte de Great Benefit en 1991, el año de la estratagema. Cuando me parezca conveniente, le gustaría pasar por mi bufete y estudiar mi ficha. En cualquier momento, le respondo, en cualquier momento.

Deck y yo almorzamos en Moe's, un viejo restaurante situado en el centro de la ciudad, cerca del juzgado, y frecuentado por abogados y personas por el estilo. Recibo unas cuantas miradas, un apretón de manos y una palmada en la espalda de un antiguo condiscípulo de la facultad. Debería comer aquí más a menudo.

La misión está prevista para esta noche, lunes, porque la tierra está seca y la temperatura es de unos cinco grados. ¿Qué clase de locos juegan al béisbol en invierno? Kelly no responde. Es evidente con qué clase de loco tratamos. Está segura de que jugarán esta noche, porque es muy importante para ellos. Han sufrido durante dos semanas sin partidos, ni fiestas de cerveza a continuación para presumir de sus hazañas. Cliff no se perdería el partido por nada del mundo.

Empieza a las siete y, para asegurarnos, nos acercamos al campo. PFX Freight está efectivamente allí. Nos alejamos velozmente. Nunca he hecho nada parecido y estoy bastante nervioso. A decir verdad, los dos estamos asustados. Hablamos poco. Cuanto más nos acercamos al piso, más de prisa conduzco. Tengo un revólver del treinta y ocho debajo del asiento y no pienso separarme de él.

En el supuesto de que no haya cambiado las cerraduras, creo que podemos entrar y salir en menos de diez minutos. Kelly quiere recoger la mayor parte de su ropa y algunas pertenencias. Diez minutos a lo sumo, le digo, porque puede que algún vecino nos vea y se le ocurra llamar a Cliff y, bueno, quién sabe.

Recibió sus heridas hace cinco noches y el dolor en gran parte ya ha desaparecido. Puede andar sin molestias. Dice que está bastante fuerte para recoger la ropa y moverse con rapidez. Los dos tendremos que cooperar.

El complejo de pisos está a quince minutos del campo de béisbol. Consiste en media docena de edificios de tres plantas, dispersos alrededor de una piscina y dos pistas de tenis. Sesenta y ocho unidades, según el cartel. Afortunadamente, su antiguo piso está en la planta baja. No puedo aparcar cerca de la puerta, de modo que decidimos entrar primero en el piso y reunir sigilosamente sus pertenencias, luego acercaré el coche sobre el césped, lo arrojaremos todo sobre el asiento trasero y desapareceremos a toda velocidad.

Aparco el coche y respiro hondo.

—¿Tienes miedo? —me pregunta.

—Sí —respondo al tiempo que cojo el revólver de debajo del asiento.

—Tranquilo, está en el campo de béisbol. No se lo perdería por nada del mundo.

—Si tú lo dices. Adelante.

Avanzamos por la oscuridad hasta su piso sin ver a nadie. Sus llaves entran en la cerradura, abre la puerta y entramos. Hay una luz encendida en la cocina y otra en el vestíbulo, que proporcionan suficiente luz. Hay dos sillas en la sala de estar cubiertas de ropa. Las mesillas y el suelo están cubiertos de latas de cerveza vacías y bolsas de patatas fritas. Cliff, como soltero, es bastante desaseado. Kelly para momentáneamente y mira a su alrededor.

—Lo siento —dice.

—Date prisa, Kelly —respondo.

Dejo el revólver sobre una pequeña barra, que separa la cocina de la sala de estar. Vamos al dormitorio, donde enciendo una pequeña lámpara. No se ha hecho la cama desde hace días. Más latas de cerveza y una caja de pizza. Un *Playboy*. Señala los cajones de una pequeña cómoda barata.

—Ésas son mis cosas —susurra.

Levanto las fundas de almohada y empiezo a llenarlas de ropa interior, calcetines y pijamas. Kelly está sacando ropa del armario. Llevo un montón de vestidos y blusas a la sala de estar, los dejo sobre una silla y regreso al dormitorio.

—No puedes llevártelo todo —digo al comprobar lo lleno que está el armario.

Me entrega otro montón de ropa sin decir nada y lo llevo a la sala de estar. Trabajamos en silencio y con rapidez.

Me siento como un ladrón. Cada movimiento es demasiado ruidoso. Me late con fuerza el corazón mientras hago viajes de ida y vuelta a la sala de estar.

—Ya basta —digo por fin.

Ella lleva una funda de almohada llena de ropa y yo la sigo con varios vestidos.

—Larguémonos —exclamo, sumamente nervioso.

Se oye un ligero ruido en la puerta. Alguien intenta entrar. Nos quedamos paralizados y nos miramos. Ella se acerca a la puerta cuando de pronto se abre y la impulsa contra la pared. Cliff Riker irrumpe en la sala.

—¡Kelly! ¡Estoy en casa! —exclama al verla caerse contra una silla.

Estoy exactamente delante de él, a menos de tres metros, y lo único que puedo ver cuando avanza con rapidez es su jersey amarillo, sus ojos irritados y su arma predilecta. Estoy paralizado de terror cuando levanta el bate de aluminio y lo impulsa directamente contra mi cabeza.

—¡Hijo de puta! —exclama al tiempo que impulsa el bate con todas sus fuerzas.

A pesar del miedo que me paraliza, logro agachar la cabeza una fracción de segundo antes de que el bate me roce el cabello. Oigo su silbido al pasar. Siento su fuerza. El bate golpea una pequeña columna de madera al borde de la barra, la destroza en mil pedazos y se precipita al suelo un montón de platos sucios. Kelly da un grito. El golpe pretendía destrozarme el cráneo y, al no haberlo alcanzado, su cuerpo ha seguido girando y está de espaldas a mí. Me lanzo contra él como un loco y lo empujo sobre la silla con ropa y colgadores. Kelly vuelve a chillar a mi espalda.

—¡Coge el revólver, Kelly!

Se recupera con fuerza y rapidez y yo logro conservar el equilibrio.

—¡Voy a matarte! —exclama al tiempo que intenta golpearme de nuevo con el bate.

Eludo el golpe por los pelos. Su segundo intento ha encontrado sólo aire.

—¡Hijo de puta! —repite.

Decido que no tendrá una tercera oportunidad. Antes de que acabe de levantar el bate, le lanzo un gancho de derecha que aterriza en su mandíbula y lo aturde lo suficiente para poder darle una fuerte patada en la horcajadura. Le he dado en el punto perfecto, porque oigo y siento la explosión de sus testículos, al tiempo que emite un quejido agonizante. Baja el bate, lo agarro, doy un tirón y se lo arrebato de las manos.

Le propino un soberano golpe con el bate sobre la oreja izquierda y el ruido es casi nauseabundo. Huesos que crujen y se rompen. Cae de gatas al suelo, con la cabeza colgando momentáneamente, y luego la vuelve para mirarme y empieza a incorporarse. Mi segundo golpe empieza en el techo y desciende con toda la fuerza a mi alcance. Le ataco con todo el odio y el miedo imaginables en plena cabeza.

Cuando empiezo a levantar nuevamente el bate, Kelly me sujeta el brazo.

—¡Para, Rudy!

Paro, la miro a ella y luego a Cliff. Está boca abajo en el suelo, estremeciéndose y gimiendo. Lo observamos horrorizados cuando deja de moverse. Hay un pequeño estremecimiento e intenta decir algo, pero de su garganta sólo emerge un nauseabundo sonido gutural. Intenta mover la cabeza, que sangra abundantemente.

—Voy a matar a ese cabrón, Kelly —digo con la respiración muy alterada, todavía asustado e iracundo.

—No.

—Sí. Él nos habría matado a nosotros.

—Dame el bate —dice Kelly.

—¿Cómo?

—Dame el bate y márchate.

Me asombra lo calmada que está en este momento. Sabe exactamente lo que hay que hacer.

—¿Cómo...? —intento preguntarle viendo cómo lo mira.

Me arrebata el bate de las manos.

—Para mí no es la primera vez. Márchate. Escóndete. Tú no has estado aquí esta noche. Te llamaré más tarde.

Permanezco inmóvil contemplando los esfuerzos de ese moribundo en el suelo.

—Por favor, Rudy —dice Kelly al tiempo que me empuja suavemente hacia la puerta—. Te llamaré luego.

—De acuerdo, de acuerdo.

Entro en la cocina, recojo mi revólver y regreso a la sala de estar. Nos miramos antes de volver la mirada al suelo. Salgo a la calle, cierro sigilosamente la puerta a mi espalda y miro a mi alrededor, por si veo a algún vecino curioso. No hay nadie. Titubeo unos instantes y no oigo ruido alguno en el interior de la casa.

Siento náuseas. Me alejo en la oscuridad, de pronto empapado de sudor.

Tarda diez minutos en llegar el primer coche de policía. Llega otro casi inmediatamente. Luego una ambulancia. Estoy acurrucado en mi Volvo, en un aparcamiento abarrotado de coches, observando lo que sucede. Los enfermeros entran en la casa. Otro coche de policía. Las luces rojas y azules iluminan la noche y atraen a los curiosos. Pasan los minutos y no hay rastro de Cliff. Aparece un enfermero en la puerta y se dirige pausadamente a recoger algo de la ambulancia. No tiene prisa.

Kelly está allí sola, asustada, respondiendo a un sinfín de preguntas sobre lo sucedido, y yo estoy aquí, convertido de pronto en el señor Gallina, oculto tras el volante con la esperanza de que nadie me vea. ¿Por qué la he dejado sola? Me siento mareado, se me turba la visión y me ciegan las luces azules y rojas.

No puede estar muerto. Tal vez malherido, pero no muerto.

Creo que volveré a la casa.

Se me pasa el susto y el miedo se apodera de mí. Quiero que saquen a Cliff en una camilla y se lo lleven a toda prisa al hospital para curarlo. De pronto quiero que viva. Puedo tratar con él si sigue vivo, aunque esté loco. Vamos, Cliff. Vamos, muchacho. Levántate y anda.

No puedo haberlo matado.

Crece la muchedumbre y un policía obliga a la gente a retroceder.

Pierdo la noción del tiempo. Llega una furgoneta del forense y eso excita los rumores de la muchedumbre. Cliff no viajará en la ambulancia. Cliff será trasladado al depósito de cadáveres.

Abro ligeramente la puerta y vomito tan discretamente como puedo, junto al coche. Nadie me oye. Luego me seco la boca y me acerco a la muchedumbre.

—Por fin la ha matado —oigo que dice alguien.

Los policías entran y salen de la casa. Estoy a treinta metros, perdido en un mar de rostros. La policía coloca una cinta amarilla alrededor del edificio. Desde la calle se ve repetidamente el resplandor del flash de la cámara dentro de la casa.

Esperamos. Necesito verla, aunque no hay nada que yo pueda hacer. Circula otro rumor entre la muchedumbre y en esta ocasión es cierto. Él está muerto. Y creen que ella lo ha matado. Escucho atentamente lo que dicen, porque si alguien ha visto salir a un desconocido de la casa, después de oír gritos y gemidos, quiero saberlo. Circulo despacio entre la gente, prestando atención a lo que dicen. No oigo nada. Me retiro unos segundos y vomito de nuevo tras unos matorrales.

Hay mucha actividad junto a la puerta y salen los enfermeros con una camilla. El cuerpo está en una bolsa plateada. Lo llevan cuidadosamente por la acera hasta la furgoneta del forense y se lo llevan. Al cabo de unos minutos aparece Kelly con un policía a cada lado. Parece diminuta y asustada. Afortunadamente no va esposada. Ha logrado cambiarse de ropa y ahora lleva unos vaqueros y un anorak.

La instalan en el asiento trasero de un coche patrulla y se retiran. Regreso inmediatamente a mi coche y me dirijo a la comisaría.

Le comunico al sargento de guardia que soy abogado, que acaban de detener a mi cliente y que insisto en estar presente cuando la interroguen. Lo digo con la suficiente autoridad y él hace una llamada a quién sabe dónde. Aparece otro sargento, que me acompaña al segundo piso, donde Kelly está sola en una sala de interrogatorio. Un detective de la brigada de homicidios llamado Smotherton la observa por una ventana unidireccional. Le entrego una de mis tarjetas. Se niega a darme la mano.

—¿Cómo se las arreglan para ir tan de prisa? —pregunta con profundo desdén.

—Me ha avisado inmediatamente, después de llamar al cero noventa y uno. ¿Qué han descubierto?

Ambos la observamos. Está al final de una larga mesa, frotándose los ojos con un pañuelo.

Smotherton refunfuña mientras piensa cuánto debe revelarme.

—Hemos encontrado a su marido muerto en el suelo de la sala de estar, con el cráneo fracturado, aparentemente de un golpe con un bate de béisbol. Ella no ha dicho gran cosa, sólo que iban a divorciarse, había entrado a escondidas en la casa para recoger su ropa, él la ha sorprendido y se han peleado. Él estaba muy borracho, de algún modo le ha arrebatado el bate y ahora está en el depósito de cadáveres. ¿Se ocupa usted del divorcio?

—Sí. Le facilitaré una copia. La semana pasada el juez le ordenó mantenerse alejado de ella. Hace años que le daba palizas.

—Hemos visto las contusiones. Sólo quiero formularle algunas preguntas, ¿de acuerdo?

—Por supuesto.

Entramos juntos en la sala. Kelly se sorprende de verme, pero conserva la serenidad. Nos saludamos educadamente como abogado y cliente. Aparece otro detective de paisano, el agente Hamlet, que trae un magnetófono. No tengo ningún inconveniente en que lo utilicen. Cuando lo ponen en funcionamiento, tomo la iniciativa.

—Para que conste, soy Rudy Baylor, abogado de Kelly Riker. Hoy es lunes, 15 de febrero de 1993. Estamos en la comisaría de policía, en el centro de la ciudad de Memphis. Estoy presente porque he recibido una llamada de mi cliente, aproximadamente a las siete cuarenta y cinco de esta tarde. Acababa de llamar al cero noventa y uno y me ha dicho que le parecía que su marido estaba muerto.

Muevo la cabeza en dirección a Smotherton, como para indicarle que puede proseguir, y me mira como si quisiera estrangularme. Los policías odian a los abogados defensores y en este momento no me importa en absoluto.

Smotherton empieza con un montón de preguntas sobre Kelly y Cliff, cosas básicas como fechas de nacimiento, boda, empleo, hijos, etcétera. Kelly responde pacientemente, con desinterés en la mirada. Ha desaparecido la hinchazón de su cara, pero su ojo izquierdo está todavía negro y azulado. Lleva un vendaje sobre la ceja. Está muerta de miedo.

Describe los malos tratos con todo detalle, lo que provoca que se nos pongan a los tres los pelos de punta. Smotherton manda a Hamlet en busca de los antecedentes de Cliff: tres detenciones por malos tratos. Habla de abusos de los que no quedó constancia ni documento alguno. Cuenta que le rompió el tobillo con un bate, también le dio puñetazos en algunas ocasiones, cuando no quería romperle ningún hueso.

Habla de la última paliza, de la decisión de abandonarle y ocultarse, y solicitar el divorcio. Lo que cuenta es perfectamente creíble, porque es verdad. Son las mentiras que vendrán a continuación las que me preocupan.

—¿Por qué ha ido esta tarde a su casa? —pregunta Smotherton.

—Para recoger mi ropa. Estaba segura de que no lo encontraría.

—¿Dónde ha estado estos últimos días?

—En un refugio para mujeres maltratadas.

—¿Cómo se llama?

—Prefiero no decírselo.

—¿Está en Memphis?

—Sí.

—¿Cómo llegó hasta su casa esta tarde?

Me da un vuelco el corazón al oír la pregunta, pero ya ha pensado en ello.

—En mi coche —responde.

—¿Qué clase de coche es?

—Un Volkswagen Rabbit.

—¿Dónde está ahora?

—En el aparcamiento, frente a mi casa.

—¿Podemos inspeccionarlo?

—No hasta que lo haga yo —interrumpo, al recordar de pronto que estoy aquí como abogado y no como conspirador.

Smotherton mueve la cabeza y me mira como si fuera a matarme.

—¿Cómo entró en su piso?

—He utilizado mi llave.

—¿Qué ha hecho cuando ha entrado?

—Me he dirigido al dormitorio y he empezado a recoger mi ropa. He llenado tres o cuatro fundas de almohada con mis pertenencias y trasladado un montón de cosas a la sala de estar.

—¿Cuánto hacía que estaba en casa cuando ha llegado el señor Riker?

—Unos diez minutos.

—¿Qué ha ocurrido entonces?

—No tiene por qué responder a esta pregunta —interrumpo—, hasta que haya hablado conmigo y yo haya podido investigar el caso. Por ahora, este interrogatorio ha concluido.

Extiendo el brazo y pulso el botón del magnetófono. Smotherton se tranquiliza mientras consulta sus notas. Hamlet regresa con la transcripción de la grabación y la estudian juntos. Kelly y yo no nos prestamos atención alguna, pero nos tocamos los pies por debajo de la mesa.

Smotherton escribe algo en un papel y me lo entrega: «Este caso se tratará como homicidio, pero pasará al departamento de abusos domésticos de la fiscalía. El nombre de la encargada es Morgan Wilson. Ella se ocupará de todo en adelante.»

—¿Pero van a encerrarla?

—No tengo otra alternativa. No puedo dejarla en libertad.

—¿De qué se la acusa?

—Homicidio involuntario.

—Puede soltarla bajo mi responsabilidad.

—No puedo —responde enojado—. ¿Qué clase de abogado es usted?

—Entonces suéltela bajo su propia palabra.

—Imposible —responde con una sonrisa de frustración a Hamlet—. Tenemos un cadáver. La fianza debe decretarla un juez. Si usted convence a su señoría de que la suelte bajo su propia palabra, estará libre. Yo soy un humilde detective.

—¿Voy a la cárcel? —pregunta Kelly.

—No tengo otra alternativa, señora —dice Smotherton, de pronto mucho más amable—. Si su abogado es competente, estará libre mañana mismo. A condición, claro está, de que pueda pagar la fianza. Pero yo no puedo soltarla aunque lo desee.

Estrecho el brazo sobre la mesa y le cojo la mano.

—No te preocupes, Kelly. Te sacaré mañana, lo antes posible.

Asiente, aprieta los dientes y procura ser fuerte.

—¿Pueden colocarla en una celda a solas? —le pregunto a Smotherton.

—Oiga, mequetrefe, no soy yo quien dirige los calabozos, ¿vale? Si sabe hacerlo mejor que ellos, hable con los celadores. Les encantan los abogados.

472

No me provoques, amigo. Hoy ya le he roto el cráneo a alguien. Nos miramos con odio.

—Gracias —digo.

—No hay de qué —responde, al tiempo que él y Hamlet apartan las sillas de un empujón y salen de la sala—. Tiene cinco minutos —agrega por encima del hombro antes de dar un portazo.

—No te muevas, ¿de acuerdo? —susurro—. Te observan a través de esa ventana. Y aquí probablemente hay micrófonos. De modo que ten cuidado con lo que dices.

No dice nada. Yo sigo con mi papel de abogado.

—Lamento lo sucedido.

—¿Qué significa homicidio involuntario?

—Puede significar muchas cosas, pero básicamente que se ha cometido un asesinato sin intención de hacerlo.

—¿A cuánto tiempo podrían sentenciarme?

—Primero deben condenarte, y eso no sucederá.

—¿Me lo prometes?

—Te lo prometo. ¿Estás asustada?

Se frota suavemente los ojos y reflexiona un buen rato.

—Tiene muchos parientes y todos son como él, borrachos y violentos. Me dan mucho miedo.

No sé qué responder. Yo también tengo miedo de ellos.

—¿Pueden obligarme a asistir al funeral?

—No.

—Me alegro.

Vienen a por ella al cabo de unos minutos y en esta ocasión utilizan esposas. Veo cómo se la llevan a lo largo del pasillo. Se detienen frente a un ascensor y Kelly vuelve la cabeza para verme. La saludo con la mano y desaparece.

CINCUENTA Y DOS

En todo asesinato se cometen veinticinco errores. Quien recuerda diez es un genio. Por lo menos eso fue lo que oí en una ocasión en una película. No ha sido exactamente un asesinato, sino un acto de defensa propia. No obstante, van apareciendo errores.

Camino alrededor de mi escritorio, que está cubierto de montones de papeles cuidadosamente ordenados. He hecho un diagrama del piso, el cuerpo, la ropa, el revólver, el bate, las latas de cerveza y todo lo que recuerdo. He dibujado la posición de mi coche, el de Kelly y el de Cliff en el aparcamiento. He escrito un montón de páginas con todos los detalles de lo sucedido aquella noche. Creo que pasé menos de quince minutos en el piso, pero escrito parece una pequeña novela. ¿Cuántos gritos o gemidos pudieron oírse desde el exterior? Cuatro a lo sumo, creo. ¿Cuántos vecinos vieron a un desconocido abandonar la casa después de los gritos? Quién sabe.

Eso, a mi parecer, fue el primer error. No debí haberme marchado tan pronto. Debí haber esperado unos diez minutos, para comprobar si alguien había oído algo, antes de escabullirme en la oscuridad de la noche.

O tal vez debí haber llamado a la policía y contarles la verdad. Kelly y yo teníamos perfecto derecho a estar en la casa. Es evidente que estaba al acecho en algún lugar cercano cuando se le suponía en otro lugar. Yo estaba en mi perfecto derecho a defenderme, desarmarlo y golpearle con su propia arma. Dada la violencia de su personalidad y sus antecedentes, ningún jurado del mundo me condenaría. Además, el único testigo presencial estaría completamente de mi parte.

¿Entonces por qué no me quedé en la casa? Por una parte, ella me empujaba hacia la puerta, y ésa parecía la mejor forma de actuar. ¿Quién puede pensar racionalmente cuando, en quince segundos, uno pasa de ser brutalmente atacado a convertirse en asesino?

El error número dos fue mentir acerca de su coche. Circulé por el aparcamiento cuando salí de la comisaría y encontré el Volkswagen Rabbit de Kelly y el cuatro por cuatro de Cliff. Esta mentira funcionará, siempre y cuando nadie le cuente a la policía que su coche no se había movido desde hacía varios días.

¿Pero y si Cliff y algún amigo habían inmovilizado su coche cuando Kelly estaba en el hogar, y el amigo aparece dentro de unas horas y se lo cuenta a la policía? Se me desboca la imaginación.

El peor error que he recordado en las últimas cuatro horas ha sido el de la mentira acerca de la llamada telefónica, que Kelly supuestamente realizó después de llamar al cero noventa y uno. Eso fue mi pretexto para estar tan pronto en la comisaría. Es una mentira estúpida, y si la policía decide comprobar las llamadas me veré en un grave aprieto.

Aparecen otros errores conforme avanza la noche. Afortunadamente, la mayoría son producto de una mente asustada, y la mayoría desaparecen después de un cuidadoso análisis y de haber tomado suficientes notas.

Dejo que Deck duerma hasta las cinco antes de despertarle. Al cabo de una hora está en el despacho con café. Le cuento mi versión de lo sucedido y su respuesta inicial es maravillosa.

—Ningún jurado del mundo la condenará —dice sin la menor duda.

—El juicio es una cosa —digo yo—. Sacarla de la cárcel, otra.

Formulamos un plan. Necesito documentos: informes de detenciones, fichas judiciales, informes médicos y una copia de su primera petición de divorcio. Deck está impaciente por reunir todo lo necesario. A las siete sale a por más café y para comprar un periódico.

La noticia aparece en la página tercera de la sección metropolitana, en tres breves párrafos sin ninguna fotografía del fallecido. Ocurrió demasiado tarde para elaborar un buen artículo. Esposa detenida por la muerte del marido dice el titular, pero en Memphis ocurren tres casos parecidos todos los meses. Si no lo buscara, no lo habría visto.

Llamo a Butch y le obligo a resucitar. Se acuesta tarde. Vive solo después de tres divorcios y le gusta cerrar los bares. Le cuento que su amigo Cliff Riker ha encontrado una muerte prematura y eso parece estimularlo. Llega al despacho poco después de las ocho y le explico que quiero que inspeccione la zona y averigüe si alguien ha visto u oído algo, y si la policía hace lo mismo. Butch me interrumpe. Él es el investigador, sabe lo que hay que hacer.

Llamo a Booker a su despacho y le explico que una cliente

para la que tramito el divorcio anoche mató a su marido, pero es una chica realmente encantadora y quiero sacarla de la cárcel. Necesito su ayuda. El hermano de Marvin Shankle es juez de un tribunal penal y quiero que la ponga en libertad bajo su propia palabra, o con una fianza muy baja.

—¿Has pasado de un veredicto de cincuenta millones a un asqueroso divorcio? —pregunta Booker bromeando.

Logro soltar una carcajada. Si lo supiera...

Marvin Shankle ha salido de la ciudad, pero Booker me promete empezar a hacer llamadas. Salgo de mi despacho a las ocho y media y me dirijo velozmente al centro de la ciudad. A lo largo de la noche, he procurado no pensar en Kelly en una celda de la cárcel.

Entro en el palacio de Justicia del condado de Shelby y voy directamente hacia el despacho de Lonnie Shankle. Al llegar me entero de que el juez Shankle, al igual que su hermano, ha salido de la ciudad y no volverá hasta esta tarde. Hago algunas llamadas e intento localizar la ficha de Kelly. No es más que una entre varias docenas de personas detenidas anoche y estoy seguro de que su ficha está todavía en la policía.

Me reúno con Deck a las nueve y media en el vestíbulo. Lleva consigo los informes de las detenciones. Le mando a la comisaría de policía en busca de la ficha de Kelly.

Las oficinas del fiscal del distrito del condado de Shelby están en el tercer piso, y consta de cinco secciones con más de setenta fiscales. En abusos domésticos hay sólo dos, Morgan Wilson y otra mujer. Afortunadamente, Morgan Wilson está en su despacho, sólo es cuestión de entrar. Coqueteo con la recepcionista durante media hora y, asombrosamente, funciona.

Morgan Wilson es una mujer asombrosa de unos cuarenta años, que me recibe con un fuerte apretón de manos y una sonrisa que sugiere: «Dese prisa, estoy muy ocupada.» Su despacho está abarrotado de sumarios, pero muy ordenado. Me canso sólo de ver todo el trabajo que hay que hacer. Nos sentamos y de pronto me reconoce.

—¿El individuo de los cincuenta millones de dólares? —pregunta ahora con una sonrisa mucho más amable.

—Ése soy yo —respondo encogiéndome de hombros, como si se tratara de algo perfectamente común.

—Le felicito —dice claramente impresionada.

El precio de la fama. Sospecho que, como todos los demás abogados, está calculando el treinta por ciento de cincuenta millones.

Ella gana cuarenta mil anuales a lo sumo y, naturalmente, quiere hablar de mi buena suerte. Le hago un breve resumen del juicio y de mi sensación cuando oí el veredicto. Me apresuro y le cuento el motivo de mi visita.

Me escucha atentamente y toma muchas notas. Le entrego copias de la petición actual de divorcio, del anterior y los informes de las tres detenciones de Cliff por malos tratos a su esposa. Le prometo facilitarle los informes médicos de Kelly por la tarde. Describo algunas de las heridas producidas durante las peores palizas.

Casi todos los sumarios a mi alrededor son de hombres que han maltratado a sus esposas, hijos o novias, de modo que es fácil pronosticar de qué lado está Morgan.

—Pobre chica —dice, refiriéndose evidentemente a Kelly—. ¿Cuánto mide? —pregunta.

—Metro sesenta aproximadamente, y debe de pesar unos cincuenta kilos.

—¿Cómo se las arregló para golpearle hasta acabar con su vida? —pregunta con asombro, sin el menor indicio acusatorio.

—Estaba asustada y él borracho. De algún modo logró hacerse con el bate.

—Estupendo —exclama.

Se me ponen los pelos de punta hasta en los muslos. ¡Esto es un fiscal como Dios manda!

—Me encantaría sacarla de la cárcel —digo.

—Necesito revisar la ficha. Llamaré al secretario de fianzas y le diré que no tenemos ningún inconveniente en que se fije una fianza muy baja. ¿Dónde vive?

—Está en un hogar, uno de esos refugios anónimos.

—Los conozco bien. Son muy útiles.

—Allí está a salvo, pero ahora esa pobre chica está en la cárcel, todavía cubierta de cardenales de la última paliza.

—Es mi vida —responde Morgan, con un ademán para mostrarme los sumarios a nuestro alrededor.

Acordamos vernos por la mañana a las nueve.

Deck, Butch y yo nos reunimos en el despacho para comer un bocadillo y planear nuestros próximos pasos. Butch ha llamado a todas las puertas de todos los pisos cercanos al de los Riker y sólo ha encontrado una persona que tal vez oyera un ruido. Vive exactamente encima y dudo que me viera salir de la casa. Sospecho que lo que oyó fue cómo se desintegraba la columna cuando el bateador falló en su primer intento. La policía no ha hablado con ella. Butch ha estado tres horas en el complejo y no ha visto ningún indicio de actividad policial. El piso está cerrado y precintado, y parece llamar la atención de los curiosos. En un momento dado, dos corpulentos jóvenes que parecían parientes de Cliff se han reunido con un grupo de compañeros del trabajo y se han quedado detrás del cordón policial contemplado la puerta y prometiendo vengarse. Una pandilla de indeseables, según Butch.

Ha hablado también con un agente de fianzas amigo suyo, que nos hará el favor de extender el cheque de la fianza por sólo el cinco por ciento, en lugar del habitual diez por ciento. Eso nos ahorrará un poco de dinero.

Deck ha pasado casi toda la mañana en la comisaría de policía para obtener los informes de las detenciones y la ficha de Kelly. Se lleva bien con Smotherton, sobre todo porque Deck le ha asegurado que odia a los abogados. Ahora se ha convertido en investigador, lejos de un seudoabogado. Curiosamente, Smotherton le ha comunicado que a partir de media mañana se habían recibido amenazas de muerte contra Kelly.

Decido ir a la cárcel para ver cómo está. Deck se ocupará de encontrar al juez adecuado para que le concedan la libertad bajo fianza. Butch estará listo con su agente de fianzas. Cuando nos disponemos a abandonar el despacho, suena el teléfono. Deck lo contesta y me lo pasa.

Es Peter Corsa, el abogado de Jackie Lemancyzk, en Cleveland. La última vez que hablé con él fue de la declaración de Jackie y le di las gracias. Me dijo que dentro de pocos días presentaría su propia demanda.

Corsa me felicita por el veredicto y me comunica que ha sido una noticia sensacional en su ciudad, en el periódico dominical. La fama aumenta. Entonces me dice que algo raro ocurre en Great Benefit. El FBI, junto con el fiscal general de Ohio y el departamento estatal de seguros, ha registrado la oficina central esta mañana y ha empezado a retirar documentos. A excepción de los analistas informáticos de contabilidad, han mandado al resto del personal a sus casas y les han dicho que no regresen en dos días. Según un reciente artículo en los periódicos, Pinn-Conn, de la que Great Benefit es subsidiaria, ha dejado de pagar algunos bonos y despedido a muchos empleados.

No puedo decir gran cosa. Hace dieciocho horas que he matado a un hombre y es difícil concentrarse en otra cosa. Charlamos. Le doy las gracias y promete mantenerme informado.

Tardan una hora en encontrar a Kelly en aquel laberinto y traerla a la sala de visitas. Estamos uno a cada lado de una pantalla de cristal y nos hablamos por teléfono. Me dice que parezco cansado. Le respondo que tiene muy buen aspecto. Está en una celda sola, a salvo, pero hay mucho ruido y no puede dormir. Lo que quiere es salir. Le digo que estoy haciendo todo lo que puedo y le hablo de mi entrevista con Morgan Wilson. Le explico cómo funciona el sistema de fianza. No menciono las amenazas.

Tenemos mucho de que hablar, pero no aquí.

Después de despedirnos, cuando abandono la sala de visitas, una celadora uniformada me llama por mi nombre. Me pregunta si soy el abogado de Kelly Riker y me entrega una copia informatizada.

—Es nuestro registro telefónico —dice—. Hemos recibido cuatro llamadas relacionadas con esa chica en las dos últimas horas.

Soy incapaz de interpretar el papel que me ha mostrado.

—¿Qué clase de llamadas?

—Amenazas de muerte. Se trata de unos locos.

El juez Lonnie Shankle llega a su despacho a las tres y media, y Deck y yo estamos esperándolo. Tiene un sinfín de cosas que hacer, pero Booker ha llamado y conquistado a su secretaria para prepararnos el terreno. Le entrego al juez un montón de documentos, le resumo el caso en cinco minutos y acabo por suplicarle una fianza mínima porque yo, el abogado, tendré que pagarla. Shankle fija la fianza en diez mil dólares. Le damos las gracias y nos retiramos.

Al cabo de treinta minutos estamos todos en la cárcel. Estoy seguro de que Butch lleva una pistola en la sobaquera y sospecho que el agente de fianzas, un individuo llamado Rick, va también armado. Estamos listos para lo que se presente.

Le extiendo a Rick un cheque de quinientos dólares por la fianza y firmo todos los papeles necesarios. Si los cargos contra ella no se retiran, o si Kelly no se presenta a cualquiera de sus citas en el juzgado, Rick tiene la opción de entregar los restantes nueve mil quinientos dólares, o encontrar a Kelly y llevarla a la cárcel. Lo he convencido de que se retirarán los cargos.

Tardan una eternidad en resolver el papeleo, pero por fin la vemos acercarse a nosotros, sin esposas, sólo con una sonrisa. La acompañamos rápidamente a mi coche. Les he pedido a Butch y a Deck que nos sigan unas manzanas, por seguridad.

Le cuento a Kelly lo de las amenazas. Sospechamos que son los locos de su familia y los fanáticos sureños con quienes trabajaba. Hablamos poco cuando abandonamos el centro de la ciudad y nos dirigimos velozmente hacia el refugio. Prefiero no hablar de anoche y a ella tampoco le apetece.

A las cinco de la tarde del martes, los abogados de Great Benefit solicitan protección al amparo del código de insolvencia en el tribunal federal de Cleveland. Peter Corsa llama al bufete mientras yo estoy ocultando a Kelly, y Deck recibe la llamada. Cuando regreso, a los pocos minutos, Deck está pálido como un cadáver.

Nos sentamos en mi despacho con los pies sobre la mesa durante mucho rato sin decir palabra. Silencio absoluto. Ninguna voz. Ningún teléfono. No se oye el tráfico de la calle. Hasta ahora hemos postergado la cuestión del porcentaje que le corresponde a Deck del caso, de modo que no está seguro de cuánto ha perdido. Pero ambos sabemos que hemos pasado de ser teóricamente millonarios, a casi insolventes. Nuestros sueños fantásticos de ayer parecen hoy bobadas.

Hay un vestigio de esperanza. La semana pasada, el extracto financiero de Great Benefit parecía lo suficientemente sólido como para convencer a un jurado de que les sobraban cincuenta millones de dólares. Sin duda, algo de verdad hay en ello. Recuerdo las advertencias de Max Leuberg. No se debe confiar jamás en las cifras de una compañía de seguros, porque crean sus propias normas de contabilidad.

Sin duda, en algún lugar, habrá un milloncejo para nosotros.

Yo no lo creo. Ni tampoco Deck.

Corsa ha dejado el número de teléfono de su casa y por fin acumulo las fuerzas necesarias para llamarlo. Se disculpa por las malas noticias, y me dice que en los círculos jurídicos y financieros la actividad es frenética. Es demasiado pronto para saber la verdad, pero parece que PinnConn ha sufrido algunos golpes muy importantes en el comercio de divisa extranjera. Entonces ha empezado a succionar las enormes reservas de sus subsidiarias, incluida Great Benefit. Las cosas han empeorado y PinnConn se ha limitado a coger el dinero y mandarlo a Europa. La mayor parte de los bienes de PinnConn están en manos de unos piratas norteamericanos que operan desde Singapur. Parece que todo el mundo conspire contra mí.

Está convirtiéndose rápidamente en un atroz revoltillo y puede que tarde meses en aclararse, pero el fiscal federal ha aparecido por televisión esta tarde y ha prometido acusaciones oficiales. De mucho nos va a servir.

Corsa me llamará por la mañana.

Se lo cuento a Deck y ambos comprendemos que no cabe

ninguna esperanza. Los que han robado el dinero son demasiado sofisticados para que los atrapen. Millares de asegurados con reclamaciones legítimas que ya han sido víctimas de una estafa lo serán ahora de otra. Deck y yo hemos sido víctimas de un fraude. Al igual que Dot y Buddy. Donny Ray ha sido la víctima definitiva. Drummond tampoco cobrará cuando presente su exorbitante minuta por servicios jurídicos. Se lo menciono a Deck, pero es difícil reírse.

Los empleados y agentes de Great Benefit serán víctimas del fraude. Las personas como Jackie Lemancyzk sufrirán.

Los males parecen menos graves cuando son compartidos, pero de algún modo tengo la sensación de haber perdido más que la mayoría de ellos. El hecho de que otros sufrirán no me consuela.

Pienso de nuevo en Donny Ray. Lo veo sentado bajo el árbol intentando ser fuerte durante la declaración. Él ha pagado el precio más elevado por el ladrocinio de Great Benefit.

He pasado la mayor parte de los últimos seis meses trabajando en este caso y ahora ese tiempo está perdido. El bufete ha ingresado unos mil dólares mensuales desde que empezamos, pero la recompensa del caso Black alimentaba nuestra esperanza. Los honorarios de los sumarios que tenemos no bastan para sobrevivir los dos próximos meses, y no estoy dispuesto a acosar a la gente. Deck tiene un buen siniestro automovilístico, que no se saldará hasta que el cliente se recupere, probablemente dentro de unos seis meses. En el mejor de los casos, supondrá unos veinte mil dólares.

Suena el teléfono y lo contesta Deck, escucha y lo cuelga rápidamente.

—Un individuo dice que va a matarte —dice tranquilamente.

—No es la peor llamada del día.

—En este momento no me importaría que me pegaran un tiro —dice Deck.

Ver a Kelly me levanta el ánimo. Volvemos a comer comida china en su habitación, con la puerta cerrada con llave y mi revólver bajo la chaqueta.

Nos embargan tantas emociones que compiten por nuestra atención que la conversación no es fácil. Le cuento lo de Great Benefit y le sabe mal, sólo porque me ve muy desilusionado. El dinero no significa nada para ella.

Unas veces nos reímos y otras casi lloramos. Le preocupa el mañana y el pasado mañana y lo que la policía haga o descubra. El clan Riker la aterra. Empiezan a cazar a los cinco años. Las armas son algo habitual en su vida. Le asusta la perspectiva de volver a la cárcel, aunque le prometo que no ocurrirá. Si la policía y la acusación se ponen duros, les contaré la verdad.

Menciono lo sucedido anoche y es incapaz de hablar de ello. Echa a llorar y pasamos mucho rato sin hablar.

Abro la puerta y avanzo sigilosamente por el oscuro pasillo y a través de la extensa casa, hasta encontrar a Betty Norvelle mirando sola la televisión en la sala de estar. Conoce los más mínimos detalles de lo sucedido anoche. Le cuento que Kelly está demasiado desanimada para dejarla sola en este momento. Debo quedarme con ella y dormiré en el suelo si es necesario. A pesar de la rigurosa prohibición respecto a la estancia de hombres en la casa, decide hacer una excepción en este caso.

Nos acostamos juntos en la pequeña cama, sobre las sábanas y las mantas, abrazados. Yo no dormí anoche, he hecho una pequeña siesta por la tarde, y me siento como si apenas hubiera dormido en una semana. No quiero abrazarla demasiado fuerte, porque temo hacerle daño. Me quedo dormido.

CINCUENTA Y TRES

Puede que la defunción de Great Benefit sea una gran noticia en Cleveland, pero en Memphis no le importa prácticamente a nadie. No se menciona en el periódico del miércoles. Aparece un breve artículo sobre Cliff Riker. La autopsia ha revelado que murió como consecuencia de varios golpes en la cabeza, con algún objeto contundente. Su viuda ha sido detenida y puesta en libertad. Su familia clama justicia. El funeral se celebrará mañana, en la pequeña ciudad de la que él y Kelly huyeron.

Mientras Deck y yo hojeamos el periódico, llega un fax del despacho de Peter Corsa. Es una copia de un largo artículo de primera plana de un periódico de Cleveland, donde se habla de los últimos sucesos en el escándalo de PinnConn. Por lo menos dos grandes jurados entran en acción. Se presentan cantidades extraordinarias de demandas contra la compañía y empresas subsidiarias, particularmente Great Benefit, cuya solicitud de insolvencia merece un considerable estudio aparte. La actividad es asombrosa entre los abogados.

M. Wilfred Keeley fue detenido ayer por la tarde en el aeropuerto de Nueva York, cuando esperaba para embarcar en un avión destino a Londres. Le acompañaba su esposa y aseguró que sólo iban de vacaciones. Sin embargo, no pudieron facilitar el nombre de un solo hotel en Europa donde los esperaran.

Al parecer, las compañías han sido saqueadas en los dos últimos meses. Al principio, el dinero se utilizó para cubrir malas inversiones, pero luego empezó a distribuirse por paraísos fiscales en el mundo entero. En todo caso, ha desaparecido.

La primera llamada del día procede de Leo Drummond. Me habla de Great Benefit como si no supiera nada. Charlamos brevemente y es difícil decidir quién está más deprimido. Ninguno de nosotros cobrará por la batalla que hemos librado. No comenta la pelea con su ex cliente sobre mi oferta. Claro que su anterior cliente tampoco está en condiciones de demandarlo por representación indebida. En realidad, Great Benefit ha eludido el veredicto del caso Black y, por consiguiente, tampoco puede alegar que la representación de Drummond haya sido indebida. Trent & Brent se ha ahorrado un buen quebradero de cabeza.

La segunda llamada es de Roger Rice, el nuevo abogado de la señorita Birdie. Me felicita por el veredicto. Si lo supiera... Dice que no ha dejado de pensar en mí desde que vio mi fotografía en el periódico dominical. La señorita Birdie intenta modificar su testamento y están hartos de ella en Florida. Delbert y Randolph consiguieron por fin su firma en un documento de elaboración casera, con el que acudieron a los abogados de Atlanta e insistieron en conocer los detalles de los bienes de su madre. Los abogados se negaron. Los hermanos siguieron en Atlanta un par de días. Uno de los abogados llamó a Roger Rice y la verdad salió a relucir. Delbert y Randolph le preguntaron a bocajarro si su madre poseía veinte millones de dólares. Él no pudo evitar echarse a reír y eso molestó a los muchachos. Por fin llegaron a la conclusión de que su madre les tomaba el pelo y regresaron a Florida.

El lunes por la noche, la señorita Birdie llamó a Roger Rice a su casa y le comunicó que regresaba a Memphis. Le dijo que había estado intentando llamarme, pero yo parecía estar muy ocupado. El señor Rice le habló del juicio y del veredicto de cincuenta millones de dólares, lo cual pareció complacerla enormemente.

—Estupendo —exclamó—. No está mal para un jardinero.

Pareció alegrarse muchísimo de que fuera rico.

En todo caso, Rice quiere advertirme que puede llegar en cualquier momento. Le doy las gracias.

Morgan Wilson ha estudiado a fondo la ficha de Riker y no es partidaria de proseguir con los cargos. Pero su jefe, Al Vance, está indeciso. Entro con ella en su despacho.

Vance fue elegido como fiscal del distrito hace muchos años y logra que le reelijan con mucha facilidad. Tiene unos cincuenta años y en otra época aspiró a ocupar altos cargos políticos. La oportunidad nunca se presentó y se ha contentado con su fiscalía. Tiene una cualidad inusual entre fiscales: no le gustan las cámaras.

Me felicita por mi veredicto. Le doy las gracias, pero prefiero no hablar del tema, por razones que ahora no vienen al caso. Sospecho que en menos de veinticuatro horas se conocerá en Memphis la noticia de Great Benefit y desaparecerá inmediatamente la admiración que ahora se me profesa.

—Esa gente está loca —dice al tiempo que arroja la ficha sobre la mesa—. Nos llaman incesantemente, dos veces esta misma mañana. Mi secretaria ha hablado con el padre de Riker y con uno de sus hermanos.

—¿Qué quieren? —pregunto.

—La muerte para su cliente. Que olvidemos el juicio y la sujetemos ahora mismo a la silla eléctrica. ¿Ha salido de la cárcel?

—Sí.

—¿Está escondida?

—Sí.

—Me alegro. Son tan estúpidos que no comprenden que es ilegal amenazarla. Están enfermos.

Los tres estamos de acuerdo en que los Riker son unos ignorantes y muy peligrosos.

—Morgan no quiere proseguir con los cargos —dice Vance al tiempo que Morgan asiente.

—Es muy sencillo, señor Vance —digo—. Si lo presenta ante el gran jurado, puede que tenga suerte y obtenga una acusación oficial. Pero si va a juicio, perderá. Les mostraré ese maldito bate de aluminio al jurado y traeré una docena de expertos en abusos domésticos. La convertiré en un símbolo y ustedes quedarán muy mal intentando condenarla. No conseguirá ni un voto entre los doce del jurado.

»No me importa lo que haga su familia —prosigo—, pero si le obligan a seguir adelante, lo lamentará. Le odiarán todavía más cuando el jurado la perdone y salga en libertad.

—Tiene razón, Al —dice Morgan—. No habrá forma de condenarla.

Al estaba dispuesto a arrojar la toalla antes de que entráramos en su despacho, pero necesitaba que ambos se lo confirmáramos. Accede a retirar todos los cargos. Morgan promete mandar un fax de confirmación a primera hora.

Les doy las gracias y me retiro inmediatamente. Los ánimos cambian rápidamente. Estoy solo en el ascensor y no puedo evitar sonreírme al verme reflejado en la placa de bronce de los botones. ¡Se retirarán todos los cargos! ¡Para siempre!

Voy casi corriendo por el aparcamiento hasta mi coche.

La bala se disparó desde la calle, perforó la ventana del vestíbulo, dejó un agujero de un centímetro de diámetro, atravesó también el tabique y se empotró en la pared. Deck estaba en la sala cuando oyó el disparo. La bala le pasó a tres metros de distancia. No se acercó inmediatamente a la ventana, sino que se ocultó bajo la mesa y esperó unos minutos.

A continuación cerró la puerta con llave y esperó a que llegara alguien, pero no vino nadie. Ocurrió alrededor de las diez y media, cuando yo estaba reunido con Al Vance. Al parecer nadie vio al pistolero. Nunca sabremos si alguien más oyó el disparo. El ruido ocasional de armas de fuego no es inusual en esta parte de la ciudad.

La primera llamada de Deck fue a Butch, que estaba dormido. Al cabo de veinte minutos llegó al despacho, armado hasta los dientes, y procuró tranquilizar a Deck.

Están examinando el agujero de la ventana cuando llego y Deck me cuenta lo sucedido. Estoy seguro de que Deck tiembla y se estremece incluso cuando está profundamente dormido, pero ahora realmente tiembla. Nos dice que está bien, pero le tiembla la voz. Butch dice que esperará debajo de la ventana y los sorprenderá si regresan. En su coche lleva dos escopetas y un rifle de asalto AK47. Que Dios ayude a los Riker si piensan pasar de nuevo para disparar.

No logro localizar a Booker por teléfono. Ha salido de la ciudad con Marvin Shankle para tomar declaraciones, por lo que decido escribirle una pequeña carta para comunicarle que lo llamaré más tarde.

Deck y yo nos decidimos por un almuerzo privado, lejos de grupos de admiradores y de balas perdidas. Compramos unos bocadillos y nos los comemos en la cocina de la señorita Birdie. Butch está aparcado en el camino de la casa, detrás de mi Volvo. Si hoy no logra disparar su AK47, se llevará una terrible decepción.

Ayer se limpió la casa, que ahora huele bien y, temporalmente, sin su habitual aire enmohecido. Está lista para la llegada de la señorita Birdie.

El trato que hemos hecho es simple y satisfactorio. Deck se queda con las fichas que quiera y yo recibo dos mil dólares, pagaderos dentro de noventa días. Se asociará con otros abogados si le parece necesario. También distribuirá los casos que no le interesen. Se le devolverán a Booker los casos de Ruffin. No le gustará, pero qué le vamos a hacer.

Organizar las fichas es fácil. Es lamentable los pocos clientes y casos que hemos acumulado en seis meses.

El bufete tiene tres mil cuatrocientos dólares en el banco y unas cuantas facturas pendientes.

Hablamos de los detalles mientras comemos y el aspecto comercial de nuestra separación es fácil. El vínculo personal ya no lo es tanto. Deck no tiene futuro. No puede aprobar el examen de colegiatura y no tiene adónde ir. Pasará unas semanas resolviendo mis casos, pero no puede ejercer sin un Bruiser o un Rudy que dé la cara. Ambos lo sabemos, pero no lo comentamos.

Me confiesa que está sin blanca.

—¿Apostando? —pregunto.

—Sí. Los casinos. No puedo mantenerme alejado de ellos.

Ahora está relajado, casi anestesiado. Le da un gran mordisco a un bocadillo y mastica ruidosamente.

Cuando abrimos nuestro bufete el verano pasado acabábamos de recibir una compensación a partes iguales del caso de Van Landel. Disponíamos de cinco mil quinientos dólares cada uno y aportamos dos mil cada uno. Yo tuve que recurrir varias veces a mis ahorros, pero tengo dos mil ochocientos en el banco, que he ahorrado viviendo austeramente, e ingresando algún dinero siempre que he podido. Deck tampoco se lo gasta. Lo desperdicia en las mesas de juego.

—Anoche hablé con Bruiser —dice, y no me sorprende.

—¿Donde está?

—En Las Bahamas.

—¿Está Prince con él?

—Sí.

Ésa es una buena noticia. Estoy seguro de que Deck lo sabía hace mucho tiempo.

—De modo que lo han logrado —digo mientras miro por la ventana, e intento imaginarlos con sombreros de paja y gafas de sol, puesto que siempre vivían a oscuras.

—Sí. No sé cómo lo lograron. Hay cosas que no se preguntan —dice Deck con la mirada en blanco y aspecto meditabundo—. ¿Sabías que el dinero está todavía aquí?

—¿Cuánto?

—Cuatro millones, al contado. Lo que ahorraron en los clubes.

—¿Cuatro millones?

—Sí. Están escondidos en el sótano de un almacén. Aquí en Memphis.

—¿Y cuánto te ofrecen?

—El diez por ciento si lo hago llegar a Miami. Bruiser dice que él puede ocuparse del resto.

—No lo hagas, Deck.

—No hay peligro.

—Te descubrirán y acabarás en la cárcel.

—Lo dudo. Los federales han dejado de vigilar. No saben nada del dinero. Se supone que Bruiser se llevó lo que quiso y no necesita más.

—¿Lo necesita?

—No lo sé. Pero estoy seguro de que lo quiere.

—No lo hagas, Deck.

—Es pan comido. El dinero cabe en una pequeña furgoneta. Bruiser dice que se tardará dos horas a lo sumo en cargarlo. Luego conduciré la furgoneta a Miami y esperaré instrucciones. En cuestión de dos días me haré rico.

En su voz hay un tono remoto. No me cabe la menor duda de que lo intentará. Él y Bruiser han estado planeándolo. He dicho lo suficiente. Además, no me escucha.

Salimos de la casa de la señorita Birdie y nos dirigimos a mi piso. Deck me ayuda a trasladar algunos bultos a mi coche, que ya tiene lleno el maletero y la mitad del asiento trasero. No voy a regresar al despacho, de modo que nos despedimos junto al garaje.

—No te reprocho que te vayas —dice.

—Ten cuidado, Deck.

Nos damos un abrazo y, durante unos segundos, se me forma un nudo en la garganta.

—¿Te das cuenta, Rudy, de que has dejado tu huella en los anales de la historia?

—Lo hemos hecho juntos.

—Sí, ¿y qué hemos ganado a fin de cuentas?

—Podemos presumir.

Nos estrechamos la mano y los ojos de Deck están húmedos. Veo cómo se aleja por el camino y sube al coche de Butch.

Le escribo una larga carta a la señorita Birdie y prometo llamarla. Se la dejo sobre la mesa de la cocina, porque estoy seguro de que no tardará en llegar. Inspecciono una vez más la casa y me despido de mi piso.

Acudo a una sucursal de mi banco y cierro mi cuenta. Un fajo de veintiocho billetes de cien dólares tiene un tacto agradable. Los oculto bajo la esterilla.

Casi ha oscurecido cuando llamo a la puerta de los Black. Dot abre y casi sonríe al verme.

La casa está oscura y silenciosa, todavía de luto. Me pregunto si jamás cambiará. Buddy está en cama con la gripe.

Mientras nos tomamos un café instantáneo, le cuento delicadamente lo de la insolvencia de Great Benefit y que una vez más ha sido víctima de un fraude. A no ser que se produzca un milagro en un futuro lejano, no recibiremos un centavo. No me sorprende su reacción.

Parece haber varias razones complejas que han provocado la

muerte de la compañía, pero en este momento Dot prefiere pensar que ha sido ella quien ha apretado el gatillo. Se le iluminan los ojos y se refleja una enorme felicidad en su rostro cuando asimila la noticia. Los ha arruinado. Una decidida mujer de Memphis, Tennessee, ha arruinado a esos hijos de perra.

Mañana acudirá a la tumba de Donny Ray y se lo contará.

Kelly espera impaciente en la sala de estar, con Betty Norvelle. Tiene en las manos una pequeña bolsa negra que le compré ayer, con algunos artículos de baño y unas prendas que le han regalado en el hogar. Contiene todas sus posesiones.

Firmamos los papeles necesarios y le damos las gracias a Betty. Nos cogemos de la mano cuando nos dirigimos al coche. Respiramos hondo cuando estamos dentro del vehículo y nos alejamos.

El revólver está debajo del asiento, pero he dejado de preocuparme.

—¿Hacia dónde, querida? —pregunto al llegar a la autopista de circunvalación.

Nos reímos porque es maravilloso. ¡No importa en absoluto el rumbo que elijamos!

—Me gustaría ver montañas —dice Kelly.

—A mí también. ¿Este u oeste?

—Grandes montañas.

—Entonces al oeste.

—Quiero ver nieve.

—Creo que la encontraremos.

Se me acerca y apoya la cabeza en mi hombro. Yo le froto las piernas.

Cruzamos el río y entramos en Arkansas. La silueta de Memphis se pierde a nuestra espalda. Es asombroso lo poco que hemos planeado lo que estamos haciendo. Hasta esta mañana no sabíamos que podría abandonar el condado. Pero se han retirado los cargos contra ella y tengo una carta del propio fiscal del distrito. Su fianza ha sido cancelada a las tres de esta tarde.

Nos instalaremos en algún lugar donde nadie pueda encontrarnos. No temo que me sigan, pero quiero que me dejen tranquilo. No quiero saber nada de Deck ni de Bruiser. No me interesa la insolvencia de Great Benefit. No quiero que la señorita Birdie me llame para pedirme consejos jurídicos. No quiero preocuparme por la muerte de Cliff y todo lo relacionado con la misma. Algún día Kelly y yo hablaremos de ello, pero no pronto.

Elegiremos una pequeña ciudad con universidad, porque quiere volver a estudiar. Tiene sólo veinte años. Incluso yo soy un chiquillo. Estamos desprendiéndonos de muchas pesadillas y ha llegado el momento de pasárselo bien. Me encantaría dar clases de historia en un instituto. No debe ser demasiado difícil. Después de todo, he estudiado siete años en la universidad.

No tendré, en modo alguno, ninguna relación con el Derecho. Dejaré que caduque mi colegiatura. No me registraré como votante, para que no puedan llamarme como jurado. Nunca volveré a pisar voluntariamente un juzgado.

Nos reímos alegremente cuando el terreno se allana y el tráfico escasea. Memphis está treinta y cinco kilómetros a nuestra espalda. Me prometo no regresar jamás.

Impreso en LITOGRAFÍA ROSÉS, S. A.
Progrés, 54-60. Polígono La Post
Gavá (Barcelona)